DYNAMIC OPTIMIZATION AND ECONOMIC APPLICATIONS

McGRAW-HILL
BOOK COMPANY
New York
St. Louis
San Francisco
Auckland
Bogotá
Hamburg
Johannesburg
London
Madrid
Mexico
Montreal
New Delhi
Panama
Paris
São Paulo
Singapore
Sydney
Tokyo
Toronto

RONALD E. MILLER
Professor of Regional Science
University of Pennsylvania

Dynamic Optimization and Economic Applications

This book was set in Times Roman 327.

British Library Cataloging in Publication Data

Miller, Ronald Eugene
Dynamic optimization and economic applications.
1. Economics, Mathematical 2. Control theory
I. Title
330′.01′51 HB135 78-40724

ISBN 0-07-042180-3

DYNAMIC OPTIMIZATION AND ECONOMIC APPLICATIONS

2 3 4 MPMP 987654321

Printed and bound in the United States of America.

CONTENTS

PREFACE

The object of this book is to provide an introduction to a set of mathematical techniques that is becoming increasingly important in the social sciences and to illustrate some of the areas where they are being employed. The techniques, broadly classed under the rubric "optimal control theory," are standard subject matter in mathematics and in engineering programs, for example, and there are many texts and reference works that are designed with those audiences in mind.

In the social sciences—particularly in economics and regional science—there is a much smaller literature on these subjects to which the interested student or researcher can turn, particularly if that person is only modestly facile with quantitative methods. And yet it is in these fields that one comes across references to such concepts as Euler-Lagrange conditions, present-value hamiltonians, and terminal transversality conditions on costate variables, for example, with increasing frequency. It is to this audience that the exposition in this book is aimed. That is, I have tried to present the fundamentals in a way that is as intuitively appealing as possible to a person who wants to be able at least to follow, if not actively contribute to, these modern developments in his or her field.

There is, of course, a base level of mathematical tolerance that is necessary for even a novice in this area, as a quick perusal of the book will suggest. Just as constrained optimization and nonlinear programming discussions require an acquaintance at least with differential calculus and generally also with matrix algebra and the essentials of quadratic forms, the subjects presented in this book rely on the reader's familiarity at least with the rudiments of integral calculus and differential equations. Integral calculus is necessary because the analogue to the objective function in mathematical programming problems here very often takes the form of an integral. Similarly, the constraints in the problems that are examined in this book often consist of (or at least contain, inter alia) differential equations (or inequalities). Moreover, the first-order conditions for optimal solutions in dynamic problems usually take the form of differential equations.

Readers for whom these topics are not new but are perhaps a little vague will find that Appendix A covers the most basic aspects of integral calculus. Appendix C begins with the same objective for differential (and difference) equations, but then goes on somewhat beyond basics, particularly to techniques for systems of equations and to analysis via phase diagrams, since these are often needed in finding solutions using the control theory approach. (Appendix B reminds the reader of the terminology in use regarding signs of quadratic forms.) In this sense, there has been an attempt to keep the book self-contained, so that a person with only a modest introduction to the mathematical methods that are now prevalent in, say, basic economics could still follow the discussions in the text, with support from these appendices, where necessary. The content of the text itself is described straightforwardly by the chapter titles, and the final appendix contains supplemental material on the discrete versus continuous approaches that may be of interest to some but not all readers.

Early drafts of this manuscript have been used for several years in various graduate classes in the Regional Science Department at the University of Pennsylvania, attended primarily by students from economics, regional science, and city and regional planning. I am happy to acknowledge here with thanks their many constructive comments (and corrections). The helpful suggestions made by Professor Richard E. Quandt of Princeton University are legion; as in the past, he alerted me to many errors, some blatant and some subtle. Also as in the past, I am grateful to my colleagues in the Regional Science Department for a congenial environment in which to work.

R.E.M.

Philadelphia, Pennsylvania
February 28, 1978

CHAPTER

ONE

INTRODUCTION

In order to maintain even a very general understanding of theoretical developments in many of the social sciences, it has become increasingly necessary to have some familiarity and facility with a number of basic mathematical concepts. In the field of economics, for example, the simplest differential calculus—first- and second-order conditions on derivatives for maxima and minima of functions of one and possibly two variables—is no longer adequate. The intuitively appealing connection between algebraic rules on derivatives and their geometric interpretations, as found, for example, in Robinson [2], has largely given way to multidimensional constrained optimization formulations (see, for example, Henderson and Quandt [1]). Geometric analogies may persist (in a small number of dimensions), but in many cases they are much more complex and hence less useful in supporting one's attempts at an intuitive understanding of the principles involved. Complications arise and complexity increases with nonlinear functions and with inequality instead of equality constraints, including nonnegativity requirements on some or all of the choice variables. Techniques such as Lagrange multipliers, analysis of quadratic forms (and hence, of course, familiarity with matrix algebra), linear programming, and nonlinear programming, with the associated Kuhn-Tucker conditions, are generally necessary. The basic optimization idea, however, is still one of selecting values of certain variables so as to maximize some function of those variables, subject to one or more constraints—e.g., amounts to purchase of various consumption goods so as to maximize an individual's total utility subject to the individual's total budget.

More recently a number of explorations have been undertaken in the social sciences—notably economics, but also in regional science and in geography, for example—which utilize an entirely different set of mathematical optimization procedures. In their original form, these techniques constitute the subject matter of the calculus of variations; a more modern treatment is found in the maximum principle with which the name of Pontryagin is most often associated. (For reasons that will become clear in later chapters, this mathematical area is covered by the name *control theory*.) The essence of the newer explorations is that instead of searching among the values of one or more *variables* for the optimal values of those variables, one looks among *functions* for an optimal function.

For example, in the setting of an economic planning problem, one might want to find the function representing an optimal amount of capital stock for an economy at every point in time, from an initial date to a terminal target date. There may be general constraints that must hold over the entire period and also there may be initial or terminal conditions. For example, at the economy-wide level of aggregation, total output, which is a function of the amount of capital employed, equals total income, which is the sum of consumption and investment, and investment, at any time, is the change in the stock of capital; moreover, there is an exogenously given stock of capital at the beginning of the planning period and/or a preestablished amount to be left available at the end of the period for the beginning of the next plan. The objective of the planning problem might be defined as maximization of total utility over the entire planning period, where utility at any point in the period is some known function of the amount of output devoted to consumption at that point.

Mathematically, let Y, C, I, and K—all functions of time—refer to output, consumption, investment, and capital stock, respectively. At any point in time, I is defined as the change in capital stock; that is, $I \equiv dK/dt$. Let t_0 and t_1 indicate the initial and terminal dates of the planning period; let $U(C)$ denote the utility function and $Y = f(K)$ be the production function for the economy. Then the planning problem consists of finding the function $K(t)$ so as to maximize

$$\int_{t_0}^{t_1} U[C(t)]\, dt$$

subject to (1) $Y = C + I$, which is $f(K) = C(t) + dK/dt$ or $C(t) = f(K) - dK/dt$ (definition of total output), (2) $K(t_0) = K_0$ (the given initial capital stock), and (3) $K(t_1) = K_1$ (the terminal capital stock).

This is clearly a different species of problem from that for which first- and second-order conditions on derivatives would be employed. It is, in fact, a calculus of variations problem. That approach to a problem such as this specifies a set of necessary conditions that an optimal function must satisfy, and often it is possible to establish sufficient conditions as well. These conditions, however, do not have the geometric appeal of those from ordinary calculus for maxima and minima of functions, where the requirement of zero slope and then investigation of the rate of change of the slope have logical appeal. Therefore, an understanding of the requirements for calculus of variations problems (and more complex ones, for which the maximum principle approach turns out to be preferable) demands comprehension of essentially more purely mathematical material. This material is the content of Chaps. 2 through 4 of this book.

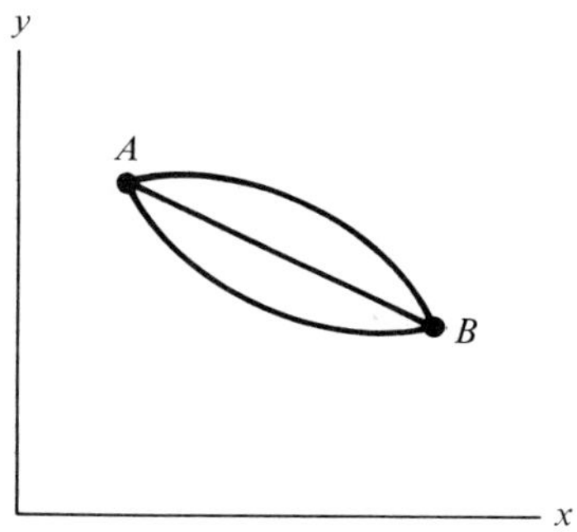

Figure 1-1 Alternative possible curves for the brachistochrone problem.

At present, most of the presentations of these fundamentals are in exclusively mathematical or else engineering texts, both of which are generally written for students with extensive mathematical training.† Also, and appropriately enough, the emphasis in these presentations tends to be on mathematical completeness, rigorous proofs, etc., and illustrative examples, when they are given, tend to come from the physical sciences.

The adjective "dynamic," as applied to these mathematical techniques, deserves comment. Clearly, in the economic planning example, the independent variable is time, and therefore in finding an optimal time path for capital stock one is dealing with a dynamic problem, by definition. In addition, the appearance of the time derivative of capital stock—its rate of change—in one of the constraints provides a dynamic flavor for the problem. Perhaps the original and historically most important problem was that of specifying the shape of the curve from A to B, several of which are illustrated in Fig. 1-1, which would have the property that a particle starting from A and traveling along it, acted upon only by gravity (i.e., no friction), would arrive at B in the shortest time possible. (The name "brachistochrone," which is attached to this problem, comes from the Greek words for shortest and time.) The specific dynamics of the problem enter (from physics) through the equation for velocity of falling objects, which is a specification of downward movement in the vertical direction y per unit of time t, that is, dy/dt.

A second historically important problem is that of connecting two points in the plane, such as A and B in Fig. 1-1, with a curve that has the property that when it is rotated about the x axis the area of the resulting surface is minimized (Fig. 1-2). While this does not have any "time" element involved explicitly, it too is a calculus of variations problem. (Both are discussed in Chap. 2 in more detail.) It does include, in the formal statement of the problem, the derivative of y with respect to x (in fact, the presence in the statement of the problem of the derivative of the function that is sought is a characteristic of many calculus of variations

† There are, of course, exceptions in the social science literature, particularly in economics. As will be noted in the chapters following, several texts covering mathematics for economists include one or more chapters on variational methods, and discussions of optimal economic growth often include self-contained brief expositions of the necessary mathematics.

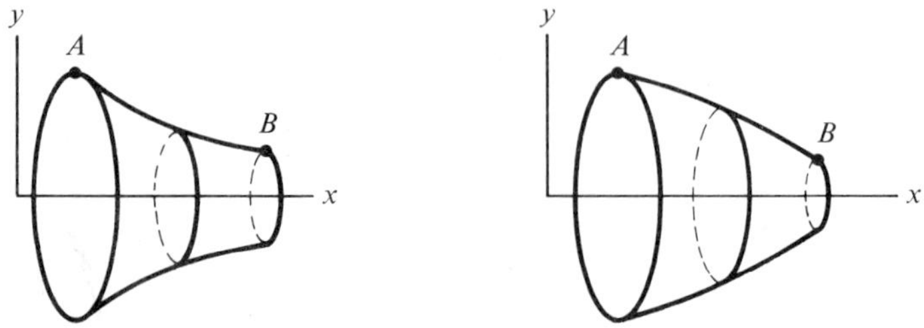

Figure 1-2 Alternative possible curves for the minimum surface of revolution problem.

problems) and, since the derivative is a rate of change, in this sense the problem is "dynamic."

In the social sciences, an example of the truly dynamic problem is the illustration from economic planning, where a function of time is sought (in the example, this was the time path of capital stock over a specified time interval). A second type of variational problem in the social sciences, e.g., in regional science, urban economics, and quantitative geography, involves finding an optimal function over space, not over time. Spatial variation is important, for example, in traffic density and congestion problems, where one might seek a representation of optimal road capacity as a function of distance from the core of an urban area. (Examples of both types are discussed in Chap. 5.) Thus, for present-day problems in the social sciences which involve finding optimal functional relationships over time or across space (or both), the "dynamic" methods discussed in this book are appropriate.

REFERENCES

1. Henderson, J., and R. E. Quandt: "Microeconomic Theory: A Mathematical Approach," 2d ed., McGraw-Hill, New York, 1971. Development of much of the material throughout this book depends upon optimization techniques for functions of more than one variable, subject to equality or inequality constraints.
2. Robinson, J.: "The Economics of Imperfect Competition," Macmillan, London, 1933. A classic exposition, relying heavily on the geometric relationships between average and marginal cost curves and average and marginal revenue curves, without calculus.

CHAPTER

TWO

THE CALCULUS OF VARIATIONS: FUNDAMENTALS

Some of the most common applications of the techniques of differential calculus are in problems of maximization or minimization of a function of either one variable, $f(x)$, or several variables, $f(x_1, \ldots, x_n)$. In the latter case, the variables may be independent or they may be connected by one or more equations or inequalities which make them dependent; this is then the problem of constrained optimization. We review some of the basic results from differential calculus as they apply to maximization and minimization problems, because of the parallels that will be found in problems requiring the calculus of variations, or variational calculus, approach.

For the single-variable, unconstrained case, the procedure is to look for one or more values of the independent variable x at which $f(x)$ may have the desired property. For functions with continuous first derivatives, these will be the points at which $f'(x) = 0$, and if there are several, maxima and minima are distinguished via second-order tests (on second derivatives) or by simply evaluating the known function $f(x)$ at each of the candidate values of the independent variable x. The essence of the problem is that one looks for values of an independent variable at which a function of that variable has desired properties.

Problems to which the calculus of variations applies have a similar object but a different character. We consider magnitudes (previously functions) that depend not on the values of variables but rather that depend on functions; such magnitudes—functions of functions—are called functionals. For example, the area between the x axis and a curve $y = f(x)$ above the x axis in x, y space, between two points $x = a$ and $x = b$, is given by a definite integral

$$A = \int_a^b f(x)\,dx \tag{2-1}$$

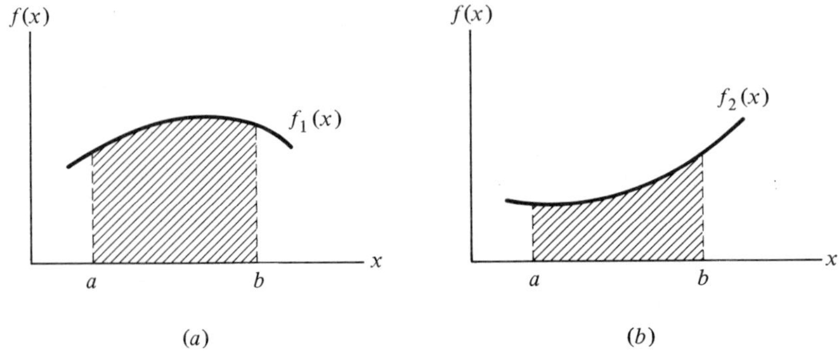

Figure 2-1 (*a*) Area between $f_1(x)$ and the x axis. (*b*) Area between $f_2(x)$ and the x axis.

Clearly, the area depends on the particular shape that $f(x)$ has (see Fig. 2-1); it will be larger for the function $f_1(x)$ than for the function $f_2(x)$. (The connection between a definite integral and an area is reviewed in App. A, especially Sec. A-2.) Thus A is a functional whose value depends on the curve $f(x)$.

If one imagines, say, 10 different curves of the sort shown in Fig. 2-1*a*,*b*, and calculates the areas in each case between $x = a$ and $x = b$, it is clear that generally there will be one function for which the area is largest.† Thus a different kind of maximization problem arises: from among the 10 given functions, find that one for which the integral A is maximized; i.e., select a function to maximize a functional.

While this illustrates the kind of problem to which we want to turn, it is a very specialized example. In the more general and interesting case where no particular curves are specified in advance, the problem would be to find that function for which A was maximized (subject to restrictions that rule out the infinite-area case). The point of the example is only to illustrate that here we are looking for a *function* of x so as to maximize a *functional*, in this case a definite integral of that function; in ordinary calculus we look for the value of a *variable* x so as to maximize (or minimize) a known *function* of that variable.

2-1 HISTORICAL BACKGROUND

The problem that led to classical development of the calculus of variations technique apparently dates to Galileo in 1630. This is the so-called brachistochrone problem, mentioned by Galileo and later solved by John Bernoulli in 1696. James

† Of course, there *may* be more than one curve with the same (largest) area. Clearly, in the absence of some restrictions on possible $f(x)$, it is obvious that the area given in (2-1) can be infinite by having a curve with a virtually vertical section at $x = a$ and another virtually vertical section at $x = b$, where the two sections are joined infinitely far above the x axis. (Imagine an infinitely elastic rubber band with one end at $x = a$, the other at $x = b$, and pull its center infinitely far upward.)

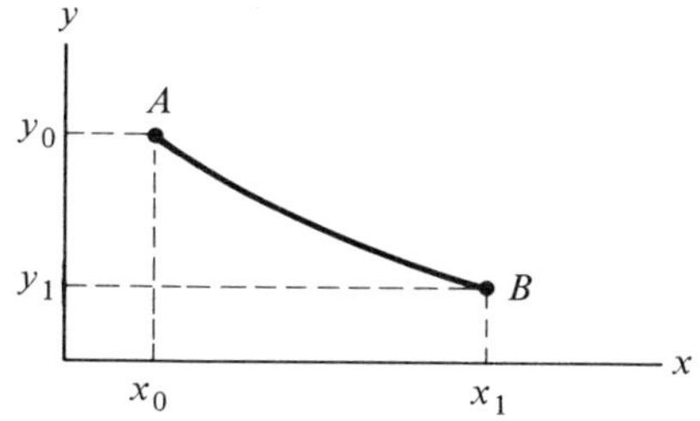

Figure 2-2 A possible solution for the brachistochrone problem.

Bernoulli and Newton also solved the problem, and further developments and generalizations of the technique engaged the attention of many of the greatest mathematicians of their time, including L'Hôpital, Lagrange, Euler, Legendre, Jacobi, and Weierstrass.† It is easily stated: imagine a bead that is to slide down a wire in the absence of any friction (i.e., under the influence of gravity alone) from an initial point A to a terminal point B, where A is higher than B. The question is: what shape should the wire have so that the time taken by the bead to fall along it from A to B is as short as possible? Figure 2-2 illustrates the problem, with one possible shape for the wire. It is obvious that the curve should not have a positive slope at A, since then gravity would keep the bead at A. It also seems obvious that it should not be concave, since then it would start from A very slowly. In fact, even a straight line from A to B does not appear to be optimal, since a strictly convex curve (as in Fig. 2-2) would appear to allow the bead to move faster sooner. What is needed (and what the calculus of variations supplies) is an approach to deal with this problem in a rigorous way.

To pose the problem precisely, we need to utilize a few simple observations from physics. Our primary interest here is more in the form of the final statement of the problem than in the derivation of that statement. One essential notion is that of the arc length along the curve. If we denote this arc length by s, then for *small* changes in x and y, dx and dy, respectively,

$$(ds)^2 = (dx)^2 + (dy)^2$$

as Fig. 2-3 suggests. That is, $ds = \sqrt{(dx)^2 + (dy)^2} = \sqrt{1 + (dy/dx)^2}\, dx$. (Here and elsewhere when a distance or length is represented as a square root, it will be understood as the positive square root.) Using $y' = dy/dx$, $ds = \sqrt{1 + (y')^2}\, dx$. It is known from physics that the velocity v of a particle when it has fallen through a distance y, due to gravity alone, is $v^2 = 2gy$ (where g is the gravitational constant). For the frictionless wire, this is the velocity along the curve, ds/dt. Thus $(ds/dt)^2 =$

† The name comes from the Greek *brachistos* (shortest) and *chronos* (time). A more detailed history of contributions to this branch of mathematics can be found in Bliss [2], Elsgolc [5], or Pars [11]. There are a great many texts and chapters in texts dealing with the fundamentals of the calculus of variations, just as there are for ordinary calculus. This is especially true of engineering texts on "optimal control." Intriligator [9, chaps. 11 and 12], Takayama [12, chap. 5], and Chakravarty [4, app. A, secs. A.1 through A.9 and sec. 3.3] provide a good introduction. Elsgolc [5] and Gelfand and Fomin [6] provide good mathematical expositions and are relatively advanced, as are Hadley and Kemp [7, chaps. 2 and 3] and Hestenes [8].

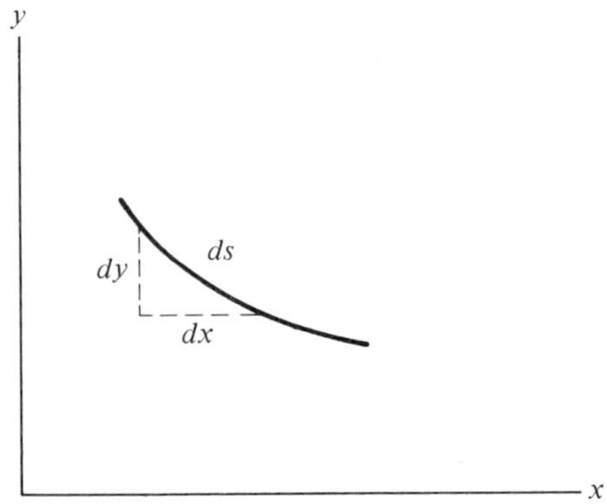

Figure 2-3 A change in s associated with small changes in x and y.

$2gy$ or, rearranging, $dt = ds/\sqrt{2gy}$. Total time t, over any segment of the curve, is just $\int dt$ along that segment. That is, $t = \int dt$ and, substituting first for dt and then for ds, $t = (1/\sqrt{2g}) \int ds/\sqrt{y} = (1/\sqrt{2g}) \int [\sqrt{1 + (y')^2}/\sqrt{y}]\, dx$. In particular, then, the total time from A (at x_0, y_0) to B (at x_1, y_1) will be

$$t = \frac{1}{\sqrt{2g}} \int_{x_0}^{x_1} \frac{\sqrt{1 + (y')^2}}{\sqrt{y}}\, dx \tag{2-2}$$

[Instead of $y = f(x)$, we now use $y = y(x)$ to indicate a function of x and avoid the introduction of another letter, f.] The brachistochrone problem is to find the function $y = y(x)$ for which t in (2-2) is minimized.† The structure of the problem is: minimize $t = \int dt$, where $dt = (1/\sqrt{2gy})\, ds$ and $ds = \sqrt{1 + (y')^2}\, dx$. Note that the integral involves y, which is a function of x, and the derivative of y with respect to x. Using $F(x, y, y')$ to denote the integrand in (2-2) and $I[y]$ to denote that the entire integral is to be minimized by a choice of y, we can represent the brachistochrone problem as:

$$\text{Minimize} \quad I[y] = \int_{x_0}^{x_1} F(x, y, y')\, dx \tag{2-3}$$

A second classical problem of similar structure is that of finding the curve connecting two points A and B that generates the smallest surface area when revolved around the x axis, as in Fig. 2-4. At any particular x, the addition to area for a small increase in x is just the area of a disc with radius y and width ds. Denoting the surface of revolution by R, we have $dR = 2\pi y\, ds$, as Fig. 2-5 suggests. The total surface area over any segment of the curve is then just $\int dR$ along that segment. Therefore the total surface area is

$$R = 2\pi \int_{x_0}^{x_1} y\sqrt{1 + (y')^2}\, dx \tag{2-4}$$

and the problem is to select a $y = y(x)$ so that R in (2-4) is minimized. Parallel

† It turns out that the minimizing curve is a cycloid through (x_0, y_0) and (x_1, y_1).

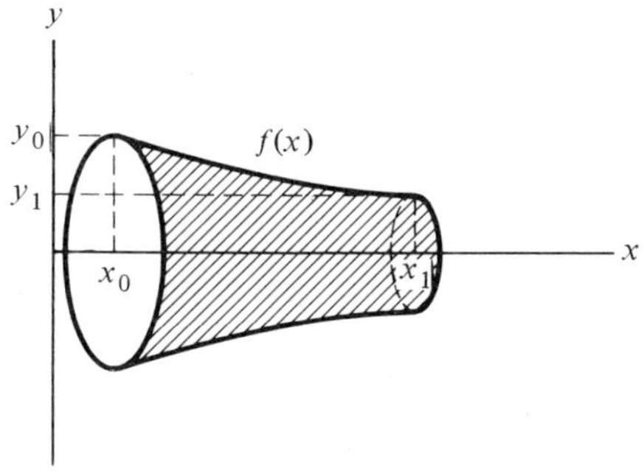

Figure 2-4 Surface generated by revolving $f(x)$ around the x axis.

to the brachistochrone problem, the structure here is: minimize $R = \int dR$, where $dR = 2\pi y\, ds$ and $ds = \sqrt{1 + (y')^2}\, dx$, as above. Clearly, this also has the structure indicated in (2-3).†

Finally, the problem of finding the shortest path between two points A and B in a plane, i.e., the curve joining them that has the shortest length, is of this same general form. From Figs. 2-2 and 2-3, we want the length L, which is $\int ds$, to be minimized, i.e.,

$$\text{Minimize} \quad L = \int_{x_0}^{x_1} ds = \int_{x_0}^{x_1} \sqrt{1 + (y')^2}\, dx \tag{2-5}$$

which again has the fundamental structure of (2-3), although in this particular case y does not appear explicitly in the integrand of (2-5).‡

These three examples happened to involve minimization, but, as with ordinary optimization problems, the calculus of variations technique is applicable to either maximization or minimization problems. In summary, the fundamental calculus of variations problem is: maximize/minimize $I[y] = \int_{x_0}^{x_1} F[x, y(x), y'(x)]\, dx$, where $y(x_0) = y_0$ and $y(x_1) = y_1$. More simply, since we will understand that y is a

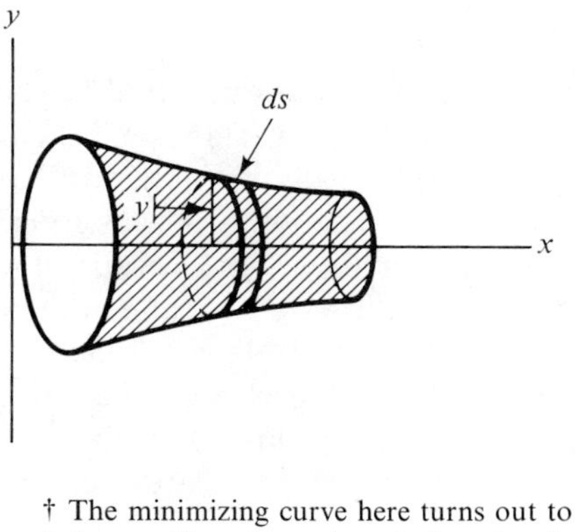

Figure 2-5 A "typical" disc on the surface of revolution.

† The minimizing curve here turns out to be a catenary through (x_0, y_0) and (x_1, y_1).

‡ As we will see later, the calculus of variations solution assures us that the minimum-length curve is the straight line joining A and B.

function of x:

$$\text{Maximize/minimize} \quad I[y] = \int_{x_0}^{x_1} F(x, y, y')\, dx \tag{2-6}$$

where $\qquad y(x_0) = y_0 \quad \text{and} \quad y(x_1) = y_1$

In words: find the function $y = y(x)$ which passes through the points (x_0, y_0) and (x_1, y_1) and which has the property that it either maximizes or minimizes a definite integral in which it and its derivative may appear. It is worth noting that in many applied problems the independent variable is time, denoted by t. In such cases, the function being sought is often denoted $x(t)$—parallel to the use of x in ordinary maximization and minimization problems. In that case, and using the convention of a centered dot for derivatives with respect to time, that is, $\dot{x} = dx/dt$, the fundamental problem is then stated as:†

$$\text{Maximize/minimize} \quad I[x] = \int_{t_0}^{t_1} F(t, x, \dot{x})\, dt \tag{2-7}$$

where $\qquad x(t_0) = x_0 \quad \text{and} \quad x(t_1) = x_1$

2-2 UNDERLYING MATHEMATICAL CONCEPTS

Particularly in the derivation of necessary conditions, there will be a number of parallels between differential calculus and variational calculus. For this reason, we should recall a few of the more fundamental results in differential calculus and also some of the conditions and conventions upon which they are based. Since discussion of the n-variable case utilizes terminology and results from the theory of quadratic forms, this material is reviewed in App. B for the interested reader.

Neighborhoods, Continuity, and Maxima or Minima in Differential Calculus

Using, for illustration, the maximum problem for a function of one variable, the function $f(x)$ is said to have a strong relative maximum at x^* if $f(x^*) > f(x)$ [or $f(x) - f(x^*) < 0$] for all x in a neighborhood of x^*. Informally, the function has a larger value at x^* than at "nearby" values of x. The maximum is a "strong" one because $f(x^*)$ is strictly larger than $f(x)$ for x near to x^*, i.e., because the inequality $f(x^*) > f(x)$ is a strong one. If the inequality were weak, namely $f(x^*) \geq f(x)$, the maximum would also be referred to as weak. It is a "relative" maximum because the value of the function at x^* is compared with the value of the function for nearby x's; x^* is best relative to other values of x that are close by. The principles for a function of several variables, $f(\mathbf{X})$, are identical

† The potential for confusion is primarily that x denotes the independent variable in (2-6) and the unknown function of time in (2-7).

but should be recalled because of the necessity of extending the concept of a neighborhood to more than one dimension.

Basically, for $f(x_1, \ldots, x_n)$, the results follow those for $f(x)$, with $\mathbf{X}^* = [x_1^*, \ldots, x_n^*]'$ replacing x^*, etc. With $f(x)$, the notion of a neighborhood of x^* is easily visualized as including all x within some distance, say δ, on the x axis on either side of x^*; for $f(\mathbf{X})$, a neighborhood of $\mathbf{X}^*$ *could* be defined when each x_i is within a δ distance of x_i^* on the x_i axis. For the two-variable case, when $\mathbf{X}^* = [x_1^*, x_2^*]'$, this neighborhood would be a $2\delta \times 2\delta$ square surrounding $\mathbf{X}^*$ in the x_1, x_2 plane. More usually, however, the δ neighborhood of a point $\mathbf{X}^*$ in two-dimensional space is defined as the circle with radius δ centered on $\mathbf{X}^*$. The generalization to more dimensions would be a sphere (or hypersphere) of radius δ. We dwell on this rather straightforward notion of neighborhoods in the ordinary maximum (or minimum) problem because we will soon need to establish a corresponding convention for neighborhoods in the rather different problem for which the calculus of variations is used.

These intuitively reasonable observations on $f(x^*) > f(x)$ or $f(\mathbf{X}^*) > f(\mathbf{X})$ are made mathematically exact for functions which are differentiable through the use of derivatives or differentials. For $f(x)$, the first-order, or necessary, condition for a maximum at x^* requires that the slope of the tangent to $f(x)$ at x^* be zero; this is achieved by setting the first derivative or the first total differential equal to zero. Since $df = f'(x)\,dx$ and letting $dx = (x - x^*)$, i.e., letting dx denote the distance of an arbitrary nearby x from x^*, setting $df = 0$ is equivalent to setting $f'(x) = 0$. The second-order condition, which distinguishes a maximum from a minimum from a point that is neither, is a requirement on the sign of $f''(x)$ at x^*. Since the second total differential for $f(x)$ is $d^2f = f''(x)(dx)^2$, a sign condition on $f''(x)$ at x^* is equivalent to a requirement on the sign of d^2f evaluated at x^*. For a maximum, $f''(x^*)$ or $d^2f(x^*)$ must be negative; for a minimum, $f''(x^*)$ or $d^2f(x^*)$ must be positive. The geometry is again appealing. Since $f''(x)$ represents the rate of change of $f'(x)$ at a point—just as $f'(x)$ gives the rate of change of $f(x)$—then the requirement that $f''(x^*) < 0$ says that the slope of the tangent, which is zero at x^*, must be positive to the left of x^* and negative to the right. This means that at x^*, $f(x)$ has a hilltop.

Recall that these rules break down when $f''(x^*) = 0$, as would be the case for $y = -3x^4 + 5$. Here $f'(x) = -12x^3$, which means $x^* = 0$; but since $f''(x) = -36x^2$, $f''(x^*) = 0$, even though a sketch will show that this function has an unambiguous maximum at $x = 0$. Such cases force one to a more general approach, using the Taylor series; the simple rules on $f'(x)$ and $f''(x)$ are in fact derived from this more general treatment. Given that $f(x)$ is a continuous function with derivatives at all points, the Taylor series expression for $f(x)$ uses terms involving the function and its derivatives evaluated at any point, say $x = a$:

$$f(x) = f(a) + f'(a)\frac{x-a}{1!} + f''(a)\frac{(x-a)^2}{2!} + f'''(a)\frac{(x-a)^3}{3!} + \cdots$$

$$+ f^{(n-1)}(a)\frac{(x-a)^{n-1}}{(n-1)!} + R_n \qquad (2\text{-}8)$$

R^n, the remainder after n terms, is $f^{(n)}(x_1)[(x-a)^n/n!]$, where x_1 lies between a and x. Therefore R^n gives the limits of error from using only n terms of the series as an approximation to the value of the function at x. Suppose that we let $a = x^*$, a point which is a candidate for a maximum because $f'(x^*) = 0$, and that the point x is in some small neighborhood of x^*, so that the $(x - a)$ terms—here $(x - x^*)$—are small; as before, we denote them by dx. Then, from (2-8),

$$f(x) - f(x^*) = f'(x^*)\,dx + f''(x^*)\frac{(dx)^2}{2!} + f'''(x^*)\frac{(dx)^3}{3!} + \cdots + f^{(n-1)}(x^*)\frac{(dx)^{n-1}}{(n-1)!} + R_n \tag{2-9}$$

The difference in the value of the function at x^* and at a nearby point is thus seen to be the sum of a series of terms involving progressively higher-order derivatives, evaluated at x^*, multiplied by dx raised to ascending powers, and divided by correspondingly higher-order factorials. Thus this difference, $f(x) - f(x^*)$, will be well approximated by only a few terms in (2-9), as long as dx is small. [The remainder, R_n, will be small for even moderately small n; if $dx = 0.01$, the remainder after using only $f'(x^*)$ and $f''(x^*)$ terms will be $R_3 = f'''(x_1)(0.000\,001)/6 = (0.000\,000\,17)f'''(x_1)$.]

For x^* to represent a strong relative maximum, $f(x) - f(x^*) < 0$ for x near to x^*. From (2-9), using as an approximation only the first two terms on the right and recalling that $f'(x^*) = 0$ (since that is what makes x^* a candidate for a maximum point), this clearly means that $f''(x^*)$ must be negative, since $(dx)^2$ will always be positive for x near to but distinct from x^*. The result in (2-9) also makes clear how one utilizes higher-order derivatives in the case where both $f'(x^*)$ and $f''(x^*)$ are zero. The value of $f(x) - f(x^*)$ then depends on the sign of $f'''(x^*)$ or, should that also be zero, on the sign of the first nonzero higher-order derivative. However, the $(dx)^2, (dx)^3, \ldots, (dx)^{n-1}$ terms add a complication. Clearly, if the first nonzero derivative is an *even* ordered one, say $f^{(4)}(x^*)$, then since $(dx)^4$ is necessarily positive, the sign of $f(x) - f(x^*)$ will be the same as that of $f^{(4)}(x^*)$. If the first nonzero derivative is of *odd* order, however, such as $f'''(x^*)$, then the sign of $(dx)^3$ will depend on whether dx is positive or negative. Since $dx = (x - x^*)$, this sign cannot be established unambiguously; it depends on whether x is near to x^* on the left or on the right. Therefore, if $f'(x^*) = f''(x^*) = \cdots = f^{(i-1)}(x^*) = 0$,and $f^{(i)}(x^*) \neq 0$, then $f(x)$ has a stationary value at x^* that is a point of inflection if i is odd; if i is even, the stationary value is a maximum if $f^{(i)}(x^*) < 0$ and a minimum if $f^{(i)}(x^*) > 0$. Figure 2-6 illustrates the possibilities for $f(x) = x^4 + 2$, $f(x) = -3x^4 + 5$, and $f(x) = x^3 + 2$, respectively. The reader should observe that for each of these functions $f'(x) = 0$ requires that $x = 0$ and then $f''(0) = 0$. However, $f^{(4)}(0) = 24$, $f^{(4)}(0) = -72$, and $f^{(3)}(0) = 6$, respectively, and hence the three functions have a minimum, a maximum, and a point of inflection, respectively, at $x = 0$.

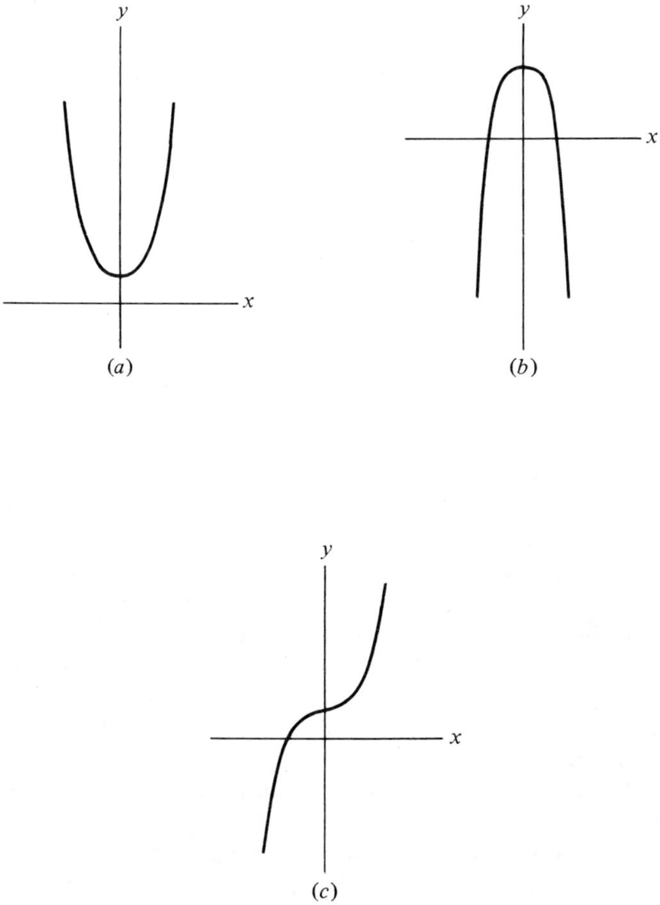

Figure 2-6 (*a*) $y = x^4 + 2$. (*b*) $y = -3x^4 + 5$. (*c*) $y = x^3 + 2$.

For the *n*-variable case, the Taylor series expression parallel to (2-9) is

$$f(\mathbf{X}) - f(\mathbf{X}^*) = df(\mathbf{X}^*) + \frac{1}{2!}\, d^2f(\mathbf{X}^*) + \frac{1}{3!}\, d^3f(\mathbf{X}^*) + \cdots + \frac{1}{(n-1)!}\, d^{(n-1)}f(\mathbf{X}^*) + R_n \tag{2-10}$$

The terms on the right are the first, second, third, etc., total differentials of $f(\mathbf{X})$, evaluated at $\mathbf{X}^*$ and divided by factorials. Recalling gradient notation, $\nabla \mathbf{f} = [\partial f/\partial x_1, \ldots, \partial f/\partial x_n]'$, or, letting $\partial f/\partial x_i = f_i$, $\nabla \mathbf{f} = [f_1, \ldots, f_n]'$, and letting $\mathbf{dX} = [dx_1, \ldots, dx_n]'$, the first term on the right-hand side of (2-10) is

$$df(\mathbf{X}^*) = [\nabla \mathbf{f}(\mathbf{X}^*)] \cdot [\mathbf{dX}]$$

Further, letting $\partial^2 f/\partial x_i\,\partial x_j = f_{ij}$ and using $\mathbf{H}$ to denote the hessian matrix of second partial derivatives and cross-partial derivatives,

$$\mathbf{H} = \begin{bmatrix} f_{11} & f_{12} & \cdots & f_{1n} \\ \cdots & \cdots & \cdots & \cdots \\ f_{n1} & f_{n2} & \cdots & f_{nn} \end{bmatrix}$$

the second total differential of $f(\mathbf{X})$, evaluated at $\mathbf{X}^*$, is given by

$$d^2 f(\mathbf{X}^*) = [\mathbf{dX}]'\mathbf{H}(\mathbf{X}^*)[\mathbf{dX}]$$

where $\mathbf{H}(\mathbf{X}^*)$ indicates that these derivatives are evaluated at $\mathbf{X}^*$. That is, $d^2 f$ is a quadratic form in the dx_i.

If $\mathbf{X}^*$ is a candidate for a maximum, then all $\partial f/\partial x_i$ have been set equal to zero, that is, $\nabla \mathbf{f}(\mathbf{X}^*) = \mathbf{0}$ and thus the approximation to $f(\mathbf{X}) - f(\mathbf{X}^*)$ using only the first two terms on the right-hand side of (2-10) shows that the sign of $f(\mathbf{X}) - f(\mathbf{X}^*)$ depends on the sign of $d^2 f(\mathbf{X}^*)$. Since this is a quadratic form, its sign is governed by the principal minors of $\mathbf{H}(\mathbf{X}^*)$. Specifically, if the principal minors alternate, beginning negative, then $d^2 f(\mathbf{X}^*) < 0$ and therefore $f(\mathbf{X}) - f(\mathbf{X}^*) < 0$ so $\mathbf{X}^*$ would represent a strong relative maximum. If the principal minors are all positive, then $d^2 f(\mathbf{X}^*) > 0$ and $\mathbf{X}^*$ would be a strong relative minimum (App. B).

To summarize, in problems of maximization or minimization of $f(x)$ or $f(\mathbf{X})$, we utilize the concepts of (1) neighborhoods around a point and (2) continuity and differentiability of a function. A definition of a neighborhood is needed so that, for example, the requirement $f(\mathbf{X}^*) - f(\mathbf{X}) > 0$ for all $\mathbf{X}$ near to $\mathbf{X}^*$ has an unambiguous meaning. The continuity of $f(\mathbf{X})$ is necessary (not sufficient) to assure differentiability of $f(\mathbf{X})$ which is, in turn, exploited in translating the inequality statement into terms involving derivatives at $\mathbf{X}^*$, e.g., in utilizing the Taylor series for $\mathbf{X}^*$ and nearby points. The approach to calculus of variations problems will parallel that to ordinary maximization and minimization problems in many respects. In particular, we will need to consider neighborhoods of a function $y(x)$, which is a candidate for the solution to a maximizing or minimizing problem as in (2-6). Further, we will require a definition of continuity for a functional. This suggests that we review the concept of continuity for functions.

Geometrically, a continuous function between two points is one that can be drawn without lifting the pencil from the paper. However, a continuous function may be smooth (everywhere differentiable) or it may not, in which case it has one or more corners, or kinks. Figure 2-7 illustrates this.

An algebraic distinction between continuous and discontinuous functions (which would be necessary, for example, for functions of many variables, when the geometry would not be straightforward) rests on the existence of certain limits for the function. We examine these. (In what follows, δ and ε are assumed to be very small positive quantities.)

1. *Right-sided limit at* x_0. Formally, if there is a number α^* and if for any $\varepsilon > 0$ there is a $\delta > 0$, such that for $x_0 < x < x_0 + \delta$, $|f(x) - \alpha^*| < \varepsilon$, then $\lim_{x \to x_0^+} f(x) = \alpha^*$. This says that if the value of the function, $f(x)$, differs

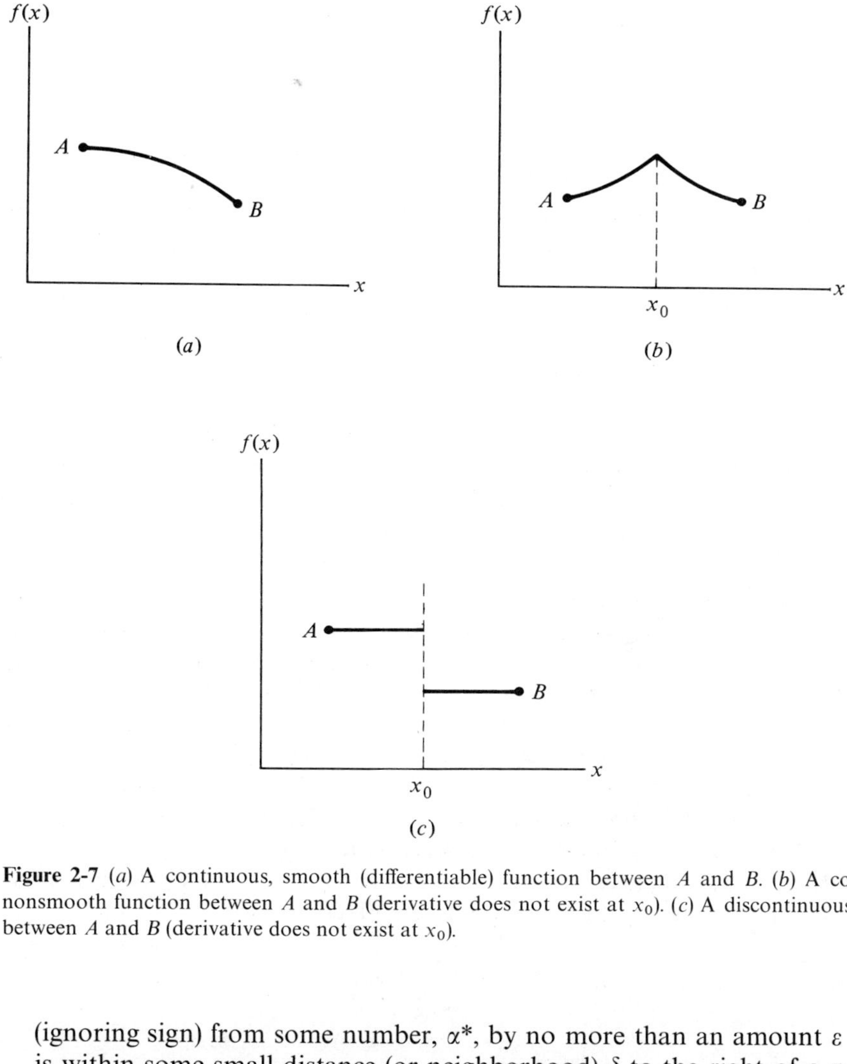

Figure 2-7 (*a*) A continuous, smooth (differentiable) function between A and B. (*b*) A continuous, nonsmooth function between A and B (derivative does not exist at x_0). (*c*) A discontinuous function between A and B (derivative does not exist at x_0).

(ignoring sign) from some number, α^*, by no more than an amount ε when x is within some small distance (or neighborhood) δ to the right of a point x_0, then the right-sided limit of $f(x)$ at x_0 is α^*. This is also written $f(x) \to \alpha^*$ as $x \to x_0^+$.

2. *Left-sided limit at* x_0. The formal statement is similar to that above, except that x now ranges in a neighborhood to the left of x_0. Namely, if for any $\varepsilon > 0$ there is a $\delta > 0$ such that for $x_0 - \delta < x < x_0$, $|f(x) - \alpha^{**}| < \varepsilon$, then $\lim_{x \to x_0^-} f(x) = \alpha^{**}$.
3. *Limit at* x_0. When $\alpha^* = \alpha^{**} = \alpha$, this common value is called the limit of $f(x)$ at x_0. Formally, if for any $\varepsilon > 0$ there is a $\delta > 0$ such that for $|x_0 - x| < \delta$, $|f(x) - \alpha| < \varepsilon$, then $\lim_{x \to x_0} f(x) = \alpha$. (The distinguishing feature is now that the δ neighborhood extends on both sides of x_0.) When $\alpha = f(x_0)$, then $f(x)$ is said to be continuous at x_0.

Continuity of the function $f(x)$ If for any $\varepsilon > 0$ there is a $\delta > 0$ such that for $|x_0 - x| < \delta$, $|f(x) - f(x_0)| < \varepsilon$, then $f(x)$ is continuous at x_0.

We examine the geometry of these concepts. In Fig. 2-8, the right-sided limit at x_0 is α, that is, $\lim_{x \to x_0^+} f(x) = \alpha$, since for all x in the range $x_0 < x < x_0 + \delta$ (horizontal axis), the value of the function is between α and $\alpha + \varepsilon$ (vertical axis). Similarly, the left-sided limit at x_0 is also α, that is, $\lim_{x \to x_0^-} f(x) = \alpha$ and hence $\lim_{x \to x_0} f(x) = \alpha$—the limit of $f(x)$ at x_0 is α. Furthermore, α is exactly the value of $f(x)$ at x_0—since $f(x_0) = \alpha$—and we say (this is obvious when we have the figure in front of us) that $f(x)$ is continuous at x_0. The reader should be convinced that even for a function with a kink at x_0, such as in Fig. 2-7*b*, the left-sided limit at x_0 equals the right-sided limit at x_0 and their common value is the value of the function at x_0.

The situation in which right- and left-sided limits exist and are unequal is illustrated by a step function; e.g., if $f(x) = 1$ when $x \leq 5$ and $f(x) = 3$ when $x > 5$, as shown in Fig. 2-9*a*. Note that at $x_0 = 5$, the right-sided limit $\lim_{x \to x_0^+} f(x) = 3$ and the left-sided limit $\lim_{x \to x_0^-} f(x) = 1$. Thus there is no number that is $\lim_{x \to x_0} f(x)$. This is easily illustrated using ε and δ distances. Consider $\alpha = 3$ as a potential limit for the function at x_0. For $\varepsilon = 4$, i.e., a range from -1 to 7 on the $f(x)$ axis, we can easily find a δ neighborhood of $x_0 = 5$, say $\delta = 2$, such that for all $|x_0 - x| < 2$, $|f(x) - 3| < 4$. This is a reflection of the fact that for x in the range from $x = 3$ to $x = 7$, $f(x)$ will be either 1 or 3, i.e., will be either 2 units or 0 units away from $\alpha = 3$. However, it is not possible to find a $\delta > 0$ for *any* $\varepsilon > 0$; consider $\varepsilon = \frac{1}{2}$ and $\alpha = 3$ as a candidate for the limit. There is no δ, irrespective of how small we make it, which will keep $f(x) = 2\frac{1}{2}$ or more for x to the left of $x_0 = 5$. Thus, the important concept in the definition of limits is that for *any* $\varepsilon > 0$ there is a $\delta > 0$ for which the inequalities hold.

Finally, we note that even when the right- and left-sided limits exist at a point x_0 and are equal, their common value may be different from $f(x_0)$; in this case,

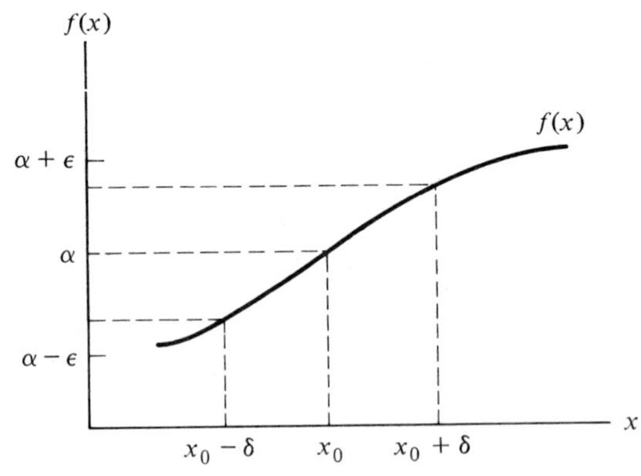

Figure 2-8 $\text{Lim}_{x \to x_0} f(x) = \alpha$.

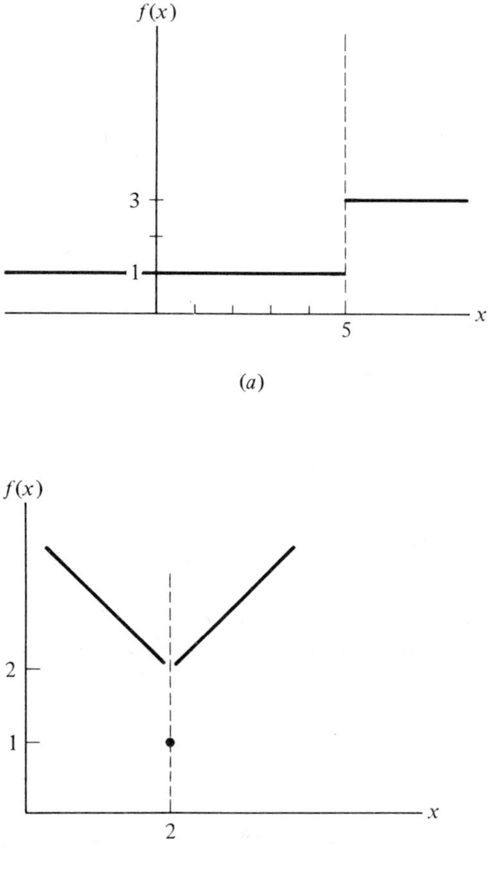

Figure 2-9 (*a*) The step function $f(x) = 1$, $x \leq 5$; $f(x) = 3$, $x > 5$. (*b*) The discontinuous function $f(x) = 4 - x$, $x < 2$; $f(x) = 1$, $x = 2$; $f(x) = x$, $x > 2$.

also, the function is discontinuous. For example,

$$f(x) = \begin{cases} 4 - x \\ 1 \\ x \end{cases} \quad \text{when } x \begin{cases} < 2 \\ = 2 \\ > 2 \end{cases}$$

which is illustrated in Fig. 2-9*b*. At $x_0 = 2$, $\lim_{x \to x_0^+} f(x) = 2$ and $\lim_{x \to x_0^-} f(x) = 2$, but $f(x_0) = f(2) = 1$. Again, for $\varepsilon = \frac{1}{2}$ around the point $f(x) = 2$, there is no δ neighborhood around x_0 such that for the x in that neighborhood, $|f(x) - 2| < \frac{1}{2}$.

Recall that the derivative of a function at a point x_0 is defined in terms of a particular limit, namely,

$$\frac{dy}{dx} = \lim_{x_1 \to x_0} \frac{f(x_1) - f(x_0)}{x_1 - x_0} \tag{2-11}$$

or, using $\Delta x = x_1 - x_0$, $dy/dx = \lim_{\Delta x \to 0} [f(x_0 + \Delta x) - f(x_0)]/\Delta x$. Geometrically, we recall that the particular limit defined in (2-11) is the slope of the tangent to $f(x)$ at x_0. The existence of the derivative at x_0 means that the function $f(x)$ is continuous there. For $x_1 \neq x_0$, write $f(x_1) - f(x_0)$ as

$$f(x_1) - f(x_0) = \frac{f(x_1) - f(x_0)}{x_1 - x_0}(x_1 - x_0)$$

Taking limits,

$$\lim_{x_1 \to x_0} f(x_1) - \lim_{x_1 \to x_0} f(x_0) = \lim_{x_1 \to x_0} \frac{f(x_1) - f(x_0)}{x_1 - x_0} \lim_{x_1 \to x_0} (x_1 - x_0)$$

or

$$\lim_{x_1 \to x_0} f(x_1) - f(x_0) = f'(x_0)(x_0 - x_0) = 0$$

that is,

$$\lim_{x_1 \to x_0} f(x_1) = f(x_0)$$

which is the definition of continuity of $f(x)$ at x_0. The converse does not hold, as Fig. 2-7*b* illustrates; a continuous function need not have a derivative everywhere. At a kink, as at x_0 in Fig. 2-7*b*,

$$\lim_{x_1 \to x_0^+} \frac{f(x_1) - f(x_0)}{x_1 - x_0} \neq \lim_{x_1 \to x_0^-} \frac{f(x_1) - f(x_0)}{x_1 - x_0}$$

Geometrically, the right-sided limit is a negative value (downward sloping tangent as x_0 is approached from the right) and the left-sided limit is a positive value (upward sloping tangent as x_0 is approached from the left). A function without kinks is called smooth. Therefore, the standard analytic procedures for defining maxima and minima using derivatives require continuous and smooth functions.

Neighborhoods, Continuity, and Maxima and Minima in Variational Calculus

We now turn to similar considerations for calculus of variations problems. A maximizing function $y(x)$ will be defined as one for which $I[z] - I[y] \leq 0$ for all functions $z(x)$ "near to" $y(x)$.† The use of concepts similar to derivatives and Taylor's series for $I[y]$ instead of $f(\mathbf{X})$ requires continuity of the functional; the definition of continuity, in turn, requires a measure of nearness for functions.

† In an attempt to maintain a parallel between variational calculus and differential calculus, one might think of using $y^*(x)$ for the maximizing function and $y(x)$ for comparison functions, in place of x^* and x. However, for notational convenience (e.g., in denoting derivatives with a prime) it is easier if the function y is not encumbered with an asterisk.

Continuity of the functional $I[y]$ If for any $\varepsilon > 0$ there is a $\delta > 0$ such that for $|y_0 - y| < \delta$, $|I[y] - I[y_0]| < \varepsilon$, then $I[y]$ is continuous at y_0.

[Compare the statement for continuity of $f(x)$, above.] What is needed now is an understanding of the measure of distance used to define functions y which are "near to" (i.e., within some distance δ of) y_0. We begin by reviewing some general notions of distance.

Distance between points In one-dimensional space, with an origin and a unit of measure, a point is located by giving its distance and direction from the origin. For example, along an x axis, $x_a = 10$ and $x_b = -3$ define two locations, the first 10 units to the right of $x = 0$ and the second 3 units to the left. The *distance* between the points is the *difference* (ignoring sign) in their values; $D = |x_a - x_b| = 13$ units. In two-dimensional space, points may be thought of as representations of two-element vectors. Conventionally, $\mathbf{A} = \begin{bmatrix} a_1 \\ a_2 \end{bmatrix}$ would be represented by a point located a_1 units along the horizontal axis and a_2 units along the vertical axis in so-called vector space. Similarly for $\mathbf{B} = \begin{bmatrix} b_1 \\ b_2 \end{bmatrix}$. Often the endpoints are connected to the origin, with an arrowhead at the endpoint. Either the endpoint alone or the complete arrow are representations of the vector. The norm of a vector is its length; i.e., the length of the line connecting its endpoint with the origin. It is denoted by double vertical bars; for two-element vectors, the pythagorean theorem defines norms. Thus $\|\mathbf{A}\| = \sqrt{a_1^2 + a_2^2}$ and $\|\mathbf{B}\| = \sqrt{b_1^2 + b_2^2}$ (see Fig. 2-10). The distance between the vectors $\mathbf{A}$ and $\mathbf{B}$ is defined simply as the length of the line connecting them. Again, by the pythagorean theorem $D = \sqrt{(a_1 - b_1)^2 + (a_2 - b_2)^2}$. Since, from matrix algebra, $\mathbf{A} - \mathbf{B} = \begin{bmatrix} a_1 - b_1 \\ a_2 - b_2 \end{bmatrix}$, $\mathbf{D} = \|\mathbf{A} - \mathbf{B}\|$; the distance between

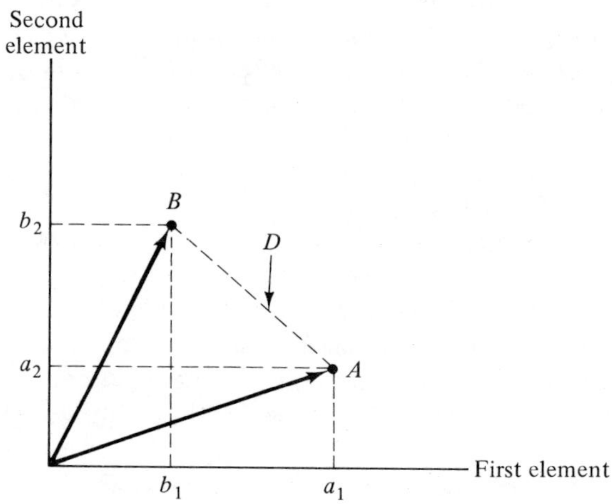

Figure 2-10 Vectors **A** and **B** in two-dimensional vector space.

the two points (vectors) is the norm (length) of their difference. This logic can be extended to higher-order vector space, i.e., to vectors that represent collections of three, four, etc., elements, although beyond three dimensions there is no geometry to support our intuition. The point is that, even when each vector represents the values of a large number of individual elements, it is representable as a single point (or a single line, if we connect the endpoint to the origin) in some space, and the distance between two such points is the length of the line connecting them.

Distance between collections of points Consider, next, matrices which may be thought of as collections of vectors. Given a $2 \times n$ matrix $\mathbf{A}$, that is, $\mathbf{A} = [A_1\ A_2 \cdots A_n]$, with $A_i = \begin{bmatrix} a_{1i} \\ a_{2i} \end{bmatrix}$, there are numerous possible definitions of the length or norm of the matrix $\mathbf{A}$. One of these is the largest of the $\| A_i \|$, that is, $\| \mathbf{A} \| = \max [\| A_1 \|, \ldots, \| A_n \|]$; in words, the "size" of a matrix is represented by the length of the longest of the column vectors of which it is made up. (The reader can easily visualize, for an $\mathbf{A}$ of size 2×3, say, the picture in two-dimensional vector space. Each column of $\mathbf{A}$ will be a vector in this space, and $\| \mathbf{A} \|$ is measured as the longest of these three lines.) Consider another $2 \times n$ matrix $\mathbf{B}$, whose n columns can also be represented in two-dimensional vector space. Then, in the same spirit, one could define the distance between *matrices* $\mathbf{A}$ and $\mathbf{B}$ as $\| \mathbf{A} - \mathbf{B} \| = \max [\| A_1 - B_1 \|, \ldots, \| A_n - B_n \|]$; in words, the distance between two matrices could be represented by the largest of the distances between corresponding columns.

Clearly many other definitions are possible, because the objects between which we want to measure a distance are collections of points. Functions also are collections of points, and taking a similar point of view, the norm of a continuous function $y_0(x)$, over some range $x_0 \le x \le x_1$, could be defined as the (absolute value of the) maximum value of the function over the range: $\| y_0(x) \| = \max_{x_0 \le x \le x_1} |y_0(x)|$. Note that this is actually the maximum distance between points along the x axis and the corresponding points along the function $y_0(x)$ (see Fig. 2-11*a*). In a similar way, the distance between two continuous functions over the same range would be the maximum distance between them; $\| y_0(x) - y(x) \| = \max_{x_0 \le x \le x_1} |y_0(x) - y(x)|$ (see Fig. 2-11*b*). By this measure, the distance between $y_0(x)$ and $y(x)$ will not exceed δ if the graph of y lies within a band of width 2δ (measured vertically) bordering y_0 (Fig. 2-12).

It is obvious that functions of many different shapes, continuous over $x_0 \le x \le x_1$, could fit within the δ band around $y_0(x)$ and thus be within a δ neighborhood of $y_0(x)$, as required in the definition of continuity of $I[y]$. To be able to utilize concepts parallel to the differential and the Taylor series in ordinary calculus requires continuity of the integral $I[y]$—in much the same way that the continuity of $f(x)$ was needed in order that the results of differential calculus could be expressed via derivatives in the Taylor series. The fact that a wide variety of differently shaped curves fall within the δ neighborhood of $y_0(x)$ in Fig. 2-12

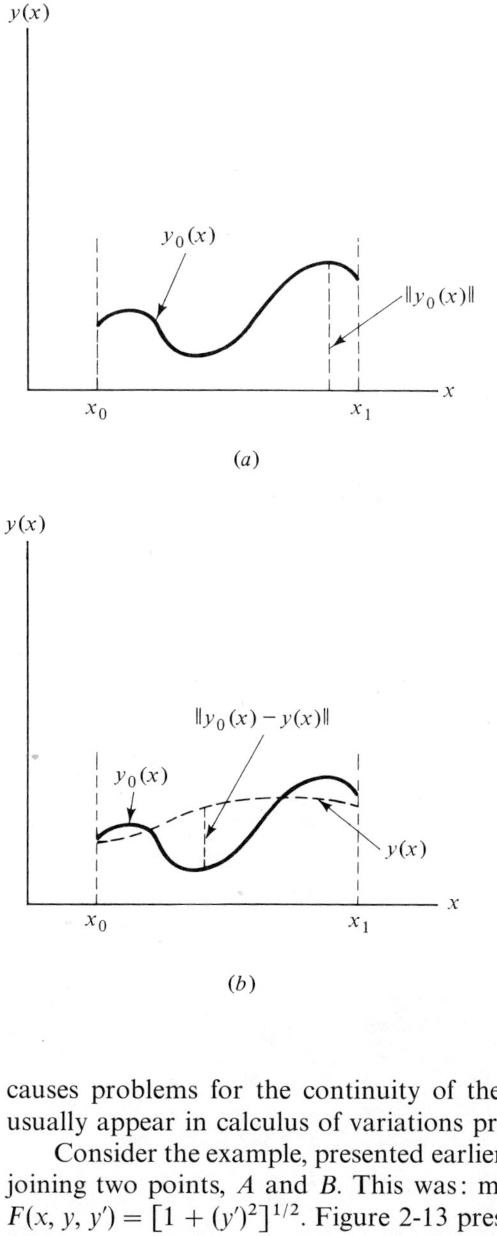

Figure 2-11 (*a*) The norm of $y_0(x)$. (*b*) The distance between $y_0(x)$ and $y(x)$.

causes problems for the continuity of the kinds of functionals (integrals) that usually appear in calculus of variations problems.

Consider the example, presented earlier, of finding the minimum length curve joining two points, A and B. This was: minimize $I[y] = \int_{x_0}^{x_1} F(x, y, y')\,dx$, where $F(x, y, y') = [1 + (y')^2]^{1/2}$. Figure 2-13 presents a function $y(x)$ which is within a δ band of $y_0(x)$ but which is much longer than $y_0(x)$; the problem, then, is that for a functional $I[y]$ such as that in the arc length problem, $|I[y] - I[y_0]|$ would not necessarily be less than ε even though $\| y_0(x) - y(x) \| < \delta$. That is, $I[y]$, the functional of interest, would not be continuous. What is needed to assure continuity, then, is a sharper measure of closeness of functions— one that would *not* define y in Fig. 2-13 as close to y_0.

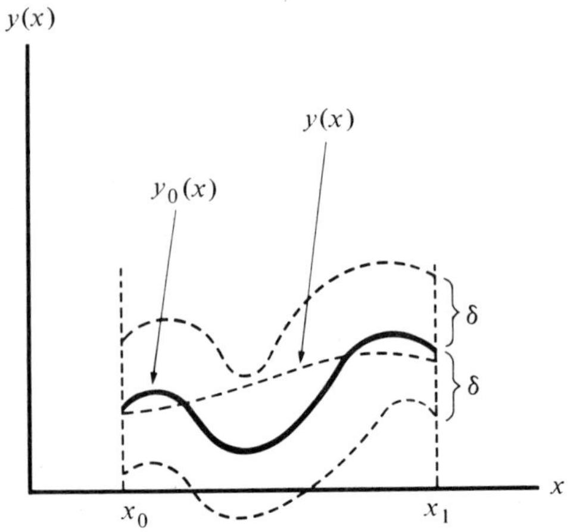

Figure 2-12 $\|y_0(x) - y(x)\| < \delta$.

An obvious difference between the two functions in Fig. 2-13 is in their derivatives. While $y_0'(x)$ appears to lie somewhere within the range between $+1$ and -1 over $x_0 \leq x \leq x_1$, the slope of $y(x)$ is at many places almost vertical [$y'(x)$ almost $+\infty$ or $-\infty$]. This suggests a second possible norm for functions, namely,

$$\max_{x_0 \leq x \leq x_1} |y(x)| + \max_{x_0 \leq x \leq x_1} |y'(x)|$$

In fact, for functions with higher-order derivatives (up to the nth, say) over the range of x, one can define norms involving sums of maxima of absolute values of the function and each of the derivatives from the first to the nth. With this in mind, we denote the particular norm that we are using by a subscript indicating the highest derivative involved; therefore what we originally had, with just $\max_{x_0 \leq x \leq x_1} |y(x)|$, would be denoted $\| y \|_0$, since no derivatives were involved.

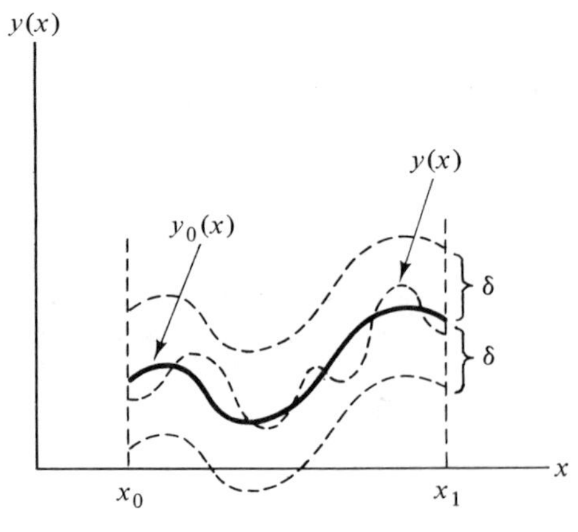

Figure 2-13 Another example of $\|y_0(x) - y(x)\| < \delta$.

In all cases, the maximum is found for x in the range $x_0 \le x \le x_1$:

$$\| y \|_0 = \max |y(x)|$$

$$\| y \|_1 = \max |y(x)| + \max |y'(x)|$$

$$\| y \|_2 = \max |y(x)| + \max |y'(x)| + \max |y''(x)|$$

$$\vdots$$

$$\| y \|_n = \max |y(x)| + \max |y'(x)| + \cdots + \max |y^{(n)}(x)|$$

Similarly, the distance between functions can be defined using any one of these norms. In particular,

$$\| y_0(x) - y(x) \|_1 = \max |y_0(x) - y(x)| + \max |y_0'(x) - y'(x)|$$

This is termed distance of order 1. Previously we were dealing with distance of order 0. Note that if we interpret distance between $y_0(x)$ and $y(x)$, in the definition of continuity, as being of order 1, then the $y(x)$ shown in Fig. 2-13 would be excluded and the problem of discontinuity of $I[y]$ in the arc length example would be removed.

Because y' enters explicitly and often importantly into the functional in a great many calculus of variations problems (of which the arc length problem was an example), it is generally useful to adopt the order-1 norm for distance between functions in order to be assured of the continuity of $I[y]$. That is, a δ neighborhood about $y_0(x)$ is defined as one for which

$$\| y_0(x) - y(x) \|_1 < \delta$$

which means, since $\max |y_0(x) - y(x)| + \max |y_0'(x) - y'(x)| < \delta$, that both

$$|y_0(x) - y(x)| < \delta \quad \text{and} \quad |y_0'(x) - y'(x)| < \delta$$

At each point in the range $x_0 \le x \le x_1$, both the value of $y(x)$ and its derivative cannot depart from the value of $y_0(x)$ and its derivative by more than δ. Geometrically, closeness of order 1 can be illustrated in three-dimensional x,y,y' space (so-called extended phase space). If $\| y_0(x) - y(x) \|_1 < \delta$, then $y(x)$ lies inside a tube of radius δ, centered on $y_0(x)$. In the x,y plane (perpendicular to the y' axis) $|y_0(x) - y(x)| < \delta$ and in the x,y' plane (perpendicular to the y axis) $|y_0'(x) - y'(x)| < \delta$. Figure 2-14 suggests the geometry in extended phase space.

The measure of closeness used distinguishes what are called weak and strong maxima and minima in the calculus of variations; this terminology differs from that for ordinary maximum and minimum problems, where weak and strong refer to the nature of the inequality used in describing the characteristics of the extreme point. Specifically:

Weak maximum If there is an $\varepsilon > 0$ such that for all $\| y_0(x) - y(x) \|_1 < \varepsilon$, $I[y_0] - I[y] \ge 0$, then y_0 provides a weak maximum to the functional I.

Strong maximum If there is an $\varepsilon > 0$ such that for all $\| y_0(x) - y(x) \|_0 < \varepsilon$, $I[y_0] - I[y] \ge 0$, then y_0 provides a strong maximum to the functional I.

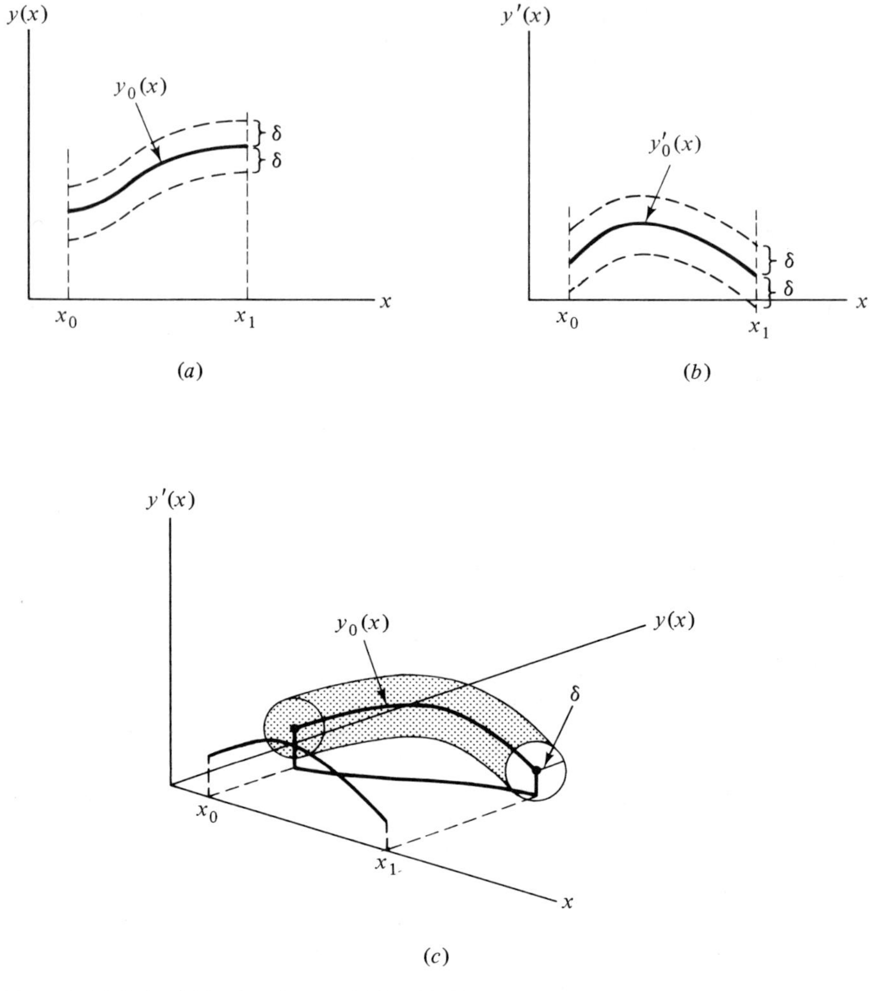

Figure 2-14 A δ neighborhood around (*a*) $y_0(x)$, (*b*) $y_0'(x)$, and (*c*) $y_0(x)$ in extended phase space.

The difference lies only in the definition of the neighborhood around $y_0(x)$, within which comparison curves are required to lie. In the weak case, $y_0(x)$ is compared with other functions $y(x)$ whose vertical distances from $y_0(x)$ are small and whose first derivatives are also close to that of $y_0(x)$; that is, $y_0(x)$ is compared with functions within a δ tube in x, y, y' space. For a strong maximum, the neighborhood about $y_0(x)$ admits for comparison all curves $y(x)$ whose vertical distances from $y_0(x)$ are small, without restriction on their slopes; that is, $y_0(x)$ is compared with functions within a δ band in x, y space. Thus to provide a strong maximum, $y_0(x)$ is compared with a larger number of nearby functions $y(x)$; it wins out over a larger number of contenders than in the weak case.

Weak and strong minima are defined analogously.

Weak minimum If there is an $\varepsilon > 0$ such that for all $\| y_0(x) - y(x) \|_1 < \varepsilon$, $I[y_0] - I[y] \leq 0$, then y_0 provides a weak minimum to the functional I.

Strong minimum If there is an $\varepsilon > 0$ such that for all $\| y_0(x) - y(x) \|_0 < \varepsilon$, $I[y_0] - I[y] \leq 0$, then y_0 provides a strong minimum to the functional I.

From the definitions of order-0 and order-1 distance, it is clear that all strong extrema are also weak extrema. The set of functions $y(x)$ over which $y_0(x)$ is judged best in the $\| y_0(x) - y(x) \|_0$ case (strong extremum) contains, as a subset, those functions $y(x)$ over which $y_0(x)$ is judged best in the $\| y_0(x) - y(x) \|_1$ case (weak extremum). Thus satisfaction of the criterion for a strong extremum assures that the criterion for a weak extremum has also been met. Generally, however, the reverse is not true; a weak extremum is not usually also a strong one.

In the next two sections of this chapter, we will be considering the simplest problem in the calculus of variations. Assume, for concreteness, that our aim is to find a function $y(x)$ that maximizes a functional I, defined as

$$I[y] = \int_{x_0}^{x_1} F(x, y, y')\, dx \tag{2-12}$$

where $y(x_0) = y_0$ and $y(x_1) = y_1$, i.e., where $y(x)$ goes through the points (x_0, y_0) and (x_1, y_1). We refer to this as the simplest problem because (1) I depends on a single function, $y(x)$, (2) in addition, only its first derivative, $y'(x)$, appears in I, (3) there is only one independent variable, x, (4) the limits of integration, x_0 and x_1, are fixed, and (5) the values of $y(x)$ at both x_0 and x_1 are specified. In later sections and in the next chapter, we will see how the relaxation of each of these conditions affects the fundamental necessary condition for a maximum of I.

Our derivations, not unexpectedly, will require differentiation and, less often, integration. These operations, in turn, assume certain properties about the functions on which they are performed; e.g., smoothness of a function at a point is necessary if its derivative is to be found at that point, as we have seen. In contrast to ordinary calculus, where we investigate the properties of one or more potentially optimal points (and therefore need derivatives at those points), we now are concerned with potentially optimal curves. This suggests that the properties, such as continuity, will be needed along the entire curve. In particular, we need to be specific about both the functions $F(x, y, y')$ and $y(x)$. We assume that F has continuous first and second partial derivatives with respect to x, y, and y' over the range $x_0 \leq x \leq x_1$. Furthermore, we assume that $y(x)$ is smooth over the same range of x [which means that $y'(x)$ exists at all points in that range]. We will later see that actually $y(x)$ need only be continuous, i.e., that it may have kinks, in which case it is often referred to as piecewise smooth. In that case, $y'(x)$ will only be piecewise continuous. We consider this possibility later when we introduce the so-called "corner conditions" for functions $y(x)$ that are nonsmooth curves. In the more modern approach to functional optimization (e.g., in the derivation of the maximum principle in Chap. 4), the continuity assumptions on

F and y can be somewhat relaxed. Whether or not the present restrictions on F and y are excessive depends entirely on the nature of the problem in which the variational calculus is being applied.

2-3 A NECESSARY CONDITION: APPROACH I

In order to avoid excessive subscripting in what follows, we denote the optimal (maximizing) curve by $y(x)$ and functions nearby, with which $y(x)$ is compared, by $z(x)$. One way to think of $z(x)$ is as a perturbation of $y(x)$ or, alternatively, as a *variation* of the function $y(x)$, denoted δy. [This is similar to Δx in ordinary calculus; however, the independent variable is often shown explicitly and the notation becomes $\delta y(x)$, which is not to be interpreted as δ times $y(x)$.] That is,

$$z(x) = y(x) + \delta y(x) \tag{2-13}$$

or $z(x) - y(x) = \delta y(x)$, which makes clear that the variation is just a measure of the (vertical) distance between $z(x)$ and $y(x)$ at any point x, $x_0 \leq x \leq x_1$ (see Fig. 2-15). Note that, for $z(x)$ near to $y(x)$ of order 1, $\delta y(x)$ represents an infinitesimal change in $y(x)$ and in its derivative $y'(x)$ for a particular value of x. In ordinary calculus problems we study the effect of an infinitesimal change in the independent variable x.

From Fig. 2-15, we see that the size of the variation is a function of x (which depends on where it is measured along the x axis). We could think of it as a function $\phi(x)$ multiplied by a small parameter, ε, that is,

$$\delta y(x) = \varepsilon\phi(x) \tag{2-14}$$

where $\phi(x_0) = 0$ and $\phi(x_1) = 0$. Figure 2-16 illustrates this, using δy from Fig. 2-15, for various ε. It appears that all we have gained is complexity, since we now write

$$z(x) = y(x) + \varepsilon\phi(x) \tag{2-15}$$

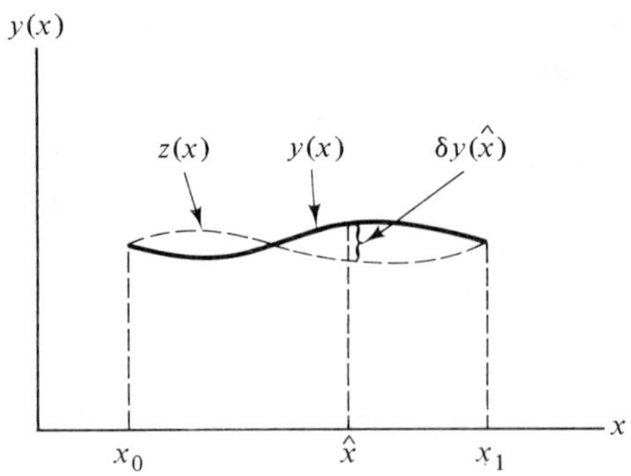

Figure 2-15 The variation $\delta y(x)$.

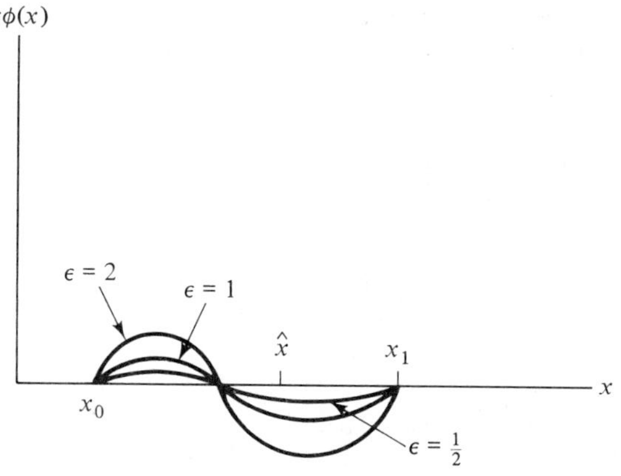

Figure 2-16 $\delta y(x) = \varepsilon\phi(x)$, for $\varepsilon = 2$, 1, and $\frac{1}{2}$.

Note, however, that as ε approaches zero, $z(x)$ approaches $y(x)$; i.e., $\lim_{\varepsilon\to 0} z(x) = y(x)$. If we express the value of I for a nearby function $z(x)$ in terms of (2-15), we have

$$I = \int_{x_0}^{x_1} F[x, y(x) + \varepsilon\phi(x), y'(x) + \varepsilon\phi'(x)]\, dx \tag{2-16}$$

which makes clear that, for any particular $\phi(x)$, I depends entirely on the size of ε. Since $y(x)$ is assumed to be the maximizing function, we also know that $dI/d\varepsilon$, evaluated at $\varepsilon = 0$, must be zero; that is,

$$\left.\frac{dI}{d\varepsilon}\right|_{\varepsilon=0} = 0 \tag{2-17}$$

This is completely analogous to the observation in ordinary maximization problems that, if x^* is the value of x that maximizes $y = f(x)$, $dy/dx\,|_{x=x^*} = 0$. Note, however, that the reasoning depends on the existence of the derivative $dI/d\varepsilon$.

In order to utilize (2-17), we need to recall two rules from differential calculus. The chain rule for functions of functions is: if $u = g(x)$, $v = h(x)$, and $f(x) = \phi(u, v)$, then $df(x)/dx = (\partial\phi/\partial u)(du/dx) + (\partial\phi/\partial v)(dv/dx)$. The rule for differentiating under an integral is: if $I(\varepsilon) = \int_{x_0}^{x_1} F(\varepsilon)\, dx$, then $dI/d\varepsilon = \int_{x_0}^{x_1} (dF/d\varepsilon)\, dx$. (This is parallel to the rule in ordinary calculus that the derivative of a sum is the sum of the derivatives.) From (2-16), let $y(x) + \varepsilon\phi(x) = \Phi(\varepsilon)$ and $y'(x) + \varepsilon\phi'(x) = \Phi'(\varepsilon)$, so that the problem is to find $dI/d\varepsilon$ for $I = \int_{x_0}^{x_1} F[x, \Phi(\varepsilon), \Phi'(\varepsilon)]\, dx$. Applying the rules on differentiation gives

$$\frac{dI}{d\varepsilon} = \int_{x_0}^{x_1} \left(\frac{\partial F}{\partial \Phi}\frac{d\Phi}{d\varepsilon} + \frac{\partial F}{\partial \Phi'}\frac{d\Phi'}{d\varepsilon}\right) dx \tag{2-18}$$

Since $d\Phi/d\varepsilon = \phi(x)$ and $d\Phi'/d\varepsilon = \phi'(x)$, (2-18) becomes

$$\frac{dI}{d\varepsilon} = \int_{x_0}^{x_1} \left[\frac{\partial F}{\partial \Phi}\phi(x) + \frac{\partial F}{\partial \Phi'}\phi'(x)\right] dx \tag{2-19}$$

The structure of the second term under the integral—one function times the derivative of another—suggests that it might be possible to simplify by the device of integration by parts.† Here, this gives

$$\int_{x_0}^{x_1} \left[\frac{\partial F}{\partial \Phi'} \phi'(x) \right] dx = \frac{\partial F}{\partial \Phi'} \phi(x) \Bigg]_{x_0}^{x_1} - \int_{x_0}^{x_1} \left[\frac{d}{dx} \frac{\partial F}{\partial \Phi'} \phi(x) \right] dx \tag{2-20}$$

The simplification comes from the fact that the varied curve, $z(x)$, must go through the two endpoints (x_0, y_0) and (x_1, y_1), so that $\phi(x_0) = 0$ and $\phi(x_1) = 0$. Therefore the first term on the right-hand side of (2-20) is zero. Thus, collecting the information in (2-19) and (2-20),

$$\frac{dI}{d\varepsilon} = \int_{x_0}^{x_1} \left(\frac{\partial F}{\partial \Phi} - \frac{d}{dx} \frac{\partial F}{\partial \Phi'} \right) \phi(x)\, dx \tag{2-21}$$

Our interest is in setting this derivative equal to zero, when it is evaluated at $\varepsilon = 0$. But when $\varepsilon = 0$, $\Phi(\varepsilon) = y(x)$ and $\Phi'(\varepsilon) = y'(x)$, so that (2-21) (when $\varepsilon = 0$) can be expressed in terms of the function $y(x)$ as

$$\left. \frac{dI}{d\varepsilon} \right|_{\varepsilon = 0} = \int_{x_0}^{x_1} \left(\frac{\partial F}{\partial y} - \frac{d}{dx} \frac{\partial F}{\partial y'} \right) \phi(x)\, dx \tag{2-22}$$

Notice that the integration by parts, used to simplify (2-19), allowed $\phi(x)$ to be factored out of the square brackets. Finally, then, we set $dI/d\varepsilon|_{\varepsilon=0}$ equal to zero:

$$\int_{x_0}^{x_1} \left(\frac{\partial F}{\partial y} - \frac{d}{dx} \frac{\partial F}{\partial y'} \right) \phi(x)\, dx = 0 \tag{2-23}$$

The function $\phi(x)$ in (2-23) is quite arbitrary, constrained only by the fact that it is continuous and by the size and type of neighborhood of $y(x)$ within which $z(x)$ is required to lie. In particular, $\phi(x)$ may be positive throughout the range $x_0 \leq x \leq x_1$, it may be negative over the same range, or it may be partly positive and partly negative (as in Fig. 2-16). It therefore seems intuitively plausible that for (2-23) to be zero for an arbitrary $\phi(x)$, the expression in parentheses must be zero. (This mathematical fact can be proven; it is sometimes known as the fundamental lemma of the calculus of variations.) Thus (2-23) means

$$\frac{\partial F}{\partial y} - \frac{d}{dx} \frac{\partial F}{\partial y'} = 0 \tag{2-24}$$

over $x_0 \leq x \leq x_1$, or, using standard notation for partial derivatives,

$$F_y - \frac{d}{dx} F_{y'} = 0 \tag{2-25}$$

† The rule is:

$$\int_{x_0}^{x_1} u(x)v'(x)\, dx = u(x)v(x) \Bigg]_{x_0}^{x_1} - \int_{x_0}^{x_1} u'(x)v(x)\, dx$$

There is a brief review of integral calculus in App. A.

This result is known as the Euler-Lagrange equation (or sometimes just the Euler equation); it constitutes a necessary condition which any maximizing function $y(x)$ must satisfy. It is also a necessary condition for a minimizing function, since the reasoning behind (2-17) holds for maxima or minima. A function $y(x)$ satisfying the Euler-Lagrange equation is called an *extremal.*

For the condition on $y(x)$ given in (2-24) or (2-25) to make sense, F_y and $F_{y'}$ must exist throughout the range $x_0 \leq x \leq x_1$. We have assumed this (and more) for F. In general, both of these functions will themselves depend on x, y, and y'. In fact, the term $(d/dx)F_{y'}$ requires the existence of the derivative of $F_{y'}$ with respect to x throughout $x_0 \leq x \leq x_1$. Note that this in turn presupposes the existence of $y'(x)$ over this range, since the derivative with respect to x of any terms in $F_{y'}$ that involve y' will lead to terms in which y'' is present.† Since we have also assumed that second partial derivatives of F are continuous, we can expand the second term in (2-25) using the chain rule. That is,

$$\frac{d}{dx}F_{y'} = \frac{\partial F_{y'}}{\partial y'}\frac{dy'}{dx} + \frac{\partial F_{y'}}{\partial y}\frac{dy}{dx} + \frac{\partial F_{y'}}{\partial x}\frac{dx}{dx}$$

or

$$\frac{d}{dx}F_{y'} = (F_{y'y'})(y'') + (F_{y'y})(y') + (F_{y'x}) \tag{2-26}$$

The Euler-Lagrange equation in (2-25) can therefore also be expressed as

$$(F_{y'y'})y'' + (F_{y'y})y' + (F_{y'x} - F_y) = 0 \tag{2-27}$$

Written out in this way, we see clearly that this necessary condition is a second-order differential equation for $y(x)$, generally nonlinear (depending on the terms $F_{y'y'}$ and $F_{y'y}$), to which the boundary conditions $y(x_0) = y_0$ and $y(x_1) = y_1$ apply. Not surprisingly, such equations are not, in general, easy to solve. The difficulties arise both from the nonlinearity (when it is present) and also from the fact that boundary values are given for $y(x)$ at both x_0 and x_1, as opposed to the usual situation for a second-order differential equation in which values for $y(x)$ and $y'(x)$ are specified at one end or the other (usually at x_0). (Appendix C reviews the usual solution procedures for, among others, second-order differential equations.)

For this reason (as well as because of the fact that the necessary conditions become much more complicated in more advanced problems) there are a number of so-called "direct methods" that attempt to approach the calculus of variations problem via discrete approximations.‡ The situation is not unlike that in nonlinear programming problems where the Kuhn-Tucker conditions, while clearly

† An alternative is available in cases where this requirement on $y'(x)$ is too severe; namely, integration of the first rather than the second term under the integral in (2-19). See, for example, Bolza [3, pp. 22–25].

‡ See, for example, Gelfand and Fomin [6, chap. 8] or Elsgolc [5, chap. 5]. Discrete approximations and discrete models are also the subject matter of App. D, to which the interested reader is referred.

characterizing the optimal solution, may not be easily solved, and therefore some kind of iterative gradient method may be used for an actual solution in a particular problem.†

2-4 A NECESSARY CONDITION: APPROACH II

Alternative Derivation of the Euler-Lagrange Equation

The derivation of the Euler-Lagrange equation in the preceding section was based on an analogy to the requirement that the first derivative be zero at a maximum or minimum point in ordinary calculus. Recall that this requirement—that the tangent to the function have zero slope—is actually embedded in an alternative view of the characteristics of extreme points, which is based on the Taylor series expansion of a function. We investigate the calculus of variations parallel to this view because of its greater generality; it provides, among other things, an approach toward sufficient conditions (to be examined in Chap. 3).

Again, considering $y(x)$ to be a maximizing curve and $z(x)$ a nearby curve, we know that

$$I[z] - I[y] \leq 0$$

or, defining $\Delta I = I[z] - I[y]$ as the increment of I or the total variation of I, the fact that $y(x)$ maximizes I means that

$$\Delta I \leq 0 \tag{2-28}$$

That is, ΔI must have the same sign (if it is not zero) for all $z(x)$ in some neighborhood of $y(x)$. More explicitly, since $I[z] = \int_{x_0}^{x_1} F(x, z, z')\, dx$, ΔI can be shown as $\int_{x_0}^{x_1} F(x, z, z')\, dx - \int_{x_0}^{x_1} F(x, y, y')\, dx$, that is,

$$\Delta I = \int_{x_0}^{x_1} [F(x, z, z') - F(x, y, y')]\, dx \tag{2-29}$$

Recall from Sec. 2-1, for a function of several variables, that the Taylor series (to a second-order approximation) gives the value of a function at a particular point in terms of values at some nearby point; namely, that

$$f(\mathbf{X}) = f(\mathbf{X}^*) + df(\mathbf{X}^*) + \tfrac{1}{2}d^2 f(\mathbf{X}^*)$$
$$= f(\mathbf{X}^*) + [\nabla \mathbf{f}(\mathbf{X}^*)]'[\mathbf{X} - \mathbf{X}^*] + \tfrac{1}{2}[\mathbf{X} - \mathbf{X}^*]'\mathbf{H}(\mathbf{X}^*)[\mathbf{X} - \mathbf{X}^*]$$

Here we are interested in $F(x, z, z')$ as given by $F(x, y, y')$ and its derivatives. That is,

$$F(x, z, z') = F(x, y, y') + [\nabla \mathbf{F}(y)]'[\mathbf{Z} - \mathbf{Y}] + \tfrac{1}{2}[\mathbf{Z} - \mathbf{Y}]'\mathbf{H}(y)[\mathbf{Z} - \mathbf{Y}]$$

or
$$F(x, z, z') = F(x, y, y') + F_y(z - y) + F_{y'}(z' - y')$$
$$+ \tfrac{1}{2}[F_{yy}(z - y)^2 + 2F_{yy'}(z - y)(z' - y') + F_{y'y'}(z' - y')^2] \tag{2-30}$$

† For a review of Kuhn-Tucker conditions and alternative approaches, see Miller [10, especially sec. 4.8 and chaps. 8 and 9].

where
$$\mathbf{\nabla F}(y) = \begin{bmatrix} \partial F/\partial y \\ \partial F/\partial y' \end{bmatrix} = \begin{bmatrix} F_y \\ F_{y'} \end{bmatrix}$$
$$[\mathbf{Z} - \mathbf{Y}] = \begin{bmatrix} z(x) - y(x) \\ z'(x) - y'(x) \end{bmatrix}$$
$$\mathbf{H}(y) = \begin{bmatrix} F_{yy} & F_{yy'} \\ F_{y'y} & F_{y'y'} \end{bmatrix}$$

In terms of our notation for the variation of $y(x)$, $z(x) - y(x) = \varepsilon\phi(x)$ and $z'(x) - y'(x) = \varepsilon\phi'(x)$. Substituting into (2-30) and moving $F(x, y, y')$ to the left-hand side:

$$F(x, z, z') - F(x, y, y') = (F_y)\varepsilon\phi(x) + (F_{y'})\varepsilon\phi'(x) + \tfrac{1}{2}\{(F_{yy})\varepsilon^2[\phi(x)]^2 + 2(F_{yy'})\varepsilon^2\phi(x)\phi'(x) + (F_{y'y'})\varepsilon^2[\phi'(x)]^2\} \tag{2-31}$$

Since this expression, $F(x, z, z') - F(x, y, y')$, appears under the integral in (2-29), we substitute and obtain the following expression for the total variation of I:

$$\Delta I = \varepsilon \int_{x_0}^{x_1} [F_y\phi(x) + F_{y'}\phi'(x)]\, dx + \varepsilon^2/2 \int_{x_0}^{x_1} \{F_{yy}[\phi(x)]^2 + 2F_{yy'}\phi(x)\phi'(x) + F_{y'y'}[\phi'(x)]^2\}\, dx \tag{2-32}$$

Using terminology similar to that for differentials, the first term in this total variation expression is called the first variation and is denoted δI. Similarly, the second term on the right-hand side of (2-32) is known as the second variation of the integral I and is denoted $\delta^2 I$. To a second-order approximation, then, $\Delta I = \delta I + \delta^2 I$; to a first-order approximation, $\Delta I = \delta I$ and therefore the requirement in (2-28) that $\Delta I \leq 0$ translates initially to the requirement that $\delta I \leq 0$, i.e., that

$$\delta I = \varepsilon \int_{x_0}^{x_1} [F_y\phi(x) + F_{y'}\phi'(x)]\, dx \leq 0 \tag{2-33}$$

Since ε is arbitrary, in terms of both magnitude and sign, (2-33) will hold if and only if

$$\int_{x_0}^{x_1} [F_y\phi(x) + F_{y'}\phi'(x)]\, dx = 0 \tag{2-34}$$

The steps now parallel those from (2-19) to (2-24). Integrating the second term under the integral sign by parts,

$$\int_{x_0}^{x_1} F_{y'}\phi'(x)\, dx = F_{y'}\phi(x)\Big]_{x_0}^{x_1} - \int_{x_0}^{x_1} \frac{d}{dx} F_{y'}\phi(x)\, dx$$

and, since $\phi(x_0) = \phi(x_1) = 0$, the first term on the right-hand side disappears so that (2-34) can be expressed as

$$\int_{x_0}^{x_1} \left(F_y - \frac{d}{dx} F_{y'} \right) \phi(x)\, dx = 0 \tag{2-35}$$

[Compare (2-23).] From the fundamental lemma, since $\phi(x)$ is arbitrary, except for its endpoints, (2-35) can only hold if

$$F_y - \frac{d}{dx} F_{y'} = 0 \tag{2-36}$$

exactly as we found before, in (2-24) or (2-25). However, as was suggested at the beginning of this section, this derivation of the Euler-Lagrange equation will allow us to investigate requirements similar to the sufficient conditions in ordinary calculus, since the $\delta^2 I$ term in ΔI allows us to look further into the sign of ΔI, much as the sign of the hessian matrix at a point $\mathbf{X}^*$, where $\nabla f(\mathbf{X}^*) = \mathbf{0}$, generally establishes the sign of $f(\mathbf{X}) - f(\mathbf{X}^*)$.

Example I: Shortest Distance between Points in a Plane

We consider further the example of the shortest distance between two points A (x_0, y_0) and B (x_1, y_1) in a plane. (Here, of course, we are looking for a *minimizing* function.) Recall that the particular functional form was given in (2-5) as:

$$\text{Minimize} \quad L = \int_{x_0}^{x_1} \sqrt{1 + (y')^2}\, dx$$

that is, $F(x, y, y') = \sqrt{1 + (y')^2}$ in this case. Moving directly to the Euler-Lagrange equation, we need F_y and $F_{y'}$; here $F_y = 0$ and $F_{y'} = y'/\sqrt{1 + (y')^2}$. Thus, using (2-36),

$$-\frac{d}{dx} \frac{y'}{\sqrt{1 + (y')^2}} = 0 \tag{2-37}$$

and integrating both sides gives

$$\frac{y'}{\sqrt{1 + (y')^2}} = k \tag{2-38}$$

where k is a constant. But if (2-38) is to hold, it must be true that y' itself is a constant.† Thus the curve $y(x)$ satisfying the Euler-Lagrange equation is one whose slope is constant; that is, $y(x)$ is a straight line. Since we require the function to go through the endpoints (x_0, y_0) and (x_1, y_1), we have satisfied ourselves that a straight line connecting two points in a plane is the shortest distance between them. (Clearly in this case we have minimized L and not maximized it, since given any A and B and the straight line between them it is always possible to draw

† Straightforward algebra leads to $(y')^2 = k^2/(1 - k^2)$.

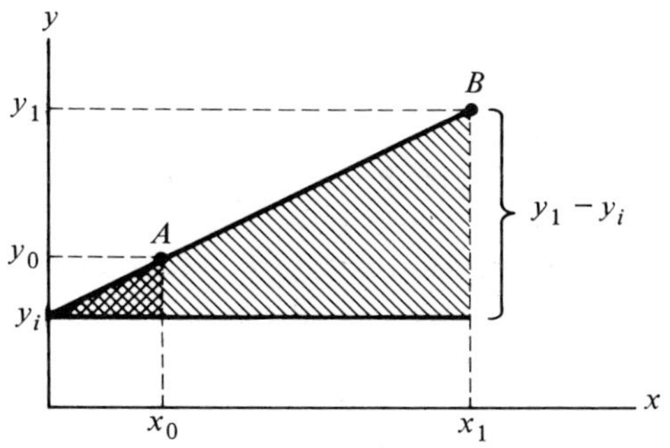

Figure 2-17 The curve of shortest length connecting A and B.

curves between A and B that are longer; hence the straight line is not the curve of maximum length.)

To see exactly how the endpoint information defines the unique straight line connecting A and B, let k_1 denote the constant value of $y'(x)$. That is, since $y'(x) = k_1$, integrating both sides gives $y(x) = k_1 x + k_2$. But at x_0, $y(x_0) = y_0$ and at x_1, $y(x_1) = y_1$, which means

$$k_1 x_0 + k_2 = y_0$$

$$k_1 x_1 + k_2 = y_1$$

This is a pair of linear equations in k_1 and k_2, since x_0, y_0, x_1, and y_1 are given. We use Cramer's rule, assuming that $\begin{vmatrix} x_0 & 1 \\ x_1 & 1 \end{vmatrix} \neq 0$; this will hold as long as $x_0 \neq x_1$, which means that the points A and B are not on the same vertical line. Then

$$k_1 = \frac{\begin{vmatrix} y_0 & 1 \\ y_1 & 1 \end{vmatrix}}{x_0 - x_1} = \frac{y_0 - y_1}{x_0 - x_1}$$

which is just the slope of $y(x)$. (See Fig. 2-17; both numerator and denominator are negative in this example, and hence the slope is still positive.)

In addition,

$$k_2 = \frac{\begin{vmatrix} x_0 & y_0 \\ x_1 & y_1 \end{vmatrix}}{x_0 - x_1} = \frac{x_0 y_1 - y_0 x_1}{x_0 - x_1}$$

It can be shown that k_2 is exactly y_i, the intercept on the y axis of the line through A and B. It is an elementary property of similar triangles that corresponding sides are proportional. Considering the large shaded triangle and the smaller (similar) cross-hatched one, $x_1/(y_1 - y_i) = x_0/(y_0 - y_i)$ or $x_1(y_0 - y_i) = x_0(y_1 - y_i)$, and straightforward rearrangement gives $y_i = (x_0 y_1 - y_0 x_1)/(x_0 - x_1)$, which is just k_2. Thus the Euler-Lagrange equation specifies the general characteristics of the minimizing function (here a straight line) and then introduction of the endpoint information defines the constants that have appeared through integration [here to identify that particular straight line which passes through (x_0, y_0) and (x_1, y_1)].

Example II: Monopolistic Pricing over Time†

This example will also illustrate exactly how the endpoint information is used in conjunction with the results that emerge from the specifics of the Euler-Lagrange necessary condition. Consider a monopolist producing each week to meet a weekly demand that depends on the price that is set and also on buyers' views on the future price of the product. This speculative element on the future course of the product's price is incorporated into the demand function via the rate of change of price with respect to time. Specifically, assume that the amount demanded at any time, $z(t)$, is the following function of price and its rate of change:

$$z(t) = -p + 100\frac{dp}{dt} + 100 \tag{2-39}$$

For illustration, we also assume that the monopolist's weekly production costs are the following specific function of the amount produced each week:

$$c(z) = (\tfrac{1}{2})z^2 + 2z + 40 \tag{2-40}$$

Thus the profits (revenue less cost) at any time t are

$$\pi(p, p', t) = z(t)p(t) - c(z) \tag{2-41}$$

Over a planning horizon from an initial point, t_0, to some terminal point, t_1, an objective that the monopolist might have would be to select a set of prices—a time path of $p(t)$ over the interval from t_0 to t_1—so as to maximize the total profits over that period, namely, so as to maximize $\int_{t_0}^{t_1} \pi(p, p', t)\, dt$. Suppose, finally, that at the beginning of the planning interval, when $t_0 = 0$, the price is set at 70 [that is, $p(t_0) = p_0 = 70$] and that the monopolist wants the price to be adjusted to 100 after 52 weeks [that is, $t_1 = 52$ and $p(t_1) = p_1 = 100$]. Substitution of (2-39) into (2-40) expresses costs as a function of $p(t)$ and $p'(t)$, and then substituting this and (2-39) into (2-41) expresses π as a function of $p(t)$ and $p'(t)$ only; namely,

$$\pi(t) = -\tfrac{3}{2}p^2 + 202p - 5000(p')^2 - 10{,}200p' + 200pp' - 5240 \tag{2-42}$$

Thus the monopolist's problem has the form: choose $p(t)$ so as to

$$\text{Maximize} \int_{t_0}^{t_1} F(p, p')\, dt \tag{2-43}$$

where $\qquad t_0 = 0, \; p(t_0) = 70 \quad \text{and} \quad t_1 = 52, \; p(t_1) = 100$

This is in the form of (2-7), with the unknown function $x(t)$, here denoted by $p(t)$, and with t not explicitly present in the integrand. Here, then, $F_p = -3p + 202 + 200p'$, $F_{p'} = -10{,}000p' - 10{,}200 + 200p$, and $(d/dt)F_{p'} = -10{,}000p'' + 200p'$, so that the Euler-Lagrange equation, (2-36), becomes

$$10{,}000p'' - 3p = -202 \tag{2-44}$$

This is a second-order, linear, nonhomogeneous differential equation in $p(t)$.

† An early version of this kind of problem is given in Allen [1, sec. 20.7].

Using straightforward procedures (App. C, Sec. C-4), the solution to the homogeneous part of (2-44) is

$$p(t) = k_1\, e^{0.0173t} + k_2\, e^{-0.0173t}$$

Trying $p(t) = k_3$ (a constant) for the nonhomogeneous solution to (2-44) gives $k_3 = 67.333$, and the general solution is thus

$$p(t) = k_1\, e^{0.0173t} + k_2\, e^{-0.0173t} + 67.333 \tag{2-45}$$

At this point the endpoint information is utilized. At $t_0 = 0$, $p_0 = 70$, and at $t_1 = 52$, $p_1 = 100$; these lead, respectively, to

$$k_1 + \quad k_2 = 2.667$$

$$2.459k_1 + 0.407k_2 = 32.667$$

which has the unique solution $k_1 = 15.391$ and $k_2 = -12.724$. Thus the complete solution to the monopolist's problem is that prices should be set over the next 52 weeks according to the function

$$p(t) = 15.391\, e^{0.0173t} - 12.724\, e^{-0.0173t} + 67.333 \tag{2-46}$$

For example, during the twentieth week, the price should be roughly 80; by the fiftieth week, the price should be 98.53. For future reference, substitution of (2-46) and the expression derived from it for $p'(t)$ into (2-42) and evaluating the profit integral from $t_0 = 0$ to $t_1 = 52$ gives a total profit of roughly 170,000.

The following example illustrates the fact that optimal pricing behavior for the monopolist need not always be as straightforward as it was in the previous case. Using the same production and demand conditions—as given in (2-39) through (2-41)—suppose that the price at the beginning of the period is 10 and that the monopolist wishes to see it doubled at the end of a year. The problem is then: choose $p(t)$ so as to

$$\text{Maximize} \int_{t_0}^{t_1} F(p, p')\, dt$$

where $\quad t_0 = 0,\ p(t_0) = 10 \quad \text{and} \quad t_1 = 52,\ p(t_1) = 20$

Clearly the Euler-Lagrange equations will be the same as in the previous example, giving (2-44) and hence

$$p(t) = k_1\, e^{0.0173t} + k_2\, e^{-0.0173t} + 67.333$$

as before, in (2-45). However, the endpoint information on $p(t)$ at t_0 and t_1 now gives

$$k_1 + \quad k_2 = -57.333$$

$$2.459k_1 + 0.407k_2 = -47.333$$

leading to $k_1 = -11.695$ and $k_2 = -45.638$. Therefore the solution is

$$p(t) = -11.695\, e^{0.0173t} - 45.638\, e^{-0.0173t} + 67.333 \tag{2-47}$$

Examining this function for maxima and/or minima shows that it has a single maximum at a value of t between 39 and 40, and that the maximum value is more than 21. Thus the monopolist's optimum pricing behavior is, starting at 10, to increase the price to more than 20 by midyear (week 27) and keep it above 20 until the final week. Table 2-1 illustrates this. Here, substitution of $p(t)$ from (2-47) and the expression for $p'(t)$ derived from it into the objective functional

Table 2-1 Selected values for $p(t)$

t	$p(t)$
0	10
10	15.04
20	18.51
26	19.89
27	20.07
30	20.52
40	21.12
50	20.34
52	20

and evaluating between $t_0 = 0$ and $t_1 = 52$ gives a total profit of approximately $-201{,}500$. Thus, given the profit function facing the monopolist, even optimal pricing policy fails to return a positive profit when $p(t_0) = 10$ and $p(t_1) = 20$.

2-5 EXTENSIONS OF THE BASIC PROBLEM

In ordinary calculus, an understanding of the first-order maximum and minimum conditions for $y = f(x)$ is generally followed by an extension of the problem to several variables—$y = f(\mathbf{X})$; this is an increase in the dimensionality of the function. Following this, constraints, first equations, and then also inequalities are added to the problem. In the present calculus of variations, we leave consideration of constraints until the next chapter. It should be clear that there are several ways in which the dimensionality of the functional $I = \int_{x_0}^{x_1} F(x, y, y')\,dx$ can be extended. That which seems most parallel to the ordinary calculus case would be when I depends on several functions $y_i(x), i = 1, \ldots, n$. Alternatively, or in conjunction with this, I may depend on higher-order derivatives, beyond just the first. Finally, there may be more than one independent variable upon which the function or functions depend. We briefly examine these extensions in turn; in the case of several $y_i(x)$, the change in the Euler-Lagrange equation (or equations) is fairly straightforward and a complete derivation is unnecessary, since it would parallel to a great extent that already used for the simplest case. The other two extensions require some additional explanation. We also examine the case in which the upper limit of integration is infinite.

Several Independent Functions and Their First Derivatives

If the integral of interest depends on the characteristics of several curves over the interval, we would have

$$I = \int_{x_0}^{x_1} F(x, y_1, \ldots, y_n, y'_1, \ldots, y'_n)\, dx \tag{2-48}$$

where $y_i(x_0) = y_{i0}$ and $y_i(x_1) = y_{i1}, i = 1, \ldots, n$; i.e., initial values and terminal values are specified for each of the individual functions. Let $\mathbf{Y} = [y_1, \ldots, y_n]'$, remembering that this is a vector of *functions* $y_1(x), \ldots, y_n(x)$ and not of variables. Also, we utilize the centered-dot notation for the derivative with respect to the independent variable; this is standard when the independent variable is "time" but can be used generally as long as there is no confusion. This is useful here in order to avoid confusion with the transposition operation in matrix algebra. Thus $\dot{\mathbf{Y}} = [y'_1, \ldots, y'_n]'$. Continuing with a maximization example, the problem is then to:

$$\text{Maximize} \quad I[\mathbf{Y}] = \int_{x_0}^{x_1} F(x, \mathbf{Y}, \dot{\mathbf{Y}})\, dx$$

where $\quad \mathbf{Y}(x_0) = \mathbf{Y}_0 \quad \text{and} \quad \mathbf{Y}(x_1) = \mathbf{Y}_1 \quad$ (2-49)

[Compare (2-6), for the case of one function only.]

Not surprisingly, an argument parallel to that in Secs. 2-3 or 2-4 shows that a necessary condition for a maximum is that each of the $y_i(x)$ satisfy an Euler-Lagrange equation:

$$\frac{\partial F}{\partial y_i} - \frac{d}{dx}\frac{\partial F}{\partial \dot{y}_i} = 0 \quad i = 1, \ldots, n \tag{2-50}$$

[Compare (2-24), (2-25), or (2-36) for the earlier case.] The derivation depends on the argument that we can examine the effect on the functional of a variation in any one of the y_i (and consequently in $\dot{y}_i$), while all other *functions* (y's) are unchanged. This is parallel to the development of the requirement in ordinary calculus for $f(x_1, \ldots, x_n)$ that $\partial f/\partial x_i = 0$ $(i = 1, \ldots, n)$. That argument considers the effect on f of a small change in any one of the x_i, all other *variables* (x's) remaining unchanged. In vector terms, where, for example, $\partial \mathbf{F}/\partial \mathbf{Y}$ $(= \mathbf{F}_{\mathbf{Y}}) = [\partial F/\partial y_1, \ldots, \partial F/\partial y_n]'$,

$$\frac{\partial \mathbf{F}}{\partial \mathbf{Y}} - \frac{d}{dx}\frac{\partial \mathbf{F}}{\partial \dot{\mathbf{Y}}} = \mathbf{0} \quad \text{or} \quad \mathbf{F}_{\mathbf{Y}} - \frac{d}{dx}\mathbf{F}_{\dot{\mathbf{Y}}} = \mathbf{0} \tag{2-51}$$

Using further matrix notation, namely,

$$\mathbf{F}_{\dot{\mathbf{Y}}\dot{\mathbf{Y}}} = \begin{bmatrix} F_{\dot{y}_1\dot{y}_1} & \cdots & F_{\dot{y}_1\dot{y}_n} \\ \cdots & \cdots & \cdots \\ F_{\dot{y}_n\dot{y}_1} & \cdots & F_{\dot{y}_n\dot{y}_n} \end{bmatrix} \qquad \mathbf{F}_{\dot{\mathbf{Y}}\mathbf{Y}} = \begin{bmatrix} F_{\dot{y}_1 y_1} & \cdots & F_{\dot{y}_1 y_n} \\ \cdots & \cdots & \cdots \\ F_{\dot{y}_n y_1} & \cdots & F_{\dot{y}_n y_n} \end{bmatrix}$$

$$\mathbf{F}_{\dot{\mathbf{Y}}\mathbf{x}} = [F_{\dot{y}_1 x}, \ldots, F_{\dot{y}_n x}]' \qquad \ddot{\mathbf{Y}} = [\ddot{y}_1, \ldots, \ddot{y}_n]'$$

the d/dx terms can be written out in full [compare (2-27)]:

$$[\mathbf{F}_{\dot{\mathbf{Y}}\dot{\mathbf{Y}}}][\ddot{\mathbf{Y}}] + [\mathbf{F}_{\dot{\mathbf{Y}}\mathbf{Y}}][\dot{\mathbf{Y}}] + [\mathbf{F}_{\dot{\mathbf{Y}}\mathbf{x}} - \mathbf{F}_{\mathbf{Y}}] = \mathbf{0} \tag{2-52}$$

These constitute a set of n second-order (generally nonlinear) differential equations with the $2n$ boundary conditions $\mathbf{Y}(x_0) = \mathbf{Y}_0$ and $\mathbf{Y}(x_1) = \mathbf{Y}_1$. In general, exact analytic solutions to these equations will not be easy to obtain, and numerical approximations are useful.

Higher-Order Derivatives

For simplicity, we return to the case of only one independent function, $y(x)$, but now imagine that the first n derivatives with respect to x—$y'(x), y''(x), \ldots, y^{(n)}(x)$—exist over $x_0 \leq x \leq x_1$ and enter explicitly into the integrand, i.e., we now have

$$I[y] = \int_{x_0}^{x_1} F(x, y, y', y'', \ldots, y^{(n)})\, dx \tag{2-53}$$

One might think that this problem could be recast in the form of (2-48), letting $y_1 = y$, $y_2 = y'$, $y_3 = y''$, ..., $y_n = y^{(n-1)}$, and $y'_1 = \cdots = y'_{n-1} = 0$ while $y'_n = y^{(n)}$. The problem is that the derivation of (2-50) or (2-51) depends upon our ability to vary one y_i (and its first derivative, y'_i) at a time, the others remaining fixed. This is clearly not possible when y_{i+1} represents the function which is the derivative (with respect to x) of y_i. However, the endpoint conditions for the integral in (2-53) *are* similar to those for (2-48). Since all n derivatives of $y(x)$ exist over the range of x, then at least the first through $(n-1)$th of them will be functions of x. Hence, parallel to the conditions on $y_i(x_0)$ and $y_i(x_1)$ for the integral in (2-48), values at x_0 and x_1 need to be specified for $y(x)$ and the first through $(n-1)$th derivatives. That is,

1. At x_0: $y(x_0) = y_0$, $y'(x_0) = y'_0, \ldots, y^{(n-1)}(x_0) = y_0^{(n-1)}$.
2. At x_1: $y(x_1) = y_1$, $y'(x_1) = y'_1, \ldots, y^{(n-1)}(x_1) = y_1^{(n-1)}$.

The expression for the first variation of the integral in (2-53) is accordingly changed (since now F depends on $y, y', y'', \ldots, y^{(n)}$) to

$$\delta I = \varepsilon \int_{x_0}^{x_1} [F_y \phi(x) + F_{y'} \phi'(x) + F_{y''} \phi''(x) + \cdots + F_{y^{(n)}} \phi^{(n)}(x)]\, dx$$

Again, for $\delta I \leq 0$, with ε arbitrary, the expression under the integral must be zero. Repeated application of the operation of integration by parts, to remove derivatives of $\phi(x)$, and incorporation of the endpoint conditions on the values of the function $y(x)$ *and* its first through $(n-1)$th derivatives, will generate the requirement that†

$$F_y - \frac{d}{dx} F_{y'} + \frac{d^2}{dx^2} F_{y''} - \cdots (-1)^n \frac{d^n}{dx^n} F_{y^{(n)}} = 0 \tag{2-54}$$

† The interested reader might work through the derivation for the case of $I[y] = \int_{x_0}^{x_1} F(x, y, y', y'')\, dx$ to see, for example, why the signs change as they do in (2-54).

This is sometimes termed the Euler-Poisson equation. Recall that the Euler-Lagrange equation in the simplest case—$F_y - (d/dx)F_{y'} = 0$—became a second-order (usually nonlinear) differential equation in $y(x)$ when the second term was expanded. Similarly with (2-54); it becomes a (generally nonlinear) differential equation of order $2n$ if the $(d/dx), (d^2/dx^2), \ldots, (d^n/dx^n)$ terms are expanded. This explains the need for the initial and terminal values of y through $y^{(n-1)}$.

Several Independent Variables

Finally, we may have the case in which the function y depends on more than one variable; e.g., a curve $y(x_1, x_2)$ connecting two points in three-dimensional space as opposed to two points in a plane. (See Fig. 2-18, where we use x_{10} for the initial value of variable x_1, x_{21} for the terminal value of variable x_2, etc.) Since there are two independent variables, we will have a double integral and parallel to y' we will have partial derivatives of y with respect to x_1 and to x_2. Thus

$$I[y] = \int_{x_{10}}^{x_{11}} \int_{x_{20}}^{x_{21}} F\left(x_1, x_2, y, \frac{\partial y}{\partial x_1}, \frac{\partial y}{\partial x_2}\right) dx_1\, dx_2 \tag{2-55}$$

with the endpoint conditions that $y(x_{10}, x_{20}) = y_0$ and $y(x_{11}, x_{21}) = y_1$; i.e., that $y(x_1, x_2)$ go through A and B. The first-order equation is a logical modification of $F_y - (d/dx)F_{y'} = 0$, from before. Using $y_{x_1} \equiv \partial y/\partial x_1$ and $y_{x_2} \equiv \partial y/\partial x_2$ (previously we had $y' \equiv dy/dx$) and also $F_{y_{x_1}} \equiv \partial F/\partial y_{x_1}$ and $F_{y_{x_2}} \equiv \partial F/\partial y_{x_2}$ (previously we had $F_{y'} \equiv \partial F/\partial y'$), the analogous requirement for the integral in (2-55) is

$$F_y - \frac{\partial}{\partial x_1} F_{y_{x_1}} - \frac{\partial}{\partial x_2} F_{y_{x_2}} = 0 \tag{2-56}$$

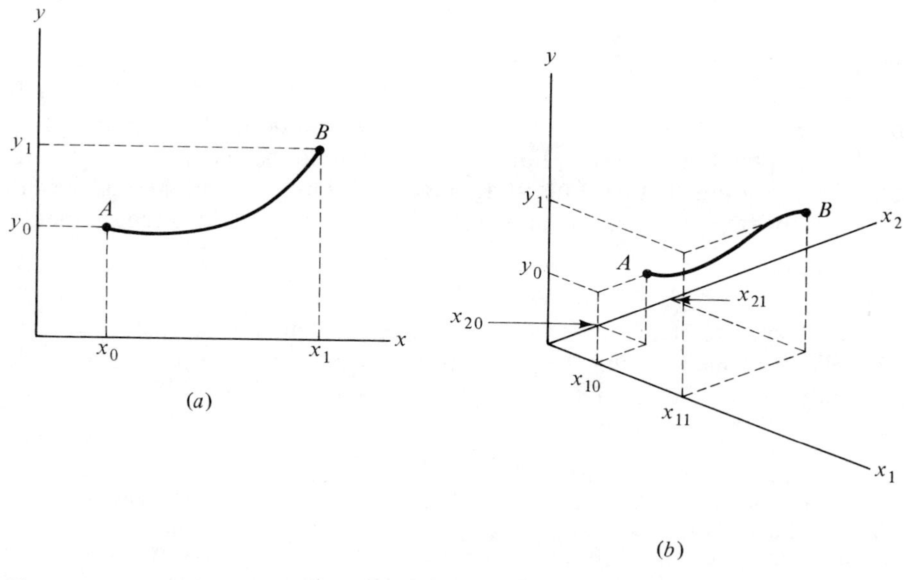

Figure 2-18 A calculus of variations problem in (*a*) two dimensions and (*b*) three dimensions.

Thus the $(-d/dx)F_{y'}$ term from the simplest case has been expanded to account for the fact that y is a function of both x_1 and x_2 and that the integrand F consequently depends on both variables. Here, then, the Euler-Lagrange equation is a second-order *partial* differential equation (because it involves partial derivatives), for which solutions are even more difficult than in the case of ordinary differential equations.

Upper Limit of Integration at Infinity

When $x_1 = +\infty$, i.e., when the functional for the simplest problem, given in (2-12), is changed to

$$I[y] = \int_{x_0}^{\infty} F(x, y, y')\, dx \tag{2-57}$$

some fundamental difficulties may arise. There is a question of the boundedness of the integral; for a maximization problem, one needs to know or be able to establish that in fact the integral is bounded from above. (For a minimization problem it must be bounded from below.) Additionally, the question of the existence of an optimal $y(x)$ can be difficult to establish when the integral is an improper one. However, assuming proper boundedness and existence, we can see that (2-34), which will now read

$$\int_{x_0}^{\infty} [F_y\phi(x) + F_{y'}\phi'(x)]\, dx = 0 \tag{2-58}$$

leads to [compare (2-35)]

$$\int_{x_0}^{\infty} \left(F_y - \frac{d}{dx}F_{y'}\right)\phi(x)\, dx + \lim_{x\to\infty} F_{y'}\phi(x) = 0 \tag{2-59}$$

since $\phi(x_0) = 0$ as before. Although the argument is more involved than that used to derive the Euler-Lagrange equation in either Approach I or Approach II, above, the Euler-Lagrange necessary condition can be derived independently of whether the upper limit of integration is finite or infinite.† The important outcome of this observation is that the Euler-Lagrange equation must still hold in the case of the improper integral in (2-57), and hence, from (2-59), the added requirement is

$$\lim_{x\to\infty} F_{y'}\phi(x) = 0 \tag{2-60}$$

If it is specified that $\lim_{x\to\infty} y(x) = y_1$, then of course $\lim_{x\to\infty} \phi(x) = 0$ and (2-60) will be satisfied, provided $F_{y'}$ is bounded. However, when there is no upper limit condition on $y(x)$, then satisfaction of (2-60) requires

$$\lim_{x\to\infty} F_{y'} = 0 \tag{2-61}$$

† This is not the classical derivation, as reflected in Approaches I and II. The interested reader can find a derivation in Hadley and Kemp [7, pp. 29–37]. When the upper limit of integration is infinite, as in (2-57), derivation of (2-58) and hence the subsequent analysis requires uniform convergence of the integrals involved. Again, see Hadley and Kemp [7, pp. 37–39].

PROBLEMS

2-1 Is each of the following functions continuous over the range indicated?

(*a*) $y = 2x^2 + 6x - 2$ over $0 \le x \le 10$

(*b*) $y = x^2/(x - 1)$ over $0 \le x \le 10$

(*c*) $y = x^2/(x - 1)$ over $10 \le x \le 100$

(*d*) $y = \sin x$ over $0 \le x \le 2\pi$

(*e*) $y = 4 - x$ for $x \le 2$ and $y = x$ for $x \ge 2$, over $0 \le x \le 10$

2-2 Find the Euler-Lagrange equation for each of the following calculus of variations problems:

(*a*) Maximize $I[y] = \int_{x_0}^{x_1} [7xy - (y')^2]\, dx$

(*b*) Maximize $I[y] = \int_{x_0}^{x_1} (x^2 - 2xy)\, dx$

(*c*) Minimize $I[y] = \int_{x_0}^{x_1} [x^2 - 2x(y')^2]\, dx$

(*d*) Maximize/minimize $I[y] = \int_{x_0}^{x_1} [(y')^2 + x^3 y]\, dx$

2-3 Find the Euler-Lagrange equations for calculus of variations problems whose integrals have each of the following integrands:

(*a*) $F(x, y_1, y_2, y_1', y_2') = (y_1')^2 + y_2 + y_1' y_2'$

(*b*) $F(x, y_1, y_2, y_1', y_2') = 2y_1' + y_1' y_2' + 2y_2' + y_1 y_2 + xy_1 + xy_2$

(*c*) $F(x, y_1, y_2, y_3, y_1', y_2', y_3') = xy_1 y_2 y_3 + 3y_1' + 2xy_2' + (y_3')^2$

(*d*) $F(x_1, x_2, y, \partial y/\partial x_1, \partial y/\partial x_2) = x_1 y^2 + x_2 y^2 + x_1(\partial y/\partial x_1) + x_1(\partial y/\partial x_2) +$
$x_2(\partial y/\partial x_1) + x_2(\partial y/\partial x_2)$

2-4 Examine the extremals in each of the following problems:

(*a*) Prob. 2-2(*a*), with $x_0 = 0$, $x_1 = 1$, $y(x_0) = 0$, and $y(x_1) = 5$

(*b*) The same problem as in (*a*), above, but with $x_0 = 1$, $x_1 = 10$, $y(x_0) = 0$, and $y(x_1) = 5$

(*c*) The same problem as in (*a*), above, with $x_0 = 0$, $x_1 = 1$, $y(x_0) = 0$, but with $y(x_1) = 500$

REFERENCES

1. Allen, R. G. D.: "Mathematical Analysis for Economists," Macmillan, London, 1938. A classic exposition of the most essential mathematical concepts in differential and integral calculus and their applications, especially in maxima and minima. Calculus of variations basics are introduced in chap. XX.
2. Bliss, G. A.: "Lectures on the Calculus of Variations," Phoenix Science Series, University of Chicago Press, Chicago, 1961 (paperback edition of the original 1946 book). A "modern classic" exposition of the mathematical basics of the calculus of variations and an historical overview of developments in the field. Extremely thorough; advanced level of mathematical difficulty.
3. Bolza, O.: "Lectures on the Calculus of Variations," University of Chicago Press, Chicago, 1904. A classic treatise on the mathematics of the calculus of variations. Generally advanced level of mathematical difficulty.
4. Chakravarty, S.: "Capital and Development Planning," MIT Press, Cambridge, Mass., 1969. Appendix A (secs. A.1 through A.9) contains a very readable account of the basics of the calculus of variations. Section 3.3 is a brief summary of fundamentals.
5. Elsgolc, L. E.: "Calculus of Variations," Addison-Wesley, Reading, Mass., 1962. A very readable and complete text covering the history of work on the classical calculus of variations problems, the mathematical details of the technique, and (in chap. 5) a discussion of direct methods for solving variational problems.

6. Gelfand, I. M., and S. V. Fomin: "Calculus of Variations," Prentice-Hall, Englewood Cliffs, N.J., 1963. A thorough exposition of the mathematics of the calculus of variations. Chapters 1 to 3 are at a moderate level of mathematical difficulty; later chapters require more advanced mathematics. Chapter 8 discusses direct methods for solution of calculus of variations problems.
7. Hadley, G., and M. C. Kemp: "Variational Methods in Economics," American Elsevier, New York, 1971. A very complete and mathematically advanced discussion of calculus of variations and maximum principle techniques and their use in economic growth models. Chapter 2 deals with fundamentals of the calculus of variations.
8. Hestenes, M. R.: "Calculus of Variations and Optimal Control Theory," Wiley, New York, 1966. A complete exposition of the calculus of variations and maximum principle approaches. Advanced level of mathematical difficulty.
9. Intriligator, M. D.: "Mathematical Optimization and Economic Theory," Prentice-Hall, Englewood Cliffs, N.J., 1971. Dynamic optimization techniques are covered in pt. IV. Chapter 11 is an overall introduction to the basic approach of control theory; chap. 12 is a concise and very readable introduction to the calculus of variations.
10. Miller, R. E.: "Modern Mathematical Methods for Economics and Business," Holt, Rinehart and Winston, New York, 1972. This text explains the Kuhn-Tucker approach to inequality constrained optimization problems in sec. 4.8 and chap. 8. Chapter 9 covers gradient methods and other direct approaches to constrained optimization.
11. Pars, L. A.: "An Introduction to the Calculus of Variations," Wiley, New York, 1962. A very readable and complete introduction to calculus of variations techniques. Moderate level of mathematical difficulty.
12. Takayama, A.: "Mathematical Economics," Dryden Press, Hinsdale, Ill., 1974. Chapter 5 of this very complete and readable text covers the essentials of the calculus of variations and illustrations of applications in economics.

CHAPTER

THREE

THE CALCULUS OF VARIATIONS: MORE ADVANCED RESULTS

We noted in Chap. 2 that the simplest problem in the calculus of variations involved only one function of a single independent variable, $y(x)$, and its first derivative, $y'(x)$, passing through two specified points, (x_0, y_0) and (x_1, y_1). After developing the Euler-Lagrange results for this problem, we investigated the changes that would be required if there were several y's, higher-order derivatives, or more than one independent variable upon which the y's depend. In this chapter we will first examine both the algebra and the geometry of various ways in which the endpoint conditions can be altered. Next, we will introduce the possibility of several kinds of constraints, restricting, for example, the set of functions from which the optimal $y(x)$ is to be selected. In addition, we note in passing how our results may be expanded to include an optimal $y(x)$ with one or more corners, or kinks, i.e., we deal with functions that are only piecewise smooth. Finally, we examine the second variation term, $\delta^2 I$, in more detail and discover additional parallels with the Taylor series approach in ordinary calculus; i.e., we derive additional necessary conditions and we sketch the reasoning behind the development of sufficient conditions. As the mathematical developments become more complex, our primary aim will be to understand the underlying logic of the additional requirements and their parallels (where possible) with ordinary maximization and minimization problems.

3-1 ENDPOINT CONDITIONS: THE BASIC TRANSVERSALITY RESULTS

General Derivation

By requiring that the maximizing curve $y(x)$ go through specified endpoints (x_0, y_0) and (x_1, y_1), we have been dealing with a problem in which both the limits

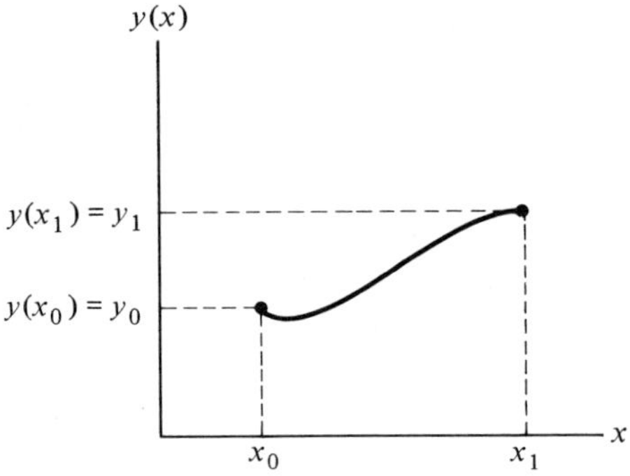

Figure 3-1 The geometry of the fixed endpoint problem (3-1).

of integration are fixed, namely, x_0 and x_1, and also the initial and terminal values of $y(x)$ are specified, namely, $y(x_0) = y_0$ and $y(x_1) = y_1$. From Chap. 2, this was the problem:

$$\text{Maximize} \quad I[y] = \int_{x_0}^{x_1} F(x, y, y')\,dx \tag{3-1}$$

where $\qquad y(x_0) = y_0 \quad \text{and} \quad y(x_1) = y_1$

We recall the geometry in Fig. 3-1.

A problem for which this formulation would be appropriate might be the following. Let x denote time; in particular, suppose that $x_0 = 1979$ and $x_1 = 1984$. Let $y(x)$ represent gross national product and $I[y]$ be some measure of aggregate utility in the nation. Then the problem in (3-1) is to find a path from the current (1979) value of GNP (y_0) to a target value of GNP (y_1) at a target date (1984), such that aggregate utility over the time period is maximized. Alternatively one might: (1) specify the terminal time, 1984, but not the target value of GNP (a so-called free right-hand boundary problem), (2) specify a target value of GNP, y_1, but not specify the year in which it is to be reached (a so-called free terminal time problem), or (3) specify neither the target GNP nor a terminal time, but rather impose some kind of more general requirement such as that the further away the terminal time turns out to be, the larger the final value of GNP must

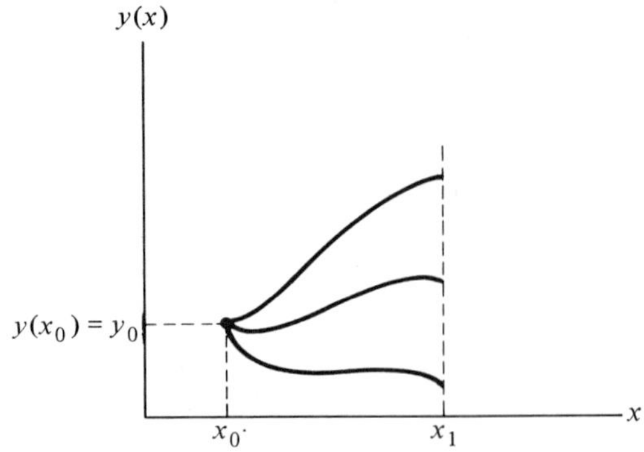

Figure 3-2 A free right-hand boundary problem.

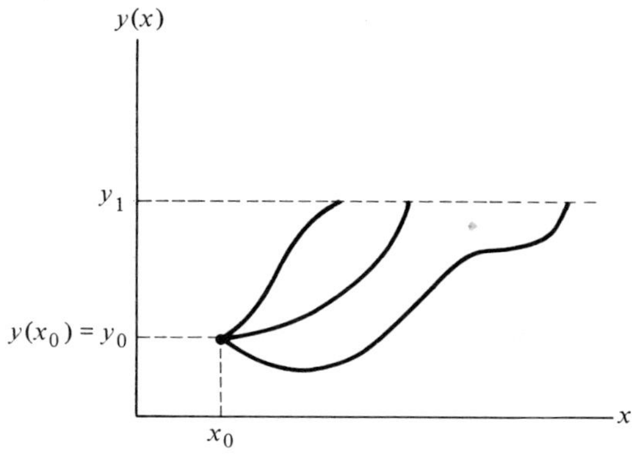

Figure 3-3 A free terminal time problem.

be (a so-called fixed terminal surface problem). The geometry of these three possibilities is presented in Figs. 3-2, 3-3, and 3-4.

In the problem illustrated in Fig. 3-4, the terminal surface is specified as some function of x—$y = \sigma(x)$. With only one independent variable and one function y, the surface is of course a curve. In fact, then, the problems illustrated in Figs. 3-2 and 3-3 are particularizations of that shown in Fig. 3-4. In Fig. 3-2, the "terminal surface" is just the vertical line $x = x_1$ and in Fig. 3-3 it is the function $y = y_1$ (that is, y = a constant, independent of x, namely, the specified terminal value of y). A more general way to specify the terminal surface—and one which will be useful in higher-dimensional space when, for example, I depends on several $y_i(x)$—is as $S(x, y) = 0$. Using this notation, we find that in Figs. 3-2, 3-3, and 3-4 we have $S(x, y) = x - x_1$, $S(x, y) = y - y_1$, and $S(x, y) = y - \sigma(x)$, respectively.†

Although the problems to which they apply are perhaps less obvious, it is also possible to consider a relaxation of the left-hand endpoint conditions in exactly the same three ways, and therefore the most general form of variable boundary problem will be one in which the endpoints of $y(x)$ are required only to lie on

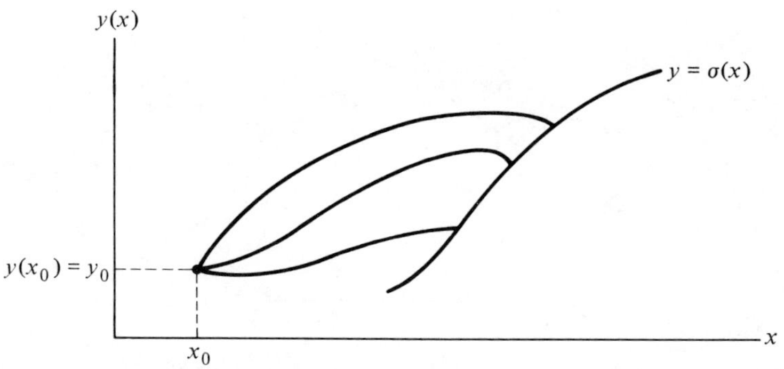

Figure 3-4 A fixed terminal surface problem.

† In this view, we might say that the fixed right-hand endpoint problem in Fig. 3-1 has a "terminal surface" specified by the *pair* of linear equations $x = x_1$ and $y = y_1$.

some initial surface and some terminal surface. Before examining the implications of this general case on the derivation of the Euler-Lagrange necessary conditions, we recall that the fixed endpoint problem in Fig. 3-1 influenced our approach in Chap. 2 in an important way. In the development of the expression for the first variation, we found that the requirement

$$\int_{x_0}^{x_1} [F_y \phi(x) + F_{y'} \phi'(x)]\, dx = 0 \tag{3-2}$$

could be simplified through integration by parts of the second term under the integral, namely,

$$\int_{x_0}^{x_1} F_{y'} \phi'(x)\, dx = F_{y'} \phi(x) \Big]_{x_0}^{x_1} - \int_{x_0}^{x_1} \frac{d}{dx} F_{y'} \phi(x)\, dx \tag{3-3}$$

Since $z(x) = y(x) + \varepsilon\phi(x)$ and any $z(x)$ must necessarily also go through the specified endpoints, $\phi(x_0) = \phi(x_1) = 0$, the first term on the right-hand side of (3-3) disappeared. This allowed (3-2) to be rewritten as

$$\int_{x_0}^{x_1} \left(F_y - \frac{d}{dx} F_{y'} \right) \phi(x)\, dx = 0 \tag{3-4}$$

from which the Euler-Lagrange requirement

$$F_y - \frac{d}{dx} F_{y'} = 0$$

followed. Now, since alternative conditions are possible for either or both of the endpoints, the transformation of (3-2) into (3-4) is not possible.

We therefore reexamine the general definition of the total and the first variation of I under the conditions that the initial and terminal points lie on the functions $y = \rho(x)$ and $y = \sigma(x)$, respectively.† In Fig. 3-5, we indicate the

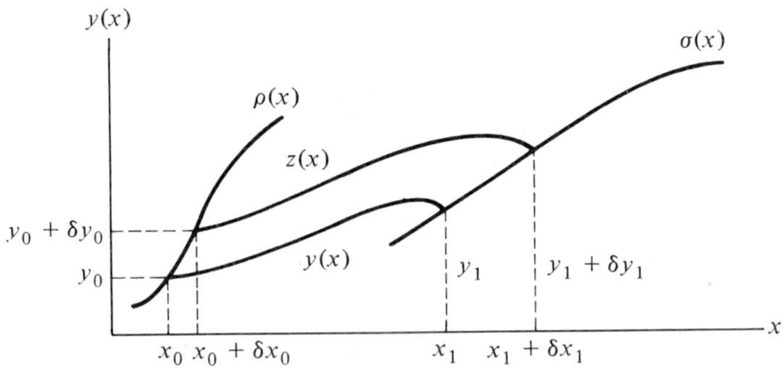

Figure 3-5 $y(x)$ and a neighboring curve $z(x)$ for the initial and terminal surfaces problem.

† Alternatively, we could specify left- and right-hand surfaces as $R(x, y) = 0$ and $S(x, y) = 0$, where $R(x, y) = y - \rho(x)$ and $S(x, y) = y - \sigma(x)$. In the initial development of this section, however, we will utilize the functional dependencies of y on x, via $\rho(x)$ and $\sigma(x)$, explicitly.

geometry of the problem. We introduce the notation δx_0 and δy_0 to indicate the displacement of the initial value of the independent variable, x_0, and the associated displacement of the initial value of the neighboring function, $z(x)$, when $z(x)$ does not begin at (x_0, y_0) but rather nearby, at $(x_0 + \delta x_0, y_0 + \delta y_0)$, on the function $y = \rho(x)$. Similarly, $y(x)$ terminates at (x_1, y_1) and $z(x)$ terminates at $(x_1 + \delta x_1, y_1 + \delta y_1)$, both on the function $y = \sigma(x)$.

The total variation in I, which was defined in Chap. 2 as

$$\Delta I = I[z] - I[y] \tag{3-5}$$

will now be

$$\Delta I = \int_{x_0 + \delta x_0}^{x_1 + \delta x_1} F(x, z, z')\, dx - \int_{x_0}^{x_1} F(x, y, y')\, dx \tag{3-6}$$

If the variation of $y(x)$ is small, so that $z(x)$ is near to $y(x)$, then without introducing much inaccuracy we can imagine $z(x)$ extended at its left-hand end [via a line that is tangent to $z(x)$ there] as far as x_0. This will allow both $y(x)$ and $z(x)$ to have x_0 as a lower limit of integration, which will be useful in what follows. Similarly, we can imagine $y(x)$ extended via a tangent at its right-hand end as far as $x_1 + \delta x_1$. Then both $y(x)$ and $z(x)$ will have $x_1 + \delta x_1$ as an upper limit of integration. Initially, with $z(x)$ extended at its left-hand end, we can both add and subtract $\int_{x_0}^{x_0 + \delta x_0} F(x, z, z')\, dx$ to (3-6), thus leaving it unchanged in value but altered in appearance:

$$\Delta I = \int_{x_0}^{x_1} [F(x, z, z') - F(x, y, y')]\, dx + \int_{x_1}^{x_1 + \delta x_1} F(x, z, z')\, dx - \int_{x_0}^{x_0 + \delta x_0} F(x, z, z')\, dx \tag{3-7}$$

It is important to notice that the first of the three integrals on the right-hand side of (3-7) is exactly the one that was defined as ΔI in the previous chapter, when we considered the fixed endpoint problem. Thus, using the Taylor series for a first-order approximation and substituting $z(x) = y(x) + \varepsilon\phi(x)$, all as in Chap. 2, this integral becomes

$$\varepsilon \int_{x_0}^{x_1} [F_y \phi(x) + F_{y'} \phi'(x)]\, dx$$

which we termed the first variation of I, δI. Therefore, (3-7) can be reexpressed (to a first-order approximation) as

$$\Delta I = \varepsilon \int_{x_0}^{x_1} [F_y \phi(x) + F_{y'} \phi'(x)]\, dx + \int_{x_1}^{x_1 + \delta x_1} F(x, z, z')\, dx - \int_{x_0}^{x_0 + \delta x_0} F(x, z, z')\, dx \tag{3-8}$$

Consider the second and third definite integrals on the right-hand side of (3-8). Geometrically, these represent two areas under $F(x, z, z')$ in F, x space, as Fig. 3-6 suggests. The second integral in (3-8) is the shaded area on the right, the

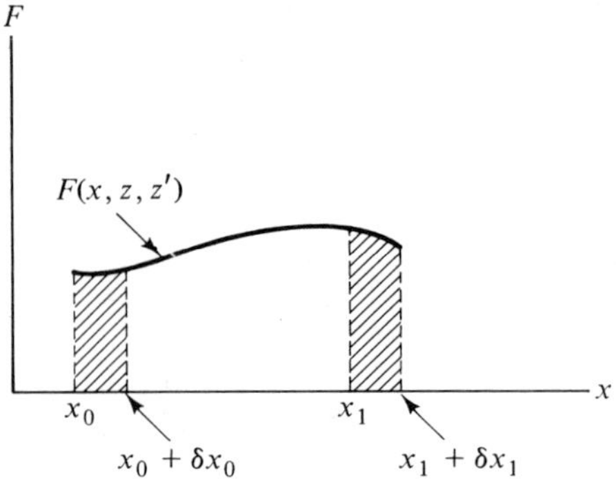

Figure 3-6 $\int_{x_1}^{x_1+\delta x_1} F(x, z, z')\,dx$ and $\int_{x_0}^{x_0+\delta x_0} F(x, z, z')\,dx$ in F,x space.

third integral is the shaded area on the left, and the difference between the two integrals is just the difference in these areas. When $z(x)$ and $y(x)$ are close of order 1, so that both $|z(x) - y(x)|$ and $|z'(x) - y'(x)|$ are small over the entire range, then $F(x, y, y')$, if it were drawn on Fig. 3-6, would be close to $F(x, z, z')$ and thus the difference of the areas in Fig. 3-6 will be approximately the same as the difference in the areas under $F(x, y, y')$, over x_0 to $x_0 + \delta x_0$ and x_1 to $x_1 + \delta x_1$. [We here are extending $y(x)$ at the right-hand end, as discussed above.] Thus (3-8) becomes

$$\Delta I \cong \varepsilon \int_{x_0}^{x_1} [F_y \phi(x) + F_{y'} \phi'(x)]\,dx + \int_{x_1}^{x_1+\delta x_1} F(x, y, y')\,dx - \int_{x_0}^{x_0+\delta x_0} F(x, y, y')\,dx \tag{3-9}$$

In addition, when δx_1 is small, so that x_1 and $x_1 + \delta x_1$ are close, the area represented by $\int_{x_1}^{x_1+\delta x_1} F(x, y, y')\,dx$ is approximated by $(\delta x_1)F(x, y, y')|_{x=x_1}$. This is the so-called first mean-value theorem of integral calculus; Fig. 3-7 illustrates the geometry of this theorem. The area of the rectangle (shaded) is an approximation to the area under the curve; the smaller the base (δx_1), the better the approximation. Similarly, at the left-hand end, $\int_{x_0}^{x_0+\delta x_0} F(x, y, y')\,dx \cong (\delta x_0)F(x, y, y')|_{x=x_0}$. These two approximations can replace the last two integrals on the right-hand side of (3-9).

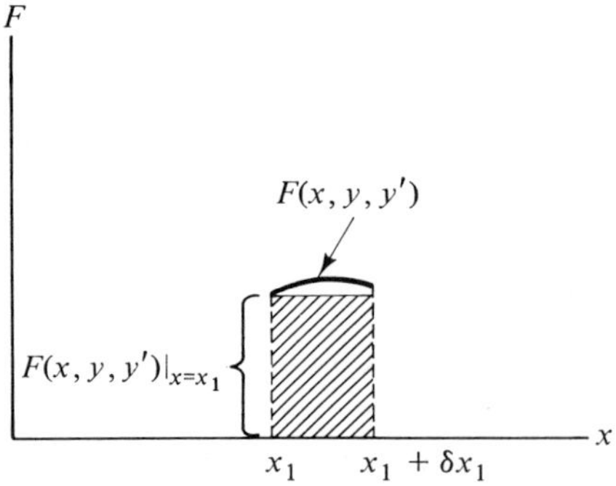

Figure 3-7 Approximation to the area under a curve.

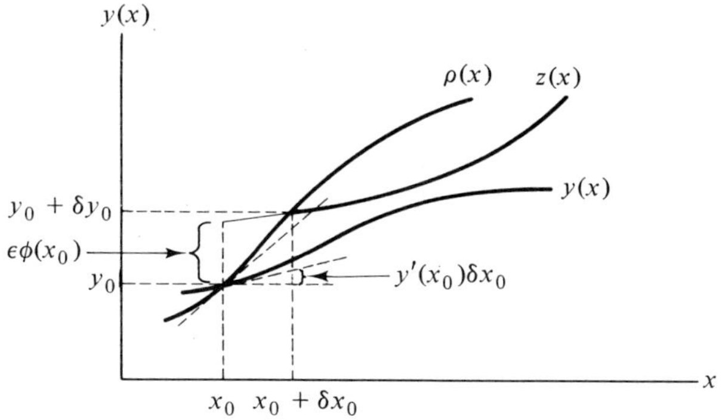

Figure 3-8 Relationships between functions at their initial points.

In addition to this, integrating the $[F_{y'}\phi'(x)]$ term under the first integral in (3-9) by parts, as before, we have, finally,

$$\Delta I \cong \varepsilon \int_{x_0}^{x_1} \left(F_y - \frac{d}{dx} F_{y'} \right) \phi(x)\, dx + \varepsilon\phi(x_1) F_{y'}\big|_{x=x_1} - \varepsilon\phi(x_0) F_{y'}\big|_{x=x_0}$$
$$+ (\delta x_1) F(x, y, y')\big|_{x=x_1} - (\delta x_0) F(x, y, y')\big|_{x=x_0} \tag{3-10}$$

We can now introduce additional geometric considerations on $\phi(x_0)$ and $\phi(x_1)$—in effect to substitute for the conditions $\phi(x_0) = \phi(x_1) = 0$ that held in the fixed endpoints case of Chap. 2. In Fig. 3-8 we enlarge the left-hand end of the curves in Fig. 3-5, having extended $z(x)$ leftwards, as necessary. For $z(x) = y(x) + \varepsilon\phi(x)$ which represent small variations of $y(x)$, δx_0 is small and the vertical distance δy_0 is approximately the sum of the two vertical segments $\varepsilon\phi(x_0)$ and $y'(x)\,\delta x_0$, that is,

$$\varepsilon\phi(x_0) \cong \delta y_0 - y'(x_0)\,\delta x_0 \tag{3-11}$$

A similar geometric argument at the right-hand endpoints would suggest that

$$\varepsilon\phi(x_1) \cong \delta y_1 - y'(x_1)\,\delta x_1 \tag{3-12}$$

We introduce these approximations into (3-10), collect terms on δx_0, δx_1, δy_0, and δy_1, and define this expression as the first variation of I:

$$\delta I = \varepsilon \int_{x_0}^{x_1} \left(F_y - \frac{d}{dx} F_{y'} \right) \phi(x)\, dx + F_{y'}\big|_{x=x_1} (\delta y_1)$$
$$+ (F - F_{y'} y')\big|_{x=x_1} (\delta x_1) - F_{y'}\big|_{x=x_0} (\delta y_0) - (F - F_{y'} y')\big|_{x=x_0} (\delta x_0) \tag{3-13}$$

In the fixed endpoint case considered in Chap. 2, there was no variation of x_0, y_0, x_1, or y_1 (that is, $\delta x_0 = \delta y_0 = \delta x_1 = \delta y_1 = 0$) and hence only the integral term appeared in the expression for δI [see (2-35) in Chap. 2, for example]. In this more general case it must still be true that $y(x)$ is superior to, among others, neighboring functions $z(x)$ which go through (x_0, y_0) and (x_1, y_1), the same endpoints as for $y(x)$. Hence, even in this more general case, $y(x)$ must be an extremal, i.e., a solution to the Euler-Lagrange equation

$$F_y - \frac{d}{dx} F_{y'} = 0 \tag{3-14}$$

Thus, for δI in (3-13) to be zero, since $y(x)$ will still be an extremal and the integral will be zero, it is necessary that

$$F_{y'}|_{x=x_1}(\delta y_1) + (F - F_{y'}y')|_{x=x_1}(\delta x_1) - F_{y'}|_{x=x_0}(\delta y_0) - (F - F_{y'}y')|_{x=x_0}(\delta x_0) = 0 \tag{3-15}$$

We now introduce specific information about the functions $\rho(x)$ and $\sigma(x)$ on which the endpoints are required to lie. This information allows us to relate the variations in y_0 to those in x_0 and also those in y_1 to variations in x_1. It is again an approximation, which is, as usual, more valid as the variation of $y(x)$ is small. Looking again at Fig. 3-8, consider the tangent to $\rho(x)$ at the point x_0. Note that

$$\delta y_0 \cong \rho'(x_0)\,\delta x_0 \tag{3-16}$$

[Assume for the moment that $0 < \rho'(x_0) < \infty$ and similarly that $0 < \sigma'(x_1) < \infty$. That is, neither curve on which the endpoints are to lie is horizontal or vertical.] Thus δy_0 and δx_0 are connected via the slope of $\rho(x)$, the left-hand curve on which the maximizing function must lie, evaluated at x_0. Similar geometric considerations at the right-hand end, where the required curve is $\sigma(x)$, show that

$$\delta y_1 \cong \sigma'(x_1)\,\delta x_1 \tag{3-17}$$

Putting this information into (3-15) and collecting terms on δx_1 and δx_0 gives

$$[F + (\sigma' - y')F_{y'}]|_{x=x_1}(\delta x_1) - [F + (\rho' - y')F_{y'}]|_{x=x_0}(\delta x_0) = 0 \tag{3-18}$$

and, finally, since δx_1 and δx_0 are arbitrary, the terms multiplying them must each be zero if (3-18) is to hold, namely,

$$[F + (\sigma' - y')F_{y'}]|_{x=x_1} = 0 \quad \text{and} \quad [F + (\rho' - y')F_{y'}]|_{x=x_0} = 0 \tag{3-19}$$

These two conditions, one at the right-hand end and one at the left-hand end, replace the simple information that $y(x_0) = y_0$ and $y(x_1) = y_1$ which we had in the fixed endpoint problem of Chap. 2. They are known as the *transversality conditions* for the variable endpoint problem. The maximizing curve $y(x)$ intersects the functions $\rho(x)$ and $\sigma(x)$, that is, $y(x)$ is a transversal of those functions. The results in (3-19), since they relate y' and ρ' at the initial point and y' and σ' at the terminal point, specify how this transversal meets the two bounding curves at the points where it intersects them.

For the problem suggested in Fig. 3-4, the conditions in (3-19) would reduce to those for the right-hand end only (when $x = x_1$), since the terms δy_0 and δx_0 in (3-15) would be zero when the left-hand endpoint is fixed at (x_0, y_0) and there would be no relation (3-16). For the problems suggested in Figs. 3-2 and 3-3 this will also be true. In fact, even further simplification of (3-15) is possible in these two cases. For the free right-hand boundary problem in Fig. 3-2, where x_1 is specified but y_1 is not, $\delta x_1 = 0$ also (as well as $\delta x_0 = 0$ and $\delta y_0 = 0$) and, therefore, since $\delta y_1 \neq 0$, (3-15) reduces to

$$F_{y'}\big|_{x=x_1} = 0 \tag{3-20}$$

[This is the case in which $\sigma'(x_1) = \infty$ and the development of the results in (3-19) is not valid because the approximation in (3-17) is not appropriate.] Similarly, for the free terminal time problem of Fig. 3-3, $\delta y_1 = 0$ (as well as $\delta x_0 = 0$ and $\delta y_0 = 0$) but $\delta x_1 \neq 0$, so condition (3-15) becomes

$$(F - F_{y'}y')\big|_{x=x_1} = 0 \tag{3-21}$$

[This is the case in which $\sigma'(x_1) = 0$, and here the development of the results in (3-19) is still valid; (3-17) specifies that $\delta y_1 = 0$ and (3-19), with $\sigma'(x_1) = 0$, is exactly (3-21), above.]

Example I: Shortest Distance in a Plane (Continued)

An illustration will suggest the geometric content of conditions (3-19), and in Sec. 3-2 we will explore the geometry in more detail. Recall the shortest-distance problem of Chap. 2, namely,

$$\text{Minimize} \quad L = \int_{x_0}^{x_1} \sqrt{1 + (y')^2}\, dx \tag{3-22}$$

where $y(x_0) = y_0$ and $y(x_1) = y_1$ [this was (2-5) in Chap. 2]. That is, find the shortest curve $y(x)$ connecting (x_0, y_0) and (x_1, y_1) in x, y space. The Euler-Lagrange equation [this was (2-37) in Chap. 2] led us to conclude that $y'(x)$ was constant, k_1, and hence that $y(x)$ was a straight line, $k_1x + k_2$. We also found that the initial and terminal values of y, y_0 and y_1, allowed us to determine the constants that arose through integration, and they assured that the line $y(x)$ had the proper slope and y-axis intercept to pass through (x_0, y_0) and (x_1, y_1). Suppose now that in place of the right-hand endpoint we only require that $y(x)$ terminate on the surface $y = \sigma(x)$. Thus we need to impose the first of the two conditions in (3-19).† For this problem, $F = \sqrt{1 + (y')^2}$ and $F_{y'} = y'/\sqrt{1 + (y')^2}$, giving the requirement that, when $x = x_1$,

$$\sqrt{1 + (y')^2} + \frac{\sigma' y'}{\sqrt{1 + (y')^2}} - \frac{(y')^2}{\sqrt{1 + (y')^2}} = 0 \tag{3-23}$$

Multiplying through by $\sqrt{1 + (y')^2}$ leaves $1 + (y')^2 + \sigma' y' - (y')^2 = 0$ at $x = x_1$, that is,

$$\sigma'(x_1)y'(x_1) = -1 \quad \text{or} \quad y'(x_1) = -\frac{1}{\sigma'(x_1)} \tag{3-24}$$

† Throughout this and the next section we will concentrate on relaxation of the *terminal* condition $y(x_1) = y_1$, in the spirit of Figs. 3-2, 3-3, and 3-4. Obviously, there are exactly parallel developments for the case in which the *initial* point is not fixed at (x_0, y_0). For a great many applications in the social sciences, however, the initial point *is* fixed and the terminal conditions are the more flexible ones.

Thus, at x_1, when $y(x)$ meets $\sigma(x)$, the two curves must be perpendicular, since the slopes of their tangents are related as shown in (3-24).† Therefore, the right-hand transversality condition for this problem represents a generalization of the well-known fact that in a plane the shortest distance to a straight line from a point not on the line is along the perpendicular from the point to the line.

Since x_1, the terminal value of the independent variable, is not determined until $y(x)$ intersects the terminal surface $\sigma(x)$, it may appear that the orthogonality result in (3-24) is inadequate to compensate for the loss of the endpoint information in the fixed case, namely, $y(x_1) = y_1$. We know, for the problem in (3-22), that $y'(x) = k_1$ and $y(x) = k_1 x + k_2$. In the fixed endpoints case, we had two equations in the unknowns k_1 and k_2 (since x_0, y_0, x_1, and y_1 were known):

$$k_1 x_0 + k_2 = y_0$$

$$k_1 x_1 + k_2 = y_1$$

In the present example, we still conclude from the Euler-Lagrange condition that the optimal $y(x)$ will be a straight line, that it will go through (x_0, y_0) (the fixed left-hand endpoint), and that [from (3-24)] at the terminal surface its slope will be $-1/\sigma'(x_1)$. We investigate exactly how to utilize this information in the example that follows.

Let it be required to find the shortest curve from the point $(x_0, y_0) = (2, 3)$ to the terminal surface $y = \sigma(x)$, where $\sigma(x) = +\sqrt{4(x-5)}$. This is the upper branch of a parabola, open to the right, with its vertex at $x = 5$, $y = 0$. The functional for the problem is that in (3-22); hence $y(x) = k_1 x + k_2$. Since the optimal $y(x)$ is linear, we know from (3-24) that its constant slope, k_1, will be $-1/\sigma'(x_1)$. For the terminal surface specified, $\sigma'(x) = 2/+\sqrt{4(x-5)} = 2/y$ and so $k_1 = -y_1/2$. Therefore: (1) putting information about the left-hand end, (x_0, y_0), into $k_1 x_0 + k_2 = y_0$ we have $2k_1 + k_2 = 3$ or, from our general knowledge about the slope, $-y_1 + k_2 = 3$; (2) at the right-hand end, $k_1 x_1 + k_2 = y_1$ or $-x_1 y_1/2 + k_2 = y_1$; and (3) we now have in addition the requirement that at the right-hand end, the terminal point must lie on the specified surface, that is, $4x_1 - y_1^2 = 20$. We have, then, three

† The reader may recall that this follows from observations on linear functions written in inner-product form. Consider any two lines in x, y space whose slopes are negative reciprocals: (1) $y = ax + b$ and (2) $y = -(1/a)x + c$. Rewriting (1) as $-ax + y = b$ and (2) as $(1/a)x + y = c$, these can be shown in inner-product form as

$$(1)\ \begin{bmatrix} -a \\ 1 \end{bmatrix} \cdot \begin{bmatrix} x \\ y \end{bmatrix} = b \quad \text{and} \quad (2)\ \begin{bmatrix} 1/a \\ 1 \end{bmatrix} \cdot \begin{bmatrix} x \\ y \end{bmatrix} = c$$

For linear functions, the (constant) gradient is the normal to the line everywhere; these normals are

$$\begin{bmatrix} -a \\ 1 \end{bmatrix} \quad \text{and} \quad \begin{bmatrix} 1/a \\ 1 \end{bmatrix}$$

for (1) and (2), respectively. But these normals are clearly perpendicular since their inner product is zero. (This comes from the fact that for two n-element vectors $\mathbf{V}$ and $\mathbf{W}$ with an included angle α, $\cos \alpha = \mathbf{V} \cdot \mathbf{W} / \|\mathbf{V}\| \|\mathbf{W}\|$ and $\cos 90° = 0$.) Hence the lines (1) and (2) are themselves perpendicular.

equations (not all linear) in the three unknowns x_1, y_1, and k_2:

$$-y_1 + k_2 = 3$$

$$-\frac{x_1 y_1}{2} + k_2 = y_1$$

$$4x_1 - y_1^2 = 20$$

Rearranging the first as $y_1 = k_2 - 3$ and substituting into the second gives $x_1 = 6/y_1$; putting this into the third gives a cubic equation for y_1: $y_1^3 + 20y_1 = 24$. By inspection, it is clear that y_1 will be slightly larger than 1. Simple trial and error leads to $y_1 = 1.128$ (to three-decimal accuracy). Therefore $x_1 = 6/y_1 = 5.319$ and $k_2 = y_1 + 3 = 4.128$. Finally, then, $k_1 = -y_1/2 = -0.564$ and hence the optimal $y(x)$ is

$$y(x) = -0.564x + 4.128$$

Figure 3-9 illustrates this. The set of equations from which k_1 and k_2 are derived will clearly in general be nonlinear and more complicated than in this example; hence it is impossible to know in advance how difficult they will be to solve.

The reader may wish to convince himself that the result obtained in (3-24) actually will hold for any functional of the form

$$I[y] = \int_{x_0}^{x_1} f(x, y)\sqrt{1 + (y')^2}\, dx$$

where $y(x_0) = y_0$ and the right-hand endpoint is to be on $y = \sigma(x)$. [In the previous example, (3-22), we had $f(x, y) = 1$.] It would be incorrect to conclude that the right-hand transversality conditions always impose a perpendicularity or orthogonality requirement on the terminal curve and the extremal $y(x)$. They depend, of course, on the exact form of the functional and are, in general, rather more subtle, although orthogonality between certain vectors is always involved. In addition, the extensions to more dimensions—where the integrand is $F(x, y_1, \ldots, y_n, y_1', \ldots, y_n')$—as well as to more complicated terminal surfaces make necessary a format that allows generalization of the results in (3-19). We will turn to these matters in Sec. 3-2.

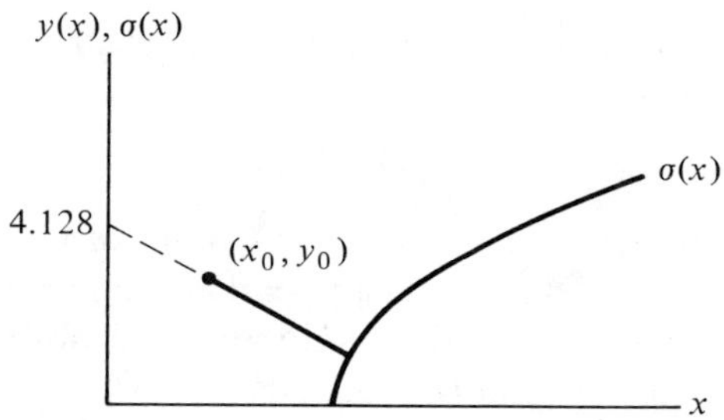

Figure 3-9 Solution for the shortest curve from (2, 3) to $\sigma(x) = +\sqrt{4(x - 5)}$.

Example II: Monopolistic Pricing over Time (Continued)

Consider again the two monopolistic pricing problems of Example II in Chap. 2, Sec. 2-4. We now examine these problems under different assumptions. For the first problem, we now assume that the producer wants to plan for a 52-week horizon but does not set any particular final price; that is, $t_1 = 52$ but $p(t_1)$ is unspecified, whereas in the original problem $p(t_1)$ was set at 100. This corresponds to the free right-hand boundary situation in Fig. 3-2. For the second problem, we now assume that the monopolist sets a final price of 20, as before, but does not specify the time at which that price should be attained; that is, $p(t_1) = 20$ but t_1 unspecified. This is the free terminal time situation depicted in Fig. 3-3.

Problem 1: Free right-hand boundary For this problem, the previous specification of the right-hand endpoint—namely, $t_1 = 52$ and $p(t_1) = 100$—is replaced by $t_1 = 52$ and the transversality condition in (3-20), which here is $F_{p'}|_{t=t_1} = 0$. From the details of this problem in Chap. 2, we find that this requirement becomes (for p and p' evaluated at t_1)

$$-10{,}000p' - 10{,}200 + 200p = 0$$

The Euler-Lagrange condition still applies; that is,

$$p(t) = k_1 e^{0.0173t} + k_2 e^{-0.0173t} + 67.333$$

This was (2-45) in Chap. 2. Consequently, also,

$$p'(t) = 0.0173k_1 e^{0.0173t} - 0.0173k_2 e^{-0.0173t}$$

Evaluating $p(t)$ and $p'(t)$ at $t_1 = 52$, we find

$$p(t_1) = 2.4586k_1 + 0.4067k_2 + 67.333$$

and $$p'(t_1) = 0.0425k_1 - 0.0070k_2$$

Putting these results for p and p' at $t_1 = 52$ into the transversality condition gives, after some algebra,

$$66.72k_1 + 151.34k_2 = -3266.667$$

The left-hand endpoint information from the original problem still holds; $t_0 = 0$ and $p(t_0) = 70$, so we have, as before,

$$k_1 + k_2 = 2.667$$

From this pair of linear equations in k_1 and k_2 it is easily established that $k_1 = 43.373$ and $k_2 = -40.706$, so that

$$p(t) = 43.373 e^{0.0173t} - 40.706 e^{-0.0173t} + 67.333$$

and, in particular, at $t_1 = 52$, $p(t_1) = 157.4$. From the monopolist's point of view, the optimal price after 52 weeks is higher than that set in the earlier version of the problem. [The reader should check that solving the monopolist's problem with the pair of fixed endpoints $t_0 = 0$, $p(t_0) = 70$ and $t_1 = 52$, $p(t_1) = 157.4$ gives the solution found here.] In addition, substituting the current $p(t)$ and the expression for $p'(t)$ derived from it into the objective functional of the problem and evaluating between $t_0 = 0$ and $t_1 = 52$ shows that the total profit can be expected to be approximately 243,000. Recall that previously, when p_1 was set at 100, the comparable figure was 170,000. Of course an increase in profits in the present case is to be expected, since we have seen that when p_1 is not restricted ahead of time, it optimally takes on the value of 157.4 and not 100.

Problem 2: Free terminal time We now consider the second monopolistic pricing problem with $t_0 = 0$, $p(t_0) = 10$, $p(t_1) = 20$ but t_1 unspecified. The previous specification of the right-hand endpoint $[p(t_1) = 20$ and $t_1 = 52]$ is replaced by $p(t_1) = 20$ and the transversality condition in (3-21), which here is $(F - F_{p'}p')|_{t=t_1} = 0$. From the details of this problem in Chap. 2, we find that this requirement becomes (for p and p' evaluated at t_1)

$$-\tfrac{3}{2}p^2 + 202p + 5000(p')^2 - 5240 = 0$$

Since $p(t_1) = 20$, we find that this transversality condition specifies that $p'(t_1) = \pm 0.6$.

The Euler-Lagrange condition still holds, so it must still be true that

$$p(t) = k_1 e^{0.0173t} + k_2 e^{-0.0173t} + 67.333$$

Consequently, also (as above),

$$p'(t) = 0.0173k_1 e^{0.0173t} - 0.0173k_2 e^{-0.0173t}$$

Evaluating $p(t)$ and $p'(t)$ at t_1, which is unspecified, we have, respectively,

$$k_1 e^{0.0173t_1} + k_2 e^{-0.0173t_1} = -47.333 \tag{3-25a}$$

and

$$k_1 e^{0.0173t_1} - k_2 e^{-0.0173t_1} = \pm 34.682 \tag{3-25b}$$

Finally, from the left-hand endpoint information that $t_0 = 0$ and $p(t_0) = 10$, we have, as in Chap. 2,

$$k_1 + k_2 = -57.333 \tag{3-25c}$$

Therefore we have two sets of three equations in k_1, k_2, and t_1 [depending on whether $+34.682$ or -34.682 is used as the right-hand side of (3-25b)]. In the former case, adding (3-25a) and (3-25b) gives

$$k_1 = -6.326 e^{-0.0173t_1}$$

and

$$k_2 = -41.008 e^{0.0173t_1}$$

Substituting into (3-25c) leads to

$$-6.326 e^{-0.0173t_1} - 41.008 e^{0.0173t_1} = -57.333$$

from which $t_1 \cong 14.15$. Then $k_1 = -4.95$, $k_2 = -52.38$, and

$$p(t) = -4.95 e^{0.0173t} - 52.38 e^{-0.0173t} + 67.333$$

Using the second set of equations [with -34.682 for the right-hand side of (3-25*b*)] leads to $t_1 \cong 122.2$, with the same values for k_1 and k_2, as the reader should check. Since the function $p(t)$ has a unique maximum at $t_* \cong 68$, with $p(t_*) = 35.13$, it is clear that there will be a value of t smaller than 68 and a value larger than 68 for which $p(t) = 20$. These are $t_1 \cong 14.15$ and $t_1 \cong 122.2$, respectively. By following $p(t)$, from above, from $t_0 = 0$ to $t_1 = 14.15$, i.e., by shortening the planning horizon (from $t_1 = 52$), the monopolist cuts losses from $-201{,}500$ to approximately $-114{,}000$.

3-2 ENDPOINT CONDITIONS: ALTERNATIVE FORMULATIONS AND GENERALIZATIONS

A More General Orthogonality Requirement

The fundamental result on endpoint requirements is given in (3-15). When the left-hand endpoint is fixed at x_0 and $y_0 = y(x_0)$, the remaining requirement is (where y', F, and $F_{y'}$ are evaluated at $x = x_1$)

$$F_{y'}(\delta y_1) + (F - F_{y'}y')(\delta x_1) = 0$$

This transversality requirement can be expressed compactly in inner-product notation as

$$\begin{bmatrix} (F - F_{y'}y') \\ F_{y'} \end{bmatrix}_{x=x_1} \cdot \begin{bmatrix} \delta x_1 \\ \delta y_1 \end{bmatrix} = 0 \tag{3-26}$$

The left-hand side of (3-26) bears something of a resemblance to the inner-product expression for the first differential for a multivariable function, $f(x_1, \ldots, x_n)$. Letting $\mathbf{\nabla f} = [f_1, \ldots, f_n]'$ and $\mathbf{dX} = [dx_1, \ldots, dx_n]'$, $df = [\mathbf{\nabla f}]' \cdot [\mathbf{dX}]$ and a first-order condition for a maximum or minimum of f is that $df = 0$, i.e., that $[\mathbf{\nabla f}]$ and $[\mathbf{dX}]$ are orthogonal vectors. We might, somewhat arbitrarily, define the first vector on the left in (3-26) as the "gradient" of I, namely,

$$\mathbf{\nabla I} = \begin{bmatrix} (F - F_{y'}y') \\ F_{y'} \end{bmatrix} \tag{3-27}$$

Evaluated at a particular value of x_1, say x_1^*, we will denote this as $\mathbf{\nabla I}(x^*)$. Then the transversality requirement in (3-26) is an orthogonality requirement, at $x = x_1$, between $\mathbf{\nabla I}$ and the vector of variations in x and y.

However, since the optimal curve must terminate on $y = \sigma(x)$, then, as stated in (3-17), the variations in x and y at the right-hand endpoint are not independent. For small variations in the independent variable at x_1, $\delta y_1 = \sigma'(x_1)\,\delta x_1$ or $\delta y_1 - \sigma'(x_1)\,\delta x_1 = 0$; the variation in y_1 is approximated by the tangent to $y = \sigma(x)$ at $x = x_1$. Alternatively, $\begin{bmatrix} \delta x_1 \\ \delta y_1 \end{bmatrix}$ and $\begin{bmatrix} 1 \\ \sigma'(x_1) \end{bmatrix}$ are parallel vectors, since the determinant of the matrix made up of these two column vectors is (approximately) zero. Thus (3-26) becomes

$$\begin{bmatrix} (F - F_{y'}y') \\ F_{y'} \end{bmatrix} \cdot \begin{bmatrix} 1 \\ \sigma'(x_1) \end{bmatrix} = 0 \tag{3-28}$$

or $F - F_{y'}y' + F_{y'}\sigma' = 0$, evaluated at $x = x_1$, exactly as in (3-19).

If we consider a more general specification of the terminal curve, the geometry of the orthogonality requirement in (3-26) will become clear. Instead of $y = \sigma(x)$, define the terminal surface by $S(x, y) = 0$, where $S(x, y) = \sigma(x) - y$. $S(x, y)$ itself is a surface in three-dimensional space whose particular value depends on the values of x and y; when the value of $S(x, y)$ is specified [as when $S(x, y) = 0$], the corresponding geometry shows the contours of $S(x, y)$ in a plane parallel to the x,y plane and perpendicular to the S axis at the specified height. The two-element gradient $\nabla \mathbf{S} = \begin{bmatrix} \partial S/\partial x \\ \partial S/\partial y \end{bmatrix}$ shows the vector perpendicular to the contours of S in that plane, and when $S(x, y) = 0$, the plane is just the original two-dimensional x,y space. Here $\nabla \mathbf{S} = \begin{bmatrix} \sigma'(x) \\ -1 \end{bmatrix}$, and hence the vector orthogonal to $\nabla \mathbf{S}$ and therefore tangent to $S(x, y)$ in the x,y plane [i.e., tangent to $y = \sigma(x)$] is $\mathbf{T} = \begin{bmatrix} 1 \\ \sigma'(x) \end{bmatrix}$,

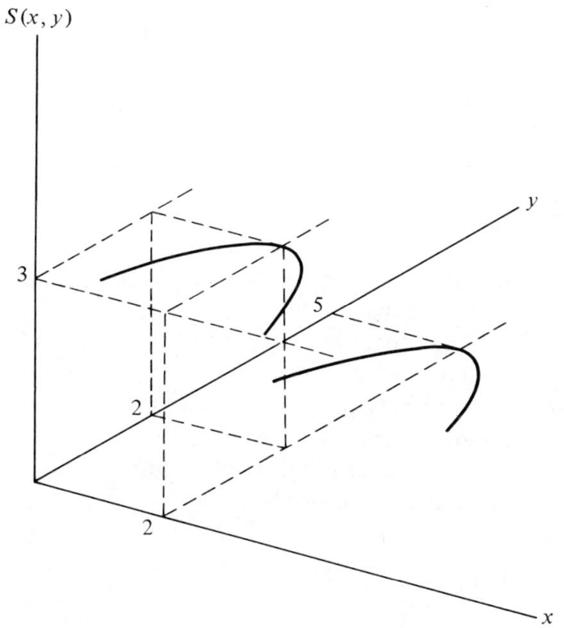

Figure 3-10 Contours of $S(x, y) = -x^2 + 4x + 1 - y$ for $S = 0$ and 3.

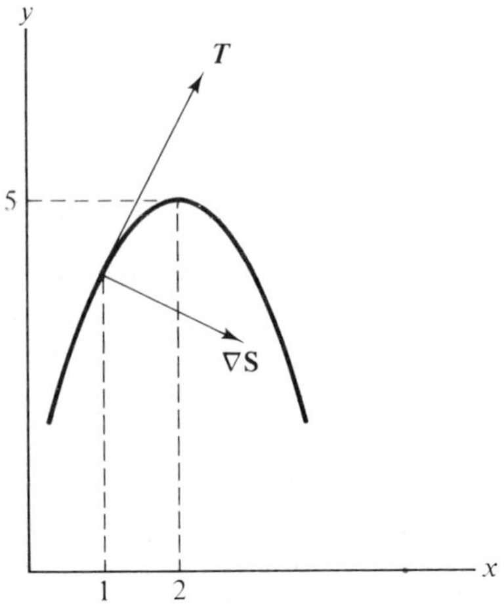

Figure 3-11 Contour of $S(x, y) = -x^2 + 4x + 1 - y$ for $S = 0$.

since then $[\nabla\mathbf{S}] \cdot [\mathbf{T}] = 0$. Following previous notation, we will denote $\nabla\mathbf{S}$ and $\mathbf{T}$, evaluated at a particular x^*, by $\nabla\mathbf{S}(x^*)$ and $\mathbf{T}(x^*)$.

Consider the function $y = -x^2 + 4x + 1$, for example, from which $S(x, y) = -x^2 + 4x + 1 - y$ and $\nabla\mathbf{S} = \begin{bmatrix} -2x + 4 \\ -1 \end{bmatrix}$. In Fig. 3-10 we show two contours of S, those associated with $S = 0$ and $S = 3$. In Fig. 3-11 we show the $S(x, y) = 0$ contours in the x,y plane and introduce the two-element vectors $\nabla\mathbf{S} = \begin{bmatrix} -2x + 4 \\ -1 \end{bmatrix}$ and $\mathbf{T} = \begin{bmatrix} 1 \\ -2x + 4 \end{bmatrix}$ at $x = 1$ (and, consequently, $y = 4$); namely, $\nabla\mathbf{S} = \begin{bmatrix} +2 \\ -1 \end{bmatrix}$ and $\mathbf{T} = \begin{bmatrix} 1 \\ 2 \end{bmatrix}$. Note that the gradient is inward pointing, reflecting the fact that if one were looking for a maximum of the function S, the move from $x = 1$, $y = 4$ should be in the direction of increasing x and decreasing y. Whether inward pointing or outward pointing, the included angle between $\nabla\mathbf{S}$ and $\mathbf{T}$ is 90°, and hence $\nabla\mathbf{S}$ and $\mathbf{T}$ are orthogonal.

Therefore, the condition given in (3-28) specifies orthogonality between $\nabla\mathbf{I}$ and $\mathbf{T}$, the tangent to the terminal curve at the point where $y(x)$ intersects $\sigma(x)$. This observation suggests that an alternative way of specifying the orthogonality in (3-28) would be to require that $\nabla\mathbf{I}$ and the gradient, $\nabla\mathbf{S}$, evaluated at $x = x_1$, be parallel. Since the two vectors go through the terminal point x_1 and $y_1 = \sigma(x_1)$ in the x,y plane, this parallelism means that the vectors $\nabla\mathbf{I}$ and $\nabla\mathbf{S}$ must, in fact, be *collinear*; i.e., one is just a multiple of the other at $x = x_1$ $[\nabla\mathbf{I}(x_1) = \alpha\nabla\mathbf{S}(x_1)]$ or

$$\begin{bmatrix} (F - F_{y'}y') \\ F_{y'} \end{bmatrix} = \alpha \begin{bmatrix} \sigma'(x) \\ -1 \end{bmatrix} \tag{3-29}$$

evaluated at $x = x_1$. This means that (1) $(F - F_{y'}y') = \alpha\sigma'(x)$ and (2) $F_{y'} = -\alpha$.

Substituting from (2) into (1) gives $(F - F_{y'}y') = -\sigma'(x)F_{y'}$ or

$$[F + (\sigma' - y')F_{y'}]\,|_{x=x_1} = 0 \qquad (3\text{-}30)$$

exactly as in (3-19).

The view of transversality as orthogonality between ∇I and the tangent to the contour of $S(x, y)$ in the x,y plane—and consequently as collinearity between ∇I and the gradient of $S(x, y)$ at $x = x_1$—is the more easily generalized for multidimensional problems in which the integral depends on several $y_i(x)$ and where, in addition, the terminal surface may be defined as the intersection of several surfaces. We now turn to these problems.

Consider the generalization of the problem in (3-1) to the case in which the integral depends on several functions $y_i(x)$ and their first derivatives, $y_i'(x)$ $(i = 1, \ldots, n)$. The functional to be maximized is

$$\int_{x_0}^{x_1} F(x, y_1, \ldots, y_n, y_1', \ldots, y_n')\, dx$$

Utilizing vector notation, where $\mathbf{Y} = [y_1, \ldots, y_n]'$ and $\dot{\mathbf{Y}} = [y_1', \ldots, y_n']'$, the problem is:

$$\text{Maximize} \quad I[\mathbf{Y}] = \int_{x_0}^{x_1} F(x, \mathbf{Y}, \dot{\mathbf{Y}})\, dx \qquad (3\text{-}31)$$

In analogy to the situation in Figs. 3-2 to 3-4 for a single function $y(x)$, we imagine that the left-hand endpoints of each of the $y_i(x)$ are fixed at $\mathbf{Y}(x_0) = \mathbf{Y}_0$ but that the right-hand endpoints are not.

It is well to pause here to visualize exactly the geometry for the case $\mathbf{Y} = [(y_1(x), y_2(x)]'$, i.e., when $I[\mathbf{Y}] = \int_{x_0}^{x_1} F(x, y_1, y_2, y_1', y_2')\, dx$. Corresponding to the fixed endpoint problem in Fig. 3-1, we have the problem of finding one curve, $y_1(x)$, from an initial point in the x,y_1 plane $[x_0, y_1(x_0) = y_{10}]$ to a terminal point $[x_1, y_1(x_1) = y_{11}]$ in that same plane and a second curve in the x,y_2 plane, $y_2(x)$, from $[x_0, y_2(x_0) = y_{20}]$ to $[x_1, y_2(x_1) = y_{21}]$. Figure 3-12 illustrates this.

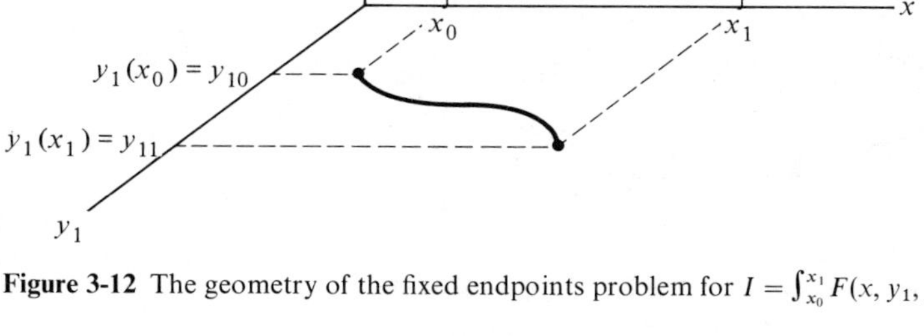

Figure 3-12 The geometry of the fixed endpoints problem for $I = \int_{x_0}^{x_1} F(x, y_1, y_2, y_1', y_2')\, dx$.

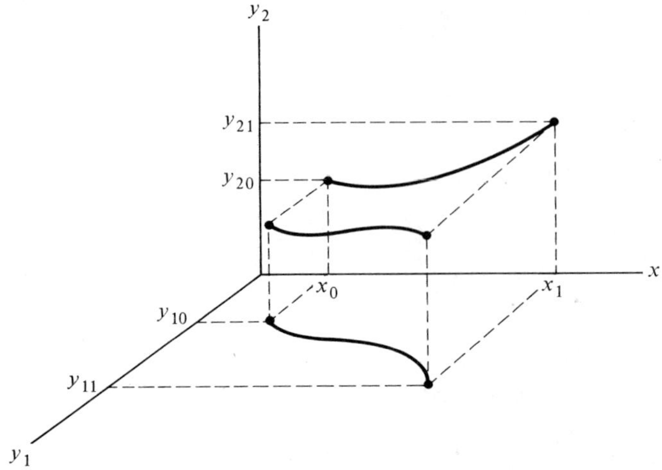

Figure 3-13 Alternative geometry for the fixed endpoints problem.

In three-dimensional x, y_1, y_2 space, we could equivalently represent the geometry as the problem of finding a function in that space connecting the initial point (x_0, y_{10}, y_{20}) and the terminal point (x_1, y_{11}, y_{21}). That is, given $y_1(x)$ and $y_2(x)$, selection of a value of x will simultaneously specify a value of $y_1(x)$ and $y_2(x)$, i.e., will identify a point in x, y_1, y_2 space. It is the projection of this function onto the x, y_1 plane and the x, y_2 plane that would give the two particular curves shown in Fig. 3-12. This alternative point of view is illustrated in Fig. 3-13. Note that a function that depends on two independent variables, x_1 and x_2 [that is, $y(x_1, x_2)$], can lead to a three-dimensional picture, as in Fig. 2-18*b* of Chap. 2.

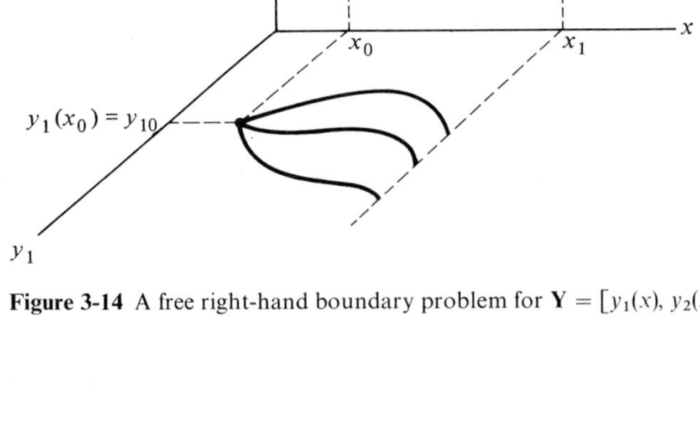

Figure 3-14 A free right-hand boundary problem for $\mathbf{Y} = [y_1(x), y_2(x)]'$.

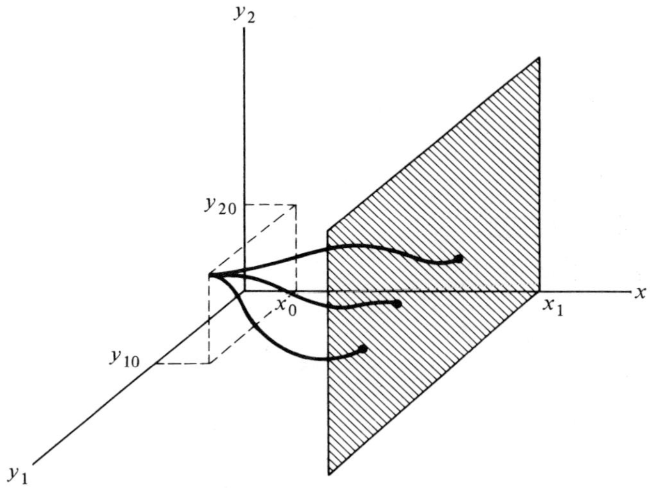

Figure 3-15 Alternative geometry for the free right-hand boundary problem.

There, however, x_1 and x_2 were two independent variables and a single function, $y(x_1, x_2)$, was to be found. Here we have a single independent variable, and two functions, $y_1(x)$ and $y_2(x)$, are to be found.

The analogue to the free right-hand boundary problem, illustrated in Fig. 3-2, is one in which only x_1 is specified, thus defining a line in both x,y_1 space and x,y_2 space that is orthogonal to the x axis (see Figs. 3-14 and 3-15).

The extension of the problem illustrated in Fig. 3-3 requires that the projections of the terminal surface $S(x, y_1, y_2)$ onto the $y_2 = 0$ plane (which defines x,y_1 space) and onto the $y_1 = 0$ plane (which defines x,y_2 space) be horizontal lines in both

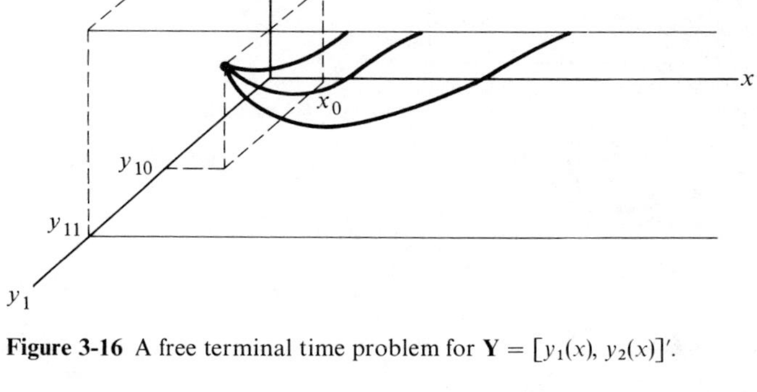

Figure 3-16 A free terminal time problem for $\mathbf{Y} = [y_1(x), y_2(x)]'$.

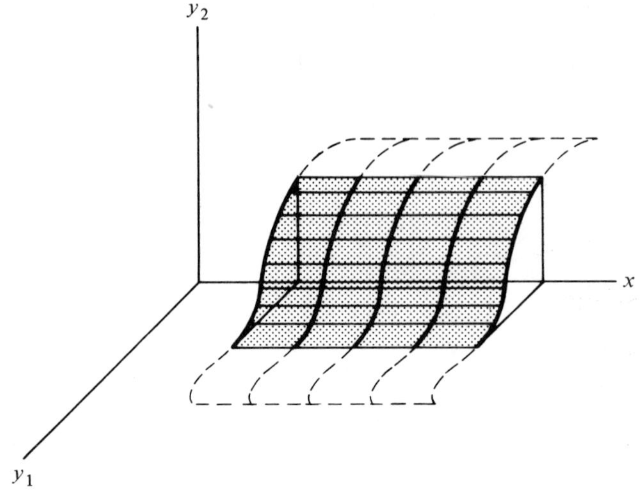

Figure 3-17 A terminal surface problem when $S(y_1, y_2) = 0$.

cases. This is only possible if the "surface," in x, y_1, y_2 space, is simply a straight line, orthogonal to the y_1, y_2 plane (see Fig. 3-16). Since the surface is independent of x, it could as well be denoted $S(y_1, y_2)$. The more general case, analogous to that represented in Fig. 3-4, is illustrated in Figs. 3-17 and 3-18. In the former case, the terminal surface is independent of x; in the latter it is not. Of course, when the terminal surface is as shown in Fig. 3-18 *and* when x_1 is also specified, then the terminal point is required to lie on a particular curve in the $x = x_1$ plane

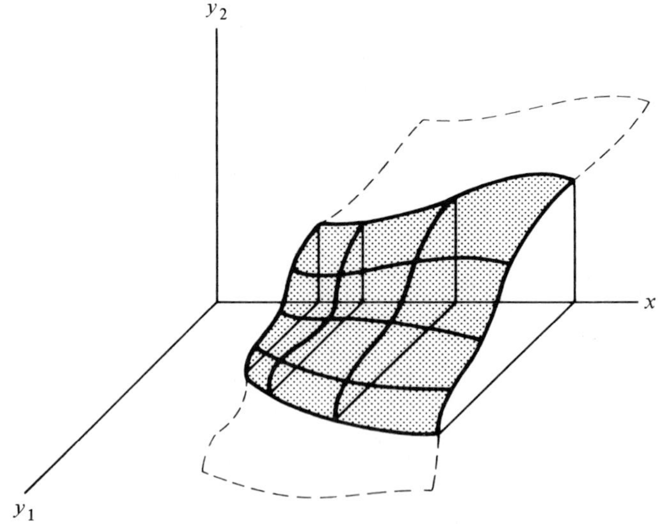

Figure 3-18 A terminal surface problem when $S(x, y_1, y_2) = 0$.

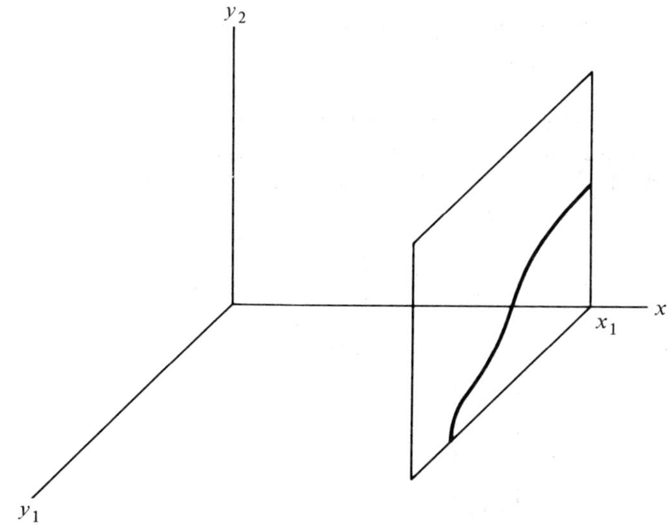

Figure 3-19 The terminal surface problem of Fig. 3-18 when $x = x_1$ is specified.

(see Fig. 3-19). Imagine that it has been generated by passing the $x = x_1$ plane through the surface in Fig. 3-18.

When an optimal $y_1(x)$ and $y_2(x)$ are found, it is possible, at least in principle, to solve for one, say y_2, in terms of the other, y_1. This would provide the representation of the solution in y_1,y_2 space; e.g., in Fig. 3-13, it would be the projection of the curve in x,y_1,y_2 space onto the y_1,y_2 plane, with both the initial and terminal points fixed. The free right-hand boundary problem (Fig. 3-15) would be one in y_1,y_2 space with no restrictions on the terminal point, since the terminal surface $x = x_1$ does not project onto y_1,y_2 space. The terminal surface in Fig. 3-16, however, would be projected as a single point (y_{11}, y_{21}) onto y_1,y_2 space. Finally, the terminal surface in Fig. 3-17 would project a single terminal curve and that in Fig. 3-18 a series of contours onto y_1,y_2 space; in the case with x_1 specified (Fig. 3-19), only one contour would be projected onto y_1,y_2 space, as from Fig. 3-17. For the most general case, Fig. 3-18, when an optimizing curve was found, it would hit the terminal surface at a point at which x_1, $y_1(x_1)$, and $y_2(x_1)$ would be simultaneously determined. On a plane through this point, parallel to the x,y_1 plane, a projection of the terminal surface in x,y_1 space would occur; similarly, on a plane through this point, parallel to the x,y_2 plane, a trace of the terminal surface in x,y_2 space would be found. These would be analogous to the terminal surface (curve) $y = \sigma(x)$ in the two-dimensional (one function) case illustrated in Fig. 3-4. We now turn to an examination of the algebraic parallels to the statements of the transversality conditions that were associated with Figs. 3-2, 3-3, and 3-4 in the simpler case of one independent variable x and one function $y(x)$.

The gradient $\nabla \mathbf{I}$ for (3-31) will be similar in form to that defined above in (3-27) for the problem with a single function $y(x)$. Now, however, there will be an

n-element vector of partial derivatives of F with respect to the y_i', namely,

$$\mathbf{F}_{\dot{\mathbf{Y}}} = [F_{y_1'}, \ldots, F_{y_n'}]'$$

and the scalar that was previously the simple product $(F_{y'})(y')$ must now be expanded to include the product of each $F_{y_i'}$ and its corresponding y_i', i.e., it becomes the inner product $[\mathbf{F}_{\dot{\mathbf{Y}}}] \cdot [\dot{\mathbf{Y}}]$. Thus $\nabla\mathbf{I}$ (which was previously a two-element vector) now becomes the $(n + 1)$-element vector

$$\nabla\mathbf{I} = \begin{bmatrix} F - [\mathbf{F}_{\dot{\mathbf{Y}}}] \cdot [\dot{\mathbf{Y}}] \\ \mathbf{F}_{\dot{\mathbf{Y}}} \end{bmatrix} \tag{3-32}$$

and the transversality condition at $x = x_1$ expressed by (3-26) becomes

$$[\nabla\mathbf{I}] \cdot \begin{bmatrix} \delta x \\ \delta y_1 \\ \vdots \\ \delta y_n \end{bmatrix} = 0 \tag{3-33}$$

evaluated at $x = x_1$.

As usual, if the right-hand endpoint were fixed at $\mathbf{Y}(x_1) = \mathbf{Y}_1$ (Figs. 3-12 and 3-13), then all $\delta y_i = 0$ and $\delta x = 0$ as well, so that (3-33) is unnecessary as an additional condition since it is automatically fulfilled. When only $x = x_1$ is specified (the free right-hand boundary problem of Figs. 3-14 and 3-15), $\delta x = 0$ but there are no restrictions on the terminal $y_i(x)$. Thus, from (3-33), there is no added requirement on the first element in $\nabla\mathbf{I}$, namely, on $F - [\mathbf{F}_{\dot{\mathbf{Y}}}] \cdot [\dot{\mathbf{Y}}]$, but since the $\delta y_i(x_1)$ are arbitrary, the second through $(n + 1)$ elements of $\nabla\mathbf{I}$ must be zero, that is,

$$[\mathbf{F}_{\dot{\mathbf{Y}}}]\big|_{x=x_1} = \mathbf{0} \tag{3-34}$$

This is the multidimensional analogue of $F_{y'}\big|_{x=x_1} = 0$, which is (3-20), above.

For the free terminal time problem of Fig. 3-16, all $\delta y_i(x_1) = 0$ but, in contrast, $\delta x \neq 0$, since the terminal value x_1 is not specified in advance. Hence, from (3-33), the second through $(n + 1)$ elements in $\nabla\mathbf{I}$ are unrestricted, but the first element must be zero:

$$(F - [\mathbf{F}_{\dot{\mathbf{Y}}}] \cdot [\dot{\mathbf{Y}}])\big|_{x=x_1} = 0 \tag{3-35}$$

This, in turn, is the n-function analogue of $(F - F_{y'}y')\big|_{x=x_1} = 0$, which is (3-21), above.

Finally, for the terminal surface problems illustrated in Figs. 3-17 and 3-18, we utilize the general $S(x, y_1, \ldots, y_n) = 0$ representation of that surface. The gradient of S, $\nabla\mathbf{S}$, will now be the $(n + 1)$-element vector

$$\nabla\mathbf{S} = \begin{bmatrix} \partial S/\partial x \\ \partial S/\partial y_1 \\ \vdots \\ \partial S/\partial y_n \end{bmatrix}$$

In the case where $n = 2$, as, for example, in Fig. 3-18, the gradient evaluated at a particular point on the surface S will be a three-element vector normal to S at that point, i.e., orthogonal to the plane tangent to S at that point. Thus, the extension of the condition in (3-29) $[\nabla \mathbf{I}(x_1) = \alpha\, \nabla \mathbf{S}(x_1)]$ is

$$\begin{bmatrix} F - [\mathbf{F}_{\dot{\mathbf{Y}}}]\cdot[\dot{\mathbf{Y}}] \\ \mathbf{F}_{\dot{\mathbf{Y}}} \end{bmatrix}_{x=x_1} = \alpha \begin{bmatrix} \partial S/\partial x \\ \partial S/\partial y_1 \\ \vdots \\ \partial S/\partial y \end{bmatrix}_{x=x_1} \tag{3-36}$$

Since direction (collinearity) and not magnitude is important, we can set $\alpha = 1$ with no loss of generality, from the point of view of the underlying geometry. As the following example illustrates, however, the constant α plays a role in the algebra of the solution. Thus the transversality requirement for the generalization of the case illustrated in Fig. 3-4 is

$$\begin{bmatrix} F - [\mathbf{F}_{\dot{\mathbf{Y}}}]\cdot[\dot{\mathbf{Y}}] \\ F_{y_1'} \\ \vdots \\ F_{y_n'} \end{bmatrix}_{x=x_1} = \alpha \begin{bmatrix} S_x \\ S_{y_1} \\ \vdots \\ S_{y_n} \end{bmatrix}_{x=x_1} \tag{3-37}$$

Example

We consider a rather straightforward extension of the shortest-distance problem for illustration. The particular functional is chosen in order to keep the mathematics as simple as possible; the logic of the application of the transversality conditions in (3-37) would be the same in more complex problems. Let $F(x, y_1, y_2, y_1', y_2') = \sqrt{1 + (y_1')^2 + (y_2')^2}$, with the initial point fixed at $x_0 = 1$, $y_1(x_0) = 2$, and $y_2(x_0) = 3$ and the requirement that the extremal terminate on the surface (plane) $S(x, y_1, y_2) = 0$, where $S = 3x + 4y_1 + 4y_2$.

Applying, first of all, the Euler-Lagrange conditions for y_1 and y_2 [(2-50) in Chap. 2] we find that $y_1(x) = k_1 x + k_2$ and $y_2(x) = k_3 x + k_4$. From initial conditions we know that

(*a*) $$k_1 + k_2 = 2$$

(*b*) $$k_3 + k_4 = 3$$

To substitute for the fixed values of y_1 and y_2 at x_1, we have the transversality requirements in (3-37) and the specification of the terminal surface. Here $F_{y_1'} = y_1'/\sqrt{1 + (y_1')^2 + (y_2')^2}$ and $F_{y_2'} = y_2'/\sqrt{1 + (y_1')^2 + (y_2')^2}$ so that (after some algebra) $F - [\mathbf{F}_{\dot{\mathbf{Y}}}]\cdot[\dot{\mathbf{Y}}] = 1/\sqrt{1 + (y_1')^2 + (y_2')^2}$. Moreover, $\nabla \mathbf{S} = \begin{bmatrix} 3 \\ 4 \\ 4 \end{bmatrix}$, so that

(3-37) requires

$$(c) \qquad \frac{1}{\sqrt{1 + (y_1')^2 + (y_2')^2}} = 3\alpha$$

$$(d) \qquad \frac{y_1'}{\sqrt{1 + (y_1')^2 + (y_2')^2}} = 4\alpha$$

$$(e) \qquad \frac{y_2'}{\sqrt{1 + (y_1')^2 + (y_2')^2}} = 4\alpha$$

Equations (*c*) through (*e*) are required to hold at $x = x_1$; however, since S is a plane and hence $\nabla \mathbf{S}$ is independent of x, and since both $y_1' = k_1$ and $y_2' = k_3$ (since both extremal curves are linear), conditions (*c*) through (*e*) hold for all x. Finally, we know that x_1, $y_1(x_1) = y_{11}$, and $y_2(x_1) = y_{21}$ must lie on S:

$$(f) \qquad 3x_1 + 4y_{11} + 4y_{21} = 0$$

In a fixed right-hand endpoint problem we would have, as complements to (*a*) and (*b*):

$$(a') \qquad k_1 x_1 + k_2 = y_{11}$$

$$(b') \qquad k_3 x_1 + k_4 = y_{21}$$

Now, however, x_1, y_{11}, and y_{21} are unknown. However, from (*d*) and (*e*) we conclude that $y_1' = y_2'$. Noting this, and substituting for $\sqrt{1 + (y_1')^2 + (y_2')^2}$ from (*d*) or (*e*) into (*c*), we find that $y_1' = \frac{4}{3} = y_2'$ and $\alpha = 1/\sqrt{41}$. But from our Euler-Lagrange results, this means $k_1 = k_3 = \frac{4}{3}$. Putting this into (*a*) and (*b*) gives $k_2 = \frac{2}{3}$ and $k_4 = \frac{5}{3}$ and hence

$$y_1(x) = \tfrac{4}{3}x + \tfrac{2}{3}$$
$$y_2(x) = \tfrac{4}{3}x + \tfrac{5}{3}$$

are the two extremals. Because of the linearity of the extremals, it was not necessary to find x_1, y_{11}, and y_{21} in the process of solving for k_1 through k_4. If we want to know the terminal point, however, it is easily established. Since $y_{11} = \frac{4}{3}x_1 + \frac{2}{3}$ and $y_{21} = \frac{4}{3}x_1 + \frac{5}{3}$, substitution into (*f*) gives $x_1 = -(28/41)$. Putting this in turn into $y_1(x)$ and into $y_2(x)$ gives $y_{11} = -(10/41)$ and $y_{21} = 31/41$. (The reader who visualize: well in three dimensions might want to sketch the terminal plane and the two extremals and notice that y_1 is orthogonal to the intersection of S and the x,y_1 plane and similarly that y_2 is orthogonal to the intersection of S and the x,y_2 plane.)

The utilization of the transversality conditions may not always be mathematically simple. For example, if we alter the functional so that $F(x, y_1, y_2, y_1', y_2') = x + \sqrt{1 + (y_1')^2 + (y_2')^2}$ (which differs from the preceding example only by the fact that the variable x has been added), while maintaining everything else from the example, we find that initial conditions, transversality requirements, and the terminal surface imply a fourth-degree equation in k_1, which is by no means simple to solve. The optimal $y_1(x)$ and $y_2(x)$ are still linear functions, and $k_1 \cong 4.05$, giving $y_1(x) = 4.05x - 2.05$ and $y_2(x) = 4.05x - 1.05$, as the interested reader may wish to check. (In addition, $x_1 = 0.35$, $y_{11} = -0.63$, $y_{21} = 0.37$, and $\alpha = 0.174$.)

More Complex Terminal Conditions

In problems with several $y_i(x)$, the terminal conditions may be defined by the requirement that $\mathbf{Y}(x_1)$ lie on several surfaces $S_1(x, y_1, \ldots, y_n) = 0$, $S_2(x, y_1, \ldots, y_n) = 0, \ldots, S_k(x, y_1, \ldots, y_n) = 0$, where, as in the case of linear equations, we have $k \leq n$. For example, with $n = 3$, there might be one terminal surface requirement involving x, $y_1(x)$, and $y_2(x)$ and a second connecting values of x, $y_1(x)$, and $y_3(x)$. It is not difficult to state the transversality condition in words: $\nabla \mathbf{I}$ must be orthogonal at $[x, \mathbf{Y}(x_1)]$ to the terminal surface S_0, where $S_0 = S_1 \cap S_2 \cap \cdots \cap S_k$.

We consider the geometry of the intersections of surfaces. For simplicity, suppose that the S_i are hyperplanes. The problem lies partly in visualizing anything of more than three dimensions. Two planes (three-dimensional surfaces) intersect in a line (a two-dimensional "surface"), provided that the planes are not parallel or identical. In general, three planes intersect in a point (a one-dimensional "surface"). Similarly, the intersection of two four-dimensional hyperplanes will, generally, be one three-dimensional plane, etc. When the surfaces are not planes, their intersections will be other surfaces or (nonlinear) curves.

Suppose that in the case of two functions, $y_1(x)$ and $y_2(x)$, we have two terminal planes $S_1(x, y_1, y_2) = 0$ and $S_2(x, y_1, y_2) = 0$. $\nabla \mathbf{S}_1$ is a vector orthogonal to S_1 (since S_1 is a plane, its gradient is a constant). Similarly, $\nabla \mathbf{S}_2$ is a vector orthogonal to S_2 (where $\nabla \mathbf{S}_2$ also is a constant). Since $S_0 = S_1 \cap S_2$ is a line lying in both S_1 and S_2, it is clear that both $\nabla \mathbf{S}_1$ and $\nabla \mathbf{S}_2$ are orthogonal to S_0 at the terminal point. In fact, $\nabla \mathbf{S}_1$ and $\nabla \mathbf{S}_2$ span a two-dimensional space (i.e., define a plane) whose origin is the terminal point $[x_1, y_1(x_1), y_2(x_1)]$ and which is orthogonal to S_0. Therefore, any two-element vector that is a linear combination of $\nabla \mathbf{S}_1$ and $\nabla \mathbf{S}_2$ will also emanate from the terminal point and be orthogonal to S_0.† Thus orthogonality between $\nabla \mathbf{I}$ and S_0 at the terminal point means that $\nabla \mathbf{I}$ must be a linear combination of $\nabla \mathbf{S}_1$ and $\nabla \mathbf{S}_2$, that is,

$$\nabla \mathbf{I}(x_1) = \alpha_1 \nabla \mathbf{S}_1 + \alpha_2 \nabla \mathbf{S}_2 \tag{3-38}$$

In the process, we introduce two new unknowns, α_1 and α_2, but we also have two new equations, namely, the terminal planes $S_1 = 0$ and $S_2 = 0$.

Example

We return to $F(x, y_1, y_2, y_1', y_2') = \sqrt{1 + (y_1')^2 + (y_2')^2}$ but now require that (1) $x_0 = 1$, $y_{10} = 2$, $y_{20} = 3$ and (2) the terminal point x_1, y_{11}, y_{21} lie on both

† The reader might try to visualize this using two intersecting pieces of paper and two pencils for the two gradients.

$S_1 = 3x + 4y_1 + 4y_2 = 0$ (from before) and $S_2 = x - y_1 - y_2 = 0$. As before, the Euler-Lagrange equations assure us that the optimal $y_1(x)$ and $y_2(x)$ are linear, that is, $y_1(x) = k_1x + k_2$ and $y_2(x) = k_3x + k_4$, so that $y_1' = k_1$ and $y_2' = k_3$. The transversality conditions (3-38) require that

$$(a)\qquad \frac{1}{\sqrt{1 + (y_1')^2 + (y_2')^2}} = 3\alpha_1 + \alpha_2$$

$$(b)\qquad \frac{y_1'}{\sqrt{1 + (y_1')^2 + (y_2')^2}} = 4\alpha_1 - \alpha_2$$

$$(c)\qquad \frac{y_2'}{\sqrt{1 + (y_1')^2 + (y_2')^2}} = 4\alpha_1 - \alpha_2$$

and hence $y_1' = y_2'$ $(= k_1 = k_3)$. The terminal planes

$$(d)\qquad 3x_1 + 4y_{11} + 4y_{21} = 0$$

$$(e)\qquad x_1 - y_{11} - y_{21} = 0$$

along with initial conditions

$$(f)\qquad k_1 + k_2 = 2$$

$$(g)\qquad k_3 + k_4 = 3$$

and the fact that $y_{11} = k_1x_1 + k_2$ and $y_{21} = k_3x_1 + k_4$ lead eventually, after a good deal of algebra, to $k_1 = 2.5$. Then it follows, from (f) and (g), that $k_2 = -0.5$ and $k_4 = 0.5$. From (a) and (b), with $k_1 = k_3 = y_1' = y_2'$, $\alpha_1 = 0.136$, $\alpha_2 = -0.136$, $x_1 = 0$, $y_{11} = -0.5$, and $y_{21} = 0.5$. That is, $y_1(x) = 2.5x - 0.5$ and $y_2(x) = 2.5x + 0.5$. The reader who works through the example will appreciate the fact that the mathematics do not generally become anything but more complicated if one or both of the terminal surfaces is nonlinear, if the integrand F is a more complex function of x, y_1, y_2, y_1', and y_2', etc.

When the terminal surfaces are nonlinear, the above argument still applies, except that in all cases we must specify that the gradients are evaluated at the terminal point. We need only recall that orthogonality between a line and a curve at a point means orthogonality between the line and the tangent to the curve at that point. Similarly with a line orthogonal to a surface; it is orthogonal to the tangent plane or hyperplane at the point of tangency.

Transversality at Infinity

When the upper limit of integration is $+\infty$, as in $\int_{x_0}^{\infty} F(x, \mathbf{Y}, \dot{\mathbf{Y}})\,dx$, the concept of transversality conditions at the "right-hand endpoint" requires modification. We saw at the end of Chap. 2 that the extension of the fixed endpoints case required simply that $\lim_{x\to\infty} y(x) = y_1$. For more variables, the requirement is $\lim_{x\to\infty} \mathbf{Y}(x) = \mathbf{Y}_1$. We also saw that when there is no condition on $y(x)$ as $x \to \infty$, then it must be true that $\lim_{x\to\infty} F_{y'} = 0$. This was (2-61) in Chap. 2. With several

$y_i(x)$, the requirement is $\lim_{x\to\infty} \mathbf{F}_{\dot{\mathbf{Y}}} = \mathbf{0}$. For most other possibilities, e.g., when $\mathbf{Y}(x)$ is required to satisfy $S(\mathbf{Y}) = 0$ as $x \to \infty$, there is a limiting form of the transversality condition in (3-36), above, with the first element eliminated as $x \to \infty$, namely, if $\lim_{x\to\infty} \mathbf{Y}(x) = \bar{\mathbf{Y}}$, then

$$\lim_{x\to\infty} \mathbf{F}_{\dot{\mathbf{Y}}} = \alpha \nabla \mathbf{S}(\bar{\mathbf{Y}})$$

Details for less well-behaved cases can be found in the references (for example, Hadley and Kemp [6, sec. 2.23, pp. 137–140] or Takayama [8, pp. 623–625]).

3-3 CONSTRAINTS

As in ordinary calculus, some of the most interesting problems in the calculus of variations include side conditions so that, for example, one does not have completely free choice in the selection of functions $y_i(x)$. For example, in the case of finding a time path of gross national product, $y(x)$, from the present to some terminal date in the future, we might require that at no point should the value of gross national product be less than some floor, $\bar{g}$, that is,

$$y(x) \geq \bar{g}$$

Geometrically, this restricts our choice of functions in x,y space to those $y(x)$ that start on or above the line $y = \bar{g}$ and never cut through it. As we will see, the possibilities for constraints are more varied than in ordinary calculus, where we may face (1) one or more, (2) linear or nonlinear, (3) equality or inequality constraints. For purposes of illustration, we return to the problem given in (3-1), namely:

$$\text{Maximize} \quad I[y] = \int_{x_0}^{x_1} F(x, y, y')\, dx$$

where $$y(x_0) = y_0 \quad \text{and} \quad y(x_1) = y_1$$

Extensions to more functions, higher-order derivatives, more independent variables, and alternative boundary conditions would parallel the discussions at the end of Chap. 2 and in the previous sections of this chapter.

A Global Constraint

A very early problem in the calculus of variations, and one which was also solved by Euler, can be very simply stated: from among all closed curves of a given length K, find that curve that encloses the largest area. This is the so-called "isoperimetric" (with the same perimeter) problem, and of course the maximizing curve is a circle. A variant of the problem is to find the curve of length K connecting two points on a line (the x axis) such that the area between that curve and the x axis is maximized (of course, K must be larger than the distance between the two points). Putting the problem more formally:

$$\text{Maximize} \quad I[y] = \int_{x_0}^{x_1} F(x, y, y')\, dx \tag{3-39}$$

where $$y(x_0) = y_0 \quad \text{and} \quad y(x_1) = y_1$$

and also where

$$\int_{x_0}^{x_1} G(x, y, y')\, dx = K \tag{3-40}$$

In the isoperimetric problem, the constraint is total arc length and so $G(x, y, y') = \sqrt{1 + (y')^2}$. The new constraint, (3-40), is called a global constraint since it specifies an overall property that $y(x)$ must have—in the isoperimetric case, a particular length. It does not refer to $y(x)$ at particular points in the range from x_0 to x_1, as would, for example, a constraint requiring that $y(x)$ never be less than a specified value, $\bar{g}$.

Global constraints are not common in applications in the social sciences, but the approach to solution of such problems is instructive and is quite similar to that which is necessary for other types of constraints. It is, in appearance, parallel to the Lagrange multiplier procedure for equality-constrained multivariable optimization problems in ordinary calculus. If we formulate a Lagrange-like function†

$$L(x, y, y', \lambda) = F(x, y, y') - \lambda G(x, y, y') \tag{3-41}$$

then the necessary condition corresponding to the Euler-Lagrange equation can be shown to be exactly that same equation, with L replacing F everywhere. That is, instead of $F_y - (d/dx)F_{y'} = 0$ we have

$$L_y - \frac{d}{dx} L_{y'} = 0 \tag{3-42}$$

In terms of the given functions $F(x, y, y')$ and $G(x, y, y')$ this is, from (3-41),

$$\frac{\partial}{\partial y}(F - \lambda G) - \frac{d}{dx}\left[\frac{\partial}{\partial y'}(F - \lambda G)\right] = 0$$

or $$F_y - \lambda G_y - \frac{d}{dx}(F_{y'} - \lambda G_{y'}) = 0$$

or $$\left(F_y - \frac{d}{dx} F_{y'}\right) - \lambda\left(G_y - \frac{d}{dx} G_{y'}\right) = 0 \tag{3-43}$$

In (3-43), the first term in parentheses is just the left-hand side of the Euler-Lagrange equation in the unconstrained case, and the second term in parentheses is the same set of partial derivatives, only from the constraining function G. Also

† As in ordinary maximization and minimization, some authors add, rather than subtract, $\lambda G(x, y, y')$.

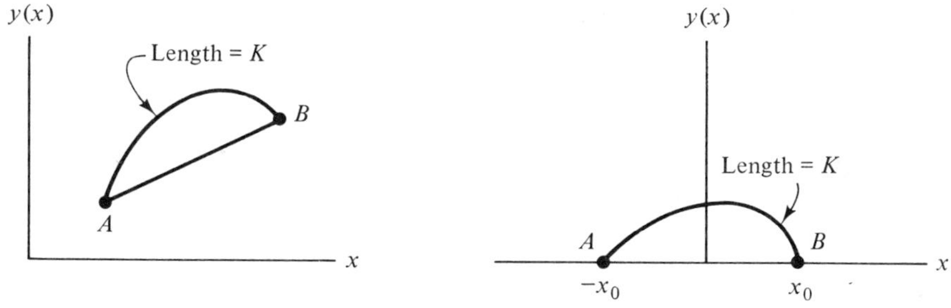

Figure 3-20 Alternative geometric representations of a maximum area, fixed perimeter problem.

as with ordinary constrained maximization and minimization problems, to these first-order conditions we must add the constraint itself. Thus an optimal $y(x)$ must satisfy (3-43) [or (3-42)] and the constraint itself, (3-40), plus the endpoint conditions given in (3-39).

Example

We want to find the curve of given length K connecting two points, A and B, in a plane, so that the area enclosed between the curve and the cord AB is maximized. This can easily be translated to align the cord AB along the x axis with its midpoint at the origin (see Fig. 3-20).

The problem is then:

$$\text{Maximize} \quad I[y] = \int_{-x_0}^{x_0} y(x)\,dx$$

$$\text{where} \qquad y(-x_0) = 0, \quad y(x_0) = 0 \quad \text{and} \quad \int_{-x_0}^{x_0} \sqrt{1 + (y')^2}\,dx = K \tag{3-44}$$

This is in the form of (3-39) and (3-40), with $F(x, y, y') = y(x)$ and $G(x, y, y') = \sqrt{1 + (y')^2}$. Applying (3-43) and noting that $F_y = 1$, $F_{y'} = 0$, $G_y = 0$, and $G_{y'} = y'/\sqrt{1 + (y')^2}$ gives

$$1 + \lambda\left[\frac{d}{dx}\frac{y'}{\sqrt{1 + (y')^2}}\right] = 0 \tag{3-45}$$

and integration of both sides gives

$$x + \lambda\left[\frac{y'}{\sqrt{1 + (y')^2}}\right] = k_1 \tag{3-46}$$

Now we want to integrate again, so as to undo the differentiation with respect to x that is present in the y' terms. This is most easily accomplished if we represent x and y parametrically, as follows.† Let $y' = \tan \alpha$. Then, since (1) $1 + (\tan \alpha)^2 = (\sec \alpha)^2$, (2) $\sec \alpha = 1/\cos \alpha$, and (3) $\sin \alpha/\cos \alpha = \tan \alpha$, (3-46) can be expressed as $(x - k_1) = -\lambda \sin \alpha$ or $x = k_1 - \lambda \sin \alpha$. By definition, $y' = \tan \alpha$ and therefore $dy = \tan \alpha\, dx$; but since $x = k_1 - \lambda \sin \alpha$, $dx = -\lambda \cos \alpha\, d\alpha$ and hence $dy = -\lambda \tan \alpha \cos \alpha\, d\alpha = -\lambda \sin \alpha\, d\alpha$, from which, integrating both sides, $y = \lambda \cos \alpha + k_2$ or $y - k_2 = \lambda \cos \alpha$. That is,

$$\begin{aligned} x - k_1 &= -\lambda \sin \alpha \\ y - k_2 &= \lambda \cos \alpha \end{aligned} \tag{3-47}$$

Squaring both sides of both equations and adding [recalling that $(\sin \alpha)^2 + (\cos \alpha)^2 = 1$] gives

$$(x - k_1)^2 + (y - k_2)^2 = \lambda^2 \tag{3-48}$$

from which it is clear that the function $y(x)$ is to be a circle whose center is at (k_1, k_2) and whose radius is λ.

Since $y(-x_0) = 0$ and $y(x_0) = 0$,

$$(-x_0 - k_1)^2 + (0 - k_2)^2 = \lambda^2$$
$$(x_0 - k_1)^2 + (0 - k_2)^2 = \lambda^2$$

and therefore $k_1 = 0$ (i.e., the center of the circle is on the y axis, as is to be expected from Fig. 3-20). Furthermore, $x_0^2 + k_2^2 = \lambda^2$ or

$$k_2 = \sqrt{\lambda^2 - x_0^2} \tag{3-49}$$

(see Fig. 3-21). The added variable, λ, provides the flexibility to adjust the location of the center of the circle, at k_2 on the y axis, so that the length of that part of the circumference of the circle that is above the x axis is equal to K. If $\lambda = x_0$, $k_2 = 0$, and $\pi x_0 = \pi\lambda$, exactly one-half of the total circumference of the circle would be above the x axis. This is only possible if $\pi x_0 = K$; otherwise, when $\lambda > x_0$—assuming $K > 2x_0$—we choose the negative root of $\sqrt{\lambda^2 - x_0^2}$ for k_2 and there

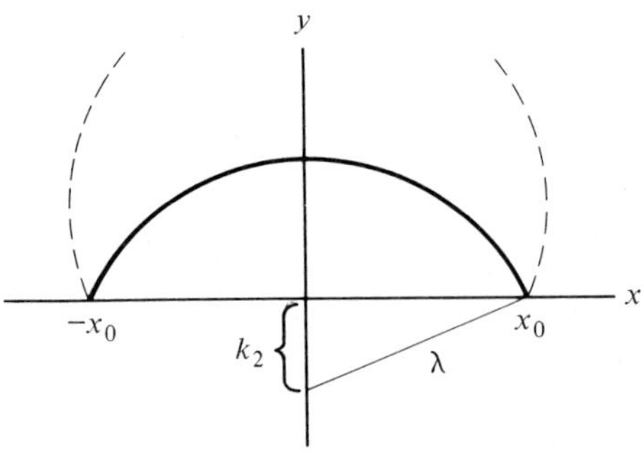

Figure 3-21 Solution curve for (3-44).

† The reader who is not interested in the details of the mathematics can proceed directly to the result, given in (3-48) and the text following.

will be less than one-half of the circumference above the x axis.† The values of λ and k_2 can be found from (3-49) and the constraint fact that the total length above the x axis should be K. The algebraic and trigonometric manipulations need not concern us further; it is clear that by varying λ—and hence k_2—the length of the curve above the axis will be varied also and therefore can be made to conform to K.

Local Constraints (Equalities)

Suppose that $I[y] = \int_{x_0}^{x_1} F(x, y_1, y_2, y_1', y_2')\, dx$, where both endpoints are fixed. Figure 3-13 illustrated the problem. If instead of being completely free to choose $\mathbf{Y}(x) = [y_1(x), y_2(x)]'$ it was required that the maximizing curve lie on a given surface in x,y_1,y_2 space, say $g(x, y_1, y_2) = c$, then we would have a different kind of constrained calculus of variations problem. (The given initial and terminal points must lie on the surface, of course.) The constraint $g(x, y_1, y_2) = c$ [or $h(x, y_1, y_2) = g(x, y_1, y_2) - c = 0$] is termed "local" because it imposes requirements on the functions $y_1(x)$ and $y_2(x)$ at every value of x from x_0 to x_1 (see Fig. 3-22).

Again quite analogously to the constrained optimization case in ordinary calculus, we formulate a function

$$L(x, \mathbf{Y}, \dot{\mathbf{Y}}, \lambda) = F(x, \mathbf{Y}, \dot{\mathbf{Y}}) - [\lambda(x)]h(x, \mathbf{Y}, \dot{\mathbf{Y}}) \tag{3-50}$$

(We include the possibility of $\dot{\mathbf{Y}}$ in the constraints h in order to accommodate a more general case, to be discussed below.) Since the constraint is imposed at all values of x from x_0 to x_1, $\lambda(x)$ depends on x (unlike the global constraint case,

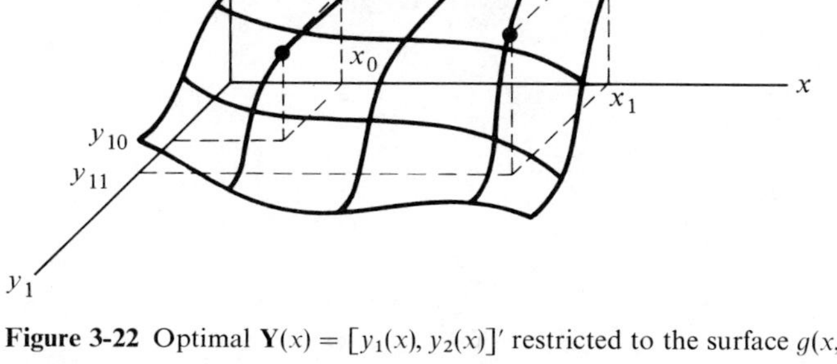

Figure 3-22 Optimal $\mathbf{Y}(x) = [y_1(x), y_2(x)]'$ restricted to the surface $g(x, y_1, y_2) = c$.

† We assume that K is not so large as to require a $k_2 > 0$, which would mean a circle, such as the dashed one in Fig. 3-21, that extended beyond the bounds of integration.

where it was a constant). It can be shown that the necessary condition corresponding to the Euler-Lagrange equation is again that same equation, with L substituted for F throughout (and $i = 1, \ldots, n$):

$$L_{y_i} - \frac{d}{dx} L_{y_i'} = 0 \tag{3-51}$$

[Compare (3-42). Note that a form parallel to (3-43) is not possible here since λ is a function of x.] The maximizing solution must satisfy (3-51), the fixed initial and terminal values, and the constraint itself. If $\mathbf{Y} = [y_1, \ldots, y_n]'$, with $n > 2$, there may be several constraints $g_1(x, \mathbf{Y}) = c_1, \ldots, g_k(x, \mathbf{Y}) = c_k$, that is, $h_1(x, \mathbf{Y}) = 0, \ldots, h_k(x, \mathbf{Y}) = 0$ $(k < n)$. In this case there would be k Lagrange multiplier functions $\lambda_1(x), \ldots, \lambda_k(x)$ connecting the constraints to $F(x, \mathbf{Y}, \dot{\mathbf{Y}})$ in the usual way; $L = F - \sum_{i=1}^{k} \lambda_i(x) h_i$. Detailed proofs of results for the general case of many constraints impose requirements on the rank of the matrix of partial derivatives $[\partial g_i / \partial y_j]$; these serve to assure nonsingularity, linear independence of columns, etc.†

As in ordinary calculus, a constraint of the sort that we are now considering does not make sense when only one function $y(x)$ is involved. That is, if $g(x, y) = c$ is specified for the functional $I[y] = \int_{x_0}^{x_1} F(x, y, y')\, dx$, then we are left with no choice but to select that $y(x)$ satisfying the constraint (see Fig. 3-23). This is similar to the problem in ordinary calculus of finding the x to maximize $f(x)$ when as a side condition we have the equation $x = c$. For essentially this same reason, when $\mathbf{Y} = [y_1, \ldots, y_n]'$ with constraints $g_i(x, \mathbf{Y}) = 0$ $(i = 1, \ldots, k)$, it is necessary that $k < n$. In Fig. 3-22, where $n = 2$ and $k = 1$, a second constraint surface would, in general, intersect the first one in a single curve. If that curve passed through the fixed endpoints $(x_0, \mathbf{Y}_0)$ and $(x_1, \mathbf{Y}_1)$, then it would represent the only possible solution; if it did not pass through both endpoints, then the problem would have no solution.

The equality constraints might also contain derivatives of some or all of the y's. For the $\mathbf{Y} = [y_1, y_2]'$ case, we might have $g(x, y_1, y_2, y_1', y_2') = 0$, which would be

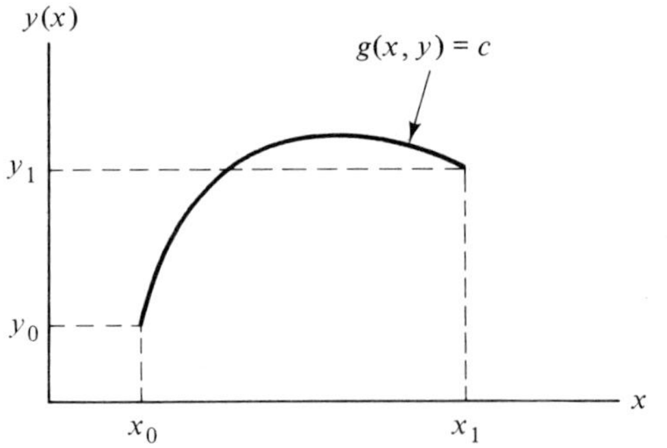

Figure 3-23 A local constraint for the one-function case.

† Hadley and Kemp [6, chap. 3] provide a thorough derivation of the results with all mathematical details.

a hypersurface in five-dimensional extended phase space. Again, a lagrangian function L, as given in (3-50), is appropriate and the resulting Euler-Lagrange equations in (3-51) constitute a set of necessary conditions for the constrained optimization problem. With more variables and more constraints $g_1(x, \mathbf{Y}, \dot{\mathbf{Y}}) = c_1, \ldots, g_k(x, \mathbf{Y}, \dot{\mathbf{Y}}) = c_k$, it is again necessary that $k < n$ and also that a rank condition hold for the matrix $[\partial g_i/\partial y_j']$.†

Local Constraints (Inequalities)

Instead of requiring that the optimal $y(x)$ or $\mathbf{Y}(x)$ lie on some particular surface, that surface may only form a boundary to the function or functions, i.e., the constraint may take the form of an inequality $g(x, y, y') \leq c$, or $h(x, y, y') = g(x, y, y') - c \leq 0$. Consider Fig. 3-23 as if it were for this case. Then the maximizing $y(x)$ would be required to begin at a point (x_0, y_0) which could be on or below the surface, terminate at (x_1, y_1) (again, on or below the surface), and never go above the curved boundary set by $g(x, y, y') \leq c$. [Here it does make sense in a problem with only one function $y(x)$ to have a local inequality constraint—or even several. Compare the ordinary calculus case of choosing x to maximize $f(x)$ subject to $x \leq c$.]

Inequality constraints can introduce complications, since $y(x)$ will generally have a kink at the points where it meets (or leaves) the constraint. Thus the derivative, $y'(x)$, will not be defined there. There are so-called corner conditions that must be met at such points; these are the subject matter of Sec. 3-4, below. It will be clear from the discussion in that section, however, that satisfaction of the corner conditions may not be possible when the kink in $y(x)$ is caused by the presence of a constraint.

In fact, inequality constraints of various kinds are far more easily handled in the maximum principle formulation; these are covered in some detail in Sec. 4-4 of Chap. 4, below. The general formulation, however, turns out to be quite analogous to the Kuhn-Tucker approach in nonlinear programming. Forming the lagrangian-like function exactly as in (3-50)—except that now we are only looking for one function $y(x)$—gives

$$L(x, y, y', \lambda) = F(x, y, y') - [\lambda(x)]h(x, y, y') \tag{3-52}$$

It can be shown that in addition to the Euler-Lagrange counterpart requirement in (3-51)

$$L_y - \frac{d}{dx} L_{y'} = 0$$

the specified endpoint values, and satisfaction of the (inequality) constraint itself, the maximizing $y(x)$ must also satisfy

$$\lambda(x)h(x) = 0 \tag{3-53}$$

and $\lambda(x) \geq 0$.

With all of these constrained problems, it is of course possible that the endpoint

† Again, Hadley and Kemp [6, chap. 3] cover all mathematical details very thoroughly.

conditions at either the left-hand end or the right-hand end may be less exactly specified. In those cases, the transversality results of Sec. 3-2 apply, with F replaced everywhere by the appropriately formulated Lagrange-like function—(3-41) or (3-50). No new principles are involved.

In formal proofs of many of the results for inequality constrained problems, both using the calculus of variations approach and also that of the maximum principle (Chap. 4), it is necessary to consider constraint qualification conditions. In the Kuhn-Tucker results for ordinary nonlinear programming problems, this condition is designed to rule out certain exceptionally troublesome behavior on the boundaries of the feasible region, such as outward-pointing "cusps" formed by the intersection of two convex constraint functions (upper bounds) in a maximization problem. As in much of the nonlinear programming and the dynamic optimization literature, we will assume throughout, unless otherwise noted, that such regularity assumptions hold.

3-4 NONSMOOTH CURVES (CORNERS)

Restatement of First Variation Conditions

Thus far, we have assumed that the function $y(x)$ is not only continuous throughout the interval $x_0 \le x \le x_1$ but also that it is smooth throughout this entire interval. Thus in the derivation of Euler-Lagrange equations, we have assumed that terms such as F_y, which will in general itself be a function of x, y, and y', exist everywhere. If $y(x)$ has one or more kinks, or corners, $y'(x)$ will not be defined at those points and consequently terms whose values depend on $y'(x)$ will also not be defined at those points. Yet this would seem to be exclusively a mathematical problem, since clearly there is no logical reason to require that an optimal path always be smooth. It might easily turn out to be optimal for $y(x)$ to follow one curve for the first part of the path, say from x_0 to x_c, and then to follow an entirely different curve over the range from x_c to x_1, as illustrated in Fig. 3-24. There will, in general, be a corner where the two functions join.

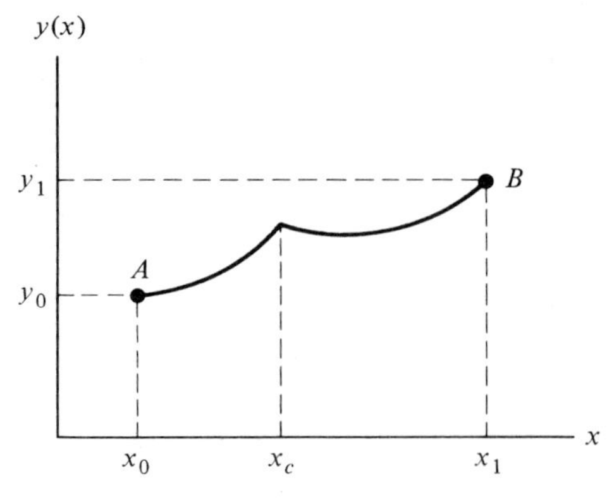

Figure 3-24 A kinked path from A to B.

If we consider the two smooth segments separately, we can write the functional as

$$I[y] = \int_{x_0}^{x_c} F(x, y, y')\,dx + \int_{x_c}^{x_1} F(x, y, y')\,dx \tag{3-54}$$

or, letting I_1 and I_2 denote the first and second integrals, respectively, on the right of (3-54),

$$I[y] = I_1 + I_2$$

Recall from our initial consideration of the transversality conditions in Sec. 3-1 that the general definition of the first variation of I [given in (3-13)] was

$$\delta I = \varepsilon \int_{x_0}^{x_1} \left(F_y - \frac{d}{dx} F_{y'} \right) \phi(x)\,dx + F_{y'}\big|_{x=x_1} (\delta y_1) + (F - F_{y'}y')\big|_{x=x_1} (\delta x_1)$$
$$- F_{y'}\big|_{x=x_0} (\delta y_0) - (F - F_{y'}y')\big|_{x=x_0} (\delta x_0) \tag{3-55}$$

and in the present case

$$\delta I = \delta I_1 + \delta I_2 \tag{3-56}$$

As before, the maximizing curve must satisfy the Euler-Lagrange equation, and hence the integral on the right-hand side of (3-55) will be zero. Consider, then, the remaining terms in the expressions for δI_1 and δI_2. We will generally use the notation $F_{y'_-}$ instead of the more standard but also more cumbersome $F_{y'}\big|_{x=x_{c^-}}$ to indicate that $F_{y'}$ is evaluated just to the left of x_c; this is necessary because $y'(x)$ does not exist at x_c and hence terms in which $y'(x)$ may appear cannot be defined at x_c either. Subscripts "$-$" and "$+$" on other terms also indicate that they are being evaluated at $x = x_{c^-}$ and $x = x_{c^+}$, respectively. Since x_c is at the right-hand end of I_1 and at the left-hand end of I_2, we have

$$\delta I_1 = F_{y'}\big|_{x=x_{c^-}} (\delta y_c) + (F - F_{y'}y')\big|_{x=x_{c^-}} (\delta x_c)$$
$$- F_{y'}\big|_{x=x_0} (\delta y_0) - (F - F_{y'}y')\big|_{x=x_0} (\delta x_0) \tag{3-57}$$

and

$$\delta I_2 = F_{y'}\big|_{x=x_1} (\delta y_1) + (F - F_{y'}y')\big|_{x=x_1} (\delta x_1)$$
$$- F_{y'}\big|_{x=x_{c^+}} (\delta y_c) - (F - F_{y'}y')\big|_{x=x_{c^+}} (\delta x_c) \tag{3-58}$$

Since we are considering the fixed endpoints case, $\delta x_0 = \delta y_0 = \delta x_1 = \delta y_1 = 0$ and the expressions for δI_1 and δI_2 are considerably simplified:

$$\delta I_1 = F_{y'_-}(\delta y_c) + (F - F_{y'}y')_-(\delta x_c) \tag{3-59}$$

$$\delta I_2 = -F_{y'_+}(\delta y_c) - (F - F_{y'}y')_+(\delta x_c) \tag{3-60}$$

Moreover, since we do require continuity (but not smoothness) of $y(x)$ at $x = x_c$, δy_c in δI_1 is the same as δy_c in δI_2, and similarly δx_c is the same in both expressions. Therefore, for $\delta I = 0$, which is our standard necessary condition for a maximizing (or minimizing) function y, we want $\delta I_1 + \delta I_2 = 0$, that is,

$$[F_{y'_-} - F_{y'_+}](\delta y_c) + [(F - F_{y'}y')_- - (F - F_{y'}y')_+](\delta x_c) = 0 \tag{3-61}$$

Finally, since δy_c and δx_c are arbitrary and therefore in general cannot in any way be expected to help balance the left-hand side of (3-61) to zero, it is necessary that

$$F_{y'_-} = F_{y'_+} \tag{3-62}$$

so that the first term on the left-hand side of (3-61) is zero and also

$$(F - F_{y'}y')_- = (F - F_{y'}y')_+ \tag{3-63}$$

so that the second term will be zero. These two equations, (3-62) and (3-63), are known as the Weierstrass-Erdmann corner conditions, after the two mathematicians who investigated them. Using our previous definition, (3-27), of the gradient of I, namely,

$$\nabla \mathbf{I} = \begin{bmatrix} (F - F_{y'}y') \\ F_{y'} \end{bmatrix}$$

these conditions could also be expressed as

$$\nabla \mathbf{I}\big|_{x=x_{c^-}} = \nabla \mathbf{I}\big|_{x=x_{c^+}} \tag{3-64}$$

The requirement that a function have the same value just to the left of x_c and just to the right of x_c is simply the requirement that that function be continuous at the point x_c. Thus (3-62) requires that $F_{y'}$ be continuous across a corner of $y(x)$, (3-63) similarly requires the continuity of $(F - F_{y'}y')$ across the corner, and (3-64) summarizes both requirements by specifying that $\nabla \mathbf{I}$ is continuous at x_c. Referring again to (3-56), (3-59), and (3-60), we see that these requirements assure that the expression for the first variation of I, as given in (3-56), will not have discontinuities.

Geometrically, the corner conditions have an interpretation in F,y' space. Consider (3-62); this requires that the derivative of the function F in F,y' space be the same at the two points $y'(x_{c^-})$ and $y'(x_{c^+})$. Figure 3-25 illustrates this for the nonsmooth curve in Fig. 3-24; assume that at x_{c^-}, $y' = 3$ and at x_{c^+}, $y' = -\frac{1}{2}$. The slopes of the dashed tangent lines at y'_- and y'_+ are $F_{y'_-}$ and $F_{y'_+}$, respectively; condition (3-62) requires that these tangents have the same slope (i.e., be parallel)

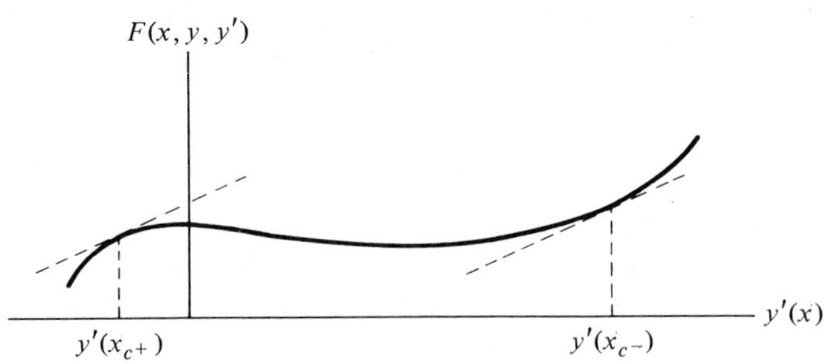

Figure 3-25 Weierstrass-Erdmann corner condition (3-62).

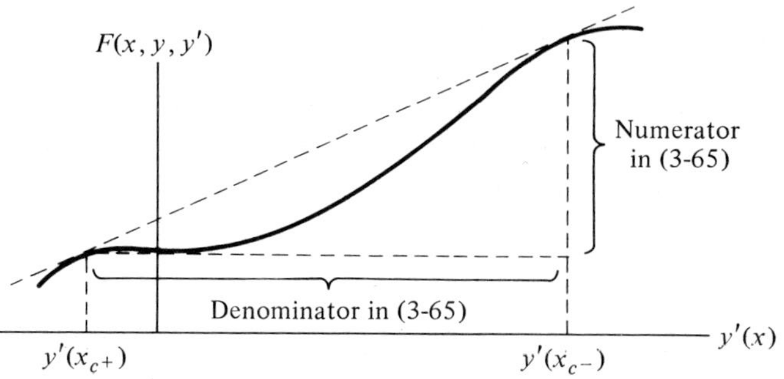

Figure 3-26 Weierstrass-Erdmann corner conditions (3-62) and (3-63).

as in Fig. 3-25. The second corner condition, (3-63), can be rewritten as

$$F_+ - F_- = (y'_+ - y'_-)F_{y'_-}$$

where, from (3-62) and Fig. 3-25, the $F_{y'}$ term on the right-hand side is the same whether evaluated at x_{c^-} or x_{c^+}. Thus

$$\frac{F_+ - F_-}{y'_+ - y'_-} = F_{y'_-} \tag{3-65}$$

The numerator is the vertical distance between F evaluated at y'_+ and y'_- in F,y' space and the denominator is the horizontal distance between the y' values. Thus, to accommodate condition (3-63) [as rewritten in (3-65)], Fig. 3-25 must be redrawn as in Fig. 3-26. In the geometry of Fig. 3-26, both numerator and denominator in the left-hand side of (3-65) will be negative, but the ratio will still be positive and must equal the slope.

Examples

Despite the geometric interpretation, it may not be obvious how one properly makes use of these corner conditions. Unless one knows in advance from the nature of the problem that nonsmooth functions are precluded (not generally likely), what is the operational usefulness of the conditions in (3-62) and (3-63)? As shown in the following example, the requirement in (3-62) that $F_{y'}$ be continuous may imply that $y'(x)$ is continuous and hence that there are no corners [recall that if $y'(x)$ is continuous throughout an interval then $y(x)$ is smooth throughout that interval].

For example, the functional in the problem of finding the curve of shortest length connecting A and B in a plane was $I[y] = \int_{x_0}^{x_1} \sqrt{1 + (y')^2}\, dx$. Here $F_{y'} = y'/\sqrt{1 + (y')^2}$ and it is clear that if $F_{y'}$ is to be continuous, y' itself must be and hence the minimizing curve will be smooth (a straight line, as we saw previously when, however, we did not consider the possibility that a nonsmooth function might be even better). Thus, when the continuity requirement on $F_{y'}$ in (3-62) can be shown to imply continuity of y', then we know that the optimal $y(x)$ will be smooth. Moreover, a corollary that follows from (3-62) and Rolle's theorem is that if x_c is the point at which the optimizing curve has a corner, then $F_{y'y'}[x_c, y(x_c), p]$ must be zero for some finite value of p.† Therefore, if one can show that $F_{y'y'}[x_c, y_c, p]$ cannot be zero, then again one has shown that the optimal $y(x)$ will be a smooth curve. Applying this test to our shortest-distance example,

$$F_{y'y'} = \frac{1}{[1 + (y')^2]^{3/2}}$$

which can never be zero and hence (as we already concluded from the continuity requirement on $F_{y'}$) the minimizing function $y(x)$ will be smooth. Similarly, in the monopolistic pricing example we found that $F_{p'} = -10{,}000p' - 10{,}200 + 200p$. Hence $F_{p'p'} = -10{,}000$, which is never zero, and the function $p(t)$ to maximize total profits will be smooth.

Consider a less clear-cut example.‡ Minimize $I[y] = \int_0^2 [(y')^2 - 1]^2\,dx$, where $y(0) = 1$ and $y(2) = 1$. In this case, $F_{y'} = 4y'[(y')^2 - 1]$, and one senses trouble since, for example, if y'_- were -1 and y'_+ were $+1$, (3-62) would hold even though $y(x)$ would have a corner at x_c. Alternatively, $F_{y'y'} = 12(y')^2 - 4$, which clearly will be zero when $y' = \pm\sqrt{1/3}$. Suppose, initially, that we were to proceed by imposing the Euler-Lagrange condition. Here $F_y = 0$ and we have already found $F_{y'}$, so the equation requires

$$-\frac{d}{dx}[4(y')^3 - 4y'] = 0$$

or

$$4(y')^3 - 4y' = \text{constant}$$

from which we conclude that $y'(x)$ is constant and hence $y(x)$ must be a straight line, $y(x) = k_1x + k_2$, connecting the two points. Since $y(x_0) = 1$ and $y(x_1) = 1$, it follows that $k_1 = 0$ and $k_2 = 1$, i.e., the line must be horizontal, $y(x) = 1$. Consequently, the minimized value of $I[y]$ when $y(x)$ is smooth is $\int_0^2 1\,dx = x]_0^2 = 2$.

Since we suspect that nonsmooth curves may be better, we utilize the corner conditions directly. From (3-62),

$$4y'[(y')^2 - 1]\,|_{x=x_c-} = 4y'[(y')^2 - 1]\,|_{x=x_c+}$$

and from (3-63),

$$\{[(y')^2 - 1]^2 - 4(y')^2[(y')^2 - 1]\}_{x=x_c-} = \{[(y')^2 - 1]^2 - 4(y')^2[(y')^2 - 1]\}_{x=x_c+}$$

† Let $f(p) = F_{y'}(x_c, y_c, p)$, and let the slopes of $y(x)$ to the left and the right of the corner be p_1 and p_2, respectively, that is, $y'_- = p_1$ and $y'_+ = p_2$, where $p_1 < p_2$. From (3-62), $f(p_1) = f(p_2)$. Rolle's theorem says that if a continuous function, such as $f(p)$, has the same value for two distinct values of p, such as p_1 and p_2, then there is a p in the open interval $p_1 < p < p_2$ at which $f'(p) = 0$. But by the definition of f, $f'(p) = F_{y'y'}(x_c, y_c, p)$. The geometry is straightforward. Let $f(p_1) = k$, $f(p_2) = k$, and $p_1 < p_2$. In $p, f(p)$ space, imagine a horizontal line at $f(p) = k$. The only way to draw a continuous function $f(p)$ so that it cuts that horizontal at p_1 and again at p_2 is if there is at least one point p between p_1 and p_2 at which the slope of $f(p)$ changes from positive to negative (or from negative to positive); i.e., if there is at least one point p at which $f'(p) = 0$.

‡ Adapted from Citron [3, pp. 41–43].

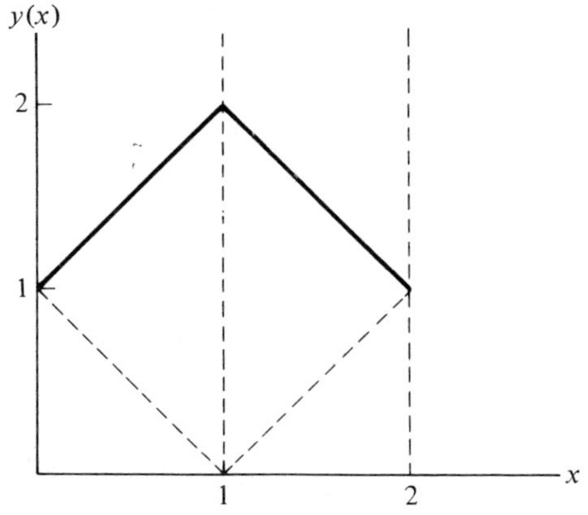

Figure 3-27 Optimal functions $y(x)$ with a corner.

Rearranging these two equations and using simplified notation gives

$$[(y')_-^3 - (y')_+^3] - [y'_- - y'_+] = 0 \tag{3-66a}$$

$$3[(y'_-)^4 - (y'_+)^4] - 2[(y'_-)^2 - (y'_+)^2] = 0 \tag{3-66b}$$

Obviously when $y'_- = y'_+$ at $x = x_c$, there is no corner and (3-66*a*) and (3-66*b*) are clearly satisfied. The question is, are there other values of y'_- and y'_+ to simultaneously satisfy (3-66*a*) and (3-66*b*)? A moment's reflection on these two equations might suggest that $+1$ and -1 are likely to be solutions. In fact, for $y'_- = -1$, $y'_+ = +1$, or for $y'_- = +1$, $y'_+ = -1$, the equations are satisfied.† This means that straight line segments with alternating slopes of $+1$ and -1 or -1 and $+1$ will be optimal extremals with corners. For example, $y(x) = x + 1$, $0 \le x \le 1$; $y(x) = -x + 3$, $1 \le x \le 2$. Figure 3-27 illustrates this solution (solid line), as well as an alternative one, $y(x) = -x + 1$, $0 \le x \le 1$; $y(x) = x - 1$, $1 \le x \le 2$ (dashed line). Clearly there are an infinite number of solutions with more than one corner; all that is required is that the slope be either $+1$ or -1 and that $y(x)$ begin at $y(0) = 1$ and end at $y(2) = 1$. The functional for the solution given by the heavy line in Fig. 3-27 is $I[y] = \int_0^1 0\,dx + \int_1^2 0\,dx = 0$, which is a better minimum than that given by the smooth straight line $y(x) = 1$. (Note that this minimum value of zero will be given by any series of lines with slopes alternating between ± 1 and ∓ 1, since the integral over each individual segment will be zero.)

The extension to functionals depending on several $y_i(x)$ $(i = 1, \ldots, n)$ is straightforward. Parallel to (3-62) we have the n conditions

$$F_{y'_i}\big|_{x=x_c-} = F_{y'_i}\big|_{x=x_c+} \tag{3-67}$$

or, using vectors as before,

$$\mathbf{F}_{\dot{\mathbf{Y}}}\big|_{x=x_c-} = \mathbf{F}_{\dot{\mathbf{Y}}}\big|_{x=x_c+} \tag{3-68}$$

† Solution requires factoring $(y'_- - y'_+)$ from both equations and then exploring the consequences of $y'_- \neq y'_+$, i.e., of a corner at x_c.

and (3-63) is expanded to

$$(F - [\mathbf{F}_{\dot{\mathbf{Y}}}] \cdot [\dot{\mathbf{Y}}])|_{x=x_c^-} = (F - [\mathbf{F}_{\dot{\mathbf{Y}}}] \cdot [\dot{\mathbf{Y}}])|_{x=x_c^+} \tag{3-69}$$

Alternatively, recalling (3-64) and our definition [in (3-32)] of $\nabla\mathbf{I}$ in the case of $y_1(x), \ldots, y_n(x)$, we have

$$\nabla\mathbf{I}\,|_{x=x_c^-} = \nabla\mathbf{I}\,|_{x=x_c^+} \tag{3-70}$$

3-5 MORE NECESSARY CONDITIONS AND THE QUESTION OF SUFFICIENCY

We continue to explore the parallel between total differentials in ordinary maximization and minimization problems and the total variation in calculus of variations problems. Recall that for a function of one variable, in addition to $f'(x) = 0$ as a necessary condition for an unconstrained maximum or a minimum, it was also *necessary* that $f''(x) \leq 0$ for a maximum or that $f''(x) \geq 0$ for a minimum. Additionally, the two conditions (1) $f'(x) = 0$ and (2) $f''(x) < 0$ were *sufficient* for a maximum or (1) $f'(x) = 0$ and (3) $f''(x) > 0$ were *sufficient* for a minimum; these were not, however, necessary and sufficient conditions, because of the possibility that $f''(x)$ may be zero at either a maximum or a minimum point. For $f(x_1, \ldots, x_n)$, the same rules pertained, replacing $f'(x)$ with df and $f''(x)$ with d^2f. In particular, the sign of d^2f, evaluated at the point (or points) in question as maxima or minima, turns out to be crucial. Recall, finally, that

$$d^2f = [\mathbf{dX}]'\mathbf{H}[\mathbf{dX}]$$

where $\mathbf{H}$ is the hessian matrix of second partial and cross-partial derivatives and $\mathbf{dX} = [dx_1, \ldots, dx_n]'$. The second total differential is thus a quadratic form in $\mathbf{dX}$, and rules for establishing the signs of quadratic forms can be developed because of the fact that these forms can be expressed as sums of squares. (This material is reviewed in App. B.) In particular,

$$d^2f = |\mathbf{H}_1|(\cdot)^2 + \frac{|\mathbf{H}_2|}{|\mathbf{H}_1|}(\cdot)^2 + \cdots + \frac{|\mathbf{H}_n|}{|\mathbf{H}_{n-1}|}(\cdot)^2$$

The squared terms, $(\cdot)^2$, contain various functions of the dx_i and of the elements of $\mathbf{H}$ (the f_{ij}), and are unimportant from the point of view of the sign of d^2f. (Since these squared terms involve the dx_i, they will not all be zero if $\mathbf{dX} \neq \mathbf{0}$, thus at least some will be strictly positive.) $|\mathbf{H}_i|$ denotes the ith principal minor of the matrix $\mathbf{H}$. Thus d^2f is unambiguously positive if all principal minors of $\mathbf{H}$ are strictly positive and d^2f is negative if the principal minors of $\mathbf{H}$ alternate in sign, beginning negative. These rules are sufficient to establish the sign of d^2f.

In the calculus of variations, the distinction between a maximizing function and a minimizing one can be shown to turn on the sign of $\delta^2 I$, the second variation of the functional I. In particular, in addition to the Euler-Lagrange equation, a *necessary* condition for a maximizing curve is that $\delta^2 I \leq 0$ (compare

$d^2f \le 0$ in ordinary calculus) and a sufficient condition for a maximum is that $\delta I = 0$ and $\delta^2 I < 0$ (compare $df = 0$ and $d^2f < 0$ in ordinary calculus). This suggests that we should look further at the structure of $\delta^2 I$ to see whether it is generally possible to say anything about its sign. Recall from Sec. 2-4 of Chap. 2, using a Taylor series expansion for ΔI, that we found

$$\delta^2 I = \frac{\varepsilon^2}{2} \int_{x_0}^{x_1} \{F_{yy}[\phi(x)]^2 + 2F_{yy'}\phi(x)\phi'(x) + F_{y'y'}[\phi'(x)]^2\}\, dx \tag{3-71}$$

[This is from (2-32) in Chap. 2.]

Since the sign of $\delta^2 I$ in (3-71) will not be affected by $\varepsilon^2/2$, we can ignore it in our investigation and concentrate on the expression under the integral, which bears a resemblance to a quadratic form. That is, we reexpress (3-71) as

$$\delta^2 I = \frac{\varepsilon^2}{2} \int_{x_0}^{x_1} [\phi(x)\ \phi'(x)] \begin{bmatrix} F_{yy} & F_{yy'} \\ F_{y'y} & F_{y'y'} \end{bmatrix} \begin{bmatrix} \phi(x) \\ \phi'(x) \end{bmatrix} dx \tag{3-72a}$$

or, alternatively,

$$\delta^2 I = \frac{\varepsilon^2}{2} \int_{x_0}^{x_1} [\phi'(x)\ \phi(x)] \begin{bmatrix} F_{y'y'} & F_{y'y} \\ F_{yy'} & F_{yy} \end{bmatrix} \begin{bmatrix} \phi'(x) \\ \phi(x) \end{bmatrix} dx \tag{3-72b}$$

where $F_{yy'} = F_{y'y}$ and hence the center matrix is symmetric, when F is continuously differentiable, i.e., when F is differentiable and $F_{yy'}$ and $F_{y'y'}$ are continuous. This suggests, parallel to the sum of squares form for d^2f, that if we had $\delta^2 I$ in the form $\int_{x_0}^{x_1} (\cdot)^2\, dx$ or as the product of a function A and the squared expression, that is, $\int_{x_0}^{x_1} A(\cdot)^2\, dx$, then conditions on the sign of A and the nonzeroness of the squared expression would be the continuous analogue to the sum of squares form for d^2f.

Our concern, then, is with the sign of the integral in (3-71), ignoring $\varepsilon^2/2$. This is, as in ordinary maximization and minimization, fundamentally a concern with the shape of the function—here $F(x, y, y')$. Recall that conditions on the sign of the second total differential, which are conditions on the principal minors of the hessian matrix in the case of more than one variable, are simply algebraic requirements to insure a particular geometric shape (concave or convex) for the function around the point (or points) where the first differential is zero.† For problems in the calculus of variations, it turns out that if $F(x, y, y')$ is a concave function with respect to (y, y') for all x in $[x_0, x_1]$, then satisfaction of the Euler-Lagrange equations (and the Weierstrass-Erdmann corner conditions, where appropriate) is also sufficient for a maximum, which is in fact a global and not just a local maximum. Similarly, if $F(x, y, y')$ is a convex function of (y, y') for all x in the range, satisfaction of these same necessary conditions is also sufficient for a minimum. When F depends on several y_i, these results hold, with $\mathbf{Y}$ and $\dot{\mathbf{Y}}$ replacing y and y' everywhere. The same is true for the case of equality constraints, as discussed in Sec. 3-3, with the Lagrange-like function $F(x, \mathbf{Y}, \dot{\mathbf{Y}}) -$

† See, for example, Miller [7, app. 8.3] for a review of these concepts.

$\lambda(x)g(x, \mathbf{Y}, \dot{\mathbf{Y}})$ [or $F(x, \mathbf{Y}, \dot{\mathbf{Y}}) - \sum_{i-1}^{k} \lambda_i(x)g_i(x, \mathbf{Y}, \dot{\mathbf{Y}})$, when there are several constraints] replacing F, above, and for $\lambda_i(x)$ satisfying the necessary conditions.† This approach to sufficient conditions is often useful in optimal economic growth models, for example, where specific assumptions about the shapes of the functions involved are generally made.

In the remainder of this section we sketch the classical approach to the development of additional necessary conditions and ultimately to sufficient conditions for a maximum or a minimum for the calculus of variations problem. To the extent possible, the more involved mathematical details have been omitted in the belief that they might intrude on a general understanding of the principles involved. These details can be found elsewhere.‡

Consider the second term under the integral in (3-71) and integrate by parts, letting $u = F_{yy'}$ and $dv = 2\phi(x)\phi'(x)\,dx$. We return to the most straightforward case, namely, the fixed endpoints problem in which $\phi(x_0) = \phi(x_1) = 0$. We find that

$$\delta^2 I = \frac{\varepsilon^2}{2}\int_{x_0}^{x_1}\left\{F_{y'y'}[\phi'(x)]^2 + \left(F_{yy} - \frac{d}{dx}F_{yy'}\right)[\phi(x)]^2\right\}dx \tag{3-73}$$

What has been gained becomes apparent if we let $M = F_{y'y'}$ and $N = [F_{yy} - (d/dx)F_{yy'}]$ so that

$$\delta^2 I = \frac{\varepsilon^2}{2}\int_{x_0}^{x_1}\{M[\phi'(x)]^2 + N[\phi(x)]^2\}\,dx \tag{3-74}$$

which is much closer to a kind of sum of squares form. In fact, it can be shown § that a necessary condition for $\delta^2 I$ in (3-74) [where $\phi(x_0) = \phi(x_1) = 0$] to be nonpositive is that $M \le 0$ in the interval $x_0 \le x \le x_1$. The logic of this condition is as follows: $\phi(x)$ must be zero at x_0 and at x_1. If, starting at $\phi(x_0) = 0$, $\phi(x)$ takes on values far from zero throughout the interval, then $\phi'(x)$ must do so also. [To get to large positive or negative values of $\phi(x)$ requires a large positive or negative slope of $\phi(x)$.] However, if $\phi(x)$ is near to zero throughout the interval, $\phi'(x)$ may or may not be small (see Fig. 3-28). Put rather loosely, and using "large" in an absolute value sense, $\phi(x)$ cannot be large without $\phi'(x)$ also being large, but $\phi'(x)$ can be large without $\phi(x)$ being large. The conclusion is that the $M[\phi'(x)]^2$ term dominates in the expression under the integral in (3-74), since $M[\phi'(x)]^2$ may be much larger than $N[\phi(x)]^2$ at one or more points in $[x_0, x_1]$, but it cannot be much smaller than $N[\phi(x)]^2$. Therefore, the sign of (3-74) is governed by the sign of M. Since $M = F_{y'y'}$ we have:

$$\text{A necessary condition for } \delta^2 I \le 0 \text{ is } F_{y'y'} \le 0. \tag{3-75}$$

† Hadley and Kemp [6, secs. 2.17 and 3.15].

‡ See, for example, Chakravarty [2, sec. A.5], Gelfand and Fomin [5, chaps. 5 and 6], Hadley and Kemp [6, secs. 2.17 and 2.18], or Bolza [1, chap. 2].

§ For example, see Gelfand and Fomin [5, p. 103] for a formal proof.

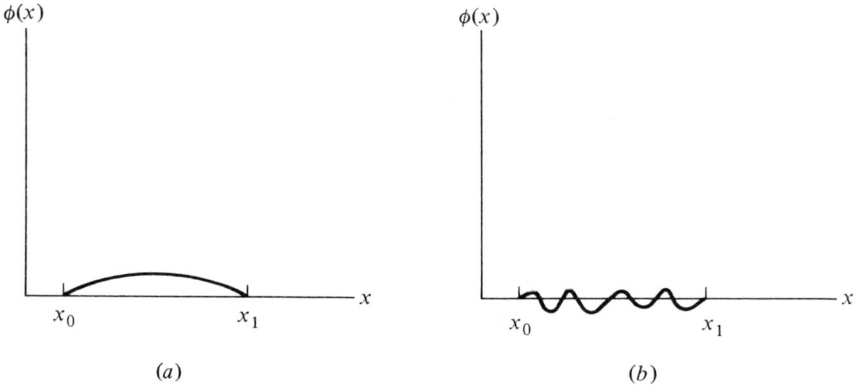

Figure 3-28 Throughout $x_0 \leqq x \leqq x_1$, (a) $\phi(x)$ and $\phi'(x)$ small, and (b) $\phi(x)$ small but $\phi'(x)$ not small.

Clearly, also, if $\delta^2 I \geq 0$, then $F_{y'y'} \geq 0$. Therefore, since $\delta^2 I \leq 0$ is a necessary condition for $y(x)$ to provide a maximum to $I[y]$, we have:

> A *necessary* condition for $y(x)$ to provide a maximum to $\int_{x_0}^{x_1} F(x, y, y')\,dx$, where $y(x_0) = y_0$ and $y(x_1) = y_1$, is that $F_{y'y'} \leq 0$ for every x in the interval $x_0 \leq x \leq x_1$. (3-76)

Similarly, a necessary condition for a minimum is $F_{y'y'} \geq 0$. These are known as the *Legendre* necessary conditions after the mathematician who first investigated them. [These are the analogues to $f''(x) \leq 0$ and $f''(x) \geq 0$ in ordinary calculus.] For a functional involving several y_i, the generalization is to the symmetric matrix

$$[\partial^2 F/\partial \dot{\mathbf{Y}}^2] = \begin{bmatrix} F_{y_1'y_1'} & \cdots & F_{y_1'y_n'} \\ \cdots & \cdots & \cdots \\ F_{y_n'y_1'} & \cdots & F_{y_n'y_n'} \end{bmatrix}$$

Necessary for a maximum is that this matrix be negative semidefinite; this means that the principal minors must be alternatively nonpositive and nonnegative, beginning nonpositive. These necessary conditions, for the case of more than one $y(x)$, are sometimes known as the Legendre-Clebsch conditions. For a minimum, it is necessary that $[\partial^2 F/\partial \dot{\mathbf{Y}}^2]$ be positive semidefinite; i.e., all principal minors must be nonnegative.

The conditions that assure *strict* negativity or *strict* positivity of $\delta^2 I$ are a good deal more complicated to derive. In particular, it is not adequate to require $F_{y'y'} < 0$ for $\delta^2 I < 0$ or $F_{y'y'} > 0$ for $\delta^2 I > 0$, primarily because when the possibility of $\delta^2 I$ being equal to zero is not allowed, one has to be certain that the $[\phi'(x)]^2$ and $[\phi(x)]^2$ terms in (3-74) are not zero over $x_0 \leq x \leq x_1$. In fact, the task is considerably simplified if the integral in (3-74) can be further reworked into the form $\int A(\cdot)^2\,dx$, since then it can be shown that if $A < 0$, then $(\cdot) \neq 0$ is a necessary *and* sufficient condition for the integral to be strictly negative. In other words, what is perfectly clear in ordinary algebra (if $a < 0$, then $x \neq 0$ is necessary and sufficient for $ax^2 < 0$) is also true for the much more complicated case of the definite integral $\int_{x_0}^{x_1} A(\cdot)^2\,dx$. A complete mathematical exposition of the results to follow is beyond the needs of this text. The material is presented primarily to give some feeling for the origins of the so-called Jacobi and Weierstrass conditions.

Consider a differentiable function $w(x)$, and note that the expression $\int_{x_0}^{x_1} (d/dx)\{w(x)[\phi(x)]^2\}\,dx$ equals zero, since in the fixed endpoint problem $\phi(x_0) = \phi(x_1) = 0$, that is,

$$\int_{x_0}^{x_1} \frac{d}{dx}\{w(x)[\phi(x)]^2\}\,dx = w(x)[\phi(x)]^2\Big]_{x_0}^{x_1} = 0 - 0 = 0$$

But, performing the differentiation under the integral sign (using the rule for a product of two functions) gives

$$\int_{x_0}^{x_1} \{w'(x)[\phi(x)]^2 + 2w(x)\phi(x)\phi'(x)\}\,dx$$

This must, as we have seen, equal zero, and therefore it can be added to the right-hand side of (3-74) without changing the value of that expression. Thus

$$\delta^2 I = \frac{\varepsilon^2}{2}\int_{x_0}^{x_1} \{M[\phi'(x)]^2 + 2w(x)\phi(x)\phi'(x) + [N + w'(x)][\phi(x)]^2\}\,dx \tag{3-77}$$

For the moment, this appears to have increased the complexity of the expression. We assume throughout the remainder of this section that $M < 0$, i.e., that $F_{y'y'} < 0$. [Recall that the Legendre necessary condition for a maximum, given in (3-76), was $F_{y'y'} \leq 0$; we are now assuming the so-called *strengthened* Legendre maximum condition.]† Since $M \neq 0$, we can divide by it and reexpress (3-77) as

$$\delta^2 I = \frac{\varepsilon^2}{2}\int_{x_0}^{x_1} M\left\{[\phi'(x)]^2 + \frac{2w(x)\phi(x)\phi'(x)}{M} + \frac{N + w'(x)}{M}[\phi(x)]^2\right\}dx \tag{3-78}$$

Notice that an algebraic expression of the form

$$x^2 + 2\frac{b}{a}xy + \frac{b^2}{a^2}y^2$$

is just $[x + (b/a)y]^2$. Comparing the expression in curly brackets in (3-78), it follows that if $[w(x)/M]^2$ were equal to $[N + w'(x)]/M$, then (3-78) could be written

$$\delta^2 I = \frac{\varepsilon^2}{2}\int_{x_0}^{x_1} M\{\phi'(x) + [w(x)/M]\phi(x)\}^2\,dx \tag{3-79}$$

† For the case of several y_i, the strengthened Legendre-Clebsch condition for a maximum requires that $[\partial^2 F/\partial \dot{\mathbf{Y}}^2]$ be negative definite—not semidefinite—and thus that the principal minors alternate in sign, beginning strictly negative. For a minimum, the strengthened condition is that the matrix be positive definite, i.e., that its principal minors all be strictly positive.

i.e., in the form $\int_{x_0}^{x_1} A(\cdot)^2\, dx$, which is exactly what we want. For example, if $M < 0$ and if the expression in curly brackets is nonzero, then $\delta^2 I < 0$. The condition on $w(x)$ under which (3-78) can be written as in (3-79) can be expressed as

$$[w(x)]^2 = M[N + w'(x)] \tag{3-80}$$

or $[w(x)]^2 = MN + Mw'(x)$.

This is a nonlinear first-order differential equation in $w(x)$. (An equation with this particular form is known as a Riccati equation, after the mathematician who studied methods and forms of its solution, particularly for more complicated extensions.) The question then becomes: does (3-80) have a finite solution for all x in the interval $x_0 \le x \le x_1$? Note that the character of $w(x)$ at x_0 and x_1 is not of particular interest, since $w(x)$ always appears multiplied by $\phi(x)$—e.g., in (3-79)—and this product will be zero in any case at x_0 and x_1 since $\phi(x_0) = \phi(x_1) = 0$. The *nonlinear* equation in (3-80) can be converted into a *linear* (although second-order) differential equation by utilizing the change of variables

$$w(x) = -[v'(x)/v(x)]M \tag{3-81}$$

provided that $v(x) \neq 0$. Finding $w'(x)$ from (3-81) and substituting into (3-80) gives

$$\frac{d}{dx}[Mv'(x)] = Nv(x) \quad \text{or} \quad Nv(x) - \frac{d}{dx}[Mv'(x)] = 0 \tag{3-82}$$

which is a second-order [since $(d/dx)[v'(x)]$ is involved] but linear differential equation in $v(x)$.

What has been established thus far is this: (1) if (3-82) has a solution for which $v(x) \neq 0$ anywhere in the open interval (x_0, x_1), then (3-81) provides a solution to the Riccati equation (3-80) over that interval; and (2) it then follows that (3-79) is a valid expression for $\delta^2 I$ and hence will be strictly negative if $M = F_{y'y'} < 0$ and $\{\phi'(x) + [w(x)/M]\phi(x)\}^2 \neq 0$. We note that the integrand in (3-74) [or (3-79)] is a function of x, $\phi(x)$, and $\phi'(x)$; that is, $\delta^2 I = \varepsilon^2 \int_{x_0}^{x_1} G[x, \phi(x), \phi'(x)]\, dx$, where $G = \frac{1}{2}\{M[\phi'(x)]^2 + N[\phi(x)]^2\}$. There is an Euler-Lagrange equation for this functional (which would be of interest, for example, if we were looking for the ϕ to maximize or minimize $\delta^2 I$), namely, $G_\phi - (d/dx)G_{\phi'} = 0$. In fact, given the definition of G, this equation is

$$N\phi(x) - \frac{d}{dx}[M\phi'(x)] = 0 \tag{3-83}$$

Comparing (3-82), we see that the function $v(x)$ that satisfies it is the same as the function $\phi(x)$ that satisfies (3-83), i.e., that $v(x)$ must be a solution to the Euler-Lagrange equation for the functional in $\delta^2 I$. This Euler-Lagrange equation is known as the Jacobi equation, again after the mathematician who studied it. There is a special name for a point at which a solution to the Jacobi equation is equal to zero; it is known as a *conjugate point*. Formally, x_a is said to be conjugate to x_0 if the Jacobi equation (3-82) has a solution $v(x)$ for which $v(x_0) = 0$ and

$v(x_a) = 0$ when $v(x)$ is not identically zero. Using this terminology, if there are no points in $[x_0, x_1]$ conjugate to x_0, then the Jacobi equation has a nonzero solution $v(x)$ throughout $(x_0, x_1]$, and therefore $w(x)$ is defined over that interval, making (3-79) a valid representation for $\delta^2 I$.

If we assume the absence of a conjugate point to x_0 in $[x_0, x_1]$ then, using (3-81), the expression for $\delta^2 I$ from (3-79) can be written as

$$\delta^2 I = \frac{\varepsilon^2}{2} \int_{x_0}^{x_1} M \left\{ \frac{\phi'(x)v(x) - \phi(x)v'(x)}{v(x)} \right\}^2 dx \tag{3-84}$$

Therefore, since we are assuming $M < 0$, $\delta^2 I$ could be zero only if the squared expression in curly brackets under the integral sign in (3-84) were equal to zero over the entire interval $[x_0, x_1]$. For this to be true, $\phi'(x)v(x) - \phi(x)v'(x) = 0$ over that interval; to satisfy this equation, $v(x) = c\phi(x)$, where c is an arbitrary constant. However, $\phi(x_0) = \phi(x_1) = 0$, leaving $v(x_0) = v(x_1) = 0$. But we have assumed no conjugate point in $[x_0, x_1]$ and hence $v(x_1) \neq 0$, so the expression in curly brackets cannot be zero. Thus we have (recall that $M = F_{y'y'}$):

> If $F_{y'y'} < 0$ over $[x_0, x_1]$ and if the interval $[x_0, x_1]$ contains no points conjugate to x_0, then $\delta^2 I < 0$ for all $\phi(x)$ with $\phi(x_0) = \phi(x_1) = 0$. (3-85)

Building upon additional and detailed reasoning along these lines, it can also be shown† that:

> If $F_{y'y'} < 0$ over $[x_0, x_1]$ and if $\delta^2 I < 0$ for all $\phi(x)$ with $\phi(x_0) = \phi(x_1) = 0$, then the interval $[x_0, x_1]$ contains no points conjugate to x_0. (3-86)

A weakened version of (3-86), calling only for nonpositivity of $\delta^2 I$, is:

> If $F_{y'y'} < 0$ over $[x_0, x_1]$ and if $\delta^2 I \leq 0$ for all $\phi(x)$ with $\phi(x_0) = \phi(x_1) = 0$, then the open interval (x_0, x_1) contains no points conjugate to x_0. (3-87)

This simply allows for the possibility that x_1 is a conjugate point. A new *necessary* condition follows directly from this:

> If $y(x)$ corresponds to a maximum of $\int_{x_0}^{x_1} F(x, y, y')\, dx$ and if $F_{y'y'} < 0$ over the interval $x_0 \leq x \leq x_1$, then the open interval (x_0, x_1) contains no points conjugate to x_0. (3-88)

This is the *Jacobi* necessary condition. To summarize: with $F_{y'y'} < 0$, the absence of conjugate points in (x_0, x_1) is necessary for $\delta^2 I \leq 0$, and $\delta^2 I \leq 0$, in turn, is necessary for a maximum. Similarly, with $F_{y'y'} > 0$, the absence of a conjugate point in (x_0, x_1) is necessary for a minimum.

† For example, Gelfand and Fomin [5, p. 109].

Summary of Necessary Conditions

If $\int_{x_0}^{x_1} F(x, y, y')\,dx$, with $y_0 = y(x_0)$, $y_1 = y(x_1)$ has a weak extremum for $y = y(x)$ then

1. $y(x)$ satisfies the *Euler-Lagrange* equation $F_y - (d/dx)F_{y'} = 0$.
2. $F_{y'y'}$ satisfies the *Legendre* condition, namely, over $x_0 \leq x \leq x_1$, $F_{y'y'} \leq 0$ for a maximum and $F_{y'y'} \geq 0$ for a minimum.
3. The open interval (x_0, x_1) satisfies the *Jacobi* condition that it contain no points conjugate to x_0.

A Sufficient Condition

A slight strengthening of the three necessary conditions above allows, finally, a sufficiency statement. What is needed is the strengthened Legendre condition in condition 2—strong inequalities only—and the strengthened Jacobi condition in condition 3—extension to the closed interval $[x_0, x_1]$. That is:

> *If*, for $\int_{x_0}^{x_1} F(x, y, y')\,dx$, there is a $y(x)$ where $y_0 = y(x_0)$ and $y_1 = y(x_1)$, which satisfies:
> 1. the Euler-Lagrange equation $F_y - (d/dx)F_{y'} = 0$,
> 2. the strengthened Legendre condition $F_{y'y'} < 0\ (F_{y'y'} > 0)$, and
> 3. the strengthened Jacobi condition that the closed interval $[x_0, x_1]$ contain no points conjugate to x_0,
>
> *then* the functional has a weak maximum (minimum) for $y = y(x)$. (3-89)

That is, the conditions in (3-89) are sufficient for a weak maximum or minimum. This follows generally from (3-85) and (3-86); namely, that the absence of a conjugate point in $[x_0, x_1]$ is both necessary and sufficient for $\delta^2 I < 0$ when $F_{y'y'} < 0$:

> If $F_{y'y'} < 0$ over $[x_0, x_1]$ then $\delta^2 I < 0$ for all $\phi(x)$ with $\phi(x_0) = \phi(x_1) = 0$ if and only if the interval $[x_0, x_1]$ contains no points conjugate to x_0. (3-90)

The problem with the Jacobi condition on conjugate points is that it is not always easy or even straightforward to apply. However, there is an alternative test which is very useful when the specific form of the extremal (or extremals) is known.† Suppose that the solution to the Euler-Lagrange equation is written as $y = \psi(x, k_1, k_2)$, where k_1 and k_2 are the two constants that necessarily will appear in the solution, since the Euler-Lagrange condition is a second-order

† See Forsyth [4, pp. 22–28].

differential equation. (See App. C, Sec. C-4, for examples when the differential equation is linear.) Recall that these constants are determined entirely from endpoint conditions in the problem. Different values of k_1 and k_2 will result from different endpoint conditions, and, clearly, different extremals will be associated with different k_1 and k_2.

Let $\psi_1 \equiv \partial\psi/\partial k_1$ and $\psi_2 \equiv \partial\psi/\partial k_2$; these are the partial derivatives that measure the sensitivity of the extremal function $y = \psi(x, k_1, k_2)$ to small changes in the constants k_1 and k_2. For any given small changes β_1 and β_2 in k_1 and k_2, respectively, using the total differential,

$$d\psi = \beta_1\psi_1 + \beta_2\psi_2$$

Forsyth shows that $d\psi$ must satisfy the Jacobi equation in (3-83); i.e., that $d\psi(x) = v(x)$. Therefore, to assure $d\psi = 0$ (that is, $v = 0$) at x_0, one can always choose β_1 and β_2 so that

$$\frac{-\beta_1}{\beta_2} = \left.\frac{\psi_2}{\psi_1}\right|_{x=x_0}$$

Thus, provided that ψ_2/ψ_1 never again assumes the value $-\beta_1/\beta_2$ over the range of integration, $d\psi(x)$ and thus $v(x)$ will not again be zero; i.e., there will not be a point conjugate to x_0 in the range of integration. This leads to

The interval $[x_0, x_1]$ contains no points conjugate to x_0 if and only if $\psi_2/\psi_1|_{x_0} \neq \psi_2/\psi_1|_x$ for $x_0 < x \leq x_1$. (3-91)

Proofs of most of the above results rely in one way or another on the closeness of the functions involved and of their first derivatives as well; this is why they constitute results for a weak extremum only. Conditions for strong extrema are largely due to the work of Weierstrass and they require, in their development, mathematical concepts beyond the scope of this book, e.g., Hilbert integrals, the theory of "fields," etc.† In the process, the function

$$E(x, y, y', z') = F(x, y, z') - F(x, y, y') - (z' - y')F_{y'}(x, y, y') \tag{3-92}$$

emerges; this is the so-called Weierstrass excess function, or E function. For admissible functions $y(x)$ and $z(x)$, it measures the difference (or excess) between the function F evaluated for z' and the first two terms of the Taylor series expansion of F about the point y'. Using this function, it turns out that

If $E(x, y, y', z') < 0$ (>0), then $\int_{x_0}^{x_1} F(x, y, y')\,dx$, where $y_0 = y(x_0)$, $y_1 = y(x_1)$, has a *strong* maximum (minimum) for $y = y(x)$. (3-93)

This is known as the Weierstrass sufficient condition for a strong maximum or minimum. Moreover, it can be shown that weakened restrictions on E, with

† As illustrated, for example, by the discussions in Gelfand and Fomin [5, chap. 6], Bolza [1, chap. 3], or Hadley and Kemp [6, sec. 2.20].

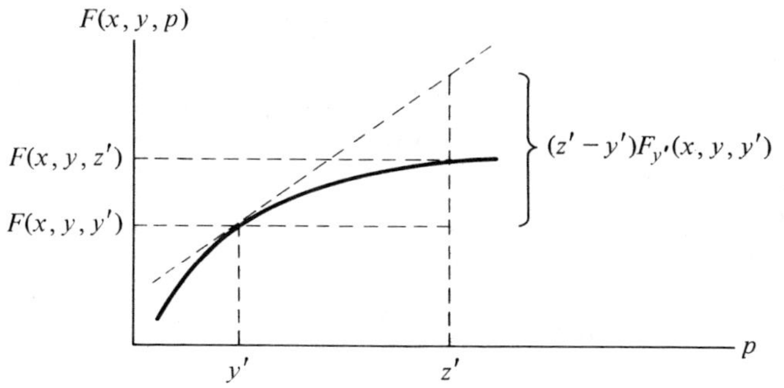

Figure 3-29 The geometry of $E(x, y, y', z') \le 0$.

weak inequalities, constitute yet another *necessary* condition for either a maximum or a minimum:

> A necessary condition for $y(x)$ to provide a maximum for $\int_{x_0}^{x_1} F(x, y, y')\, dx$, where $y_0 = y(x_0)$ and $y_1 = y(x_1)$, is that $E(x, y, y', z') \le 0$. (3-94)

Similarly, a necessary condition for a minimum is $E(x, y, y', z') \ge 0$.

Geometrically, (3-93) and (3-94) are requirements on the concavity (convexity) of the function F when considered for fixed x and y. Consider the maximum case: from (3-94) and (3-92), the Weierstrass necessary condition is $F(x, y, y') + (z' - y')F_{y'}(x, y, y') \ge F(x, y, z')$ (see Fig. 3-29). For a maximum, the function F must be nowhere above the tangent drawn at y'. Notice that a *necessary* condition for $E \le 0$ is that, in the geometry of Fig. 3-29, the function F be concave at y', i.e., that $F''(y') \le 0$, which is that $F_{y'y'}(x, y, y') \le 0$, the Legendre condition. Alternatively, a *sufficient* condition for $E \le 0$ is that the function F be *everywhere* concave, i.e., that $F''(p) \le 0$ for all p, or $F_{y'y'}(x, y, y', p) \le 0$.

Example I: Shortest Distance between Points in a Plane (Continued)

Consider again the shortest-distance problem whose functional, $\int_{x_0}^{x_1} \sqrt{1 + (y')^2}\, dx$, we last saw in (3-22). With fixed endpoints, we know that $y(x_0) = y_0$ and $y(x_1) = y_1$. Also, $F_{y'} = y'/\sqrt{1 + (y')^2}$ and the Euler-Lagrange equation leads to the conclusion that $y'(x)$ is a constant and hence that $y(x)$ is the straight line $y(x) = k_1 x + k_2$. The initial and terminal points, (x_0, y_0) and (x_1, y_1), establish k_1 and k_2 so that the line in fact goes through both points, as we saw in Sec. 2-4 of Chap. 2. We now turn to the additional conditions developed in this section.

Legendre The Legendre condition for a minimum, given in (3-76), is that $F_{y'y'} \ge 0$. For this example, $F_{y'y'} = 1/[1 + (y')^2]^{3/2}$, which is clearly always strictly positive (recall from Chap. 2 that for this problem the positive square root of $[1 + (y')^2]$ is always taken, since it represents distance). In fact, the strengthened Legendre condition is always met.

Jacobi The Jacobi equation [(3-82) in terms of $v(x)$] for this problem is $Nv(x) - (d/dx)[Mv'(x)] = 0$, where $N = [F_{yy} - (d/dx)F_{yy'}]$ and $M = F_{y'y'}$. Moreover, $F_{yy} = 0$ and $F_{yy'} = 0$, and $F_{y'y'} = k$, a constant, since the Euler-Lagrange condition has already established that $y' = k_1$. Therefore the Jacobi equation is just $(k)(d/dx)[v'(x)] = 0$. Integration gives $v(x) = k_3 x + k_4$; the condition $v(x_0) = 0$ means $k_3 x_0 + k_4 = 0$ or $k_3 = -k_4/x_0$. Thus $v(x) = (-k_4/x_0)x + k_4 = k_4(1 - x/x_0)$ and hence $v(x)$ will be zero only at $x = x_0$; i.e., there is no conjugate point in (x_0, x_1), and Jacobi's necessary condition, given in (3-88), is satisfied. (In fact, the strengthened Jacobi condition is satisfied, since the closed interval $[x_0, x_1]$ contains no points conjugate to x_0.)

Alternatively, using (3-91), we know that $y(x) = \psi(x, k_1, k_2) = k_1 x + k_2$. Therefore, $\partial\psi/\partial k_1 \equiv \psi_1 = x$ and $\partial\psi/\partial k_2 \equiv \psi_2 = 1$, and $\psi_2/\psi_1 = x$. This ratio clearly has the value x_0 at $x = x_0$ and never again; hence, in particular, there are no points conjugate to x_0 in $[x_0, x_1]$.

Weierstrass For this problem, the Weierstrass E function, given in (3-92), is $E(x, y, y', z') = \sqrt{1 + (z')^2} - \sqrt{1 + (y')^2} - (z' - y')[y'/\sqrt{1 + (y')^2}]$. Straightforward algebra gives

$$E(x, y, y', z') = \frac{\sqrt{1 + (y')^2 + (z')^2 + (y'z')^2} - \sqrt{1 + 2y'z' + (y'z')^2}}{\sqrt{1 + (y')^2}}$$

The denominator is always positive. The numerator is nonnegative, being zero only in the uninteresting case when $y' = z'$. Thus, for $y' \neq z'$, $E > 0$ and the Weierstrass condition for a strong minimum, given in (3-93), is satisfied also.

Example II: Monopolistic Pricing over Time (Continued)

For this example, the integrand in the objective functional used p and p', for price and its rate of change, instead of y and y'; it was given in (2-42) of Chap. 2, namely,

$$F(p, p') = -\tfrac{3}{2}p^2 + 202p - 5000(p')^2 - 10{,}200p' + 200pp' - 5240$$

The general solution was found, in (2-45) of Chap. 2, using t as the independent variable instead of x, as

$$p(t) = k_1\, e^{0.0173t} + k_2\, e^{-0.0173t} + 67.333$$

Recall that the two monopolistic pricing problems differed only in endpoint conditions, i.e., in values that determined k_1 and k_2.

Legendre In this example we want the extremal to provide a maximum; from (3-76), we want $F_{p'p'} \leq 0$. Here $F_{p'p'} = -10{,}000$ which is clearly always negative and hence the strengthened Legendre condition is always met.

Jacobi The extremal is $p(t) = \psi(t, k_1, k_2) = k_1 e^{0.0173t} + k_2 e^{-0.0173t} + 67.333$. Thus $\psi_1 = e^{0.0173t}$ and $\psi_2 = e^{-0.0173t}$ and for the condition in (3-91) we find that

$$\frac{\psi_2}{\psi_1} = e^{-0.0346t}$$

which is a monotonically decreasing function of t. Whatever the value at t_0, ψ_2/ψ_1 will not attain that value again. Thus there are no points conjugate to t_0 in $[t_0, t_1]$.

Weierstrass After some algebraic manipulation, the E function, given in (3-92), is

$$E(t, p, p', z') = -5000(z' - p')^2$$

which is always negative for $p' \neq z'$. Thus the Weierstrass condition for a strong maximum, given in (3-93), is satisfied also.

Clearly, these results for the Legendre, Jacobi, and Weierstrass conditions for the monopolistic pricing problem hold for both versions of that problem since (1) $F_{p'p'}$ is a constant and hence is unaffected by the specifics of the extremal, (2) the extremals for the two problems differ only in the values of the two arbitrary constants, and hence ψ_1 and ψ_2 are the same for both, and (3) the sign of the E function is also unaffected by the specific form of the extremal.

3-6 ALTERNATIVE FORMULATIONS

The fundamental feature of the problems that we have examined thus far is that the objective is maximization or minimization of an *integral* of a known function, perhaps with constraints and/or endpoint conditions. The objective functional has been of the form

$$\int_{x_0}^{x_1} F(x, \mathbf{Y}, \dot{\mathbf{Y}})\, dx \qquad (3\text{-}95)$$

In some problems, however, one might be interested instead, or in addition, in a function of the terminal values, e.g., the final valuation of an accumulated stock of capital goods, $K(x_1, \mathbf{Y}_1)$. Similarly, some function of both initial and terminal values might enter into the objective, as, for example, the change in the value of the stock of capital goods over the period, or final value minus initial value, $K_1(x_1, \mathbf{Y}_1) - K_0(x_0, \mathbf{Y}_0)$. Thus, quite generally, the objective functional in (3-95) might be expanded to

$$\int_{x_0}^{x_1} F(x, \mathbf{Y}, \dot{\mathbf{Y}})\, dx + K(x_0, \mathbf{Y}_0, x_1, \mathbf{Y}_1) \qquad (3\text{-}96)$$

What we have been dealing with until now may be thought of as the form in (3-96), with $K = 0$. Expressed in this way [i.e., as in (3-95)], the problem is known as the *problem of Lagrange*. If, in (3-96), neither F nor K is identically zero, we have the so-called *problem of Bolza*. Finally, when $F \equiv 0$ in (3-96), so that the objective contains only functions of one or both of the endpoint values, we have what is known as the *problem of Mayer*:

$$K(x_0, \mathbf{Y}_0, x_1, \mathbf{Y}_1) \tag{3-97}$$

(All names, of course, come from the mathematicians who explored the problem in that particular form.) The main reason for mentioning these alternative expressions is to point out that, while (3-96) may appear at first glance to be the most general of the three, they are all actually equivalent; any problem form can be translated into either of the others. Thus, for example, the problem of Mayer, (3-97), is no more nor less general than either of the others.

To translate from the Bolza form to the Mayer form, i.e., from (3-96) to (3-97), define an additional function of x, $y_{n+1}(x)$ as

$$y_{n+1}(x) = \int_{x_0}^{x} F(\chi, \mathbf{Y}, \dot{\mathbf{Y}})\, d\chi \tag{3-98}$$

which means $y'_{n+1}(x) = F(x, \mathbf{Y}, \dot{\mathbf{Y}})$ and also $y_{n+1}(x_0) = \int_{x_0}^{x_0} F(\chi, \mathbf{Y}, \dot{\mathbf{Y}})\, d\chi = 0$. Therefore, a problem with the Bolza functional

$$\int_{x_0}^{x_1} F(x, \mathbf{Y}, \dot{\mathbf{Y}})\, dx + K(x_0, \mathbf{Y}_0, x_1, \mathbf{Y}_1)$$

becomes a problem with the functional

$$y_{n+1}(x_1) + K(x_0, \mathbf{Y}_0, x_1, \mathbf{Y}_1)$$

i.e., of the Mayer form, dependent only on functions of the initial and terminal conditions, with an added differential constraint for the motion of the new variable $y'_{n+1}(x) = F(x, \mathbf{Y}, \dot{\mathbf{Y}})$, and an initial condition for the new variable, $y_{n+1}(x_0) = 0$. Equivalence of the Lagrange and either Mayer or Bolza forms can also be shown (the reader may wish to do this).

PROBLEMS

3-1 Examine the extremals in each of the following problems:

(*a*) Prob. 2-2(*a*) of Chap. 2, with $x_0 = 0$, $x_1 = 1$, $y(x_0) = 0$, but y_1 unspecified (a free right-hand boundary problem).

(*b*) The same problem as in (*a*), above, with $x_0 = 0$, $y(x_0) = 0$, $y(x_1) = 5$, but x_1 unspecified (a free terminal time problem).

(*c*) The same problem as in (*a*), above, with $x_0 = 0$, $y(x_0) = 0$, but also with the requirement that the extremal $y(x)$ terminate on the line $y = 2x$.

3-2 (*a*) Find the extremal for the problem of minimizing the distance between the functions $x^2 + y^2 = 4$ and $y = -5x + 20$.

(*b*) Solve the same problem as in (*a*), above, except that now the left-hand endpoint is required to lie on $y = -x^2 + 2$.

(*c*) Minimum distance problems, as in (*a*) and (*b*), above, lead to linear extremals, $y(x) = c_1x + c_2$. We saw above that when the right-hand surface, $y = \sigma(x)$, is a straight line, the right-hand transversality conditions establish c_1, the slope of the extremal. Suppose, however, that the left-hand surface, $y = \rho(x)$, were also a straight line. How would the transversality (orthogonality) requirements at *both* the initial and terminal points operate?

3-3 (*a*) Find the function $y(x)$ that maximizes $\int_{x_0}^{x_1} [7xy - (y')^2]\, dx$, where $x_0 = 0$, $y(x_0) = 0$, $x_1 = 1$, $y(x_1) = 5$ [as in Prob. 2-4(*a*) in Chap. 2] and where the area under $y(x)$ is constrained to be 10 square units.

(*b*) Do part (a) of this problem two more times, first with the right-hand side of the area constraint at 9 and then with the right-hand side of the constraint at 11. Find the value of $I[y]$ using the three extremals for the constraint at 10 [part (*a*)] and at 9 and 11. Compare the difference in the optimal values of $I[y]$ and the value of λ, the Lagrange-like multiplier, found in part (*a*) of this problem. This illustrates the parallel between the optimal values of Lagrange multipliers in ordinary constrained optimization and here, in a dynamic constrained optimization context.

3-4 (*a*) Find $y_1(x)$ and $y_2(x)$ so as to maximize $I[y_1, y_2] = \int_{x_0}^{x_1} [7xy_1 - (y_1')^2 - (y_2')^2]\, dx$, subject to the constraint that the sum of the two functions at all points be 100, i.e., where $y_1 + y_2 = 100$, and given that $x_0 = 0$, $y_1(x_0) = 0$, $y_2(x_0) = 100$ and $x_1 = 1$, $y_1(x_1) = 5$, $y_2(x_1) = 95$.

(*b*) Compare the results in (*a*) for $y_1(x)$ and $y_2(x)$ with the case in which the functions must go through the same endpoints as in (*a*) but are otherwise unconstrained.

(*c*) Evaluate $I[y_1, y_2]$ using the extremals found in (*a*) and in (*b*), above, to quantify the effect of the constraint on the optimum. Confirm this result by examining $y_1(x) + y_2(x)$ in the unconstrained case [part (*b*)].

3-5 Consider the problem in 3-4(*a*), above, with the same objective functional and the same fixed endpoints, but with the constraint an inequality, namely, $y_1 + y_2 \leq 100$.

3-6 Demonstrate that the optimal functions for each of the preceding problems in this chapter will be smooth, i.e., that the extremals will not have corners. (Do not use the actual solutions that you have found.)

3-7 Examine the Legendre, Jacobi, and Weierstrass conditions for each of the preceding problems.

3-8 Investigate the extremal of $I[y] = \int_0^1 [(y')^2 + y^2 + 2y\, e^{2x}]\, dx$, where $y(0) = \frac{1}{3}$ and $y(1) = \frac{1}{3}e^2$.

REFERENCES

1. Bolza, O.: "Lectures on the Calculus of Variations," University of Chicago Press, Chicago, 1904. A classic treatise on the mathematics of the calculus of variations at a generally advanced level of mathematical difficulty. Chapters 2 and 3 deal with the classical approach to the second variation and sufficient conditions.
2. Chakravarty, S.: "Capital and Development Planning," MIT Press, Cambridge, Mass., 1969. Section A.5 of app. A presents an overview of second-order conditions for variational problems at a very readable level.
3. Citron, S. J.: "Elements of Optimal Control," Holt, Rinehart and Winston, New York, 1969. An engineering text that is very readable. Chapter 2 covers the calculus of variations basics, including an analysis of the second variation.
4. Forsyth, A. R.: "Calculus of Variations," Cambridge University Press, Cambridge, 1927. A thorough and extremely well written account of the subject. Chapter I presents the Euler-Lagrange, Legendre, Jacobi, and Weierstrass conditions in a very readable way.
5. Gelfand, I. M., and S. V. Fomin: "Calculus of Variations," Prentice-Hall, Englewood Cliffs, N.J., 1963. A thorough exposition of the mathematics of the calculus of variations. Chapters 5 and 6 deal with sufficiency conditions at an advanced mathematical level.
6. Hadley, G., and M. C. Kemp: "Variational Methods in Economics," American Elsevier, New York, 1971. A very complete and mathematically advanced discussion of calculus of variations and maximum principle techniques and their use in economic growth models. Sufficiency is covered in later sections of both chaps. 2 and 3.

7. Miller, R. E.: "Modern Mathematical Methods for Economics and Business," Holt, Rinehart and Winston, New York, 1972. The relationships between concave and convex functions and the associated quadratic forms is covered in app. 8.3.
8. Takayama, A.: "Mathematical Economics," Dryden Press, Hinsdale, Ill., 1974. Chapter 5 discusses the fundamentals of the calculus of variations and includes examples of applications from economics. Problems with transversality at infinity are mentioned in chap. 8, sec. A.d.

CHAPTER

FOUR

THE MAXIMUM PRINCIPLE

In the last two chapters we have investigated the treatment of variational problems by classical methods whose origins reach back to the seventeenth century. The more modern approach, which has largely developed since 1950, is generally termed the theory of optimal control, or optimal control theory. This terminology reflects the point of view that the fundamental problem is one of optimally guiding or controlling a variable (or several variables) over time or space; the criterion of optimality is the requirement that a specified functional be maximized or minimized.

The newer formulation turns out to be more suited to certain kinds of constraints, especially inequalities. In addition, it places less stringent continuity and smoothness restrictions on some of the functions involved. Also it is more general in the sense of being able to deal with constraints and/or integrands that are linear; the Euler-Lagrange condition from the calculus of variations cannot be used in a case where, for example, F_y and $F_{y'}$ are both constants.†

4-1 THE CONTROL FORMULATION

The simplest problem in the calculus of variations was that of finding the function $y(x)$ to maximize or minimize $I[y] = \int_{x_0}^{x_1} F(x, y, y')\,dx$, where $y(x_0) = y_0$ and

† This is analogous to the failure of Lagrange multiplier methods in constrained optimization problems—say, maximize $f(\mathbf{X})$ subject to $g(\mathbf{X}) = c$, when both $f(\mathbf{X})$ and $g(\mathbf{X})$ are linear.

$y(x_1) = y_1$. This can be cast as a control problem in the following way: if, starting at the known initial point (x_0, y_0) and ending at the known terminal point (x_1, y_1), we were to specify the slope of the function $y(x)$ at every point in the interval $[x_0, x_1]$, then $y(x)$ itself would be specified over that entire interval. That is, the choice of $y'(x)$ would *control* $y(x)$ from (x_0, y_0) to (x_1, y_1). In the terminology of control theory, the variables (functions) in a problem are divided into those which represent the condition or state of the objective functional [the so-called *state* variables, usually denoted by $y(x)$] and those which guide or control the state variables [the so-called *control* variables, usually denoted by $u(x)$]. The simplest calculus of variations problem could thus be rephrased as:

$$\text{Maximize/minimize} \quad I[y, u] = \int_{x_0}^{x_1} F(x, y, u)\, dx \tag{4-1}$$

where $\qquad y(x_0) = y_0, \quad y(x_1) = y_1 \quad$ and where $\quad y'(x) = u(x)$

That is, the control variable makes its influence felt via a (here very simple) differential equation relating u and the rate of change of y.

In terms of the calculus of variations approach, we have a two "variable" problem, in which y and u (but neither y' nor u') appear in the integrand and in which there is one equality constraint. In the notation of Chap. 3, the constraint can be expressed as $h(x, y, u, y') = y' - g(x, y, u) = 0$, where $g(x, y, u) = u$. For the moment we continue to view this as a two-function, one-constraint calculus of variations problem; in particular, this means that we ignore the fact that while y is piecewise smooth, u (which is y') need only be piecewise continuous. We explored functionals with more than one function in Chap. 2, Sec. 2-5 and equality constraints in Chap. 3, Sec. 3-3. Combining the results in these sections gives, for the problem in (4-1),

$$\begin{aligned} L(x, y, u, y') &= F(x, y, u) - \lambda(x)h(u, y') \\ &= F(x, y, u) - \lambda(x)[y' - g(u)] \end{aligned}$$

The Euler-Lagrange conditions are applied to the augmented function L above—recall (3-51) in Chap. 3. Here these are

$$L_y - \frac{d}{dx} L_{y'} = 0 \tag{4-2}$$

$$L_u - \frac{d}{dx} L_{u'} = 0 \tag{4-3}$$

In addition, recall that the constraint itself is a part of the set of necessary conditions; as in ordinary Lagrange multiplier analysis, it can be generated by treating the added function $\lambda(x)$ in the same manner as $y(x)$ and $u(x)$, i.e., by requiring

$$L_\lambda - \frac{d}{dx} L_{\lambda'} = 0 \tag{4-4}$$

Recognizing that for this problem $L_{y'} = -\lambda(x)$, $L_{u'} = 0$, and $L_{\lambda'} = 0$, (4-2) through (4-4) become

$$L_y = -\lambda'(x) \quad \text{that is,} \quad -\frac{\partial L}{\partial y} = \lambda'(x) \tag{4-5}$$

$$L_u = 0 \quad \text{that is,} \quad \frac{\partial L}{\partial u} = 0 \tag{4-6}$$

$$L_\lambda = 0 \quad \text{that is,} \quad \frac{\partial L}{\partial \lambda} = 0 \tag{4-7}$$

Thus far, except for the exchange of $y'(x)$ for $u(x)$, the treatment of the problem follows the calculus of variations approach. We now introduce a new function which plays a central role in the control theory formulation of the problem. Ignoring the particular arguments of each of the functions, $L = F - \lambda(y' - g) = F - \lambda y' + \lambda g$. If we define a new function H as

$$H = F + \lambda g$$

then $L = H - \lambda y'$. It is worth noting that H depends upon x, y, u, and λ; in particular, y' is absent as an argument of H. Furthermore, $\partial L/\partial y = \partial H/\partial y$, $\partial L/\partial u = \partial H/\partial u$, and $\partial L/\partial \lambda = \partial H/\partial \lambda - y'$; thus the necessary conditions above in (4-5) through (4-7) can be further reexpressed as

$$-\frac{\partial H}{\partial y} = \lambda' \tag{4-8}$$

$$\frac{\partial H}{\partial u} = 0 \tag{4-9}$$

$$\frac{\partial H}{\partial \lambda} = y' \tag{4-10}$$

Equations (4-8) and (4-10) present the dynamics of the original variable y and the added variable λ in terms of partial derivatives of the function H. These are a pair of first-order differential equations and the endpoint conditions in (4-1) provide both initial and terminal values for $y(x)$ and specify nothing about λ at either x_0 or x_1. This new function is known as the hamiltonian function for the problem (hence the H); (4-8) and (4-10) parallel certain dynamic equations in classical mechanics which are due to the work of Hamilton. In control theory, the Lagrange multiplier-like variable λ is generally known as the *costate* or *adjoint* variable. [Note the symmetry, except for the minus sign, of (4-8) and (4-10).]

Consider the condition given in (4-9). Setting derivatives equal to zero is of course necessary for an unconstrained maximum or an unconstrained minimum, so it would appear that (4-9) requires u to be chosen so as to maximize or minimize H. However, in Chap. 3, Sec. 3-5 [(3-93) and (3-94)], we saw that the Weierstrass conditions that distinguished maxima from minima (since the Euler-Lagrange conditions are necessary for either kind of extremal) were a specification of the concavity or convexity of the function F for fixed x and y. But with x and y fixed, $H = F(u) + \lambda g(u)$ and since $g(u) = u$ for the problem given in (4-1), $H = F(u) + \lambda u$.

Thus when F is a concave function of u—the Weierstrass condition for a maximum of the integral—H will also be a concave function of u; hence the condition in (4-9), $\partial H/\partial u = 0$, characterizes a maximum of H. Similarly, when F is a convex function of u—the Weierstrass condition for a minimum—H will also be a convex function of u and the $\partial H/\partial u = 0$ condition will be associated with a minimum of H. Therefore, when the problem as given in (4-1) is to maximize I, condition (4-9) will be interpreted as choosing u to maximize H; when the problem as given in (4-1) is to minimize I, condition (4-9) directs that u be chosen to minimize H. It is from condition (4-9), and its extension to cases with many state and control variables as well as constraints, that the terminology of the "maximum principle"† or "Pontryagin's maximum principle"‡ comes. To simplify terminology, the general examples that we will consider in the remainder of this chapter will usually be ones involving maximization of an integral, and hence the conditions that parallel (4-9) will be referred to as maximum principles.

Example I: Shortest Distance in a Plane (Continued)

We can approach the shortest-distance problem from this point of view. Instead of minimization of $\int_{x_0}^{x_1} \sqrt{1 + (y')^2}\, dx$, with fixed endpoints $y(x_0) = y_0$ and $y(x_1) = y_1$, we now write:

$$\text{Minimize} \quad \int_{x_0}^{x_1} \sqrt{1 + u^2}\, dx$$

where $\qquad y(x_0) = y_0,\ y(x_1) = y_1 \quad \text{and} \quad y' = u$

For this problem, $L = \sqrt{1 + u^2} - \lambda(y' - u)$, $H = \sqrt{1 + u^2} + \lambda u$, and the necessary conditions, (4-8) through (4-10), become

$$0 = \lambda' \tag{4-11}$$

$$\frac{u}{\sqrt{1 + u^2}} + \lambda = 0 \tag{4-12}$$

† Clearly, this could also be referred to (and often is) as a "minimum principle." When there is no constraint on the control variable, the distinction is immaterial, since the operation in either case requires setting $\partial H/\partial u = 0$. In cases in which the control variable is constrained, however, the distinction is important, as we will see later in this chapter. Although it complicates the discussion unnecessarily at this point, we will see in Sec. 4-6 that the "maximum principle" for a maximization problem is also sometimes presented as a "minimum principle" (for the maximization problem), primarily depending on whether a positive or a negative sign is used in the statement of certain transversality conditions.

‡ The basic theory is developed and presented in Pontryagin et al. [8]. Intriligator [6, chaps. 11 and 14] provides a general introduction; Hadley and Kemp [4, chaps. 4 and 5], Hestenes [5], Rozonoer [9], or Takayama [10, chap. 8] contain derivations and many details.

$$u = y' \tag{4-13}$$

In this rather straightforward problem, the implications of (4-11) through (4-13) work out easily. From (4-12), $u/\sqrt{1+u^2} = -\lambda$ but from (4-11), $\lambda' = 0$. Therefore $\lambda = k$, a constant, and so $u/\sqrt{1+u^2} = -k$. From (4-13), this means $y'/\sqrt{1+(y')^2} = -k$ which, as in the calculus of variations approach, leads to the conclusion that y' = a constant and hence that $y(x)$ is a straight line, $y = k_1 x + k_2$. The fixed endpoints, as usual, will allow determination of k_1 and k_2.

A more general route to this conclusion proceeds as follows. From (4-12), one solves for u as a function of λ; here $u = \pm\sqrt{\lambda^2/(1-\lambda^2)}$. This accomplished, (4-11) and (4-13) become a pair of first-order differential equations in λ and y, namely,

$$\lambda' = 0$$

$$y' = \pm\sqrt{\lambda^2/(1-\lambda^2)}$$

In general, these will be nonlinear and not easy to solve exactly (see App. C). Moreover, instead of initial conditions on both y and λ [$y(x_0) = y_0$ and $\lambda(x_0) = \lambda_0$], we have, as noted earlier, initial and terminal values for y and neither initial nor terminal values for λ. This does not usually make the equations any easier to deal with. In the present case, however, the equations lead immediately to: (1) λ = a constant, therefore (2) y' = a constant, therefore (3) $y(x) = k_1 x + k_2$, exactly as before. What is worth noting is the sequence in which conditions (4-8) through (4-10) are utilized—at least in principle. Requirement (4-9) that $\partial H/\partial u = 0$ leads to one or more u, which may be functions of both λ and y. This depends entirely on the particular structure of H, which in turn depends on the original F and the constraint. When substituted into (4-8) and (4-10), we have a system (a pair when there is only one y and one λ) of first-order differential equations, usually nonlinear, in λ and y only. Recall that in the calculus of variations, the Euler-Lagrange condition for this problem was a single second-order differential equation.

Example II: Monopolistic Pricing over Time (Continued)

In control theory terms, the monopolistic pricing problem [(2-42) and (2-43) in Chap. 2] can be expressed as:

$$\text{Maximize} \quad \int_{t_0}^{t_1} \left(-\tfrac{3}{2}p^2 + 202p - 5000u^2 - 10{,}200u + 200pu - 5240\right) dt$$

where $\quad t_0 = 0, \quad p(t_0) = 70, \quad t_1 = 52, \quad p(t_1) = 100, \quad \text{and} \quad p' = u$

For this problem,

$$L = -\tfrac{3}{2}p^2 + 202p - 5000u^2 - 10{,}200u + 200pu - 5240 - \lambda(p' - u)$$

and the hamiltonian is

$$H = -\tfrac{3}{2}p^2 + 202p - 5000u^2 - 10{,}200u + 200pu - 5240 + \lambda u$$

Conditions (4-8) through (4-10) are

$$3p - 202 - 200u = \lambda' \tag{4-14}$$

$$-10{,}000u - 10{,}200 + 200p + \lambda = 0 \tag{4-15}$$

$$u = p' \tag{4-16}$$

As in the shortest-distance example, one need not solve these equations in the general way, since (4-15) can be solved for λ, the resulting equation differentiated with respect to t, and set equal to the expression for λ' given in (4-14). Substituting p' for u and p'' for u' [from (4-16)] gives $10{,}000p'' - 3p = -202$, which is exactly (2-44) from Chap. 2. Since the initial and terminal conditions are the same, the solution is the same as in the calculus of variations approach, namely,

$$p(t) = 15.391\, e^{0.0173t} - 12.724\, e^{-0.0173t} + 67.333 \tag{4-17}$$

This was (2-46) in Chap. 2.

Alternatively, we can follow the more general procedure. From (4-15),

$$u = 0.02p + 0.0001\lambda - 1.02 \tag{4-18}$$

Putting this into (4-14) and (4-16) gives the following pair of first-order differential equations (in this case the equations are also linear):

$$\begin{aligned} p' &= 0.02p + 0.0001\lambda - 1.02 \\ \lambda' &= \quad -p - \quad 0.02\lambda + 2 \end{aligned} \tag{4-19}$$

Utilizing standard procedures for such equations (App. C, Sec. C-7), the eigenvalues of the coefficient matrix

$$A = \begin{bmatrix} 0.02 & 0.0001 \\ -1 & -0.02 \end{bmatrix}$$

are found to be 0.0173 and -0.0173, and a pair of associated eigenvectors are found to be

$$V_1 = \begin{bmatrix} 1 \\ -27 \end{bmatrix} \quad \text{and} \quad V_2 = \begin{bmatrix} 1 \\ -373 \end{bmatrix}$$

so that

$$\begin{bmatrix} p \\ \lambda \end{bmatrix} = k_1 V_1\, e^{0.0173t} + k_2 V_2\, e^{-0.0173t} + \begin{bmatrix} h_1 \\ h_2 \end{bmatrix}$$

where $\begin{bmatrix} h_1 \\ h_2 \end{bmatrix}$ represents a solution to the pair of equations in their nonhomogeneous form. That is,

$$p = k_1\, e^{0.0173t} + k_2\, e^{-0.0173t} + h_1 \tag{4-20}$$

$$\lambda = -27k_1\, e^{0.0173t} - 373k_2\, e^{-0.0173t} + h_2 \tag{4-21}$$

Letting both p and λ be constants, the nonhomogeneous form equations (4-19) are

$$0.02p + 0.0001\lambda = 1.02$$
$$-p - \quad 0.02\lambda = -2$$

which have the unique solution $p = 67.333$ and $\lambda = -3266.667$; these are h_1 and h_2, respectively, in (4-20) and (4-21). Thus

$$p = k_1\, e^{0.0173t} + k_2\, e^{-0.0173t} + 67.333 \tag{4-22}$$

$$\lambda = -27k_1\, e^{0.0173t} - 373k_2\, e^{-0.0173t} - 3266.667 \tag{4-23}$$

Utilizing the endpoint information $[t_0 = 0,\ p(t_0) = 70,\ t_1 = 52$, and $p(t_1) = 100]$ in (4-22) leads to exactly the same result as in the calculus of variations approach, since (4-22) is the same as (2-45) in Chap. 2 and the endpoint conditions are also the same. Again, then,

$$p(t) = 15.391\, e^{0.0173t} - 12.724\, e^{-0.0173t} + 67.333$$

In addition, we find that

$$\lambda(t) = -415.557\, e^{0.0173t} + 4746.052\, e^{-0.0173t} - 3266.667$$

We will find that the value of the costate variable, particularly at the right-hand endpoint, is often important information in inequality constrained problems.

In both of these examples, a problem that was easily dealt with in the calculus of variations framework was seen to be amenable to a control theory formulation, with no apparent advantage (or disadvantage). In fact, the derivation of the maximum principle, (4-9), and the associated pair of differential equations, (4-8) and (4-10), can be carried out with only the following requirements on the functions involved:

1. $F(x, y, u)$ need only have continuous first partial derivatives. Recall (Chap. 2, Sec. 2-2) that in the calculus of variations approach F was required to have continuous first and second partial derivatives.†
2. $y(x)$, the state variable, needs to be piecewise smooth, as in the calculus of variations analysis.
3. $u(x)$, the control variable, need only be piecewise continuous; e.g., it may undergo jump changes. For the example just completed, $u = y'$ and so the relaxed condition on u is natural; however, in more general problems in the control theory format, where the constraint is $y' = g(x, y, u)$, this represents a relaxation on the character of the variable $u(x)$.
4. $g(x, y, u)$, the constraint function, should in certain cases have continuous first and second partial derivatives. The same is true if there are inequality constraints.

† In fact, in the Jacobi equation [(3-82) or (3-83) in Chap. 3] the term $(d/dx)[M]$, where $M = F_{y'y'}$, will involve third partial derivatives of F.

The complete derivation and discussion is in Pontryagin et al. [8]. (Rozonoer [9] offers a somewhat briefer introduction to the theory including most of the mathematical details, as do Hadley and Kemp [4].) The purpose of the discussion in this chapter is only to provide an introduction to the logic and the structure of the optimality conditions when expressed in the control formulation, and not to provide detailed mathematical proofs and derivations.

With the more general statement of the equality constraint, the problem in (4-1) becomes:

$$\text{Maximize} \quad I[y, u] = \int_{x_0}^{x_1} F(x, y, u)\, dx \tag{4-24}$$

where $\qquad y(x_0) = y_0, \quad y(x_1) = y_1 \quad$ and where $\quad y'(x) = g(x, y, u)$

The extension to problems with n state variables and m control variables is straightforward. As in previous chapters, let $\mathbf{Y} = [y_1(x), \ldots, y_n(x)]'$ and $\dot{\mathbf{Y}} = [y_1'(x), \ldots, y_n'(x)]'$. Further, let $\mathbf{U} = [u_1(x), \ldots, u_m(x)]'$, $\mathbf{G}(x, \mathbf{Y}, \mathbf{U}) = [g_1(x, \mathbf{Y}, \mathbf{U}). \ldots, g_n(x, \mathbf{Y}, \mathbf{U})]'$, $\mathbf{\Lambda}(x) = [\lambda_1(x), \ldots, \lambda_n(x)]'$, and $\dot{\mathbf{\Lambda}} = [\lambda_1'(x), \ldots, \lambda_n'(x)]'$. Then the extension of problem (4-1) to more variables and more general equality constraints can be written as:

$$\text{Maximize} \quad I[\mathbf{Y}, \mathbf{U}] = \int_{x_0}^{x_1} F(x, \mathbf{Y}, \mathbf{U})\, dx \tag{4-25}$$

where $\qquad \mathbf{Y}(x_0) = \mathbf{Y}_0, \quad \mathbf{Y}(x_1) = \mathbf{Y}_1, \quad$ and $\quad \dot{\mathbf{Y}} = \mathbf{G}(x, \mathbf{Y}, \mathbf{U})$

The Lagrange-like function, similar to (4-2) in the simplest case, is

$$L(x, \mathbf{Y}, \mathbf{U}, \dot{\mathbf{Y}}) = F(x, \mathbf{Y}, \mathbf{U}) - [\mathbf{\Lambda}(x)] \cdot [\dot{\mathbf{Y}} - \mathbf{G}(x, \mathbf{Y}, \mathbf{U})] \tag{4-26}$$

and the hamiltonian is

$$H(x, \mathbf{Y}, \mathbf{U}, \mathbf{\Lambda}) = F(x, \mathbf{Y}, \mathbf{U}) + [\mathbf{\Lambda}(x)] \cdot [\mathbf{G}(x, \mathbf{Y}, \mathbf{U})] \tag{4-27}$$

Using $\mathbf{H_Y} = [\partial H/\partial y_1, \ldots, \partial H/\partial y_n]'$, $\mathbf{H_\Lambda} = [\partial H/\partial \lambda_1, \ldots, \partial H/\partial \lambda_n]'$, and $\mathbf{H_U} = [\partial H/\partial u_1, \ldots, \partial H/\partial u_m]'$, the extension of the necessary conditions in (4-8) through (4-10) is

$$-\mathbf{H_Y} = \dot{\mathbf{\Lambda}} \tag{4-28}$$

$$\mathbf{H_U} = \mathbf{0} \tag{4-29}$$

$$\mathbf{H_\Lambda} = \dot{\mathbf{Y}} \tag{4-30}$$

Equations (4-28) and (4-30) constitute a set of $2n$ differential equations with initial and terminal conditions on the $\mathbf{Y}$, namely, $\mathbf{Y}(x_0) = \mathbf{Y}_0$ and $\mathbf{Y}(x_1) = \mathbf{Y}_1$, and the m equations in (4-29) specify, as before, that the u should be chosen so as to maximize H.

4-2 ENDPOINT CONDITIONS

In Chap. 3, Sec. 3-2, we found that endpoint requirements could be expressed in terms of an orthogonality requirement. For the simplest case, $I = \int_{x_0}^{x_1} F(x, y, y')\, dx$, with fixed left-hand endpoint, we defined

$$\nabla \mathbf{I} = \begin{bmatrix} (F - F_{y'}y') \\ F_{y'} \end{bmatrix}$$

and found that at the right-hand end

$$[\nabla \mathbf{I}] \cdot \begin{bmatrix} \delta x_1 \\ \delta y_1 \end{bmatrix} = 0$$

[This was (3-26) in Chap. 3.] The specifics of the right-hand endpoint requirement, e.g., that the terminal point lie on the function $y = \sigma(x)$, were then incorporated into the vector $\begin{bmatrix} \delta x_1 \\ \delta y_1 \end{bmatrix}$, as in (3-28) in Chap. 3. With an equality constraint of the form $y' = g(x, y, u)$, $I[y, u] = \int_{x_0}^{x_1} L(x, y, u, y', \lambda)\, dx$, where

$$L(x, y, u, y', \lambda) = F(x, y, u) - \lambda(x)[y' - g(x, y, u)]$$

and
$$\nabla \mathbf{I} = \begin{bmatrix} (L - L_{y'}y') \\ L_{y'} \end{bmatrix}$$

In the control theory formulation, when the hamiltonian is defined as $H = F + \lambda g$, we have $L = H - \lambda y'$ and in particular the elements of $\nabla \mathbf{I}$ are: (1) $L_{y'} = -\lambda(x)$ and (2) $(L - L_{y'}y') = F - \lambda y' + \lambda g + \lambda y' = F + \lambda g = H$. Therefore,

$$\nabla \mathbf{I} = \begin{bmatrix} H \\ -\lambda \end{bmatrix}$$

We recall the possibilities for specification of the right-hand endpoint that were illustrated in Figs. 3-1 through 3-4 in Chap. 3.

Fixed Endpoints (Fig. 3-1 in Chap. 3)

When $y(x_0) = y_0$ and $y(x_1) = y_1$, then, as we saw before in Chap. 3, both $\delta x_1 = 0$ and $\delta y_1 = 0$. The requirement that at x_1, $[\nabla \mathbf{I}] \cdot \begin{bmatrix} \delta x_1 \\ \delta y_1 \end{bmatrix} = 0$, i.e., that

$$\begin{bmatrix} H(x_1) \\ -\lambda(x_1) \end{bmatrix} \cdot \begin{bmatrix} \delta x_1 \\ \delta y_1 \end{bmatrix} = 0 \tag{4-31}$$

imposes no restrictions at all on the value of either the hamiltonian H or the costate variable λ at the right-hand endpoint x_1.

Free Right-Hand Boundary (Fig. 3-2 in Chap. 3)

Here $\delta x_1 = 0$ but, since $y(x)$ is only required to terminate at $x = x_1$, $\delta y_1 \neq 0$. Therefore the transversality condition in (4-31) imposes no restrictions on $H(x_1)$ but requires that $-\lambda(x_1) = 0$, that is, $\lambda(x_1) = 0$. In this case, the pair of first-order differential equations in (4-8) and (4-10) ($-\partial H/\partial y = \lambda'$ and $\partial H/\partial \lambda = y'$) has an initial value specified for y at the fixed left-hand endpoint, namely, $y(x_0) = y_0$, and a terminal value specified for λ, namely, $\lambda(x_1) = 0$. As usual, the absence of initial values for both variables in such a pair of equations may complicate their solution.

In Sec. 3-1 of Chap. 3 we considered the free right-hand boundary version of the first monopolist's pricing problem in which the original specification of $t_1 = 52$ and $p(t_1) = 100$ was replaced by $t_1 = 52$ but $p(t_1)$ unspecified. In the control version of this problem, the transversality requirement is $\lambda(t_1) = 0$, and thus the pair of equations in (4-22) and (4-23), above, now must be solved with the endpoint information that (1) $t_0 = 0$, $p(t_0) = 70$ and (2) $t_1 = 52$, $\lambda(t_1) = 0$, respectively. Using (1) in (4-22) gives, exactly as before, $k_1 + k_2 = 2.667$. Using (2) in (4-23) gives $-66.383k_1 - 151.711k_2 = 3266.667$. Except for rounding errors in the coefficients multiplying k_1 and k_2 in (4-23), this is just (the negative of) the equation in k_1 and k_2 that was derived in Sec. 3-1 of Chap. 3 from the calculus of variations transversality condition for the free right-hand boundary problem. Here $k_1 = 43.026$ and $k_2 = -40.358$; before the results were $k_1 = 43.373$ and $k_2 = -40.706$.

Free Terminal Time (Fig. 3-3 in Chap. 3)

In this case $\delta y_1 = 0$ but $\delta x_1 \neq 0$, and therefore, again from (4-31), there is no restriction on λ at $x = x_1$ but the value of the hamiltonian function there must be zero, that is, $H(x_1) = 0$. Again, for the free terminal time version of the second monopolist's pricing problem in Sec. 3-1 of Chap. 3, we replaced the original specification of $t_1 = 52$ and $p(t_1) = 20$ with $p(t_1) = 20$ but t_1 unspecified. In the control version of this problem, the transversality requirement is $H(t_1) = 0$. Here

$$H = -\tfrac{3}{2}p^2 + 202p - 5000u^2 - 10{,}200u + 200pu - 5240 + \lambda u$$

From (4-15), $\lambda = 10{,}000u + 10{,}200 - 200p$; hence the λu term in the hamiltonian is

$$10{,}000u^2 + 10{,}200u - 200pu$$

and substituting into $H(t_1) = 0$ gives

$$-\tfrac{3}{2}p_1^2 + 202p_1 + 5000u_1^2 - 5240 = 0$$

Since, from (4-16), $u = p'$ and $p_1 = 20$, we have the requirement that

$$p'(t_1) = \pm 0.6$$

exactly as in the calculus of variations approach, and the solution proceeds as before.

From the Euler-Lagrange equation

$$p(t) = k_1 e^{0.0173t} + k_2 e^{-0.0173t} + 67.333$$

and

$$p'(t) = 0.0173k_1 e^{0.0173t} - 0.0173k_2 e^{-0.0173t}$$

At t_1, which is unspecified,

$$p(t_1) = k_1 e^{0.0173t_1} + k_2 e^{-0.0173t_1} = -47.333$$

and, after dividing by 0.0173,

$$p'(t_1) = k_1 e^{0.0173t_1} - k_2 e^{-0.0173t_1} = \pm 34.682$$

From the left-hand endpoint information that $t_0 = 0$ and $p(t_0) = 10$, we have, as before,

$$k_1 + k_2 = -57.333$$

This parallels exactly the information in (3-25*a*,*b*,*c*) of Chap. 3 and thus leads to $k_1 = -4.95$, $k_2 = -52.38$ with $t_1 \cong 14.15$ and 122.2, as before.

Fixed Terminal Surface (Fig. 3-4 in Chap. 3)

As before, the requirement is orthogonality between ∇I and the terminal surface, $y = \sigma(x)$, at the point of intersection, x_1:

$$\begin{bmatrix} H(x_1) \\ -\lambda(x_1) \end{bmatrix} \cdot \begin{bmatrix} 1 \\ \sigma'(x_1) \end{bmatrix} = 0$$

or $H = \lambda\sigma'$, all evaluated at $x = x_1$.

In Example I in Sec. 3-1 of Chap. 3 we found the shortest distance in the plane from $(x_0, y_0) = (2, 3)$ to the function $y = \sigma(x) = +\sqrt{4(x-5)}$. We utilized the right-hand transversality condition in (3-19) of Chap. 3, that $[F - (\sigma' - y')F_{y'}]\,|_{x=x_1} = 0$. For the shortest-distance problem, this reduced to

$$\sigma'(x_1)y'(x_1) = -1$$

Consider now the transversality requirement in the control version of the problem, namely, $H(x_1) = \lambda(x_1)\sigma'(x_1)$. We have seen earlier in this chapter (Example I of Sec. 4-1) that the hamiltonian for the shortest-distance problem is

$$H = \sqrt{1 + u^2} + \lambda u$$

and that included in the necessary conditions [(4-12) and (4-13), above] are $\lambda = -u/\sqrt{1+u^2}$ and $u = y'$. Thus the transversality requirement becomes (all evaluated at x_1)

$$\sqrt{1 + u^2} + \lambda(u - \sigma') = 0$$

Replacing λ by its expression in u and multiplying both sides of the equation by $\sqrt{1+u^2}$ gives

$$1 + u(x_1)\sigma'(x_1) = 0$$

Since $u = y'$, this is

$$y'(x_1)\sigma'(x_1) = -1$$

exactly as before in the calculus of variations approach.

The extension to n state variables and m control variables is, again, fairly straightforward. We need only investigate the composition of $\nabla\mathbf{I}$. Recalling L from (4-26) and observing that there are now n costate variables $\lambda_1(x), \ldots, \lambda_n(x)$, we see that $\nabla\mathbf{I}$ will be an $(n+1)$-element vector:

$$\nabla\mathbf{I} = \begin{bmatrix} L - [\mathbf{L}_{\dot{\mathbf{Y}}}] \cdot [\dot{\mathbf{Y}}] \\ \mathbf{L}_{\dot{\mathbf{Y}}} \end{bmatrix}$$

Less compactly, since $L = F - \sum_{j=1}^{n} \lambda_j(x)[y_j' - g_j] = F - \sum_{j=1}^{n} \lambda_j(x) y_j' + \sum_{j=1}^{n} \lambda_j(x) g_j$ and $H = F + \sum_{j=1}^{n} \lambda_j(x) g_j$, the first element in $\nabla\mathbf{I}$, $L - [\mathbf{L}_{\dot{\mathbf{Y}}}] \cdot [\dot{\mathbf{Y}}]$, simply represents $F - \sum_{j=1}^{n} \lambda_j(x) y_j' + \sum_{j=1}^{n} \lambda_j(x) g_j + \sum_{j=1}^{n} \lambda_j(x) y_j' = F + \sum_{j=1}^{n} \lambda_j(x) g_j$, which is H. [This was written in compact matrix form in (4-27).] This term has grown "wider" by the need to subtract, from L, a sum of the λ times the corresponding y'. Correspondingly, the rest of $\nabla\mathbf{I}$ has grown "deeper" since in place of simply $y'(x)$ there are now n state variables with derivatives $y_1'(x), \ldots, y_n'(x)$. Therefore, with n state variables,

$$\nabla\mathbf{I} = \begin{bmatrix} H \\ -\lambda_1 \\ \vdots \\ -\lambda_n \end{bmatrix} = \begin{bmatrix} H \\ -\mathbf{\Lambda} \end{bmatrix} \tag{4-32}$$

Consider the fixed terminal surface case, where that surface is specified as $S(x, \mathbf{Y}) = 0$. The set of necessary conditions then contains the set of n equations of motion for the λ, given in (4-28), the n equations of motion for the y, given in (4-30), the fixed initial values $\mathbf{Y}(x_0) = \mathbf{Y}_0$, and the terminal transversality condition $\nabla\mathbf{I}(x_1) = \alpha\,\nabla\mathbf{S}(x_1)$, which means

$$H(x_1) = \alpha \left.\frac{\partial S}{\partial x}\right|_{x=x_1} \tag{4-33}$$

and

$$-\mathbf{\Lambda}(x_1) = \alpha \nabla\mathbf{S}_{\mathbf{Y}} \big|_{x=x_1} \tag{4-34}$$

This is the control theory analogue of (3-36) in Chap. 3. In particular, (4-34) supplies an additional n boundary conditions on the λ (although at the right-hand end) to supplement the initial values for the y given by $\mathbf{Y}(x_0) = \mathbf{Y}_0$. The additional possibilities provided by several terminal surfaces $S_1(x, \mathbf{Y}) = 0, \ldots, S_k(x, \mathbf{Y}) = 0$ are exactly parallel to those discussed above in Chap. 3, Sec. 3-2; in place of the $\nabla\mathbf{I}$ of Chap. 3 we now have the expanded version defined in (4-32).

4-3 CONTINUITY AND SMOOTHNESS ONCE AGAIN

We have approached the control theory formulation of dynamic optimization problems via an extension of calculus of variations techniques. In the simplest problem we treated the control variable u in exactly the same way as the state variable y, even though the constraint $y' = u$ made clear that when $y(x)$ was required to be piecewise smooth, $y'(x) = u(x)$ could only be assumed to be piecewise continuous. In developing the calculus of variations analysis for $I = \int_{x_0}^{x_1} F(x, y, u)\, dx$ in this chapter as a two-variable problem, therefore, we apparently have been ascribing more to $u(x)$—namely, piecewise smoothness—than is proper. By utilizing a change of variables, however, we will see that the results in this chapter are nonetheless valid.

Let $v(x)$ be defined so that $v'(x) = u(x)$. Then in place of: maximize $\int_{x_0}^{x_1} F(x, y, u)\, dx$, with the constraint $y' = g(x, y, u)$ and with fixed endpoints $y(x_0) = y_0$ and $y(x_1) = y_1$, we have:

$$\text{Maximize} \quad \int_{x_0}^{x_1} F(x, y, v')\, dx \tag{4-35}$$

where $\qquad y(x_0) = y_0, \quad y(x_1) = y_1, \quad \text{and} \quad y' = g(x, y, v')$

Viewing this as a calculus of variations problem in the two piecewise smooth variables y and v, in which y' and v do not happen to appear in the integrand F, we proceed in the usual way: $L = F - \lambda[y' - g] = F - \lambda y' + \lambda g$, $H = F + \lambda g$, and therefore, as before, $L = H - \lambda y'$. The necessary conditions parallel to (4-2) through (4-4) are

$$L_y - \frac{d}{dx} L_{y'} = 0 \tag{4-36}$$

$$L_v - \frac{d}{dx} L_{v'} = 0 \tag{4-37}$$

$$L_\lambda - \frac{d}{dx} L_{\lambda'} = 0 \tag{4-38}$$

Since $L_y = H_y$, $L_{y'} = -\lambda$, $L_v = 0$, $L_{v'} = H_{v'}$, $L_\lambda = H_\lambda - y'$, and $L_{\lambda'} = 0$, these reduce to

$$-H_y = \lambda' \tag{4-39}$$

$$\frac{d}{dx} H_{v'} = 0, \quad \text{that is, } H_{v'} = \text{constant} \tag{4-40}$$

$$H_\lambda = y' \tag{4-41}$$

Equations (4-39) and (4-41) are the usual first-order differential equations for λ and y—compare (4-8) and (4-10), above. The results in (4-40), however, appear to differ from the maximum principle earlier in which $H_u = 0$—as in (4-9). The transversality conditions turn out to provide the needed connection. For this problem

$$\nabla \mathbf{I} = \begin{bmatrix} H \\ L_{y'} \\ L_{v'} \end{bmatrix}$$

and, as we have seen, $L_{y'} = -\lambda$ and $L_{v'} = H_{v'}$. Therefore

$$\nabla \mathbf{I} = \begin{bmatrix} H \\ -\lambda \\ H_{v'} \end{bmatrix} \tag{4-42}$$

and the transversality requirement is

$$\begin{bmatrix} H(x_1) \\ -\lambda(x_1) \\ H_{v'}(x_1) \end{bmatrix} \cdot \begin{bmatrix} \delta x_1 \\ \delta y_1 \\ \delta v_1 \end{bmatrix} = 0$$

[which is the extension of (4-31) to two variables, $y(x)$ and $v(x)$]. Since x_1 and $y(x_1)$ are fixed but $v(x_1)$ is free, $\delta v_1 \neq 0$ and so $H_{v'}(x_1) = 0$. But from (4-40), this means $H_{v'} = 0$ for all x in $[x_0, x_1]$, and since $v' = u$, (4-40) becomes $H_u = 0$, exactly as before.

4-4 CONSTRAINTS

The essence of even the simplest problem in the control theory formulation is that the control variables influence the rates of change of the state variables through equality constraints of the form $y_i' = g_i(x, \mathbf{Y}, \mathbf{U})$; therefore this form of equality constraint is dealt with from the beginning. In this section we investigate the treatment of (1) additional equality constraints involving the control variables, with or without the state variables, (2) inequality constraints on the control variables, with or without the state variables, and (3) equality or inequality constraints on the state variables alone. We will see that some of these situations may present added complications.

Control Variable Equalities

In a problem with n state variables and m control variables, suppose that there is a constraint of the form $c(x, \mathbf{U}) = 0$ on the control variables. [Clearly this kind of restriction is only interesting if there is more than one control variable, since otherwise the single $u(x)$ would be determined by the constraint and there would be no problem of choice for the control variable.] The new constraint on the u is easily accommodated in straightforward lagrangian fashion by attaching it directly to the hamiltonian, forming an expanded function [compare (4-27)]

$$H^* = F + \mathbf{\Lambda} \cdot \mathbf{G} - vc$$

and proceeding as before in (4-28) through (4-30). Since $H^* = H - vc(x, \mathbf{U})$, $\mathbf{H}_{\mathbf{Y}}^* = \mathbf{H}_{\mathbf{Y}}$ and (4-28) will be exactly as before. Similarly, $\mathbf{H}_{\Lambda}^* = \mathbf{H}_{\Lambda}$ and (4-30) will reproduce the original constraints $\dot{\mathbf{Y}} = \mathbf{G}(x, \mathbf{Y}, \mathbf{U})$, also as before. Now, however, **U** will be chosen, as in (4-29), so that

$$\mathbf{H}_{\mathbf{U}}^* = \mathbf{0}$$

and here

$$\mathbf{H}_{\mathbf{U}}^* = \mathbf{F}_{\mathbf{U}} + \mathbf{\Lambda} \cdot \mathbf{G}_{\mathbf{U}} - vc_{\mathbf{U}} = \mathbf{0}$$

That is, the place where the new constraint on the u makes itself felt is in the equations for determining the optimal values of the u, exactly as would be expected. Now, the m equations in $\mathbf{H}_{\mathbf{U}}^* = \mathbf{0}$ plus the constraint itself, $c(x, \mathbf{U}) = 0$, serve to determine the optimal values of the m control variables and the value of the Lagrange-like multiplier v. Similarly, if there were several constraints $c_j(x, \mathbf{U}) = 0$, these would be attached to the hamiltonian, each with a corresponding multiplier v_j, and only the expression for $\mathbf{H}_{\mathbf{U}}^*$ would be altered.

If there were an equality constraint of the form $p(x, \mathbf{Y}, \mathbf{U}) = 0$, involving both state and control variables, a similar procedure can be followed. Forming

$$H^* = F + \mathbf{\Lambda} \cdot \mathbf{G} - vp$$

and following (4-28) through (4-30) will lead to

$$-\mathbf{H}_{\mathbf{Y}}^* = -\mathbf{H}_{\mathbf{Y}} + vp_{\mathbf{Y}} = \dot{\mathbf{\Lambda}} \qquad (4\text{-}28')$$

$$\mathbf{H}_{\mathbf{U}}^* = \mathbf{H}_{\mathbf{U}} - vp_{\mathbf{U}} = \mathbf{0} \qquad (4\text{-}29')$$

and

$$\mathbf{H}_{\Lambda}^* = \mathbf{H}_{\Lambda} = \dot{\mathbf{Y}} \qquad (4\text{-}30')$$

Thus, again as might be expected, the choice of the optimal u is governed by an expanded set of equations in (4-29′) and moreover the equations of motion for the λ, (4-28′), are changed from what was given in (4-28) because the state variables are now explicitly included in the constraint. Again, with several constraints $p_l(x, \mathbf{Y}, \mathbf{U}) = 0$, each would be attached to the hamiltonian with a multipler v_l and the expressions for both $\mathbf{H}_{\mathbf{Y}}^*$ and $\mathbf{H}_{\mathbf{U}}^*$ would be "widened." Equality constraints on the control variables, with or without the presence of state variables, do not fundamentally alter the maximum principle approach.

Control Variable Inequalities: I

The maximum principle allows easily for the possibility of inequality constraints on the control variables. For example, if $0 \leq u \leq k$, then of course it may not be possible to find a u within these bounds, for which $\partial H/\partial u = 0$. Denote the set of feasible u by $\bar{u}$. In fact, the maximum principle, as embodied in (4-9), for example, actually only requires that u be chosen so as to:

$$\underset{u \in \bar{u}}{\text{Maximize}} \; H(x, y, u, \lambda)$$

[When the original problem is one of minimization of an integral, the requirement is to minimize$_{u \in \bar{u}}$ $H(x, y, u, \lambda)$.] This is a constrained optimization problem in its own right, which may require utilization of some type of nonlinear programming technique. The fact that u, y, and λ are themselves functions (of x) may influence the approach. With many y, $\mathbf{Y} = [y_1, \dots, y_n]'$, and u, $\mathbf{U} = [u_1, \dots, u_m]'$, if $\bar{U}$ defines the closed and bounded feasible set of $u_1, \dots, u_m$ (each of which is constrained by a requirement of the form $b_j \leq u_j \leq t_j$), then the maximum principle requires that the u be chosen to maximize$_{\mathbf{U} \in \bar{U}}$ $H(x, \mathbf{Y}, \mathbf{U}, \mathbf{\Lambda})$.

For example, in the Kuhn-Tucker approach to selection of u so as to maximize $H(x, y, u, \lambda)$, subject to $u(x) \leq k$, we would attach to H a $\mu(x)[u(x) - k]$ term to form, say, $J = H - \mu(u - k)$. Note that μ will be a function of x just as λ is, for the same reasons, namely, that the condition in the constraint $u(x) \leq k$ must hold at each value of x in $[x_0, x_1]$. The Kuhn-Tucker necessary conditions would include a requirement on the partial derivative of the expanded function J, with respect to u—namely, $\partial J/\partial u = \partial H/\partial u - \mu = 0$, the inequality constraint itself, $u(x) \leq k$, and the conditions

$$\mu(x)[u(x) - k] = 0 \quad \mu(x) \geq 0 \tag{4-43}$$

Since the added term $\mu(u - k)$ contributes $-\mu$ to the partial derivative with respect to u, one could as well, following the earlier logic of $H = F + \lambda g$, define an expanded hamiltonian

$$\mathscr{H} = F + \lambda g - \mu u = H - \mu u$$

and then the partial derivative condition could be expressed simply as

$$\mathscr{H}_u = 0$$

This, along with $u(x) \leq k$ and (4-43), would constitute the necessary conditions for the constrained maximization of H. In addition, the complete set of necessary conditions for the variational problem includes $-H_y = \lambda'$ and $H_\lambda = y'$, as usual. However, since $\mathscr{H} = H - \mu u$, these can as well be expressed as $-\mathscr{H}_y = \lambda'$ and $\mathscr{H}_\lambda = y'$, respectively.

The procedure is the same for a more general inequality constraint of the form $c(x, u) \leq 0$; the illustration above is simply the special case in which $c(x, u) = u - k$, but it is of some interest since very often in the social sciences the constraint on a control variable occurs as an upper (and/or lower) limit on the value of that variable. Furthermore, extension to more state variables, more control variables, and/or more constraints is logically straightforward but notationally cumbersome.

To continue the case of a single control variable, when there is a terminal inequality only on the control variable [for example, $u(x_1) \leq k$], the conditions in (4-43) become simply the endpoint conditions

$$\mu(x_1)[u(x_1) - k] = 0 \quad \mu(x_1) \geq 0 \tag{4-44}$$

And, of course, if the endpoint requirement on the control variable is one of nonnegativity $[u(x_1) \geq 0]$, these conditions reduce to

$$\mu(x_1)u(x_1) = 0 \quad \mu(x_1) \geq 0 \tag{4-45}$$

As we will see in the examples below, these endpoint conditions establish whether or not the unconstrained optimal solution satisfies the terminal inequality on the control variable. If it does, then no change in the optimal control function is necessary; if it does not, then there will be a jump in the optimal control function at the final moment to satisfy the inequality there.

Example II: Monopolistic Pricing over Time (Continued)

We examine the effects of control variable constraints on the dynamic pricing problems for the two monopolists. Consider the first case, with $t_0 = 0$, $p(t_0) = 70$, $t_1 = 52$, and $p(t_1) = 100$, but now also with the constraint that $u \leq 0.6$, throughout. We found earlier that profits over the year would be maximized by following the pricing schedule given by

$$p(t) = 15.391\, e^{0.0173t} - 12.724\, e^{-0.0173t} + 67.333$$

Since $u = p'$, we find here that $p'(t) = 0.266\, e^{0.0173t} + 0.220\, e^{-0.0173t}$. This function for $p'(t)$ has a minimum at $t < 0$, and it increases over $0 \leq t \leq 52$ from $p' = 0.486$ at $t = 0$ to $p' = 0.744$ at $t = 52$. That is, the original solution in which the control variable was unconstrained violates the new constraint $u \leq 0.6$ over some part of the interval $0 \leq t \leq 52$. In fact, from $t = 33.8$ onward, $u > 0.6$.

From before, the hamiltonian is

$$H = -\tfrac{3}{2}p^2 + 202p - 5000u^2 - 10{,}200u + 200pu - 5240 + \lambda u$$

Forming $\mathscr{H} = H - \mu u$ gives, for this problem,

$$\mathscr{H} = -\tfrac{3}{2}p^2 + 202p - 5000u^2 - 10{,}200u + 200pu - 5240 + \lambda u - \mu u$$

and the constrained optimization problem of choosing u to maximize H subject to $u \leq 0.6$ leads to:

(*a*) $$\mathscr{H}_u = -10{,}000u - 10{,}200 + 200p + \lambda - \mu = 0$$

(*b*) $$u \leq 0.6$$

(*c*) $$\mu(u - 0.6) = 0$$

(*d*) $$\mu \geq 0$$

We consider the implications of (*c*), in which at least one of the two terms must be zero:

1. Let $(u - 0.6) = 0$, that is, $u = 0.6$. That is, $p'(t) = 0.6$. Thus the solution would be of the form $p(t) = 0.6t + k$. But since $p(t_0) = 70$, this suggests that $k = 70$, while from $p(t_1) = 100$ we find $k = 68.8$. This simply reflects the obvious fact

that a line with slope 0.6 cannot connect the points $p = 70$ at $t = 0$ and $p = 100$ at $t = 52$. (The slope of the unique line connecting these two points is 0.577.)

2. If $\mu = 0$, then (*a*) reduces to exactly $H_u = 0$ from the unconstrained version of the problem; this is (4-15), above. In addition we have the usual conditions that $H_p = \lambda'$ and $H_\lambda = p'$ (as usual, the latter simply gives the constraint $u = p'$); these are (4-14) and (4-16), above. Thus we have exactly the situation examined in Sec. 4-1 and hence the solution is $p(t) = 15.391\, e^{0.0173t} - 12.724\, e^{-0.0173t} + 67.333$, which violates condition (*b*) over $33.8 \leq t \leq 52$, as we have seen.

Thus neither the straight line with a slope of 0.6 nor the original unconstrained solution can be optimal over the entire 52-week period. The profit-maximizing pricing policy will follow the exponential function that solved the unconstrained problem, starting at $t = 0$, and it will finish on the straight line, at $t = 52$. Thus the constant in $p(t) = 0.6t + k$ is established to be 68.8, and the optimal function will have a corner at the value of t for which

$$15.391\, e^{0.0173t} - 12.724\, e^{-0.0173t} + 67.333 = 0.6t + 68.8$$

This is at approximately $t = 11.3$, where $p(t) = 75.58$, evaluated by either function.

Total profits are found by integrating the profit function using $p(t) = 15.391\, e^{0.0173t} - 12.724\, e^{-0.0173t} + 67.333$ over the interval from 0 to 11.3 and adding the integral of the profit function using $p(t) = 0.6t + 68.8$ over the interval from 11.3 to 52. This gives a total profit for the year of roughly 169,000. [Recall that in the original problem, with no constraint on the control variable, this figure was approximately 170,000. Thus the penalty imposed by this particular control variable constraint is not great in this problem; this is not surprising since, as we saw above, the optimal $p(t)$ is a rather gentle smooth curve with a slope of 0.486 at t_0 and 0.744 at t_1.] Notice that even though the original solution to the unconstrained problem did not violate the new control variable constraint until $t = 33.8$, the ultimate impact of this added requirement on u is to force abandonment of the original optimal curve much earlier, namely, at $t = 11.3$.

A similar kind of solution arises for the second monopolist if we impose the control variable constraint that $u \geq 0$. Recall that this was the problem with the same objective functional as in the previous problem but with $t_0 = 0$, $p(t_0) = 10$, $t_1 = 52$, and $p(t_1) = 20$. The optimal price function was

$$p(t) = -11.695\, e^{0.0173t} - 45.638\, e^{-0.0173t} + 67.333$$

As before, since $u = p'$, we examine the function $p'(t)$. Here $p'(t) = -0.202\, e^{0.0173t} + 0.790\, e^{-0.0173t}$, which is monotonic decreasing over $0 \leq t \leq 52$. At $t_0 = 0$, $p'(t_0) = 0.588$ and at $t_1 = 52$, $p'(t_1) = -0.176$. In fact, from $t = 39.4$ onward, $u < 0$.

Again, we form $\mathscr{H} = H - \mu u$:

$$\mathscr{H} = -\tfrac{3}{2}p^2 + 202p - 5000u^2 - 10{,}200u + 200pu - 5240 + \lambda u - \mu u$$

and, as before, constrained maximization of H leads to

$$(a) \qquad \mathscr{H}_u = -10{,}000u - 10{,}200 + 200p + \lambda + \mu = 0$$
$$(b) \qquad u \geq 0$$
$$(c) \qquad \mu u = 0$$
$$(d) \qquad \mu \geq 0$$

From (*c*), at least one of the two terms must be zero:

1. If $u = 0$, then $p'(t) = 0$ and $p(t) = k$. Since $p(t_0) = 10$ and $p(t_2) = 20$, this is impossible; a straight line with zero slope cannot connect $p = 10$ at $t = 0$ and $p = 20$ at $t = 52$. (The line connecting the points would have a slope of 0.192.)
2. If $\mu = 0$, then we have exactly the unconstrained version of this problem, for which the control variable constraint is violated from $t = 39.4$ onward.

Therefore the optimal pricing policy will be to begin on the exponential function that is the solution to the unconstrained problem, end on the straight line $p = 20$, and have a corner where these two functions intersect. This will be at the value of t for which

$$-11.695\, e^{0.0173t} - 45.638\, e^{-0.0173t} + 67.333 = 20$$

which is at approximately $t = 26.6$. Thus the optimal policy is to follow the exponential function over the interval $0 \leq t \leq 26.6$ and then keep p at 20 from that point onward. Again, although the control variable constraint is not violated until after $t = 39.4$, the original optimal function for $p(t)$ must be abandoned earlier, at $t = 26.6$, to accommodate the constraint. This is simply because, at $t = 39.4$, $p(\mathrm{t}) = 21.127$ and hence to have $p(t) = 20$ at $t = 52$ requires that $p'(t)$, which is $u(t)$, be negative in at least some of the interval between $t = 39.4$ and $t = 52$. Total profits will be roughly $-202{,}700$, as opposed to approximately $-201{,}500$ in the unconstrained case.

Finally, consider the impact of only a terminal inequality on the control variable; e.g., in the first problem, suppose the constraint were only $u_1 \leq 0.6$. We know, from earlier, that $u_1 = 0.744$ and hence that this constraint is violated by the unconstrained solution. Form $J = H - \mu(u - k)$ and $\mathscr{H} = H - \mu u$ as in the $u \leq 0.6$ case, but note that J and $\mathscr{H}$ are evaluated only at $t = t_1$. Thus the constrained optimization conditions are "terminal" ones only, namely,

$$(a) \qquad -10{,}000u_1 - 10{,}200 + 200p_1 + \lambda_1 - \mu_1 = 0$$
$$(b) \qquad u_1 \leq 0.6$$
$$(c) \qquad \mu_1(u_1 - 0.6) = 0$$
$$(d) \qquad \mu_1 \geq 0$$

In fact, since there are no new conditions anywhere but at $t = 52$, the optimal functions will continue to be $p(t) = 15.391\, e^{0.0173t} - 12.724\, e^{-0.0173t} + 67.333$, $\lambda(t) = -415.557\, e^{0.0173t} + 4746.052\, e^{-0.0173t} - 3266.667$, and $u(t) = p'(t) = 0.266$

$e^{0.0173t} + 0.220\,e^{-0.0173t}$, over $0 \le t \le 52$. Moreover, since there can be jumps in the control variables, it is clear that the optimal control will follow $u(t)$ until the last moment, when u will drop to $u = 0.6$, since without the constraint, $u(t_1) = 0.744$.

Whether or not a terminal constraint of this sort on $u(t)$ will be binding is established through the conditions above. For example, from (c) either $\mu_1 = 0$ or $u_1 = 0$ (or both) at $t = 52$.

1. If $\mu_1 = 0$, then the problem is unconstrained at $t = 52$ as well as earlier, and we have seen that $u_1 \ge 0.6$ in this case, so (b) is violated.
2. If $u_1 = 0.6$, then evaluating (a) at t_1, where $p_1 = 100$ and $\lambda_1 = -2358$, gives $\mu_1 = 1442 > 0$, so (d) and in fact all conditions (a) through (d) are met. Similarly, for example, if the final condition were $u_1 \le 0.3$, for the $u_1 = 0.3$ case we would find $\mu_1 = 4442 > 0$ and again all conditions are satisfied (with 0.6 replaced by 0.3). On the other hand, if the constraint were $u_1 \le 0.8$, then the $u_1 = 0.8$ case in (c) would lead to $\mu_1 = -558 < 0$, violating (d); conversely, the $\mu_1 = 0$ case, which is the unconstrained problem, leads to $u_1 = 0.744$, and (a) through (d) are satisfied (with 0.6 replaced by 0.8). In this case, there would be no terminal jump in the control variable.

Control Variable Inequalities: II

As with equality constraints, the conditions on u may vary more generally with x and/or with y; this can be represented as

$$p(x, y, u) \le 0 \tag{4-46}$$

With more variables, we would have $p(x, \mathbf{Y}, \mathbf{U}) \le 0$, and with more constraints as well as variables, $\mathbf{P}(x, \mathbf{Y}, \mathbf{U}) \le \mathbf{0}$, where

$$\mathbf{P} = [p_1(x, \mathbf{Y}, \mathbf{U}), \ldots, p_s(x, \mathbf{Y}, \mathbf{U})]'$$

There are two requirements on the characteristics of the control variable inequality constraints that are necessary for a complete derivation of the results; these will only be sketched below. The first is not unlike a kind of nondegeneracy requirement in linear programming; if s, the number of constraints, is greater than m, the number of control variables, then there are no points at which all inequality constraints are satisfied and at which more than m are actually equations. For $m = 2$, imagine $s = 4$ constraints in u_1, u_2 space. The requirement is that not more than 2 ($= m$) of the constraints intersect in any point on the boundaries of the feasible region. The second requirement is that at least one of the u appears in each of the inequality constraints; this distinguishes the constraints that we are now considering from those on the state variables only, which require a somewhat different treatment.† This condition is stated formally

† For a complete discussion of various kinds of constraint requirements and their relationship to the constraint qualification for nonlinear programming problems, see Takayama [10, chap. 8, especially secs. A(c) and C(a)].

in terms of the rank of a certain matrix. Suppose that a particular $(x, \mathbf{Y}, \mathbf{U})$ satisfies $\mathbf{P}(x, \mathbf{Y}, \mathbf{U}) \leq \mathbf{0}$ and that $k \leq s$ of the constraints are met as equalities at that point. Form an $(m \times k)$ matrix $[\partial \mathbf{P}/\partial \mathbf{U}]$ whose ith column is $[\partial p_i/\partial u_1, \ldots, \partial p_i/\partial u_m]'$, where the p_i are the equality constraints. Then the rank of $[\partial \mathbf{P}/\partial \mathbf{U}]$ must be k. If $m = 3$ and $k = 2$, where p_1 and p_2 are the constraints that are equalities, then the matrix is

$$\begin{bmatrix} \partial p_1/\partial u_1 & \partial p_2/\partial u_1 \\ \partial p_1/\partial u_2 & \partial p_2/\partial u_2 \\ \partial p_1/\partial u_3 & \partial p_2/\partial u_3 \end{bmatrix}$$

and requiring the rank to be 2 $(= k)$ assures, among other things, that neither column will contain all zero elements. This, in turn, means that at least one u appears in each of the constraints $p_1(x, \mathbf{Y}, \mathbf{U}) = 0$ and $p_2(x, \mathbf{Y}, \mathbf{U}) = 0$.

A complete derivation of the results in the case of control variable inequality constraints can be found in the references.† Our interest here is to provide the reader with a general feeling for the logic of the results. The basic idea, due to Valentine, is to convert the inequalities into equations by adding a nonnegative slack variable to the left-hand side of each $p_i(x, \mathbf{Y}, \mathbf{U}) \leq 0$. This is very much in the spirit of the simplex method approach in linear programming and the derivation of Kuhn-Tucker results in nonlinear programming. It is, however, more complicated because of the fact that functions, not simply variables, are involved.

We return to the calculus of variations setting, in which the simplest control theory problem is converted from $\int_{x_0}^{x_1} F(x, y, u)\, dx$ to $\int_{x_0}^{x_1} F(x, y, v')\, dx$, where $u = v'$, so that the problem involves two piecewise smooth functions $y(x)$ and $v(x)$ and their piecewise continuous derivatives $y'(x)$ and $v'(x)$. Consider only one differential inequality constraint (4-46) which, with $u(x) = v'(x)$, will be written $p(x, y, v') \leq 0$. The slack to be added to the left-hand side of this inequality will clearly be a function of x, since it must be able to vary as $y(x)$ and $v'(x)$ vary. Since it must be nonnegative, this suggests that we will add the function squared. Finally, since it will be appropriate to treat the new function in a manner parallel to $y(x)$ and $v(x)$, we need to be certain that it too is piecewise smooth; this is the requirement that causes a certain amount of trouble.

Let $\omega(x) = -p(x, y, v')$; $\omega(x)$ is nonnegative and piecewise continuous [since $v'(x)$ need only be piecewise continuous]. Next, define $\psi(x) = \sqrt{\omega(x)}$; $\psi(x)$ is also piecewise continuous. Third, define $w(x) = \int_{x_0}^{x_1} \psi(x)\, dx$. Since $\psi(x)$ is piecewise continuous, $w(x)$ will be piecewise smooth and $w'(x) = \psi(x)$. But $[w'(x)]^2 = [\psi(x)]^2 = \omega(x) = -p(x, y, v')$ and thus $w(x)$ is precisely the piecewise smooth function needed, and $[w'(x)]^2$ will balance the left- and right-hand sides of $p(x, y, v') \leq 0$. That is, the differential inequality constraint is converted to the equality

$$p(x, y, v') + [w'(x)]^2 = 0 \tag{4-47}$$

† For example, Hadley and Kemp [4, chap. 5].

This accomplished, we can now treat the problem as one in three piecewise continuous functions y, v, and w, with a new equality constraint, namely,

$$\text{Maximize} \quad \int_{x_0}^{x_1} F(x, y, v')\, dx$$

where

$$y(x_0) = y_0$$

$$y(x_1) = y_1 \tag{4-48}$$

$$y' = g(x, y, v')$$

and

$$p(x, y, v') + [w'(x)]^2 = 0$$

[Compare (4-35), where there was no differential inequality constraint.] The augmented lagrangian function will be (ignoring the arguments of each function)

$$L = F - \lambda(y' - g) - \mu[p + (w')^2] \tag{4-49}$$

and we define a hamiltonian function, following the same logic as earlier, to be

$$\mathscr{H} = F + \lambda g - \mu p = H - \mu p \tag{4-50}$$

Parallel to (4-39) through (4-41), we now want Euler-Lagrange equations for y, v, w, λ, and μ. Here $L = \mathscr{H} - \lambda y' - \mu(w')^2$, so that $L_y = \mathscr{H}_y$, $L_{y'} = -\lambda$, $L_v = 0$, $L_{v'} = \mathscr{H}_{v'}$, $L_w = 0$, $L_{w'} = -2\mu w'$, $L_\lambda = \mathscr{H}_\lambda - y'$, $L_{\lambda'} = 0$, $L_\mu = \mathscr{H}_\mu - (w')^2$, and $L_{\mu'} = 0$. Thus the Euler-Lagrange equations reduce to

$$-\mathscr{H}_y = \lambda' \tag{4-51}$$

$$\frac{d}{dx}\mathscr{H}_{v'} = 0 \tag{4-52}$$

$$\frac{d}{dx}(-2\mu w') = 0 \tag{4-53}$$

$$\mathscr{H}_\lambda = y' \tag{4-54}$$

$$\mathscr{H}_\mu - (w')^2 = 0 \tag{4-55}$$

The results in (4-51) and (4-54) parallel (4-39) and (4-41) from earlier; these are the usual first-order differential equations describing the dynamics of λ and y. From (4-55), $p + (w')^2 = 0$, which just reproduces the new constraint in (4-48). From (4-52), as before, $\mathscr{H}_{v'} = k_1$, a constant, and from (4-53), $2\mu w' = k_2$, a constant. Also as before, determination of these constants comes from a consideration of endpoint conditions. In (4-42) we expanded the gradient of I, $\nabla \mathbf{I}$, to account for the (then) new function $v(x)$. Now we expand it further to include the new function $w(x)$. For the problem given in (4-48),

$$\nabla \mathbf{I} = [\mathscr{H}, L_{y'}, L_{v'}, L_{w'}]'$$

Since we have seen that $L_{y'} = -\lambda$, $L_{v'} = \mathscr{H}_{v'}$, and $L_{w'} = -2\mu w'$, we have

$$\mathbf{VI} = \begin{bmatrix} \mathscr{H} \\ -\lambda \\ \mathscr{H}_{v'} \\ -2\mu w' \end{bmatrix} \tag{4-56}$$

[Compare (4-42).] In this problem, $v(x_1)$ and $w(x_1)$ are free, although x_1 and $y(x_1)$ are fixed. The transversality requirement

$$\begin{bmatrix} \mathscr{H}(x_1) \\ -\lambda(x_1) \\ \mathscr{H}_{v'}(x_1) \\ -2\mu w'(x_1) \end{bmatrix} \cdot \begin{bmatrix} \delta x_1 \\ \delta y_1 \\ \delta v_1 \\ \delta w_1 \end{bmatrix} = 0 \tag{4-57}$$

means, since $\delta v(x_1) \neq 0$ and $\delta w(x_1) \neq 0$, that

$$\mathscr{H}_{v'}(x_1) = 0 \tag{4-58}$$

and

$$-2\mu w'(x_1) = 0 \tag{4-59}$$

Since (4-52) and (4-53) require that the left-hand sides of both of these equations be constant for all x in $[x_0, x_1]$, it is clear that $\mathscr{H}_{v'} = 0$ and $\mu(x)w'(x) = 0$ for all x in $[x_0, x_1]$. Since $u = v'$, the requirement in (4-52) is once again the maximum principle, namely,

$$\mathscr{H}_u = 0$$

exactly as expected, except that of course now the hamiltonian function has been augmented by a $-\mu(x)p(x, y, v')$ term, that is, $\mathscr{H} = H - \mu p$. The only really new condition—except for the new constraint given in (4-55)—is

$$\mu(x)w'(x) = 0 \tag{4-60}$$

Reasoning as in the derivation of Kuhn-Tucker conditions for mathematical programming problems, (4-60) means that if $\mu(x) \neq 0$, $w'(x) = 0$ and if $w'(x) \neq 0$, $\mu(x) = 0$. But if $w'(x) = 0$ then $[w'(x)]^2 = 0$ which means, from (4-47), that $p(x, y, v') = 0$. Thus (4-60) can be expressed as

$$\mu(x)p(x, y, v') = 0 \tag{4-61}$$

The Legendre-Clebsch conditions, for a maximum or minimum for a function of several variables, were an extension of (3-76) in Chap. 3. In a constrained problem, L replaces F in the hessian-like matrix of second partial and cross-partial derivatives. Forming

$$\begin{bmatrix} L_{w'w'} & L_{w'y'} & L_{w'v'} \\ L_{y'w'} & L_{y'y'} & L_{y'v'} \\ L_{v'w'} & L_{v'y'} & L_{v'v'} \end{bmatrix}$$

we find that $L_{w'w'} = -2\mu(x)$ and all other elements are zero. To be negative semidefinite, which is the Legendre-Clebsch necessary condition for a maximum, it is necessary that the principal minors alternate between nonpositive and nonnegative, beginning nonpositive. Therefore $-2\mu(x) \leq 0$ or

$$\mu(x) \geq 0 \tag{4-62}$$

which is a sign condition on the Lagrange multiplier-like term in (4-60); again this is similar to Kuhn-Tucker results in nonlinear programming.†

The results for an inequality constraint on u alone [(4-43) through (4-45), above] are seen to be simply special cases of those above in (4-61) and (4-62) with $p(x, y, u) = u(x) - k$. In addition, since $\mathscr{H} = H - \mu p$ [from (4-50)], setting $\mathscr{H}_u = 0$ with $\mu p = 0$, $\mu \geq 0$, and $p \leq 0$, is equivalent to maximization of H with the inequality constraint $p(x, y, u) \leq 0$ using the Kuhn-Tucker approach.

Consider the Weierstrass condition, distinguishing maxima from minima, for the problem in (4-48), which is more constrained than the original problem, given in (4-1). The Weierstrass E function was given in (3-92) of Chap. 3, for the case of one variable $y(x)$. The extension to several variables is

$$E(x, \mathbf{Y}, \dot{\mathbf{Y}}, \dot{\mathbf{Z}}) = F(x, \mathbf{Y}, \dot{\mathbf{Z}}) - F(x, \mathbf{Y}, \dot{\mathbf{Y}}) - [\dot{\mathbf{Z}} - \dot{\mathbf{Y}}] \cdot [\mathbf{F}_{\dot{\mathbf{Y}}}(x, \mathbf{Y}, \dot{\mathbf{Y}})]$$

and, when there are constraints, the function F from (4-48) is replaced by L, given in (4-49), as usual. Thus for the current problem we have

$$E(x, \mathbf{Y}, \dot{\mathbf{Y}}, \dot{\mathbf{Z}}) = L(x, \mathbf{Y}, \dot{\mathbf{Z}}) - L(x, \mathbf{Y}, \dot{\mathbf{Y}}) - [\dot{\mathbf{Z}} - \dot{\mathbf{Y}}] \cdot [\mathbf{L}_{\dot{\mathbf{Y}}}(x, \mathbf{Y}, \dot{\mathbf{Y}})] \tag{4-63}$$

Recall that, in the simpler version, $z(x)$ was also an admissible function, and the necessary condition for $y(x)$ to provide a maximum was that $E \leq 0$. Here we have $\mathbf{Y} = [y(x), v(x), w(x)]'$ and $\dot{\mathbf{Y}} = [y'(x), v'(x), w'(x)]'$; suppose that we choose $\dot{\mathbf{Z}}$ so that only the second element differs from $\dot{\mathbf{Y}}$, that is, $\dot{\mathbf{Z}} = [y'(x), t'(x), w'(x)]'$. For $\mathbf{Z}$ (and hence $\dot{\mathbf{Z}}$) to be admissible, $t'(x)$ must satisfy the constraints in the problem given in (4-48), when $t'(x)$ is substituted for $v'(x)$. By this choice of $\dot{\mathbf{Z}}$, notice that the last term on the right-hand side of (4-63) becomes simply $(t' - v')L_{v'}$. But $L_{v'} = \mathscr{H}_{v'}$, and we know that for an optimal control variable v, $\mathscr{H}_{v'} = 0$. Thus (4-63) reduces to

$$E(x, \mathbf{Y}, \dot{\mathbf{Y}}, \dot{\mathbf{Z}}) = L(x, \mathbf{Y}, \dot{\mathbf{Z}}) - L(x, \mathbf{Y}, \dot{\mathbf{Y}}) \tag{4-64}$$

Examination of the structures of L and $\mathscr{H}$, given in (4-49) and (4-50), makes clear that $L(x, \mathbf{Y}, \dot{\mathbf{Z}}) - L(x, \mathbf{Y}, \dot{\mathbf{Y}}) = \mathscr{H}(x, \mathbf{Y}, \dot{\mathbf{Z}}) - \mathscr{H}(x, \mathbf{Y}, \dot{\mathbf{Y}})$. In particular, when the only difference between $\dot{\mathbf{Y}}$ and $\dot{\mathbf{Z}}$ is in their second elements, the Weierstrass condition that $E \leq 0$, in conjunction with (4-64), becomes

$$\mathscr{H}(x, y, t', \lambda, \mu) - \mathscr{H}(x, y, v', \lambda, \mu) \leq 0 \tag{4-65}$$

† As usual, if the function L is formulated by *adding* $\lambda[y' - g]$ and $\mu[p + (w')^2]$, then the sign requirement on $\mu(x)$ will be reversed. With inequality constraints, also, there is an additional possibility of a sign change. If the constraint in (4-46) had been written $p(x, y, u) \geq 0$, then conversion to an equation would require subtraction of the nonnegative slack, $[w'(x)]^2$, with corresponding changes in L and $\mathscr{H}$ and, ultimately, a reversal of the sign requirement for $\mu(x)$.

Just as $v'(x)$ was defined to be equal to the control variable $u(x)$, we may think of $t'(x)$ as equal to an alternative control variable, say $s(x)$. Then (4-65) specifies that

$$\mathscr{H}(x, y, s, \lambda, \mu) \leq \mathscr{H}(x, y, u, \lambda, \mu) \tag{4-66}$$

which is to say that u is chosen so as to maximize the hamiltonian function, for given x, y, λ, and μ. If problem (4-48) were to minimize the functional, then u would be chosen to minimize $\mathscr{H}$. Again, when the minimum is not on a boundary of u, this is done via $\partial\mathscr{H}/\partial u = 0$. Otherwise, however, u is chosen so as to $\text{minimize}_{u \in \bar{u}} \mathscr{H}$.†

If, instead of $y(x_1) = y_1$ in (4-48), there is some specified terminal surface on which $y(x_1)$ must lie, then the transversality condition (4-57) leads to, as before, the requirement of orthogonality between $\begin{bmatrix} \mathscr{H}(x_1) \\ -\lambda(x_1) \end{bmatrix}$ and the terminal surface. With more state variables, control variables, and inequality constraints, the lagrangian function is expanded by having $-\sum_{j=1}^{n} \lambda_j(x)[y'_j - g_j]$ and $-\sum_{i=1}^{s} \mu_i(x) \times [p_i + (w'_i)^2]$ terms instead of just $-\lambda(y' - g)$ and $-\mu[p + (w')^2]$. The hamiltonian is similarly changed. No new principles are involved. Finally, if the terminal surface is defined by the intersection of several functions $S_1(x, \mathbf{Y}, \mathbf{U}), \ldots, S_k(x, \mathbf{Y}, \mathbf{U})$, then $\begin{bmatrix} \mathscr{H}(x_1) \\ -\mathbf{\Lambda}(x_1) \end{bmatrix}$ must be a linear combination of $\nabla\mathbf{S}_1(x_1), \ldots, \nabla\mathbf{S}_k(x_1)$, exactly as before (Chap. 3, Sec. 3-2).

We summarize these results for the problem:

$$\text{Maximize} \quad \int_{x_0}^{x_1} F(x, y, u)\, dx$$

where

$$y(x_0) = y_0$$

$$y(x_1) \text{ lies on } S(x, y, u)$$

$$y' = g(x, y, u) \tag{4-67}$$

and

$$p(x, y, u) \leq 0$$

Defining $\mathscr{H} = F + \lambda g - \mu p = H - \mu p$, the necessary conditions that $\lambda(x)$ and a maximizing $y(x)$ and $u(x)$ must satisfy are:

$$-\mathscr{H}_y = \lambda' \tag{4-68a}$$

$$\mathscr{H}_\lambda = y' \tag{4-68b}$$

† Again, as is sometimes done, if $\mathscr{H}$ were defined as $-F - \lambda g + \mu p$, i.e., as $-\mathscr{H}$ in (4-50), then the inequality in (4-66) would be reversed and we would want u chosen so as to minimize $\mathscr{H}$ in order to maximize the original functional, etc. We return to this point briefly in Sec. 4-6.

u is chosen so as to maximize H subject to $p(x, y, u) \leq 0$, which is equivalent (via Kuhn-Tucker reasoning) to setting $\mathscr{H}_u = 0$, with the conditions $\mu p = 0$, $\mu \geq 0$, and $p \leq 0$. (4-68c)

$$\begin{bmatrix} \mathscr{H}(x_1) \\ -\lambda(x_1) \end{bmatrix} = \alpha \nabla \mathbf{S}(x_1) \tag{4-68d}$$

Sufficiency

For the specific cases in which (1) the endpoints are fixed, as in (4-48), or (2) if either endpoint is not fixed, so that it has a free boundary [for example, x_1 established but no restrictions on $y(x_1)$], then it is possible to derive a set of sufficient conditions based on the shape of $H = F(x, y, u) + \lambda(x)g(x, y, u)$ and of the function $p(x, y, u)$. Assume that $p(x, y, u)$ is a convex function of (y, u) for all x in $[x_0, x_1]$, so that the (y, u) satisfying $p(x, y, u) \leq 0$ constitute a convex set. Then for the $\lambda(x)$ that satisfies the necessary conditions above, if $H(x, y, u)$ is a concave function of (y, u) for all x in $[x_0, x_1]$, the $y(x)$ satisfying the same necessary conditions above provides a global maximum to the functional. That is, under these convexity/concavity restrictions, the necessary conditions (4-68a, b, c) are also sufficient for a maximum. Similarly, if H is a convex function of (y, u), subject to all of the other restrictions, then the necessary conditions are also sufficient for a global minimum of the functional. These "geometrical" statements are reminiscent of results for maxima and minima of functions in ordinary calculus and of some of the results in Sec. 3-5 of Chap. 3 for the calculus of variations problem. Proofs are more involved, however. See Hadley and Kemp [4, secs. 2.17, 3.15, and 5.7] for details.

State Variable Equality Constraints

When there is a constraint of the sort $r(x, \mathbf{Y}) = 0$ involving state variables but not control variables, a new kind of problem arises. [As in the case of control variable constraints of the sort $c(x, \mathbf{U}) = 0$, it is only interesting to consider a state variable equality constraint when there is more than one state variable; otherwise the single state variable $y(x)$ would be specified by the constraint and there would be nothing to control via choice of the control variable or variables.] The problem is that there is no apparent direct connection between the control variables, which the decision maker is choosing, and the constraint in the problem, which involves state but not control variables. Given $r(x, \mathbf{Y}) = 0$, however, it is certainly true that dr/dx must equal zero during the period that the constraint is in effect, i.e., over $[x_0, x_1]$. Since

$$\frac{dr}{dx} = \frac{\partial r}{dx} + \frac{\partial r}{\partial y_1}\frac{dy_1}{dx} + \cdots + \frac{\partial r}{\partial y_n}\frac{dy_n}{dx}$$

we can express the $dr/dx = 0$ condition as

$$r_x + [\mathbf{r_Y}] \cdot [\dot{\mathbf{Y}}] = 0$$

Since $\dot{\mathbf{Y}} = \mathbf{G}(x, \mathbf{Y}, \mathbf{U})$, the influence of the control variables is now made explicit in the equality constraint

$$r_x + [\mathbf{r_Y}] \cdot [\mathbf{G}(x, \mathbf{Y}, \mathbf{U})] = 0 \tag{4-69}$$

To this equality constraint we add the condition that

$$r[x_0, \mathbf{Y}(x_0)] = 0 \tag{4-70}$$

to compensate for the information lost in differentiating the original constraint. [That is, $dr/dx = 0$ for any constraint $r(x, \mathbf{Y}) = k$, where k is any constant. Notice, also, that we could as well add the condition $r[x_1, \mathbf{Y}(x_1)] = 0$ to specify precisely the original constraint.] Having made the conversion to (4-69) and (4-70), we proceed as earlier in this section in the case of control and state variable equality constraints of the form $p(x, \mathbf{Y}, \mathbf{U}) = 0$.

State Variable Inequality Constraints

Constraints of the form $r(x, \mathbf{Y}) \leq 0$ can be approached via a combination of techniques described above. Clearly, in those intervals during which the state variables $\mathbf{Y}(x)$ are such that $r(x, \mathbf{Y}) = 0$, the conversion described in (4-69) and (4-70) is effective. However, when the state variables are such that $r(x, \mathbf{Y}) < 0$, it is not possible to conclude anything about dr/dx; i.e., this derivative may be either positive, negative, or zero. On the other hand, during these intervals the constraint is being satisfied and hence could be ignored.

Figure 4-1 indicates a possible optimal $y(x)$ for the case of several inequality constraints on the state variable. Let $r_1(x, y) = 2x + y - 10 \leq 0$, $r_2(x, y) = x^2 + y^2 - 25 \leq 0$, and $r_3(x, y) = -y \leq 0$. In x, y space these constraints define a feasible region for $y(x)$, as suggested in Fig. 4-1. An optimal $y(x)$ may contain portions completely interior to the feasible region and portions that lie along a boundary; the trajectories connect at what are called junction points. The full problem, then, is:

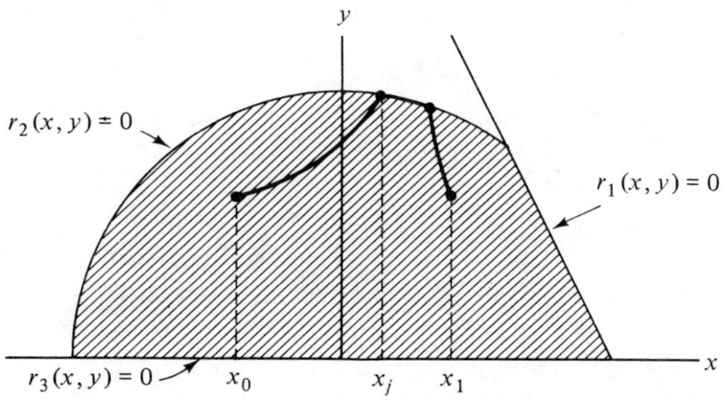

Figure 4-1 Feasible region for a problem with state variable inequality constraints.

$$\text{Maximize} \int_{x_0}^{x_1} F(x, y, u)\, dx$$

where

$$y(x_0) = y_0$$
$$y(x_1) = y_1$$
$$y' = g(x, y, u) \tag{4-71}$$
$$p(x, y, u) \leq 0$$

and

$$r(x, y) \leq 0$$

Clearly, if y_0 and/or y_1 violate the constraint, the problem has no solution.

Interior segments For those portions of the optimal $y(x)$ along which $r(x, y) < 0$, the presence of this new constraint is immaterial and the necessary conditions are those summarized above in (4-68*a*, *b*, *c*). The question of endpoint conditions arises if the segment is the final one. Then, if the terminal condition requires $y(x_1)$ on some surface, rather than $y(x_1) = y_1$, the usual transversality requirements apply, as given in (4-68*d*), above. In other words, if a segment of the optimal $y(x)$ ends at an interior point of the feasible region, then it must be the final segment, to which endpoint conditions will apply.

Boundary segments When the optimal $y(x)$ lies, for a time, on the boundary given by $r(x, y) = 0$, the constraint $r_x + r_y y' = 0$ or $r_x + r_y g(x, y, u) = 0$, as in (4-69), must be satisfied, and the "endpoint" information, as in (4-70), $r[x_j, y(x_j)] = 0$ is added. Then the hamiltonian [compare (4-50)] is further expanded to

$$\mathscr{H}^* = F + \lambda g - \mu p - \pi(r_x + r_y g) = \mathscr{H} - \pi(r_x + r_y g) \tag{4-72}$$

and the necessary conditions parallel those in (4-68*a*, *b*, *c*), with the new $\mathscr{H}^*$ and consequently with the possibility of additional terms in $\mathscr{H}_y^*$. In more dimensions, with several state variables, control variables, and numerous constraints of various sorts, faces and edges of the feasible region will be defined where different subsets of the constraints are met as equalities, and therefore the hamiltonian will vary, depending on the particular edge or surface, since only active constraints are included in $\mathscr{H}^*$, each with a multiplier π_i.

In practice, the distinction between interior segments and boundary segments can be characterized by the Kuhn-Tucker-like device of requiring

$$\pi(x)[r(x, y)] = 0 \quad \pi(x) \geq 0 \tag{4-73}$$

so that, when $r(x, y) < 0$ (i.e., along an interior segment), $\pi(x)$ must be zero; therefore $\mathscr{H}^* = \mathscr{H}$ and conditions (4-68*a*, *b*, *c*, *d*) apply, as we have seen should be the case. Conversely, when $r(x, y) = 0$ (a boundary segment), then $(r_x + r_y y') = 0$. In this case, although $\mathscr{H}_y^*$ in (4-68*a*) may have additional terms (compared with $\mathscr{H}_y$), maximization of $\mathscr{H}^*$ with respect to u is the same as maximization of $\mathscr{H}$ subject to the constraint $r_x + r_y y' = 0$. We will investigate the sign requirement on $\pi(x)$ in more detail below.

Results for the problem in (4-71) with $r(x, y) \le 0$ are therefore [compare (4-68a, b, c), above]

$$-\mathscr{H}_y^* = \lambda' \tag{4-74a}$$

$$\mathscr{H}_\lambda^* = y' \tag{4-74b}$$

u is chosen so as to maximize H subject to $p(x, y, u) \le 0$ and $r(x, y) \le 0$, which is equivalent to setting $\mathscr{H}_u^* = 0$, with the conditions $\mu p = 0, \mu \ge 0, p \le 0; \pi r = 0, \pi \ge 0$, and $r \ge 0$. (4-74c)

If $y(x_1)$ is not fixed at y_1, then appropriate transversality requirements apply.

Consider the specific and quite common state variable inequality requiring nonnegativity of $y(x)$, for $x_0 \le x \le x_1$. [Obviously, if the specification of y_1 or of the terminal surface $S(x, y, u)$ on which $y(x_1)$ is to lie is inconsistent with the nonnegativity requirement the problem has no solution.] Here, then, $r(x, y) \le 0$ is $y(x) \ge 0$, that is, $r(x, y) = -y(x)$. Thus $r_x + r_y y' = -y'$ and when the constraint is binding, from (4-72),

$$\mathscr{H}^* = \mathscr{H} + \pi y' = \mathscr{H} + \pi g$$

Results for the case of nonnegative state variables are therefore [compare (4-74a, b, c), above]

$$-\mathscr{H}_y^* = \lambda' \tag{4-75a}$$

$$\mathscr{H}_\lambda^* = y' \tag{4-75b}$$

u is chosen so as to maximize H subject to $p(x, y, u) \le 0$ and $y(x) \ge 0$. As before, this is equivalent to setting $\mathscr{H}_u^* = 0$, with the conditions $\mu p = 0$, $\mu \ge 0$, $p \le 0$; $\pi y = 0$, $\pi \ge 0$, and $y \ge 0$. (4-75c)

Again, less definite specification of $y(x_1)$ leads to alternative transversality requirements at $x = x_1$.

Finally, when the only constraint on the state variable is a *terminal* nonnegativity requirement, $y(x_1) \ge 0$, the new $\pi(x)y(x) = 0$ conditions above collapse to $\pi(x_1)y(x_1) = 0$ and $\pi(x_1) \ge 0$. However, the constraint $y(x_1) \ge 0$ is clearly simply a restriction on the right-hand endpoint for $y(x)$ and hence transversality considerations apply. Assume that this is all that is specified about the right-hand boundary, i.e., there is no additional terminal surface specification of the sort $S(x, y, u) = 0$. Consider the two possibilities:

1. $y(x_1) = 0$. This is a fixed endpoint problem, and from (4-31), $H(x_1)\,\delta x_1 - \lambda(x_1)\,\delta y_1 = 0$, since both $\delta x_1 = 0$ and $\delta y_1 = 0$. Hence no restrictions are placed on $\lambda(x_1)$ when $y(x_1) = 0$.
2. $y(x_1) > 0$. Again, from (4-31), we know that $\lambda(x_1)\,\delta y_1$ must be zero, since $\delta x_1 = 0$; now, however, δy_1 need not be zero.

Combining these two observations leads to the requirement

$$\lambda(x_1)[y(x_1)] = 0$$

Thus $\lambda(x)$ serves exactly the role of $\pi(x)$ at $x = x_1$. Therefore, to:

$$\text{Maximize} \int_{x_0}^{x_1} F(x, y, u)\, dx$$

where
$$y(x_0) = y_0$$
$$y(x_1) \geq 0$$
$$y' = g(x, y, u)$$

and
$$p(x, y, u) \leq 0$$

[compare (4-67)], we have $\mathscr{H} = F + \lambda g - \mu p = H - \mu p$, and the necessary conditions that $\lambda(x)$ and a maximizing $y(x)$ and $u(x)$ must satisfy are

$$-\mathscr{H}_y = \lambda' \tag{4-76a}$$

$$\mathscr{H}_\lambda = y' \tag{4-76b}$$

u is chosen so as to maximize H subject to $p(x, y, u) \leq 0$ and $y(x_1) \geq 0$, which is equivalent to setting $\mathscr{H}_u = 0$, with the conditions $\mu p = 0$, $\mu \geq 0$, $p \leq 0$; $\lambda(x_1)y(x_1) = 0$, $\lambda(x_1) \geq 0$, and $y(x_1) \geq 0$. (4-76*c*)

When the terminal inequality on $y(x)$ is specified as $y(x_1) \geq y_1$, exactly similar reasoning leads to a restatement of (4-76*c*) only. This now becomes:

u is chosen so as to maximize H subject to $p(x, y, u) \leq 0$ and $y(x_1) \geq y_1$, which is equivalent to setting $\mathscr{H}_u = 0$, with the conditions $\mu p = 0$, $\mu \geq 0$, $p \leq 0$; $\lambda(x_1)[y_1 - y(x_1)] = 0$, $\lambda(x_1) \geq 0$, and $y(x_1) \geq y_1$. (4-76*c*′)

It might seem logical to deal with a terminal state variable constraint in the following way. Solve the problem with no restrictions on the state variable at the right-hand endpoint. If $y(x_1)$ satisfies the constraint, then of course the constrained problem has also been solved. If $y(x_1)$ fails to satisfy the terminal constraint, follow the unconstrained optimal path until "just before" the last moment and then zoom in on the appropriate terminal value along a straight line. In the illustrations of further variations on the monopolistic pricing problem, below, we will see that this is *not* an optimal strategy.

Junction points Formally, such a point is defined as one on the boundary of the feasible region where either (1) the set of constraints that are active just to its left is different from the set that is active just to its right, or (2) all constraints

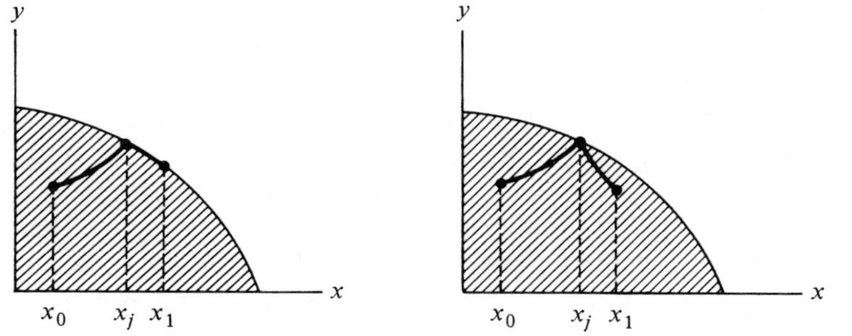

Figure 4-2 Junction points, x_j.

are inactive both just to its left and just to its right. Figure 4-2 illustrates the two kinds of junction points.

Define the converted constraint as $\rho(x, y, u) = r_x + r_y y' = r_x + r_y g$. Then if there are several such constraints, in a problem with more state and control variables, we will have $\rho_1(x, \mathbf{Y}, \mathbf{U}) = 0, \ldots, \rho_k(x, \mathbf{Y}, \mathbf{U}) = 0$. For a particular junction point x_j, denote by A^- the set of these constraints that are *inactive* to the left of x_j but *active* to the right of x_j and by A^+ the set of constraints that are active to the left of x_j but inactive to the right. Then at each junction point, the following so-called jump condition must hold:

$$\mathbf{\Lambda}(x_j^-) - \sum_{\rho_j \in A^-} \pi_j(x) \frac{\partial \rho_j}{\partial \mathbf{Y}} = \mathbf{\Lambda}(x_j^+) - \sum_{\rho_j \in A^+} \pi_j(x) \frac{\partial \rho_j}{\partial \mathbf{Y}} \tag{4-77}$$

For the situation depicted on the right in Fig. 4-2, for which $\mathbf{\Lambda}$ becomes λ, $\mathbf{Y}$ becomes y, and there is only one $\rho(x, y, u)$, the sets A^- and A^+ are both empty. Thus (4-77) reduces to the requirement that $\lambda(x_j^-) = \lambda(x_j^+)$, which is to say that λ is continuous across the junction point.†

Interpretation of the Costate Variables

Often the multipliers associated with constraints in the problems discussed in this chapter have interpretations as dynamic analogues of Lagrange multipliers in ordinary static constrained optimization problems. In particular, evaluated at their optimal values, they may represent the sensitivity of the optimal value of the objective functional to small changes in parameters of the original problem.‡

For example, $\lambda(x_0)$ describes the effect on the objective functional of a small change in y_0, the initial value of the state variable. Of more interest, usually, is

† The conditions in (4-77) are in general not easy to apply or to interpret. See, for example, Hadley and Kemp [4, sec. 5.14] or Arrow and Kurz [1, sec. II.7].

‡ Interpretations of some of the adjoint or costate variables are suggested in Benavie [2, secs. 5.3 to 5.5], Dorfman [3], and Intriligator [6, sec. 14.2]. A very complete discussion is to be found in Peterson [7].

the fact that $-\lambda(x_1)$ describes the effect on the objective functional of a small change in y_1, the terminal value of the state variable, in problems in which this value is specified a priori. Since equality or inequality constraints on terminal values of state variables tend to be quite common in problems in the social sciences, we utilize this last result on $-\lambda(x_1)$ to make some observations on sign rules for $\lambda(x_1)$ when constrained problems are stated in various forms.

Recall that in ordinary (static) inequality constrained maximization and minimization problems the Kuhn-Tucker results on the sign of the multiplier depend upon the form in which the problem is stated. We consider the case of one constraint only; extension to several constraints involves no new principles. For a maximization problem to be in so-called standard form, the constraint should be expressed as $g(\mathbf{X}) \leq c$, and then it is usually converted to $h(\mathbf{X}) \leq 0$, where $h(\mathbf{X}) = g(\mathbf{X}) - c$. Similarly, for minimization problems, in standard form, the constraint should be expressed as $h(\mathbf{X}) \geq 0$. When this convention is followed, then the sign requirement on the optimal value of the Lagrange multiplier is that it must be nonnegative, for either kind of problem, maximization or minimization. The logic is straightforward. In a maximization problem with $g(\mathbf{X}) = c$, if $\lambda > 0$, then larger c would allow a larger value for the objective function. Recall that among the Kuhn-Tucker necessary conditions for inequality constrained problems is the requirement that $\lambda[h(\mathbf{X})] = 0$. In a maximization problem with $g(\mathbf{X}) \leq c$, if $\lambda \neq 0$, then in $\lambda[h(\mathbf{X})] = 0$, $h(\mathbf{X}) = 0$ or $g(\mathbf{X}) = c$; one is on the upper-limit boundary specified by $g(\mathbf{X}) \leq c$. But the only way in which it might be optimal to be on a boundary of that sort is if the unconstrained maximum point is located outside that boundary. That is, if a larger c would bring about a larger objective function value; i.e., if $\lambda > 0$. (When $\lambda = 0$ the maximum is on the boundary exactly, and hence it is immaterial whether or not the constraint is considered in the maximization calculations.) Thus $\lambda \geq 0$ for maximization problems with $g(\mathbf{X}) \leq c$. The same kind of reasoning shows that $\lambda \geq 0$ for minimization problems with $g(\mathbf{X}) \geq c$, as well. And if the direction of the inequality is reversed in the statement of either problem, the sign rule on λ is reversed also. The situation for dynamic optimization problems is similar.

Starting with the result on $-\lambda(x_1) = \partial I^*/\partial y_1$ for the control problem with $y(x_1) = y_1$, if $\lambda(x_1) < 0$ in a maximization problem, then a small increase in y_1 will lead to an increase in the maximum value of I. In a maximization problem with a terminal *inequality* constraint of the sort $y(x_1) \leq y_1$, we have the Kuhn-Tucker necessary condition $\lambda(x_1)[y_1 - y(x_1)] = 0$. Then if it is optimal to be on the boundary of $y(x_1) \leq y_1$ it must be because $\lambda(x_1) \leq 0$, so that $-\lambda(x_1) = \partial I^*/\partial y_1 \geq 0$. The optimal value of the objective functional would be larger if the terminal upper bound on the state variable were larger. Similarly for a minimization problem with $y(x_1) \geq y_1$, the optimality rule is $\lambda(x_1) \leq 0$, for the same kinds of reasons as in the static case. And also for the same kinds of reasons, when the terminal constraint is $y(x_1) \geq y_1$ in a maximization problem (as, for example, with a terminal nonnegativity requirement where $y_1 = 0$) or when the constraint is $y(x_1) \leq y_1$ in a minimization problem, then the sign rule is $\lambda(x_1)$

Table 4-1 Sign rules on $\lambda(x_1)$ for problems with terminal inequality constraints on state variables

Form of terminal constraint	Objective of problem	
	Maximization	Minimization
$y(x_1) \geq y_1$	$\lambda(x_1) \geq 0$	$\lambda(x_1) \leq 0$
$y(x_1) \leq y_1$	$\lambda(x_1) \leq 0$	$\lambda(x_1) \geq 0$

≥ 0. See Table 4-1 for a summary. The nonnegativity rules on $\lambda(x_1)$ in (4-76c, c') are seen to be consistent with the case described in the upper left quadrant of this table.

Example II: Monopolistic Pricing over Time (Continued)

Consider again the original monopolistic pricing problem with $t_0 = 0$, $p(t_0) = 70$, $t_1 = 52$, and $p(t_1) = 100$. In Sec. 4-1, above, we found $\lambda(t) = -415.557\, e^{0.0173t} + 4746.052\, e^{-0.0173t} - 3266.667$. Evaluating $\lambda(t)$ at $t_1 = 52$ gives $\lambda(t_1) = -2358$. Also, for the optimal pricing function, $p(t)$, we found that the monopolist's total profit would be approximately 170,000. Following the logic just presented $-\lambda(t_1) = 2358$ should represent the increase in total maximized profits if $p(t_1)$ is changed to 101. Also, the amount 2358 should approximate the decrease in profits that would accompany a change of $p(t_1)$ to 99. Using both of these alternative terminal values for $p(t_1)$ leads to the following pair of optimal price functions:

$$p(t) = \begin{cases} 15.878\, e^{0.0173t} - 13.211\, e^{-0.0173t} + 67.333 & \text{for } p(t_1) = 101 \\ 14.903\, e^{0.0173t} - 12.236\, e^{-0.0173t} + 67.333 & \text{for } p(t_1) = 99 \end{cases}$$

Total profits in the former case are increased to 172,350; this represents an increase of 2350. In the second case—where $p(t_1) = 99$—total profits are found to be 167,640, which is a decrease of 2360. In particular, the *average* change for a one-unit increase or decrease is 2355; and $-\lambda(t_1) = 2358$. This illustrates the marginal valuation property of $-\lambda(x_1)$ with respect to changes in the terminal value of the state variable.

Next we examine the effects of a terminal inequality constraint on the state variable in the dynamic monopoly pricing problem. The free right-hand boundary version of the first problem had $t_0 = 0$, $p(t_0) = 70$, $t_1 = 52$ but $p(t_1)$ unspecified, and in the optimal solution it was found that $p(t_1) = 157.4$. Suppose that instead of a free right-hand boundary value for the state variable, we specify only that $p(t_1) \geq 150$. From the unconstrained version of the problem, we know that this constraint will be satisfied; the object here is to show that this result is also produced by the apparatus of (4-76), especially (4-76c'). Here there are no constraints of the sort $p(x, y, u) \le 0$, and hence $\mathscr{H} = H$. In Sec. 4-1 we found that the hamiltonian for the control version of the problem is

$$H = -\tfrac{3}{2}p^2 + 202p - 5000u^2 - 10{,}200u + 200pu - 5240 + \lambda u$$

From (4-76c′) we have [ignoring conditions on μ and p, because there are no constraints $p(x, y, u) \le 0$]

$$(a) \qquad \mathscr{H}_u = H_u = -10{,}000u - 10{,}200 + 200p + \lambda = 0$$

$$(b) \qquad p(t_1) \ge 150$$

$$(c) \qquad \lambda(t_1)[150 - p(t_1)] = 0$$

$$(d) \qquad \lambda(t_1) \ge 0$$

As usual with conditions of this sort, we consider the implications of the restrictions in (*c*), where at least one of the two terms in the product must be zero:

1. Let $[150 - p(t_1)] = 0$, that is, $p(t_1) = 150$. Then we have a fixed endpoints problem, since now $t_0 = 0$, $p(t_0) = 70$, $t_1 = 52$, and $p(t_1) = 150$. From (4-76*a*, *b*) we have

$$3p - 202 - 200u = \lambda'$$

and
$$u = p'$$

This pair of equations, plus (*a*), above, reproduces exactly (4-14) through (4-16) in Sec. 4-1. This leads, in turn, to

$$p(t) = k_1\, e^{0.0173t} + k_2\, e^{-0.0173t} + 67.333$$

which was (4-22), above. Utilizing the current fixed endpoint information on $p(t)$ at $t_0 = 0$ and $t_1 = 52$ leads to the following pair of equations:

$$k_1 + \qquad k_2 = 2.667$$

$$2.459k_1 + 0.407k_2 = 82.667$$

from which $k_1 = 39.757$ and $k_2 = -37.090$. Thus

$$p(t) = 39.757\, e^{0.0173t} - 37.090\, e^{-0.0173t} + 67.333$$

However, at $t_1 = 52$, $p'(t_1) = u(t_1) = 1.952$, and putting this into (*a*), above, gives $\lambda(t_1) = -280$, which violates (*d*).

2. In (*c*), let $\lambda(t_1) = 0$. Then this is exactly the free right-hand boundary case where information on $p(t)$ at t_1 is replaced by the condition on $\lambda(t)$ at t_1 that $\lambda(t_1) = 0$. Thus (*a*) becomes

$$\mathscr{H}_u = H_u = -10{,}000u_1 - 10{,}200 + 200p_1 = 0$$

and, since $u = p'$, this is exactly the version of the transversality requirement used in Sec. 3-1 for this problem. Thus we find, as there, that $p(t_1) = 157.4$ and since (*b*) and (*d*) are also met, this solution satisfies all the necessary conditions of (4-76a, b, c'). This is, of course, what we expected from our observations on the earlier solution to the unconstrained version of the problem. Again, also, $-\lambda(t_1)$ approximates the change in total profits that would accompany an increase in $p(t_1)$ from 150 to 151. In fact, finding $p(t)$ for $p(t_1) = 151$ and $p(t_1) = 149$, and evaluating the total profits in both cases, leads to $I^* =$ 235,370 and 234,860, for an *average* change [from $I^* = 235{,}130$ for $p(t_1) = 150$] of 255. Here $-\lambda(t_1)$ was 280.

Alternatively, consider the same problem but with the terminal state variable inequality $p(t_1) \geq 200$. Again, in the unconstrained version of the problem we found $p(t_1) = 157.4$ and so we expect that this new constraint will be met as an equality. In what follows we see that this result emerges from application of the conditions in (4-76). Here

(*a*) $$\mathscr{H}_u = H_u = -10{,}000u - 10{,}200 + 200p + \lambda = 0$$

(*b*) $$p(t_1) \geq 200$$

(*c*) $$\lambda(t_1)[200 - p(t_1)] = 0$$

(*d*) $$\lambda(t_1) \geq 0$$

Note that (*a*) and (*d*) are unchanged from the $p(t_1) \geq 150$ case:

1. Letting $[200 - p(t_1)] = 0$, that is, $p(t_1) = 200$, gives a fixed endpoints problem in which again $p(t) = k_1\, e^{0.0173t} + k_2\, e^{-0.0173t} + 67.333$. From $t_1 = 0$, $p(t_1) = 70$, $t_2 = 52$, and $p(t_2) = 200$, we have

$$k_1 + \qquad k_2 = 2.667$$

$$2.459k_1 + 0.407k_2 = 132.667$$

and so $k_1 = 64.124$ and $k_2 = -61.457$. Thus

$$p(t) = 64.124\, e^{0.0173t} - 61.457\, e^{-0.0173t} + 67.333$$

At $t_1 = 52$, $p'(t_1) = u(t_1) = 3.157$ and thus, from (*a*), $\lambda(t_1) = 1790$, clearly satisfying (*d*). Hence all necessary conditions are satisfied by the case in which $p(t_1) = 200$.

2. In (*c*), let $\lambda(t_1) = 0$. Then, as before, this is the free right-hand boundary case in which we have already found that $p(t_1) = 157.4$, violating (*b*). This is, again, as we expected. For the problem with $p(t_1) \geq 200$, the solution with $p(t_1) = 200$ satisfies all necessary conditions in (4-76a, b, c').

The reader may wish to find $p(t)$ for the alternative endpoint conditions $p(t_1) = 201$ and $p(t_1) = 199$ and then evaluate the objective functional in these two cases. It turns out that

$$p(t) = \begin{cases} 64.611\, e^{0.0173t} - 61.944\, e^{-0.0173t} + 67.333 & \text{for } p(t_1) = 201 \\ 63.636\, e^{0.0173t} - 60.969\, e^{-0.0173t} + 67.333 & \text{for } p(t_1) = 199 \end{cases}$$

and the optimal values of the objective functional are 193,650 and 197,360, respectively. Thus the average of the changes in the value of the objective functional is 1855; for this problem $-\lambda(t_1) = -1790$. When $p(t_1)$ increases, the value of the objective functional decreases; when $p(t_1)$ decreases, the objective functional is increased.

Next we evaluate the effectiveness of a solution to this problem that follows the unconstrained optimal path

$$p(t) = 43.373\, e^{0.0173t} - 40.706\, e^{-0.0173t} + 67.333$$

over, say, $0 \leq t \leq 51$, and then rushes in on $p(t_1) = 200$ from below, along a steep straight line. At $t = 51$, $p(t) = 155.3$ on this path. The equation for the straight line joining $p(t) = 155.3$ at $t = 51$ and $p(t) = 200$ at $t = 52$ is

$$p(t) = 44.7t - 2124.4$$

Total profits under this plan would be

$$\int_0^{51} P_1\, dt + \int_{51}^{52} P_2\, dt$$

where P_1 and P_2 represent the profit functions with the unconstrained function $p(t)$ and the straight line function for $p(t)$, respectively.

Evaluating the second integral only for the profit function of this problem is tedious but straightforward; it turns out to be approximately -8.87 million (!), and hence total profits under this two-part solution will be (extremely) negative.

It is clear that if the terminal constraints had been $p(t_1) \leq 150$ and $p(t_1) \leq 200$, respectively, then our conclusions would be exactly reversed, in accordance with the results in Table 4-1. Namely, $\lambda(t_1) < 0$ in the case of $p(t_1) \leq 150$ indicates that indeed we want to be at the upper limit when the unconstrained optimum is $p(t_1) = 157.4$ and $\lambda(t_1) > 0$ in the case of $p(t_1) \leq 200$ signals that this constraint should be ignored, since the unconstrained optimal $p(t_1)$ satisfies it as a strict inequality.

Consider, finally, the first monopolistic pricing problem with a free right-hand boundary, where $t_0 = 0$, $p(t_0) = 70$, $t_1 = 52$, and $p(t_1)$ is unspecified, but with the state variable inequality constraint $p(t) \leq 140$, over the entire planning period, $t_0 \leq t \leq t_1$. We know from the unconstrained version of this problem that

$$p(t) = 43.373\, e^{0.0173t} - 40.706\, e^{-0.0173t} + 67.333$$

with $p(t_0) = 70$ and $p(t_1) = 157.4$. Thus, over a range, the constraint is violated. Since $p'(t) = 0.750\, e^{0.0173t} + 0.704\, e^{-0.0173t}$, $p(t)$ is monotonic increasing over $0 \leq t \leq 52$, and since $p''(t) = 0.0130\, e^{0.0173t} - 0.0122\, e^{-0.0173t}$, which is positive over $0 \leq t \leq 52$, $p(t)$ is convex over the interval.

Setting $p(t) = 140$, we find that the critical value of t is $t_c = 43.5$. Over $0 \leq t \leq 43.5$, the new constraint is satisfied by the unconstrained solution; over $4.35 \leq t \leq 52$, this is not true. Employing the results in (4-74), with $\mathscr{H}^* = H - \pi p' = F + \lambda u - \pi p'$, we have

$$(a) \qquad 3p - 202 - 200u = \lambda'$$

$$(b) \qquad u = p'$$

$$(c) \qquad -10{,}000u - 10{,}200 + 200p + \lambda - \pi = 0$$

with the additional conditions $\pi[p - 140] = 0$, $\pi \geq 0$, $p \leq 140$:

1. If $p \neq 140$, then $\pi = 0$, and this is the unconstrained problem, since (a) and (b) are exactly as in (4-14) and (4-16) and, when π disappears from (c), the condition is the same as in (4-15). As we have seen, $p(t) > 140$ for t in the range [43.5, 52].
2. If $\pi \neq 0$, then $p = 140$, which is impossible at the initial point, since $p(t_0) = 70$ is specified.

Thus, as might be expected, neither the unconstrained solution in condition 1 nor the boundary solution in condition 2 is effective over the entire range $0 \leq t \leq 52$. If we imagine the ceiling imposed by the line $p(t) = 140$, then one possible solution would be to follow the unconstrained optimal function until $t = 43.5$ and thereafter let $p(t) = 140$. This is the strategy of hitting the ceiling at the earliest time necessary. The opposite strategy would be to hit the ceiling at the latest time necessary, i.e., at $t = 52$. [Since we know that $p(t_1) = 157.4$ in the unconstrained problem, we know that the constraint $p(t) \leq 140$ will be met as an equation at least at t_1, if not sooner.] We examine these two possibilities in turn.

Let $p(t) = 43.373\, e^{0.0173t} - 40.706\, e^{-0.0173t} + 67.333$ over $0 \leq t \leq 43.5$ and $p(t) = 140$ over $43.5 \leq t \leq 52$. We examine $\lambda(t)$ for this solution. For the unconstrained range, $\lambda(t) = -1171.071\, e^{0.0173t} + 15{,}183.338\, e^{-0.0173t} - 3266.667$— from (4-23), for example. Over the constrained range, $p(t) = 140$, $p'(t) = u(t) = 0$; from (a), above, $\lambda'(t) = -202$ and so $\lambda(t) = -202t + k$. Since here the constraint $p(t) - 140 \leq 0$ becomes $p'(t) = 0$ in the form shown in (4-69), the junction point condition given in (4-77), since $\rho(t, p, u) = p'$, is simply that $\lambda(t)$ be continuous across the junction point. Thus the two functions for $\lambda(t)$ must be equal at $t = 43.5$; this leads to $k = 11{,}793$, so

$$\lambda(t) = -202t + 11{,}793$$

over $43.5 \leq t \leq 52$. From (c), however, this means

$$\pi(t) = -202t + 1593$$

with $\pi(43.5) = -7194$ and $\pi(52) = -8911$. Thus the constraint $\pi(t) \geq 0$ is violated by this solution.

Alternatively, then, consider the original problem with the added condition $p(t_1) = 140$. This gives $p(t) = 34.884\, e^{0.0173t} - 32.217\, e^{-0.0173t} + 67.333$ over $0 \leq t \leq 52$. As before, this function is monotonic increasing and convex over $0 \leq t \leq 52$ and hence does not violate the constraint $p(t) \leq 140$. Thus, (a) and (b) are satisfied, as is (c), with $\pi(t) = 0$, except possibly at $t_1 = 52$, where $p(t_1) = 140$. But from (c), with $p(t)$, $u(t)$, and $\lambda(t)$ evaluated at $t_1 = 52$ ($p = 140$, $u = 1.709$, and $\lambda = -695$), $\pi(t_1) = 15 > 0$, so all conditions in (*c*) are also satisfied. The optimal pricing function, in the face of the constraint $p(t) \leq 140$, is thus

$$p(t) = 34.884\, e^{0.0173t} - 32.217\, e^{-0.0173t} + 67.333$$

Total maximized profits are approximately 230,480, $\lambda(t_1) = -695$, and, as we have seen in several earlier examples, $-\lambda(t_1)$ approximates the effect on these profits if $p(t_1)$ is increased by one unit. As the reader may wish to check, for $p(t_1) = 141$, $p(t) = 35.371\, e^{0.0173t} - 32.704\, e^{-0.0173t} + 67.333$ and total profits are increased to approximately 231,130, which is an increase of 650.

Upper Limit of Integration at Infinity

As is suggested by our earlier discussions for the calculus of variations approach (at the end of Sec. 2-5, Chap. 2, and of Sec. 3-2, Chap. 3), some of the necessary conditions are modified when $x_1 = \infty$. This is also true when there are constraints, in either the calculus of variations or the control theory formulation, but the results are often a good deal more complicated and are not always obtained by simply replacing F with the related Lagrange-like function L. For details, the reader is referred to Hadley and Kemp [4, in particular sec. 3.13 (pp. 223–225) and pp. 245–246 and 292].

4-5 LINEAR EXAMPLES: THE MINIMUM TIME PROBLEM

Example I

Suppose that the independent variable x is time and that the objective in a control problem is to find a $y(x)$ connecting $y(x_0) = y_0$ and $y(x_1) = y_1$, where x_1 is unspecified, that minimizes the elapsed time. (This is a free terminal time problem, as pictured in Fig. 3-3 of Chap. 3, reproduced as Fig. 4-3.) Here, then, $F(x, y, u) = 1$, since $\int_{x_0}^{x_1} 1\, dx = x_1 - x_0$, which is exactly the elapsed time from

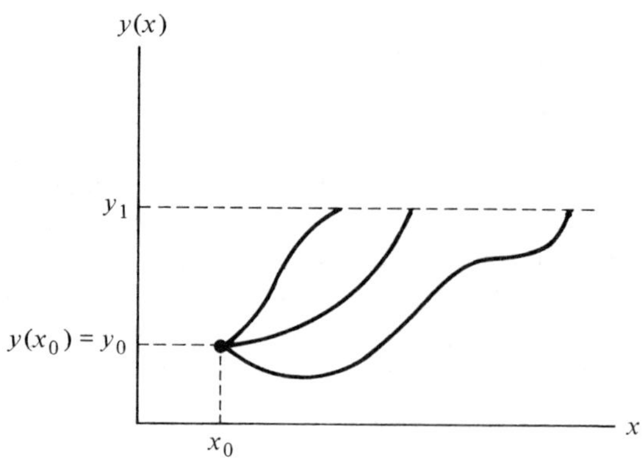

Figure 4-3 A free terminal time problem.

x_0 to the terminal time x_1. In addition, assume that the constraint $g(x, y, u) = ay + bu$, i.e., the full constraint is $y' = ay + bu$.† Imagine, finally, that there are upper and lower limits on the control variable and that these have been normalized so that they can be represented as $-1 \leq u(x) \leq 1$. The full problem is then to:

$$\text{Minimize} \quad \int_{x_0}^{x_1} dx$$

where

$$\begin{aligned} y(x_0) &= y_0 \\ y(x_1) &= y_1 \text{ (but } x_1 \text{ unspecified)} \\ y' &= ay + bu \end{aligned} \tag{4-78}$$

and

$$-1 \leq u \leq 1$$

Forming the hamiltonian in the usual way, namely $H = F + \lambda g$, we find that for this problem

$$H = 1 + \lambda(ay + bu) = 1 + \lambda ay + \lambda bu \tag{4-79}$$

Since (4-78) requires minimization of the integral, we want to choose u so as to minimize H, and because H is a linear function of the control variable u, the problem to $\text{minimize}_{u \in \bar{u}} H$ becomes extremely simple:

1. If $\lambda b > 0$, then to minimize H, set u at its minimum possible value, namely, -1.
2. If $\lambda b < 0$, then to minimize H, set u at its maximum possible value, namely $+1$.

Denoting the optimal u by u^*, we have

$$u^* = \begin{cases} -1 & \text{if } \lambda b > 0 \\ +1 & \text{if } \lambda b < 0 \end{cases}$$

Define the *signum* function, sgn x, as

$$\text{sgn } x = \begin{cases} +1 & \text{if } x > 0 \\ \text{undefined} & \text{if } x = 0 \\ -1 & \text{if } x < 0 \end{cases}$$

For example, if $x = 42$, sgn $x = 1$, if $x = -3$, sgn $x = -1$. Then

$$u^* = -\text{sgn}\,(\lambda b) \tag{4-80}$$

The clear implication of (4-80) is that u^* is always at one of its two boundary values, depending entirely on the sign of (λb). Since b is a parameter of the

† That is, the size of the control variable depends upon the present value of the state variable and its rate of change. We will see in Chap. 5, Sec. 5-1, that this is precisely the form of the constraint in a version of the optimal economic growth problem in which the production function exhibits constant marginal productivity.

model, the behavior over time of $u^*(x)$ depends on the behavior over time of $\lambda(x)$, and in particular on how often (if at all) $\lambda(x)$ changes sign. This "either-or" character of the optimal $u(x)$ that is associated with minimum time problems with linear constraints has come to be known, not very elegantly, as the "bang-bang" principle or the outcome as "bang-bang" control. A furnace thermostat is an oft-cited example of a device that exercises bang-bang control, since it is either off or on, depending on a temperature setting. The practical advantage of such control problems, of course, is that one need not worry about the intensity of $u(x)$. At any point x, $u(x)$ is either as large as it can be or as small.

Even when $u(x)$ is not constrained to the interval $[-1, 1]$, this character will emerge if the problem is otherwise the same. Thus u may be the amount of money to devote to unemployment relief in a particular region each month, with an upper limit of \$25,000 per month (and a lower limit of no help, that is, \$0). Then $0 \leq u(x) \leq 25{,}000$. The problem of choosing $u(x)$ to $\text{minimize}_{u \in \bar{u}} H$, where H is defined as in (4-79), still leads to the rules (1) if $\lambda b < 0$, $u(x)$ should be at its maximum possible value (now 25,000) and (2) if $\lambda b > 0$, $u(x)$ should be at its minimum possible value (now 0). Bounds on $u(x)$ other than $+1$ and -1 simply remove the possibility of the compact signum function representation of $u^*(x)$, as in (4-80).

Returning to (4-78), we know that an additional necessary condition for an optimal $y(x)$ and $u(x)$ is that $\lambda' = -\partial H/\partial y$, which here means $\lambda' = -a\lambda$. This is an extremely simple first-order linear differential equation whose solution (see App. C, Sec. C-3) is $\lambda = c_0\, e^{(-a)x}$. The value of c_0 depends on $\lambda(x_0)$, an initial condition which may or may not be given by the problem or its transversality conditions. Nonetheless, since $e^{(-a)x}$ is positive, the sign of $\lambda(x_0)$ will be the same as that of c_0. Therefore, although the value of $\lambda(x)$ for various x will depend on the initial condition, it is clear that its sign *will not change* over $[x_0, x_1]$. It will always be positive if $c_0 > 0$ and always negative if $c_0 < 0$. Therefore, the optimal control $u^*(x)$ will be the same throughout the interval $[x_0, x_1]$, constantly at either its lowest or its highest level. An optimal decision on $u(x)$ made on the basis of facts at the beginning of the period will remain optimal during the entire period.

Figure 4-4 illustrates the problem in (4-78) when $y' = 3y + 2u$. Here $b > 0$, so if $\lambda(x_0) < 0$, we will always want $u(x) = 1$ and hence move in the upper plane in x,y,u space. Alternatively, if $\lambda(x_0) > 0$, we will move in the lower plane. In either plane, the trajectory will move from (x_0, y_0) to its intersection with $y = y_1$ along a curve with slope $y' = 3y + 2$. In the illustration $y_0 > 0$, so $y'(x_0) > 0$ and gets larger as y_1 is approached.

Consider the problem in (4-78) once again. Since minimization of the integral is equivalent to maximization of the negative of the integral, the objective in (4-78) could as well be written as:

$$\text{Maximize} \quad -\int_{x_0}^{x_1} dx$$

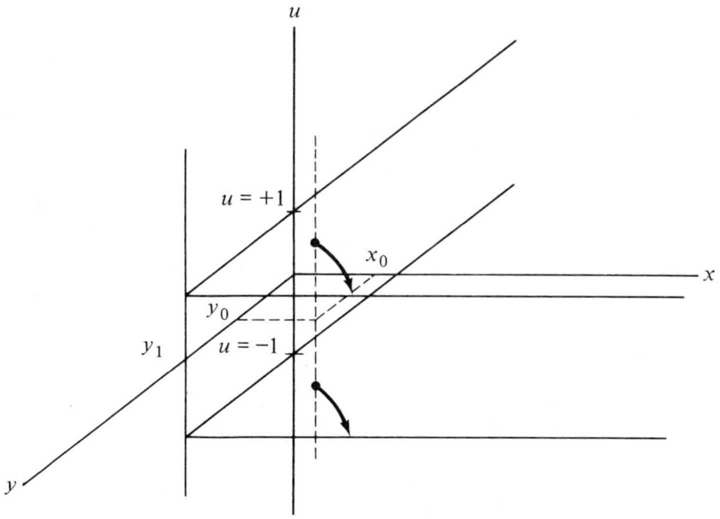

Figure 4-4 Constant control.

with the remainder of the problem unchanged. In this case, the hamiltonian will be

$$H = -1 + \lambda ay + \lambda bu$$

[compare (4-79)], and our objective is to choose u so as to maximize H. Although the sign on the first term of this hamiltonian is reversed from before, the other terms are identical, and hence to $\text{maximize}_{u \in \bar{u}} H$ we would have:

1. If $\lambda b > 0$, set u at its maximum value, namely $+1$.
2. If $\lambda b < 0$, set u at its minimum value, namely -1.

Compared with the rules given following the hamiltonian in (4-79), these appear to be just reversed.

In fact, by examining the transversality condition for this free terminal time problem, we will see that the function $\lambda(x)$ in the original minimization problem as given in (4-78) becomes $-\lambda(x)$ in the restated maximization problem. Recall that the transversality condition is that the terminal value of the hamiltonian function must be zero. For the original problem, this is

$$H(x_1) = 0 = 1 + \lambda(x_1)ay(x_1) + \lambda(x_1)bu(x_1)$$

To be specific, assume that $a > 0$, $b > 0$ and $y(x_1) = y_1 > 0$. Thus, for example, if $u(x_1) = 1$, $\lambda(x_1) = -1/[ay(x_1) + b]$, which is negative. And since we have seen that the sign of $\lambda(x)$ will not change over $[x_0, x_1]$, this is the situation of $u(x) = 1$ throughout that interval.

Application of the terminal transversality condition to the hamiltonian for the maximization version of this problem gives

$$H(x_1) = 0 = -1 + \lambda(x_1)ay(x_1) + \lambda(x_1)bu(x_1)$$

Again, with $a > 0, b > 0$ and $y_1 > 0$, for $u(x_1) = 1$, we have $\lambda(x_1) = 1/[ay(x_1) + b]$ which is positive. It has the same absolute value and the opposite sign from $\lambda(x_1)$ for the original version of the problem. Since $\lambda(x)$ does not change sign over $[x_0, x_1]$, this is the situation under which $u(x) = 1$ over the entire interval. Thus the costate variable in the rewritten problem is just the negative of the costate variable for the original problem.

This is analogous to the situation in ordinary constrained optimization problems. Consider the problem of maximizing $6x_1x_2$ subject to $2x_1 + x_2 = 10$. Using the Lagrange multiplier approach leads to $x_1 = 2\frac{1}{2}$, $x_2 = 5$, and $\lambda = 15$. Rewriting the problem as one of minimizing $-6x_1x_2$ subject to the same constraint leads to $x_1 = 2\frac{1}{2}$, $x_2 = 5$, and $\lambda = -15$, as would be expected. Relaxation of the right-hand side of the constraint allows an increase in the value of the function being maximized ($\lambda = 15$) or it allows a decrease in the value of the function being minimized ($\lambda = -15$).

The next two examples illustrate problems in which the optimal control generally *will* switch at least once from one boundary to the other.†

Example II

Consider the case in which the control variable is the acceleration (not velocity) of the state variable; instead of $y' = u$, we have $y'' = u$.‡ This can be expressed in terms of first-order differential equations (where $y = y_1$) as (1) $y_1' = y_2$, that is, $g_1(x, y_1, y_2, u) = y_2$, and (2) $y_2' = u$, that is, $g_2(x, y_1, y_2, u) = u$. If we continue to constrain u to $[-1, +1]$, the problem is:

$$\text{Minimize} \int_{x_0}^{x_1} dx$$

where

$$y_1(x_0) = y_{10}$$

$$y_1(x_1) = y_{11} \text{ (but } x_1 \text{ unspecified)}$$

$$y_1' = y_2 \tag{4-81}$$

$$y_2' = u$$

and

$$-1 \le u \le 1$$

† From Pontryagin et al. [8, pp. 23–35].

‡ Again, to anticipate illustrations in Chap. 5, if investment at time t, $I(t)$, is defined as the rate of change of capital at t, $K'(t)$, then one might wish to define the control variable in an optimal economic growth problem as the rate of change of investment, $I'(t)$, i.e., as $K''(t)$.

Here $H = F + \lambda_1 g_1 + \lambda_2 g_2 = 1 + \lambda_1 y_2 + \lambda_2 u$, again linear in the u, and parallel to the conclusion for the problem given in (4-78) we have

$$u^*(x) = -\operatorname{sgn}(\lambda_2) \tag{4-82}$$

It is thus of interest to know what the behavior of λ_2 is over time; in particular, is it likely to change sign, and if so, how often? For this problem

$$\lambda_1' = -\frac{\partial H}{\partial y_1} = 0$$

$$\lambda_2' = -\frac{\partial H}{\partial y_2} = -\lambda_1$$

This extremely simple pair of first-order linear differential equations can be solved without using matrix methods, which are appropriate for systems of first-order equations. Clearly $\lambda_1 = k_1$ (a constant) and therefore $\lambda_2 = -k_1 x + k_2$, where k_1 and k_2 are determined from initial or terminal conditions. The important observation is that since λ_2 is a linear function of x, the *sign* of λ_2 can change at most *once* over $[x_0, x_1]$—if λ_2 starts negative, with a positive slope, and cuts through the x axis (from below) before x_1 is reached, or if it starts positive, with a negative slope, and cuts the x axis (from above) before x_1. Since $u^*(x) = -\operatorname{sgn}[\lambda_2(x)]$, $u^*(x)$ will "switch" at most once (from one boundary value to the other); $\lambda_2(x)$ is known as the *switching function* for $u^*(x)$.

An interesting view of the geometry of the problem is provided by a phase diagram for $y\ (= y_1)$. This has $y\ (= y_1)$ on the horizontal axis and $y'\ (= y_1' = y_2)$ on the vertical axis.

Case a: $u = +1$ From (4-81), the differential equations for y_1 and y_2 are $y_1' = y_2$ and $y_2' = 1$. Thus $y_2 = x + k_3$ and $y_1 = \frac{1}{2}x^2 + k_3 x + k_4$. Expressing y_1 as a function of y_2, so as to have a curve in y_1,y_2 space (i.e., in y,y' space) we substitute $x = y_2 - k_3$ into y_1 and find

$$y_1 = \tfrac{1}{2}y_2^2 + k_5$$

(where $k_5 = -\frac{1}{2}k_3^2 + k_4$).

Case b: $u = -1$ Similar procedures, where now $y_2' = -1$, lead to

$$y_1 = -\tfrac{1}{2}y_2^2 + k_6$$

(where $k_6 = \frac{1}{2}k_3^2 + k_4$). These represent parabolas in y_1,y_2 space. With no loss of generality, we can "normalize" the problem by specifying that $y_1(x_1) = 0$ and $y_2(x_1) = 0$. This simply moves the axes so that the origin in the phase diagrams represents the *terminal* point.

Figure 4-5 illustrates Case a, where $u = +1$. Notice that only the heavily shaded lower branch leads to the origin; only if the original y $[y(x_0)]$ lies along this particular curve will control start at $u = +1$ and not switch. Figure 4-6

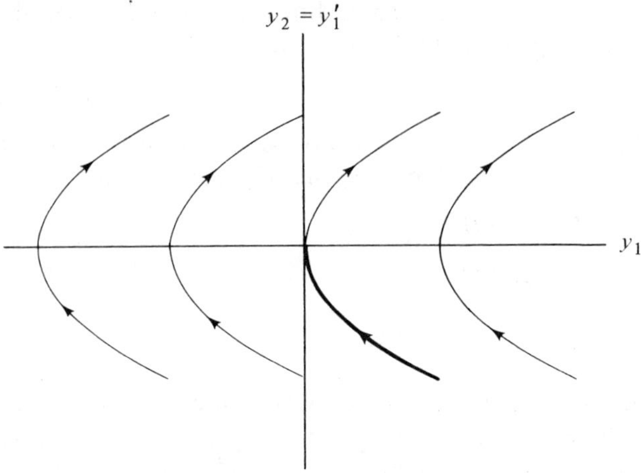

Figure 4-5 Phase diagram for y_1 and y_2 in (4-81) when $u = +1$.

illustrates the situation for Case b, where $u = -1$. Notice that only the heavily shaded upper branch leads to the origin.

The complete path followed by y when it is not initially on one of these two branches can be observed if we combine the two figures, as is done in Fig. 4-7. When y does not begin on the switching curve, it travels along a parabolic path until it hits the switching curve, along which it moves to the origin. For example, from point A, movement is upward, under $u = +1$ control; this is a parabola from Fig. 4-5. At A', u switches to $u = -1$ and y moves along the heavy curve to the origin. From B, movement is downward, under $u = -1$ control (Fig. 4-6)

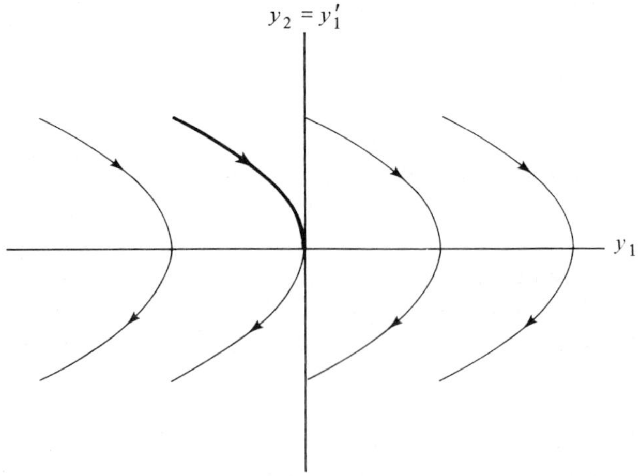

Figure 4-6 Phase diagram for y_1 and y_2 in (4-81) when $u = -1$.

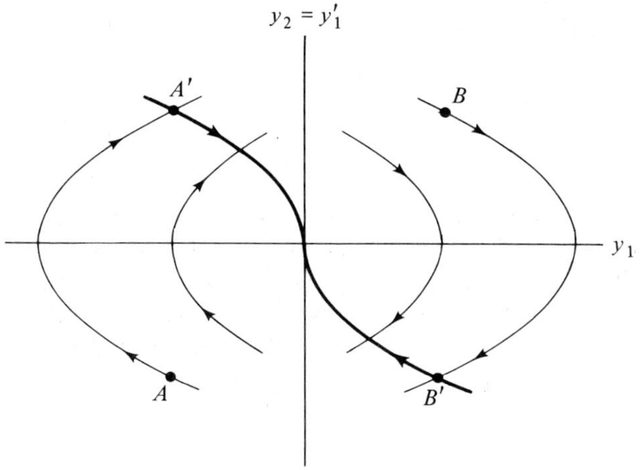

Figure 4-7 Phase diagram and switching curve for y_1 and y_2 in (4-81).

until B', where u becomes $u = +1$ and y moves to the origin from below, along the heavy line. Thus, movement from *any* initial point to the origin (terminal point) will require at most one switch in the value of the control variable.

Example III

An apparently slight modification of the problem above in (4-81) will illustrate a case in which possibly more than one switch in the optimal control will occur. This comes from a modification of $u = y''$ (where control was exercised via acceleration) to $u = y'' + y$. Using the definitions of y_1 and y_2 from above, that is, $y = y_1$ and $y_2 = y_1'$, this leads to:

$$\text{Minimize} \int_{x_0}^{x_1} dx$$

where

$$\begin{aligned} y_1(x_0) &= y_{10} \\ y_1(x_1) &= y_{11} \ (x_1 \text{ unspecified}) \\ y_1' &= y_2 \\ y_2' &= -y_1 + u \end{aligned} \tag{4-83}$$

and

$$-1 \le u \le 1$$

Proceeding as usual, $H = 1 + \lambda_1 y_2 + \lambda_2(-y_1 + u)$, and as before

$$u^*(x) = -\operatorname{sgn}(\lambda_2) \tag{4-84}$$

since H is linear in u. The associated first-order conditions giving the time paths of λ_1 and λ_2 come, as usual, from $\lambda_1' = -\partial H/\partial y_1$ and $\lambda_2' = -\partial H/\partial y_2$. Here these are

$$\lambda_1' = \lambda_2$$
$$\lambda_2' = -\lambda_1$$

Again, because of the extremely simple nature of this system—and because our ultimate interest is in the behavior of $\lambda_2(x)$—we do not use full-scale matrix methods. Instead, observe that $\lambda_2'' = -\lambda_1'$ but $\lambda_1' = \lambda_2$; therefore $\lambda_2'' = -\lambda_2$, or $\lambda_2'' + \lambda_2 = 0$. The solution of second-order linear differential equations such as this one in λ_2 depends on the roots of its characteristic equation; these turn out in this case to be $\pm\sqrt{-1}$ and hence

$$\lambda_2(x) = k \cos(x + \delta)$$

where k and δ are constants determined from initial conditions.† Irrespective of the values of these constants, the behavior of the cosine function is such that it changes sign every 180° (π rad).‡ Thus, since $u^*(x) = -\operatorname{sgn}(\lambda_2)$, the number of times that the optimal control switches depends on the distance between x_0 and x_1.

Turning now to the phase-space geometry, we consider the $u = +1$ and $u = -1$ cases separately, as before.

Case a: $u = +1$ From (4-83), the differential equations for y_1 and y_2 are $y_1' = y_2$ and $y_2' = -y_1 + 1$. By a simple change of variables, namely, $v_1 = y_1 - 1$ and $v_2 = y_2$, the original equations become

$$v_1' = v_2$$
$$v_2' = -v_1$$

which are identical in structure to the pair of equations for λ_1' and λ_2', above. Again, as before, it is easily shown that

$$v_2(x) = A \cos(x + \gamma) \tag{4-85}$$

for constants A and γ to be determined; and since $v_2' = -v_1$, simple differentiation shows

$$v_1(x) = A \sin(x + \gamma) \tag{4-86}$$

from which, since $(\sin\alpha)^2 + (\cos\alpha)^2 = 1$,

$$[v_1(x)]^2 + [v_2(x)]^2 = A^2$$

which says that the points in v_1,v_2 space satisfying (4-85) and (4-86) lie on a

† Appendix C, Sec. C-4. In the discussion of difference and differential equations, the λ were the characteristic roots of the coefficient matrix of the equation system. Here, of course, they are the costate variables in the control theory problem.

‡ Appendix C, Fig. C-4.

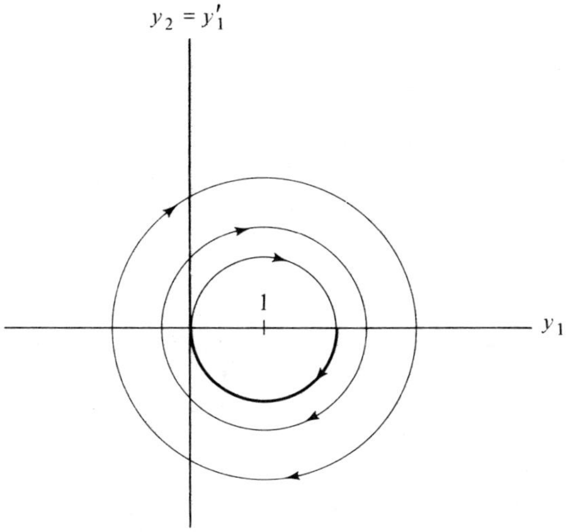

Figure 4-8 Phase diagram for y_1 and y_2 in (4-83) when $u = +1$.

circle, centered at the origin, with radius A. Thus, in y_1, y_2 space, since $v_1 = y_1 - 1$ and $v_2 = y_2$, we have

$$\begin{aligned} y_1(x) &= A \sin(x + \gamma) + 1 \\ y_2(x) &= A \cos(x + \gamma) \end{aligned} \tag{4-87}$$

which represents a circle centered at (1, 0) with radius A. Figure 4-8 illustrates this for various values of A, i.e., various radii.

Case b: $u = -1$ When $y_1' = y_2$ and $y_2' = -y_1 - 1$, the analysis is similar to that for $u = +1$, and the phase diagram turns out to be a family of circles centered on $(-1, 0)$ in y_1, y_2 space. These are shown in Fig. 4-9.

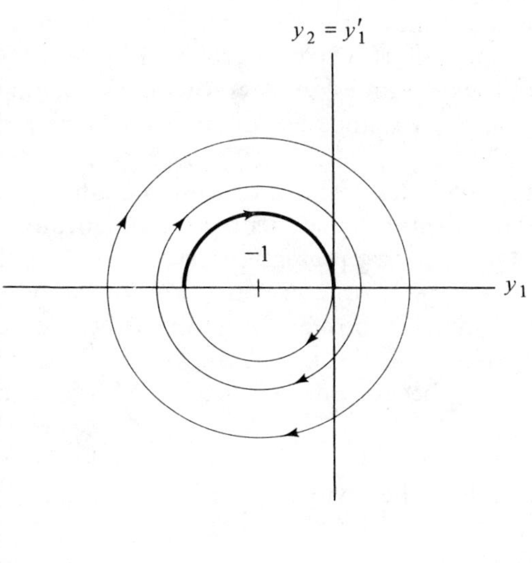

Figure 4-9 Phase diagram for y_1 and y_2 in (4-83) when $u = -1$.

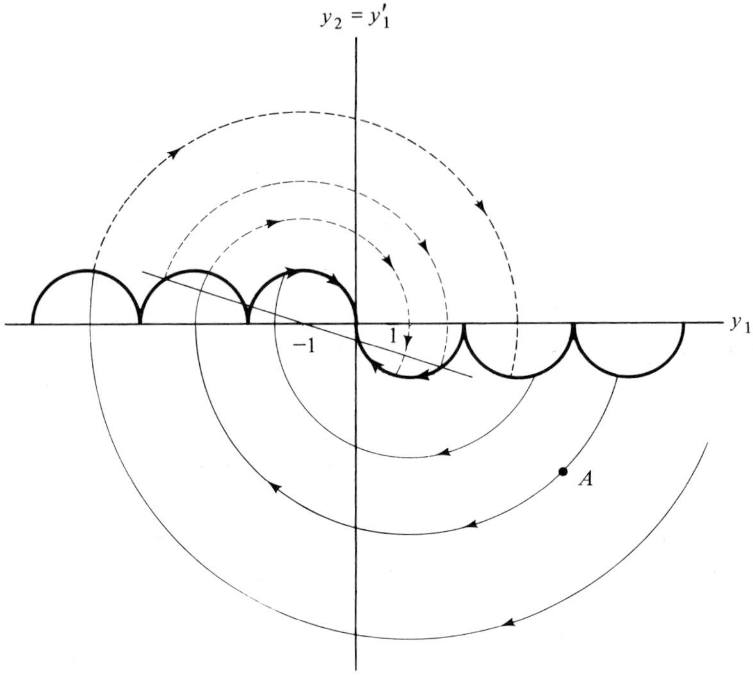

Figure 4-10 Phase diagram and switching curve for y_1 and y_2 in (4-83).

As x increases by 2π rad (360°), $y_1(x)$ would travel around the circumference of a given circle. But $u^*(x)$ changes sign every time x increases by π rad. Therefore $y_1(x)$ will not follow any particular circle for longer than π rad, i.e., for longer than one-half of its circumference. When y reaches the origin, it will have been following all or part of the shaded circumference in Fig. 4-8 (if $u = +1$) or Fig. 4-9 (if $u = -1$). Prior to that, it must have been under the influence of the opposite control, but again for no longer than one-half of a circumference. Figure 4-10, which combines some of the paths from Figs. 4-8 and 4-9, also shows the switching curve, which here turns out to be a series of semicircles of radius 1, centered along the horizontal axis.

In the phase diagram, the lower semicircles (solid) are centered on $(1, 0)$, meaning $u = +1$; the upper ones (dashed) are centered on $(-1, 0)$, meaning $u = -1$. The small semicircles along the y_1 axis represent the switching curve, where motion changes from $u = +1$ to $u = -1$, or vice versa. For the middle one of the three dashed semicircles, the diameter through $(-1, 0)$ is shown; note that it intersects the second switching circle on the left of the origin and the first one on the right of the origin. This is because the dashed trajectories are centered at $(-1, 0)$.

Starting at the large dot, labeled A, y_1 would move along the middle one of the lower semicircles (solid) until it hits the switching curve, then travels along the lowest of the upper semicircles (dashed) until it hits the switching curve adjacent to the origin, along which it would then travel to the origin. (The other small semicircles along the axes represent the loci of switching points; there is no motion *along* them. Only the two on either side of the origin represent true trajectories.)

4-6 ALTERNATIVE FORMULATIONS

Autonomous versus Nonautonomous Problems

The work of Pontryagin and his associates dealt with a formulation of the control problem in which the independent variable does not appear explicitly as an argument in the integrand of the objective functional or in the differential constraints for the state variables. That is, the type of problem that they studied was:

$$\text{Maximize} \int_{x_0}^{x_1} F(\mathbf{Y}, \mathbf{U})\, dx$$

where $\mathbf{Y}(x_0) = \mathbf{Y}_0$

$\mathbf{Y}(x_1)$ lies on some specified terminal surface (4-88)

and $\dot{\mathbf{Y}} = \mathbf{G}(\mathbf{Y}, \mathbf{U})$

Since in much control theory work the independent variable is time, a formulation like (4-88), in which the independent variable does not appear explicitly, is known as an autonomous problem. Alternatively, the problem presented in (4-25) is termed nonautonomous, since the independent variable is included as an argument in both the integrand F and the differential constraints $\mathbf{G}$. We repeat (4-25) here:

$$\text{Maximize} \int_{x_0}^{x_1} F(x, \mathbf{Y}, \mathbf{U})\, dx$$

where

$$\mathbf{Y}(x_0) = \mathbf{Y}_0$$
$$\mathbf{Y}(x_1) = \mathbf{Y}_1 \tag{4-89}$$

and $\dot{\mathbf{Y}} = \mathbf{G}(x, \mathbf{Y}, \mathbf{U})$

This is the fixed endpoints problem. The extension of results below to terminal (or initial) surfaces parallels earlier discussions of transversality conditions.

Assume that $\mathbf{Y}$ is an n-element vector of state variables, and add a new variable, $y_{n+1}(x)$, defined simply as $y_{n+1}(x) = x$. This new variable is easily specified by means of a differential equation and initial condition:

$$y'_{n+1}(x) = 1 \quad \text{and} \quad y_{n+1}(x_0) = x_0 \tag{4-90}$$

Then (4-89) can be expressed as follows, defining $\mathbf{Y}^* = [y_1, \ldots, y_n, y_{n+1}]'$:

$$\text{Maximize} \int_{x_0}^{x_1} F(\mathbf{Y}^*, \mathbf{U})\, dx$$

where

$$\begin{aligned} \mathbf{Y}(x_0) &= \mathbf{Y}_0 \\ y_{n+1}(x_0) &= x_0 \\ \mathbf{Y}(x_1) &= \mathbf{Y}_1 \\ y_{n+1}(x_1) &= x_1 \\ \dot{\mathbf{Y}} &= \mathbf{G}(\mathbf{Y}^*, \mathbf{U}) \end{aligned} \tag{4-91}$$

and

$$y'_{n+1} = 1$$

or, alternatively:

$$\text{Maximize} \int_{x_0}^{x_1} F(\mathbf{Y}^*, \mathbf{U})\, dx$$

where

$$\mathbf{Y}^*(x_0) = \begin{bmatrix} \mathbf{Y}_0 \\ x_0 \end{bmatrix}$$

$$\mathbf{Y}^*(x_1) = \begin{bmatrix} \mathbf{Y}_1 \\ x_1 \end{bmatrix} \tag{4-91$'$}$$

and

$$\dot{\mathbf{Y}}^* = \begin{bmatrix} \mathbf{G}(\mathbf{Y}^*, \mathbf{U}) \\ 1 \end{bmatrix}$$

Therefore, necessary conditions for the autonomous formulation of the problem can be translated to conditions for a nonautonomous version, and vice versa.

Different Forms of the Objective Functional

In Sec. 3-6 of Chap. 3, where we examined the Lagrange and Mayer forms of the calculus of variations problem, we saw that the objective functional in the classical calculus of variations problem could be reexpressed as a function of terminal values of the y. Much of the definitive work in modern control theory has treated a particular version of the Mayer form of the problem.

We start with:

$$\text{Maximize} \int_{x_0}^{x_1} F(x, \mathbf{Y}, \mathbf{U})\, dx$$

where

$$\mathbf{Y}(x_0) = \mathbf{Y}_0 \quad \text{and} \quad \dot{\mathbf{Y}} = \mathbf{G}(x, \mathbf{Y}, \mathbf{U}) \tag{4-92}$$

$\mathbf{Y}(x_1)$ is not specified; i.e., we are dealing with the so-called free right-hand boundary problem. The conversion proceeds by defining a new variable $y_{n+1}(x)$ as

$$y_{n+1}(x) = \int_{x_0}^{x} F(\chi, \mathbf{Y}, \mathbf{U})\, d\chi \tag{4-93}$$

which means that $y'_{n+1}(x) = F(x, \mathbf{Y}, \mathbf{U})$ and that $y_{n+1}(x_0) = 0$. Thus the integral in (4-92) becomes $y_{n+1}(x_1)$ and that problem is equivalent to:

$$\text{Maximize} \quad y_{n+1}(x_1)$$

where

$$\begin{aligned} \mathbf{Y}(x_0) &= \mathbf{Y}_0 \\ y_{n+1}(x_0) &= 0 \\ \dot{\mathbf{Y}} &= \mathbf{G}(x, \mathbf{Y}, \mathbf{U}) \end{aligned} \tag{4-94}$$

and

$$y'_{n+1} = F(x, \mathbf{Y}, \mathbf{U})$$

In fact, an objective of maximization of some function of the terminal values of several or all state variables can also be converted to the objective of maximization of the terminal value of a single variable. Suppose that the objective in (4-92) had been in the general Mayer form, namely:

$$\begin{aligned} &\text{Maximize} \quad K[y_1(x_1), \ldots, y_n(x_1)] \\ &\text{where} \quad \mathbf{Y}(x_0) = \mathbf{Y}_0 \quad \text{and} \quad \dot{\mathbf{Y}} = \mathbf{G}(x, \mathbf{Y}, \mathbf{U}) \end{aligned} \tag{4-95}$$

Define

$$y_{n+1}(x) = K[y_1(x), \ldots, y_n(x)] \tag{4-96}$$

As in (4-93), the conversion begins by defining $y_{n+1}(x_1)$ to be the objective function in the given problem. Provided that K is differentiable, we have a differential equation and initial condition for the new variable, namely,

$$y'_{n+1}(x) = \sum_{j=1}^{n} \frac{\partial K}{\partial y_j} \frac{dy_j}{dx} = \sum_{j=1}^{n} \frac{\partial K}{\partial y_j} (y'_j)$$

and

$$y_{n+1}(x_0) = K[y_1(x_0), \ldots, y_n(x_0)]$$

Let $[\partial K/\partial \mathbf{Y}] = [\partial K/\partial y_1, \ldots, \partial K/\partial y_n]'$. Then the new problem, equivalent to (4-95), is:

$$\text{Maximize} \quad y_{n+1}(x_1)$$

where

$$\begin{aligned} \mathbf{Y}(x_0) &= \mathbf{Y}_0 \\ y_{n+1}(x_0) &= K[y_1(x_0), \ldots, y_n(x_0)] \end{aligned} \tag{4-97}$$

and

$$y'_{n+1}(x) = [\partial K/\partial \mathbf{Y}] \cdot [\dot{\mathbf{Y}}] = [\partial K/\partial \mathbf{Y}] \cdot [\mathbf{G}(x, \mathbf{Y}, \mathbf{U})]$$

Notice that $y_{n+1}(x_1)$ in (4-97)—which, by (4-96), is $K[y_1(x_1), \ldots, y_n(x_1)]$—in fact specifies a great deal about the terminal surface for the $y_i(x)$ at $x = x_1$. That is, at $x = x_1$, the optimal $y_1(x), \ldots, y_n(x)$ will be on the surface $S(x, \mathbf{Y}, y_{n+1}) = 0$, where $S = K[y_1(x), \ldots, y_n(x)] - y_{n+1}(x)$. As before, let $\mathbf{Y}^* = [y_1, \ldots, y_n, y_{n+1}]'$.

Then $\nabla \mathbf{S}_{\mathbf{Y}^*} = [\partial K/\partial y_1, \ldots, \partial K/\partial y_n, -1]'$. Similarly, let $\mathbf{\Lambda}^* = [\lambda_1, \ldots, \lambda_n, \lambda_{n+1}]'$. The transversality condition for such a problem is that $\mathbf{\Lambda}^*$ be orthogonal to the terminal surface at $x = x_1$, which is to say that $\mathbf{\Lambda}^*(x_1)$ must be parallel to the gradient at x_1. Since both $\mathbf{\Lambda}^*$ and $\nabla \mathbf{S}_{\mathbf{Y}^*}$ emanate from the origin, the requirement of parallelism is one of collinearity, and since orientation and not magnitude is important, the collinearity condition can be specified as either $\mathbf{\Lambda}^*(x_1) = \nabla \mathbf{S}_{\mathbf{Y}^*}(x_1)$ or $\mathbf{\Lambda}^*(x_1) = -\nabla \mathbf{S}_{\mathbf{Y}^*}(x_1)$, i.e., as

$$\begin{bmatrix} \lambda_1(x_1) \\ \vdots \\ \lambda_n(x_1) \\ \lambda_{n+1}(x_1) \end{bmatrix} = \begin{bmatrix} \partial K/\partial y_1 \\ \vdots \\ \partial K/\partial y_n \\ -1 \end{bmatrix}_{x=x_1} \tag{4-98}$$

or as

$$\begin{bmatrix} \lambda_1(x_1) \\ \vdots \\ \lambda_n(x_1) \\ \lambda_{n+1}(x_1) \end{bmatrix} = \begin{bmatrix} -\partial K/\partial y_1 \\ \vdots \\ -\partial K/\partial y_n \\ 1 \end{bmatrix}_{x=x_1} \tag{4-99}$$

This turns out to be of interest mostly for what appears at first to be a very special case.

Consider a particularly simple form of the objective function $K[\mathbf{Y}(x_1)]$ in (4-95), namely,

$$K[\mathbf{Y}(x_1)] = \sum_{j=1}^{n} c_j y_j(x_1) \tag{4-100}$$

i.e., a linear function of the terminal values of the state variables. Thus, as in (4-96),

$$y_{n+1}(x) = c_1 y_1(x) + \cdots + c_n y_n(x) \tag{4-101}$$

Here $S(x, \mathbf{Y}^*) = c_1 y_1(x) + \cdots + c_n y_n(x) - y_{n+1}(x)$ and the gradient is constant, that is, $\nabla \mathbf{S}_{\mathbf{Y}^*} = [c_1, \ldots, c_n, -1]'$, and therefore the orthogonality requirement at x_1 can be specified as either

$$\begin{bmatrix} \lambda_1(x_1) \\ \vdots \\ \lambda_n(x_1) \\ \lambda_{n+1}(x_1) \end{bmatrix} = \begin{bmatrix} c_1 \\ \vdots \\ c_n \\ -1 \end{bmatrix} \tag{4-102}$$

or

$$\begin{bmatrix} \lambda_1(x_1) \\ \vdots \\ \lambda_n(x_1) \\ \lambda_{n+1}(x_1) \end{bmatrix} = \begin{bmatrix} -c_1 \\ \vdots \\ -c_n \\ 1 \end{bmatrix} \tag{4-103}$$

For the case in which the general problem of (4-92) has been converted to the form given in (4-94), the present representation is valid, with $c_1 = \cdots = c_n = 0$. Thus

$$\begin{bmatrix} \lambda_1(x_1) \\ \vdots \\ \lambda_n(x_1) \end{bmatrix} = \begin{bmatrix} 0 \\ \vdots \\ 0 \end{bmatrix} \tag{4-104}$$

exactly as we saw before for the free right-hand boundary problem in Sec. 4-2. The terminal requirement on λ_{n+1} will be either $\lambda_{n+1}(x_1) = -1$ or $\lambda_{n+1}(x_1) = 1$, depending on how the collinearity condition was specified.

Forming the hamiltonian for the problem in (4-94) gives

$$H = \sum_{j=1}^{n} \lambda_j(x) g_j(x, \mathbf{Y}, \mathbf{U}) + \lambda_{n+1}(x) F(x, \mathbf{Y}, \mathbf{U})$$

At $x = x_1$, $\lambda_1(x), \ldots, \lambda_n(x)$ are all zero, and

1. If $\lambda_{n+1}(x_1) = -1$, then $H = -F$.
2. If $\lambda_{n+1}(x_1) = 1$, then $H = F$.

This suggests that if the original problem (4-92) had been, for example, to minimize $\int_{x_0}^{x_1} F(x, \mathbf{Y}, \mathbf{U})\, dx$, then if terminal conditions were specified as $\mathbf{\Lambda}^*(x_1) = \nabla S_{\mathbf{Y}^*}(x_1)$ in the rewritten problem [i.e., as in (4-98)] leading to $\lambda_{n+1}(x_1) = -1$, we would want to maximize H. Conversely, with terminal conditions $\mathbf{\Lambda}^*(x_1) = -\nabla S_{\mathbf{Y}^*}(x_1)$ [as in (4-99)] leading to $\lambda_{n+1}(x_1) = 1$, we would want to minimize H. Thus, in fact, in certain reformulations of a problem involving maximization of an integral, one may want either to maximize or minimize the hamiltonian, and similarly for minimization of an integral. In this sense, then, the terms "maximum principle" and "minimum principle" are equally appropriate. (This was alluded to in the footnote on page 100 above.)

The potential for confusion is probably compounded in view of one further aspect of the formulation of Pontryagin and his colleagues. They suggest that one consider the simple relabeling in which $y_n(x)$ in (4-100) is considered as $y_{n+1}(x)$ in (4-101). This means that $S = c_1 y_1(x) + \cdots + c_n y_n(x)$, $\nabla \mathbf{S} = [c_1, \ldots, c_n]'$, and therefore the $(n+1)$th element in both vectors in (4-102) or (4-103) disappears. Similarly, the nth element in both vectors in (4-104) disappears. In this view, c_n in (4-100) is 1, and thus the terminal requirement on $\lambda_n(x_1)$—the costate variable associated with the "added" variable $y_n(x)$—will be $\lambda_n(x_1) = 1$ in (4-102) or $\lambda_n(x_1) = -1$ in (4-103). Hence the same possibilities of $H = -F$ or $H = F$ occur. Pontryagin et al. [8] use the specification

$$\begin{bmatrix} \lambda_1(x_1) \\ \vdots \\ \lambda_n(x_1) \end{bmatrix} = \begin{bmatrix} -c_1 \\ \vdots \\ -c_n \end{bmatrix}$$

and also begin with the problem of minimizing $\int_{x_0}^{x_1} F\, dx$. Hence for them $\lambda_n(x_1) = -1$, $H = -F$, and thus they derive their maximum principle.

PROBLEMS

4-1 Solve Prob. 2-4(*a*) of Chap. 2 using the control formulation, i.e., letting $y'(x) = u(x)$.

4-2 Solve Probs. 3-1(*a*), (*b*), and (*c*) of Chap. 3 using the control formulation, i.e., letting $y'(x) = u(x)$.

4-3 Solve Probs. 3-2(*a*) and (*b*) of Chap. 3 using the control formulation.

4-4 (*a*) Consider Prob. 4-1 with the added constraint on the control variable that $u \leq 8$.
(*b*) Consider Prob. 4-1 with the added constraint $u \leq 5.3$.

4-5 (*a*) Solve Prob. 3-4(*b*) in Chap. 3 using the control approach of the present chapter.
(*b*) Solve the problem in (*a*), above, if, in addition, it is required that $u_1 \leq 5$ and $u_2 \leq 10$ over $0 \leq x \leq 1$.

4-6 Minimize $I = \int_0^1 \frac{1}{2}(3y^2 + 5u^2)\,dx$ where $y' = y + 4u$ and $y(x_0) = 1$.

4-7 (*a*) Consider Prob. 4-6 with the additional condition that $y(x_1) = 0.5$.
(*b*) Consider Prob. 4-6 with the terminal value of the state variable constrained to be nonnegative.
(*c*) Consider Prob. 4-6 with the inequality constraint on the terminal value of the state variable requiring that $y(x_1) \geq 0.5$.

4-8 (*a*) Consider Prob. 4-1 again, now with the added constraint on the state variable and the control variable that $y + u \leq 10$.
(*b*) As in (*a*), above, except that the constraint is now $y + u \leq 7$.

REFERENCES

1. Arrow, K. J., and M. Kurz: "Public Investment, the Rate of Return, and Optimal Fiscal Policy," Johns Hopkins Press for Resources for the Future, Baltimore, 1970. A thorough discussion of the basic maximum principle results is given in chap. II at a moderate level of mathematical difficulty.
2. Benavie, A.: "Mathematical Techniques for Economic Analysis," Prentice-Hall, Englewood Cliffs, N.J., 1972. Static optimization techniques and examples of economic applications are given in pt. I. Part II covers dynamic analysis, including difference and differential equations and, in chap. 5, the maximum principle. Emphasis is on discrete, not continuous, formulations; moderate level of mathematical difficulty.
3. Dorfman, R.: An Economic Interpretation of Optimal Control Theory, *American Economic Review*, vol. 59, pp. 817–831, December, 1969. An extremely readable account of the basic results of the maximum principle, with economic parallels and interpretations of costate variables.
4. Hadley, G., and M. C. Kemp: "Variational Methods in Economics," American Elsevier, New York, 1971. A very complete and mathematically advanced discussion of calculus of variations and maximum principle techniques and their use in economic growth models. Chapters 4 and 5 deal with the maximum principle.
5. Hestenes, M. R.: "Calculus of Variations and Optimal Control Theory," Wiley, New York, 1966. A complete exposition of the calculus of variations and maximum principle approaches; advanced level of mathematical difficulty.
6. Intriligator, M. D.: "Mathematical Optimization and Economic Theory," Prentice-Hall, Englewood Cliffs, N.J., 1971. Dynamic optimization techniques are covered in pt. IV. Chapter 11 is an overall introduction to the basic approach of control theory; chap. 14 is a compact and readable introduction to the maximum principle results.
7. Peterson, D. W.: The Economic Significance of Auxiliary Functions in Optimal Control, *International Economic Review*, vol. 14, pp. 234–252, February, 1973. A thorough examination of costate variables and their economic interpretation.
8. Pontryagin, L. S., V. G. Boltyanskii, R. V. Gamkrelidze, and E. F. Mishchenko: "The Mathematical Theory of Optimal Processes," (K. N. Trirogoff, trans.), Interscience, New York, 1962.

This is the basic source for the derivation and development of maximum principle results; the mathematical level is advanced.

9. Rozonoer, L. I.: L. S. Pontryagin's Maximum Principle in the Theory of Optimal Systems, *Automation and Remote Control*, vol. 20, pp. 1288–1302, 1405–1421, and 1517–1532, 1959. Also reprinted in R. Oldenburger (ed.), "Optimal and Self-Optimizing Control," MIT Press, Cambridge, Mass., 1966. A thorough but readable account of the maximum principle results; moderate to fairly advanced level of mathematics.
10. Takayama, A.: "Mathematical Economics," Dryden Press, Hinsdale, Ill., 1974. This very complete and readable text covers many of the derivations and details for the maximum principle in chap. 8.

CHAPTER

FIVE

MODELS IN ECONOMICS AND REGIONAL SCIENCE

For the social scientist, the mathematical results of the preceding three chapters are primarily of interest because of the insights that they may provide in particular applications. For that reason, we turn in this chapter to some illustrative examples using the calculus of variations and maximum principle approaches in economics and in regional science. The "classical" application in economics is in growth models, dating from Ramsey's 1928 paper [20]. This is truly a "dynamic" model insofar as the independent variable is time and the object is to derive an optimal time path over a planning horizon for the stock of capital in a society. Models of this sort are presented in Sec. 5-1.

In Sec. 5-2 we examine a typical model of a more recent and rather different type, in which the independent variable is a spatial rather than a temporal one, namely, distance from the center of an urban area. Models of urban form deal with optimal allocations of land to alternative uses—most simply, production, housing and transport facilities. Based on a number of simplifying assumptions dealing with the topography of the urban area, one objective is to derive an optimal function across space ("space path" as opposed to time path) from the center of the city to its boundaries for the amount of land devoted to transportation.

A second temporal application in economics deals not with a stock that (generally) grows but rather with one that is depleted over time—exhaustible resources. The problem here (Sec. 5-3) is to determine an optimal extraction program over a planning horizon. When the optimal economic growth problem (Sec. 5-1) is examined for a nation composed of distinct and disparate regions, one can pose questions such as: how should investment funds be allocated over time and between regions so as to achieve some national goal? A model for regional allocation of investment is presented in Sec. 5-4. Finally, in Sec. 5-5, we introduce briefly the notions of space-time models in regional science which incorporate both independent variables—location in space and location in time. Standard results in both capital theory and location theory are obtained from this combined point of view.

5-1 OPTIMAL ECONOMIC GROWTH

In dynamic economic models, or models of economic growth, time paths of economic variables (e.g., capital stock, consumption) are generated. Such models are fundamentally descriptive. However, if one introduces a criterion by which to evaluate alternative paths, one has an optimal growth model. A classic problem of this sort in economics arises from the observation that resources devoted to current production of capital goods are by definition diverted from the current production of consumption goods. But currently produced capital goods can be utilized in some future period for consumption-good production. Hence the problem of intertemporal allocation of resources between production of capital goods and consumption goods. From society's point of view, this is the question of how much to save and how much to spend on consumption goods in each period.

Several very simplified approaches to the problem are sketched in this section. The object is entirely to illustrate the connection with the optimization techniques of earlier chapters. There are numerous refinements of the economic specifications and the details of the optimization problem, and these constitute the large and growing literature on optimal economic growth models.† A pioneering investigation of some of the questions that are now the concern of this field was carried out by Frank Ramsey [20] and published in 1928. We first present an oversimplified version of Ramsey's work.

The macroeconomic relationships in an economy in which population, and hence labor supply, is held constant are fairly straightforward. Disregarding technical change, output at any time t, $Y(t)$, depends upon the amount of capital employed at that time, $K(t)$; specifically, $Y(t) = f[K(t)]$. The usual national income identity, involving aggregate consumption and aggregate investment, is

$$Y(t) = C(t) + I(t)$$

Investment at time t is just the change in capital stock at that time, $I(t) = dK(t)/dt \equiv \dot{K}(t)$, and therefore the differential equation

$$\dot{K}(t) = f[K(t)] - C(t)$$

† Representative examples of this literature include Arrow and Kurz [1], Burmeister and Dobell [2], Chakravarty [4], Hadley and Kemp [8], Intriligator [10, chap. 16], Phelps [17], and Shell [24]. A clear introduction is provided by Dorfman [5]. The forefront of explorations of this type can be found in Cass and Shell [3].

describes how the economy moves over time. Alternatively, since $C(t) = f[K(t)] - \dot{K}(t)$, knowing how $K(t)$ changes over time (and $f[K(t)]$) would determine how consumption changes over time.

If one assumes that consumption is engaged in for the utility that it provides, then the question can be posed: what is the "best" investment program for the economy, i.e., the best path for $K(t)$ over some planning period? Assume that a utility function $U[C(t)]$ can be specified that is twice differentiable, such that $U_C > 0$ and $U_{CC} < 0$ (diminishing marginal utility). Assume also that we are concerned with a planning period from the present $t = 0$ to some future time $t = T$. To simplify, for the moment, assume also that both the initial ($t = 0$) and terminal ($t = T$) amounts of capital are known or specified, that is, $K(0) = K_0$ and $K(T) = K_T$.† Ignoring possible constraints on $C(t)$ or $K(t)$, the planning problem could be posed as: find $K(t)$ so as to

$$\text{Maximize} \quad \int_0^T U[C(t)]\,dt$$

where
$$K(0) = K_0 \quad \text{and} \quad K(T) = K_T \tag{5-1}$$
and where
$$C(t) = f[K(t)] - \dot{K}(t)$$

This is, of course, a straightforward fixed-endpoint calculus of variations problem (Chap. 2) of the sort: find $y(x)$ to

$$\text{Maximize} \quad \int_{x_0}^{x_1} F(x, y, y')\,dx$$
where
$$y(x_0) = y_0 \quad \text{and} \quad y(x_1) = y_1 \tag{5-2}$$

with $F(x, y, y') = U[C(t)] = U[f(K) - \dot{K}]$, where $x = t$, $y(x) = K(t)$, and $y'(x) = \dot{K}(t)$.

The elements of the Euler-Lagrange equation for this case are F_y and $(d/dx)F_{y'}$, or (using primes for derivatives with regard to K and dots, as usual, for derivatives with regard to time)

$$U_K = \frac{\partial U}{\partial C}\frac{dC}{dK} = U_C f'(K) \tag{5-3a}$$

$$U_{\dot{K}} = \frac{\partial U}{\partial C}\frac{dC}{d\dot{K}} = U_C(-1) \tag{5-3b}$$

Therefore the Euler-Lagrange condition $F_y - (d/dx)F_{y'} = 0$, or $U_K - (d/dt)U_{\dot{K}} = 0$, requires

$$U_C f'(K) + \dot{U}_C = 0 \quad \text{or} \quad -f'(K) = \frac{\dot{U}_C}{U_C} \tag{5-4}$$

† There are many alternative specifications of terminal conditions on $K(t)$. The logic here is simply that it may be appropriate to leave future generations (starting at $t = T$) an amount of "initial" capital for their planning period.

In words, the Ramsey "optimal savings rule" says that the relative rate of change in the marginal utility of consumption should equal (in absolute value) the marginal product of capital.

The basic Ramsey result is often presented somewhat differently. For the particular calculus of variations problem (5-2) in which the independent variable x does not appear explicitly in the integrand, the Euler-Lagrange equation can be rearranged so that direct integration is possible. (When the independent variable is time, t, this is the "autonomous" case.) The requirement $F_y - (d/dx)F_{y'} = 0$ becomes

$$F_y - F_{y'y}y' - F_{y'y'}y'' = 0$$

Multiplying through by y' gives

$$F_y y' - F_{y'y}(y')^2 - F_{y'y'}y'y'' = 0$$

which the reader can verify to be

$$\frac{d}{dx}[F - y'F_{y'}] = 0 \tag{5-5}$$

Therefore, integrating both sides of (5-5) gives

$$F - y'F_{y'} = \text{constant} \tag{5-6}$$

which is an alternative way of expressing the Euler-Lagrange requirement for the case in which x does not appear explicitly in the integrand.

For the simplified version of the Ramsey problem given in (5-1), where $F(y, y') = U[C] = U[f(K) - \dot{K}]$, $y(x) = K(t)$, and $y'(x) = \dot{K}(t)$, (5-6) becomes (simplifying notation by dropping arguments of functions)

$$U + \dot{K}U_C = \text{constant} \tag{5-7}$$

Since Ramsey was concerned with a mathematical theory of saving, the rule is generally stated as: the rate of saving ($\dot{K}$) at any time t, multiplied by the marginal utility of consumption at that time, should always equal a constant minus the total utility at time t.†

To obtain further insights into these results, consider the concrete cases of (1) a production function $f(K)$ exhibiting constant marginal productivity, that is, $f'(K) = b$ $(b > 0)$, and (2) a utility function $U[C]$ exhibiting constant elasticity. (Recall that the elasticity of any function $f(x)$ at a point x_0 is defined as $\varepsilon(x_0) = -[f'(x_0)/f(x_0)]x_0$.) A utility function having this property is $U(C) = aC^v$ $(a > 0,$ $1 > v > 0)$. Here $U_C = vaC^{(v-1)}$ (marginal utility of consumption is always positive) and $U_{CC} = (v - 1)vaC^{(v-2)}$ (diminishing marginal utility). The elasticity of utility is $-[U_C/U]C = -[vaC^{(v-1)}/aC^v]C = -v$ (a constant); the elasticity of marginal

† Ramsey actually worked with an integrand of the form $B - U[C(t)]$, where B was defined as the "bliss" level of maximum attainable and sustainable utility. In his formulation, then, one wants to minimize the integral of the difference between actual utility and bliss, and the constant on the right-hand side of (5-7)—and in the verbal statement of the rule—becomes B.

utility is constant also, since $-[U_{CC}/U_C]C = -[(v-1)va C^{(v-2)}/vaC^{(v-1)}]C = 1-v$. Using these specific functional forms for $f(K)$ and $U(C)$, the Euler-Lagrange condition in (5-4) becomes $(v-1)vaC^{(v-2)}\dot{C}/vaC^{(v-1)} = -b$, or

$$\frac{(v-1)\dot{C}}{C} = -b \tag{5-8}$$

or, finally, $\dot{C}/C = b/(1-v)$, suggesting, plausibly, that the optimal relative rate of growth of consumption is a constant, larger for larger b (marginal productivity of capital) and larger also for larger v (recall that the larger the v, the larger the utility associated with a given amount of consumption).

The simple first-order differential equation for the time path of consumption,

$$\dot{C}(t) = \frac{b}{1-v}\,C(t)$$

follows immediately from (5-8), and therefore (App. C, Sec. C-3)

$$C(t) = A_1\,e^{[b/(1-v)]t} \tag{5-9}$$

The time path of capital is given in the fundamental relation $\dot{K}(t) = f[K(t)] - C(t)$, which is now

$$\dot{K}(t) = bK - A_1\,e^{[b/(1-v)]t} \tag{5-10}$$

Considering first the homogeneous part, $\dot{K}(t) = bK(t)$, we have

$$K(t) = A_2\,e^{bt} \tag{5-11}$$

Next, a particular solution to (5-10) is easily shown to be

$$K(t) = \frac{-A_1}{b/(1-v)-b}\,e^{[b/(1-v)]t} \tag{5-12}$$

so that the complete solution is the sum of the solutions in (5-11) and (5-12):

$$K(t) = A_2\,e^{bt} - \frac{A_1}{b/(1-v)-b}\,e^{[b/(1-v)]t} \tag{5-13}$$

and the boundary conditions $K(0) = K_0$ and $K(T) = K_T$ allow determination of A_1 and A_2 in (5-13); $A_1 = [b/(1-v)-b](K_0 e^{bT} - K_T)/(e^{[b/(1-v)]T} - e^{bT})$ and $A_2 = (K_0\,e^{[b/(1-v)]T} - K_T)/(e^{[b/(1-v)]T} - e^{bT})$.

Consider the additional necessary conditions in the calculus of variations approach. The Legendre necessary condition [(3-76) in Chap. 3] $F_{y'y'} \le 0$ for a maximum, clearly holds here in its strengthened (strong inequality) form, since $F_{y'y'}$ in this example is $(\partial/\partial\dot{K})U_{\dot{K}} = (\partial/\partial\dot{K}) - U_C = (-U_{CC})(-1) = U_{CC}$ which has been assumed negative (diminishing marginal utility). The Jacobi condition from (3-91) in Chap. 3 requires the partial derivatives of $K(t)$ with respect to A_1 and A_2, the two constants that emerge in the solution to the Euler-Lagrange condition. From (5-13), these derivatives are $\psi_1 = -\{1/[b/(1-v)-b]\}\,e^{[b/(1-v)]t}$ and $\psi_2 = e^{bt}$. It is easily established that the ratio ψ_2/ψ_1 equals a constant times

$e^{bt[v/(v-1)]}$ and therefore the condition in (3-91) is met. Finally, the Weierstrass necessary condition on the sign of the E function [(3-94) in Chap. 3] is fulfilled since $F_{y'y'} = U_{CC} < 0$ everywhere, by assumption. In fact, the assumption $U_{CC} < 0$ serves to assure the concavity of the integrand, and hence the above necessary conditions for a maximum of the intertemporal utility function are also sufficient.

The problem posed in (5-1) could be approached via the control framework of Chap. 4. There is no particular advantage in doing so, since the problem is straightforward, e.g., since no inequality constraints have been imposed on any of the functions involved. However, more complex problems later in this section will benefit from being cast in the control theory format, so we introduce that approach here.

Rewrite (5-1) as:

$$\text{Maximize} \quad \int_0^T U[C(t)]\, dt$$

where $$K(0) = K_0 \quad \text{and} \quad K(T) = K_T \tag{5-14}$$

and where $$\dot{K}(t) = f[K(t)] - C(t)$$

Then one can pose the problem as: find a control function $C(t)$ so as to maximize the integral in (5-14), given the endpoint conditions on the state variable, $K(t)$, and its movement over time, $\dot{K}(t)$. The general control problem with one state variable and one control variable was given in (4-24) in Chap. 4; it is repeated here:

$$\text{Maximize} \quad I[y, u] = \int_{x_0}^{x_1} F(x, y, u)\, dx$$

where $y(x_0) = y_0, \quad y(x_1) = y_1$ and where $y' = g(x, y, u)$

The correspondence between C and u and between K and y should be clear.

Forming the hamiltonian, $H = F + \lambda g$,

$$H = U[C(t)] + \lambda\{f[K(t)] - C(t)\} \tag{5-15}$$

and the results of Chap. 4—specifically (4-8) through (4-10)—require that

$$\dot{\lambda} = -\frac{\partial H}{\partial K} = -\lambda f'(K) \tag{5-16a}$$

$$\dot{K} = \frac{\partial H}{\partial \lambda} = f[K(t)] - C(t) \tag{5-16b}$$

and that $C(t)$ be chosen so as to maximize H, i.e., so that

$$\frac{\partial H}{\partial C} = U_C - \lambda = 0 \tag{5-16c}$$

The second-order condition for a maximum of H, $\partial^2 H/\partial C^2 = U_{CC} < 0$, is satisfied by assumption (that the utility function exhibits diminishing marginal utility everywhere). Clearly, (5-16*b*) reproduces the state variable differential equation from the problem in (5-14). From (5-16*a*), $\dot{\lambda}/\lambda = -f'(K)$, and from (5-16*c*), $\lambda = U_C$, so that

$$\frac{\dot{U}_C}{U_C} = -f'(K)$$

exactly as in (5-4), from the calculus of variations approach to the problem. In addition, however, the hamiltonian function and the costate variable λ, which appear in the maximum principle approach to the problem, have economic interpretations. The second term in (5-15) is the costate variable at time t multiplied by net investment at t. Since the first term in (5-15) is utility at time t, this suggests that $\lambda(t)$ be viewed as the shadow price (imputed value) in utility terms of an additional unit of investment at t. Thus the sum in (5-15) is the total imputed value of output, in utility terms, at time t. The result in (5-16*c*), $\lambda = U_C$, expresses the optimality requirement that, at time t and measured in utility terms, the shadow price on a unit of investment be equal to the utility arising from a unit of consumption.

Introduction of Discounting

If future utility is discounted, the integrand in the fundamental planning problem (5-1) would be

$$\int_0^T e^{-\delta t} U[C(t)]\, dt$$

where $\delta > 0$ is the discount rate, putting future returns in present-value terms.† Reasoning exactly as above, the first Euler-Lagrange result, parallel to (5-4), is

$$\frac{\dot{U}_C}{U_C} = -[f'(K) - \delta] \tag{5-17}$$

Again assuming $f'(K) = b$ and $U(C) = aC^v$, we now would have $\dot{C}/C = (b - \delta)/(1 - v)$, i.e., the effect of discounting is to reduce the optimal relative growth rate of consumption by an amount equal to δ. Similarly,

$$C(t) = B_1\, e^{[(b-\delta)/(1-v)]t} \tag{5-18}$$

and

$$K(t) = B_2\, e^{bt} - \frac{B_1}{(b-\delta)/(1-v) - b}\, e^{[(b-\delta)/(1-v)]t} \tag{5-19}$$

[Compare (5-9) and (5-13).] Initial and terminal conditions on $K(t)$ allow determination of B_1 and B_2, as before.

† There is a large literature on the appropriateness of a discount rate in intertemporal planning. See, for example, Chakravarty [4, sec. 2.3] or Koopmans [13, especially sec. 7].

Also as before, the problem could be cast in control theory terms: find $C(t)$ so as to

$$\text{Maximize} \int_0^T e^{-\delta t}\, U[C(t)]\, dt$$

where $$K(0) = K_0 \quad \text{and} \quad K(T) = K_T \tag{5-20}$$

and where $$\dot{K}(t) = f[K(t)] - C(t)$$

Formulating the hamiltonian in the usual way, although using q rather than λ to denote the costate variable, and using H_d since this is the discounting case,

$$H_d = e^{-\delta t}\, U[C(t)] + q\{f[K(t)] - C(t)\} \tag{5-21}$$

would lead to

$$\dot{q} = \frac{-\partial H_d}{\partial K} = -\, qf'(K) \tag{5-22a}$$

$$\dot{K} = \frac{\partial H_d}{\partial q} = f[K(t)] - C(t) \tag{5-22b}$$

and $$\frac{\partial H_d}{\partial C} = 0 = e^{-\delta t}\, U_C - q \tag{5-22c}$$

or $q = e^{-\delta t} U_C$. [Again, diminishing marginal utility, $U_{CC} < 0$, assures that (5-22*c*) specifies a maximum and not a minimum of H_d.]

Except for the change from λ to q for the costate variable in the discounting case, the results in (5-22*a*) and (5-22*b*) are the same as (5-16*a*) and (5-16*b*) in the undiscounted case; the difference between (5-22*c*) and (5-16*c*) is of course the discounting term in (5-22*c*). The form of the hamiltonian in this case with discounting, (5-21), appears somewhat asymmetric, when compared with (5-15), above, since utility at each time t is discounted back to $t = 0$ whereas the imputed value of investment [the second term in (5-21)] is not. However, (5-22*c*) suggests that the optimal shadow price on investment at t must equal the *discounted* marginal utility at t. Thus it has become common in the economics literature to interpret q, the costate variable in (5-21) and (5-22), as a *discounted* shadow price, i.e., as if

$$q(t) = e^{-\delta t}\, \lambda(t)$$

In terms, then, of the current, not discounted, shadow price of investment, the hamiltonian is

$$H_d = e^{-\delta t}\big\{U[C(t)] + \lambda\{f[K(t)] - C(t)\}\big\} \tag{5-21$'$}$$

The term in the large curly brackets is the hamiltonian in the undiscounted case, (5-15), which is known as the current-value hamiltonian. Thus

$$H_d = e^{-\delta t} H \tag{5-21$''$}$$

One often finds the standard equations of motion and optimality conditions for the discounted case [the problem in (5-20)] expressed in *current-value* terms, i.e., in terms of λ and H.† Consider (5-22*a*). Since $q = e^{-\delta t}\lambda$, $\dot{q}$ (the left-hand side) is equal to $(d/dt)\,e^{-\delta t}\lambda = -\delta\,e^{-\delta t}\lambda + e^{-\delta t}\dot{\lambda}$; since $H_d = e^{-\delta t}H$, $-\partial H_d/\partial K$ (the right-hand side) is equal to $e^{-\delta t}(-\partial H/\partial K)$. Dividing by $e^{-\delta t}$,

$$\dot{\lambda} = \delta\lambda - \frac{\partial H}{\partial K} \qquad (5\text{-}22a')$$

Recall (5-16*a*) in the undiscounted case, namely, $\dot{\lambda} = -\partial H/\partial K$. Inspection of the respective hamiltonians makes clear that $\partial H_d/\partial q$ is the same as $\partial H/\partial\lambda$, so (5-22*b*) is unaltered:

$$\dot{K} = \frac{\partial H}{\partial \lambda} \qquad (5\text{-}22b')$$

This is the same as (5-16*b*) in the undiscounted case. Finally, $\partial H_d/\partial C = e^{-\delta t}(\partial H/\partial C)$, so that (5-22*c*) becomes

$$e^{-\delta t}(U_C - \lambda) = 0 \qquad (5\text{-}22c')$$

or $\lambda = U_C$, exactly as in (5-16*c*) from the undiscounted case.

As in the undiscounted problem, the basic results from the control theory formulation are the same as those using the calculus of variations. From (5-22*a*′),

$$\dot{\lambda} = \delta\lambda - \lambda f'(K) = \lambda[-f'(K) + \delta]$$

and since $\lambda = U_C$ along an optimal path, this means

$$\frac{\dot{U}_C}{U_C} = -[f'(K) - \delta]$$

exactly as in (5-17), arrived at from the Euler-Lagrange calculus of variations conditions.

Notice that we have ignored an obvious inequality that must hold over any feasible path of consumption or capital accumulation; namely, that $f(K) \geq \dot{K}$, i.e., that $C(t) \geq 0$. From (5-9) and observations on A_1, and since $1 > v > 0$ and $b > 0$, we discover that whether or not $C(t) \geq 0$ depends upon whether or not $K_T \leq K_0\,e^{bT}$, i.e., it depends on the specification of the terminal capital stock. We introduce flexibility in the specification of $K(T)$ and the explicit constraint $C(t) \geq 0$ in the next section.

Depreciation and Population Growth

Suppose now that, although ignoring discounting, we introduce (1) capital depreciation and (2) a growing population. This alters the fundamental macroeconomic

† In addition to facilitating the economic interpretation in many cases, there are rather subtle mathematical advantages to working with current-value functions, e.g., in investigating questions of stability of optimal growth paths via saddle-point characteristics of the hamiltonian. This is dealt with extensively in Cass and Shell [3].

relationships as follows. The fundamental income identity is unchanged: $Y(t) = C(t) + I(t)$. Aggregate output is now an explicit function of both labor input and capital input

$$Y(t) = f[K(t), L(t)]$$

Assuming constant returns to scale in production, and using lower-case letters for per-capita variables,

$$y(t) = f[k(t), 1] = f[k(t)]$$

Aggregate investment at any time t must now cover both net change in the capital stock and replacement of depreciated capital. If μ is the depreciation rate, we have

$$I(t) = \dot{K}(t) + \mu K(t)$$

and, in per-capita terms,

$$i(t) = \frac{\dot{K}(t)}{L(t)} + \mu k(t)$$

Since $\dot{k} = (d/dt)(K/L) = (\dot{K}L - K\dot{L})/L^2 = \dot{K}/L - k(\dot{L}/L)$, we have

$$i(t) = \dot{k}(t) + \left(\mu + \frac{\dot{L}}{L}\right)k(t)$$

Let the population (and labor force) grow at a constant proportional rate n, that is, $\dot{L}/L = n$ [which means that $L(t) = L_0 e^{nt}$, as the reader can verify by straightforward differentiation and substitution]. Then

$$i(t) = \dot{k}(t) + (\mu + n)k(t)$$

and the fundamental income identity, in per-capita terms, is

$$f(k) = y(t) = c(t) + \dot{k}(t) + (\mu + n)k(t)$$

Rearranging, and omitting reference to t,

$$\dot{k} = f(k) - c - (\mu + n)k$$

Therefore, the planning problem may be stated as: find $c(t)$ so as to

$$\text{Maximize} \quad \int_0^T U[c(t)]\, dt$$

where $$\dot{k} = f(k) - c - (\mu + n)k \tag{5-23}$$

and $$k(0) = k_0, \quad k(T) \geq k_T, \quad \text{and} \quad c(t) \geq 0$$

Because of the inequality constraint on $c(t)$ and the initial and terminal conditions on $k(t)$, this is most conveniently viewed as a control problem in which $c(t)$ is the control variable and $k(t)$ is the state variable, as in (5-14) and (5-20), above.

The current-value hamiltonian for this problem is

$$H = U(c) + \lambda[f(k) - c - (\mu + n)k]$$

The equations of motion for k and λ are given as usual by

$$\dot{\lambda} = -H_k = -[f'(k) - (\mu + n)]\lambda \tag{5-24a}$$

and

$$\dot{k} = H_\lambda = f(k) - c - (\mu + n)k \tag{5-24b}$$

(The latter is, as usual, the original differential equation for the state variable.) The boundary conditions for (5-24*b*) are the given initial conditions, $k(0) = k_0$. The boundary conditions for (5-24*a*) come from the transversality requirement that

$$\lambda(T)[k_T - k(T)] = 0 \quad \text{and} \quad \lambda(T) \geq 0$$

[These results are presented in (4-76*a*), (4-76*b*), and (4-76*c*′) in Chap. 4 for the case of a more general and complicated constraint on the control variable.] Finally, it is necessary that, along an optimal path, $c(t)$

$$\underset{c(t)\geq 0}{\text{Maximize}}\ H \tag{5-24c}$$

The inequality constraint on the maximization operation in (5-24*c*) can be handled in either of two ways. The unconstrained maximization can be carried out and the outcome examined to see if the constraint is satisfied, or the general Kuhn-Tucker necessary conditions can be applied from the beginning. Using the former approach, we assume initially an interior maximum, i.e., one at which $c(t) > 0$. Thus we have $H_c = 0$, and, as before,

$$U_c - \lambda = 0 \quad \text{or} \quad \lambda = U_c$$

Also, parallel to the earlier examples, from (5-24*a*),

$$\frac{\dot{U}_c}{U_c} = -[f'(k) - (\mu + n)] \tag{5-25}$$

Recall that this ratio was equal to $-f'(K)$ in the original example, (5-14) (without discounting and not in per-capita terms), and was equal to $-f'(K) + \delta$ in the discounting case, (5-20). The essentials are identical, except that now the rate of population growth and capital depreciation enter into the optimal savings rule, and the results are expressed in per-capita terms.

We continue to assume a utility function for which $U_c > 0$ and $U_{cc} < 0$. In addition, assume the (logical) limiting conditions that

$$\underset{\lim c\to 0}{U_c} = \infty \quad \text{and} \quad \underset{\lim c\to\infty}{U_c} = 0$$

Then it is clear that c will be strictly positive when $U_c = \lambda$, and hence the control variable inequality constraint in (5-24*c*), $c(t) \geq 0$, is satisfied.

Recall the definition of elasticity of marginal utility (now in per-capita terms), $\varepsilon(c) = -(U_{cc}/U_c)c$. Since $\dot{U}_c = (d/dt)U_c = (\partial/\partial c)U_c(dc/dt) = U_{cc}\dot{c}$, we have

$$\frac{\dot{U}_c}{U_c} = \frac{U_{cc}}{U_c}\dot{c} = -\varepsilon(c)\frac{\dot{c}}{c}$$

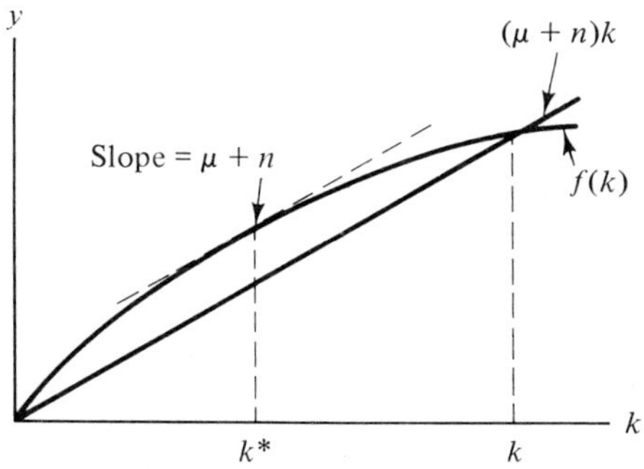

Figure 5-1 Determination of k^*.

and, from (5-25),

$$\dot{c} = \frac{1}{\varepsilon}\left[f'(k) - (\mu + n)\right]c \tag{5-26}$$

This replaces information on the time path of the costate variable, $\lambda(t)$, in (5-24*a*), with information on the time path of the control variable, $c(t)$. In conjunction with (5-24*b*) this constitutes a pair of homogeneous first-order differential equations in the control and state variables, $c(t)$ and $k(t)$.

Being homogeneous, one solution to the equations is $\dot{c}(t) = 0$ and $\dot{k}(t) = 0$. From (5-26), $\dot{c} = 0$ requires $f'(k) = \mu + n$; define k^* as the k for which this equation holds (see Fig. 5-1). Thus, $\dot{c}\{\gtreqless\}\ 0$ as $f'(k)\{\gtreqless\}(\mu + n)$, which means as $k\{\lesseqgtr\}k^*$. From (5-24*b*), with $k = k^*$, $\dot{k} = 0$ requires $c = f(k^*) - (\mu + n)k^*$. Define this as c^*. Thus, $\dot{k}\{\gtreqless\}\ 0$ as $c\{\lesseqgtr\}[f(k) - (\mu + n)k]$. This information allows us to construct a phase diagram (App. C, Sec. C-8) for the two differential equations in (5-24*b*) and (5-26) (see Fig. 5-2). This is clearly the situation in which the equilibrium is a saddle point; the heavy line in Fig. 5-2 denotes the loci of equilibrium initial values of c_0 and k_0. That is, given the initial value $k(0) = k_0$, there is a unique c_0 associated with that value which will lead to the (k^*, c^*) equilibrium values.

Utilizing standard methods for linearization via the Taylor series around the

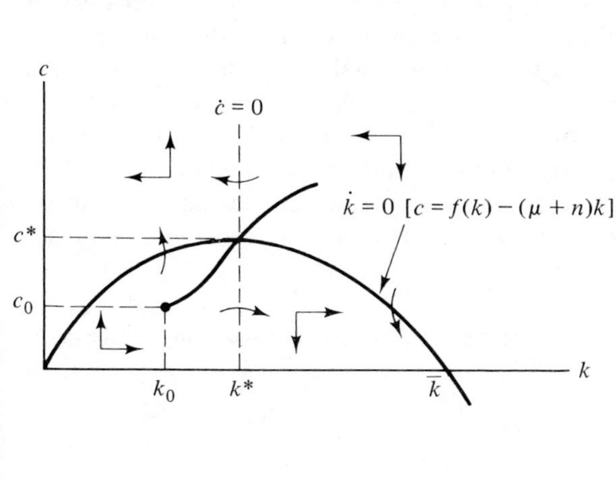

Figure 5-2 Phase diagram for Eqs. (5-24*b*) and (5-26).

equilibrium point (App. C, Sec. C-8), we find that

$$\begin{aligned} \dot{k} &= [f'(k^*) - (\mu + n)](k - k^*) - (c - c^*) \\ &= 0k - c + [c^*] \end{aligned} \tag{5-27}$$

and

$$\begin{aligned} \dot{c} &= \frac{c^*}{\varepsilon}[f''(k^*)](k - k^*) + \frac{1}{\varepsilon}[f'(k^*) - (\mu + n)](c - c^*) \\ &= \frac{c^*}{\varepsilon}[f''(k^*)]k + 0c + \frac{c^*}{\varepsilon}[f''(k^*)]k^* \end{aligned} \tag{5-28}$$

where the final terms on the right-hand sides of both equations are constants. In matrix notation

$$\begin{bmatrix} \dot{k} \\ \dot{c} \end{bmatrix} = \begin{bmatrix} 0 & -1 \\ (c^*/\varepsilon)[f''(k^*)] & 0 \end{bmatrix} \begin{bmatrix} k \\ c \end{bmatrix} + \text{constants} \tag{5-29}$$

and the coefficient matrix for the homogeneous part of the equations fails a basic stability test, since $\operatorname{tr}(A) = 0$, when a necessary requirement for stability is $\operatorname{tr}(A) < 0$. Furthermore, the eigenvalues of A are found from the characteristic equation† $\lambda^2 + (c^*/\varepsilon)f''(k^*) = 0$, as

$$\lambda = \pm\sqrt{-\frac{c^*}{\varepsilon}f''(k^*)}$$

[Since $c^* > 0$, $\varepsilon > 0$, and $f''(k^*) < 0$ (see Fig. 5-1), the expression under the square root sign is strictly positive.] When the eigenvalues of A are real and of opposite sign, the equilibrium of the pair of differential equations is known to be a saddle point (App. C, Sec. C-8).

As a brief digression, we note that the level k^* of capital per worker, namely, the k for which $f'(k) = \mu + n$, associated with maximum consumption per worker, is known as the "golden rule" level. Since the characteristic of the equilibrium at (k^*, c^*) is that k and c are constant ($\dot{k} = 0$ and $\dot{c} = 0$), this equilibrium is known as the "balanced growth path," since it is true that aggregate consumption, capital, and output grow at the same rate along it. This follows since $C = cL$, $K = kL$, and $Y = yL$; given constant c and k and $L(t) = L_0 e^{nt}$, C, K, and Y all grow at the same rate as the labor force n. (This is what makes the growth "balanced.")

The terminal requirement that $k(T) \geq k_T$, which makes itself felt in the terminal condition on the costate variable, $\lambda(T)[k_T - k(T)] = 0$, simply requires that if the final amount of capital exceeds its minimum allowed, then $\lambda(T) = 0$. This primal-dual kind of relation from linear programming (and the lagrangian flavor of the costate variables as they appear in the objective functional) lends support to the interpretation of $\lambda(t)$ as a kind of shadow price on capital formation and specifically

† The notational use of the λ here for eigenvalues should not be confused (or connected) with the $\lambda(t)$ notation for the costate variable in the control theory version of the utility maximization problem.

that this shadow price be zero if there is an "excess" of capital at the terminal time. Generally, of course, k^* and k_T will not be equal, and in particular when $k^* < k_T$, there will be a conflict between following the balanced growth path and satisfying the terminal inequality on capital. In this situation (as opposed, for example, to no terminal capital constraint) a so-called turnpike property of the optimal growth path has been derived. As the time interval $[0, T]$ increases, the optimal time paths of consumption and capital spend "most" of the interval "close" to the balanced growth equilibrium values. Thus, $k(t)$ begins at k_0, moves toward k^*, and stays there until near to the end of the period, when (if necessary) it diverts away in order to satisfy the terminal inequality.

Maximization of the Consumption Stream

Consider, finally, the objective of maximizing total per-capita consumption over the period, i.e., the special case in which $U[c(t)] = c(t)$. Note that $c(t)$, the control variable, has an upper bound of $f[k(t)]$, i.e., of $y(t)$; similarly, $c(t) \geq 0$. (Alternatively, one might specify a positive subsistence level of per-capita consumption, c_s, so that $c(t) \geq c_s$.) The problem is therefore to find $c(t)$ so as to

$$\text{Maximize} \int_0^T c(t)\,dt$$

where
$$\dot{k} = f(k) - c - (\mu + n)k \tag{5-30}$$

and
$$k(0) = k_0, \quad k(T) \geq k_T, \quad \text{and} \quad 0 \leq c(t) \leq f[k(t)]$$

The hamiltonian is

$$\begin{aligned} H &= c + \lambda[f(k) - c - (\mu + n)k] \\ &= (1 - \lambda)c + [\lambda f(k) - \lambda(\mu + n)k] \end{aligned} \tag{5-31}$$

which is a *linear* function of the control variable c; that is, $H_c = 1 - \lambda$. This is a so-called bang-bang control problem (Chap. 4, Sec. 4-5). Thus when $\lambda > 1$, H is maximized by setting c at its minimum value and, when $\lambda < 1$, H is maximized by setting c at its upper limit. From $-H_k = \dot{\lambda}$ and $H_\lambda = \dot{k}$, we have the same differential equations as in the previous case, (5-24*a*,*b*),

$$\dot{\lambda} = -[f'(k) - (\mu + n)]\lambda \tag{5-32}$$

and
$$\dot{k} = f(k) - c - (\mu + n)k \tag{5-33}$$

From the maximization of H with respect to c

$$c^* = \begin{Bmatrix} 0 \\ c(t) \\ f(k) \end{Bmatrix} \quad \text{as} \quad \lambda \begin{Bmatrix} > \\ = \\ < \end{Bmatrix} 1 \tag{5-34}$$

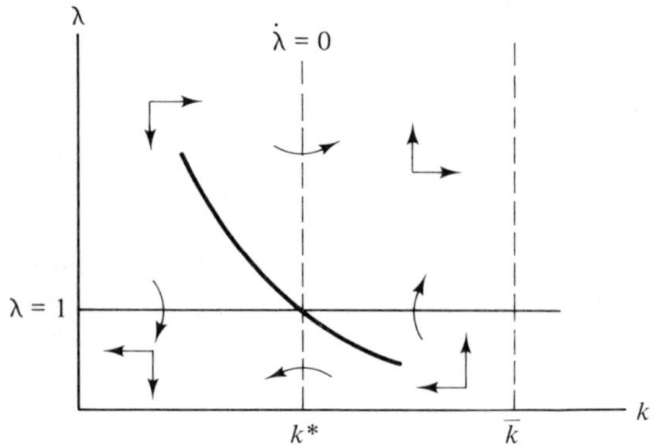

Figure 5-3 Phase diagram for Eqs. (5-32) and (5-33).

The k^* and c^* for an equilibrium solution ($\dot{k} = 0$, $\dot{\lambda} = 0$) would satisfy

$$f'(k^*) = \mu + n$$

$$c^* = f(k^*) - (\mu + n)k^*$$

$$\lambda^* = 1$$

In the (λ, k) phase space of the two differential equations, $\dot{\lambda} = 0$ when $f'(k) = (\mu + n)$, i.e., at $k = k^*$. For $k < k^*$, $f'(k) > (\mu + n)$—see Fig. 5-1—and hence λ decreases, from (5-32). The opposite is true for $k > k^*$. Thus the vertical arrows in Fig. 5-3 are established. When $\lambda < 1$, $c^* = f(k)$ in (5-34) so that, from (5-33), $\dot{k} = -(\mu + n)k$, which is negative. Above $\lambda = 1$, $c^* = 0$ and $\dot{k} = f(k) - (\mu + n)k$, which is positive up to some point $\bar{k}$ (again, see Fig. 5-1). Thus the horizontal arrows are established.

The heavy line denotes the optimal path.† The general nature of the time paths of k and c can be deduced; in particular, we have seen that this is a

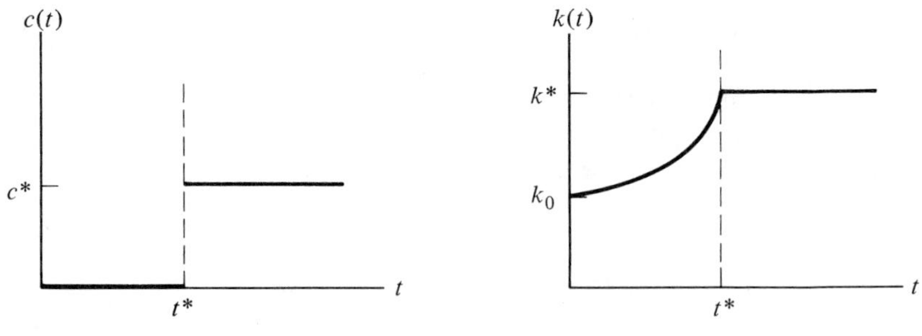

Figure 5-4 Time paths for $c(t)$ and $k(t)$ when $k_0 < k^*$.

† Note that (5-24*b*) and (5-33) for $\dot{k}$ are identical and that (5-26) for $\dot{c}$ and (5-32) for $\dot{\lambda}$ are very similar, except for sign and the constant ε. Thus the two phase diagrams (except for the $\lambda = 1$ line in Fig. 5-3) are constructed similarly and have similar properties. In particular, the equilibrium point is a saddle point in both cases.

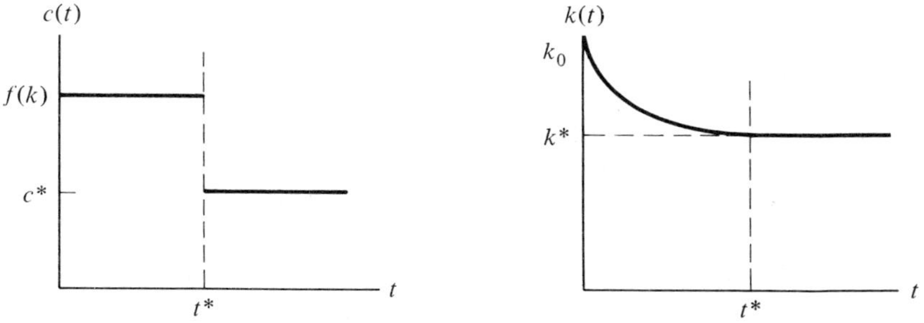

Figure 5-5 Time paths for $c(t)$ and $k(t)$ when $k_0 > k^*$.

problem in which we expect "bang-bang" control. If $k_0 < k^*$, then $\lambda > 1$, so $c(t)$ starts out at $c = 0$, its minimum value, with capital increasing at its maximal rate, $\dot{k} = f(k) - (\mu + n)k$. When $k = k^*$ (at time t^*), $\lambda = 1$ and consumption would switch to the constant level $c^* = f(k^*) - (\mu + n)k^*$ (see Fig. 5-4).

Similarly, if $k_0 > k^*$, $\lambda < 1$ and $c(t)$ begins at $c = f(k)$, its maximum value, remaining there until $k = k^*$ (at $t = t^*$), during which time capital is being used up as quickly as possible; $\dot{k} = -(\mu + n)k$ (see Fig. 5-5). Consider the switching time, t^*, in the case illustrated in Fig. 5-5. When $\lambda < 1$, i.e., when $0 \leq t \leq t^*$, $\dot{k} = -(\mu + n)k$ and hence $k^*(t) = k_0 e^{-(\mu + n)t^*}$. Taking natural logarithms, $-(\mu + n)t^* = \ln(k^*/k_0)$ and so $t^* = -[1/(\mu + n)]\ (\ln k^* - \ln k_0)$. Since $k_0 > k^*$, $(\ln k^* - \ln k_0) < 0$ and the switching time t^* is positive, as it must be.

Again, the turnpike property can be shown to hold, so that for a sufficiently long interval $[0, T]$, k will remain at k^* most of the time and then diverge, to satisfy $k(T) \geq k_T$. Of course, if $k^* \geq k_T$, no change from the horizontal line $k = k^*$ is necessary.

There are a great many variants of optimal economic growth models, and the solutions reflect their particular features. For example, in formulating a model one has to make decisions on (among others):

1. The specification of the utility function. At a minimum, it is both economically reasonable and mathematically helpful to consider a $U(C)$ for which marginal utility is always positive and diminishing, $U_C > 0$, $U_{CC} < 0$. The limiting properties of no added utility when consumption is very large and a very large addition to utility when there is no consumption ($\lim_{C \to \infty} U_C = 0$ and $\lim_{C \to 0} U_C = \infty$) are also reasonable and useful in the case of a nonnegativity constraint on $C(t)$, assuring that the optimal $C(t)$ will always be positive. [Note that the conditions $U_C > 0$ and $U_{CC} < 0$ rule out the bang-bang case just considered, where, in per-capita terms, $U(c) = c$, $U_c = 1$, and $U_{cc} = 0$.] Of course, completely specified time paths for the optimal $C(t)$ are only possible when a particular utility function is assumed, as with the case of $U(C) = aC^v$ ($a > 0$, $1 > v > 0$) in the early parts of this section.
2. The specification of the production function. Again, at a minimum, it is usual and reasonable to assume a function $Y = f(K, L)$, depending on inputs of both

capital and labor, for which the marginal products are positive and also diminishing ($f_K > 0, f_L > 0, f_{KK} < 0, f_{LL} < 0$), and also for which the logical limiting properties are $\lim_{K \to 0} f_K = \infty$, $\lim_{K \to \infty} f_K = 0$, $\lim_{L \to 0} f_L = \infty$, $\lim_{L \to \infty} f_L = 0$, with interpretations very parallel to those for the utility function. When population and hence labor supply is held constant, as in the original Ramsey model, $Y = f(K)$ only. With a growing population, if one assumes constant returns to scale and uses lower-case letters for per-capita variables, $Y = f(K, L) = Lf(K/L, 1) = Lf(k)$ so that $y = f(k)$. Again, it is usual to assume $f'(k) > 0, f''(k) < 0$, $\lim_{k \to 0} f'(k) = \infty$, and $\lim_{k \to \infty} f'(k) = 0$. A more severe assumption about the production function in the constant-population case gave $f'(K) = b > 0$ [from $f(K) = bK$, having positive and constant marginal productivity]. This level of specificity, along with $U(C) = aC^v$, allowed the exact results for $C(t)$ and $K(t)$ in (5-9) and (5-13) or in (5-18) and (5-19), above.

3. Whether or not to include discounting. To a large extent, this is a philosophical question, although Koopmans [13] and others have demonstrated basic logical difficulties that can arise in certain cases in which there is no discounting. Once introduced, one then has the choice of working with present-value (discounted) variables or current-value (undiscounted) ones. The simplest introduction of an $e^{-\delta t}$ term into the objective functional leads to the logical outcome that the optimal relative growth rate of consumption is reduced from that in the undiscounted case by an amount equal to δ, the discount rate; this is shown in (5-17).
4. Whether population and hence labor force should be held constant or be assumed to grow and, if growing, whether it is possible and convenient to express variables in per-capita terms. The usefulness of the latter, in turn, depends to some degree upon whether or not the production function is assumed to exhibit constant returns to scale. When constant returns are assumed, we have seen that the effect of a growing population [where $L(t) = L_0 e^{nt}$] is to alter the optimal rule for the relative growth rate of consumption—now in per-capita terms—by an amount equal to the population growth rate n. This is shown in (5-25), ignoring the depreciation term μ.
5. Whether or not capital depreciation is taken into account and, if so, how. We have seen above that one straightforward method of doing so influences the basic optimality results in a very logical way, through a reduction in the optimal relative growth rate of consumption by an amount equal to the depreciation rate. [This is (5-25), ignoring n, the population growth rate.]
6. Whether the time interval should be finite or infinite. This influences the kinds of restrictions that one establishes for the terminal values of the variables. In the finite-time case, should some non-zero terminal amount of capital be prespecified so as to be available as an initial stock for the next period's planning problem—that is, $K(T) \geq K_T$? If the terminal time is infinitely far into the future, one needs to be concerned with convergence of the integral that is the objective functional and also with limiting forms of terminal transversality conditions.

7. Finally, certain kinds of inequality constraints will suggest a maximum principle as opposed to a calculus of variations approach. In these cases, the hamiltonian function and/or the costate variables may have economic significance in much the same way, for example, that dual variables may have in a linear programming problem.

5-2 OPTIMAL URBAN FORM

Since about 1970 a so-called "new urban economics" has been developing, in which variational methods are applied to the analysis of optimal land use in and around an urban area.† Space (distance), not time, is the independent variable—usually distance from the center of a central business district (CBD). Functions are sought that specify optimal allocations of available land to alternative uses, e.g., transport facilities, housing, at varying distances from the CBD. In this section we illustrate the general approach by presenting one of the earliest of these models, due to Mills and de Ferranti [14]. Later papers have elaborated upon this framework, but the essential ideas remain the same.

A city has a central business district, where production takes place, and a suburban area, devoted to residential use. The urban area (CBD plus suburbs) is essentially circular. There are N workers (households) who work in the CBD, the size of which is specified by its radius ε; both N and ε are exogenous. Distances are measured from the center of the CBD. Land outside the CBD is used for only two purposes: housing and transport facilities (e.g., roadways); denote these as activities 1 and 2, respectively. Since land use may be expected to vary with distance from the CBD, we represent the two land uses as functions of distance u (for $u > \varepsilon$). The amount of land devoted to housing at any distance u outside the CBD is $L_1(u)$ and the amount of land used for transport facilities is $L_2(u)$. Also, at any distance u ($> \varepsilon$) from the center, there are θ rad of land available for these two purposes, where $0 \leq \theta \leq 2\pi$. (When $\theta < 2\pi$, a wedge has been taken out of the otherwise circular city to account for topographical features; this is why the city is "essentially" circular.) Thus

$$L_1(u) + L_2(u) = \theta u \tag{5-35}$$

Housing (per worker) requires a fixed amount of land, so $N(u)$ workers live on the $L_1(u)$ units of land at distance u from the center, where

$$N(u) = aL_1(u) \tag{5-36}$$

(a is the residential density coefficient). Production in the CBD requires that workers travel there from their residences. At any distance (ring) u, the number of travelers (workers) crossing that ring to go to the CBD, $T(u)$, is the number who

† Mills and MacKinnon [15] present an overview and relevant bibliography of the pioneering articles.

live there or beyond, namely,

$$T(u) = \int_u^{\bar{u}} N(\chi)\, d\chi \tag{5-37}$$

where $\bar{u}$ is the radius of the city (to be determined in the overall land-use modeling problem).

There are two kinds of costs considered: travel costs associated with commuting between place of residence and place of work (the CBD) and opportunity costs connected with land use outside the CBD for purposes other than residential or transport facilities. With respect to commuting costs, there is a certain amount of empirical support for a cost function per mile (or whatever the measure of linear distance) for an individual worker of the form

$$p(u) = \bar{p} + \rho_1 \left[\frac{T(u)}{L_2(u)} \right]^{\rho_2} \tag{5-38}$$

where $\bar{p}$ represents travel cost per unit distance when there is no congestion and $[T(u)/L_2(u)]$ is a measure of congestion (travelers at u per unit of transport facility at u). For the entire population of workers, then, total travel cost per mile at u is $p(u)\,T(u)$. The second urban cost is an opportunity cost associated with an alternative land use. Denoting this use as "agriculture," with a per-unit rental of R_A, this cost at each distance u from the center is $R_A \theta u$. Thus the total "cost" of the city is

$$\int_\varepsilon^{\bar{u}} [p(u)T(u) + R_A \theta u]\, du \tag{5-39}$$

and the optimization problem is to select a land-use policy that minimizes (5-39), given (5-38), and subject to (5-35), (5-36) and (5-37). From (5-37) and a fundamental theorem of the calculus [that $(d/dx) \int_a^x f(\chi)\, d\chi = f(x)$ and hence $(d/dx) \int_x^a f(\chi)\, d\chi = -f(x)$]

$$T'(u) = -N(u) \tag{5-40}$$

but from (5-35) and (5-36), (5-40) can be expressed as

$$T'(u) = aL_2(u) - a\theta u \tag{5-41}$$

The problem can therefore be expressed as: find $T(u)$ and $L_2(u)$ so as to

$$\text{Minimize} \quad \int_\varepsilon^{\bar{u}} \left\{ \bar{p}T(u) + \rho_1 \left[\frac{T(u)}{L_2(u)} \right]^{\rho_2} T(u) + R_A \theta u \right\} du$$
$$\text{subject to} \quad T'(u) = aL_2(u) - a\theta u, \text{ with } \bar{u} \text{ unspecified} \tag{5-42}$$

i.e., as a calculus of variations problem with two functions of the independent variable, $T(u)$ and $L_2(u)$, and one differential (equality) constraint. Such problems were investigated in Chap. 3, Sec. 3-3. Forming the lagrangian

$$L = \bar{p}T(u) + \rho_1 \left[\frac{T(u)}{L_2(u)} \right]^{\rho_2} T(u) + R_A \theta u - \lambda(u)[T'(u) - aL_2(u) + a\theta u] \tag{5-43}$$

as in (3-50) of Chap. 3, and applying the Euler-Lagrange equations [(3-51) in Chap. 3] gives, for $T(u)$ and $L_2(u)$, respectively,

$$\bar{p} + \rho_1(1+\rho_2)\left[\frac{T(u)}{L_2(u)}\right]^{\rho_2} + \lambda'(u) = 0 \tag{5-44}$$

$$-\rho_1\rho_2\left[\frac{T(u)}{L_2(u)}\right]^{1+\rho_2} + a\lambda(u) = 0 \tag{5-45}$$

Differentiating (5-45), setting the two expressions for $\lambda'(u)$ equal, and simplifying, leads finally to

$$\frac{d}{du}\frac{T(u)}{L_2(u)} = \frac{-a}{\rho_2} - \frac{a\bar{p}}{\rho_1\rho_2(1+\rho_2)}\left[\frac{T(u)}{L_2(u)}\right]^{-\rho_2} \tag{5-46}$$

In order to simplify the subsequent analysis, it is then assumed that $\bar{p} = 0$, i.e., that there is no cost to travel when there is no congestion.† Thus, from (5-46),

$$\frac{d}{du}\frac{T(u)}{L_2(u)} = \frac{-a}{\rho_2} \tag{5-47}$$

or, integrating,

$$\frac{T(u)}{L_2(u)} = \frac{-a}{\rho_2}u + k_1 \tag{5-48}$$

The next task is determination of the constant term k_1. Differentiation of (5-45), which was necessary in order to arrive at (5-46), loses information, as usual, with respect to constant terms that may be present in $T(u)$ and/or $L_2(u)$. Returning, then, to (5-45), we have

$$\frac{T(u)}{L_2(u)} = \left[\frac{a\lambda(u)}{\rho_1\rho_2}\right]^{1/(1+\rho_2)} \tag{5-49}$$

so that

$$\frac{-a}{\rho_2}u + k_1 = \left[\frac{a\lambda(u)}{\rho_1\rho_2}\right]^{1/(1+\rho_2)} \tag{5-50}$$

There is a transversality condition on the original problem, (5-42), which has not yet been introduced. With the upper limit of integration unspecified, it was shown in Chap. 3 that $(L - [\mathbf{L}_{\dot{\mathbf{Y}}}]\cdot[\dot{\mathbf{Y}}])|_{x=x_1} = 0$ was required. [This is (3-35) in Chap. 3 with F replaced by L, since the problem is a constrained one.] In the present problem, this requirement is

$$[L - (L_{T'})(T') - (L_{L_2'})(L_2')]\,|_{u=\bar{u}} = 0 \tag{5-51}$$

Recalling that $T(\bar{u}) = 0$, this becomes

$$R_A\theta\bar{u} - \lambda(\bar{u})[-aL_2(\bar{u}) + a\theta\bar{u}] = 0 \tag{5-52}$$

† Mills and de Ferranti [14] recognize how extreme this assumption is, but suggest that it at least provides an initial view of the problem.

Equivalently, from (5-41),

$$R_A\theta\bar{u} + \lambda(\bar{u})T'(\bar{u}) = 0 \tag{5-53}$$

or, finally,

$$\lambda(\bar{u}) = \frac{-R_A\theta\bar{u}}{aL_2(\bar{u}) - a\theta\bar{u}} \tag{5-54}$$

From (5-49), $T(u) = [a\lambda(u)/\rho_1\rho_2]^{1/(1+\rho_2)}L_2(u)$; from (5-54), we see that $\lambda(\bar{u}) \neq 0$. Since $T(\bar{u}) = 0$, it follows that $L_2(\bar{u}) = 0$ so that

$$\lambda(\bar{u}) = \frac{R_A}{a}$$

Finally, then, from (5-50), evaluated at $u = \bar{u}$,

$$k_1 = \left[\frac{R_A}{\rho_1\rho_2}\right]^{1/(1+\rho_2)} + \frac{a}{\rho_2}\bar{u}$$

so that the complete solution to (5-47) can be expressed as

$$\frac{T(u)}{L_2(u)} = \frac{a}{\rho_2}(H + \bar{u} - u) \tag{5-55}$$

where $H = (\rho_2/a)(R_A/\rho_1\rho_2)^{1/(1+\rho_2)}$. This suggests, for example, that the optimal amount of congestion, measured by $T(u)/L_2(u)$, decreases in a simple, linear way with distance from the urban center, as measured by u. Furthermore, from (5-55) and (5-41), simple substitution gives the following first-order (nonlinear) differential equation in $T(u)$:

$$T'(u) = \frac{\rho_2}{H + \bar{u} - u}T(u) - a\theta u \tag{5-56}$$

Given the endpoint condition $T(\bar{u}) = 0$, the solution can be found to be†

$$T(u) = \frac{a\theta}{\rho_2 + 1}Q^{-\rho_2}\left(uQ^{\rho_2+1} - \bar{u}H^{\rho_2+1} + \frac{Q^{\rho_2+2} - H^{\rho_2+2}}{\rho_2 + 2}\right) \tag{5-57}$$

where $Q = H + \bar{u} - u$. By substitution, the solution for $L_2(u)$ can also be found; it is

$$L_2(u) = \frac{\theta\rho_2}{\rho_2 + 1}\left[u - \bar{u}\left(\frac{H}{Q}\right)^{\rho_2+1} + \frac{Q - H(H/Q)^{\rho_2+1}}{\rho_2 + 1}\right] \tag{5-58}$$

† The equation is in the form $T'(u) + P(u)T(u) = Q(u)$, where $P(u) = -\rho_2/(H + \bar{u} - u)$ and $Q(u) = -a\theta u$. It can be shown that $\exp\left[\int P(u)\,du\right]$ is an integrating factor for such an equation and that

$$T(u)\exp\left[\int P(u)\,du\right] = \int Q(u)\exp\left[\int P(u)\,du\right]du + C$$

Here $\exp\left[\int P(u)\,du\right] = (H + \bar{u} - u)^{\rho_2}$. Using integration by parts on the right-hand side and utilizing the condition $T(\bar{u}) = 0$ gives the result shown.

From the fact that $T(\varepsilon) = N$—i.e., all workers travel across the boundary of the CBD—it is possible to solve (5-57) for $\bar{u}$ entirely in terms of the parameters of the model.

Thus an optimal city size (geographical) for a given N is established, along with optimal transport investment, $L_2(u)$, throughout the commuting area. Through examination of the derivatives of (5-57) and (5-58), the effects of variations in the parameters of the model can be found and ultimately questions such as the optimal city population size, i.e., optimal N, can be investigated. Further refinements are of course possible; e.g., one can also deal with alternative uses of land in the CBD (allocation of land for transport in the CBD is not dealt with in the original Mills-de Ferranti work) and hence seek to establish an optimal CBD radius, treating ε as a variable and not an exogenous parameter.†

5-3 RESOURCES AND ENVIRONMENTAL MODELING

Just as variational methods are useful for questions of economic growth, i.e., the accumulation of positive factors such as capital stock, they can also be used for studying the accumulation of negative factors, e.g., the build-up of pollution elements. Likewise, these techniques can be used for problems of negative accumulation, e.g., extraction of natural and exhaustible resources. Again, only the basic structures of the problems are sketched, since a great many variations are possible and appear in the literature.‡

Consider the extraction problem. One may have in mind an underground mine, for example, for which the essential question is the optimal rate of mining, where environmental spoilage is not an issue. On the other hand, decisions on the cutting of timber should no doubt take into account the damage (aesthetic and ecologic) caused by denuding of hillsides.

Hotelling [9] posed the mining problem as follows. A mine owner receives a net profit p per unit extracted at any time t, which depends both upon the current rate of production (extraction) and also upon past production. The latter affects both present extraction costs (present depth of the mine) and current demand. Let $y(t)$ be the amount that has been extracted by time t; then $y'(t)$ is the extraction rate at time t. Discounting at the rate δ, the mine owner's discounted total profit from the initial time period is

$$\int_0^\infty e^{-\delta t} p(y, y')y' \, dt$$

† Sheshinski [25] addresses this problem. See also Rothenberg's discussion [21].

‡ Following Ramsey [20] by only three years, Hotelling [9] presented what is generally considered to be the classical article on the economics of exhaustible resources employing calculus of variations techniques. For a thorough overview and extensive bibliography of environmental analyses, largely by economists, see Fisher and Peterson [7]. A variety of models is presented in Schulze [23].

By definition $y(0) = 0$. Assume that there is a finite and known total (remaining) reserve, R, in the mine. Define $t = T$ as the time of exhaustion (to be determined, clearly, by the rate of exploitation); then $y'(t) = 0$ for $t > T$ and the mine owner's problem is to select $y(t)$ so as to

$$\text{Maximize} \quad \int_0^T e^{-\delta t} p(y, y') y'(t)\, dt$$

$$\text{where} \qquad y(0) = 0 \quad \text{and} \quad y(T) = R \tag{5-59}$$

This is a standard free-terminal-time calculus of variations problem (Chap. 3).†

The relevant transversality condition, as in the previous section, is $(F - F_{y'} y')\big|_{t=T} = 0$. Here, since

$$F_{y'} = e^{-\delta t}\left(\frac{\partial p}{\partial y'} y' + p\right)$$

and assuming that $\partial p/\partial y' < 0$ throughout, i.e., that profit decreases with an increasing rate of extraction, the terminal transversality condition

$$e^{-\delta T}\left[\frac{\partial p}{\partial y'}(y')^2\right]\Bigg|_{t=T} = 0$$

translates into the logically appealing requirement that

$$y'(T) = 0 \tag{5-60}$$

The Euler-Lagrange condition is

$$e^{-\delta t}\left(\frac{\partial p}{\partial y} y'\right) - \frac{d}{dt}\left[e^{-\delta t}\left(\frac{\partial p}{\partial y'} y' + p\right)\right] = 0 \tag{5-61}$$

Integrating (5-61) from any time τ to T and multiplying through by $e^{\delta\tau}$, to convert from discounted to "current" values, gives

$$\left(\frac{\partial p}{\partial y'} y' + p\right) = \int_\tau^T e^{-\delta(t-\tau)}\left(\frac{\partial p}{\partial y} y'\right) dt \tag{5-62}$$

The left-hand side is $(\partial/\partial y')(py')$, and recalling that y' is current output, this is marginal (unit) profit at τ. Consider the bracketed term on the right-hand side of (5-62). Since unit profit, p, is a function of y and of y', $dp/dt = (\partial p/\partial y)(dy/dt) + (\partial p/\partial y')(dy'/dt) = (\partial p/\partial y)(y') + (\partial p/\partial y')(y'')$. But $(\partial p/\partial y)$ requires that y' be held constant, i.e., $y'' = 0$. So $(\partial p/\partial y)(y') = dp/dt$ and thus the integral in (5-62) is

† In more complex formulations, exhaustion of capacity might be appended in the form of a standard isoperimetric constraint

$$\int_0^T y'\, dt = R$$

The left-hand side, however, is just $y(T) - y(0)$; hence the constraint is $y(T) - y(0) = R$, and given the initial condition $y(0) = 0$, we have simply that $y(T) = R$.

$\int_\tau^T e^{-\delta(t-\tau)}(dp/dt)\,dt$. Assume, plausibly, that $\partial p/\partial y < 0$; since $y' \geq 0$, then $dp/dt \leq 0$. The right-hand side is thus the discounted (to the "current" τ, not to $t = 0$) stream of future changes (decreases) in unit profits, starting at time τ with an extraction rate of $y'(\tau)$. Thus the Euler-Lagrange rule in (5-62) says that extraction at time τ should be carried on up to the point where the addition to profit at τ from the last unit extracted just equals (in absolute value) the discounted loss in future unit profits caused by adding that final unit to the amount extracted at τ.

Environmental damage, e.g., from strip mining without restoration of the landscape, can be incorporated into such models. Denote by $D(y)$ a "damage function" which depends on the amount of extraction in such a way that both $D'(y)$ and $D''(y)$ are positive. (Damage increases at an increasing rate as y increases.) The objective functional in (5-59) can then be modified to

$$\int_0^T e^{-\delta t}[py' - D(y)]\,dt$$

and optimality conditions derived in the usual way. If the resource is truly exhaustible—i.e., if replacement is not considered a possibility (as with a mine as opposed to a forest)—then $y'(t)$ cannot be negative. Therefore the more modern control theory approaches, allowing explicit consideration of the control variable inequality constraint $y'(t) \geq 0$, should be utilized. Obviously, also, alternative objective functionals can be used, involving utility measures, to better reflect social rather than private benefits and costs.

The pollution-accumulation problem can also be considered in this framework. Let total utility at t depend upon total consumption, $C(t)$, and the total stock of waste or pollution, $P(t)$. Assume that a scarce resource, S, is employed both for production of the consumption good, in amount S_1, and pollution abatement or reduction, in amount S_2. In particular, $C(t) = f_1(S_1)$ and $P(t) = f_2(S_2)$, where $S_1(t) + S_2(t) = S(t)$. Pollution accumulates from the process of production of consumption goods in proportion to the amount of production; it also may disappear naturally (biodegradation) in proportion to the amount of pollution remaining. Thus

$$\dot{P} = \alpha f_1(S_1) - f_2(S_2) - \beta P$$

where α and β are the two proportions.

Thus one can pose the problem: choose a consumption path $C(t)$ so as to

$$\text{Maximize} \quad \int_0^T e^{-\delta t} U(C, P)\,dt$$

$$\begin{aligned} &\text{subject to} && \dot{P} = \alpha f_1(S_1) - f_2(S_2) - \beta P \\ &\text{and} && S_1(t) + S_2(t) = S(t) \\ &\text{where} && C(t) = f_1[S_1(t)] \quad \text{and} \quad P(t) = f_2[S_2(t)] \end{aligned} \tag{5-63}$$

Utilizing the maximum principle approach, the present-value (discounted) hamiltonian† can be written

$$H_d = e^{-\delta t} U(C, P) + q(t)[\alpha f_1(S_1) - f_2(S_2) - \beta P] \tag{5-64}$$

As earlier, letting $q(t) = e^{-\delta t}\lambda(t)$, the corresponding current-value hamiltonian, $H = e^{\delta t} H_d$, is

$$H = U(C, P) + \lambda(t)[\alpha f_1(S_1) - f_2(S_2) - \beta P] \tag{5-65}$$

The equations of motion for the current-value version of the problem with discounted utility were given in (5-22a') and (5-22b'); here these are

$$\dot{\lambda} = -U_P + \lambda\beta + \lambda\delta = -U_P + (\beta + \delta)\lambda \tag{5-66}$$

and

$$\dot{P} = \alpha f_1(S_1) - f_2(S_2) - \beta P \tag{5-67}$$

which, as expected, reproduces the original constraint.

This is a pair of first-order differential equations whose time paths, as usual, can be sketched and the nature of the equilibrium solutions $\dot{\lambda}(t) = 0$ and $\dot{P}(t) = 0$ can be analyzed, depending on assumptions regarding the functions and parameters in (5-63). Finally, the maximum principle requires that $C(t)$ be chosen so as to maximize H, subject to the constraint $S_1 + S_2 = S$. A choice of $C(t)$ is a choice of $S_1(t)$, given the production function $C(t) = f_1[S_1(t)]$. Therefore, formulate a lagrangian

$$L = H - \mu(S_1 + S_2 - S) \tag{5-68}$$

and require that $\partial L/\partial S_1 = 0$, i.e., that

$$U_C \frac{dC}{dS_1} + \lambda\alpha\left(\frac{df_1}{dS_1}\right) - \mu = 0$$

Since $dC/dS_1 = df_1/dS_1$, this is

$$U_C = \frac{\mu}{df_1/dS_1} - \lambda\alpha \tag{5-69}$$

The optimal behavioral result is thus that at each point t resources should go into production of $C(t)$ up to the point where the marginal utility of $C(t)$ equals (1) marginal resource cost, which is μ, the shadow price on the scarce resource, times the resource content of a marginal unit of consumption good, dS_1/df_1, minus (2) the marginal value of pollution, λ, (negative) times the amount of pollution generated by the marginal consumption good, α.

As with previous sections, the models sketched here are meant only to be representative of a large and growing literature. In this case they serve to illustrate some of the ways in which resource and environmental concerns can be approached using the mathematical techniques of the previous chapters. For much more detail, the reader is again referred to Fisher and Peterson [7] or Schulze [23] (each with extensive references).

† Recall the discussion on discounted and current-value hamiltonians in Sec. 5-1, above.

5-4 REGIONAL ALLOCATION OF INVESTMENT

A variation of the problem of optimal economic growth, from Sec. 5-1, considers the question of optimal allocation of investment over time and *among regions* in a national economy. This in fact appears to add a spatial dimension to the problem, but, as will be clear in what follows in this section, space does not enter as an explicit independent variable (as in the optimal urban form models of Sec. 5-2 or, as we will see below, in the space-time models of Sec. 5-5). Pioneering early work is due to Rahman [18]; further elaboration and development can be found in Dorfman [6], Intriligator [11], Ohtsuki [16], Rahman [19], Sakashita [22], and Takayama [26 to 28].

The basic problem is very similar to that discussed in Sec. 5-1, namely, how to decide upon an investment plan over time so as to optimize some target functional for the national economy. Two common objective functionals for this kind of problem are (1) total national income at the end of the planning period and (2) the stream of (possibly discounted) utilities associated with consumption in all regions over the planning period. The fundamental macroeconomic relationships are essentially the same as in Sec. 5-1, except that now we wish to take into explicit account the fact that the status of national income at any time is the composite of *regional* economic activity. Insofar as regions of a nation may differ with respect to such basics as investment productivity and savings rates—as is markedly the case in less-developed countries—a policy question for a central government may be how to channel or allocate investment among the regions over time so as to achieve the national (i.e., aggregate regional) objective.

A two-region example illustrates the fundamental structure of the analysis. Extension to n regions seems to be more cumbersome than instructive.† National income Y at any time t is made up of income generated in region 1 and region 2:

$$Y(t) = Y_1(t) + Y_2(t) \tag{5-70}$$

Suppose that output (income) in region i ($i = 1, 2$) is represented as the product of the regional capital stock K_i and a constant regional output-capital ratio b_i, so that (for $i = 1, 2$) $Y_i = b_i K_i$ and therefore

$$Y(t) = b_1 K_1(t) + b_2 K_2(t) \tag{5-71}$$

Aggregate national investment at any time t is the sum of regional investment which, in each region, equals changes in capital stock in that region, $I_i(t) = \dot{K}_i(t)$, so that

$$I(t) = I_1(t) + I_2(t) = \dot{K}_1(t) + \dot{K}_2(t) \tag{5-72}$$

National saving at any time t is the sum of regional savings amounts, which are represented as the products of each region's income and its (constant) savings ratio

$$S(t) = S_1(t) + S_2(t) = s_1 Y_1(t) + s_2 Y_2(t) \tag{5-73}$$

† See Ohtsuki [16] for the flavor of the n-region case.

From the equality of aggregate savings and investment, (5-72) and (5-73) may be equated, giving

$$\dot{K}_1(t) + \dot{K}_2(t) = s_1 Y_1(t) + s_2 Y_2(t)$$

Since $Y_i = b_i K_i$, and letting $g_i = s_i b_i$ for notational simplicity,

$$I(t) = \dot{K}_1(t) + \dot{K}_2(t) = g_1 K_1(t) + g_2 K_2(t) \tag{5-74}$$

This represents the total amount of investment available nationally at any time t as a function of the two regional capital stocks at that time.

Define $\beta(t)$ as an allocation parameter, representing the *proportion* of total national investment available at time t that is allocated to region 1, so that $1 - \beta(t)$ is the proportion left for region 2 at time t. [In the n-region case at time t, $\beta_1(t)$ is the proportion for region 1, $\beta_2(t)$ for region 2, ..., $\beta_n(t)$ for region n, with $0 \leq \beta_i(t) \leq 1$ $(i = 1, \ldots, n)$, and the added condition that $\sum_{i=1}^{n} \beta_i(t) = 1$.] Therefore, omitting reference to t,

$$I_1 = \dot{K}_1 = \beta(g_1 K_1 + g_2 K_2) \tag{5-75}$$

and

$$I_2 = \dot{K}_2 = (1 - \beta)(g_1 K_1 + g_2 K_2) \tag{5-76}$$

The planning problem is then to choose $\beta(t)$ over a planning period $0 \leq t \leq T$ so as to optimize some measure of national economic welfare, subject to the constraints given in (5-75) and (5-76) and the boundary values on $\beta(t)$. Also, capital stocks in the two regions at the beginning of the planning period, $K_1(0)$ and $K_2(0)$, are given.

A Terminal Objective

Consider the objective of maximum total income at the terminal time.† The problem is then to choose $\beta(t)$ so as to

$$\underset{0 \leq \beta(t) \leq 1}{\text{Maximize}} \quad Y(T) = b_1 K_1(T) + b_2 K_2(T)$$

where

$$K_1(0) = K_{10} \quad \text{and} \quad K_2(0) = K_{20} \tag{5-77}$$

and where

$$\dot{K}_1 = \beta(g_1 K_1 + g_2 K_2)$$

$$\dot{K}_2 = (1 - \beta)(g_1 K_1 + g_2 K_2)$$

This problem has the structure of the control formulation in Chap. 4. In particular, it is in the general Mayer form [see (4-95) in Chap. 4]. Here $K_1(t)$ and $K_2(t)$ are the state variables, $\beta(t)$ is the control variable (which is subject to inequality constraints), and the rates of change of the state variables, $\dot{K}_1$ and $\dot{K}_2$, are simple functions of the control and state variables. Since $K_1(0)$ and $K_2(0)$ are given but $K_1(T)$ and $K_2(T)$ are not, this is a free right-hand boundary problem.

† This is the objective initially proposed by Rahman [18].

In Mayer form, with no integrand in the objective function, the hamiltonian is just

$$H = \lambda_1 \beta(g_1 K_1 + g_2 K_2) + \lambda_2(1 - \beta)(g_1 K_1 + g_2 K_2)$$

or, rearranging,

$$H = [\beta(\lambda_1 - \lambda_2) + \lambda_2](g_1 K_1 + g_2 K_2) \tag{5-78}$$

Standard results for the control formulation specify the dynamics of the state and costate variables [for example, (4-8) and (4-10) in Chap. 4]. Here these equations are

$$\dot{\lambda}_i = -\frac{\partial H}{\partial K_i} = -[\beta(\lambda_1 - \lambda_2) + \lambda_2]g_i \quad i = 1, 2 \tag{5-79a}$$

and

$$\dot{K}_i = \frac{\partial H}{\partial \lambda_i} = \begin{cases} \beta(g_1 K_1 + g_2 K_2) & i = 1 \\ (1 - \beta)(g_1 K_1 + g_2 K_2) & i = 2 \end{cases} \tag{5-79b}$$

As usual, the results in (5-79*b*) reproduce the state variable dynamics from the original problem. The costate variables, λ_1 and λ_2, are governed by (5-79*a*), and in addition are subject to endpoint restrictions that arise from the transversality conditions on the problem. In the present case of a problem in Mayer form with a free right-hand boundary, these are conditions on the λ_i at time $t = T$:

$$\lambda_i(T) = b_i \quad i = 1, 2 \tag{5-80}$$

[recall (4-102) in Chap. 4]. Finally, the maximum principle directs that β be chosen so as to maximize H, subject to $0 \le \beta \le 1$. Since H in (5-78) is a very simple linear function of β, it is clear that this maximization is achieved by setting

$$\beta = \begin{cases} 0 \\ 1 \end{cases} \text{when } (\lambda_1 - \lambda_2) \begin{cases} <0, \text{ that is, } \lambda_1 < \lambda_2 \\ >0, \text{ that is, } \lambda_1 > \lambda_2 \end{cases} \tag{5-81}$$

As expected from the structure of H as a function of β, this is a problem in which there may be "bang-bang" control, i.e., all investment may be allocated to one region for a time and then switched to the other region.

Since the relative sizes of λ_1 and λ_2 govern which boundary value β assumes, it is of interest to explore the behavior of λ_1 and λ_2 over time, as specified by the differential equations in (5-79*a*) and the terminal conditions in (5-80). From the simple structure of the equations in (5-79*a*), it easily follows that $\dot{\lambda}_2/\dot{\lambda}_1 = g_2/g_1$ or

$$\dot{\lambda}_2 = \frac{g_2}{g_1}\dot{\lambda}_1$$

and thus, integrating, that

$$\lambda_2 = \frac{g_2}{g_1}\lambda_1 + c \tag{5-82}$$

From the terminal conditions in (5-80), it is easily established that $c = (g_1 b_2 - g_2 b_1)/g_1$. Ultimately we are interested in conditions under which $\lambda_1 > \lambda_2$ (and hence $\beta = 1$) or $\lambda_1 < \lambda_2$ (and hence $\beta = 0$). As might be expected, this means that the signs of the terms in (5-82) will be important. For this reason, recall that $g_i = s_i b_i$ and rewrite c as

$$c = \frac{b_1 b_2}{g_1}(s_1 - s_2) \tag{5-83}$$

so that, finally, from (5-82) and (5-83),

$$\lambda_2 = \frac{g_2}{g_1}\lambda_1 + \frac{b_1 b_2}{g_1}(s_1 - s_2) \tag{5-84}$$

By definition $b_i > 0$, $s_i > 0$, and hence $g_i > 0$ ($i = 1, 2$). Consider the case for which $g_1 > g_2$. (This is in no way restrictive, since the numbering of the two regions is perfectly arbitrary.) Equation (5-84) is, of course, a linear relation between λ_1 and λ_2 in λ_1,λ_2 space, with a positive slope less than unity and an intercept whose sign depends on the relative sizes of s_1 and s_2. Thus, by making assumptions about the size of s_1 relative to s_2, one can sketch the equation in (5-84).

In addition, only the positive quadrant of λ_1,λ_2 space is relevant. Consider again equations (5-79*a*), assuming now throughout that $g_1 > g_2 > 0$. We examine these equations for the two possible values of β. With $\beta = 0$, the equations in (5-79*a*) become $\dot{\lambda}_1 = -(\lambda_2)g_1$ and $\dot{\lambda}_2 = -(\lambda_2)g_2$. Suppose $\lambda_2 < 0$; then $\dot{\lambda}_1 > 0$ and $\dot{\lambda}_2 > 0$. So, in particular, λ_2 starts negative but is increasing. But as soon as λ_2 reaches 0, $\dot{\lambda}_2 = 0$ and hence λ_2 could never reach $b_2 > 0$ at time T. Thus λ_2 cannot be negative anywhere in $0 \le t \le T$, and in fact $\lambda_2(t) \ge b_2 > 0$. Similarly, since $\dot{\lambda}_1 = -(\lambda_2)g_1$ and $\lambda_2 > 0$ and $g_1 > 0$, $\dot{\lambda}_1 < 0$ and thus, for λ_1 to reach $b_1 > 0$ at $t = T$, $\lambda_1(t) \ge b_1 > 0$. This is the $\beta = 0$ case. On the other hand, with $\beta = 1$, the equations in (5-79*a*) become $\dot{\lambda}_1 = -(\lambda_1)g_1$ and $\dot{\lambda}_2 = -(\lambda_1)g_2$, and a similar analysis applies. In particular, $\lambda_1 < 0$ is impossible for the same kinds of reasons, since $\lambda_1(T) = b_1 > 0$; hence $\lambda_1(t) \ge b_1 > 0$ and from this it also follows that $\lambda_2(t) \ge b_2 > 0$. This concludes the $\beta = 1$ case. Therefore we consider only the positive quadrant of λ_1,λ_2 space and sketch (5-84) for the two cases of $s_1 < s_2$ and $s_1 > s_2$.

Equation (5-84) with $s_1 < s_2$ The line in (5-84) will have a negative intercept on the λ_2 axis, as in Fig. 5-6. Note that the 45° line, along which $\lambda_1 = \lambda_2$, divides the positive quadrant into a $\lambda_1 > \lambda_2$ region where $\beta = 1$ (below the 45° line) and a $\lambda_1 < \lambda_2$ region where $\beta = 0$ (above the 45° line). Rewriting (5-79*a*) as

$$\begin{aligned}\dot{\lambda}_1 &= -[\beta\lambda_1 + (1-\beta)\lambda_2]g_1 \\ \dot{\lambda}_2 &= -[\beta\lambda_1 + (1-\beta)\lambda_2]g_2\end{aligned} \tag{5-79a'}$$

it is clear that for g_1, g_2, λ_1, and λ_2 all positive, and for $\beta = 0$ or 1, both λ_1 and λ_2 *decrease* over time. Therefore, over time, movement along the line in Fig. 5-6 is inward, as indicated by the arrowhead. Finally, straightforward algebra shows

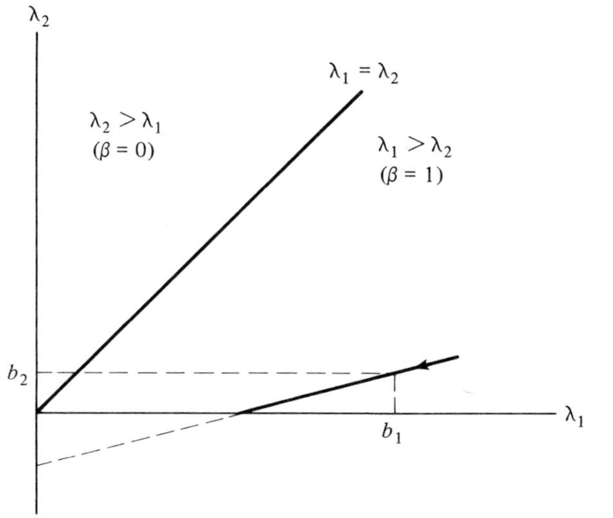

Figure 5-6 Equation (5-84) with $s_1 < s_2$.

that the terminal values of b_1 and b_2 are as shown in the figure.† Thus λ_1 and λ_2 either begin further out on the line and move inward to b_1 and b_2 over time or else they begin exactly at b_1 and b_2 and remain there during the entire interval $0 \le t \le T$. In any event, $\beta = 1$ throughout, meaning that all investment is allocated to region 1 during the entire period. No switching occurs.

Viewing the costate variables as marginal values, in utility terms, of additional investment in each of the two regions, the hamiltonian in this problem has the character of the total utility at any time associated with the allocation of investment between the regions at that time. Thus it is not surprising, in a problem for which $\lambda_1(t) > \lambda_2(t)$ throughout the period $0 \le t \le T$, that investment funds

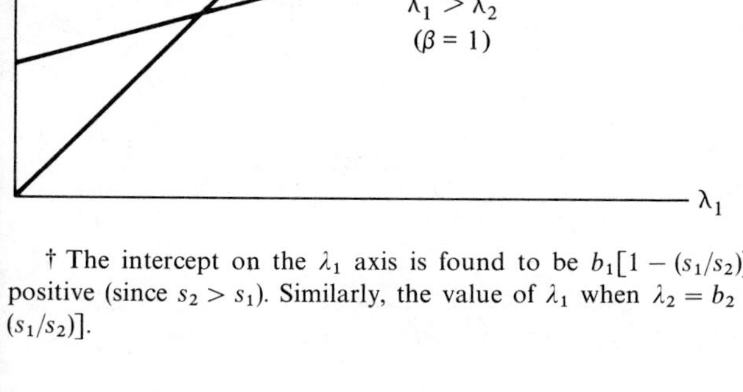

Figure 5-7 Equation (5-84) with $s_1 > s_2$.

† The intercept on the λ_1 axis is found to be $b_1[1 - (s_1/s_2)]$ which is clearly less than b_1 but positive (since $s_2 > s_1$). Similarly, the value of λ_1 when $\lambda_2 = b_2$ is found to be larger than $b_1[1 - (s_1/s_2)]$.

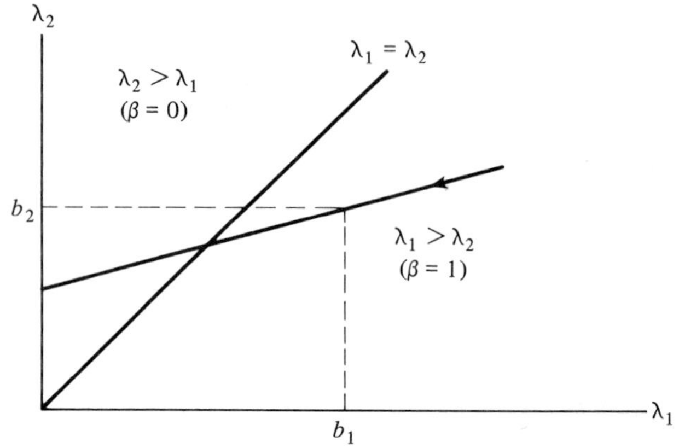

Figure 5-8 Equation (5-84) with $s_1 > s_2$ and $b_1 > b_2$.

are always allocated entirely to region 1. Also, the terminal conditions $\lambda_1(T) = b_1$ and $\lambda_2(T) = b_2$ are consistent with this interpretation of the λ; the investment program should be carried out so that at the end of the planning period the marginal utilities of investment in each region are equal to the productivities of capital in each region, as measured by the regional output-capital ratios.

Equation (5-84) with $s_1 > s_2$ The equation in (5-84) now has a positive intercept on the λ_2 axis, as well as a positive slope less than unity (see Fig. 5-7). Clearly, it is possible that a switch from $\beta = 1$ to $\beta = 0$ will occur. This will depend on b_1 and b_2 and on the initial values of λ_1 and λ_2. If $b_1 > b_2$, the terminal point appears as in Fig. 5-8. Here, as in the previous example, $\beta = 1$ throughout. Investment is always allocated entirely to region 1 and no switch occurs.†

Finally, then, suppose $b_1 < b_2$, as illustrated in Fig. 5-9. Denote by λ_1^* $(= \lambda_2^*)$ the value of λ_1 and λ_2 where a switch occurs, and denote by t^* the switching time. Note that if there is a switch, it can only be from $\beta = 1$ to $\beta = 0$. That is, if λ_1 and λ_2 at the beginning of the planning period are in the $\beta = 0$ area of Fig. 5-9, then there can be no switch and region 2 will receive all investment funds throughout the period. It is therefore of interest to find t^*.

Consider the equation for $\dot{\lambda}_2$ in the period $[t^*, T]$, i.e., in the area for which $\beta = 0$. From (5-79*a*), for $i = 2$,

$$\dot{\lambda}_2 = -g_2 \lambda_2 \tag{5-85}$$

which is a simple first-order linear differential equation whose solution is

$$\lambda_2 = k\, e^{-g_2 t}$$

† This is hardly surprising. Since in this case $s_1 > s_2$ and $b_1 > b_2$, region 1 is clearly more productive, and with an objective of maximum total income at $t = T$, investment would logically always all go to that region.

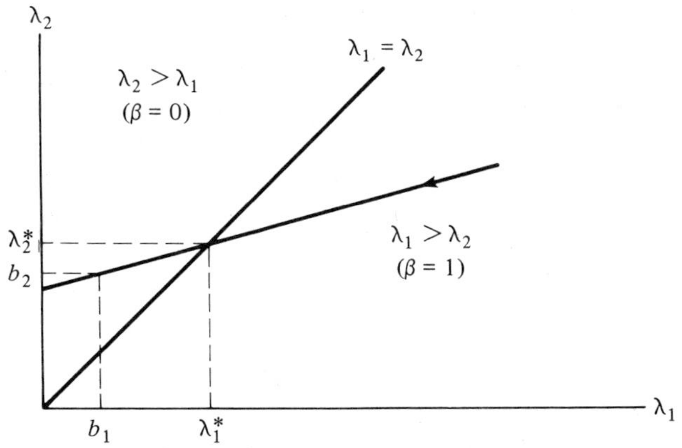

Figure 5-9 Equation (5-84) with $s_1 > s_2$ and $b_1 < b_2$.

Since $\lambda_2(T) = b_2$, the constant is established; $k = b_2\, e^{g_2 T}$ and the complete solution to (5-85) is

$$\lambda_2 = b_2\, e^{g_2(T-t)} \tag{5-86}$$

This describes the dependence of λ_2 on t toward the end of the planning period, i.e., from t^* to T. In particular, at $t = t^*$,

$$\lambda_2^* = b_2\, e^{g_2(T-t^*)} \tag{5-87}$$

From (5-84), at t^*, since $\lambda_1 = \lambda_2$, we have $\lambda_2^* = (g_2/g_1)\lambda_2^* + (b_1 b_2/g_1)(s_1 - s_2)$, or

$$\lambda_2^* = b_1 b_2\, \frac{s_1 - s_2}{g_1 - g_2} \tag{5-88}$$

Therefore, equating the right-hand sides of (5-87) and (5-88),

$$b_2\, e^{g_2(T-t^*)} = b_1 b_2\, \frac{s_1 - s_2}{g_1 - g_2}$$

Using ordinary algebra and taking logarithms (since our interest is in finding an expression for t^*),

$$t^* = T - \frac{1}{g_2} \ln\,(b_1)\, \frac{s_1 - s_2}{g_1 - g_2} \tag{5-89}$$

Thus, if the right-hand side of (5-89) is positive, there is a switch at t^* from $\beta = 1$ to $\beta = 0$. On the other hand, if the parameters of the problem—the b, s, and g—are such that the right-hand side of (5-89) is negative, then the switching time is "before" the beginning of the planning period, which means that λ_1 and λ_2 begin in the $\beta = 0$ area of Fig. 5-9 and decrease to b_1 and b_2, respectively, during the interval $[0, T]$. In that case, no switch occurs and investment is concentrated throughout the period entirely in region 2.

An Alternative Objective: The Discounted Consumption Stream

Instead of concentrating only on income at the terminal time, an objective in national investment allocation policy among regions might be the maximization of a stream (discounted or not) of consumption or of utility from consumption.† We consider here, as an example of this kind of alternative, the discounted stream of total consumption in the two-region economy. Letting δ represent the discount factor, as usual, the discounted stream of consumption over the period is $\int_0^T e^{-\delta t}(c_1 Y_1 + c_2 Y_2)\,dt$ or, since $c_i = (1 - s_i)$ and $Y_i = b_i K_i$,

$$\int_0^T e^{-\delta t}[(1 - s_1)b_1 K_1 + (1 - s_2)b_2 K_2]\,dt$$

The integrand is simply the sum of that amount of total income in each of the two regions at each time t that is not saved but rather consumed, discounted to the start of the planning period, time $t = 0$. The constraints are identical to those in the previous example, (5-77), and therefore the problem is to

$$\underset{0 \le \beta(t) \le 1}{\text{Maximize}} \int_0^T e^{-\delta t}[(1 - s_1)b_1 K_1 + (1 - s_2)b_2 K_2]\,dt$$

where $\quad K_1(0) = K_{10} \quad \text{and} \quad K_2(0) = K_{20} \quad$ (5-90)

and where

$$\dot{K}_1 = \beta(g_1 K_1 + g_2 K_2)$$
$$\dot{K}_2 = (1 - \beta)(g_1 K_1 + g_2 K_2)$$

The current-value hamiltonian for this problem is

$$H = [(1 - s_1)b_1 K_1 + (1 - s_2)b_2 K_2] + \lambda_1 \beta(g_1 K_1 + g_2 K_2) + \lambda_2(1 - \beta)(g_1 K_1 + g_2 K_2)$$

or, rearranging,

$$H = (b_1 K_1 + b_2 K_2) + [\beta(\lambda_1 - \lambda_2) + \lambda_2 - 1](g_1 K_1 + g_2 K_2) \qquad (5\text{-}91)$$

As in the previous case, it is clear that the maximum principle, requiring maximization of H by choice of β, subject to $0 \le \beta \le 1$, will lead to a "bang-bang" kind of control in which

$$\beta = \begin{cases} 0 \\ 1 \end{cases} \text{when } (\lambda_1 - \lambda_2) \begin{cases} <0, \text{ that is, } \lambda_1 < \lambda_2 \\ >0, \text{ that is, } \lambda_1 > \lambda_2 \end{cases} \qquad (5\text{-}92)$$

[See (5-81) for the preceding regional allocation example.]

As usual, equations of motion for the state variables K_1 and K_2 are $\dot{K}_1 = \partial H/\partial \lambda_1$ and $\dot{K}_2 = \partial H/\partial \lambda_2$. [Recall (5-22$b'$), above.] These reproduce the original equations in (5-90), the statement of the problem. For the costate variables in the current-value formulation [see (5-22a'), above], we have

† This is an objective initially proposed by Intriligator [11].

$$\dot{\lambda}_1 = \delta\lambda_1 - \frac{\partial H}{\partial K_1} = \delta\lambda_1 - b_1 - [\beta(\lambda_1 - \lambda_2) + \lambda_2 - 1]g_1$$
$$\dot{\lambda}_2 = \delta\lambda_2 - \frac{\partial H}{\partial K_2} = \delta\lambda_2 - b_2 - [\beta(\lambda_1 - \lambda_2) + \lambda_2 - 1]g_2 \qquad (5\text{-}93)$$

As in the previous example, since β depends on the relative sizes of λ_1 and λ_2, we are interested in the values of these variables over the period $0 \le t \le T$. Unfortunately, and unlike the case represented by (5-79*a*), the equations in (5-93) do not lend themselves to a straightforward solution of the sort developed above in (5-82) through (5-84). (This is because the ratio $\dot{\lambda}_2/\dot{\lambda}_1$ is not, in this case, a simple function of only the parameters of the problem; here λ_2 and λ_1 remain on the right-hand sides of the ratio, unlike the situation in the preceding subsection, where $\dot{\lambda}_2/\dot{\lambda}_1 = g_2/g_1$.)

Note that the transversality conditions on the costate variables in this example are

$$\lambda_1(T) = 0 \quad \text{and} \quad \lambda_2(T) = 0 \qquad (5\text{-}94)$$

This is the usual terminal condition for the free right-hand boundary problem (see Chap. 4, Sec. 4-2). As in the previous example, it is possible here also to show that $\lambda_1(t) > 0$ and $\lambda_2(t) > 0$ for all $0 \le t < T$, for either of the values that β will have, namely, for $\beta = 0$ or for $\beta = 1$.

For example, for $\beta = 1$, from (5-93),

$$\dot{\lambda}_1 = \delta\lambda_1 - b_1 - (\lambda_1 - 1)g_1 = (g_1 - b_1) - (g_1 - \delta)\lambda_1 \qquad (5\text{-}95)$$

By setting the right-hand side of (5-95) equal to zero, we find the value of λ_1 at which $\dot{\lambda}_1 = 0$. Denote this value of λ_1 by λ_1^c; here

$$\lambda_1^c = \frac{g_1 - b_1}{g_1 - \delta} \qquad (5\text{-}96)$$

Since $g_1 = s_1 b_1$ and $0 < s_1 < 1$, $(g_1 - b_1) < 0$. Assume that $g_1 > \delta$; then $\lambda_1^c < 0$. From (5-95), if $\lambda_1 < \lambda_1^c$, then $\dot{\lambda}_1 > 0$ and if $\lambda_1 > \lambda_1^c$, $\dot{\lambda}_1 < 0$, so if the terminal transversality condition on λ_1 in (5-94), $\lambda_1(T) = 0$, is to be met, λ_1 must be strictly positive throughout the period $0 \le t < T$.

For λ_2, when $\beta = 1$, (5-93) requires

$$\dot{\lambda}_2 = \delta\lambda_2 - b_2 - (\lambda_1 - 1)g_2 = (g_2 - b_2) - \lambda_1 g_2 + \delta\lambda_2 \qquad (5\text{-}97)$$

Equating the right-hand side of (5-97) to zero, we find that λ_2^c, the value of λ_2 at which $\dot{\lambda}_2 = 0$, is

$$\lambda_2^c = \frac{(b_2 - g_2) + \lambda_1 g_2}{\delta} \qquad (5\text{-}98)$$

Since $g_2 = s_2 b_2$ and $0 < s_2 < 1$, and since $\lambda_1 > 0$ (as well, of course, as g_2 and δ), $\lambda_2^c > 0$. From (5-97), if $\lambda_2 < \lambda_2^c$, $\dot{\lambda}_2 < 0$ and if $\lambda_2 > \lambda_2^c$, then $\dot{\lambda}_2 > 0$, so for the terminal transversality condition $\lambda_2(T) = 0$ to be met, λ_2 must be strictly positive (but less than λ_2^c) throughout $0 \le t < T$. A similar analysis applies for the $\beta = 0$ case, and there one assumes that $g_2 > \delta$. (With that assumption, and with $g_1 > g_2$, then $g_1 > \delta$ follows.)

Therefore, both λ_1 and λ_2 begin at positive values and decrease over time to $\lambda_1 = 0$ and $\lambda_2 = 0$ at $t = T$. Hence $\dot{\lambda}_1 < 0$ and $\dot{\lambda}_2 < 0$ throughout the entire period. Insight into the relative sizes of λ_1 and λ_2—which continues to be our major interest, because of (5-92)—may therefore come from observations on the behavior of $\dot{\lambda}_1 - \dot{\lambda}_2$ over time. From (5-93), after some algebra, we have

$$\dot{\lambda}_1 - \dot{\lambda}_2 = (\lambda_1 - \lambda_2)\delta - [\beta(\lambda_1 - \lambda_2) + \lambda_2](g_1 - g_2) + C \tag{5-99}$$

where $C = (1 - s_2)b_2 - (1 - s_1)b_1$. Continuing with the assumption that $g_1 > g_2$, we can examine the behavior of the expression in (5-99) under various assumptions about C (as always, $\beta = 0$ or 1 and of course $\delta > 0$).

Case 1: $C = 0$ If $\lambda_1 < \lambda_2$, then, from (5-92), $\beta = 0$ and $\dot{\lambda}_1 - \dot{\lambda}_2 < 0$, that is, $\dot{\lambda}_1 < \dot{\lambda}_2$. But this is impossible, since if $\lambda_1 < \lambda_2$, the requirement that $\lambda_1(T) = 0$ and $\lambda_2(T) = 0$ would make it necessary that λ_2 decrease faster than λ_1, i.e. (since both $\dot{\lambda}_1 < 0$ and $\dot{\lambda}_2 < 0$), that $\dot{\lambda}_2 < \dot{\lambda}_1$. Therefore $\lambda_1 < \lambda_2$ is impossible. Instead, $\lambda_1 > \lambda_2$ and hence for this case $\beta = 1$ throughout.

Case 2: $C < 0$ The analysis is the same as that for Case 1, above; $\lambda_1 < \lambda_2$ leads to a contradiction. Hence $\lambda_1 > \lambda_2$ and $\beta = 1$ throughout.

Case 3: $C > 0$ Here the situation is more complicated, since neither $\lambda_1 < \lambda_2$ or $\lambda_1 > \lambda_2$ leads to a contradiction.

Case 3a: $C > 0$ **and** $\lambda_1 < \lambda_2$ From (5-92), $\beta = 0$ and, from (5-99),

$$\dot{\lambda}_1 - \dot{\lambda}_2 = (\lambda_1 - \lambda_2)\delta - \lambda_2(g_1 - g_2) + C \tag{5-100}$$

Consider the locus in λ_1,λ_2 space of points along which $\dot{\lambda}_1 - \dot{\lambda}_2 = 0$. Setting (5-100) equal to zero, after rearrangement we find

$$\lambda_2 = \frac{\delta}{g_1 - g_2 + \delta}\lambda_1 + \frac{C}{g_1 - g_2 + \delta} \tag{5-101}$$

That is, the curve along which $\dot{\lambda}_1 - \dot{\lambda}_2 = 0$ is a straight line. Since $g_1 > g_2$, the line has a positive slope less than unity and a positive intercept on the vertical axis (see Fig. 5-10). As in the previous example, we are only interested in non-negative λ_1 and λ_2, and so only the positive quadrant of λ_1,λ_2 space is relevant. Figure 5-10 also includes the 45° line, along which $\lambda_1 = \lambda_2$. This line, along with that given by (5-101), divides the figure into four areas.

Above the $\lambda_1 = \lambda_2$ line, $\lambda_1 < \lambda_2$, and below it, $\lambda_1 > \lambda_2$. Similarly, from (5-100), it is easily established that above the $\dot{\lambda}_1 = \dot{\lambda}_2$ line, $\dot{\lambda}_1 < \dot{\lambda}_2$, and below it, $\dot{\lambda}_1 > \dot{\lambda}_2$. Since we are considering the $\lambda_1 < \lambda_2$ case here, these two variables must lie in the area above the 45° line. Moreover, we have seen that with $\lambda_1 < \lambda_2$ and the

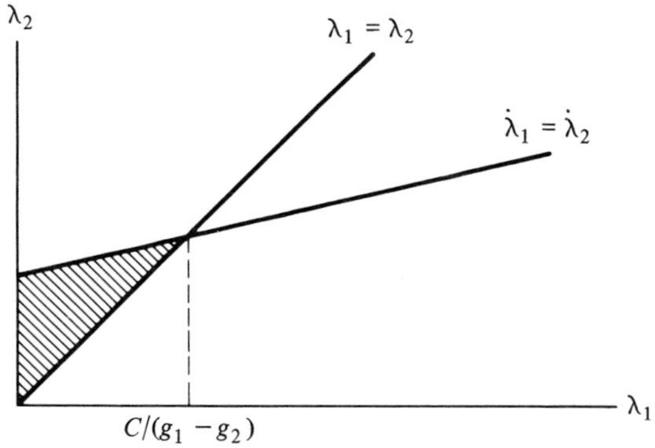

Figure 5-10 Feasible area for λ_1 and λ_2 when $\lambda_1 < \lambda_2$ and $C > 0$.

terminal conditions (5-94), $\dot{\lambda}_1 > \dot{\lambda}_2$. Hence λ_1 and λ_2 must also lie below the $\dot{\lambda}_1 = \dot{\lambda}_2$ line. This feasible area for values of λ_1 and λ_2 in the present case is shaded in Fig. 5-10.

Case 3b: $C > 0$ and $\lambda_1 > \lambda_2$ From (5-92), $\beta = 1$ and from (5-99)

$$\dot{\lambda}_1 - \dot{\lambda}_2 = (\lambda_1 - \lambda_2)\delta - \lambda_1(g_1 - g_2) + C \tag{5-102}$$

The locus of points in this case along which $\dot{\lambda}_1 - \dot{\lambda}_2 = 0$ is found to be

$$\lambda_2 = \frac{-(g_1 - g_2 - \delta)}{\delta}\lambda_1 + \frac{C}{\delta} \tag{5-103}$$

Assume $(g_1 - g_2 - \delta) > 0$ (if this does not hold, only the geometry of the example changes). This is then a straight line in λ_1,λ_2 space with a negative slope and a positive intercept. This is shown in Fig. 5-11, and the feasible area for values of λ_1 and λ_2 is again shaded. Note that the intersection of the two lines in Figs. 5-10 and 5-11 occurs at the same λ_1 value.

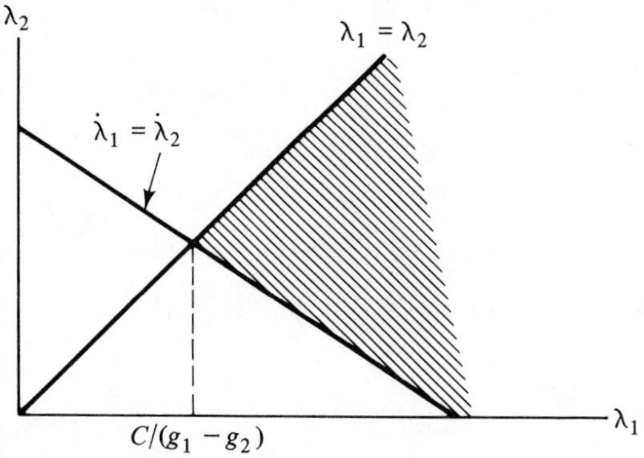

Figure 5-11 Feasible area for λ_1 and λ_2 when $\lambda_1 > \lambda_2$ and $C > 0$.

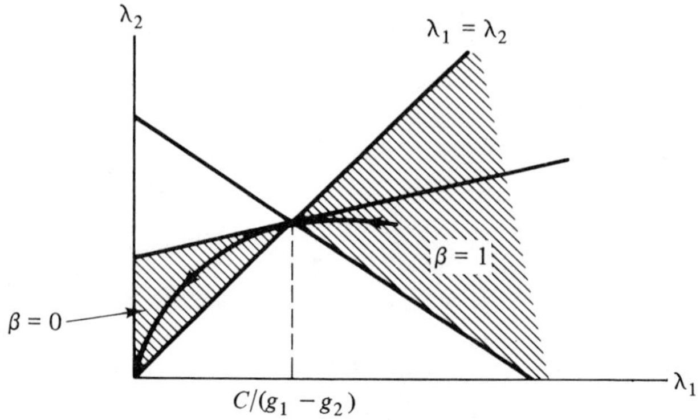

Figure 5-12 Feasible areas and possible trajectory for λ_1 and λ_2 when $C > 0$.

In Fig. 5-12, Figs. 5-10 and 5-11 are combined and a possible trajectory for λ_1 and λ_2 is sketched. As in the problem with the terminal objective, it is now of interest to note that if there is any switch at all, it will be from $\beta = 1$ (allocate all investment to region 1) to $\beta = 0$ (allocate all to region 2). Conversely, if the system begins in the $\beta = 0$ region, no switch can occur. As before, then, the problem of interest is to determine t^*, the switching time, when the trajectory crosses the 45° line. Denote the values of the λ at t^* by λ_1^* and λ_2^*.

To take advantage of the terminal condition $\lambda_2(T) = 0$, consider the equation for $\dot{\lambda}_2$ in the $\beta = 0$ area. From (5-93), this is

$$\dot{\lambda}_2 = \delta\lambda_2 - b_2 - (\lambda_2 - 1)g_2 = -(g_2 - \delta)\lambda_2 + (g_2 - b_2) \qquad (5\text{-}104)$$

[Recall that $(g_2 - \delta)$ is assumed positive.] Regular procedures for this first-order linear nonhomogeneous differential equation (App. C) give, for the homogeneous part,

$$\lambda_2(t) = k\,e^{-(g_2 - \delta)t}$$

and for the nonhomogeneous part

$$\lambda_2 = \frac{g_2 - b_2}{g_2 - \delta}$$

The full solution to (5-104) is therefore

$$\lambda_2(t) = k\,e^{-(g_2 - \delta)t} + \frac{g_2 - b_2}{g_2 - \delta} \qquad (5\text{-}105)$$

Taking into account the terminal condition $\lambda_2(T) = 0$ gives

$$k = -\frac{g_2 - b_2}{g_2 - \delta}\,e^{(g_2 - \delta)T}$$

Therefore, after some algebra, (5-105) becomes

$$\lambda_2(t) = \frac{(1 - s_2)b_2}{g_2 - \delta}(e^{(g_2 - \delta)(T - t)} - 1) \tag{5-106}$$

This represents the dependence of λ_2 on t in the range $t^* \leq t \leq T$.

In particular, from (5-106), at t^*,

$$\lambda_2^* = \frac{(1 - s_2)b_2}{g_2 - \delta}(e^{(g_2 - \delta)(T - t^*)} - 1)$$

But at t^*, we find from Fig. 5-12 that

$$\lambda_2^* = \frac{C}{g_1 - g_2}$$

Thus, equating the right-hand sides of these two expressions for λ_2^*,

$$\frac{C}{g_1 - g_2} = \frac{(1 - s_2)b_2}{g_2 - \delta}(e^{(g_2 - \delta)(T - t^*)} - 1) \tag{5-107}$$

Rewriting,

$$\frac{g_2 - \delta}{(1 - s_2)b_2} \frac{C}{g_1 - g_2} = e^{(g_2 - \delta)(T - t^*)} - 1$$

Denote the left-hand side of this equation, which is a constant, by N. Then, taking natural logarithms,

$$(g_2 - \delta)(T - t^*) = \ln (N + 1)$$

and hence

$$t^* = T - \frac{1}{g_2 - \delta} \ln (N + 1) \tag{5-108}$$

Therefore, if the right-hand side of (5-108) is positive, there is a switch at t^* from $\beta = 1$ to $\beta = 0$. However, if the parameters of the problem—the b, s, g, and δ—are such that the right-hand side of (5-108) is negative, then the system operates entirely in the $\beta = 0$ area, since the switching time is "before" the start of the planning period. Investment would be concentrated entirely in region 2 throughout $[0, T]$. [Recall the discussion of equation (5-89) in the terminal objective problem, above.]

To summarize, for the problem in (5-90), with $g_1 > g_2 > \delta$: (1) if $C \leq 0$, then investment is concentrated in region 1 ($\beta = 1$) throughout the entire planning period and (2) if $C > 0$, either investment will be concentrated in region 2 ($\beta = 0$) throughout, or else it will initially be concentrated in region 1 ($\beta = 1$) and then switch to concentration in region 2 ($\beta = 0$) at time t^*, given in (5-108).

An Alternative Objective: The Undiscounted Consumption Stream

If discounting is inappropriate, the objective functional for the problem in (5-90) becomes:

$$\underset{0 \le \beta(t) \le 1}{\text{Maximize}} \int_0^T [(1 - s_1)b_1 K_1 + (1 - s_2)b_2 K_2]\, dt$$

and the rest of the problem remains the same. As might be expected, the results are very similar to those for the problem in (5-90).† With $g_1 > g_2$, (1) if $C \le 0$, $\beta = 1$ throughout and (2) if $C > 0$, there may be a switch, from $\beta = 1$ to $\beta = 0$. The switching time t^* is given by

$$t^* = T - \frac{1}{g_2} \ln (N' + 1) \tag{5-109}$$

Here $N' = [C/(g_1 - g_2)][g_2/(1 - s_2)b_2]$, which is just N with $\delta = 0$, and the expression in (5-109) is t^* from (5-108) with $\delta = 0$. If the right-hand side of (5-109) is negative, then the system is in the $\beta = 0$ area throughout $[0, T]$.

Clearly there are many directions in which regional allocation of investment models should be extended. Some work has been done for the n-region problem (e.g., Ohtsuki [16]). The constancy of the b and s is a gross oversimplification. The simple objectives in the examples here have ignored any considerations of equity, e.g., of the disparity between incomes in the two regions. The intent, as with previous sections, has been to illustrate the kinds of results that may be expected if dynamic optimization techniques are applied to a particular type of (economic) problem.

5-5 SPACE-TIME MODELS

In a number of papers, Isard and Liossatos have focused attention on processes that evolve both through time (as in economic growth models) and across space (as in urban form models).‡ Simultaneous consideration of a temporal variable and a spatial variable necessarily means that the Euler-Lagrange first-order conditions will assume the form of *partial* differential equations. [Recall the discussion surrounding (2-55) and (2-56) in Chap. 2.] In general, this means that there are even more formidable barriers to numerical solution in specific cases; however, some interesting interpretations of the optimality conditions are possible.

Expanding upon the Ramsey type of framework from Sec. 5-1, we now posit that the various functions have as arguments both time (t), measured along a single axis, from $t = 0$, and space, i.e., location (x), measured along another single

† The interested reader might wish to work through the details as an exercise.

‡ Isard and Liossatos [12] is representative of this work. See also other references by the same authors cited in [12], as well as subsequent articles in later volumes of the *Regional Science Association Papers*.

axis, from $x = 0$. Thus, for example, consumption is now the function $C(x, t)$, depending on both *when* and *where*, relative to an initial time and origin point. Since space is now an explicit feature of the analysis, it is appropriate to expand the fundamental macroeconomic income equation, $Y(t) = C(t) + I(t)$, to incorporate movement over space, i.e., exports and imports. That is, at any space-time point (x, t),

$$Y(x, t) + \text{Imp}(x, t) = C(x, t) + I(x, t) + \text{Exp}(x, t) \tag{5-110}$$

where $\text{Imp}(x, t)$ and $\text{Exp}(x, t)$ are imports and exports, respectively, at point x and at time t. Parallel to the simplest of the Ramsey-type formulations, an optimal capital accumulation function is sought (in the initial version of the problem); therefore "imports" and "exports" are of capital. That is, the temporal and spatial variation of capital stock is examined.

Reasoning as previously, investment is the time rate of change of capital: $I(x, t) = \partial K(x, t)/\partial t$. We can still use the $\dot{K}(x, t)$ notation, realizing however that this now represents a *partial* derivative, since K is a function of both t and x. Further, as before, let the specific production function be $Y(x, t) = f[K(x, t)] = bK(x, t)$ (constant marginal productivity). In the simplest version of these models, imports and exports of capital goods are specified as follows.† In a Δx neighborhood on either side of any point x, it is assumed that imports are a simple linear function of the capital stock already available, or in place, at the import point $(x - \Delta x/2)$, namely, $\text{Imp}(x, t) = \rho K(x - \Delta x/2, t)$, and that exports are very similarly related to the capital stock already available, or in place, at the export point $(x + \Delta x/2)$, namely, $\text{Exp}(x, t) = \rho K(x + \Delta x/2, t)$. [The reason for this particularly simple representation of imports and exports will be apparent in (5-112), below.] Thus, over a small interval, from (5-110),

$$bK(x, t)\Delta x + \rho K\left(x - \frac{\Delta x}{2}, t\right) = C(x, t)\Delta x + \dot{K}(x, t)\Delta x + \rho K\left(x + \frac{\Delta x}{2}, t\right) \tag{5-111}$$

In the limit, as $\Delta x \to 0$ (after division by Δx),

$$C(x, t) = bK(x, t) - \dot{K}(x, t) - \rho \frac{\partial K(x, t)}{\partial x} \tag{5-112}$$

where

$$\frac{\partial K(x, t)}{\partial x} = \lim_{x \to 0} \frac{\left[K\left(x + \frac{\Delta x}{2}, t\right) - K\left(x - \frac{\Delta x}{2}, t\right)\right]}{\Delta x}$$

(Thus the convenience of the particular import and export specifications is clear.) For notational simplicity, following the work of Isard and Liossatos and parallel

† It is assumed that flows of capital are outward (rightward) from the origin (urban center) of the economic region, along the one-dimensional line representing location.

to the convention that $\dot{K}(x, t) \equiv \partial K(x, t)/\partial t$, let

$$\overset{\times}{K}(x, t) = \frac{\partial K(x, t)}{\partial x}$$

Thus

$$C(x, t) = bK(x, t) - \dot{K}(x, t) - \rho \overset{\times}{K}(x, t) \tag{5-113}$$

[Recall the formulation of Sec. 5-1, where $C(t) = bK(t) - \dot{K}(t)$.]

Given a utility function $U[C(x, t)]$ and assuming an outer limit of both spatial and temporal interest—denoted by X and T, respectively—the planning problem could be posed as: find $K(x, t)$ so as to

$$\text{Maximize} \quad \int_0^X \int_0^T U[C(x, t)]\, dx\, dt$$

$$\text{where} \quad C(x, t) = bK(x, t) - \dot{K}(x, t) - \rho \overset{\times}{K}(x, t) \tag{5-114}$$

[Compare (5-1), above. For the moment we ignore endpoint conditions.] This problem has the structure of (2-55) in Chap. 2, which was: find $y(x_1, x_2)$ so as to

$$\text{Maximize} \quad \int_{x_{10}}^{x_{11}} \int_{x_{20}}^{x_{21}} F\left(x_1, x_2, y, \frac{\partial y}{\partial x_1}, \frac{\partial y}{\partial x_2}\right) dx_1\, dx_2 \tag{5-115}$$

where, clearly, in the present problem $x_1 = x$, $x_2 = t$, $y = K$, etc. Parallel to the general Euler-Lagrange result [(2-56) in Chap. 2],

$$F_y - \frac{\partial}{\partial x_1} F_{y_{x_1}} - \frac{\partial}{\partial x_2} F_{y_{x_2}} = 0 \tag{5-116}$$

we have as a necessary condition for an optimal function $K(x, t)$ the requirement that

$$U_K - \frac{\partial}{\partial x} \frac{\partial U}{\partial \overset{\times}{K}} - \frac{\partial}{\partial t} \frac{\partial U}{\partial \dot{K}} = 0 \tag{5-117}$$

Here $U_K = (\partial U/\partial C)(\partial C/\partial K) = (U_C)(b)$, $\partial U/\partial \overset{\times}{K} = (\partial U/\partial C)(\partial C/\partial \overset{\times}{K}) = (U_C)(-\rho)$, and $\partial U/\partial \dot{K} = (\partial U/\partial C)(\partial C/\partial \dot{K}) = (U_C)(-1)$. Thus, (5-117) requires that

$$bU_C = -\dot{U}_C - \rho \overset{\times}{U}_C \tag{5-118}$$

[Compare (5-4), above, recalling that here $f'(K) = b$, and spatial considerations have added the term $-\rho \overset{\times}{U}_C$.]

Interpretation of a partial differential equation such as (5-118) is generally not very straightforward. Isard and Liossatos suggest the following. Multiplying both sides of (5-118) by $d\tau$ and then integrating from t to T and rearranging, we have

$$U_C(x, t) - \rho \int_t^T \overset{\times}{U}_C(x, \tau)\, d\tau = \int_t^T bU_C(x, \tau)\, d\tau + U_C(x, T) \tag{5-119}$$

The interpretation of this necessary condition for an optimal $K(x, t)$ is that investment in capital at any point (x, t) should proceed to the point where there is equality between (1) the left-hand side of (5-119) which is: (*a*) the marginal utility lost because of not consuming the last unit (which was instead invested as capital), $U_C(x, t)$, less (*b*) the gain in utility from the added unit of capital put in place at time t, over the entire planning horizon from t onward, $\rho \int_t^T \overset{\times}{U}_C(x, \tau)\, d\tau$; and (2) the right-hand side of (5-119) which is: (*a*) the gain in utility from t onward resulting from the productive use of the added unit of capital, $\int_t^T bU_C(x, \tau)\, d\tau$, plus (*b*) the "scrap value" or utility at the end of the planning period associated with not having to divert consumption goods then in order to generate a unit of capital then. Thus capital investment at (x, t) should proceed until net utility loss associated with the last unit equals net utility gain.

The actual solution function, $K(x, t)$, must be established by (1) finding a solution $C(x, t)$ for (5-118) and then (2) putting this result into (5-113). Clearly, in general, neither of these steps is likely to be easy because of the partial nature of the differential equations; of course, they depend on the form of the utility function that is assumed. Using $U(C) = C^\alpha$ $(0 < \alpha < 1)$, along with some reasonable boundary conditions, Isard and Liossatos show (the derivation is an involved one) that a general solution to (5-118) is

$$C(x, t) = \begin{cases} C(x - \rho t, 0)\, e^{[b/(1-\alpha)]t} & \text{for } x - \rho t > 0 \\ C(0, t - x/\rho)\, e^{[b/(1-\alpha)\rho]x} & \text{for } x - \rho t < 0 \end{cases} \tag{5-120}$$

which requires the "initial values," $C(x, 0)$ and $C(0, t)$. Finally, further manipulation, via (5-113), leads to specification of $K(x, t)$ as a function of the same parameters α, b, and ρ.

As an expansion upon the above analysis, account is taken of the fact that goods for consumption purposes (as well as for capital purposes) must move over space to satisfy demand and such movement over space incurs transport costs. Letting $V(x, t)$ denote the flow of consumption goods per unit of time through the space-time point (x, t) and reasoning as before for capital movement, $V(x - \Delta x/2, t)$ represents imports and $V(x + \Delta x/2, t)$ represents exports of consumption goods at (x, t). Further, let transport cost be represented in physical terms by $\sigma V(x, t)$, where σ represents the rate per unit length of consumption goods used up in transport. Thus, (5-111) is modified as follows. To the left-hand side, the imported supply $V(x - \Delta x/2, t)$ is added; to the right-hand side, the exported amount $V(x + \Delta x/2, t)$ is added as well as the demand incurred (goods used up) by transport, $\sigma V(x, t)\Delta x$. Division by Δx, taking limits [letting $\overset{\times}{V}(x, t) \equiv \partial V(x, t)/\partial x$] and rearranging, leads to

$$C(x, t) = bK(x, t) - \dot{K}(x, t) - \rho \overset{\times}{K}(x, t) - \overset{\times}{V}(x, t) - \sigma V(x, t) \tag{5-121}$$

[Compare (5-113).] The welfare-maximization problem now becomes: find $K(x, t)$

and $V(x, t)$ so as to

$$\text{Maximize} \quad \int_0^X \int_0^T U[C(x, t)]\, dx\, dt$$

where $\qquad C(x, t)$ is defined as in (5-121) $\qquad$ (5-122)

Since two functions, K and V, of two independent variables, x and t, are sought, the approach requires a combination of that for several functions† and that for several independent variables.‡ Specifically, we want to find $y_1(x_1, x_2)$ and $y_2(x_1, x_2)$ so as to

$$\text{Maximize} \quad \int_{x_{10}}^{x_{11}} \int_{x_{20}}^{x_{21}} F\left(x_1, x_2, y_1, y_2, \frac{\partial y_1}{\partial x_1}, \frac{\partial y_1}{\partial x_2}, \frac{\partial y_2}{\partial x_1}, \frac{\partial y_2}{\partial x_2}\right) dx_1\, dx_2 \qquad (5\text{-}123)$$

where in the present problem $x_1 = x$, $x_2 = t$, $y_1 = K$, $y_2 = V$, etc. [Compare (5-115).] For this problem, the Euler-Lagrange results require

$$F_{y_i} - \frac{\partial}{\partial x_1} F_{y_{ix_1}} - \frac{\partial}{\partial x_2} F_{y_{ix_2}} = 0 \quad \text{for } i = 1, 2 \qquad (5\text{-}124)$$

where $y_{ix_1} = \partial y_i / \partial x_1$ and $F_{y_{ix_1}} = \partial F / \partial y_{ix_1}$, etc. [Compare (5-116).]

For $y_1 = K$, the requirements in (5-124) are precisely those from the previous example, namely,

$$bU_C = -\dot{U}_C - \rho \overset{\times}{U}_C \qquad (5\text{-}125)$$

[This was (5-118), above.] For $y_2 = V$, (5-124) requires

$$U_V - \frac{\partial}{\partial x} \frac{\partial U}{\partial \overset{\times}{V}} - \frac{\partial}{\partial t} \frac{\partial U}{\partial \dot{V}} = 0 \qquad (5\text{-}126)$$

Here $U_V = (\partial U/\partial C)(\partial C/\partial V) = (U_C)(-\sigma)$, $\partial U/\partial \overset{\times}{V} = (\partial U/\partial C)(\partial C/\partial \overset{\times}{V}) = (U_C)(-1)$ and $\partial U/\partial \dot{V} = (\partial U/\partial C)(\partial C/\partial \dot{V}) = (U_C)(0) = 0$. Thus (5-126) becomes

$$\sigma U_C = \overset{\times}{U}_C \qquad (5\text{-}127)$$

Interpreting (5-127) in a manner similar to (5-118) in (5-119) requires multiplication of both sides by dx and then integration over an interval:

$$\int_{x_1}^{x_2} \sigma U_C\, dx = U_C(x_2, t) - U_C(x_1, t) \qquad (5\text{-}128)$$

The left-hand side represents the value of goods used up in transporting a unit of consumption good from x_1 to x_2, i.e., the transport cost, and the right-hand side is the difference in the marginal (welfare) value of a consumption good at

† The problem was illustrated in (2-48) or (2-49) of Chap. 2; the Euler-Lagrange conditions are given in (2-50) of that chapter.

‡ As illustrated in (2-55) of Chap. 2; the Euler-Lagrange conditions are given in (2-56) of that chapter.

x_2 and at x_1, i.e., the net marginal value of moving a consumption good from x_1 to x_2. Thus, consumption goods should be arranged over space so that the difference in value of having a consumption good at any two places is equal to the cost of transportation between those two places. Put loosely, for a consumption good, the value there less the value here should equal the cost of getting it from here to there. This is a "dynamic" version of the familiar transportation principle from location theory as demonstrated, for example, in the primal-dual optimality conditions from the linear programming transportation model.

Similarly to the integrated form of (5-125) from the first example, substitution from (5-127) for $\overset{\times}{U}_C$ into (5-125) gives

$$(b + \sigma\rho)U_C = -\dot{U}_C \tag{5-129}$$

Multiplying both sides by dt and integrating between t_1 and t_2 gives

$$\int_{t_1}^{t_2} (b + \sigma\rho)U_C \, dt = U_C(x, t_1) - U_C(x, t_2) \tag{5-130}$$

The left-hand side represents the gain over the period $[t_1, t_2]$ of having a unit of output as capital, not for consumption: bU_C measures the unit contribution to productive capacity and $\sigma\rho U_C$ represents the transport cost savings per unit of consumption good not transported. The right-hand side of (5-130) is the difference in the marginal (welfare) value of a unit for consumption at t_2 and t_1. Thus, investment in capital goods should be carried out over time so that the loss in utility associated with not having a consumption good between two time periods is equal to the utility of the gain, over that period, in capacity to produce consumption goods. Again, put loosely, the utility now less the utility then should be equal to the utility gained by waiting from now until then.

The similarity in the two optimality principles, (5-128) and (5-130), has led Isard and Liossatos to the term "transfer principle" to describe both, one for movement over time, (5-130), and one for movement across space, (5-128). Noting that

$$U_C(x_1, t_1) - U_C(x_2, t_2) = U_C(x_1, t_1) + U_C(x_2, t_1) - U_C(x_2, t_1) - U_C(x_2, t_2) \tag{5-131}$$

and substituting from (5-128) and (5-130), we have

$$U_C(x_1, t_1) - U_C(x_2, t_2) = -\int_{x_1}^{x_2} \sigma U_C(x, t_1)\, dx + \int_{t_1}^{t_2} (b + \sigma\rho)U_C(x_2, t)\, dt \tag{5-132}$$

which generalizes the previous interpretations of (5-128) and (5-130) to movement across both time and space. Considering the removal of a good from consumption at (x_1, t_1), either shipping it elsewhere or embodying it instead in capital for later consumption, or both, the optimality criterion is that the difference in value of the good at the two space-time points must equal the total net sum of benefits (from capital productivity gain over time) and costs (from transport over space).

Actual solutions, i.e., optimal functions $K(x, t)$ and $V(x, t)$, are not so easily found, even though consideration of (5-127) and (5-129)—and recollection of the procedure for derivatives of exponential functions—suggests a solution of the form

$$U_C(x, t) = U_C(0, 0)\, e^{[\sigma x - (b + \sigma\rho)t]} \tag{5-133}$$

Again, if one takes $U(C) = C^\alpha$, then straightforward differentiation and rearrangement [taking the $(\alpha - 1)$th root] gives

$$C(x, t) = C(0, 0)\, e^{[1/(\alpha - 1)][\sigma x - (b + \sigma\rho)t]} \tag{5-134}$$

which depends, as usual, on the specification of initial conditions $C(0, 0)$.

REFERENCES

1. Arrow, K. J., and M. Kurz: "Public Investment, the Rate of Return, and Optimal Fiscal Policy," Johns Hopkins Press for Resources for the Future, Baltimore, 1970. The application of maximum principle results to problems of optimal economic growth is begun in chap. III and continues throughout the book.
2. Burmeister, E., and A. R. Dobell: "Mathematical Theories of Economic Growth," Macmillan, New York, 1970. Optimal economic growth models, utilizing both the calculus of variations and maximum principle approaches, are presented in chap. 11.
3. Cass, D., and K. Shell (eds.): "The Hamiltonian Approach to Dynamic Economics," Academic Press, New York, 1976. This collection of papers represents the forefront of work in the application of control theory results to problems in economic theory; very advanced mathematical level.
4. Chakravarty, S.: "Capital and Development Planning," MIT Press, Cambridge, Mass., 1969. The basic concern of the entire book is application of variational methods to problems of economic growth and planning.
5. Dorfman, R.: An Economic Interpretation of Optimal Control Theory, *American Economic Review*, vol. 59, pp. 817–831, December, 1969. An extremely readable account of the basic results of the maximum principle, with economic parallels and interpretations of costate variables.
6. ———: Regional Allocation of Investment: Comment, *Quarterly Journal of Economics*, vol. 77, pp. 162–165, February, 1963. A very straightforward demonstration of the difference between an optimal investment program for one twenty-year period and a sequence of four optimal five-year plans.
7. Fisher, A. C., and F. M. Peterson: The Environment in Economics: A Survey, *Journal of Economic Literature*, vol. 14, pp. 1–33, March, 1976. A very readable overview of approaches to modeling environmental phenomena in economics.
8. Hadley, G., and M. C. Kemp: "Variational Methods in Economics," American Elsevier, New York, 1971. A very complete and mathematically advanced discussion of calculus of variations and maximum principle techniques and their use in economic growth models. Such models are the subject matter of chaps. 1 and 6, but illustrative applications are discussed throughout the other chapters as well.
9. Hotelling, H.: The Economics of Exhaustible Resources, *Journal of Political Economy*, vol. 39, pp. 137–175, April, 1931. The classic article applying dynamic optimization techniques to problems of resource depletion.
10. Intriligator, M. D.: "Mathematical Optimization and Economic Theory," Prentice-Hall, Englewood Cliffs, N.J., 1971. The application of dynamic optimization techniques to problems of optimal economic growth is the subject matter of pt. V (chap. 16).
11. ———: Regional Allocation of Investment: Comment, *Quarterly Journal of Economics*, vol. 78, pp. 659–662, November, 1964. A reformulation of the original Rahman article in terms of calculus of variations results.

12. Isard, W., and P. Liossatos: Space-Time Development and a General Transfer Principle, *Papers, Regional Science Association*, vol. 30, pp. 17–38, 1973. A representative article in a series of investigations by these authors on applications and interpretations of variational methods to spatial (and temporal) questions; advanced mathematics and notation.
13. Koopmans, T. C.: On the Concept of Optimal Economic Growth, in *Study Week on the Econometric Approach to Development Planning*, October 7–13, 1963, North-Holland, Amsterdam, and Rand-McNally, Chicago, 1965, pp. 225–287. Contains a discussion of the mathematical and philosophical implications of a discounting term in the objective functional.
14. Mills, E. S., and D. M. de Ferranti: Market Choices and Optimum City Size, *American Economic Review*, vol. 61, pp. 340–345, May, 1971. A pioneering article in the study of urban form via variational methods.
15. ———, and J. MacKinnon: Notes on the New Urban Economics, *Bell Journal of Economics and Management Science*, vol. 4, pp. 593–601, Autumn, 1973. An introduction to and summary of the current work in modeling optimal urban land use.
16. Ohtsuki, Y.: Regional Allocation of Investment in an n-Region Economy, *Journal of Regional Science*, vol. 11, pp. 225–233, August, 1971. An extension to more than two regions of the Rahman-Intriligator-Takayama regional allocation of investment model.
17. Phelps, E.: "Golden Rules of Economic Growth," Norton, New York, 1966. An introduction to the area of optimal economic growth models.
18. Rahman, M. A.: Regional Allocation of Investment, *Quarterly Journal of Economics*, vol. 77, pp. 26–39, February, 1963. The original article in a series on regional allocation of investment; variational methods are not utilized here.
19. ———: Regional Allocation of Investment: The Continuous Version, *Quarterly Journal of Economics*, vol. 80, pp. 159–160, February, 1966. A correction and extension of the Intriligator formulation of the regional allocation of investment model, using variational techniques.
20. Ramsey, F. P.: A Mathematical Theory of Saving, *Economic Journal*, vol. 38, pp. 543–559, December, 1928. The classic article applying calculus of variations techniques to a problem of optimal economic planning over time.
21. Rothenberg, J.: Discussion of "Congestion and the Optimum City Size," *American Economic Review*, vol. 63, pp. 67–69, May, 1973. Comments on some of the problems with assumptions made by Sheshinski in a paper that extends the Mills and de Ferranti analysis.
22. Sakashita, N.: Regional Allocation of Public Investment, *Papers, Regional Science Association*, vol. 19, pp. 161–182, 1967. An extension of the basic model of regional allocation of investment to include public as well as private investment decisions.
23. Schulze, W. D.: The Optimal Use of Non-Renewable Resources, *Journal of Environmental Economics and Management*, vol. 1, pp. 53–73, May, 1974. Presents a variety of models for resource depletion using variational techniques.
24. Shell, K. (ed.): "Essays on the Theory of Optimal Economic Growth," MIT Press, Cambridge, Mass., 1967. An early collection of papers treating the problem of optimal economic growth largely by variational techniques. Contains many examples of the use of phase diagrams.
25. Sheshinski, E.: Congestion and the Optimum City Size, *American Economic Review*, vol. 63, pp. 61–66, May, 1973. Extends the original Mills and de Ferranti article; determines the optimal CBD radius.
26. Takayama, A.: Regional Allocation of Investment: A Further Analysis, *Quarterly Journal of Economics*, vol. 81, pp. 330–337, May, 1967. Extension and correction of the Intriligator and Rahman versions of the regional allocation of investment model.
27. ———: Regional Allocation of Investment: Corrigendum, *Quarterly Journal of Economics*, vol. 82, pp. 526–527, August, 1968. Correction of some of the mathematical analysis in Takayama [26].
28. ———: "Mathematical Economics," Dryden Press, Hinsdale, Ill., 1974. Chapter 8, sec. B summarizes the entire discussion of regional allocation of investment modeling using variational methods. It covers, in particular, references [11], [18], [26], and [27].

APPENDIX

A

INTEGRAL CALCULUS

Two of the distinguishing mathematical characteristics of the problems that are examined in this book are (1) that the objective is maximization or minimization of an integral and (2) that the constraints consist (sometimes exclusively) of differential equations. In this appendix we review, very quickly, the rudiments of integration and in App. C we take up differential (and difference) equations in more detail. It is expected that the reader is at least familiar with the fundamentals of differential calculus, including the rules for finding derivatives of common functions.

A-1 DIFFERENTIATION AND INTEGRATION

The Indefinite Integral

In differential calculus, we find derivatives of functions, employing rules that are derived from the basic "delta process" in which the difference in the value of $y = f(x)$ at x_0 and at $x_0 + \Delta x$ is "averaged" by division by Δx and then the limit as $\Delta x \to 0$ is examined. For continuous and smooth functions, the derivative exists everywhere and so for any x_0 in the interval over which $f(x)$ is defined we obtain $\Delta y/\Delta x = [f(x + \Delta x) - f(x)]/\Delta x$, and in the limit

$$\frac{dy}{dx} \equiv f'(x) = \lim_{\Delta x \to 0} \frac{\Delta y}{\Delta x} \tag{A-1}$$

Geometrically, $f'(x)$ evaluated at a specified value of x turns out to be the slope of the tangent to $y = f(x)$ at that point. Recall also that the differential of y, dy, denotes the approximation to the change in y for a small change in x, dx, as

$$dy = f'(x)\,dx \tag{A-2}$$

Geometrically, the change in the function is approximated by the change along the tangent; i.e., the approximation in (A-2) is a linear one. With a function of several independent variables, one finds partial derivatives by imagining that all variables but one are held constant at a particular point and then utilizing the same delta process reasoning for the only varying variable.

For $y = 4x^2 + 5x + 10$, elementary differentiation gives $y' = 8x + 5$. Similarly, a second derivative, $d(dy/dx)/dx \equiv d^2y/dx^2 \equiv y''$, is found by differentiating y'; in this example $y'' = 8$. In terms of differentials, $d^2y \equiv d(dy) = d[f'(x)\,dx] = f''(x)\,dx^2$; here $dy = (8x + 5)\,dx$ and $d^2y = 8\,dx^2$. In integral calculus we are concerned with finding a function when its derivative is known; i.e., with undoing the process of differentiation. Given that $dy/dx = 8x + 5$, we ask: what was the original function $y = f(x)$? By simply "reversing" the rules for finding derivatives, we see that $y = 4x^2 + 5x + 10$ has the required derivative, as does $y = 4x^2 + 5x - 480$, or indeed most generally $y = 4x^2 + 5x + c$, where c is any constant whatsoever, since the derivative of a constant is zero.

For reasons that will soon be apparent, the undoing of a derivative is denoted as follows: if $dy/dx \equiv y' \equiv f'(x)$, i.e., if $dy \equiv f'(x)\,dx$, then the original function y is represented as $y = \int dy = \int f'(x)\,dx$. In terms of the example, $y = \int dy = \int (8x + 5)\,dx = 4x^2 + 5x + c$. (The $\int$ is known as the integral sign.) The function under the integral sign (here $8x + 5$) is known as the integrand. Similarly, to undo a second derivative (or second differential) requires integrating twice. The notation is straightforward. Since $d(dy/dx)/dx = 8$ or $d(dy/dx) = 8\,dx$, integrating both sides gives $dy/dx = \int 8\,dx = 8x + c_1$, where c_1 denotes any constant; that is, $dy = (8x + c_1)\,dx$. Further, $y = \int dy = \int (8x + c_1)\,dx = 4x^2 + c_1x + c_2$. The process of moving from $d^2y/dx^2 = 8$ to $y = 4x^2 + c_1x + c_2$ is represented as $dy/dx = \int 8\,dx$ or $dy = \int 8\,dx\,dx$ and $y = \int dy = \int\int 8\,dx\,dx$ [or $\int\int 8\,dx^2$ or $\int dx\,(\int 8\,dx)$]. This is called a double integral, since it denotes moving backward (relative to differential calculus) from a *second* derivative to the underlying function y. Triple integration unravels a third derivative, etc. More generally, with more than just a first derivative and a single integral, the problem is said to be one involving multiple integrals or an iterated integral. Multiple integrals also arise with functions of several independent variables. The notation $\int\int \phi(x_1, x_2)\,dx_1\,dx_2$—or, to clarify the operations, $\int [\int \phi(x_1, x_2)\,dx_1]\,dx_2$—directs that initially x_1 be considered the only variable and $\phi(x_1, x_2)$ be integrated with respect to x_1; in general, the result will be a new function of x_1 and x_2, say $\int \phi(x_1, x_2)\,dx_1 = g(x_1, x_2)$. Then this function is integrated with respect to x_2.

Notice that just as we could not go from $y' = 8x + 5$ to $y = 4x^2 + 5x + 10$ without additional information serving to specify the value of the constant, we also cannot go from $y'' = 8$ to $y' = 8x + 5$ without more information. Each level of integration introduces an unknown constant precisely because of the elementary observation that the derivative of a constant is zero.† Therefore, moving from y'' to y introduces two unknown constants; e.g., the function $y = 4x^2 - 56x - 698$ also has $y'' = 8$.

Thus when we speak of finding y as $\int dy$ or as $\int \int d^2y$, we are using *indefinite* integrals or performing *indefinite* integration. For obvious reasons, the integral of a function is sometimes known as the antiderivative of the function and the process as antidifferentiation.

Techniques of Integration

Reversing the process of differentiation is not always straightforward. However, since (1) if $y = c$, $y' = 0$, (2) if $y = ax$, $y' = a$, (3) if $y = ax^n$, $y' = nax^{n-1}$, and (4) the derivative of a sum is the sum of the derivatives, our example of $y' = 8x + 5$ easily integrated to $y = 4x^2 + 5x + c$.

When the derivative is less simple, however, problems arise. If $y' = xe^x$, that is, $dy = xe^x\,dx$, discovery that $y = xe^x - e^x + c$ is more complicated. In fact, some functions cannot be integrated exactly at all. However, there are a number of standard computational approaches to the problem of finding an exact integral or of approximating the integral of a complicated function.‡ We consider only one technique, that of integration by parts, largely because it is utilized in the derivation of the fundamental Euler-Lagrange equation (first-order condition) in the calculus of variations. Since the rule for the derivative or differential of a product of two functions is $d(uv) = u\,dv + v\,du$, then integrating both sides gives $\int d(uv) = \int (u\,dv + v\,du)$. The left-hand side is just uv and since the integral of a sum is the sum of the integrals

$$uv = \int u\,dv + \int v\,du \tag{A-3}$$

Therefore

$$\int u\,dv = uv - \int v\,du \tag{A-4}$$

This suggests an approach if we are looking for the integral of a product—as in $dy = xe^x\,dx$ and therefore $y = \int xe^x\,dx$. If we can define a function dv which is easy to integrate, so as to give v, and for which $\int v\,du$ is easier to find than

† This fact is reflected in the analysis of differential equations where it turns out that additional information (often in the form of so-called initial conditions) must be specified in order to remove exactly this uncertainty. For $dy/dx = 8x + 5$, that is, $y = 4x^2 + 5x + c$, if we also know that $y = 10$ when $x = 0$, then c is determined exactly: $c = 10$.

‡ These are featured in virtually any standard text on integral calculus. Primary among the approaches are integration by parts, transformations and substitutions, partial fractions, the trapezoidal rule, Simpson's rule, and, finally, the use of tables of integrals.

$\int u\,dv$, then (A-4) tells us how to avoid trying to integrate $u\,dv$ directly. For example, with $\int xe^x\,dx$, let $u = x$ and $dv = e^x\,dx$; this converts the problem to finding $\int u\,dv$. Then $du = dx$ and $v = \int e^x\,dx = e^x + c_1$, so, applying (A-4),

$$\int xe^x\,dx = x(e^x + c_1) - \int (e^x + c_1)\,dx$$

But $\int (e^x + c_1)\,dx$ is easy to evaluate; it is $e^x + c_1 x + c_2$. Hence

$$\int xe^x\,dx = xe^x + c_1 x - (e^x + c_1 x + c_2) = xe^x - e^x + c$$

where we designate by c the unknown constant $-c_2$. The integration by parts transformation is useful only when, in the particular problem, $\int u\,dv$ is complicated and $\int v\,du$ is not (or is less so).

A-2 THE DEFINITE INTEGRAL

The indefiniteness in integration that is associated with the unknown constant (or constants) that we observed in Sec. A-1 is removed when we deal with so-called definite integrals. The definition of a definite integral constitutes what is known as the fundamental theorem of the calculus. (This is not to be confused with fundamental theorems of integral calculus, to be noted below.) Suppose that $f(x)$ is continuous and defined on an interval $a \leq x \leq b$ and that the function $F(x)$ has the property that $F'(x) = f(x)$, so that $\int f(x)\,dx = F(x) + c$. Then the definite integral of $f(x)$ from a to b is denoted $\int_a^b f(x)\,dx$ and defined

$$\int_a^b f(x)\,dx = [F(b) + c] - [F(a) + c] \equiv F(x)]_a^b = F(b) - F(a) \qquad \text{(A-5)}$$

That is, it is the difference between the value of $F(x)$ evaluated at $x = b$ and the value of $F(x)$ evaluated at $x = a$. (Notice in particular that the indefiniteness associated with the arbitrary constant of integration, c, has disappeared.)

Geometric interpretations can also be associated with a definite integral. Consider a smooth, continuous function $f(x)$ as in Fig. A-1. Define as A the

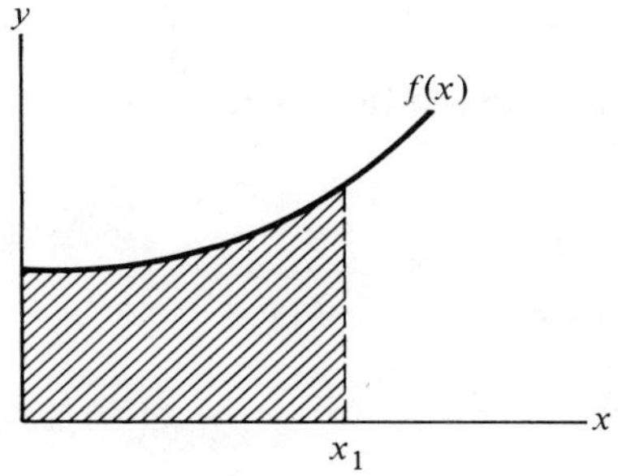

Figure A-1 Area under $f(x)$.

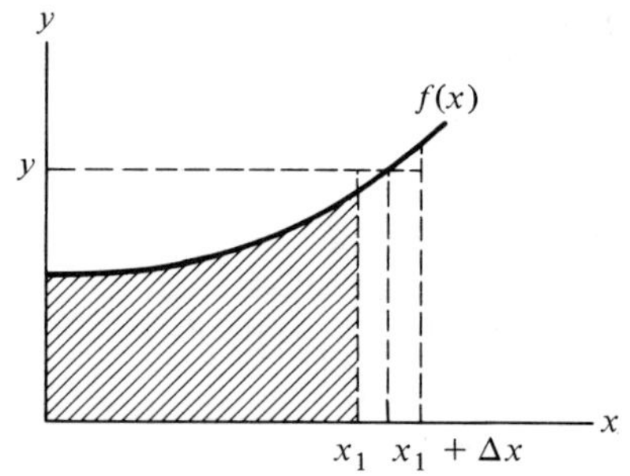

Figure A-2 $\Delta A = \bar{y}\,\Delta x$.

shaded area below $f(x)$, above the x axis and between the verticals at $x = 0$ and an arbitrary point x_1. Consider the change in area (ΔA) that would accompany a small change (Δx) in the location of the right-hand vertical line, from x_1 to $x_1 + \Delta x$. As suggested in Fig. A-2, there is some height, $\bar{y}$, for which $\Delta A = \bar{y}\,\Delta x$. That is,

$$\frac{\Delta A}{\Delta x} = \bar{y} \tag{A-6}$$

As we imagine smaller and smaller values for Δx, i.e., as $\Delta x \to 0$, the change in area gets smaller and the height $\bar{y}$ approaches the height of the function y evaluated at x_1. Thus

$$\lim_{\Delta x \to 0} \frac{\Delta A}{\Delta x} = \frac{dA}{dx} = y \tag{A-7}$$

Since $dA = y\,dx$,

$$A = \int dA = \int y\,dx = \int f(x)\,dx = F(x) + c \tag{A-8}$$

Consider two values of x, $x = a$ and $x = b$, where $b > a$. From (A-8), the area under $f(x)$ and from the y axis out to the vertical at $x = a$ (Fig. A-3a), is

$$A_a = F(a) + c$$

Similarly, the area under $f(x)$, above the x axis from the y axis out to the vertical at $x = b$ (Fig. A-3b), is

$$A_b = F(b) + c$$

Therefore, the area under $f(x)$, above the x axis and between the verticals at $x = a$ and $x = b$ (Fig. A-3c), is

$$A = A_b - A_a = F(b) + c - [F(a) + c] = F(b) - F(a) \tag{A-9}$$

Since (A-5) defines this difference as the definite integral of $f(x)$ from a to b, we have

$$A = \int_a^b f(x)\,dx \tag{A-10}$$

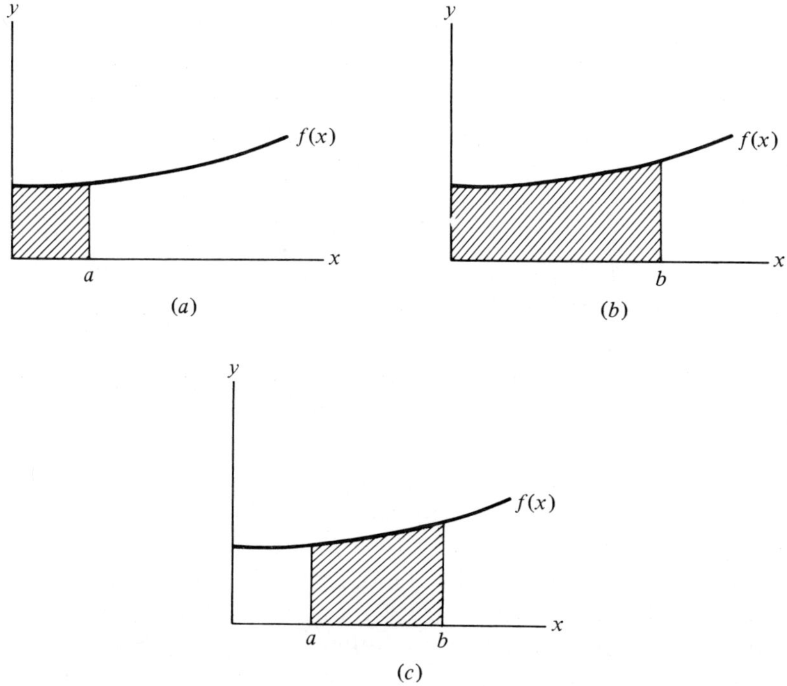

Figure A-3 Area under $f(x)$ between (*a*) $x = 0$ and $x = a$, (*b*) $x = 0$ and $x = b$, and (*c*) $x = a$ and $x = b$.

When $f(x)$ is below the x axis, the area given in (A-10) would be negative, since $\bar{y}$ and y in (A-6) and (A-7) would be negative, and therefore the actual area would be given by $-\int_a^b f(x)\,dx$. It also follows from (A-5) that $\int_a^b f(x)\,dx = -\int_b^a f(x)\,dx$. Similarly, the area between two curves can be found, as suggested in Fig. A-4, as the area under the higher one less the area under the lower one, i.e., as $\int_a^b f(x)\,dx - \int_a^b g(x)\,dx$ which is the same as $\int_a^b [f(x) - g(x)]\,dx$.

If one or both of the limits of integration is infinite, the integral is termed

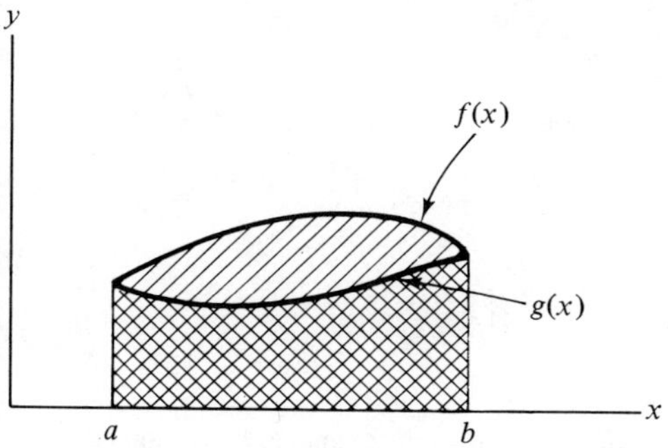

Figure A-4 Area between $f(x)$ and $g(x)$.

improper. For example, $\int_a^{+\infty} f(x)\,dx$ is an improper integral, and it is defined to be $\lim_{b\to+\infty} \int_a^b f(x)\,dx$, if such a limit exists. If it does not—if the limit is infinite—the improper integral does not exist. Similarly, $\int_{-\infty}^b f(x)\,dx = \lim_{a\to-\infty} \int_a^b f(x)\,dx$.

As might be expected, since limits are involved, the problems can become a bit subtle and intuition can be misleading. The following convergence test takes care of the matter. Let $f(x)$ be continuous. If for some $r > 1$, $\lim_{x\to+\infty} x^r|f(x)|$ and $\lim_{x\to-\infty} |x|^r|f(x)|$ both exist and are finite, then $\int_{-\infty}^{+\infty} f(x)\,dx$ converges absolutely. If for some $r \leq 1$, either limit exists and is not equal to zero, the integral does not converge absolutely. Similarly, if $f(x)$ is continuous over $c \leq x \leq +\infty$, the test for convergence of $\int_c^{+\infty} f(x)\,dx$ is only that $\lim_{x\to+\infty} x^r|f(x)|$ exist and be finite; and if for some $r \leq 1$ the limit exists and is not equal to zero, the integral does not converge absolutely. Consider $\int_1^{+\infty}(1/x^2)\,dx$. This is $\lim_{b\to+\infty} \int_1^b (1/x^2)\,dx = \lim_{b\to+\infty} [-1/x]_1^b = \lim_{b\to+\infty} [-1/b + 1] = 1$. Geometrically, this is the area between $f(x) = 1/x^2$ and the x axis, from $x = 1$ outward. However, if we investigate the superficially similar-looking improper integral $\int_1^{+\infty} (1/x)\,dx$, which equals $\lim_{b\to+\infty} \int_1^b (1/x)\,dx$, we find that it is equal to $\lim_{b\to+\infty} [\log x]_1^b = \lim_{b\to+\infty} \log b - \log 1 = \lim_{b\to+\infty} \log b = +\infty$. This, too, represents an area, namely, that between $f(x) = 1/x$ and the x axis, from $x = 1$ outward. However, for $f(x) = 1/x^2$, letting $r = 2$, $\lim_{x\to+\infty} x^r|f(x)| = 1$ and for $r \leq 1$, $\lim_{x\to+\infty} (1/x^{2-r}) = 0$, and thus convergence of $\int_1^{+\infty} (1/x^2)\,dx$ is assured. On the other hand, for $f(x) = 1/x$ $(1 \leq x \leq +\infty)$, $\lim_{x\to+\infty} x^r(1/x) = \infty$ for any $r > 1$ and for $r = 1$, $\lim_{x\to+\infty} x(1/x) = 1$ $(\neq 0)$ and so $\int_1^{+\infty} (1/x)\,dx$ does not converge. Thus, although both $1/x^2$ and $1/x$ approach the x axis asymptotically, the improper integral $\int_1^{+\infty} (1/x^2)\,dx$ exists whereas $\int_1^{+\infty} (1/x)\,dx$ does not.

A-3 THE INTEGRAL AS THE LIMIT OF A SUM

Consider an alternative approach to the problem of finding the area shown in Fig. A-3. Divide the interval along the x axis into a number of subintervals, $\Delta x_1, \Delta x_2, \ldots, \Delta x_n$, with midpoints $x_1, x_2, \ldots, x_n$, respectively, as in Fig. A-5. An approximation to the area under $f(x)$ from a to b would be given by the sum

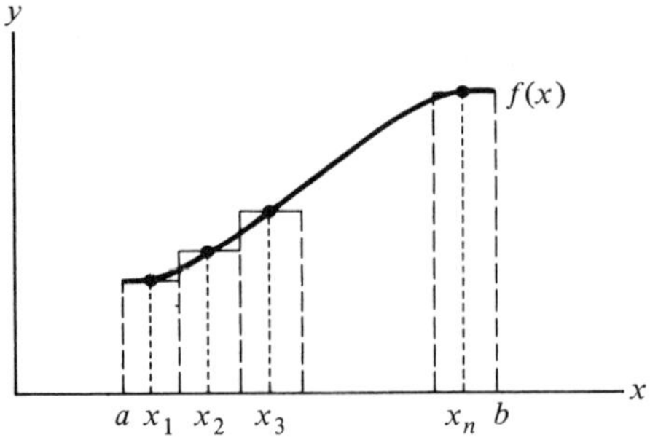

Figure A-5 Area approximated by rectangles.

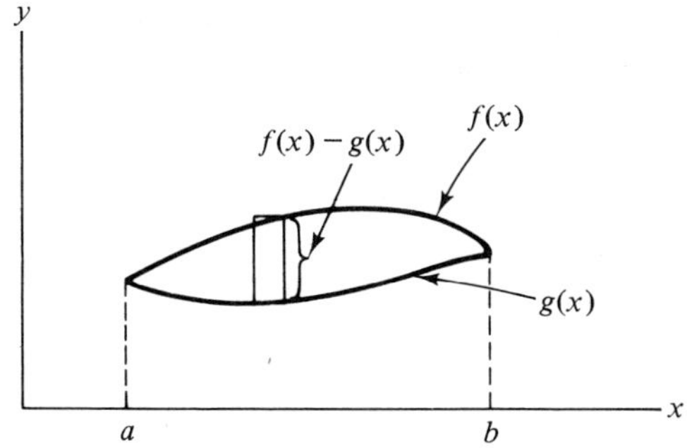

Figure A-6 Alternative approach to the area between $f(x)$ and $g(x)$.

of the area of each of the rectangles that are formed. That is, $A \cong f(x_1)\,\Delta x_1 + f(x_2)\,\Delta x_2 + \cdots + f(x_n)\,\Delta x_n = \sum_{i=1}^{n} f(x_i)\,\Delta x_i$. Clearly the approximation will be more accurate as the number of rectangles increases, i.e., as the bases, Δx_i, become smaller. This geometrically appealing argument is made specific in what is generally known as the (first) fundamental theorem of integral calculus, which is that

$$\lim_{\substack{n\to\infty \\ \Delta x_i \to 0}} \sum_{i=1}^{n} f(x_i)\,\Delta x_i = \int_a^b f(x)\,dx \tag{A-11}$$

An approach to finding areas, therefore, is to divide the figure in question into a number of "typical strips," the sum of whose areas would approximate the total area, and then to pass to the limit, i.e., to replace a summation sign with an integral sign. (The notion of a definite integral as the limit of a summation process explains the origin of the integral sign, which was originally just an elongated S, for sum.) This approach to areas could equally well be used, for example, on the problem of the area between two curves. In Fig. A-6 we use the same curves as in Fig. A-4; the area in question is approximated by the sum of the areas of the rectangles with base Δx_i and height $f(x_i) - g(x_i)$. That is, $A \cong \sum_{i=1}^{n} [f(x_i) - g(x_i)]\,\Delta x_i$ and in the limit, as $n \to \infty$ and $\Delta x_i \to 0$, $A = \int_a^b [f(x) - g(x)]\,dx$, exactly as before. This approach is also useful for surface areas and volumes of solids that are generated by revolving curves around an

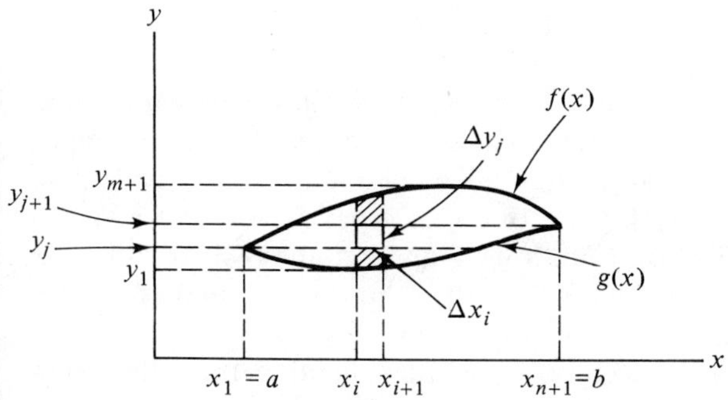

Figure A-7 Another alternative approach to the area between $f(x)$ and $g(x)$.

axis. (With volumes, one finds the volume of a "typical disc," instead of the area of a "typical strip," and then passes to the limit, replacing $\sum$ with $\int$, Δx with dx, etc.)

Areas and volumes can also be found using multiple integrals. We consider once again the curves from Fig. A-6, now shortening the "typical strip" to something closer to a "typical square." Using an argument parallel to that associated with Fig. A-5, the sum $\sum_{j=1}^{m} \Delta y_j \, \Delta x_i$ can be shown to give the area of the shaded column, and then $\sum_{i=1}^{n} \sum_{j=1}^{m} \Delta y_j \, \Delta x_i$ sums all of the column to give an approximation to the entire area (see Fig. A-7). Again, in the limit,

$$\lim_{\substack{m,n \to \infty \\ \Delta y_j, \Delta x_i \to 0}} \sum_{i=1}^{n} \sum_{j=1}^{m} \Delta y_j \, \Delta x_i = \int_a^b \int_{g(x)}^{f(x)} dy \, dx \tag{A-12}$$

This is generally known as the second fundamental theorem of integral calculus.

A-4 PRESENT-VALUE CALCULATIONS AND DISCOUNTING: AN EXAMPLE OF SUMS AND INTEGRALS

Consider an amount A_0 (of money, for example) that doubles in value every year. If the initial investment, A_0, was made on January 1, 1976, and if measurements are made on January 1 of each year thereafter, then on January 1, 1977, the investment will have grown to $2A_0$; it will be $2(2A_0) = 2^2 A_0 = 4A_0$ two years later, on January 1, 1978, etc. On January 1 n years later, it will be $2^n A$. We can denote this as A_n; that is, $A_n = 2^n A_0$. Clearly, if, instead of doubling, A is multiplied by k every period, then $A_n = k^n A_0$. In percentage terms, if A_0 increases by 6 percent each period, which means that it is multiplied by $(1 + 0.06)$, $A_n = (1.06)^n A_0$. More generally,

$$A_n = (i + 1)^n A_0 \tag{A-13}$$

represents the value n years hence of an amount A_n invested now at an annual rate of $100i$ percent. (The 100 simply converts a number like 0.06, which is 6/100, to 6, a percentage, since "percent" means "divided by 100.") Viewed alternatively,

$$A_0 = \frac{A_n}{(i + i)^n} = (1 + i)^{-n} A_n \tag{A-14}$$

represents the *present value* of an amount A_n due to be available n years hence, when the annual interest rate is $100i$ percent, calculated annually. For example, if the interest rate is 7 percent, \$100 at the end of two years is equivalent in value now to \$87.34 [= \$100/(1.07)^2], since one year from now the \$87.34 will have grown to \$93.46 [= \$87.34(1.07)] and one year later the \$93.46 will have grown to \$100 [= \$93.46(1.07) = \$87.34(1.07)^2]. (All are to two-decimal accuracy.)

If one considers the value at time T, V_T, of a flow of yields—A_1 at the end of the first year, A_2 at the end of the second, ..., A_T at the end of the Tth year—

all earning 100i percent per year, an extension of the reasoning above suggests that

$$V_T = (1+i)^{T-1}A_1 + (1+i)^{T-2}A_2 + \cdots + (1+i)A_{T-1} + A_T$$

or
$$V_T = \sum_{t=1}^{T} (1+i)^{T-t}A_t \tag{A-15}$$

Similarly, the *present value*, V_0, of this stream of yields is

$$V_0 = \frac{A_1}{1+i} + \frac{A_2}{(1+i)^2} + \cdots + \frac{A_{T-1}}{(1+i)^{T-1}} + \frac{A_T}{(1+i)^T}$$

or
$$V_0 = \sum_{t=1}^{T} \frac{A_t}{(1+i)^t} = \sum_{t=1}^{T} (1+i)^{-t}A_t \tag{A-16}$$

For example, with $i = 0.07$, \$100 at the end of year 1 and \$150 at the end of year 2 will be worth \$257 [= \$100(1.07) + \$150] at the end of year 2, from (A-15). Similarly, the present value of this stream of earnings, from (A-16), is \$224.48 (= \$100/1.07 + \$150/1.1449). The check is that \$224.48 invested now, at 7 percent per annum, will grow to \$257 after two years, that is, \$224.48(1.07) + \$224.48(1.07)^2 = \$257.

Geometrically, (A-16) can be thought of as representing the sum of a number of rectangular areas, each with height $A_t/(1+i)^t$ and base $\Delta t = 1$ year. That is, $V_0 = \sum_{t=1}^{T} [(1+i)^{-t}A_t]\,\Delta t$ (see Fig. A-8).

When the yields are the same each period, i.e., when $A_1 = A_2 = \cdots = A_T = A$, then (A-16) simplifies to

$$V_0 = A\sum_{t=1}^{T} \frac{1}{(1+i)^t} \tag{A-17}$$

Geometrically, the case of constant yields is illustrated in Fig. A-9. Recalling that the first T terms in a *geometric progression* are representable as $a + ar + ar^2 + \cdots + ar^{T-1}$ and that $S_T = a[(1-r)^T/(1-r)]$ gives the sum of these terms,

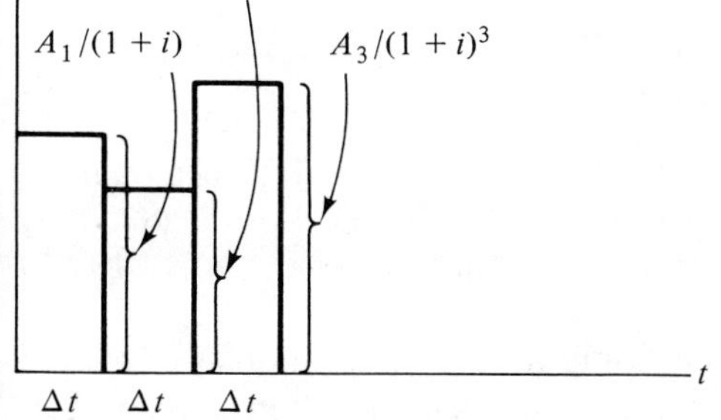

Figure A-8 Present value of A_1, A_2, A_3, . . . as a sum of areas (discrete case).

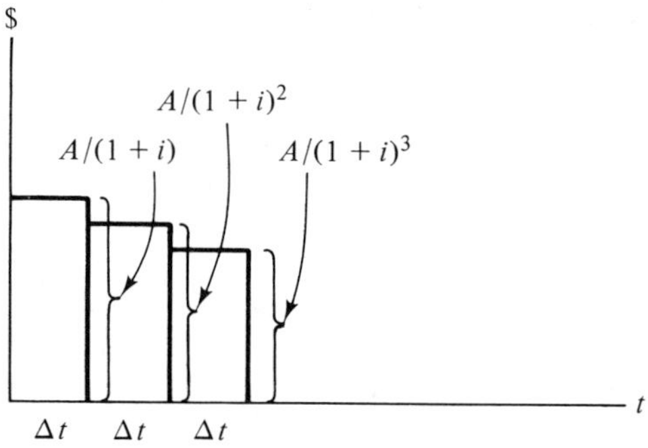

Figure A-9 Present value of A each year as a sum of areas (discrete case).

we can rewrite V_0 in (A-17) as

$$V_0 = \frac{A}{1+i}\left[1 + \frac{1}{1+i} + \frac{1}{(1+i)^2} + \cdots + \frac{1}{(1+i)^{T-1}}\right]$$

Letting $a = 1$ and $r = 1/(1 + i)$, we see that the sum in brackets is indeed a geometric progression and therefore that it equals $1\{1 - [1/(1 + i)]^T\}/\{1 - [1/(1 + i)]\}$. Thus (A-17) can be reexpressed as

$$V_0 = \frac{A}{i}\left[1 - \left(\frac{1}{1+i}\right)^T\right] \tag{A-18}$$

This, in turn, makes clear that the present value of an *infinite* stream of constant yields A would be found from (A-18) as $T \to \infty$, namely, as

$$V_0 = \frac{A}{i} \tag{A-19}$$

Returning to the case of an initial investment A_0, if the interest amounts are registered ("compounded") oftener than once a year, the modification is straightforward. Suppose that interest is compounded four times per year (i.e., quarterly). That means that $(100i/4)$ percent is applied four times during each year, so that $A_n = (1 + i/4)^{4n} A_0$. For compounding m times a year, the corresponding result is

$$A_n = \left(1 + \frac{i}{m}\right)^{mn} A_0 \tag{A-20}$$

and

$$A_0 = \left(1 + \frac{i}{m}\right)^{-mn} A_n \tag{A-21}$$

For example, 7 percent per annum, compounded quarterly, is 1.75 per quarter. After one year, \$100 will have grown to $A_1 = \$107.19$ $[= (1.0175)^4(\$100) = (1.0719)(\$100)]$. If the 7 percent is compounded 12 times per year, $A_1 = \$107.23$ $[= (1.005833)^{12}(\$100) = (1.0723)(\$100)]$.

In the limiting case, interest may be compounded continuously; i.e., the distance, Δt, between successive points in time at which the interest is applied approaches zero, which means mathematically that $m \to \infty$ in (A-20). In this case $A_n = \{\lim_{m\to\infty} [1 + (i/m)^m]\}^n A_0$. The expression for A_n can be simplified, and in the process a definition for e emerges. Let $z = (1 + i/m)^{mn}$, so that $A_n = [\lim_{m\to\infty} z] A_0$. Taking logarithms, $\ln z = mn \ln (1 + i/m) = \ln (1 + i/m)/(1/mn) = h(m)/g(m)$. We are interested in the limit of this ratio as $m \to \infty$. Since $\ln 1 = 0$, both $h(m) \to 0$ and $g(m) \to 0$ as $m \to \infty$. L'Hôpital's rule states that $\lim_{m\to\infty} h(m)/g(m) = \lim_{m\to\infty} h'(m)/g'(m)$. But $h'(m) = (-i/m^2)/(1 + i/m)$ and $g'(m) = (-1/m^2 n)$, so $\lim_{m\to\infty} (\ln z) = \lim_{m\to\infty} in/(1 + i/m) = in$. Taking antilogarithms, $\lim_{m\to\infty} z = e^{in}$, that is,

$$\lim_{m\to\infty} \left(1 + \frac{i}{m}\right)^{mn} = e^{in}$$

Thus $$A_n = e^{in} A_0 \tag{A-22}$$

and, from $\lim_{m\to\infty} (1 + i/m)^{mn} = e^{in}$, when $i = 1$ and $n = 1$, we see that

$$\lim_{m\to\infty} \left(1 + \frac{1}{m}\right)^{m} = e$$

The expression in (A-22) is the continuous analogue of (A-13). If the 7 percent is compounded continuously, \$100 grows to \$107.25 in one year, since $e^{0.07} = 1.0725$. From (A-22), the present value of an amount A_n, available in n years' time, discounting continuously at the annual rate of $100i$, is

$$A_0 = e^{-in} A_n \tag{A-23}$$

This is the continuous analogue of (A-14).

If there is a continuous flow of yields, Δt approaches zero and becomes dt. At time t, there is a yield $A(t)$. For the present-value calculation, parallel to (A-16) we will have $\sum_{t=1}^{T} [(1 + i/m)^{-mn} A_n] \Delta t$, as $m \to \infty$ and $\Delta t \to 0$. Thus, from our understanding of the integral as the limit of a sum, the present value is represented as

$$V_0 = \int_0^T e^{-it} A(t)\, dt \tag{A-24}$$

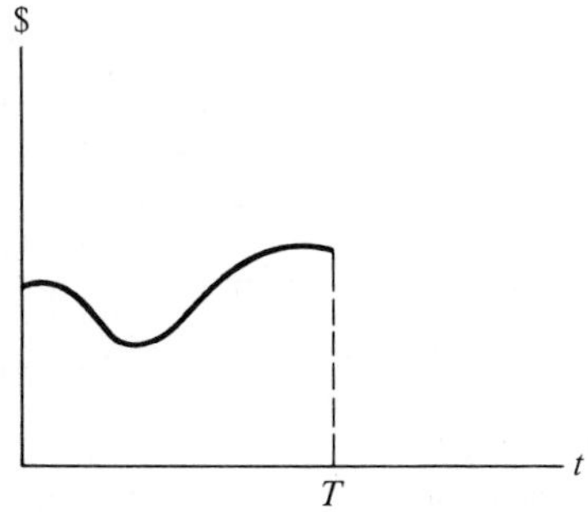

Figure A-10 Present value of $A(t)$ as an integral (continuous case).

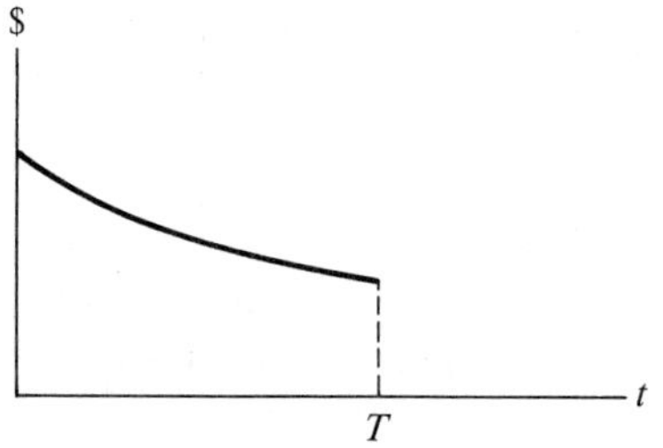

Figure A-11 Present value of A as an integral (continuous case).

Geometrically, this is the area under the function $e^{-it}A(t)$ from 0 to T, as in Fig. A-10. (Compare Fig. A-8.) In the case of constant yields, i.e., when $A(t) = A$, this becomes

$$V_0 = A \int_0^T e^{-it}\,dt \tag{A-25}$$

as in Fig. A-11. (Compare Fig. A-9.) By straightforward integration, (A-25) is

$$V_0 = \frac{A}{i}(1 - e^{-iT}) \tag{A-26}$$

Again, as $T \to \infty$, this is

$$V_0 = \frac{A}{i} \tag{A-27}$$

exactly as in the case of discrete time intervals, in (A-19). The objective in optimal economic growth problems is often to maximize an integral of the form of (A-24) or (A-25), where $A(t)$ or A represent some measure of utility.

PROBLEMS

A-1 Find each of the following indefinite integrals:
(*a*) $\int (1 + x^2 + 3x^4)\,dx$
(*b*) $\int (5x^4 - 2)\,dx$
(*c*) $\int e^{-3x}\,dx$
(*d*) $\int 3x^2 e^{2x}\,dx$
(*e*) $\int\int (x^2 + e^{3x})\,dx^2$

A-2 Evaluate each of the following:
(*a*) $\int_0^2 (1 + x^2 + 3x^4)\,dx$
(*b*) $\int_1^2 (1 + x^2 + 3x^4)\,dx$
(*c*) $\int_{-1}^1 (5x^4 - 2)\,dx$
(*d*) $\int_0^1 e^{-3x}\,dx$
(*e*) $\int_{-1}^1 \int_0^2 (x^2 + e^{3x})\,dx^2$

A-3 Find the following areas:
(*a*) Under $y = 1 + x^2 + 3x^4$, above the x axis, from $x = 0$ to $x = 2$.
(*b*) Under the same curve as in (*a*), above, between $x = 0$ and $x = 1$.

(*c*) Between the function $y = 5x - 10$ and the x axis, between $x = 1$ and $x = 3$. Verify by elementary geometry.

(*d*) Under one arc of $y = \sin x$.

(*e*) Between $y = 1 + x^2 + 3x^4$ [from (*a*), above] and $y = 5x - 10$ [from (*c*), above], between $x = 1$ and $x = 2$.

(*f*) Between $y = x^2$ and $y = 2 - x$ using double integration. Check the result using a single definite integral, as in (*e*), above.

A-4 Find each of the following improper integrals, if they exist:

(*a*) $\int_{-\infty}^{0} e^x \, dx$

(*b*) $\int_{1}^{\infty} xe^{-x^2} \, dx$

(*c*) $\int_{0}^{\infty} \cos x \, dx$

A-5 Compare the present value of \$10,000 seven years from now when the interest rate is 5 percent per annum and it is compounded (*a*) annually, (*b*) quarterly, (*c*) continuously.

APPENDIX

B

QUADRATIC FORMS

B-1 BASIC STRUCTURE OF QUADRATIC FORMS

A quadratic form of, say, two variables, x_1 and x_2, is any function of x_1 and x_2 in which each of the variables may appear in only two ways: (1) squared and (2) multiplied by the other variable. For example: $2x_1^2 + 6x_1x_2 + 5x_2^2$ is a quadratic form in x_1 and x_2. The name simply describes a particular algebraic structure. A quadratic form may be a function of any number of variables, as we shall see below. From elementary rules of matrix multiplication, this function of x_1 and x_2 can be written as

$$[x_1 \quad x_2] \begin{bmatrix} 2 & 3 \\ 3 & 5 \end{bmatrix} \begin{bmatrix} x_1 \\ x_2 \end{bmatrix}$$

where the 3 is 6/2—i.e., one-half of the coefficient attached to x_1x_2.

The general quadratic form for two variables, $Q(x_1, x_2)$, can be represented as

$$Q(x_1, x_2) = a_{11}x_1^2 + (a_{12} + a_{21})x_1x_2 + a_{22}x_2^2 \tag{B-1}$$

Since any coefficient multiplying the x_1x_2 term can always be represented as the sum of two equal terms, this could as well be written for the general case as

$$Q(x_1, x_2) = a_{11}x_1^2 + 2a_{12}x_1x_2 + a_{22}x_2^2 \tag{B-2}$$

In matrix terms:

$$[x_1 \quad x_2] \begin{bmatrix} a_{11} & a_{12} \\ a_{21} & a_{22} \end{bmatrix} \begin{bmatrix} x_1 \\ x_2 \end{bmatrix} \tag{B-3}$$

or, letting $\mathbf{X} = \begin{bmatrix} x_1 \\ x_2 \end{bmatrix}$ and denoting by $\mathbf{A}$ the *symmetric* matrix

$$\begin{bmatrix} a_{11} & a_{12} \\ a_{21} & a_{22} \end{bmatrix}$$

where $a_{12} = a_{21}$, (B-3) is just

$$\mathbf{X}'\mathbf{A}\mathbf{X} \tag{B-4}$$

The beauty of (B-4) is that it represents a quadratic form of any number of variables; nothing changes but the dimensions of the matrices involved. Thus

$$Q(x_1, x_2, x_3) = \mathbf{X}'\mathbf{A}\mathbf{X}$$

where

$$\mathbf{X} = \begin{bmatrix} x_1 \\ x_2 \\ x_3 \end{bmatrix} \quad \text{and} \quad \mathbf{A} = \begin{bmatrix} a_{11} & a_{12} & a_{13} \\ a_{21} & a_{22} & a_{23} \\ a_{31} & a_{32} & a_{33} \end{bmatrix}$$

and $\mathbf{A}$ is symmetric. One final representation is

$$Q(x_1, x_2, x_3) = \sum_{i=1}^{3} \sum_{j=1}^{3} a_{ij}x_i x_j$$

This makes clear the quadratic nature of the function. When $i = j$, a variable is squared; otherwise (when $i \neq j$) *pairs* of variables are multiplied together. (The number of variables influences only the range of the subscripts i and j.)

For n variables,

$$Q(x_1, \ldots, x_n) = \sum_{i=1}^{n} \sum_{j=1}^{n} a_{ij}x_i x_j = \mathbf{X}'\mathbf{A}\mathbf{X}$$

where $\mathbf{X}$ is an n-element column vector of the variables and $\mathbf{A}$ is an $(n \times n)$ symmetric matrix of the coefficients a_{ij}.

B-2 REWRITTEN STRUCTURE OF QUADRATIC FORMS

Consider $Q(x_1, x_2)$ as written in (B-2):

$$a_{11}x_1^2 + 2a_{12}x_1x_2 + a_{22}x_2^2$$

Suppose that we were trying to determine conditions on the values of the a_{ij} under which this expression would *always* be positive or *always* be negative, regardless of the values of x_1 and x_2. One reason for doing so is that second total differentials of functions of any number of variables can be expressed as quadratic forms, and of course the sign of the second total differential at a critical point helps to distinguish whether the function in question has a relative maximum, or a relative minimum at that point. In the form of (B-2) the question could not be answered. The middle term, $2a_{12}x_1x_2$, would take on differing signs depending on the signs of x_1 and x_2, even though $a_{11}x_1^2$ and $a_{22}x_2^2$ present no problem. What is needed, then, is an expression in which the x all appear in terms that are squared; this removes any ambiguity about signs. We thus want to modify (B-2), and specifically we employ the device of "completing the square." Consider the first two terms, $a_{11}x_1^2 + 2a_{12}x_1x_2$. If $(a_{12}^2/a_{11})x_2^2$ were added to these terms, the entire expression would be

$$a_{11}x_1^2 + 2a_{12}x_1x_2 + \frac{a_{12}^2}{a_{11}}x_2^2 = a_{11}\left(x_1^2 + 2\frac{a_{12}}{a_{11}}x_1x_2 + \frac{a_{12}^2}{a_{11}^2}x_2^2\right)$$

$$= a_{11}\left(x_1 + \frac{a_{12}}{a_{11}}x_2\right)^2$$

But then the added term $(a_{12}^2/a_{11})x_2^2$ must also be subtracted from (B-2) if the expression is to remain unchanged. Thus the third term in (B-2), $a_{22}x_2^2$, must absorb the loss of $(a_{12}^2/a_{11})x_2^2$:

$$a_{22}x_2^2 - \frac{a_{12}^2}{a_{11}}x_2^2 = \left(a_{22} - \frac{a_{12}^2}{a_{11}}\right)x_2^2 = \left(\frac{a_{11}a_{22} - a_{12}^2}{a_{11}}\right)x_2^2$$

Therefore (B-2) is now

$$Q(x_1, x_2) = a_{11}\left(x_1 + \frac{a_{12}}{a_{11}}x_2\right)^2 + \left(\frac{a_{11}a_{22} - a_{12}^2}{a_{11}}\right)x_2^2 \tag{B-5}$$

That is, it is a *sum of squares*. The sign of $Q(x_1, x_2)$ when x_1 and x_2 are both nonzero thus depends entirely on the two terms multiplying the squared expressions.

Recall the **A** matrix in (B-3) and (B-4). The first critical term in (B-5) is just a_{11}, the element in the upper left corner of **A**. The second critical term is the determinant of **A** divided by a_{11}. Since the determinant of the (1×1) matrix $[a_{11}]$ is just a_{11}, we could represent the critical terms as $|a_{11}|$ and $|\mathbf{A}|/|a_{11}|$, respectively. These determinants are called the *principal minors* of **A**. The first principal minor of a square matrix **A** is the determinant of the matrix formed by deleting *all but* the first row and column from **A**; i.e., it is always simply a_{11}. It is denoted $|\mathbf{A}_1|$. The second principal minor, $|\mathbf{A}_2|$, is the determinant of the matrix formed by removing all but the first *two* rows and columns of **A**. Thus

$$|\mathbf{A}_2| = \begin{vmatrix} a_{11} & a_{12} \\ a_{21} & a_{22} \end{vmatrix} = a_{11}a_{22} - a_{12}a_{21}$$

For a symmetric matrix this is also $a_{11}a_{22} - a_{12}^2$. For an $(n \times n)$ matrix, therefore, the nth principal minor is the determinant of the entire matrix; for the (2×2) case here, $|\mathbf{A}_2| = |\mathbf{A}|$. Thus (B-5) may be written

$$Q(x_1, x_2) = |\mathbf{A}_1|\left(x_1 + \frac{a_{12}}{a_{11}}x_2\right)^2 + \frac{|\mathbf{A}_2|}{|\mathbf{A}_1|}x_2^2 \tag{B-6}$$

Although the process of completing squares is more involved, the general quadratic form for three variables can be shown to be

$$Q(x_1, x_2, x_3) = |\mathbf{A}_1|(\cdot)^2 + \frac{|\mathbf{A}_2|}{|\mathbf{A}_1|}(\cdot)^2 + \frac{|\mathbf{A}_3|}{|\mathbf{A}_2|}(\cdot)^2 \tag{B-7}$$

The squared terms contain functions of the x and a which, from the point of view of the *sign* of (B-7), are unimportant. And for n variables,

$$Q(x_1, \ldots, x_n) = |\mathbf{A}_1|(\cdot)^2 + \frac{|\mathbf{A}_2|}{|\mathbf{A}_1|}(\cdot)^2 + \cdots + \frac{|\mathbf{A}_n|}{|\mathbf{A}_{n-1}|}(\cdot)^2 \tag{B-8}$$

B-3 THE SIGN OF A QUADRATIC FORM

The following terminology is in general use for describing quadratic forms. If a quadratic form Q is always positive ($Q > 0$) for *any* values that the x assume, except when all x are zero, it is termed *positive definite.*† If Q is always negative ($Q < 0$) except when all x are zero, it is *negative definite.* If Q is either positive or zero ($Q \geq 0$) for all values of x, except when all are zero (that is, $Q = 0$ for some set of x not all zero), it is termed *positive semidefinite.*‡. And if the inequality is reversed ($Q \leq 0$), it is said to be *negative semidefinite.* For example:

1. $x_1^2 + 6x_2^2$ is positive definite.
2. $-x_1^2 - 6x_2^2$ is negative definite.
3. $x_1^2 - 4x_1x_2 + 4x_2^2 + x_3^2 = (x_1 - 2x_2)^2 + x_3^2$ is positive semidefinite. (It is never negative, but equals zero at $x_1 = 2$, $x_2 = 1$, $x_3 = 0$; $x_1 = 10$, $x_2 = 5$, $x_3 = 0$, and so on.)
4. $-(x_1 - 2x_2)^2 - x_3^2$ is therefore negative semidefinite.
5. $x_1^2 - 6x_2^2$ cannot be classed as either definite or semidefinite; it is *indefinite.*

For the general quadratic form of two variables, $Q(x_1, x_2)$, to be *positive definite* it is therefore both necessary and sufficient that the coefficients on both squared terms be strictly positive, i.e., from (B-6), that (1) $|\mathbf{A}_1| > 0$ and (2) $|\mathbf{A}_2|/|\mathbf{A}_1| > 0$. Since the denominator in (2) is covered by the rule in (1), this can be put simply as (1) $|\mathbf{A}_1| > 0$ and (2) $|\mathbf{A}_2| > 0$. Similarly (B-6) will be *negative definite* if and only if (1) $|\mathbf{A}_1| < 0$ and (2) $|\mathbf{A}_2|/|\mathbf{A}_1| < 0$ or, more simply, (1) $|\mathbf{A}_1| < 0$ and (2) $|\mathbf{A}_2| > 0$, since if the numerator of a fraction is always positive, the sign of the fraction will be governed by the denominator.

† "Definitely positive" would seem to be more logical, and just "positive" would be in keeping with the "greater than zero" notation in general use in algebra.

‡ Again, "nonnegative" would seem to do as well.

Because of the generalization of the sum-of-squares form in (B-7) and (B-8), it is clear that:

> A quadratic form of n variables, $Q(x_1, \ldots, x_n)$, will be (*a*) *positive definite* if and only if all principal minors of A are positive (that is, $|\mathbf{A}_1| > 0,\ |\mathbf{A}_2| > 0, \ldots, |\mathbf{A}_n| > 0$) and (*b*) *negative definite* if and only if the principal minors of A *alternate* in sign, *beginning negative* (that is, $|\mathbf{A}_1| < 0,\ |\mathbf{A}_2| > 0, \ldots, |\mathbf{A}_n| < 0$ if n is odd and $|\mathbf{A}_n| > 0$ if n is even). (B-9)

To return to the previous examples, where

$$\mathbf{X} = \begin{bmatrix} x_1 \\ x_2 \end{bmatrix} \quad \text{or} \quad \begin{bmatrix} x_1 \\ x_2 \\ x_3 \end{bmatrix}$$

as appropriate:

1. $x_1^2 + 6x_2^2 = \mathbf{X}'\begin{bmatrix} 1 & 0 \\ 0 & 6 \end{bmatrix}\mathbf{X}$; $|\mathbf{A}_1| = 1 > 0,\ |\mathbf{A}_2| = 6 > 0$. Thus the quadratic form is positive definite.

2. $-x_1^2 - 6x_2^2 = \mathbf{X}'\begin{bmatrix} -1 & 0 \\ 0 & -6 \end{bmatrix}\mathbf{X}$; $|\mathbf{A}_1| = -1 < 0,\ |\mathbf{A}_2| = 6 > 0$. Thus the quadratic form is negative definite.

3. $x_1^2 - 4x_1x_2 + 4x_2^2 + x_3^2 =$

$$\mathbf{X}'\begin{bmatrix} 1 & -2 & 0 \\ -2 & 4 & 0 \\ 0 & 0 & 1 \end{bmatrix}\mathbf{X}$$

$|\mathbf{A}_1| = 1 > 0,\ |\mathbf{A}_2| = 0,\ |\mathbf{A}_3| = 0$. Thus this quadratic form is neither positive definite nor negative definite. (Note that the general rule in (B-9) on signs of principal minors is relevant for definiteness only and not for *semi*definiteness.)

4. $-x_1^2 + 4x_1x_2 - 4x_2^2 - x_3^2 =$

$$\mathbf{X}'\begin{bmatrix} -1 & 2 & 0 \\ 2 & -4 & 0 \\ 0 & 0 & -1 \end{bmatrix}\mathbf{X}$$

$|\mathbf{A}_1| = -1 < 0,\ |\mathbf{A}_2| = 0,\ |\mathbf{A}_3| = 0$; again, this is neither positive nor negative definite.

5. $x_1^2 - 6x_2^2 = \mathbf{X}'\begin{bmatrix} 1 & 0 \\ 0 & -6 \end{bmatrix}\mathbf{X}$; $|\mathbf{A}_1| = 1 > 0,\ |\mathbf{A}_2| = -6 < 0$; so this is neither positive nor negative definite.

The reader will recognize that the rules on signs of principal minors, (B-9), may allow early judgment that a quadratic form of n variables is neither positive definite nor negative definite. For example, if $|\mathbf{A}_1| < 0$ and $|\mathbf{A}_2| < 0$, we can stop; also, if $|\mathbf{A}_1| > 0$ and $|\mathbf{A}_2| < 0$, we can stop. If $|\mathbf{A}_1| > 0$, then no change of sign of higher principal minors is allowed, whereas if $|\mathbf{A}_1| < 0$, then signs must alternate continuously from that point onward. Hence in (3) and (4) above it would have been sufficient, in examining for positive or negative *definiteness*, to stop at $|\mathbf{A}_2|$ in both cases.

B-4 THE SIGN OF d^2f FOR $y = f(x_1, x_2)$

The general form of the second total differential for a function of two independent variables is

$$d^2f = f_{11}(dx_1)^2 + 2f_{12}\,dx_1\,dx_2 + f_{22}(dx_2)^2$$

This is a quadratic form in the variables dx_1 and dx_2, the independent small changes in x_1 and x_2. Thus, for $y = f(x_1, x_2)$, we can use the generalized notation for quadratic forms:

$$d^2f = [dx_1 \quad dx_2] \begin{bmatrix} f_{11} & f_{12} \\ f_{21} & f_{22} \end{bmatrix} \begin{bmatrix} dx_1 \\ dx_2 \end{bmatrix} \tag{B-10}$$

Letting

$$\mathbf{dX} = \begin{bmatrix} dx_1 \\ dx_2 \end{bmatrix} \quad \text{and} \quad \mathbf{H} = \begin{bmatrix} f_{11} & f_{12} \\ f_{21} & f_{22} \end{bmatrix}$$

(where $\mathbf{H}$ is symmetric, since we assume that we are dealing with functions for which $f_{ij} = f_{ji}$), this is

$$d^2f = [\mathbf{dX}]'\,\mathbf{H}[\mathbf{dX}] \tag{B-11}$$

For $d^2f > 0$ (i.e., for the quadratic form to be positive definite), we know that the principal minors of $\mathbf{H}$ must all be positive: $|\mathbf{H}_1| > 0$ and $|\mathbf{H}_2| > 0$. For the form to be negative definite, $d^2f < 0$, the requirements are $|\mathbf{H}_1| < 0$ and $|\mathbf{H}_2| > 0$. Thus the problem of establishing the sign of the second total differential is just a particular case of the general problem of determining the sign of a quadratic form. For the second total differential, the variables are the dx, and the symmetric matrix of coefficients is composed of second partial and cross-partial derivatives. This matrix is termed the *hessian* of the function f, which is why $\mathbf{H}$ is often used to denote it. The sign of d^2f thus depends on the signs of the principal minors of the hessian.

B-5 THE SIGN OF d^2f FOR $y = f(x_1, \ldots, x_n)$

The second total differential for $y = f(x_1, \ldots, x_n)$ is exactly as in (B-11), where

$$\mathbf{dX} = \begin{bmatrix} dx_1 \\ \vdots \\ dx_n \end{bmatrix} \quad \text{and} \quad \mathbf{H} = \begin{bmatrix} f_{11} & f_{12} & \cdots & f_{1n} \\ f_{21} & f_{22} & \cdots & f_{2n} \\ \cdots & \cdots & \cdots & \cdots \\ f_{n1} & f_{n2} & \cdots & f_{nn} \end{bmatrix}$$

Thus $d^2f < 0$ (a maximum) if and only if $|\mathbf{H}_1| < 0$, $|\mathbf{H}_2| > 0$, $|\mathbf{H}_3| < 0, \ldots, |\mathbf{H}_n| < 0$ if n is odd and $|\mathbf{H}_n| > 0$ if n is even. For $d^2f > 0$ (a minimum) we must have $|\mathbf{H}_1| > 0$, $|\mathbf{H}_2| > 0, \ldots, |\mathbf{H}_n| > 0$. To apply the second-order condition on the sign of d^2f, we evaluate the principal minors of $\mathbf{H}^*$, the hessian matrix in which f_{ij} for all i and j are evaluated at the one or more $\mathbf{X}^* = [x_1^*, \ldots, x_n^*]'$ where $df = 0$. The rules for maxima and minima of functions of one or of two variables can thus be looked upon as special cases of the general results for a function of n variables.

PROBLEMS

B-1 Write each of the following in $\mathbf{X}'\mathbf{AX}$ form:

(*a*) $-x_1^2 - x_2^2 - 4x_3^2 + x_1x_2 + 2x_2x_3$
(*b*) $2x_1^2 + 6x_2^2 - 6x_1x_2$
(*c*) $x_1^2 + x_2^2 + x_3^2 - x_1x_2 - x_2x_3 - x_1x_3$
(*d*) $5x_1^2 + x_3^2 - 6x_2x_3$

B-2 Determine whether each of the quadratic forms in Prob. B-1 is positive definite, negative definite, or neither.

B-3 For each of the following functions, examine whether $d^2f > 0$, $d^2f < 0$, or neither:

(*a*) $f(x_1, x_1) = 6x_1^2 + 5x_2^2$
(*b*) $f(x_1, x_2, x_3) = -x_1^2 - x_2^2 - x_3^2 + 4x_1 + 6x_2 + 2x_3$
(*c*) $f(x_1, x_2) = x_1^2 + x_2^2 - 3x_1x_2$
(*d*) $f(x_1, x_2, x_3) = 4x_1^2 - 2x_2^2 + x_3^2 - 4x_1x_2$

APPENDIX

C

DIFFERENCE AND DIFFERENTIAL EQUATIONS

Models of economic growth deal with the values of economic variables (e.g., consumption, investment, etc.) at various points in time. Relationships between the variables and across time are expressed in terms of equations (or inequalities). In the study of algebraic equations, *linear* relations are more easily solved or at least analyzed than *nonlinear* ones. For the single-equation case, compare $ax = b$ and $ax^2 + \ln x = b$; for systems of equations we are faced with $\mathbf{AX} = \mathbf{B}$ instead of $f_1(\mathbf{X}) = b_1, \ldots, f_m(\mathbf{X}) = b_m$ (where **A**, **X**, and **B** are matrices or vectors of appropriate size). The same relative ease of solution attaches to linear difference or differential equations, and as a consequence this appendix will be primarily concerned with the linear (or first-degree) cases. When we investigate the usefulness of phase diagrams, however, we will see how that analytical method for linear differential equations can be used in nonlinear situations as well.

The distinction between difference equations and differential equations is made entirely on whether the independent variable is discrete or continuous, respectively. (In general, we will speak of time as the independent variable; this is quite common in economic applications but, depending on the particular setting of the problem, some other variable may act as the independent one.) Letting y denote a dependent variable (e.g., regional income), then the difference equation case utilizes the concept of y_t (the value of y at "time t"), y_{t+1} (the value of y one period after time t), y_{t-1}, etc. In particular, $y_{t+1} - y_t$ would represent the *difference* or change in the value of regional income between time t and the succeeding period. Defining the length of the time period as Δt, then the *average* rate of change in y over the interval from t to $t + 1$ is $(y_{t+1} - y_t)/\Delta t$. On the other hand, in differential equations derivatives of y with respect to time appear (i.e., *instantaneous* rates of change). These instantaneous rates are, of course, the limits of the average rates, as $\Delta t \to 0$, which is to say, as time is measured continuously rather than at fixed intervals only.

Difference Equations: Example and General Notation

Suppose that the value of y is related to its values in three preceding periods in the following way:

$$y_t = 5y_{t-1} + 7y_{t-2} - 15y_{t-3} + 10 \tag{C-1}$$

This is a third-order, first-degree difference equation. Values of y as far back as *three* periods ago contribute an influence on the current value; this is why the equation is a third-order one. That is, the order is the difference between the earliest and latest period at which the variable appears in the equation; if $t = 1975$ and $\Delta t = 1$ year, $t - 3 = 1972$. The equation is a first-degree, or linear, one in exactly the same sense as ordinary algebraic equations would be; the variables involved are not multiplied together, raised to powers, and nor do they appear as arguments in trigonometric or exponential functions. [In four-dimensional space, with one axis for each of the y, the equation (C-1) would be represented as a hyperplane.] Since only the dependence of one value of y on its preceding three values (and a constant) is depicted in (C-1), two alternative presentations of the same information are

$$y_{t+1} = 5y_t + 7y_{t-1} - 15y_{t-2} + 10 \tag{C-2}$$

and

$$y_{t+3} = 5y_{t+2} + 7y_{t+1} - 15y_t + 10 \tag{C-3}$$

By defining the *operator* E as "the value of the variable one period later," we can represent y_{t+1} as $E(y_t)$. Further, using this same notion, $y_{t+2} = E(y_{t+1}) = E[E(y_t)] = E^2(y_t)$, etc. Thus, for example, (C-3) can be rewritten, after moving all y to the left-hand side, as

$$(E^3 - 5E^2 - 7E + 15)y_t = 10 \tag{C-4}$$

In correspondence with ordinary terminology, if the right-hand side were zero, the difference equation would be *homogeneous*; if there is a constant term, as here, it is a *nonhomogeneous* difference equation. If we adopt the convenient convention of always representing a difference equation so that "t" is the *earliest* period [i.e., writing (C-1) or (C-2) as (C-3)], then we recognize that in operator notation, the order of the equation will be the highest power to which the operator E is raised. Therefore, the general nth order linear difference equation can be written

$$(a_0 E^n + a_1 E^{n-1} + \cdots + a_{n-1}E + a_n)y_t = k \tag{C-5}$$

which is the operator form of

$$a_0 y_{t+n} + a_1 y_{t+n-1} + \cdots + a_{n-1} y_{t+1} + a_n y_t = k$$

For this to be an nth order equation, it is necessary that $a_0 \neq 0$; thus one can always divide all coefficients (as well as the right-hand side) by a_0, leaving y_{t+n} with a coefficient of 1. Many texts use that convention.

Considering (C-3), we see that if we knew three consecutive values of y, we could find the "next" value and, consequently, all subsequent values. For example, starting at $t = 0$ (the "initial" observation), if $y_0 = 2$, $y_1 = 1$, and $y_2 = 3$, we see from (C-3) that

$$y_3 = 5y_2 + 7y_1 - 15y_0 + 10 = 5(3) + 7(1) - 15(2) + 10 = 2$$

Similarly,

$$y_4 = 5(2) + 7(3) - 15(1) + 10 = 26$$

$$y_5 = 5(26) + 7(2) - 15(3) + 10 = 109$$

$$y_6 = 5(109) + 7(26) - 15(2) + 10 = 707$$

etc. Thus, if one wanted the value of y at $t = 100$, that is, 100 periods after the initial observation, successive application of this same procedure—94 more times—would produce it. In the process, we would have found the value of y for each and every one of the intervening periods, which in many cases would be more information than we really wanted. If, on the other hand, we had an expression in which y was shown as some function of time t, then by simply setting $t = 100$ in that expression, we would have y_{100}. Such an expression would be a solution to the difference equation (C-4).

Differential Equations: Example and General Notation

Suppose that two successive values of y are related by the following first-order difference equation:

$$(E - 3)y_t = 1$$

or

$$y_{t+1} = 3y_t + 1 \tag{C-6}$$

Subtracting y_t from both sides gives the change in y during one period (say one year),

$$y_{t+1} - y_t = 2y_t + 1$$

If our time frame were to change and we were interested in the value of y six months after time t, we might estimate that in one-half of the time from t to $t + 1$, y_t would have grown by one-half of the total change, that is,

$$y_{t+1/2} - y_t = (2y_t + 1)(\tfrac{1}{2})$$

Consider any small increment of time, Δt, which is less than one period (here, less than one year). We would have

$$y_{t+\Delta t} - y_t = (2y_t + 1)(\Delta t)$$

Dividing by Δt gives the *average* rate of change

$$\frac{y_{t+\Delta t} - y_t}{\Delta t} = \frac{(2y_t + 1)(\Delta t)}{\Delta t} \tag{C-7}$$

[If $\Delta t = \frac{1}{4}$, (C-7) gives the change in y over a three-month period.] Taking the limit, as $\Delta t \to 0$, gives

$$\frac{dy}{dt} = 2y + 1 \quad \text{or} \quad \frac{dy}{dt} - 2y = 1 \tag{C-8}$$

which is a nonhomogeneous first-order, first-degree differential equation. Put simply, a differential equation is one in which a variable and one or more of its derivatives appear. The order of the equation is simply the order of the highest derivative that appears; the degree of a differential equation is the power to which the highest-order derivative is raised. If the right-hand side were zero, the equation would be homogeneous. As with difference equations, our concern will be primarily with first-degree or linear differential equations.

By defining an *operator D* as "the derivative of" and by writing $y(t)$ to indicate with respect to what variable the derivative is being taken, we can represent dy/dt as $Dy(t)$.† Further, $d^2y/dt^2 = d/dt(dy/dt) = D[Dy(t)] = D^2y(t)$, etc. Therefore we can rewrite (C-8) as

$$(D - 2)y(t) = 1 \tag{C-9}$$

Thus the order of a differential equation will be the highest power to which the operator D is raised. The general nth order linear differential equation can be written

$$(a_0D^n + a_1D^{n-1} + \cdots + a_{n-1}D + a_n)y(t) = k \tag{C-10}$$

[Compare with (C-5), the general nth-order difference equation.] This is the operator form of

$$a_0\frac{d^ny}{dt^n} + a_1\frac{d^{n-1}y}{dt^{n-1}} + \cdots + a_{n-1}\frac{dy}{dt} + a_ny = k$$

These equations are so-called *ordinary* differential equations; if y were a function of more than one independent variable, so that partial derivatives would be necessary, we would have *partial* differential equations, whose solutions are more difficult. Our concern will be with ordinary differential equations only.

Given one particular value of y at some "initial" observation point, we see from (C-6) that succeeding values could be found via successive application of that equation. We also see from (C-8) that, given some value of y, the derivative would be known and hence the path of y through time would be established. As in the case of difference equations, the most useful kind of expression relating y to time would be if y could be found as an explicit function of t; such an expression would be a solution to the differential equation.

† When the independent variable is unambiguous, we would simply write Dy.

A great many texts emphasize the numerous special techniques for finding either exact or approximate solutions to difference and differential equations; these tend to be essentially algebraic procedures. We will touch upon a few of them only briefly, primarily in order to see in a general way what solutions to these kinds of equations will be like. A second area of investigation for difference and differential equations is that of the stability of the time path of the dependent variable (or variables); i.e., the question of whether the values get ever larger, ever smaller, oscillate, approach zero, etc., as time (the independent variable) increases. It is often possible to analyze the stability question for one or more difference or differential equations, without actually finding an explicit solution, using either algebraic or geometric techniques. We will examine these topics.

C-1 FIRST-ORDER LINEAR DIFFERENCE EQUATIONS

The general homogeneous first-order difference equation is, in operator form, from (C-5), $(a_0E + a_1)y_t = 0$, that is,

$$a_0 y_{t+1} + a_1 y_t = 0 \tag{C-11}$$

Rearrangement gives

$$y_{t+1} = -\frac{a_1}{a_0} y_t$$

or, letting $b = -(a_1/a_0)$,

$$y_{t+1} = by_t \tag{C-12}$$

Suppose that we know the value of y at some "initial" period, $t = 0$, that is, $y_0 = c_0$. Applying (C-12) successively, we find that

$$y_1 = by_0 = bc_0$$
$$y_2 = by_1 = b^2 y_0 = b^2 c_0$$
$$y_3 = by_2 = b^3 y_0 = b^3 c_0$$

and therefore that

$$y_t = b^t y_0 = b^t c_0 \tag{C-13}$$

The relationship in (C-13) constitutes a *solution* to the difference equation in (C-12), with the initial condition $y_0 = c_0$. That is, (C-13) gives the value of y at *any* time t as a function of t and two parameters, b and c_0. Recall that b is just $-(a_1/a_0)$, i.e., it is determined entirely by the coefficients of the original difference relationship in (C-11), and c_0 is exactly the value that is necessary to make (C-13) consistent with the initial observation, y_0. That is, from (C-13), with $t = 0$, $y_0 = b^0 c_0 = c_0$.

The result in (C-13) is completely general and thus expresses the form of solution for any homogeneous first-order linear difference equation. (Generally the constant term is written first, that is, $y_t = c_0 b^t$.) Much of the study of difference equations is concerned with finding solutions to higher-order and/or nonhomogeneous and/or nonlinear equations, as well as to systems of such equations. Even with a general solution as simple as that in (C-13), however, a good deal of qualitative analysis—analysis of the movement of the dependent variable over time—is possible because of the particular way in which time enters in the equation. For example, we assume $c_0 > 0$ and examine the possibilities for behavior of y over time, i.e., as t increases.

Case a: $b > 0$

1. If $b > 1$, then, since successive values of y are given by a function involving b raised to ever-increasing positive powers and multiplied by $c_0 > 0$, y_t increases by increasing amounts, or explodes toward $+\infty$ over time. (For example, if $b = 1.8$, $b^2 = 3.24$, $b^3 = 5.83$, $b^4 = 10.50$, $b^5 = 18.90$, etc.)
2. If $b = 1$, then $y_t = c_0$ for all future time periods.
3. If $b < 1$, then y_t decreases by decreasing amounts, diminishing toward zero over time. (For example, if $b = 0.7$, $b^2 = 0.49$, $b^3 = 0.34$, $b^4 = 0.24$, $b^5 = 0.17$, etc.)

Case b: $b < 0$ If b is negative, then the sign of y_t will alternate between negative and positive, since b raised to odd powers will be negative but b raised to even powers will be positive.

1. If $b < -1$, the absolute values of successive values of y_t will increase by increasing amounts, i.e., the alternations will be explosive.
2. If $b = -1$, then y_t alternates between $+c_0$ and $-c_0$.
3. If $b > -1$, the alternations will be dampened; y_t will approach zero over time.

Figure C-1 illustrates these six possibilities, for the particular case $c_0 = 2$. In sketching the evolution of y_t over time, we connect the individual values at successive points in time only as a visual aid. The paths traced out by the various solutions actually consist only of series of dots. Clearly, if $c_0 < 0$, the signs of all of the above results will be reversed. For example, if $b > 1$ [Case a(1)] and $c_0 < 0$, y_t will decrease by increasing amounts over time, i.e., it will explode toward negative infinity. Or, if $0 < b < 1$ [Case a(3)] and $c_0 < 0$, y_t will begin at a negative value (namely c_0) and increase by decreasing amounts, approaching zero (from below) over time. The signs of the other cases are similarly altered if the initial observation is negative rather than positive. (If $c_0 = 0$, then clearly y_t will remain at zero for all future periods.)

In the case of the homogeneous first-order linear difference equation, then, one can make several general observations about what the path of y_t over time will be: (1) the size of b (more correctly, the absolute value of b) relative to 1 determines whether the path will be of an explosive, constant, or diminishing nature, and (2) the *sign* of b determines whether or not y_t will alternate between

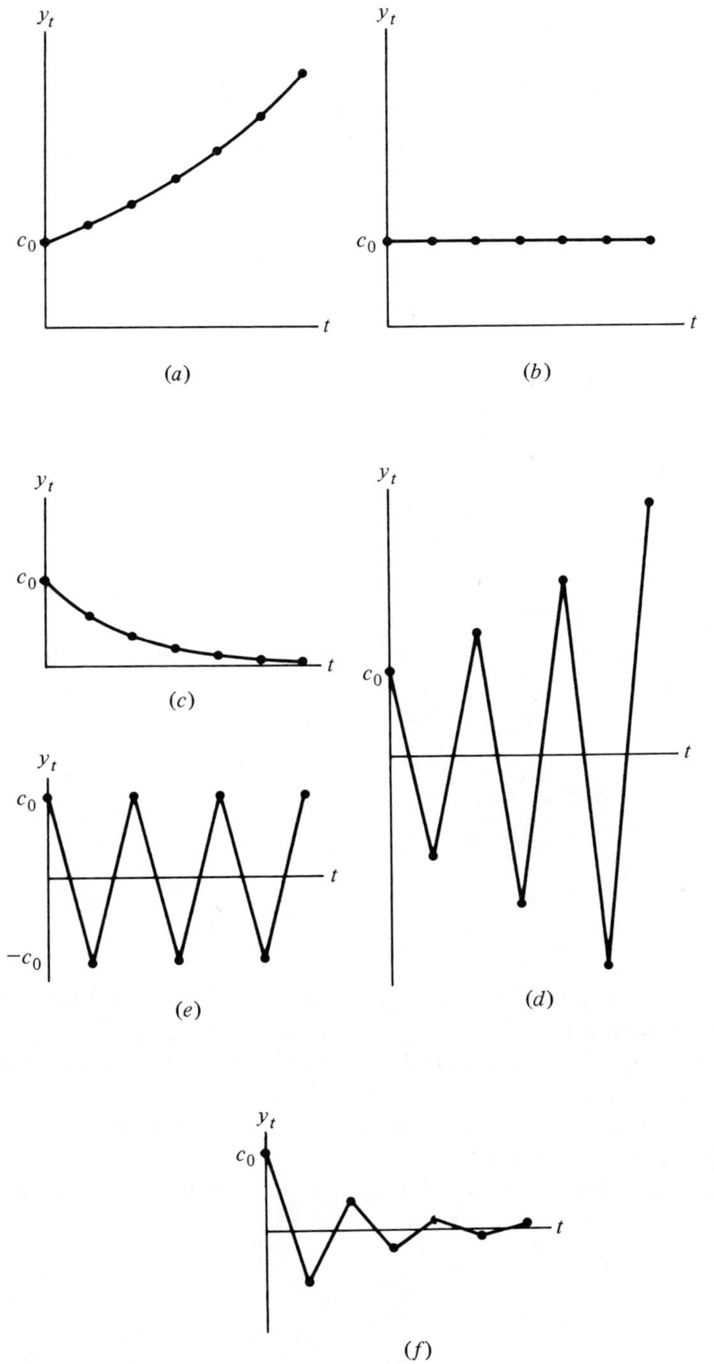

Figure C-1 Time paths for $y_t = 2b^t$, for various values of b. (a) $b = 1.2$. (b) $b = 1$. (c) $b = 0.6$. (d) $b = -1.2$. (e) $b = -1$. (f) $b = -0.6$.

positive and negative values. But since $b = -(a_1/a_0)$, this information is obtainable directly by inspection from the difference equation. The *sign* of c_0 influences the sign of the values of y_t over time, and the *size* of c_0 accelerates (if $|c_0| > 1$) or decelerates (if $|c_0| < 1$) the tendency toward explosion or diminution. It does not, however, influence the fundamental nature of the time path; that is governed exclusively by b. We will return to these notions in Sec. C-5, when we will be concerned with questions of stability and equilibrium.

C-2 HIGHER-ORDER LINEAR DIFFERENCE EQUATIONS

Second-Order Equations: Introduction

The general homogeneous second-order linear difference equation, in operator form, is

$$(a_0 E^2 + a_1 E + a_2)y_t = 0$$

that is,

$$a_0 y_{t+2} + a_1 y_{t+1} + a_2 y_t = 0 \tag{C-14}$$

Recall that the first-order equation $(a_0 E + a_1)y_t = 0$ was reexpressed as $(E - b)y_t = 0$, where $b = -(a_1/a_0)$, the root of the equation $a_0 b + a_1 = 0$, and its solution was found to be $y_t = c_0 b^t$. Similarly, $(a_0 E^2 + a_1 E + a_2)y_t = 0$ can be reexpressed as either

$$(E - x_1)(E - x_2)y_t = 0$$

or

$$(E - x_2)(E - x_1)y_t = 0$$

where x_1 and x_2 are the roots of

$$a_0 x^2 + a_1 x + a_2 = 0 \tag{C-15}$$

which is the so-called *characteristic* or *auxiliary* equation to this general second-order linear difference equation.

However, if a solution $y_t = f(t)$ is found that satisfies $(E - x_1)y_t = 0$, it clearly also satisfies $(E - x_2)(E - x_1)y_t = 0$. Similarly, if $y_t = g(t)$ satisfies $(E - x_2)y_t = 0$, it also satisfies $(E - x_1)(E - x_2)y_t = 0$. From the results for first-order linear difference equations, we know that a solution to $(E - x_1)y_t = 0$ is $y_t = k_1(x_1)^t$, where k_1 is some constant. Similarly, $y_t = k_2(x_2)^t$ is a solution to $(E - x_2)y_t = 0$. It is easily verified that the sum $f(t) + g(t)$, that is,

$$y_t = k_1(x_1)^t + k_2(x_2)^t \tag{C-16}$$

also satisfies (C-15).†

† The interested reader can easily show this by substituting $y_t = k_1(x_1)^t + k_2(x_2)^t$ into (C-14), rearranging, and remembering that both $k_1(x_1)^t$ and $k_2(x_2)^t$ are themselves solutions to (C-14).

Reasoning similarly to the first-order case, it is clear that now a *pair* of "initial" conditions, values for y at $t = 0$ and $t = 1$, are necessary in order to determine all further values of y from the relationship given in (C-14). In general, there will be two distinct roots to the quadratic auxiliary equation given in (C-15), from the formula $x = \left(-a_1 \pm \sqrt{a_1^2 - 4a_0a_2}\right)/2a_0$. The general solution given in (C-16) allows this initial condition information to be taken into account completely, through determination of the values of the two constants, k_1 and k_2.

Let the two initial conditions be $y_0 = c_0$ and $y_1 = c_1$. Then, from (C-16), for $t = 0$ and $t = 1$, respectively,

$$\begin{aligned} k_1 + \quad k_2 &= c_0 \\ x_1k_1 + x_2k_2 &= c_1 \end{aligned} \tag{C-17}$$

Since c_0 and c_1 are known from initial conditions and x_1 and x_2 are known from the a in (C-15), this is a pair of linear equations in k_1 and k_2, for which a unique solution can be found as long as the determinant of $\begin{bmatrix} 1 & 1 \\ x_1 & x_2 \end{bmatrix}$ is not zero, which is to say, as long as the two roots, x_1 and x_2, are not equal.†

Second-Order Equations: Distinct Roots

For example, consider the particular case where (C-14) is

$$y_{t+2} - 8y_{t+1} + 12y_t = 0 \tag{C-18}$$

or, in operator form,

$$(E^2 - 8E + 12)y_t = 0$$

along with initial conditions $y_0 = 57$ and $y_1 = 334$. The operator form makes particularly clear exactly what the auxiliary equation is, since it is only necessary to substitute the unknown x for the operator E. We have $x^2 - 8x + 12 = 0$, which factors easily to $(x - 6)(x - 2) = 0$, from which $x = 6$ or 2. Therefore

$$y_t = k_1(6)^t + k_2(2)^t$$

Setting $t = 0$ and then $t = 1$ in this equation, and from the observations on y_0 and y_1, we have

$$\begin{aligned} k_1 + \quad k_2 &= \quad 57 \\ 6k_1 + 2k_2 &= 334 \end{aligned}$$

† Of course, if $c_0 = c_1 = 0$ (that is, $y_0 = 0$, $y_1 = 0$) so that (C-17) is a pair of homogeneous equations, then one might be interested in nontrivial solutions, which would require a zero-valued determinant. But, as reference to (C-14) shows, y_2 would then be zero also and hence y would be zero for all future time, irrespective of the values of a_0, a_1, and a_2. This is not a very interesting case.

and therefore $k_1 = 55$ and $k_2 = 2$. The final solution of (C-18), giving y_t as a function of t, is therefore

$$y_t = 55(6)^t + 2(2)^t = 55(6)^t + (2)^{t+1} \tag{C-19}$$

Two problems may arise in the second-order case, because of the fact that the auxiliary equation is quadratic; these are that x_1 and x_2 may be equal (multiple roots) or that x_1 and x_2 may involve imaginary numbers—when $(a_1^2 - 4a_0 a_2) < 0$. These problems can occur in any linear difference equation of higher than first order, and we examine them in turn.

Second-Order Equations: Multiple Roots

Consider the second-order equation

$$y_{t+2} - 10y_{t+1} - 25y_t = 0 \tag{C-20}$$

that is, $(E^2 - 10E + 25)y_1 = 0$, with $y_0 = 3$ and $y_1 = 25$. Forming the auxiliary equation as usual gives $x^2 - 10x + 25 = 0$, which factors to $(x-5)(x-5) = 0$ and from which it follows that $x_1 = 5$ and $x_2 = 5$. The problem caused by non-unique roots comes about when introducing the information contained in the initial conditions. Using (C-16), we have

$$\begin{aligned} k_1 + k_2 &= 3 \\ 5k_1 + 5k_2 &= 25 \end{aligned} \tag{C-21}$$

i.e., an inconsistent pair of linear equations. Recalling the $\mathbf{AX} = \mathbf{B}$ form for linear equations, the rank of the coefficient matrix $\mathbf{A}$ is 1 and the rank of the augmented matrix $(\mathbf{A} \mid \mathbf{B})$ is 2; geometrically, the system is a pair of parallel lines in two-dimensional solution space. It can be shown† that when a second-order linear difference equation has multiple roots the form of the general solution, as was previously given in (C-16), is altered to

$$y_t = k_1(x_1)^t + k_2 t(x_2)^t \tag{C-22}$$

In terms of (C-21), this has the effect of removing the inconsistency in the pair of equations, since they now become (for $t = 0$ and $t = 1$, respectively)

$$\begin{aligned} k_1 \qquad &= 3 \\ 5k_1 + 5k_2 &= 25 \end{aligned}$$

from which it follows that $k_1 = 3$ and $k_2 = 2$. Thus, the solution to (C-20) is

$$y_t = 3(5)^t + 2t(5)^t$$

† This is done in many texts that are concerned primarily with difference (and/or differential) equations as a mathematical subject, e.g., Levy and Lessman [15].

Second-Order Equations: Complex Roots

With second-order equations, we have the quadratic auxiliary equation $a_0x^2 + a_1x + a_2 = 0$. The solutions are always given by $x = (-a_1 \pm \sqrt{a_1^2 - 4a_0a_2})/2a_0$. When the expression under the square root is negative, it is customary to employ the definition $i = \sqrt{-1}$ in the solution. For example, given $x^2 - 2x + 5 = 0$, we find that $x = 1 \pm 2\sqrt{-1} = 1 \pm 2i$, that is, $x_1 = 1 + 2i$, $x_2 = 1 - 2i$. The nature of the solution formula assures that complex numbers as solutions to quadratic equations will always occur in pairs; these are called complex conjugate numbers. In general notation, we can write them as $x_1 = \alpha + \beta i$ and $x_2 = \alpha - \beta i$, where α is the so-called real part and βi the imaginary part of the complex number. Here $\alpha = -(a_1/2a_0)$ and $\beta = (\sqrt{4a_0a_2 - a_1^2})/2a_0$.

The roots of the auxiliary equation therefore will be complex conjugate whenever $(a_1^2 - 4a_0a_2)$ is negative. These two roots, x_1 and x_2, can be substituted into the general solution (C-16)

$$y_t = k_1(\alpha + \beta i)^t + k_2(\alpha - \beta i)^t \tag{C-23}$$

where α and β are related to the coefficients of the original difference equation exactly as above. The problem is that the time path implied by this result is not very clear, because of the imaginary part of the solution. For this reason, we review a few facts about imaginary and complex numbers; we will see that alternative and more meaningful representations of (C-23) are possible.

Any complex number can be represented in two-dimensional cartesian coordinates if one adopts the convention that the magnitude of α is measured along one axis (the "real" axis, usually the horizontal) and the magnitude of β is measured along the other (vertical) axis (the "imaginary" axis). Any point in two-dimensional space may also be interpreted as the endpoint of a vector (in two-dimensional vector space) emanating from the origin, and vectors in two-dimensional space can also be identified uniquely by their length and orientation, i.e., the angle that they make with the positive half of the horizontal axis. Therefore, as Fig. C-2 suggests, the vector whose endpoint has coordinates α and β can also be identified as having length r and making an angle θ with the horizontal axis.

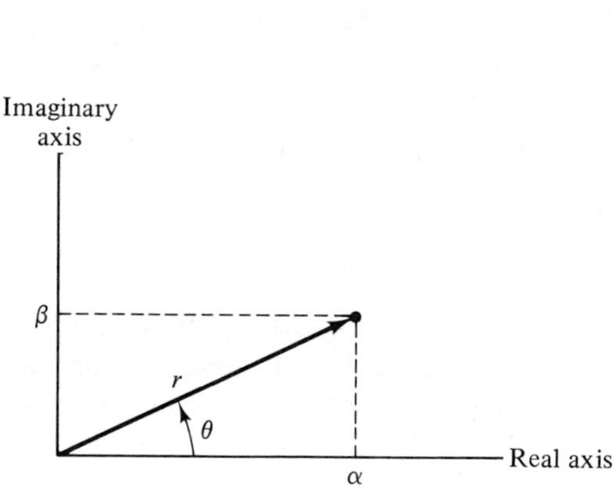

Figure C-2 Cartesian and polar coordinates for $\alpha + \beta i$.

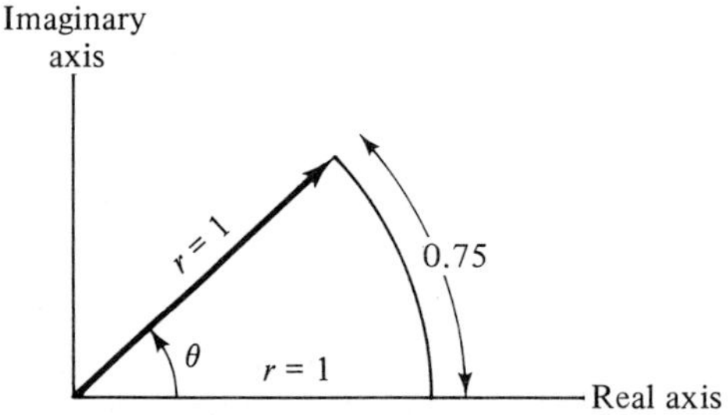

Figure C-3 Arc length uniquely associated with angle θ.

These coordinates, r and θ, simply serve to locate the point using polar coordinates. Of course, the two sets of coordinates are related, as Fig. C-2 clearly indicates, since $r^2 = \alpha^2 + \beta^2$ and $\sin\theta = \beta/r$ or $\cos\theta = \alpha/r$; in particular, $\beta = r\sin\theta$ and $\alpha = r\cos\theta$. Therefore, by simple substitution, $\alpha \pm \beta i = r(\cos\theta \pm i\sin\theta)$.

It is now appropriate to recall the use of radians, rather than degrees, as a measure of the size of an angle. If the vector in Fig. C-2 were (1) thought of as the radius of a circle whose center is at the origin and (2) arbitrarily "normalized" so that its length were defined to be unity (define $r = 1$), then the size of θ would be uniquely given by the length of the arc on the circumference of that circle that is subtended by the horizontal axis and the vector shown. This is done in Fig. C-3. Since the radius constitutes a unit of measure of length 1, the length of the arc is measured in that same unit. In the figure, the arc is approximately 0.75 radii (or, more commonly, 0.75 rad) long. Many variables, e.g., distance between two objects on a plane, are more logically measured in units along a line (linearly), like yards, than in circular units, like degrees. Therefore this measure of angle size, which is one of length, not degrees, is useful in cases when an independent variable which is logically measured in linear units is also an argument in a trigonometric function; e.g., the variable x in the expression $3x^2 + \cos x$. Since the total circumference of a circle is $2\pi r$, for the case of $r = 1$ (the so-called unit circle), the length of the circumference is just 2π. The angle associated with an entire circumference is 360°; thus 2π rad = 360° (π rad = 180°, 1 rad = 360°/2π = 57.3°, etc.).

An alternative representation for (C-23), therefore, is

$$y_t = k_1[r^t(\cos\theta + i\sin\theta)^t] + k_2[r^t(\cos\theta - i\sin\theta)^t] \tag{C-24}$$

A theorem, due to de Moivre, states that

$$(\cos\theta \pm i\sin\theta)^n = (\cos n\theta \pm i\sin n\theta)$$

This is quite easily shown, starting with $x = r(\cos\theta \pm i\sin\theta)$ and finding $x^2 = r^2[\cos 2\theta \pm i\sin 2\theta]$, using the trigonometric identities for the sine and for the cosine of the sum of two angles. This leads to $x^n = r^n(\cos n\theta \pm i\sin n\theta)$; but clearly, from the original definition of x, $x^n = r^n(\cos\theta \pm i\sin\theta)^n$ as well, and de Moivre's result follows. Therefore, (C-24) can be equally well expressed as

$$y_t = r^t[k_1(\cos \theta t + i \sin \theta t) + k_2(\cos \theta t - i \sin \theta t)] \tag{C-25}$$

and, even more neatly, letting $A_1 = k_1 + k_2$ and $A_2 = (k_1 - k_2)i$, as

$$y_t = r^t(A_1 \cos \theta t + A_2 \sin \theta t) \tag{C-26}$$

Here it is appropriate for θ to be measured in linear units, as is t; that is, θ is measured in radians.

In this form, the solution to the second-order linear difference equation is clearly seen to involve a *cyclical* path for y over time, from the simple observation that both the sine and cosine functions are periodic. (See Table C-1 and Fig. C-4.)

As a final variation on the trigonometric representation of y_t in the case of complex roots to the auxiliary equation, find the angle whose tangent is given by $-A_2/A_1$—recall that we set $A_1 = k_1 + k_2$ and $A_2 = (k_1 - k_2)i$ in order to simplify (C-25) to the form shown in (C-26).† That is, find the δ for which $\tan \delta = -A_2/A_1$.‡ Since different numerators and denominators can give the same ratio, and since $\tan \delta = \sin \delta / \cos \delta$, an additional parameter is needed. That is, δ is determined as the angle whose tangent is $-A_2/A_1$. But then $\sin \delta$ and $\cos \delta$ are also determined; yet these may only be proportional to $-A_2$ and A_1, respectively. Thus we must introduce a scale factor, A_3, such that $A_1 = A_3 \cos \delta$ and $-A_2 = A_3 \sin \delta$. (For example, let $A_2 = -3$, $A_1 = 5.196$; then $\tan \delta = 0.577$ and $\delta = 0.524$ rad, $\sin \delta = 0.5$, $\cos \delta = 0.866$, and therefore $A_3 = 6$.)

These definitions of δ and A_3 are not as arbitrary as they appear; in (C-26), substituting for A_1 and A_2 in $(A_1 \cos \theta t + A_2 \sin \theta t)$ gives $A_3 \cos \delta \cos \theta t -$

Table C-1 Values of $\sin \phi$ **and** $\cos \phi$

ϕ	Degrees	0	90	180	270	360
	Radians	0	$\pi/2$	π	$3\pi/2$	2π
$\sin \phi$		0	1	0	-1	0
$\cos \phi$		1	0	-1	0	1

† The reader may wonder if $-A_2/A_1$ will contain imaginary numbers, because of the way in which A_1 and A_2 were defined. It does not. By assuming two initial values, c_0 and c_1, for y at $t = 0$ and $t = 1$, one can solve for k_1 and k_2 in (C-23). (The reader may wish to do this.) Both k_1 and k_2 contain i but in such a way that it disappears (through cancellation) in both $k_1 + k_2$ and $(k_1 - k_2)i$. This is illustrated in the example at the end of this section.

‡ The tangent function repeats itself every π rad. At $\delta = 0$, $\tan \delta = 0$, and as δ increases toward $\pi/2$, $\tan \delta \to +\infty$; moreover, $\tan(-\delta) = -\tan \delta$, so as δ decreases toward $-\pi/2$, $\tan \delta \to -\infty$. The pattern repeats to the right of $\pi/2$ and to the left of $-\pi/2$; $\tan(\delta + \pi) = \tan \delta$ and $\tan(\delta - \pi) = \tan \delta$. Thus we can always take δ, as defined in $\tan \delta = -A_2/A_1$, to lie between $-\pi/2$ and $\pi/2$.

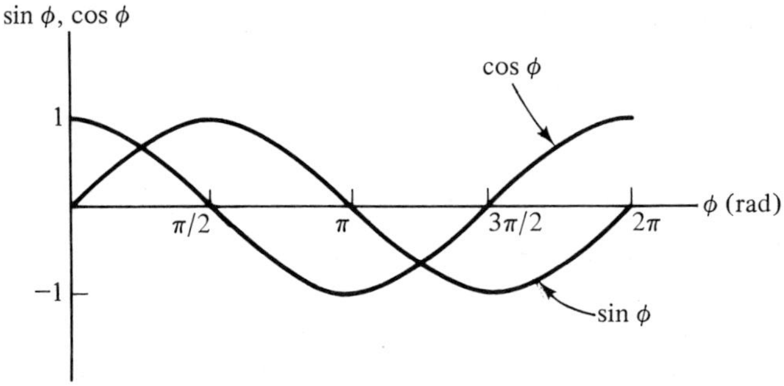

Figure C-4 Sine and cosine functions for angles from 0 to 2π rad.

$A_3 \sin \delta \sin \theta t$. From the trigonometric identity for the cosine of the sum of two angles, this is just $A_3 \cos (\theta t + \delta)$. Therefore (C-26) can also be expressed as

$$y_t = r^t[A_3 \cos (\theta t + \delta)] \qquad \text{(C-27)}$$

which again highlights the periodic or cyclical nature of the time path of y. In either (C-26) or (C-27), the values of r and θ come from the structure of the original difference equation (i.e., from the coefficients of its auxiliary equation). Specifically, $r^2 = \alpha^2 + \beta^2 = (-a_1/2a_0)^2 + (\sqrt{4a_0a_2 - a_1^2}/2a_0)^2 = a_2/a_0$ and $\cos \theta = -a_1/2\sqrt{a_0a_2}$ (or $\tan \theta = \beta/\alpha = -\sqrt{4a_0a_2 - a_1^2}/a_1$). The values of A_3 and δ in (C-27) are derived, as we have just seen, from A_1 and A_2 in (C-26) which come, in turn, from the initial conditions c_0 and c_1.

A periodic function has three characteristics, determined by the three parameters, A_3, θ, and δ, in (C-27). The *amplitude* of the function is the height of the peak above (or depth of the trough below) the average level. For the cosine function the average level is zero; as ϕ ranges from 0 to 2π rad, $\cos \phi$ ranges from 1 through 0 to -1 and back to 1 (see Table C-1 and Fig. C-4). Since A_3 multiplies the values of the cosine in (C-27), it determines the amplitude of the cycles. The *period* of the function is the range of the independent variable during which one complete oscillation occurs. For $\cos \phi$ we know that this is 2π (refer again to Table C-1 and Fig. C-4); for $\cos t$ this would also be for a range of t of 2π but for $\cos \theta t$ the period will be $2\pi/\theta$, which simply reflects the fact that if $\theta > 1$ repetitions will occur oftener and if $\theta < 1$ they will happen less often, since θ has the effect of stretching or shrinking the influence of t. Finally, the *phase* of the function is the value of the independent variable at which the first peak or trough occurs. For $\cos \phi$, this is at $\phi = 0$; it would clearly be at $t = 0$ for $\cos t$ or for $\cos \theta t$. For $\cos (t + \delta)$ it would occur at $t = -\delta$ and for $\cos (\theta t + \delta)$ at $-\delta/\theta$. Thus δ simply shifts the function rightward or leftward along the horizontal axis. The influence of r^t is to magnify or dampen the amplitude, depending on whether $r > 1$ or $r < 1$.

The results for y_t when there are complex roots to the auxiliary equation are sometimes expressed in yet another form; it is mentioned here primarily for completeness and also because it is useful when there are complex conjugate roots in the differential equation case. We need to recall several series results, all of which are particularizations of the general Taylor series. These are:

(*a*)
$$e^x = 1 + x + \frac{x^2}{2!} + \frac{x^3}{3!} + \cdots$$

(*b*)
$$e^{ax} = 1 + ax + \frac{(ax)^2}{2!} + \frac{(ax)^3}{3!} + \cdots$$

(*c*)
$$\cos x = 1 - \frac{x^2}{2!} + \frac{x^4}{4!} - \frac{x^6}{6!} + \cdots$$

(*d*)
$$\sin x = 1 - \frac{x^3}{3!} + \frac{x^5}{5!} - \frac{x^7}{7!} + \cdots$$

Applying (*b*) to the particular cases of e^{ix} and e^{-ix}, then finding

(*e*)
$$\tfrac{1}{2}(e^{ix} + e^{-ix})$$

and

(*f*)
$$\frac{1}{2i}(e^{ix} - e^{-ix})$$

it turns out that the series in (*e*) and (*c*) are the same and also that those in (*f*) and (*d*) are the same. That is, $\cos x = \frac{1}{2}(e^{ix} + e^{-ix})$ and $\sin x = (1/2i)(e^{ix} - e^{-ix})$. From this it follows that $(\cos x + i \sin x) = e^{ix}$ and $(\cos x - i \sin x) = e^{-ix}$, i.e., that $(\cos x \pm i \sin x) = e^{\pm ix}$. Thus, from (C-25),

$$y_t = r^t(k_1 e^{i\theta t} + k_2 e^{-i\theta t}) \tag{C-28}$$

In some fields, this exponential form of the difference equation solution is useful; for most applications in the social sciences, the forms in (C-26) or (C-27) are utilized, in part because they make so apparent the periodic or cyclical nature of the path of y over time.

A second-order equation that introduces the complication of complex roots is

$$y_{t+2} - 12y_{t+1} + 100y_t = 0 \tag{C-29}$$

that is, $(E^2 - 12E + 100)y_t = 0$, whose auxiliary equation is $x^2 - 12x + 100 = 0$. In addition, let $y_0 = 5$ and $y_1 = 12$. Using the general formula for solution of a quadratic equation, $x = (12 \pm \sqrt{144 - 400})/2 = 6 \pm 8\sqrt{-1} = 6 \pm 8i$.

Considering the solution form in (C-25),

$$y_t = k_1(6 + 8i)^t + k_2(6 - 8i)^t$$

and, given the two initial conditions

$$\begin{aligned} k_1 + \qquad\qquad k_2 &= 5 \\ (6 + 8i)k_1 + (6 - 8i)k_2 &= 12 \end{aligned}$$

from which it follows that $k_1 = (20i - 9)/8i$ and $k_2 = (20i + 9)/8i$. The complete solution is thus

$$y_t = \frac{20i - 9}{8i}(6 + 8i)^t + \frac{20i + 9}{8i}(6 - 8i)^t$$

Turning to the trigonometric forms of solution in (C-26) and (C-27), we find here that $A_1 = 5$ and $A_2 = -\frac{9}{4}$. In addition, $r^2 = 100$ and, since $\cos\theta = \frac{6}{10}$, $\theta = 0.927$ rad. Thus (C-26) is

$$y_t = 10^t[5\cos(0.927)t - \tfrac{9}{4}\sin(0.927)t]$$

Finally, $\tan\delta = -(-\frac{9}{4})/5 = 0.45$, $\delta = 0.423$ rad; $\sin\delta = 0.40136$, $\cos\delta = 0.91192$, and therefore $A_3 = 5.48$. Solution form (C-27) becomes

$$y_t = 10^t[5.48\cos(0.927)t + 0.423]$$

Second-Order Equations: The Nonhomogeneous Case

Another complication, which is possible with equations of any order, arises when the equation is not homogeneous. In the general notation of (C-5), this is the case of $k \neq 0$; this is shown in equation (C-4). As is shown in texts on difference equations,† the solution procedure for the nonhomogeneous case involves two steps: (1) find a solution to the so-called "reduced equation" that results when k is set equal to zero, i.e., when the difference equation is converted into a homogeneous one by ignoring the constant term, and denote this solution by y_t^h; and (2) find *any* "particular solution" that satisfies the nonhomogeneous difference equation; denote this by y_t^n. Then the general solution to the nonhomogeneous equation is the sum of the solutions found in steps (1) and (2); that is,

$$y_t = y_t^h + y_t^n \tag{C-30}$$

Only the process in (2) is new, since we have been concerned with homogeneous-case solutions (step 1) in most of this section. Consider the general nonhomogeneous second-order linear case

$$a_0 y_{t+2} + a_1 y_{t+1} + a_2 y_t = k \tag{C-31}$$

Would $y_t = c$, where c is a constant, satisfy (C-31)? This would mean $y_{t+2} = y_{t+1} = y_t = c$, that is, $a_0 c + a_1 c + a_2 c = k$ or $c = k/(a_0 + a_1 + a_2)$. Therefore, provided that $(a_0 + a_1 + a_2) \neq 0$, a solution to (C-31) is given by $y_t = k/(a_0 + a_1 + a_2)$. In cases where the coefficients of (C-31) *do* add to zero, one must try $y_t = ct$ as a possible particular solution; if this also generates a zero-valued denominator, one tries $y_t = ct^2$. It *will* provide a particular solution. This is an illustration of the general rule that for an nth-order equation, if one tries $y_t = c$, $y_t = ct$, $y_t = ct^2, \ldots$, there will always be a solution by $y_t = ct^n$ at the latest.

† The interested reader might consult Baumol [2], Gandolfo [10], or Goldberg [11].

Consider the second-order case. If $(a_0 + a_1 + a_2) = 0$, one tries $y_t = ct$, in which case $y_{t+1} = c(t+1)$ and $y_{t+2} = c(t+2)$. Substituting into (C-31),

$$a_0 c(t+2) + a_1 c(t+1) + a_2 ct = k$$

and, rearranging,

$$(a_0 + a_1 + a_2)ct + (2a_0 + a_1)c = k$$

Since $(a_0 + a_1 + a_2) = 0$ (otherwise we would not be trying the solution $y_t = ct$), this too will fail if and only if $(2a_0 + a_1) = 0$. In that case, $y_t = ct^2$ is used. Then $y_{t+1} = c(t+1)^2$, $y_{t+2} = c(t+2)^2$; substituting into (C-31) and rearranging gives

$$(a_0 + a_1 + a_2)ct^2 + 2(2a_0 + a_1)ct + (4a_0 + a_1)c = k$$

which will fail if and only if $(4a_0 + a_1) = 0$, since $y_t = ct^2$ is only being tried because $(a_0 + a_1 + a_2) = 0$ and $(2a_0 + a_1) = 0$.

Therefore, for all three solutions ($y_t = c$, $y_t = ct$, and $y_t = ct^2$) to fail, the following set of homogeneous linear equations in a_0, a_1, and a_2 must have nontrivial solutions [i.e., other than the obvious and trivial solution $a_0 = a_1 = a_2 = 0$ which is incompatible with the general equation given in (C-31)]:

$$\begin{aligned} a_0 + a_1 + a_2 &= 0 \\ 2a_0 + a_1 \quad\;\; &= 0 \\ 4a_0 + a_1 \quad\;\; &= 0 \end{aligned}$$

In matrix form, $\mathbf{AX} = \mathbf{B}$, these are

$$\begin{bmatrix} 1 & 1 & 1 \\ 2 & 1 & 0 \\ 4 & 1 & 0 \end{bmatrix} \begin{bmatrix} a_0 \\ a_1 \\ a_2 \end{bmatrix} = \begin{bmatrix} 0 \\ 0 \\ 0 \end{bmatrix}$$

and for nontrivial solutions $\mathbf{A}$ must be singular, that is, $|\mathbf{A}| = 0$.

From the second row of $\mathbf{A}$, let $x_1 = 2$, $x_2 = 1$, and $x_3 = 0$; then the structure of $\mathbf{A}$ can be shown as

$$\begin{bmatrix} 1 & 1 & 1 \\ x_1 & x_2 & x_3 \\ x_1^2 & x_2^2 & x_3^2 \end{bmatrix}$$

This is known as a Vandermonde matrix. Evaluating the determinant of the (3×3) Vandermonde matrix by expansion down the first column gives $x_2 x_3^2 - x_3 x_2^2 - x_1(x_3^2 - x_2^2) + x_1^2(x_3 - x_2)$ or, factoring out $(x_3 - x_2)$,

$$|\mathbf{A}| = (x_3 - x_2)[x_2 x_3 - x_1 x_3 - x_1 x_2 + x_1^2]$$

But the expression in brackets is just $(x_2 - x_1)(x_3 - x_1)$, so that the determinant can be expressed as

$$|\mathbf{A}| = (x_3 - x_2)(x_2 - x_1)(x_3 - x_1)$$

This can only be zero if at least two of the x are equal, which is clearly not the case for the second-order equation here, where x_1, x_2, and x_3 are the distinguishably different integers 2, 1, and 0, respectively. Therefore the coefficient matrix of the homogeneous equation system cannot be singular, the equations cannot have nontrivial solutions, and the three equations that serve to disqualify $y_t = c$, $y_t = ct$, and also $y_t = ct^2$ cannot all hold.

For an nth order equation, the coefficient matrix in the homogeneous equation system would be

$$\begin{bmatrix} 1 & 1 & \cdots & 1 \\ x_1 & x_2 & \cdots & x_{n+1} \\ \cdots & \cdots & \cdots & \cdots \\ x_1^n & x_2^n & \cdots & x_{n+1}^n \end{bmatrix}$$

In this case, $x_1, \ldots, x_n$ will be $(n-1), \ldots, 0$, respectively, and the Vandermonde determinant can be shown to be the logical extension of $|\mathbf{A}|$ above for the second-order case; it is

$$|\mathbf{A}| = \prod_{i>j} (x_i - x_j)$$

As an example of the nonhomogeneous case, consider

$$y_{t+2} - 3y_{t+1} - 10y_t = -12 \tag{C-32}$$

with $y_0 = 9$ and $y_1 = -1$. In operator form, the homogeneous version of this equation (i.e., ignoring the -12) is $(E^2 - 3E - 10)y_t = 0$ whose auxiliary equation is $x^2 - 3x - 10 = 0$, from which $(x-5)(x+2) = 0$ and $x = 5, -2$. Therefore $y_t^h = k_1(5)^t + k_2(-2)^t$. The information provided by the initial conditions is not utilized until we have the complete general solution, $y_t^h + y_t^n$. For the nonhomogeneous part, try $y_t = c$. For (C-32), this means $(1 - 3 - 10)c = -12$, or $c = 1$, so $y_t^n = 1$. Therefore the general solution is

$$y_t = k_1(5)^t + k_2(-2)^t + 1 \tag{C-33}$$

It is now appropriate to introduce the information provided by the two initial conditions

$$\begin{aligned} k_1 + k_2 + 1 &= 9 \\ 5k_1 - 2k_2 + 1 &= -1 \end{aligned}$$

from which $k_1 = 2$ and $k_2 = 6$, so that, finally,

$$y_t = 2(5)^t + 6(-2)^t + 1 \tag{C-34}$$

represents the complete general solution to (C-32).

nth-Order Equations

For the second-order linear difference equation (C-14), general solutions for the various cases have been presented, e.g., in (C-16), (C-22), (C-27), and (C-30). The varieties of behavior that are possible for the path of the dependent variable over time result from the varieties of possible solutions to the quadratic auxiliary equation—distinct, multiple, or complex conjugate roots. These alternatives are not possible, of course, in the first-order case; they (and no others) can arise in all higher-order cases, however, since the degree of the auxiliary equation is always the same as the order of the difference equation. Thus a third-order linear difference equation will have a cubic auxiliary equation whose three roots may be distinct, multiple, or complex conjugate, in various combinations; and similarly for even higher-order equations.

The solution for the homogeneous nth-order linear difference equation, as shown in (C-5)—with $k = 0$—is a logical extension of that for the second-order case, shown in (C-16). The auxiliary equation will be an nth-degree equation in x, and hence it will have n roots, $x_1, \ldots, x_n$ (not usually easily found and not necessarily distinct). When these roots are distinct, the solution is

$$y_t = k_1(x_1)^t + \cdots + k_n(x_n)^t \tag{C-35}$$

The values of $k_1, \ldots, k_n$ are found from the n initial conditions that an nth-order equation requires, namely, $y_0 = c_0, y_1 = c_1, \ldots, y_{n-1} = c_{n-1}$. If two or more x_i are equal (but real), some of the terms in (C-35) will be multiplied by t, or by some power of t. And if some of the x_i are complex conjugate roots, they will contribute cosine terms, multiplied by r^t, e.g., as in (C-27).

The second-order case, therefore, adequately illustrates all possibilities. Since our primary concern is not with the details of various computational approaches in particular special cases of higher-order equations, we need not investigate solution forms for single difference equations further. In addition, as we will see in Sec. C-6, high-order linear difference equations can be expressed as *systems* of first-order linear difference equations, and therefore the analysis of systems of first-order equations will be adequate to deal with higher-order single equations as well.

C-3 FIRST-ORDER LINEAR DIFFERENTIAL EQUATIONS

The general homogeneous first-order linear differential equation is, in operator form, from (C-10), $(a_0 D + a_1)y(t) = 0$, that is,

$$a_0 \frac{dy}{dt} + a_1 y = 0 \tag{C-36}$$

with an initial observation $y(0) = c_0$. It is general practice to denote derivatives with respect to time by dots centered over the variable. In particular, $\dot{y} \equiv dy/dt$, $\ddot{y} \equiv d^2y/dt^2$; equation (C-36) is thus also written $a_0\dot{y} + a_1y = 0$. We will use the two representations of time derivatives interchangeably.

Rearranging (C-36), dividing both sides by a_0, and letting $b = -(a_1/a_0)$ gives

$$\frac{dy}{dt} = by \tag{C-37}$$

To find the solution to this first-order differential equation is to find the function, $y = f(t)$, whose first derivative is the function itself, y, multiplied by a constant, b, and which in addition equals c_0 when $t = 0$. Recalling that the derivative of $y = e^{ax}$ is $dy/dt = a\,e^{ax}$ suggests that the function needed might be $y = e^{bt}$ for which $dy/dt = b\,e^{bt} = by$, as required by (C-37). Recalling also, however, that the derivative of $y = k\,e^{ax}$ is $dy/dt = ak\,e^{ax}$ (for k = any constant) suggests that $y = k\,e^{bt}$ would also be a possible choice, since $dy/dt = bk\,e^{bt} = by$. In fact, in order to accommodate the initial condition information that, at $t = 0$, $y = c_0$, we must utilize the second form for $y = f(t)$. That is, for the earlier function ($y = e^{bt}$) at $t = 0$, $y = 1$; but we want $y = c_0$ at $t = 0$, where c_0 will not, in general, be 1. Using $y = k\,e^{bt}$ and setting $t = 0$ gives $y = k$; thus $k = c_0$ and the function that satisfies both (C-37) [or (C-36)] and the initial condition is

$$y = c_0\,e^{bt} \tag{C-38}$$

As with first-order difference equations, the straightforward form of the solution in (C-38) makes possible a complete qualitative analysis of the nature of the path of y over time. Assume $c_0 > 0$.

Case a: $b > 0$ Unlike the difference equation case, here it is clear that for any positive value of b (and with $c_0 > 0$), the function $c_0\,e^{bt}$ will explode as $t \to \infty$, since e (2.71828) will be being raised to larger and larger positive powers. (For example, if $b = 0.8$, for $t = 0, 1, 2, 3, 4$, and 5 we have $e^{(0.8)0} = 1$, $e^{(0.8)1} = 2.226$, $e^{(0.8)2} = e^{1.6} = 4.953$, $e^{(0.8)3} = e^{2.4} = 11.02$, $e^{(0.8)4} = e^{3.2} = 24.53$, $e^{(0.8)5} = e^{4} =$ 54.60.)

Case b: $b = 0$ Here, y will be equal to c_0 for all values of t.

Case c: $b < 0$ A negative b has the effect of dividing c_0, in (C-38), by e^{-bt}, i.e., of dividing it by increasingly large numbers. Therefore, y diminishes toward zero over time. (For $b = -0.8$, for $t = 0, 1, 2, 3, 4$, and 5 we have $1/e^{(0.8)0} =$ 1, $1/e^{(0.8)1} = 0.449$, $1/e^{(0.8)2} = 0.202$, $1/e^{(0.8)3} = 0.091$, $1/e^{(0.8)4} = 0.041$, $1/e^{(0.8)5}$ $= 0.018$.)

If $c_0 < 0$, the above results are altered as follows. In the case of $b > 0$, y begins at a negative value (c_0) and decreases by increasing amounts, i.e., explodes toward $-\infty$, over time. When $b = 0$, y remains at its initial value, as before; now, however, this initial value is negative. When $b < 0$, y starts at its

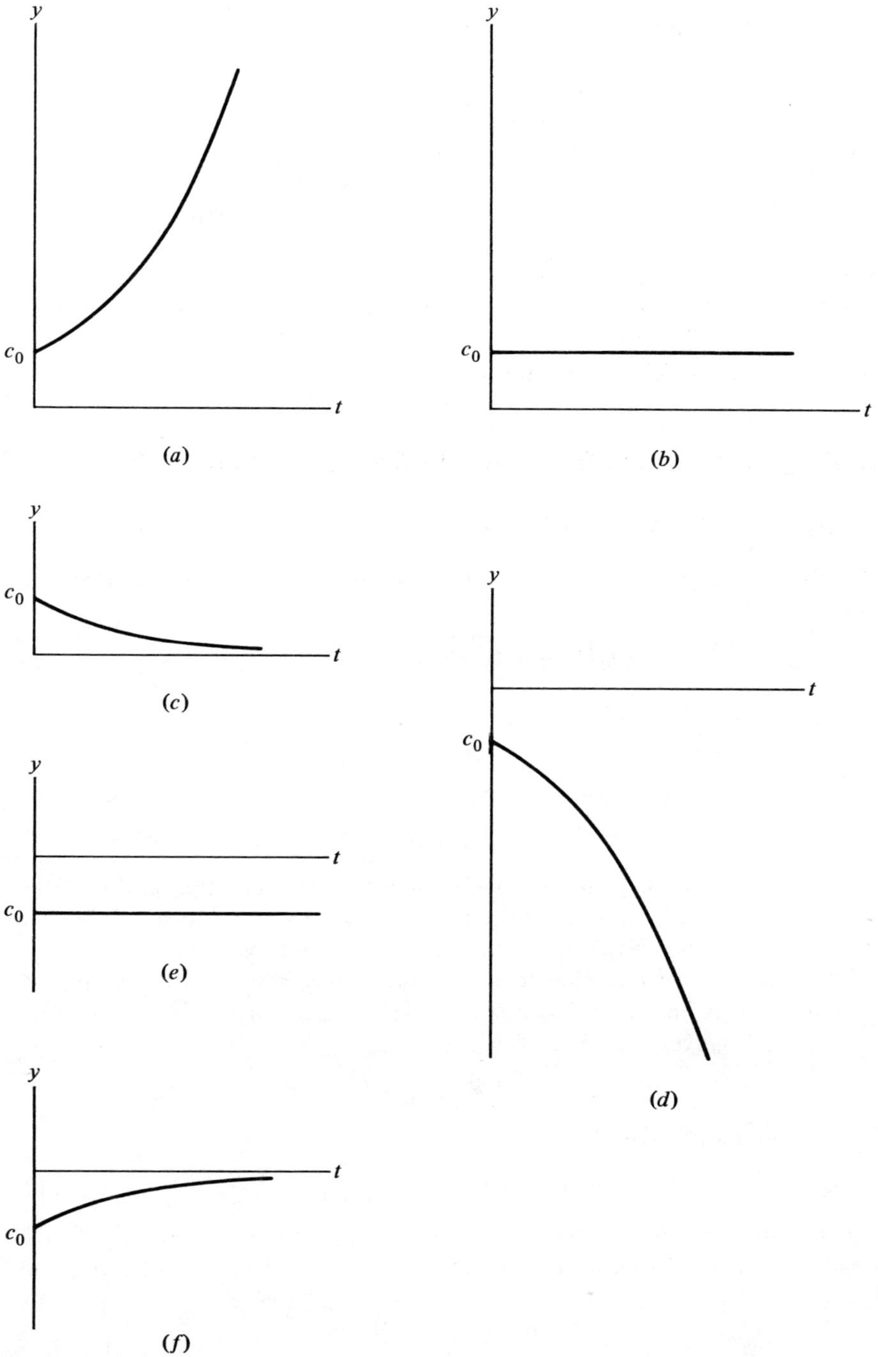

Figure C-5 Time paths for $y = c_0 e^{bt}$. (*a*) $c_0 > 0$, $b > 0$. (*b*) $c_0 > 0$, $b = 0$. (*c*) $c_0 > 0$, $b < 0$. (*d*) $c_0 < 0$, $b > 0$. (*e*) $c_0 < 0$, $b = 0$. (*f*) $c_0 < 0, b < 0$.

initial negative value and increases by decreasing amounts, toward zero, over time. The cases are illustrated in Fig. C-5.

As in the case of first-order difference equations, the *size* of b determines whether or not the time path of y will be of an explosive, constant, or diminishing nature. For differential equations, however, the critical comparison is the size of b relative to 0 (whereas for difference equations it was the size of b relative to 1 or -1).† Again, since $b = -(a_1/a_0)$, the nature of the time path for any first-order linear differential equation, as given by (C-36), can be known in advance, by inspection of the coefficients. We will return to this kind of exploration in more detail in Sec. C-5. The *sign* of c_0 simply establishes whether or not, over time, all values of y will be positive ($c > 0$) or negative ($c < 0$). (The case of $c_0 = 0$ is uninteresting, since $y = 0$ for all values of t.)

C-4 HIGHER-ORDER LINEAR DIFFERENTIAL EQUATIONS

Second-Order Equations: Introduction

The general homogeneous second-order linear differential equation, in operator form, is

$$(a_0 D^2 + a_1 D + a_2) y(t) = 0$$

that is,

$$a_0 \frac{d^2 y}{dt^2} + a_1 \frac{dy}{dt} + a_2 y = 0 \tag{C-39}$$

or

$$a_0 \ddot{y} + a_1 \dot{y} + a_2 y = 0$$

In Sec. C-2, we found a very straightforward parallel between the nature of the solution for a second-order difference equation and that for a first-order difference equation. To determine whether or not the same kind of parallel exists for differential equations, we ask what form b would have to take in order that e^{bt} satisfy (C-39). That is, letting $y = e^{bt}$, $dy/dt = b\,e^{bt}$ and $d^2y/dt^2 = b^2\,e^{bt}$, and substituting into (C-39) gives

$$a_0 b^2\, e^{bt} + a_1 b\, e^{bt} + a_2\, e^{bt} = 0$$

Dividing through by e^{bt} gives

$$a_0 b^2 + a_1 b + a_2 = 0 \tag{C-40}$$

Therefore, if $y = e^{bt}$ is to satisfy the general equation (C-39), b must satisfy (C-40). This is exactly the same quadratic equation that we saw in Sec. C-2 [equation

† Since zero is the critical number for b for differential equations, it is clear that concern about the *size* of b is equivalent to concern about the *sign* of b. With difference equations, these were separate considerations.

(C-15)] for the second-order difference equation case, when, of course, the a were coefficients of the difference equation. As before, (C-40) is termed the *characteristic* or *auxiliary* equation. We replace b by x, the variable to be determined from (C-40), and also, as before, there will in general be two roots to this equation, x_1 and x_2. Parallel to the first-order differential equation case, given two initial conditions, which now means given the value of y and of dy/dt both at a specific time $t = 0$, we can determine two constants, k_1 and k_2. Then both $y = k_1 e^{x_1 t}$ and $y = k_2 e^{x_2 t}$ are solutions to (C-39), as well as their sum. That is, the general solution to (C-39) is†

$$y = k_1 e^{x_1 t} + k_2 e^{x_2 t} \tag{C-41}$$

The values for k_1 and k_2 are determined in a straightforward manner. Let $y(0) = c_0$ and $\dot{y}(0) = c_1$. Then, from (C-41) and from $\dot{y}$ [found by differentiating (C-41) with respect to t], both evaluated at $t = 0$,

$$\begin{aligned} k_1 + \quad k_2 &= c_0 \\ x_1 k_1 + x_2 k_2 &= c_1 \end{aligned} \tag{C-42}$$

These are identical to equations (C-17) for the difference equation case. As before, knowing the x and c makes this a simple pair of linear equations in k_1 and k_2, for which a unique solution can be found as long as the determinant of the coefficient matrix is not zero, which means as long as $x_1 \neq x_2$.

Second-Order Equations: Distinct Roots

For example, suppose that the particular form of (C-39) is

$$\frac{d^2y}{dt^2} - 3\frac{dy}{dt} - 10y = 0 \tag{C-43}$$

or, in operator form,

$$(D^2 - 3D - 10)y = 0$$

with initial conditions $y = 8$ and $dy/dt = -2$ (at $t = 0$). The values of x for which $y = k_1 e^{x_1 t} + k_2 e^{x_2 t}$ [from equation (C-41)] will satisfy (C-43) are found from the auxiliary equation, which is particularly clear from the operator form of (C-43), namely,

$$x^2 - 3x - 10 = 0$$

† This can be verified directly by taking first and second derivatives of y in (C-41), substituting for x_1 and x_2 from the general quadratic formula, and then substituting into the left-hand side of (C-39), which will be found (although the algebra is a bit tedious) to be exactly zero. Proofs of many of the results to be presented here for differential equations can be found in texts that deal with such equations. For example, Baumol [2], Gandolfo [10], Kreider, Kuller, and Ostberg [13], Ritger and Rose [16], or Sanchez [18].

This leads easily to $(x-5)(x+2)=10$, that is, $x_1=5$, $x_2=-2$, and therefore

$$y = k_1 e^{5t} + k_2 e^{-2t}$$

From the initial conditions on y and dy/dt at $t=0$ we have, using (C-42),

$$\begin{aligned} k_1 + k_2 &= 8 \\ 5k_1 - 2k_2 &= -2 \end{aligned}$$

and hence $k_1 = 2$, $k_2 = 6$.

The final solution of (C-43), giving y as a function of t, is therefore†

$$y = 2e^{5t} + 6e^{-2t} \qquad \text{(C-44)}$$

As was true for the second-order difference equation case, two problems may result because of the fact that the auxiliary equation is quadratic: multiple roots and complex conjugate roots involving imaginary numbers.

Second-Order Equations: Multiple Roots

If the specific form of (C-39) were

$$2\frac{d^2y}{dt^2} - 28\frac{dy}{dt} + 98y = 0 \qquad \text{(C-45)}$$

or $(2D^2 - 28D + 98) = 0$, the auxiliary equation is $2x^2 - 28x + 98 = 0$, which factors into $(2x-14)(x-7)=0$, giving $x_1 = 7$ and $x_2 = 7$.‡ If, in addition, the initial conditions were that, at $t=0$, $y=5$ and $dy/dt=1$, then the problem of identical (multiple) roots is seen when we try to satisfy these conditions. Using (C-42),

$$\begin{aligned} k_1 + k_2 &= 5 \\ 7k_1 + 7k_2 &= 1 \end{aligned} \qquad \text{(C-46)}$$

which, as in the difference equation case, is a pair of inconsistent linear equations. Again, parallel to the difference equation case, it can be shown that the form of the general solution, given for differential equations in (C-41), is altered to

$$y = k_1 e^{x_1 t} + k_2 t e^{x_2 t} \qquad \text{(C-47)}$$

[Compare equation (C-22) for the difference equation case.] This removes the

† The reader can easily check this result: (1) by finding dy/dt and d^2y/dt^2 from (C-44) and substituting into (C-43), and (2) by evaluating y in (C-44) and dy/dt from (C-44) at $t=0$ to see that the initial conditions are indeed met.

‡ Clearly this same result can be found by direct application of the formula for the solution of a quadratic equation, or by first dividing both sides of (C-45) by 2 and then factoring.

inconsistency in the initial condition equations (C-46), since they now become† (for $t = 0$)

$$k_1 \qquad = 5$$

$$7k_1 + k_2 = 1$$

giving $k_1 = 5$ and $k_2 = -34$. Hence the solution to (C-45) is

$$y = 5\,e^{7t} - 34t\,e^{7t}$$

Second-Order Equations: Complex Roots

For the case in which the coefficients of the second-order differential equation, given in (C-39), are such that $(a_1^2 - 4a_0a_2) < 0$, the solution to the auxiliary equation will be a pair of complex conjugate roots. We denote these, as before (in Sec. C-2), by $x_1 = \alpha + \beta i$ and $x_2 = \alpha - \beta i$. Therefore, from the general solution given in (C-41), we have

$$y = k_1\,e^{(\alpha+\beta i)t} + k_2\,e^{(\alpha-\beta i)t} \tag{C-48}$$

or, factoring $e^{\alpha t}$ from both terms,

$$y = e^{\alpha t}(k_1\,e^{\beta it} + k_2\,e^{-\beta it}) \tag{C-49}$$

Recalling, from Sec. C-2, that $e^{\pm ix} = \cos x \pm i \sin x$, (C-49) can be reexpressed as

$$y = e^{\alpha t}[(k_1 + k_2)\cos \beta t + (k_1 - k_2)i \sin \beta t]$$

and, letting $A_1 = k_1 + k_2$ and $A_2 = (k_1 - k_2)i$, this is

$$y = e^{\alpha t}(A_1 \cos \beta t + A_2 \sin \beta t) \tag{C-50}$$

The reader should compare this with (C-26) for the difference equation case, noting the differences in both the factor multiplying the parenthetical expression as well as the angle whose sine and cosine are involved.

The similarity to the difference equation case is, of course, that here, too, the time path of y will be periodic, i.e., involve cycles. An alternative form of the trigonometric representation of the path of y in the complex conjugate roots case arises when, as with difference equations, we define an angle δ for which $\tan \delta = -A_2/A_1$ and such that $A_1 = A_3 \cos \delta$ and $-A_2 = A_3 \sin \delta$. This allows (C-50) to be expressed as

$$y = e^{\alpha t}[A_3 \cos(\beta t + \delta)] \tag{C-51}$$

[Compare with (C-27) for difference equations.]

† Note that the second term on the right-hand side of (C-47) is the product of two functions of t and hence that dy/dt will now involve the sum of three terms, one of which becomes zero at $t = 0$.

In this form, the three characteristics of the periodic motion of y over time are easily established: A_3 determines the amplitude, the period is $2\pi/\beta$, and the phase is governed by δ. The term $e^{\alpha t}$ serves to magnify or dampen the amplitude, depending on whether $\alpha > 0$ or $\alpha < 0$.

A second-order differential equation that introduces the complication of complex roots is

$$\frac{d^2y}{dt^2} - 6\frac{dy}{dt} + 13y = 0 \tag{C-52}$$

that is, $(D^2 - 6D + 13)y = 0$, with $y = 2$ and $\dot{y} = -2$ at $t = 0$. Here the auxiliary equation is $(x^2 - 6x + 13) = 0$, which does not factor, so that $x = \left(6 \pm \sqrt{36 - 52}\right)/2 = 3 \pm 2i$. Using (C-50),

$$y = e^{3t}(A_1 \cos 2t + A_2 \sin 2t) \tag{C-53}$$

Initial conditions determine A_1 and A_2 in the same straightforward way. Given y in (C-53) and $\dot{y}$, found by differentiating (C-53) with respect to t, we have, at $t = 0$, when $y = 2$ and $\dot{y} = -2$ (and when $\cos 2t = 1$, $\sin 2t = 0$, and $e^{3t} = 1$),

$$\begin{aligned} A_1 \qquad &= 2 \\ 3A_1 + 2A_2 &= -2 \end{aligned}$$

that is, $A_1 = 2$ and $A_2 = -4$, so that the final solution to (C-52) is

$$y = e^{3t}(2 \cos 2t - 4 \sin 2t)$$

Alternatively, defining δ by $\tan \delta = -A_2/A_1 = 2$ and $2 = A_3 \cos \delta$, $4 = A_3 \sin \delta$ gives $\delta = 1.107$ rad and $A_3 = 4.47$, from which (C-51) becomes

$$y = e^{3t}[4.47 \cos (2t + 1.107)]$$

Second-Order Equations: The Nonhomogeneous Case

The general nonhomogeneous nth-order linear differential equation is given in (C-10), with k specifically nonzero. For a second-order equation, this is $(a_0 D^2 + a_1 D + a_2)y = k$, that is,

$$a_0 \frac{d^2y}{dt^2} + a_1 \frac{dy}{dt} + a_2 y = k \tag{C-54}$$

As with difference equations, the solution procedure involves two steps: (1) find a solution to the reduced equation that results when k is set equal to zero and denote this solution to the homogeneous equation by y^h; and (2) find any particular solution, y^n, that satisfies the nonhomogeneous equation. Then the general solution is the sum of these two:

$$y = y^h + y^n \tag{C-55}$$

For y^n, consider the most straightforward solution $y = c$, where c is a constant to be determined. Substituting in (C-54), for this case in which both dy/dt and

d^2y/dt^2 are zero gives $a_2c = k$ or $c = k/a_2$. Thus $y^n = k/a_2$ is to be added to the solution obtained when k is set equal to zero, y^h. Clearly this form of particular solution for (C-54) will always be possible provided that $a_2 \neq 0$ (or, in the nth-order case, provided $a_n \neq 0$). As with the difference equations, if $y = c$ is not a particular solution, one tries $y = ct$; if this fails, try $y = ct^2$. For an nth-order equation there will always be a particular solution by $y = ct^n$ at the latest.

As an example of the nonhomogeneous case consider

$$\frac{d^2y}{dt^2} - 6\frac{dy}{dt} + 8y + 9 = 0 \tag{C-56}$$

with $y = 3$ and $\dot{y} = 2$ at $t = 0$. For y^h, the auxiliary equation is $(x^2 - 6x + 8) = 0$, from which $(x - 4)(x - 2) = 0$ and $x_1 = 4$, $x_2 = 2$. Therefore $y = k_1 e^{4t} + k_2 e^{2t}$. For y^n, try $y = c$, that is, $8c = -9$ or $c = -\frac{9}{8}$; thus $y^n = -\frac{9}{8}$. Therefore the general solution is

$$y = k_1 e^{4t} + k_2 e^{2t} - \tfrac{9}{8}$$

Now the initial condition information is introduced. At $t = 0$,

$$k_1 + k_2 - \tfrac{9}{8} = 3$$

$$4k_1 + 2k_2 = 2$$

which has the unique solution $k_1 = -\frac{25}{8}$ and $k_2 = \frac{29}{4}$ and therefore, finally,

$$y = -\tfrac{25}{8} e^{4t} + \tfrac{29}{4} e^{2t} - \tfrac{9}{8} \tag{C-57}$$

represents the complete general solution to (C-56).

nth-Order Equations

As was true for difference equations, the second-order differential equation case, with its quadratic auxiliary equation, illustrates adequately the varieties of behavior that are possible in the time path of the dependent variable as t grows. These depend on whether the solution to the auxiliary equation consists of distinct, multiple, or complex conjugate roots; the resulting form of solution to the differential equation is shown in (C-41), (C-47), and (C-50) [or (C-51)], respectively.

Higher-order differential equations will have higher-degree auxiliary equations whose solutions will be combinations of distinct, multiple, and pairs of complex conjugate roots. The general solution is

$$y = k_1 e^{x_1 t} + \cdots + k_n e^{x_n t} \tag{C-58}$$

The k, as usual, are determined from initial conditions. For the nth-order differential equation these conditions are the values of y and its first through $(n - 1)$th derivative (with respect to t) at $t = 0$.

There are special computational techniques for certain classes of higher-order equations, but these are not our primary concern. In addition, higher-order linear differential equations can be expressed as *systems* of first-order linear differential equations; we will consider methods for analyzing systems of first-order differential equations in Sec. C-7.

C-5 STABILITY FOR SINGLE EQUATIONS

The concept of stability for a single difference or differential equation that we will adopt is quite straightforward and intuitively appealing. Since solutions to the difference and differential equations that we have investigated thus far are functions that show y depending on time in some explicit way, one may ask about the path that y will trace out over time, i.e., for increasing values of t. In particular, our interest may center on whether the value of y (1) explodes over time (increases by constant or increasing amounts or decreases by constant or increasing amounts), (2) stays constant for all values from $t = 0$ onward, or (3) is dampened toward some value, which it approaches asymptotically. Recall that for both difference and differential equations, the general solution for the nonhomogeneous case was $y = y^h + y^n$, where y^n is any particular solution (often a constant) to the nonhomogeneous equation. If $y^h \to 0$ as $t \to \infty$, then y approaches an *equilibrium* value given by the particular solution. This value, once achieved, would persist. If the particular solution is itself a function of t, as, for example, when $(a_0 + a_1 + a_2) = 0$ in the second-order case, then one refers to a *moving equilibrium*. In the case of homogeneous equations, of course, $y^n = 0$ and hence zero is the equilibrium value for such equations.

Denote the equilibrium value of y by y^e. Then a difference or differential equation (or, more correctly, its solution) is said to be globally (or asymptotically) stable if $y \to y^e$ as $t \to \infty$, irrespective of the initial value of y. On the other hand, if all initial y in some "small" region near to y^e approach that value as $t \to \infty$, the solution is said to be locally stable. Otherwise, it is unstable.† Referring to Figs. C-1 and C-5, we see that Figs. C-1*c*, C-1*f*, C-5*c*, and C-5*f* represent globally stable solutions.‡

Difference Equations

Consider the homogeneous first-order linear difference equation $y_{t+1} - \frac{3}{10}y_t = 0$, or $(E - \frac{3}{10})y_t = 0$, whose solution we know, from Sec. C-1, will be $y_t = c_0(\frac{3}{10})^t$. Suppose that the initial condition is $y_0 = 10$, then the complete solution is $y_t = 10(\frac{3}{10})^t$. This is the type of situation that is depicted in Fig. C-1*c*, since as t increases, $(\frac{3}{10})^t$ decreases and, despite the influence of $c_0 = 10$, y_t approaches zero, its equilibrium value (see Table C-2).

† There are a number of ways to define stability for difference and/or differential equations; these are covered in texts on these subjects and the distinctions are not essential for our interests.

‡ The cases illustrated in Figs. C-1*b* and C-5*b*, *e* are thus not stable by this definition; while the value of y does not "explode" in any of these three cases, neither does it approach the equilibrium value, which is zero for homogeneous equations.

Table C-2 $y_t = 10(\frac{3}{10})^t$, **for various** t

t	0	1	2	5	10
y_t	10	3	0.9	0.0243	0.000058

On the other hand, consider a nonhomogeneous version of the previous equation, namely, $y_{t+1} - (\frac{3}{10})y_t = 50$. Regular solution procedures give $y_t^h = c_0(\frac{3}{10})^t$ and $y_t^n = \frac{500}{7} = 71.429$, so that $y_t = c_0(\frac{3}{10})^t + \frac{500}{7}$; and if $y_0 = 10$, we find that $c_0 = -\frac{430}{7}$ and therefore the complete solution is $y_t = -\frac{430}{7}(\frac{3}{10})^t + \frac{500}{7}$. While c_0 is different here from the homogeneous case, and while there is a new (constant) term added on, the influence of time is still felt as an exponent on $\frac{3}{10}$; as in the previous case, this term diminishes over time (see Table C-3). As t increases, the first term in the solution becomes negligible and hence y_t approaches $\frac{500}{7} = 71.429$, the constant found as the particular solution, which is the equilibrium value for this nonhomogeneous difference equation.

For second-order equations, one could sketch the time path in the t,y plane similarly. The solution given in (C-19) for the case of distinct roots indicates that the path of y over time will be found as the sum of two terms, each of which corresponds to the general solution type for a first-order equation, namely, $c_0(x)^t$.

First-order equations Since $y_t = c_0 b^t + y^n$, the nature of the time path clearly is governed by the size of (the absolute value of) b relative to 1, as we have seen in some detail in Sec. C-1. For stability, it is both necessary and sufficient that $|b| < 1$.

Second-order equations Here $y_t = k_1(x_1)^t + k_2(x_2)^t + y^n$, for the case of distinct and real roots, and thus for stability both $|x_1| < 1$ and $|x_2| < 1$. The rule is sometimes stated in terms of the largest root. Let $\rho = \max(|x_1|, |x_2|)$; then a necessary and sufficient condition for stability is $\rho < 1$. When the roots are complex conjugates, the same rule applies, since the solution will also have the form $y_t = k_1(x_1)^t + k_2(x_2)^t + y^n$, although we have seen, in Sec. C-2, that this can be rearranged into trigonometric form. Recall that complex numbers, $\alpha \pm \beta i$, are represented as vectors in two-dimensional space, with a real axis (horizontal), along which α is measured, and an imaginary axis (vertical), along which β is measured. The absolute value of either $x_1 = \alpha + \beta i$ or $x_2 = \alpha - \beta i$ is defined to be the norm (length) of the vector, namely, $\sqrt{\alpha^2 + \beta^2}$. (Recall that we always use the

Table C-3 $y_t = -\frac{430}{7}(\frac{3}{10})^t + \frac{500}{7}$, **for various** t

t	0	1	2	5	10
y_t	10	53.0	65.9	71.280	71.429

Table C-4 $kt(x)^t$ **for** $x = 0.9$

t	1	2	5	10	20	30	40	50
$kt(0.9)^t$	$0.9k$	$1.62k$	$2.95k$	$3.49k$	$2.43k$	$1.27k$	$0.59k$	$0.26k$

positive square root for vector norms, since we are defining a length.) In Fig. C-2, we denoted this length as r, and in trigonometric form [(C-26) or (C-27)] it was r^t that multiplied the trigonometric part and which therefore will contribute a dampening trend if $r < 0$. Finally, with multiple roots, we saw [in (C-22)] that the solution would be of the form $y_t = k_1(x_1)^t + k_2 t(x_2)^t$. Even in this case, the behavior of y over time is ultimately governed by the largest root. Clearly, if $x_1 > 1$ and $x_2 > 1$, y_t will explode. Less clear, however, is the contribution of the second term if x_2 is quite large but less than 1. Table C-4 illustrates the diminishing influence of this kind of term. In the multiple roots case, also, $|x_1| < 1$ and $|x_2| < 1$ are necessary and sufficient conditions for a stable solution.

Higher-order equations The auxiliary equation for the nth-order case is $a_0 x^n + a_1 x^{n-1} + \cdots + a_{n-1}x + a_n = 0$. Our interest is in whether or not $|x_i| < 1$ ($i = 1, \ldots, n$). There is a theorem, due to Schur, which exactly answers this question by examination of certain relationships among the coefficients $a_0, \ldots, a_n$ rather than by solution of the equation. For large n, the theorem is difficult and tedious to apply, but then so is the solution of an nth-degree equation when n is large.

Schur's theorem For $a_0 x^n + a_1 x^{n-1} + \cdots + a_{n-1}x + a_n = 0$, $|x_i| < 1$ ($i = 1, \ldots, n$) if and only if the following determinants, $\boldsymbol{\Delta}_1, \ldots, \boldsymbol{\Delta}_n$, are all positive:

$$\boldsymbol{\Delta}_1 = \left|\begin{array}{c|c} a_0 & a_n \\ \hline a_n & a_0 \end{array}\right|$$

$$\boldsymbol{\Delta}_2 = \left|\begin{array}{cc|cc} a_0 & 0 & a_n & a_{n-1} \\ a_1 & a_0 & 0 & a_n \\ \hline a_n & 0 & a_0 & a_1 \\ a_{n-1} & a_n & 0 & a_0 \end{array}\right|$$

$$\vdots$$

$$\boldsymbol{\Delta}_n = \left|\begin{array}{cccc|cccc} a_0 & 0 & \cdots & 0 & a_n & a_{n-1} & \cdots & a_1 \\ a_1 & a_0 & \cdots & 0 & 0 & a_n & \cdots & a_2 \\ \cdots & \cdots & \cdots & \cdots & \cdots & \cdots & \cdots & \cdots \\ a_{n-1} & a_{n-2} & \cdots & a_0 & 0 & 0 & \cdots & a_n \\ \hline a_n & 0 & \cdots & 0 & a_0 & a_1 & \cdots & a_{n-1} \\ a_{n-1} & a_n & \cdots & 0 & 0 & a_0 & \cdots & a_{n-2} \\ \cdots & \cdots & \cdots & \cdots & \cdots & \cdots & \cdots & \cdots \\ a_1 & a_2 & \cdots & a_n & 0 & 0 & \cdots & a_0 \end{array}\right|$$

The dashed lines are included to give some visual suggestion of the symmetry involved in construction of the matrices whose determinants are required. (Note that the size of the largest matrix will be $2n \times 2n$.) In cases $\mathbf{\Delta}_2$ onward, the general structure is

$$\mathbf{\Delta}_i = \left|\begin{array}{c|c} \mathbf{A} & \mathbf{B}' \\ \hline \mathbf{B} & \mathbf{A}' \end{array}\right|$$

where **A** and **B** are both of order i and are lower triangular. The construction of these two submatrices follows a rather straightforward pattern, if one begins by inserting the elements on their main diagonals and then works downward. The interested reader might wish to work out more exact implications for particular cases (e.g., the general second-order difference equation) by evaluating the necessary determinants, although even here a 4×4 matrix will be involved.†

Differential Equations

As we saw in Sec. C-3, the behavior of the solution of a first-order differential equation was governed by the sign of the root of the auxiliary equation. Since the root, multiplied by t, appears as an exponent on e, a positive root necessarily produces explosive behavior, and the solutions of higher-order equations involve sums of such terms.

First-order equations Since $y = c_0\, e^{bt} + y^n$, the solution will approach the equilibrium value y^n if and only if $b < 0$, as Fig. C-5 suggested.

Second-order equations Here $y = k_1\, e^{x_1 t} + k_2\, e^{x_2 t} + y^n$, for distinct, real roots, and thus both x_1 and x_2 must be negative. Alternatively, the rule is that the largest root must be negative. With complex conjugate roots, $x_1 = \alpha + \beta i$ and $x_2 = \alpha - \beta i$, the alternative trigonometric forms given in (C-50) and (C-51) show that only α, the real part of the complex number, enters as an exponent of e, and thus for stability in this case we require $\alpha < 0$. In general, in differential equations, we do not consider absolute values of the roots, as was necessary in the difference equation cases, since the crucial boundary for differential equations is 0 and not ± 1. Finally, there is the multiple root case, with a solution of the form $y = k_1\, e^{x_1 t} + k_2 t\, e^{x_2 t}$. As with difference equations (Table C-4), the second term does not explode as long as $x_2 < 0$ (see Table C-5).

Table C-5 $kt\, e^{xt}$ **for** $x = -0.1$

t	1	2	5	10	20	30	40	50
$kt\, e^{xt}$	$0.905k$	$1.637k$	$3.033k$	$3.679k$	$2.707k$	$1.494k$	$0.733k$	$0.337k$

† For alternative rules, not all of which are both necessary and sufficient, see Gandolfo [10], Goldberg [11, pp. 169–174], or Samuelson [17, app. B]. Some writers prefer to present all difference and differential equations with $a_0 = 1$, by dividing both sides of the original equation by a_0. This tends to simplify at least the appearance of some of the stability conditions.

Higher-order equations The auxiliary equation here, as with difference equations, is $a_0 x^n + a_1 x^{n-1} + \cdots + a_{n-1}x + a_n = 0$. Fortunately, parallel to the Schur theorem, there is a rule for establishing when the roots of such an equation will all be negative. Also parallel to the difference equation case, for large n the theorem is difficult and tedious to apply, since it involves a series of determinants (although the underlying matrices are not as large as those in the Schur theorem).

Routh's theorem For $a_0x^n + a_1x^{n-1} + \cdots + a_{n-1}x + a_n = 0$, the real parts of all n roots will be negative if and only if the following determinants, $\mathbf{D}_1, \ldots, \mathbf{D}_n$, are all positive:

$$\mathbf{D}_1 = |a_1|$$

$$\mathbf{D}_2 = \begin{vmatrix} a_1 & a_3 \\ a_0 & a_2 \end{vmatrix}$$

$$\mathbf{D}_3 = \begin{vmatrix} a_1 & a_3 & a_5 \\ a_0 & a_2 & a_4 \\ 0 & a_1 & a_3 \end{vmatrix}$$

$$\vdots$$

$$\mathbf{D}_n = \begin{vmatrix} a_1 & a_3 & a_5 & a_7 & \cdots & 0 \\ a_0 & a_2 & a_4 & a_6 & \cdots & 0 \\ 0 & a_1 & a_3 & a_5 & \cdots & 0 \\ \cdots & \cdots & \cdots & \cdots & \cdots & \cdots \\ 0 & 0 & 0 & 0 & \cdots & a_n \end{vmatrix}$$

and where all a_i for $i > n$ are set equal to zero. Thus $\mathbf{D}_3 = \begin{vmatrix} a_1 & a_3 & a_5 \\ a_0 & a_2 & a_4 \\ 0 & a_1 & a_3 \end{vmatrix}$, but if $n = 3$, $\mathbf{D}_3 = \begin{vmatrix} a_1 & a_3 & 0 \\ a_0 & a_2 & 0 \\ 0 & a_1 & a_3 \end{vmatrix}$

The construction is quite simple. Columns are headed by a_i, for $i = 1, 3, 5$, etc., and remaining elements in a given column are successively lower-subscripted a's, except that below a_0 all further column elements are zero.

Again, alternative formulations, and alternative rules, generally either necessary *or* sufficient, are available in the literature.† The reader might wish to apply the Routh theorem to the general second- or third-order case to derive more specific rules on the coefficients of the original differential equation.

† For example, Gandolfo [10], Samuelson [17], and Sanchez [18, p. 57].

C-6 SYSTEMS OF LINEAR DIFFERENCE EQUATIONS

General Notation and Form of Solution

In Sec. C-2 we considered the solution of the second-order linear difference equation $(E^2 - 8E + 12)y_t = 0$, that is, $y_{t+2} - 8y_{t+1} + 12y_t = 0$, as given in (C-18). Introduce a new variable, x_t, defined simply to be y_{t+1}, that is,

$$x_t = y_{t+1} \tag{C-59}$$

or $x_t = E(y_t)$. This implies that x_{t+1}, which is $E(x_t)$, will be $E^2(y_t) = E(y_{t+1})$, that is,

$$x_{t+1} = y_{t+2}$$

The original second-order equation can thus be written

$$x_{t+1} - 8x_t + 12y_t = 0 \tag{C-60}$$

where x_t is defined in (C-59).

Rearranging (C-59) and (C-60) gives the following pair of first-order linear difference equations in the two variables x_t and y_t:

$$\begin{aligned} x_{t+1} &= 8x_t - 12y_t \\ y_{t+1} &= x_t \end{aligned} \tag{C-61}$$

Since these are linear equations, matrix notation can be used:

$$\begin{bmatrix} x_{t+1} \\ y_{t+1} \end{bmatrix} = \begin{bmatrix} 8 & -12 \\ 1 & 0 \end{bmatrix} \begin{bmatrix} x_t \\ y_t \end{bmatrix} \tag{C-62}$$

Exactly the same principles can be used for higher-order single equations; e.g., a fourth-order equation can be reexpressed as a system of four first-order equations, through the introduction of three new variables. If we continue to denote variables by y's, the general first-order system representation for an nth-order equation will be

$$\begin{aligned} y_{1,t+1} &= a_{11}y_{1,t} + \cdots + a_{1n}y_{n,t} \\ y_{2,t+1} &= a_{21}y_{1,t} + \cdots + a_{2n}y_{n,t} \\ &\cdots\cdots\cdots\cdots\cdots\cdots\cdots\cdots \\ y_{n,t+1} &= a_{n1}y_{1,t} + \cdots + a_{nn}y_{n,t} \end{aligned}$$

or, using the obvious matrix definitions,

$$\mathbf{Y}_{t+1} = \mathbf{A}\mathbf{Y}_t \tag{C-63}$$

In the nonhomogeneous case, an n-element column vector $\mathbf{K}$ would be added to the right-hand side of (C-63). Systems of first-order difference equations may arise quite naturally in representations of the time paths of several interrelated variables. Thus the structure represented in (C-63) need not be viewed exclusively as a reexpression of a single, higher-order equation.

A solution to the set of equations in (C-63) can be found using an approach parallel to that used for the single-equation case in Sec. C-1. That is, given a set of initial observations for each of the n variables, $\mathbf{Y}_0 = \mathbf{C}_0$, (C-63) suggests that

$$\mathbf{Y}_1 = \mathbf{A}\mathbf{Y}_0 = \mathbf{A}\mathbf{C}_0$$

$$\mathbf{Y}_2 = \mathbf{A}\mathbf{Y}_1 = \mathbf{A}(\mathbf{A}\mathbf{Y}_0) = \mathbf{A}^2\mathbf{C}_0$$

$$\mathbf{Y}_3 = \mathbf{A}\mathbf{Y}_2 = \mathbf{A}^3\mathbf{Y}_0 = \mathbf{A}^3\mathbf{C}_0$$

and finally

$$\mathbf{Y}_t = \mathbf{A}\mathbf{Y}_{t-1} = \mathbf{A}^t\mathbf{Y}_0 = \mathbf{A}^t\mathbf{C}_0 \tag{C-64}$$

[Compare (C-13) in Sec. C-1.] Parallel to the definition that $a^0 = 1$, let $\mathbf{A}^0 = \mathbf{I}$; then $\mathbf{Y}_t = \mathbf{A}^t\mathbf{C}_0$ holds for all $t = 0, 1, \ldots$. While the logic is parallel to that for a single first-order equation, the calculations are a good deal more cumbersome. If one wants the values of $\mathbf{Y}_t$ for large t, this requires raising an arbitrary square matrix to a high power. However, when $\mathbf{A}$ is a *diagonal* matrix, then calculation of $\mathbf{A}^t$ is a simple matter, since it requires only raising each individual element on the diagonal to the tth power; no matrix multiplications are needed.† It is not likely, in general, that $\mathbf{A}$ will be diagonal, however, since the system (C-63) would then simply be $y_{i,t+1} = a_i y_{i,t}$; i.e., each variable at $t+1$ would depend only on its own value at t and not on the values of any other variables at t.

The problem is therefore: can the variables y be transformed so that the matrix in the representation of the transformed difference equation system *is* diagonal? More specifically, consider the possibility of finding a set of n variables $\mathbf{Z} = \begin{bmatrix} z_1 \\ \vdots \\ z_n \end{bmatrix}$, connected to the y by the relation $\mathbf{Y}_t = \mathbf{P}\mathbf{Z}_t$, where $\mathbf{P}$ must be an $n \times n$ matrix. Given (C-63),

$$\mathbf{P}\mathbf{Z}_{t+1} = \mathbf{A}\mathbf{P}\mathbf{Z}_t$$

from which

$$\mathbf{Z}_{t+1} = (\mathbf{P}^{-1}\mathbf{A}\mathbf{P})\mathbf{Z}_t$$

provided that $\mathbf{P}$ is nonsingular. Define $\mathbf{D} = \mathbf{P}^{-1}\mathbf{A}\mathbf{P}$; then

$$\mathbf{Z}_{t+1} = \mathbf{D}\mathbf{Z}_t \tag{C-65}$$

Thus we have a new system of first-order linear difference equations in the variables $\mathbf{Z}$. Now, *if* $\mathbf{P}$ had been chosen so that $\mathbf{D}$ were a *diagonal* matrix, then the solution to the equations in (C-65) would be straightforward, since, from (C-64),

$$\mathbf{Z}_t = \mathbf{D}^t\mathbf{Z}_0 \tag{C-66}$$

† The skeptical reader can easily convince himself, using a small example.

and, since $\mathbf{Y}_0 = \mathbf{P}\mathbf{Z}_0$, then $\mathbf{Z}_0 = \mathbf{P}^{-1}\mathbf{Y}_0$ and

$$\mathbf{Z}_t = \mathbf{D}^t\mathbf{P}^{-1}\mathbf{Y}_0$$

Finally, from $\mathbf{Y}_t = \mathbf{P}\mathbf{Z}_t$, it follows that

$$\mathbf{Y}_t = (\mathbf{P}\mathbf{D}^t\mathbf{P}^{-1})\mathbf{Y}_0 \tag{C-67}$$

Therefore, given an initial set of values of the y variables, $\mathbf{C}_0$,

$$\mathbf{Y}_t = (\mathbf{P}\mathbf{D}^t\mathbf{P}^{-1})\mathbf{C}_0 \tag{C-68}$$

In words, if we could find a nonsingular matrix $\mathbf{P}$, which would transform $\mathbf{A}$ into a *diagonal* matrix $\mathbf{D}$ by the multiplicative operations $\mathbf{D} = \mathbf{P}^{-1}\mathbf{A}\mathbf{P}$, then the solution to (C-63) would be easily found utilizing the tth power of $\mathbf{D}$, premultiplied by $\mathbf{P}$ and postmultiplied by $\mathbf{P}^{-1}$. Instead of multiplying $\mathbf{A}$ by itself $t - 1$ times, to get $\mathbf{A}^t$, we would need one inverse, $\mathbf{P}^{-1}$, and then two matrix multiplications, $\mathbf{P}\mathbf{D}^t$ and $(\mathbf{P}\mathbf{D}^t)\mathbf{P}^{-1}$, in addition to raising each of the n elements in $\mathbf{D}$ to the tth power. Along with this computational advantage, the form of solution in (C-67) or (C-68) will allow us to analyze the question of stability for the *system* of first-order equations (C-63), after we review a few results from matrix algebra.

Characteristics of Square Matrices: A Review

We recall terminology associated with nonsingular square matrices and illustrate some of the concepts with the general 2×2 case.

1. The *characteristic matrix* of a nonsingular $n \times n$ matrix $\mathbf{A}$ is given by $[\mathbf{A} - \lambda\mathbf{I}]$, where, for conformability, $\mathbf{I}$ is the $n \times n$ identity matrix and λ is a scalar.
2. The *characteristic determinant* of $\mathbf{A}$ is the determinant of the characteristic matrix, that is, $|\mathbf{A} - \lambda\mathbf{I}|$.
3. The *characteristic function* of $\mathbf{A}$ results from expansion of the characteristic determinant.
4. The *characteristic equation* of $\mathbf{A}$ is formed by setting the characteristic function of $\mathbf{A}$ equal to zero.

Let $\mathbf{A} = \begin{bmatrix} a_{11} & a_{12} \\ a_{21} & a_{22} \end{bmatrix}$. Then $\begin{bmatrix} a_{11} - \lambda & a_{12} \\ a_{21} & a_{22} - \lambda \end{bmatrix}$ is the characteristic matrix of $\mathbf{A}$, $\begin{vmatrix} a_{11} - \lambda & a_{12} \\ a_{21} & a_{22} - \lambda \end{vmatrix}$ is the characteristic determinant of $\mathbf{A}$, $(a_{11} - \lambda) \times (a_{22} - \lambda) - a_{12}a_{21}$ or $\lambda^2 - (a_{11} + a_{22})\lambda + (a_{11}a_{22} - a_{12}a_{21})$ is the characteristic function of $\mathbf{A}$, and

$$\lambda^2 - (a_{11} + a_{22})\lambda + (a_{11}a_{22} - a_{12}a_{21}) = 0$$

is the characteristic equation of $\mathbf{A}$. For $\mathbf{A}$ of order 2, this is a second-degree equation in λ; for $\mathbf{A}$ of order n, this will be an nth-degree equation in λ.

5. The *characteristic roots* of **A** are the values of λ satisfying the characteristic equation of **A**. These are also known as the *latent roots* or the *eigenvalues* of **A**. We note in particular that the elements of a diagonal matrix are the eigenvalues of that matrix. The 2×2 case illustrates this. Let $\mathbf{D} = \begin{bmatrix} d_1 & 0 \\ 0 & d_2 \end{bmatrix}$; then the characteristic equation of **D** is $|\mathbf{D} - \lambda\mathbf{I}| = 0$, that is,

$$\begin{vmatrix} d_1 - \lambda & 0 \\ 0 & d_2 - \lambda \end{vmatrix} = 0$$

which is $(d_1 - \lambda)(d_2 - \lambda) = 0$, from which it follows that the two eigenvalues are $\lambda = d_1, d_2$.
6. The *characteristic vectors* of **A** are those vectors **V** that satisfy the equation $[\mathbf{A} - \lambda\mathbf{I}]\mathbf{V} = \mathbf{0}$, i.e., for which $\mathbf{AV} = \lambda\mathbf{V}$. Since $[\mathbf{A} - \lambda\mathbf{I}]\mathbf{V} = \mathbf{0}$ represents a set of homogeneous linear equations, we know that for nontrivial solutions (solutions in which $\mathbf{V} \neq \mathbf{0}$) it is necessary that $|\mathbf{A} - \lambda\mathbf{I}| = 0$. But this requirement is just the characteristic equation of **A**. Thus, for each λ_i satisfying the characteristic equation, which is to say for each characteristic root of **A**, we can find an associated characteristic vector. In obvious parallel, these are also known as the *latent vectors* or as the *eigenvectors* of **A**. Since they are determined by solving a system of homogeneous linear equations with a singular coefficient matrix, the eigenvectors are of course not unique. They are determined at most up to a factor of proportionality.

There are two aspects of the characteristic function of **A**, as illustrated for the 2×2 case, that carry over to square matrices of any size. The final term in the characteristic function, $(a_{11}a_{22} - a_{12}a_{21})$, is just the determinant of **A**, $|\mathbf{A}|$. The term multiplying λ, $(a_{11} + a_{22})$, is the sum of the elements on the main diagonal of **A**; for any square matrix, this sum is known as the trace of **A**, denoted tr(**A**). Thus the characteristic equation in the 2×2 case could also be represented as $\lambda^2 - \text{tr}(\mathbf{A})\lambda + |\mathbf{A}| = 0$.

Two square matrices, **A** and **B**, are said to be *similar* if a nonsingular matrix **P** can be found such that $\mathbf{B} = \mathbf{P}^{-1}\mathbf{AP}$. Thus the diagonal matrix **D**, used earlier in this section and defined as $\mathbf{D} = \mathbf{P}^{-1}\mathbf{AP}$, is *similar* to **A**. Very shortly we will make use of several facts about similar matrices.

1. Similar matrices have the same characteristic function and therefore the same eigenvalues.† Therefore if **A** is similar to a diagonal matrix **D**, then the elements of **D** (which are the eigenvalues of **D**) are the eigenvalues of **A**.

† The proof is straightforward. $\mathbf{B} = \mathbf{P}^{-1}\mathbf{AP}$. Thus $[\mathbf{B} - \lambda\mathbf{I}] = [\mathbf{P}^{-1}\mathbf{AP} - \lambda\mathbf{I}]$ which, by the rules of matrix multiplication, equals $[\mathbf{P}^{-1}(\mathbf{A} - \lambda\mathbf{I})\mathbf{P}]$. Therefore $|\mathbf{B} - \lambda\mathbf{I}| = |\mathbf{P}^{-1}(\mathbf{A} - \lambda\mathbf{I})\mathbf{P}| = |\mathbf{P}^{-1}||\mathbf{A} - \lambda\mathbf{I}||\mathbf{P}|$, by the rules for determinants of products. Furthermore, since $|\mathbf{P}^{-1}| = 1/|\mathbf{P}|$, $|\mathbf{P}^{-1}||\mathbf{A} - \lambda\mathbf{I}||\mathbf{P}| = |\mathbf{A} - \lambda\mathbf{I}|$. That is, **A** and **B** have the same characteristic determinant and hence the same characteristic function, characteristic equation, and thus characteristic roots.

2. Similar matrices have the same determinant.†
3. Similar matrices have the same trace.‡

Consider once again the similar matrices **A** and **D**, defined by $\mathbf{P}^{-1}\mathbf{A}\mathbf{P} = \mathbf{D}$ or $\mathbf{A}\mathbf{P} = \mathbf{P}\mathbf{D}$. Let P_i $(i = 1, \ldots, n)$ denote the columns of **P**. Then the defining relationship between **A** and **D** can be expressed less compactly as

$$\mathbf{A}[P_1 \quad P_2 \quad \cdots \quad P_n] = [P_1 \quad P_2 \quad \cdots \quad P_n] \begin{bmatrix} d_1 & 0 & \cdots & 0 \\ 0 & d_2 & \cdots & 0 \\ \cdots & \cdots & \cdots & \cdots \\ 0 & 0 & \cdots & d_n \end{bmatrix} \tag{C-69}$$

which is to say, for $i = 1, \ldots, n$,

$$\mathbf{A}P_i = d_i P_i \tag{C-70}$$

But since the d_i are the eigenvalues of **D** and hence of **A**, i.e., since $d_i = \lambda_i$ $(i = 1, \ldots, n)$, (C-70) can be expressed as

$$\mathbf{A}P_i = \lambda_i P_i \quad i = 1, \ldots, n \tag{C-71}$$

which means that the columns that make up the matrix **P** are precisely the eigenvectors of **A**. This matrix, whose columns are the eigenvectors of **A**, is sometimes called the modal matrix of **A**.

Note that no two columns of **P** may be equal if **P** is to be nonsingular. That is, the eigenvectors of **A** must all be different, which in turn means that the eigenvalues of **A** must all be different. In particular, this analysis rules out the case of repeated roots of the characteristic equation of **A**. (For the modifications necessary when there are repeated roots, see Boyce and di Prima [5, pp. 312–316] or Sanchez [18, pp. 58–65].)

Stability for Systems of First-Order Difference Equations

We now know how to construct the matrix **P** which will transform **A** in (C-63) into the similar diagonal matrix **D** in (C-67); **P** contains the eigenvectors of **A** as columns. Moreover, the elements of **D**, into which **A** is transformed, are the eigenvalues of **A**. We examine the form that the solution for the 2 × 2 case will therefore take, from (C-67), denoting elements of **P** by p_{ij} and elements of $\mathbf{P}^{-1}$ by q_{ij}:

$$\begin{bmatrix} y_{1,t} \\ y_{2,t} \end{bmatrix} = \begin{bmatrix} p_{11} & p_{12} \\ p_{21} & p_{22} \end{bmatrix} \begin{bmatrix} \lambda_1^t & 0 \\ 0 & \lambda_2^t \end{bmatrix} \begin{bmatrix} q_{11} & q_{12} \\ q_{21} & q_{22} \end{bmatrix} \begin{bmatrix} y_{1,0} \\ y_{2,0} \end{bmatrix} \tag{C-72}$$

† $|\mathbf{B}| = |\mathbf{P}^{-1}||\mathbf{A}||\mathbf{P}| = |\mathbf{A}|$ since, as noted in the previous footnote, $|\mathbf{P}^{-1}| = 1/|\mathbf{P}|$.
‡ When matrix products **XY** and **YX** are both defined, $\text{tr}(\mathbf{XY}) = \text{tr}(\mathbf{YX})$. Given that $\mathbf{B} = \mathbf{P}^{-1}\mathbf{AP}$, $\text{tr}(\mathbf{B}) = \text{tr}(\mathbf{P}^{-1}\mathbf{AP}) = \text{tr}(\mathbf{AP})(\mathbf{P}^{-1}) = \text{tr}(\mathbf{A})$.

and, from straightforward matrix multiplication and collection of terms on λ_1^t and λ_2^t,

$$
\begin{aligned}
y_{1,t} &= (p_{11}q_{11}y_{1,0} + p_{11}q_{12}y_{2,0})\lambda_1^t + (p_{12}q_{21}y_{1,0} + p_{12}q_{22}y_{2,0})\lambda_2^t \\
y_{2,t} &= (p_{21}q_{11}y_{1,0} + p_{21}q_{12}y_{2,0})\lambda_1^t + (p_{22}q_{21}y_{1,0} + p_{22}q_{22}y_{2,0})\lambda_2^t
\end{aligned} \tag{C-73}
$$

or, making the obvious definitions of the constants k_{11}, k_{12}, k_{21}, and k_{22}.

$$
\begin{aligned}
y_{1,t} &= k_{11}\lambda_1^t + k_{12}\lambda_2^t \\
y_{2,t} &= k_{21}\lambda_1^t + k_{22}\lambda_2^t
\end{aligned} \tag{C-74}
$$

By an exactly parallel argument, it can be shown that the general form of solution in an $n \times n$ system will be

$$y_{i,t} = k_{i1}\lambda_1^t + k_{i2}\lambda_2^t + \cdots + k_{in}\lambda_n^t \tag{C-75}$$

for $i = 1, \ldots, n$. Hence the nature of the path of each y_i over time depends on the magnitudes of the eigenvalues of **A**, the coefficient matrix of the equation system (C-63). Note the similarity between the form of the solution in (C-75) and that for the single nth-order equation given in (C-35), namely,

$$y_t = k_1(x_1)^t + k_2(x_2)^t + \cdots + k_n(x_n)^t$$

By reasoning parallel to that for the single-equation case, it is clear that for the system (C-63) to be stable—i.e., for the time path of each y_i $(i = 1, \ldots, n)$ to be dampened over time—the absolute value of each λ_i must be less than unity. In the case of a single nth-order difference equation it was necessary that the absolute values of the roots of the auxiliary equation be less than unity; now we see that for a system of first-order difference equations there is a very similar requirement, namely, that all eigenvalues of the coefficient matrix **A** must be less than unity in absolute value.

Furthermore, a pair of necessary conditions can be developed that do not require calculation of the eigenvalues of **A**. They depend on the observation that if $|\lambda_i| < 1$ $(i = 1, \ldots, n)$ then (1) $\left|\sum_{i=1}^n \lambda_i\right| < n$ and (2) $\left|\prod_{i=1}^n \lambda_i\right| < 1$. That is, (1) and (2) are both necessary conditions for the stability of system (C-63). Since the sum of the eigenvalues is the trace of the matrix **D**, and since **D** and **A** are similar and hence, as we have seen, must have the same trace, condition (1) can be stated as

$$-n < \text{tr}(\mathbf{A}) < n \tag{C-76}$$

Also, since the product of the eigenvalues is the determinant of the matrix **D** and since similar matrices have the same determinant, condition (2) can be stated as

$$-1 < |\mathbf{A}| < 1 \tag{C-77}$$

Therefore it is possible to determine something about the stability of the system (C-63) by simple and direct observations on its coefficient matrix **A**, *without* calculating the eigenvalues of **A**. Namely, if the absolute value of $\text{tr}(\mathbf{A}) \geq n$ *or* if the absolute value of $|\mathbf{A}| \geq 1$ (or both), we know that the equation system is *unstable*. Further inferences are not possible, however, since these are only necessary conditions, not also sufficient conditions, for stability; satisfaction of conditions (C-76) and (C-77) does not assure stability. For example, a three-equation system with $\lambda_1 = 2$, $\lambda_2 = \frac{1}{4}$, and $\lambda_3 = \frac{1}{8}$ satisfies both conditions on eigenvalues but is clearly unstable since $|\lambda_1| > 1$.

As was true for the Schur theorem on roots of the auxiliary equation being less than unity in absolute value, here too there are alternative and additional conditions regarding eigenvalues. For example, when **A** is a nonnegative matrix, a *sufficient* condition for stability is that all column sums of **A** be less than unity.†

C-7 SYSTEMS OF LINEAR DIFFERENTIAL EQUATIONS

General Notation and Form of Solution

The notation and development of methods of analysis of stability for systems of differential equations is very similar to that used for systems of difference equations in the previous section. For that reason, the present section will be briefer. In Sec. C-4 we considered the second-order linear differential equation $(D^2 - 3D - 10)y = 0$, that is, $d^2y/dt^2 - 3(dy/dt) - 10y = 0$, as given in (C-43). If we define x as dy/dt, that is,

$$x = \frac{dy}{dt} \tag{C-78}$$

then $dx/dt = (d/dt)(dy/dt) = d^2y/dt^2$ and the original equation can be rewritten

$$\frac{dx}{dt} - 3x - 10y = 0 \tag{C-79}$$

Rearranging (C-78) and (C-79) gives the following pair of first-order differential equations in the two variables, x and y:

$$\begin{aligned} \frac{dx}{dt} &= 3x + 10y \\ \frac{dy}{dt} &= x \end{aligned} \tag{C-80}$$

Using matrix notation, and $\dot{x}$ and $\dot{y}$ for dx/dt and dy/dt,

$$\begin{bmatrix} \dot{x} \\ \dot{y} \end{bmatrix} = \begin{bmatrix} 3 & 10 \\ 1 & 0 \end{bmatrix} \begin{bmatrix} x \\ y \end{bmatrix} \tag{C-81}$$

† For details on this and other rules, as well as proofs, see, for example, Gandolfo [10, pp. 131–134].

Parallel to the development for systems of difference equations, the general representation for a homogeneous n-equation first-order system will be

$$\begin{aligned}\dot{y}_1 &= a_{11}y_1 + a_{12}y_2 + \cdots + a_{1n}y_n \\ \dot{y}_2 &= a_{21}y_1 + a_{22}y_2 + \cdots + a_{2n}y_n \\ &\cdots\cdots\cdots\cdots\cdots\cdots\cdots\cdots \\ \dot{y}_n &= a_{n1}y_1 + a_{n2}y_2 + \cdots + a_{nn}y_n\end{aligned}$$

or, using obvious matrix definitions [compare (C-63)],

$$\dot{\mathbf{Y}} = \mathbf{AY} \tag{C-82}$$

As before, consider the advantages of the case in which $\mathbf{A}$ is a diagonal matrix with elements $d_1, \ldots, d_n$. Then a typical equation in (C-82) would be $\dot{y}_i = d_i y_i$ which we know, from Sec. C-3, would have a solution of the form $y_i = y_{i,0}\, e^{d_i t}$, where $y_{i,0}$ is the known initial value of y_i. Further, since the elements of a diagonal matrix are the eigenvalues of that matrix, the solution could as well be written $y_i = y_{i,0}\, e^{\lambda_i t}$. Defining a new $n \times n$ diagonal matrix

$$\mathbf{e}^{\Lambda t} = \begin{bmatrix} e^{\lambda_1 t} & 0 & \cdots & 0 \\ 0 & e^{\lambda_2 t} & & \vdots \\ \vdots & & \ddots & \\ 0 & & & e^{\lambda_n t} \end{bmatrix}$$

we could express the solution to the system (C-82)—for the case where $\mathbf{A}$ is diagonal—as

$$\mathbf{Y} = \mathbf{e}^{\Lambda t}\mathbf{Y}_0 \tag{C-83}$$

Of course, in general $\mathbf{A}$ will not be diagonal, but then the same transformation of variables that was used for the difference equation system is appropriate. That is, let $\mathbf{Y} = \mathbf{PZ}$, with $\mathbf{Y}_0 = \mathbf{PZ}_0$ so that $\dot{\mathbf{Y}} = \mathbf{P}\dot{\mathbf{Z}}$. This leads from $\dot{\mathbf{Y}} = \mathbf{AY}$ in (C-82) to

$$\dot{\mathbf{Z}} = \mathbf{P}^{-1}\mathbf{APZ} \tag{C-84}$$

As before, defining $\mathbf{D} = \mathbf{P}^{-1}\mathbf{AP}$, and using the (distinct) eigenvectors of $\mathbf{A}$ to form the columns of $\mathbf{P}$, so that $\mathbf{D}$ will be a diagonal matrix whose elements are the eigenvalues of $\mathbf{A}$,

$$\dot{\mathbf{Z}} = \mathbf{DZ} \tag{C-85}$$

will have a solution

$$\mathbf{Z} = \mathbf{e}^{\Lambda t}\mathbf{Z}_0$$

and, by substitution, (C-82) will have a solution†

$$\mathbf{Y} = \mathbf{P}\mathbf{e}^{\Lambda t}\mathbf{P}^{-1}\mathbf{Y}_0$$

† An alternative approach to this solution depends upon the series limit definition of $\mathbf{e}^A$, where $\mathbf{A}$ is any square matrix, as an extension of the definition of $\mathbf{e}^x$ as the limit of an infinite series. From this, an interpretation of $\mathbf{e}^{tA}$ and then $(d/dt)(\mathbf{e}^{tA})$ follows.

and therefore, given an initial set of values for the y variables,

$$\mathbf{Y} = \mathbf{P}e^{\Lambda t}\mathbf{P}^{-1}\mathbf{C}_0 \tag{C-86}$$

Stability for Systems of First-Order Differential Equations

To illustrate with the general 2×2 case, again using p_{ij} and q_{ij} for the elements of $\mathbf{P}$ and $\mathbf{P}^{-1}$,

$$\begin{bmatrix} y_1 \\ y_2 \end{bmatrix} = \begin{bmatrix} p_{11} & p_{12} \\ p_{21} & p_{22} \end{bmatrix} \begin{bmatrix} e^{\lambda_1 t} & 0 \\ 0 & e^{\lambda_2 t} \end{bmatrix} \begin{bmatrix} q_{11} & q_{12} \\ q_{21} & q_{22} \end{bmatrix} \begin{bmatrix} y_{1,0} \\ y_{2,0} \end{bmatrix} \tag{C-87}$$

which leads, by matrix multiplication and collection of terms on $e^{\lambda_1 t}$ and $e^{\lambda_2 t}$ [which here play exactly the role of λ_1^t and λ_2^t in the difference equation case—(C-72) and (C-73)]:

$$\begin{aligned} y_1 &= (p_{11}q_{11}y_{1,0} + p_{11}q_{12}y_{2,0})e^{\lambda_1 t} + (p_{12}q_{21}y_{1,0} + p_{12}q_{22}y_{2,0})e^{\lambda_2 t} \\ y_2 &= (p_{21}q_{11}y_{1,0} + p_{21}q_{12}y_{2,0})e^{\lambda_1 t} + (p_{22}q_{21}y_{1,0} + p_{22}q_{22}y_{2,0})e^{\lambda_2 t} \end{aligned} \tag{C-88}$$

and, defining k_{ij} exactly as in (C-74),

$$\begin{aligned} y_1 &= k_{11}\, e^{\lambda_1 t} + k_{12}\, e^{\lambda_2 t} \\ y_2 &= k_{21}\, e^{\lambda_1 t} + k_{22}\, e^{\lambda_2 t} \end{aligned} \tag{C-89}$$

By a similar argument, it can be shown that the general form of solution in an $n \times n$ system will be

$$y_i = k_{i1}\, e^{\lambda_1 t} + k_{i2}\, e^{\lambda_2 t} + \cdots + k_{in}\, e^{\lambda_n t} \tag{C-90}$$

for $i = 1, \ldots, n$. Hence, again, the eigenvalues of $\mathbf{A}$ determine the fundamental characteristics of the time path of the system and therefore its stability. Also, the parallel between the solution in (C-90) and that for the single nth-order equation given in (C-58), namely,

$$y = k_1\, e^{x_1 t} + k_2\, e^{x_2 t} + \cdots + k_n\, e^{x_n t}$$

should be apparent. Thus, for stability of the first-order system (C-82), all eigenvalues of $\mathbf{A}$ must be negative. Two necessary conditions for stability are therefore: (1) $\sum_{i=1}^{n} \lambda_i < 0$ and (2) $\prod_{i=1}^{n} \lambda_i > 0$ if n is an even number or $\prod_{i=1}^{n} \lambda_i < 0$ if n is an odd number. From our previous observations on the traces and the determinants of $\mathbf{A}$ and $\mathbf{D}$, these conditions translate directly into requirements on the elements of $\mathbf{A}$, namely,

$$\operatorname{tr}(\mathbf{A}) < 0 \tag{C-91}$$

and

$$\begin{aligned} |\mathbf{A}| &> 0 \quad (n \text{ even}) \\ |\mathbf{A}| &< 0 \quad (n \text{ odd}) \end{aligned} \tag{C-92}$$

Therefore it is possible to deduce something about the stability of the system (C-82) from observations on the elements of $\mathbf{A}$ itself, without finding the eigenvalues of $\mathbf{A}$. As is always the case with necessary conditions, we know that a system that fails (C-91) or (C-92) (or both) will be unstable. Satisfaction of both conditions does not insure stability, as is illustrated for the $n = 3$ system by $\lambda_1 = -2$, $\lambda_2 = \frac{1}{4}$, and $\lambda_3 = \frac{1}{8}$. This meets the two conditions on eigenvalues but is clearly unstable since $\lambda_2 > 0$ and $\lambda_3 > 0$.†

An Example

We conclude with a small illustration. Let $\mathbf{A} = \begin{bmatrix} 7 & -4 \\ 3 & -1 \end{bmatrix}$ and $\mathbf{Y}_0 = \begin{bmatrix} 4 \\ 8 \end{bmatrix}$ in the system $\dot{\mathbf{Y}} = \mathbf{AY}$. Note that we realize immediately that the system will be unstable since $\text{tr}(\mathbf{A}) = 6$ and thus (C-91) is violated. [The fact that $|\mathbf{A}| = 5$, which means that the system satisfies (C-92) for $n = 2$, is of no consequence to the question of stability since the other necessary condition, (C-91), is not satisfied.] The eigenvalues of $\mathbf{A}$ are found from

$$\begin{vmatrix} 7-\lambda & -4 \\ 3 & -1-\lambda \end{vmatrix} = 0$$

or from $\lambda^2 - \text{tr}(\mathbf{A})\lambda + |\mathbf{A}| = 0$. That is, from $\lambda^2 - 6\lambda + 5 = 0$, from which $\lambda_1 = 1$, $\lambda_2 = 5$.

The eigenvector associated with λ_1 (call it $\mathbf{V}_1$) is found as a solution vector to the pair of equations $[\mathbf{A} - \lambda_1\mathbf{I}]\mathbf{V}_1 = \mathbf{0}$. Let $\mathbf{V}_1 = \begin{bmatrix} v_1^1 \\ v_2^1 \end{bmatrix}$. Then

$$\left\{\begin{bmatrix} 7 & -4 \\ 3 & -1 \end{bmatrix} - \begin{bmatrix} 1 & 0 \\ 0 & 1 \end{bmatrix}\right\} \begin{bmatrix} v_1^1 \\ v_2^1 \end{bmatrix} = \begin{bmatrix} 0 \end{bmatrix}$$

or

$$6v_1^1 - 4v_2^1 = 0$$

and

$$3v_1^1 - 2v_2^1 = 0$$

which is clearly a "pair" of homogeneous linear equations having nontrivial (and therefore nonunique) solutions. One such solution is $v_1^1 = 2$, $v_2^1 = 3$, that is, $\mathbf{V}_1 = \begin{bmatrix} 2 \\ 3 \end{bmatrix}$. This qualifies, therefore, as the eigenvector of $\mathbf{A}$ associated with λ_1. Similarly, let $\mathbf{V}_2$ be the eigenvector in $[\mathbf{A} - \lambda_2\mathbf{I}]\mathbf{V}_2 = \mathbf{0}$; it is found to be $\mathbf{V}_2 = \begin{bmatrix} 2 \\ 1 \end{bmatrix}$. These column vectors form the modal matrix

$$\mathbf{P} = \begin{bmatrix} 2 & 2 \\ 3 & 1 \end{bmatrix}$$

and therefore

$$\mathbf{P}^{-1} = \begin{bmatrix} -\frac{1}{4} & \frac{1}{2} \\ \frac{3}{4} & -\frac{1}{2} \end{bmatrix}$$

† Again, for alternative formulations of stability rules, the reader is referred to, for example, Gandolfo [10].

The solution, then, is found from (C-86) as $\mathbf{Y} = \mathbf{P}\mathbf{e}^{\Lambda t}\mathbf{P}^{-1}\mathbf{Y}_0$:

$$\mathbf{Y} = \begin{bmatrix} 2 & 2 \\ 3 & 1 \end{bmatrix} \begin{bmatrix} e^t & 0 \\ 0 & e^{5t} \end{bmatrix} \begin{bmatrix} -\frac{1}{4} & \frac{1}{2} \\ \frac{3}{4} & -\frac{1}{2} \end{bmatrix} \begin{bmatrix} 4 \\ 8 \end{bmatrix}$$

that is,

$$\begin{bmatrix} y_1 \\ y_2 \end{bmatrix} = \mathbf{Y} = \begin{bmatrix} 6e^t - 2e^{5t} \\ 9e^t - e^{5t} \end{bmatrix}$$

Note that the solution can also be expressed directly in terms of the eigenvectors of $\mathbf{A}$, as observation of (C-86) suggests. Since the term $\mathbf{P}^{-1}\mathbf{Y}_0$ merely generates a column of constants, $[c_1, \ldots, c_n]'$, and since $\mathbf{P}$ can be expressed in terms of its columns as $[P_1 \quad P_2 \quad \cdots \quad P_n]$, $\mathbf{Y}$ can be written, by the rules of matrix multiplication (where $\mathbf{e}^{\Lambda t}$ is diagonal), as

$$\mathbf{Y} = c_1 P_1 e^{\lambda_1 t} + c_2 P_2 e^{\lambda_2 t} + \cdots + c_n P_n e^{\lambda_n t}$$

In the example, we see that

$$\mathbf{Y} = \begin{bmatrix} 6 \\ 9 \end{bmatrix} e^t + \begin{bmatrix} -2 \\ -1 \end{bmatrix} e^{5t} = (3) \begin{bmatrix} 2 \\ 3 \end{bmatrix} e^t + (-1) \begin{bmatrix} 2 \\ 1 \end{bmatrix} e^{5t}$$

where $\begin{bmatrix} 2 \\ 3 \end{bmatrix}$ was found to be $\mathbf{V}_1$ and hence P_1 and $\begin{bmatrix} 2 \\ 1 \end{bmatrix}$ was $\mathbf{V}_2$ and hence P_2.

C-8 STABILITY FOR SYSTEMS OF EQUATIONS ONCE MORE: THE GEOMETRY OF PHASE DIAGRAMS

The general structure of the solutions for single difference or differential equations and also for systems of equations makes clear the requirements for stability of the equations. For difference equations, the results in (C-35) and (C-75) show that for a single equation the roots of the auxiliary equation must all be less than unity in absolute value and for systems of equations the characteristic roots of the coefficient matrix of the system must similarly all be less than unity in absolute value. For differential equations, the results in (C-58) and (C-90) indicate that these same roots must be negative for stability. We have also seen that there are various rules that help us to determine from the coefficients of the equations themselves—i.e., without actually finding the required roots—whether or not the equation or equations are stable. Not all of these rules are easy to apply (e.g., for large n in the single-equation case) and not all are both necessary *and* sufficient tests for stability.

For the single-equation cases, we saw that a geometric representation of the solution, in t,y space, confirmed the algebraic rules for stability. Time paths that were dampened over time were associated with roots less than unity (in absolute value) or less than zero, in the difference and differential cases, respectively. We now turn to an investigation of possibilities for geometric representation of the time paths of pairs of variables in systems of equations. In fact, our attention will focus almost exclusively on pairs of differential equations. One justification for this rather restrictive concern is that in many economic applications (e.g., growth models) there are only a small number of variables (frequently only two) whose equations of motion are involved. In addition, the first-order conditions that evolve from a maximum principle approach to a dynamic optimization problem consist of a pair of differential equations. While we initially investigate the geometry for systems (pairs) of *linear* equations, we will note the nature of the extension to nonlinear equations, which is an important qualitative aid for a difficult quantitative (computational) problem.

Phase Diagrams for Linear Differential Equations

The simple homogeneous first-order linear differential equation $(a_0 D + a_1)y = 0$ [given in (C-36)] has a general solution $y = f(t)$, where $f(t) = c_0 e^{bt}$, $b = -(a_1/a_0)$, and $c_0 = y_0$. Time paths of this solution—i.e., representations of this particular $f(t)$ in the t,y plane—were presented in Fig. C-5, for various c_0 and b. The stable case (dampened time path) was clearly that in which $b < 0$. Rewriting the original differential equation as (again where $b = -a_1/a_0$) $dy/dt = by$, or $\dot{y} = by$, suggests an alternative geometric approach; one could represent the original equation [not its solution $y = f(t)$] in $y,\dot{y}$ space. Clearly the differential equation is a straight line through the origin (when $y = 0$, $\dot{y} = 0$) with slope b. Two alternatives are suggested in Fig. C-6.

The important observation to be made about $y,\dot{y}$ space (so-called *phase space*) is that at all points *above* the horizontal axis $\dot{y} > 0$, that is, $dy/dt > 0$, and therefore the direction of motion of y as t increases is rightward, in the direction of increasing y. Similarly, at all points *below* the horizontal axis, $\dot{y} < 0$ and hence y decreases (moves leftward) as t increases. This observation allows us to introduce the influence of t in this two-dimensional space (neither of whose

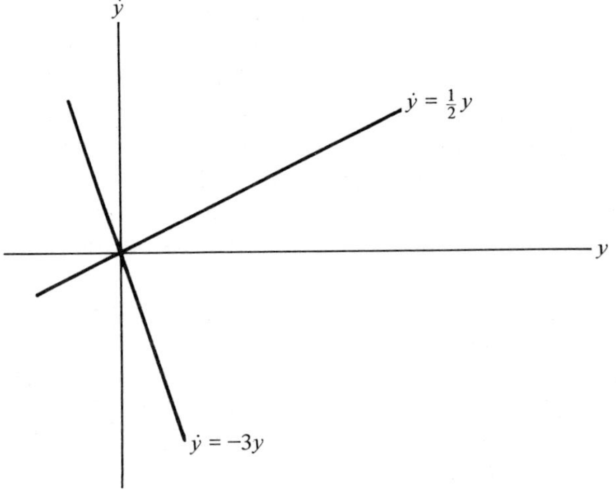

Figure C-6 $\dot{y} = \frac{1}{2}y$ and $\dot{y} = -3y$ in $y,\dot{y}$ space.

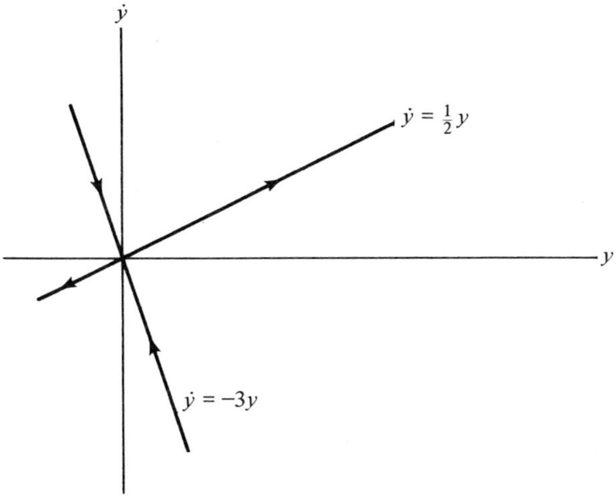

Figure C-7 The influence of t on $\dot{y} = \frac{1}{2}y$ and $\dot{y} = -3y$.

axes is t) by using arrowheads on the function $\dot{y} = by$ to indicate the direction in which y would move (i.e., increase or decrease) as t increases. These arrowheads are added to the functions shown in Fig. C-7.

It is clear that for $\dot{y} = by$ (whatever the value of b), the origin represents the only *equilibrium* point, since once $y = 0$, then $\dot{y} = 0$ and the system does not move away from $y = 0$. For the $\dot{y} = \frac{1}{2}y$ line, any strictly positive value of y (which means a value of y that is *larger* than the equilibrium value) is translated into a positive $\dot{y}$ (meaning that y gets even larger as t increases). A negative y (a value *smaller* than equilibrium) implies a negative $\dot{y}$ (i.e., further decreases). In other words, if y begins at *any* nonzero value, it will move further and further away from its equilibrium value ($y = 0$) over time. This is exactly what the arrowheads on $\dot{y} = \frac{1}{2}y$ show, since they point *away* from the origin. On the other hand, with $\dot{y} = -3y$, a positive y (larger than equilibrium value) generates a negative $\dot{y}$ (a decrease in y over time) and conversely a negative y translates into a positive $\dot{y}$. Hence, regardless of where y begins, it moves toward its equilibrium value over time. This is what the arrowheads on $\dot{y} = -3y$ show, since they point *toward* the origin.

This simple observation on representing the influence of time in $y,\dot{y}$ space (phase space) is the basis for the fundamental usefulness of such *phase diagrams*. This geometry makes clear that for the homogeneous first-order linear case a necessary and sufficient condition for stability is a negative slope to the line in phase space, that is, $b < 0$. This is exactly the result that we arrived at earlier when we examined the geometry of the *solution* to this case in t,y space. The usefulness of the phase space approach is, of course, that it involves a picture of the *given* differential equation, $\dot{y} = by$, and not of its *derived* solution, $y = c_0 e^{bt}$. Also, as we will soon see, it also suggests an approach for the case of a system of two equations.

For nonhomogeneous equations, the effect of the constant term is simply

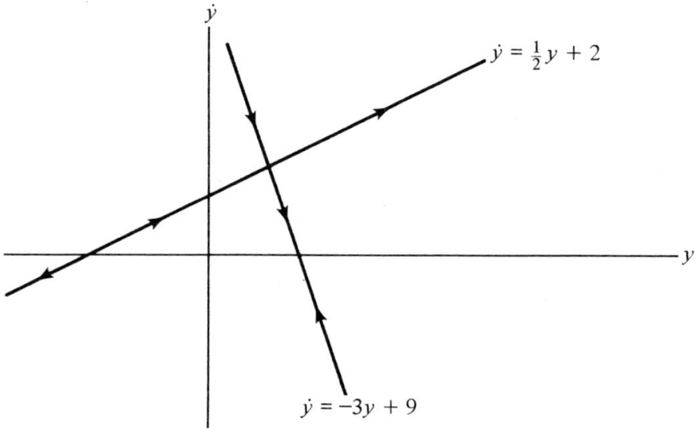

Figure C-8 $\dot{y} = \frac{1}{2}y + 2$ and $\dot{y} = -3y + 9$ in $y, \dot{y}$ space.

to shift the equilibrium value of y rightward or leftward, away from the origin, along the horizontal axis. For $\dot{y} = by + c$, $\dot{y} = 0$ when $y = -c/b$. The phase space representation will again be a straight line with a slope of b; only the intercept will vary. Figure C-8 illustrates this for $\dot{y} = \frac{1}{2}y + 2$ and $\dot{y} = -3y + 9$. The equilibrium values, as before, are when $\dot{y} = 0$, and thus the y axis continues to separate the phase space into the $\dot{y} > 0$ region (above the horizontal axis) and the $\dot{y} < 0$ region (below that axis). The logic is identical to that for the homogeneous case. A higher-order equation would present a problem, of course, since it describes a relationship between more than just y and dy/dt; e.g., a second-order equation also contains a d^2y/dt^2 term (or $\ddot{y}$), suggesting three-dimensional geometry. However, we saw that such equations can also be expressed in systems of first-order equations, so it is to such systems that we now turn.

A pair of linear homogeneous differential equations

$$\begin{aligned} \dot{y}_1 &= a_{11}y_1 + a_{12}y_2 \\ \dot{y}_2 &= a_{21}y_1 + a_{22}y_2 \end{aligned} \tag{C-93}$$

has, as we saw in Sec. C-7, a solution of the form

$$\begin{aligned} y_1 &= k_{11}\, e^{\lambda_1 t} + k_{12}\, e^{\lambda_2 t} \\ y_2 &= k_{21}\, e^{\lambda_1 t} + k_{22}\, e^{\lambda_2 t} \end{aligned} \tag{C-94}$$

From this we concluded that stability hinged on the sign of the two eigenvalues, λ_1 and λ_2. Geometrically, (C-94) could be shown in a pair of two-dimensional figures: one in t, y_1 space (for the first equation) and one in t, y_2 space (for the second). And each equation in (C-93) would need a three-dimensional phase space, since in general both y_1 and y_2 influence both $\dot{y}_1$ and $\dot{y}_2$.

Given the solution, (C-94), one could also construct a picture in two-dimensional y_1, y_2 space. With the k_{ij} and λ_j known, select a value of t, say t^*,

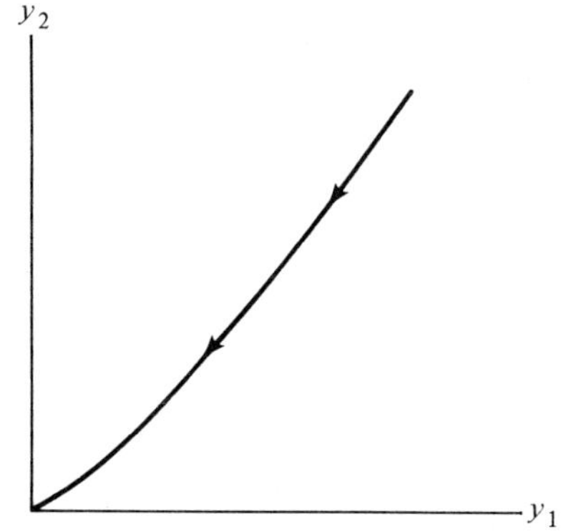

Figure C-9 $y_1 = 5e^{-t} + 6e^{-2t}$ and $y_2 = 2e^{-t} + 10e^{-2t}$ in y_1,y_2 space.

and find the y_1 and y_2 associated with that t^*, via (C-94); call these y_1^* and y_2^*. Select a second, larger, value of t, t^{**}, and find y_1^{**} and y_2^{**}, etc. Eventually a curve or trajectory will be traced out in y_1,y_2 space; the influence of increasing t can be shown by arrowheads along the curve, reflecting the sequence in which points along it were found.† Figure C-9 shows the following specific example of (C-94):

$$y_1 = 5\,e^{-t} + 6\,e^{-2t}$$

$$y_2 = 2\,e^{-t} + 10\,e^{-2t}$$

The four values of y_1 and y_2 used to plot the curve are shown explicitly in Table C-6.

Different values of the k_{ij} will lead to different trajectories in y_1,y_2 space, but as long as $\lambda_1 < 0$ and $\lambda_2 < 0$ (the stability conditions from our previous analysis) the arrowheads will point inward toward the origin. Figures C-10 and C-11 illustrate the kinds of curves that might result.

Table C-6 Values of y_1 and y_2 for $t = 0, \ldots, 3$.

t	0	1	2	3
y_1	11	2.65	0.78	0.26
y_2	12	2.09	0.45	0.12

† For a pair of differential equations, such as (C-93), y_1,y_2 space is known as phase space or the phase plane. Trajectories in phase space are often called phase paths or phase curves and the phase plane plus the path are often referred to as a phase diagram. This offers potential for a slight amount of confusion, since phase diagrams for single equations were drawn in $y,\dot{y}$ space.

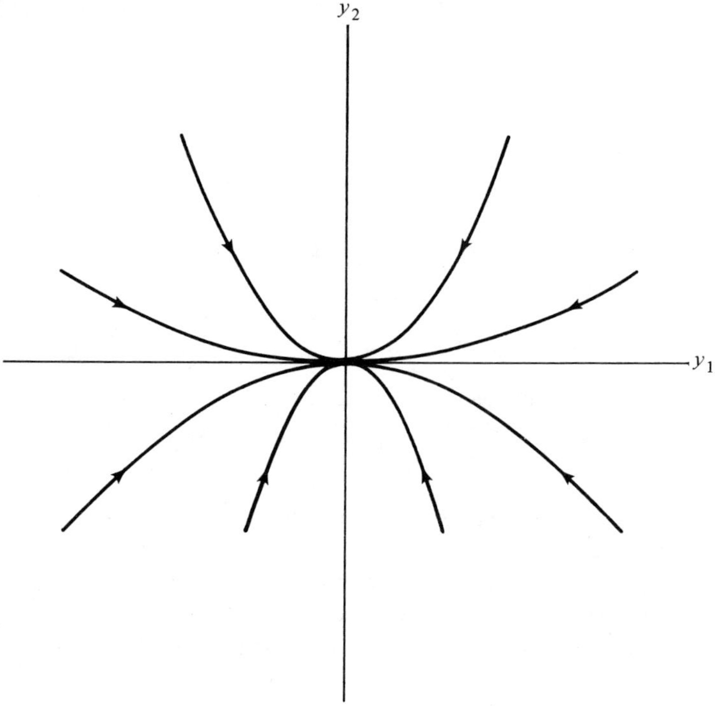

Figure C-10 Stable systems (convex trajectories in the positive quadrant of phase space).

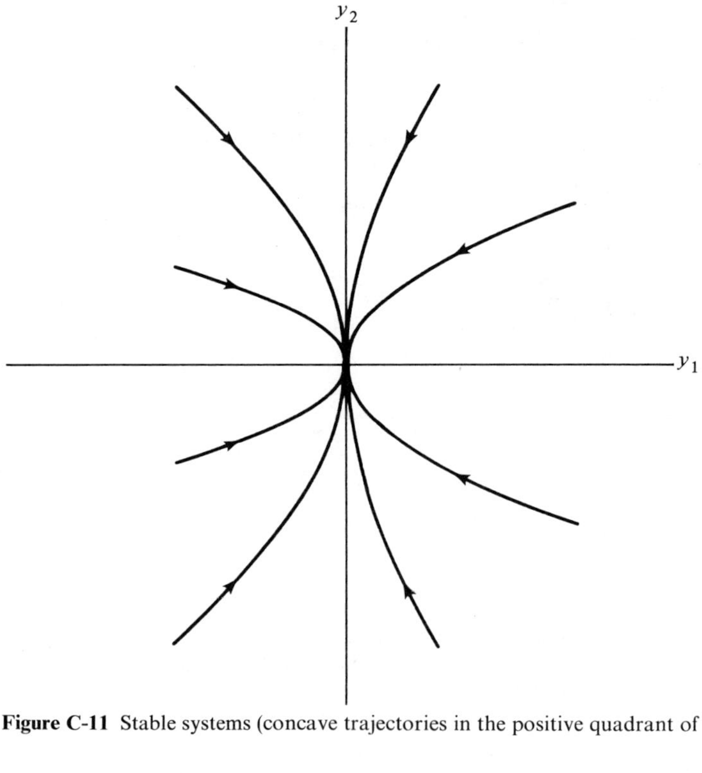

Figure C-11 Stable systems (concave trajectories in the positive quadrant of phase space).

Note that for any particular system with the solution given in (C-94), the complete trajectory will be the branch in one quadrant only, starting at some point in phase space (when $t = 0$) and terminating at the origin. Although the figures suggest parabolas, only one branch represents any given pair of differential equations. Movement along the horizontal axis occurs when $k_{21} = 0$ and $k_{22} = 0$ in (C-94), so that $y_2 = 0$ for all t; movement on the vertical axis represents the case of $k_{11} = 0$ and $k_{12} = 0$ in (C-94).

The preceding figures represent the *solution*, (C-94), to a pair of linear differential equations in a new way, utilizing the geometry of y_1,y_2 space. As we have already seen, however, if we have found the λ in the solution, then we have algebraic rules to determine whether or not the system is stable. What would be more useful would be a means of establishing at least the general shape of the phase curve and the orientation of the arrowheads without having to find the eigenvalues of **A**. We have also seen that certain rules on the elements in **A**—specifically on the trace of **A** and on the determinant of **A**—can sometimes be useful. How can the system itself, (C-93), help us develop the geometry in phase space?

From (C-93), $\dot{y}_1 = dy_1/dt$ gives the slope of the first solution equation in (C-94) in t,y_1 space and $\dot{y}_2 = dy_2/dt$ gives the slope of the second solution equation in t,y_2 space. Furthermore, $\dot{y}_2/\dot{y}_1 = (dy_2/dt)/(dy_1/dt) = dy_2/dy_1$ gives the slope of the solution function in y_1,y_2 space, i.e., the slope of functions such as those in Figs. C-9, C-10, and C-11. But this information comes directly from the system in (C-93) and not its solution in (C-94).

Consider a specific example of (C-93):

$$\begin{aligned} \dot{y}_1 &= 5y_1 + \ \ 3y_2 \\ \dot{y}_2 &= 2y_1 + 10y_2 \end{aligned} \tag{C-95}$$

The slope of a curve in phase space is $\dot{y}_2/\dot{y}_1 = (2y_1 + 10y_2)/(5y_1 + 3y_2)$. Lines through the origin in y_1,y_2 space have the general representation $y_2 = ky_1$. Along the line $y_2 = \frac{1}{5}y_1$, the slope of the phase path is given (substituting into the expression $\dot{y}_2/\dot{y}_1$) by $4y_1/\frac{28}{5}y_1 = \frac{5}{7}$; the slope will be constant, equal to $(2 + 10k)/(5 + 3k)$ along any line $y_2 = ky_1$. Thus we see how the *shape* of the phase diagram begins to emerge, independent of knowledge of the solution values in (C-94). Lines (or, more generally, curves) along which the slopes of the phase paths are constant are called *isoclines*. Along the horizontal axis ($y_2 = 0$), $\dot{y}_2/\dot{y}_1 = \frac{2}{5}$; along the vertical axis ($y_1 = 0$), $\dot{y}_2/\dot{y}_1 = \frac{10}{3}$, etc. Figure C-12 represents these facts, for the two axes and for $y_2 = \frac{1}{5}y_1$.

While the general shape of the phase curve is potentially useful information, it is the direction of motion through the phase space (along the curve) that we need to know in order to determine whether or not the system is a stable one. That is, we need to be able to place arrowheads on the phase curves of the sort suggested in Figs. C-9, C-10, and C-11. Fortunately, this is not difficult to do.

From the first equation in (C-95), we see that $\dot{y}_1 = 0$ when $5y_1 + 3y_2 = 0$, i.e., along the line $y_2 = -\frac{5}{3}y_1$. Above this line, e.g., when both y_1 and y_2 are positive, $\dot{y}_1 > 0$, and below this line, as when both y_1 and y_2 are negative,

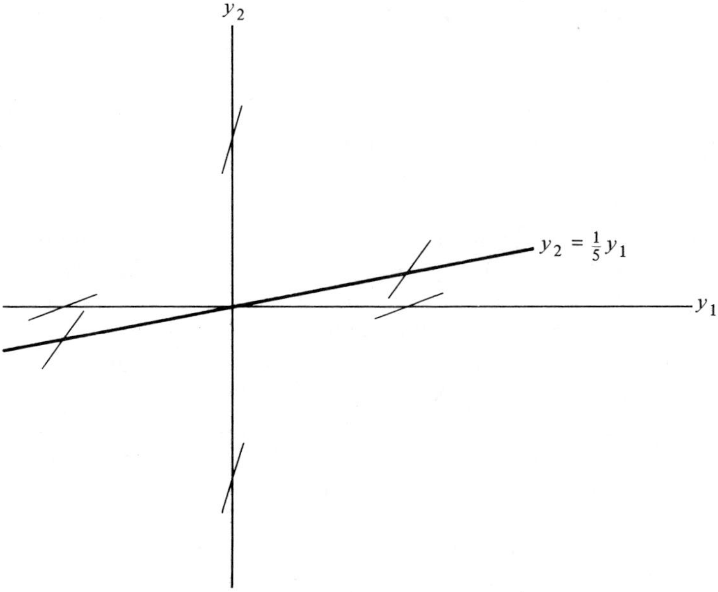

Figure C-12 Three isoclines in the phase plane.

$\dot{y}_1 < 0$. We introduce this information into the phase plane by using small horizontal arrows to indicate the movement of y_1 (the variable measured on the horizontal axis) in the two half spaces produced by the line $y_2 = -\frac{5}{3}y_1$ (Fig. C-13). Similarly, from the second equation in (C-95), $\dot{y}_2 = 0$ when $2y_1 + 10y_2 = 0$, i.e., along the line $y_2 = -\frac{1}{5}y_1$. Above this line, $\dot{y}_2 > 0$ and below it $\dot{y}_2 < 0$. We add

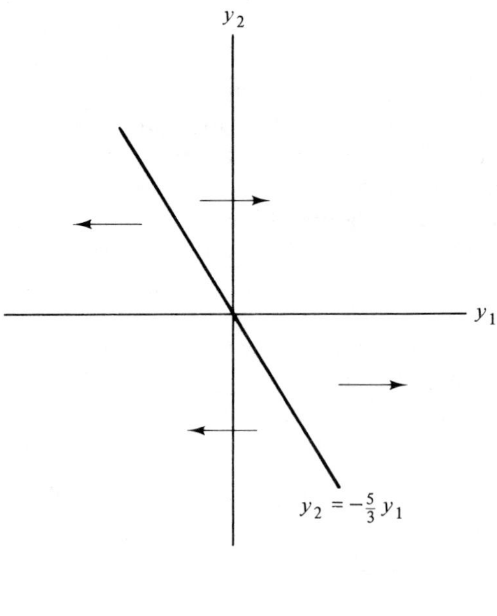

Figure C-13 Areas of increasing and decreasing y_1 in the phase plane.

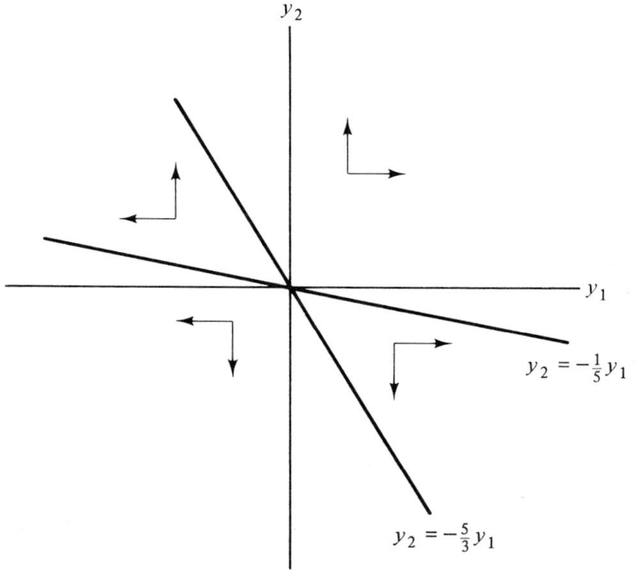

Figure C-14 Areas of increasing and decreasing y_1 and areas of increasing and decreasing y_2 in the phase plane.

this line to Fig. C-13, along with vertical arrows (y_2 is measured on the vertical axis), to show how y_2 moves as t increases. The lines defining the areas of differing directions of movement over time are the heavy lines $y_2 = -\frac{5}{3}y_1$ and $y_2 = -\frac{1}{5}y_1$, in Fig. C-14. Notice that here the axes, along which $y_1 = 0$ and $y_2 = 0$, play no significant role in delineating the *dynamically* different areas in y_1, y_2 space.

The information contained in this arrow diagram allows us to put arrowheads on the isoclines in Fig. C-12. Since instantaneous motion from any point in the upper right area of the figure must be due north, due east, or northeasterly, rightward-pointing arrowheads can be placed on the slopes along the positive halves of the y_1 axis and the y_2 axis, as well as on the slopes along that part of the line $y_2 = \frac{1}{5}y_1$ which falls in the positive quadrant. Similar considerations lead to leftward-pointing arrowheads on the other halves of these three lines. This is done in Fig. C-15. The figure clearly gives the impression that if y_1 and y_2 are not initially zero, so that, from (C-95), $\dot{y}_1 = 0$ and $\dot{y}_2 = 0$, then over time y_1 and y_2 will move further and further away from their equilibrium values.†

If we want additional help in sketching the curves in the phase diagram, we can find the lines in phase space with the property that along them the slope of the phase curve is the same as that of the line, i.e., boundaries in phase space

† A fact that could be checked by finding the eigenvalues of the system in (C-95). They are 4 and 11, thus violating the stability requirement that both be negative. The point of the geometry, of course, is to be able to make the instability conclusion without finding the eigenvalues.

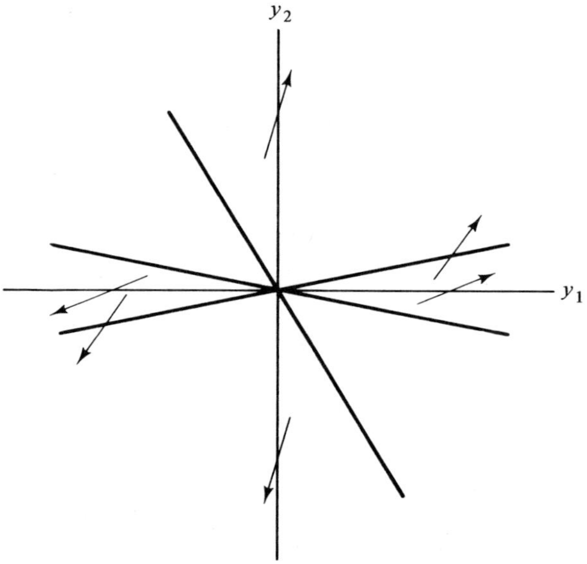

Figure C-15 Orientation of motion along three isoclines in the phase plane.

that the phase curves can never cross. In y_1,y_2 space, if a point were on one of these lines, any one of which is called a separatrix, it would continue its motion through time along the line, inward or outward, depending on the arrowhead orientation.

Such lines are easily found for this example from the fundamental definition that their slope, k, and that of the phase curve along them, $(2 + 10k)/(5 + 3k)$, must be equal. That is,

$$\frac{2 + 10k}{5 + 3k} = k$$

from which $(3k^2 - 5k - 2) = 0$ and $k = -\frac{1}{3}, 2$. Thus the lines $y_2 = -\frac{1}{3}y_1$ and $y_2 = 2y_1$ form boundaries in y_1,y_2 space, for the pair of differential equations in (C-95). They are added to the previous figure in Fig. C-16, and some representative curves are sketched.

Figure C-16 represents a generalization of the untilted figures that one has in simpler cases. For example, with

$$\begin{aligned} \dot{y}_1 &= -5y_1 \\ \dot{y}_2 &= \qquad -10y_2 \end{aligned} \tag{C-96}$$

i.e., the matrix system $\dot{\mathbf{Y}} = \mathbf{AY}$, with $\mathbf{A} = \begin{bmatrix} -5 & 0 \\ 0 & -10 \end{bmatrix}$, the axes in phase space are also the boundaries of the arrow diagram. That is, $\dot{y}_1 = 0$ along the line $y_1 = 0$ (the vertical axis); to the right, when $y_1 > 0$, $\dot{y}_1 < 0$, and to the left, when $y_1 < 0$, $\dot{y}_1 > 0$. Similarly, the horizontal axis, along which $y_2 = 0$, divides the

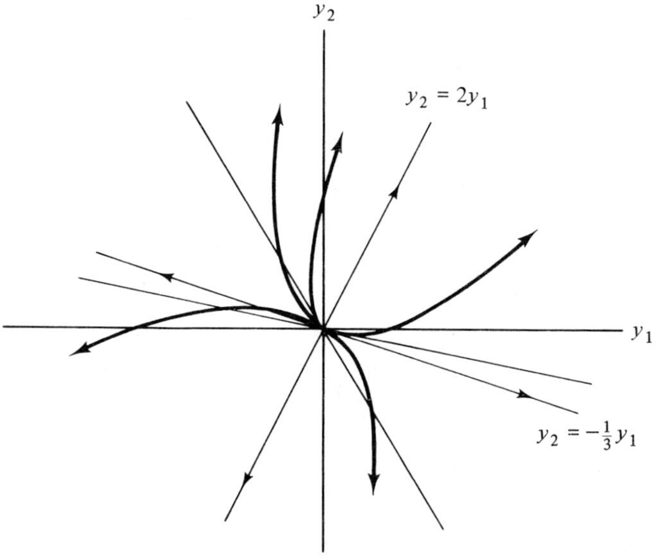

Figure C-16 The phase diagram for (C-95).

phase space into the half space above that axis, where $y_2 > 0$ and $\dot{y}_2 < 0$, and the half space below, where $\dot{y}_2 > 0$. Therefore, in this particular example, the axes *do* define the four areas of differing motion for the phase diagram.†

Moreover, they are also the two separatrices in this example. Along the horizontal axis, $y_2 = 0y_1$ and hence $\dot{y}_2/\dot{y}_1 = 2(y_2/y_1) = 2(0y_1/y_1) = 0$; i.e., the y_1 axis is the isocline along which the slope of the phase curve is zero. Since zero is also the slope of that line (the y_1 axis), this is a separatrix. Along the vertical axis, $y_1 = 0$ and hence $\dot{y}_2/\dot{y}_1 = 2(y_2/y_1)$ is not defined. However, the vertical axis can be thought of as the line $y_2 = ky_1$, when $k \to \infty$. Then by L'Hôpital's rule,‡ $\lim_{y_1 \to 0} 2(y_2/y_1) = \lim_{y_1 \to 0} 2(ky_1/y_1) = 2k$, which goes to infinity as $k \to \infty$; thus the y_2 axis is the isocline along which the slope of the phase curve is vertical. Since the y_2 axis is also vertical, this is a separatrix.

The diagram, then, has the shape of that in Fig. C-10, with inward-pointing arrowheads. Similar reasoning would show the system

$$\begin{aligned} \dot{y}_1 &= 5y_1 \\ \dot{y}_2 &= \qquad 10y_2 \end{aligned} \tag{C-97}$$

† The reader may wish to convince himself that this will always be true for a system (C-93) in which either $a_{12} = a_{21} = 0$ or $a_{11} = a_{22} = 0$. Of course, the orientation of the arrows will differ in these two general cases and in addition will depend on the signs of the nonzero elements.

‡ Given $f(x)$ and $g(x)$ continuous with continuous first derivatives, and if $\lim_{x \to a} f(x) = 0$ and $\lim_{x \to a} g(x) = 0$, but $\lim_{x \to a} g'(x) \neq 0$, then $\lim_{x \to a} f(x)/g(x) = \lim_{x \to a} f'(x)/g'(x)$. Here, for $x = y_1$, $f(x) = 2ky_1$ and $g(x) = y_1$.

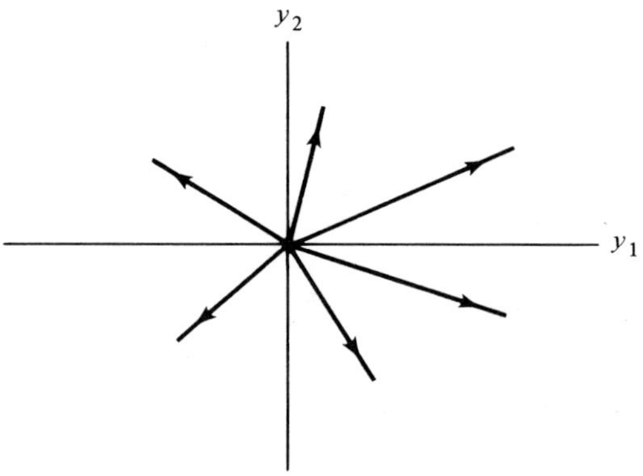

Figure C-17 The phase diagram for (C-98).

to have the shape suggested by Fig. C-11, although with outward-pointing arrowheads.

Finally, the particular example

$$\begin{aligned} \dot{y}_1 &= 5y_1 \\ \dot{y}_2 &= \qquad 5y_2 \end{aligned} \tag{C-98}$$

will have a phase diagram with isocline slopes given by $\dot{y}_2/\dot{y}_1 = 5ky_1/5y_1 = k$; i.e., the slope of the trajectory is always the same as that of the isocline, for any k. Hence the phase diagram is one of lines, not curves, in phase space, as in Fig. C-17.

These results, for the case of $a_{12} = a_{21} = 0$ in (C-93), can be easily generalized. When $a_{11} > a_{22}$, the curves are convex; when $a_{11} < a_{22}$, they are concave, and when $a_{11} = a_{22}$, they are straight lines. When a_{11} and a_{22} are positive, the arrowheads point outward; when negative, they point inward.

The important point to note is that (1) the general shape of the phase curves and (2) the orientation of the arrowheads on these curves are both obtained from the given system, as in (C-93), and do not require its specific solution, as in (C-94). That is, conclusions about the *stability* of the system are possible from information contained in the parameters of the system itself.

The interested reader can study the tilting effect of alterations of the system with $\mathbf{A} = \begin{bmatrix} a_{11} & 0 \\ 0 & a_{22} \end{bmatrix}$. For example, with $a_{12} = 0$ but $a_{21} \neq 0$, the locus of points along which $\dot{y}_2 = 0$ is no longer the y_1 axis. When this is true, the separatrix that was formerly also the y_1 axis is also tilted, and differs from the tilted $\dot{y}_2 = 0$ line. When $a_{12} \neq 0$ but $a_{21} = 0$, the same remarks apply to the y_2 axis only. When both $a_{12} \neq 0$ and $a_{21} \neq 0$, these remarks apply to both; this was the original general case we considered in (C-95).

Finally, consider

$$\begin{aligned} \dot{y}_1 &= -5y_1 + 3y_2 \\ \dot{y}_2 &= -2y_1 + 10y_2 \end{aligned} \tag{C-99}$$

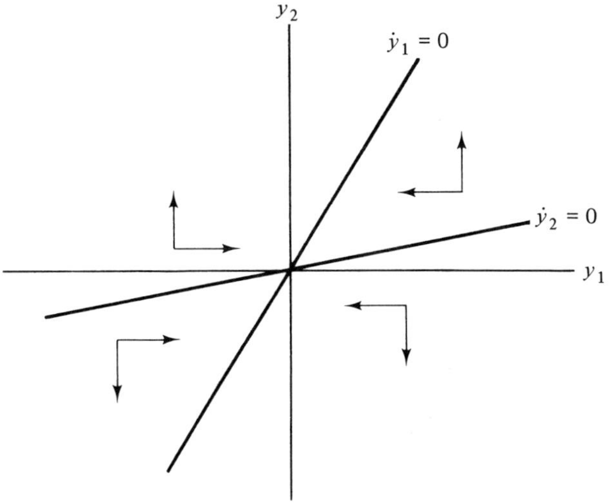

Figure C-18 Areas of the phase plane for system (C-99).

for which the direction of the arrowheads is inward along one separatrix and outward along the other; hence we have a saddle point. [This will always be the geometric character of two-dimensional phase space for systems like (C-93) when the eigenvalues of **A** are real and of opposite sign; for the system in (C-99), the eigenvalues are $\lambda_1 = 9.6$ and $\lambda_2 = -4.6$.] For $\dot{y}_1 = 0$, $-5y_1 + 3y_2 = 0$ or $y_2 = \frac{5}{3}y_1$. Above this line, e.g., when $y_1 < 0$ and $y_2 > 0$, $\dot{y}_1 > 0$; conversely, $\dot{y}_1 < 0$ below the line. Similarly, $\dot{y}_2 = 0$ when $y_2 = \frac{1}{5}y_1$; above the line, $\dot{y}_2 > 0$ and below it $\dot{y}_2 < 0$. Thus the phase space is divided into the four regions shown in Fig. C-18. Using the usual rule for separatrices,

$$\frac{-2y_1 + 10ky_1}{-5y_1 + 3ky_1} = k$$

leading to $(3k^2 - 15k + 2) = 0$ and from which, using the general rule for quadratic equations, $k = (15 \pm 14.18)/6 = 4.86, 0.14$. The separatrices ($y_2 = 4.86y_1$ and $y_2 = 0.14y_1$) are added to Fig. C-18 and representative curves are sketched in Fig. C-19. In such a case, initial values of y_1 and y_2 that lie precisely along the line $y_2 = 0.14y_1$ are the *only* ones that would converge to equilibrium; all other initial values lead to divergence from (0, 0), the equilibrium point.

The geometry for the case of complex conjugate eigenvalues can also be shown in y_1,y_2 space. For a single second-order differential equation, we saw that the time path would involve oscillations—either explosive, dampened, or constant (cycles). These possibilities are nicely reflected in the phase space diagrams. We illustrate with specific examples:

$$\begin{aligned} \dot{y}_1 &= -y_1 + 2y_2 \\ \dot{y}_2 &= -2y_1 - y_2 \end{aligned} \tag{C-100}$$

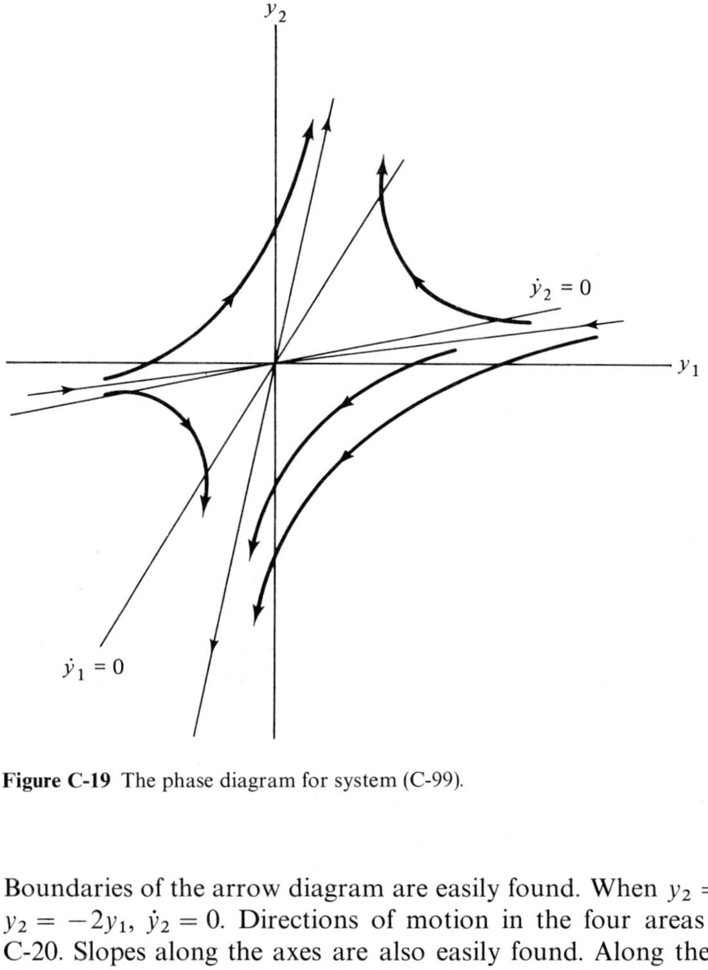

Figure C-19 The phase diagram for system (C-99).

Boundaries of the arrow diagram are easily found. When $y_2 = \frac{1}{2}y_1$, $\dot{y}_1 = 0$; when $y_2 = -2y_1$, $\dot{y}_2 = 0$. Directions of motion in the four areas are shown in Fig. C-20. Slopes along the axes are also easily found. Along the y_1 axis, $\dot{y}_2/\dot{y}_1 = 2$; along the y_2 axis, $\dot{y}_2/\dot{y}_1 = -\frac{1}{2}$. These slopes are added to Fig. C-20 and a representative trajectory is sketched in Fig. C-21. The reader should start at any point in the figure and move in the direction indicated by the set of arrows governing that area, in addition satisfying the slopes indicated. To do so, one travels along a decreasing spiral, into the origin, which is in this case known as a *focal point*.†

For the system

$$\begin{aligned} \dot{y}_1 &= y_1 - 2y_2 \\ \dot{y}_2 &= 2y_1 + y_2 \end{aligned} \tag{C-101}$$

† This geometry is consistent with algebraic fact. This is the case of complex conjugate roots with $\alpha < 0$. The solution to (C-100) is $y_1 = e^{-t}(k_1 \cos 2t + k_2 \sin 2t)$ and $y_2 = e^{-t}(k_2 \cos 2t - k_1 \sin 2t)$. Squaring, rearranging, and using the trigonometric identity $(\sin)^2 + (\cos)^2 = 1$, we have $y_1^2 + y_2^2 = (e^{-2t})4c_1c_2$, where c_1 and c_2 come from initial conditions. This describes a circle centered at the origin in y_1, y_2 space whose radius, however, decreases as t increases.

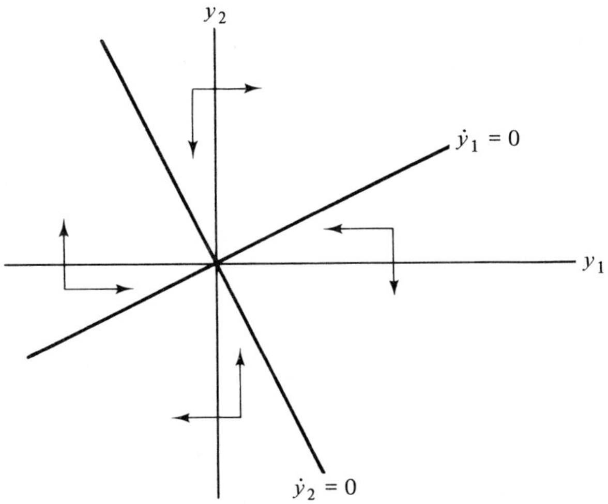

Figure C-20 Areas of the phase plane for system (C-100).

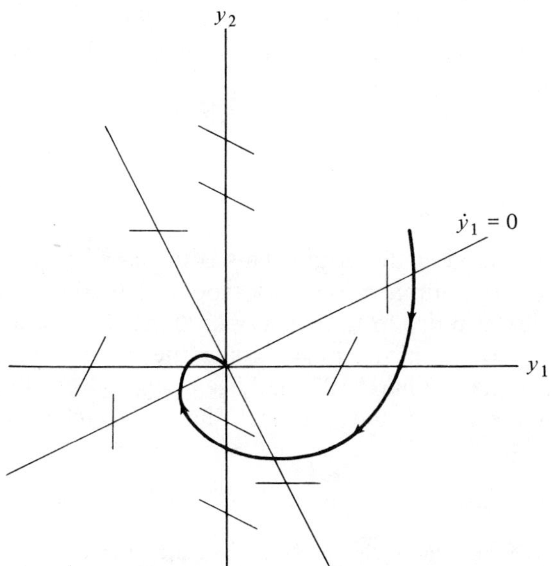

Figure C-21 The phase diagram for system (C-100).

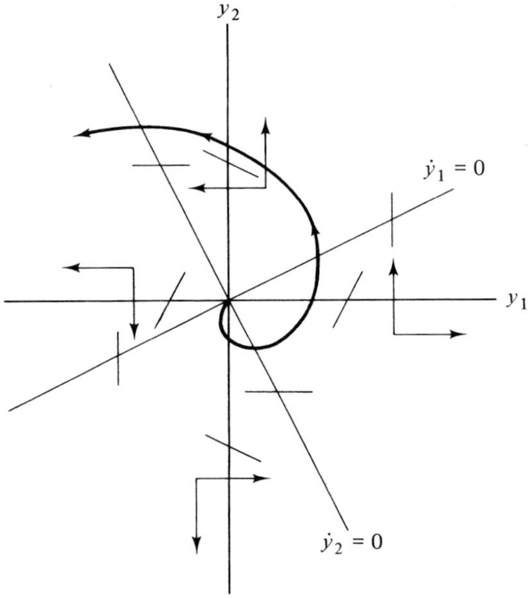

Figure C-22 The phase diagram for system (C-101).

the diagram will contain expanding spirals, as sketched in Fig. C-22. Note that the $\dot{y}_1 = 0$ and $\dot{y}_2 = 0$ lines are the same as for (C-100), and that the slopes are the same, but that the orientation of each of the arrowheads in the arrow diagram is reversed (180°). The origin is known as a *spiral point* in this case. (Algebraically, $\alpha > 0$ in the complex conjugate roots.)†

Finally, for

$$\begin{aligned} \dot{y}_1 &= \quad\quad 2y_2 \\ \dot{y}_2 &= -2y_1 \end{aligned} \tag{C-102}$$

the phase lines are closed curves, centered at the origin. This is the case of cyclic behavior. (Algebraically, $\alpha = 0$ in the complex conjugate roots.) Whether the curves are circles or ellipses can be determined from their slopes along the isocline $y_2 = y_1$, i.e., the 45° line. Here $\dot{y}_2/\dot{y}_1 = -1$ along $y_2 = y_1$, and the phase curves are circles.‡ However, if the second equation in (C-102) had been, say, $\dot{y}_2 = -4y_1$, $\dot{y}_2/\dot{y}_1 = -4$, which is compatible only with the elliptical shape§ sketched in Fig. C-23.

† Here $y_1^2 + y_2^2 = (e^{2t})4c_1c_2$, which means that the radius of the circle centered at the origin increases as t increases.

‡ Now $y_1^2 + y_2^2 = 4c_1c_2$, i.e., the circle has a constant radius whose size is determined by initial conditions.

§ The algebra of the solution would produce $y_1^2/4c_1c_2 + y_2^2/16c_1c_2 = 1$, which is indeed an ellipse centered at (0, 0) with intercepts on the y_1 axis at $\pm 2\sqrt{c_1c_2}$ and on the y_2 axis at $\pm 4\sqrt{c_1c_2}$.

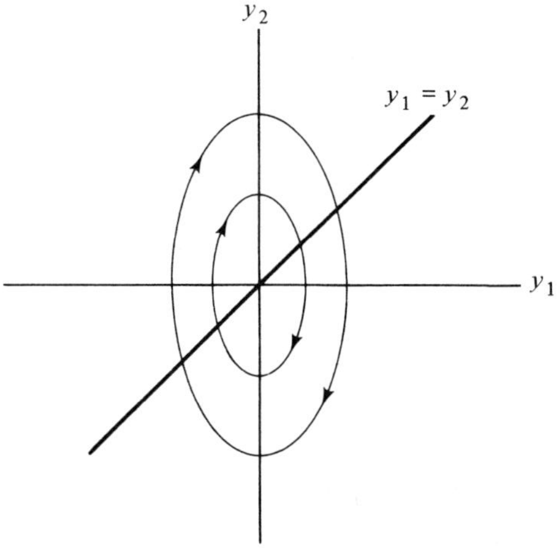

Figure C-23 The phase diagram for $\dot{y}_1 = 2y_2$ and $\dot{y}_2 = -4y_1$.

In closing, we might note that in converting a second-order linear differential equation to a system (pair) of first-order linear differential equations, we facilitate geometric analysis of the equation. Given $\ddot{y}_1 + a\dot{y}_1 + by_1 = 0$, we would need the solution, showing y_1 as a function of time, in order to sketch the behavior of y_1 over time, i.e., in the t,y_1 plane. However, (1) defining $\dot{y}_1 = y_2$ and (2) re-expressing the original equation as $\dot{y}_2 = -ay_2 - by_1$ gives us a pair of first-order equations which can be represented in y_1,y_2 space, as we have been doing in the preceding examples. Note that here, because of (1), this is exactly $y_1,\dot{y}_1$ space, i.e., true phase space for the original variable, y_1. (Recall the footnote on terminology on page 265).

Phase Diagrams for Linear Difference Equations

The simple homogeneous first-order linear difference equation $(a_0E + a_1)y_t = 0$ [given in (C-11)] has a general solution $y_t = f(t)$, where $f(t) = c_0b^t$, $b = -(a_1/a_0)$, and $c_0 = y_0$. Various time paths—curves in the t,y plane—were presented in Fig. C-1, for different c_0 and b. Alternatively, the original equation [again where $b = -(a_1/a_0)$] could be rewritten as $y_{t+1} = by_t$ and we could turn to the two-dimensional geometry of y_t,y_{t+1} space in order to represent the original equation (not its solution $y_t = c_0b^t$). Clearly the difference equation is a straight line through the origin with slope b. Two alternatives are suggested in Fig. C-24.

The line $y_{t+1} = y_t$, the 45° line, facilitates the construction of a sequence of values for y_t. For example, for the $y_{t+1} = \frac{1}{2}y_t$ case, shown in Fig. C-25, each successive "next" value (vertical axis) is translated to a "current" value (horizontal axis) via this line. The sequence is as follows: (1) y_0 (horizontal) generates y_1 (vertical), via the lower line (which represents the functional relationship between y_{t+1} and y_t), (2) y_1 (vertical) becomes y_1 (horizontal) via the upper line ($y_{t+1} = y_t$, the 45° line), (3) y_1 (horizontal) generates y_2 (vertical) via the lower line, (4) y_2

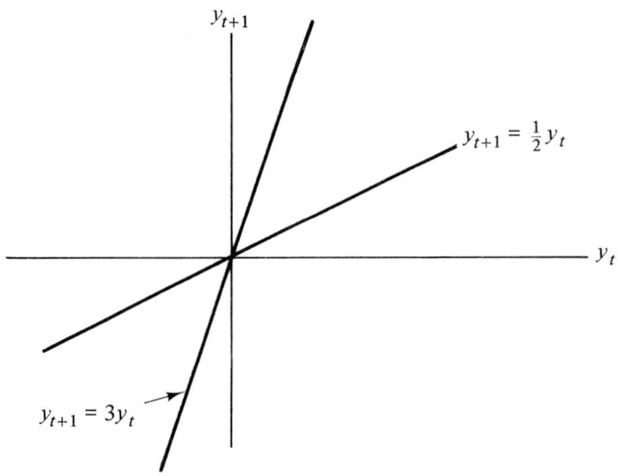

Figure C-24 $y_{t+1} = \frac{1}{2}y_t$ and $y_{t+1} = 3y_t$ in y_t, y_{t+1} space.

(vertical) becomes y_2 (horizontal) via the upper line, etc. The "time path" of y_t consists of the succession of points along either axis—the horizontal begins with y_0, the vertical with y_1. The heavily dashed lines suggest the approach of y_t toward the origin.

In addition, the 45° line plays a role here that is in some ways analogous to the horizontal axis in the $y, \dot{y}$ phase space for single differential equations. It is the locus of points for which $y_{t+1} - y_t = 0$, that is, $\Delta y_t = 0$. (In differential equations we were concerned with the locus of points for which $\dot{y} = 0$.) This means that if successive values of y_t approach the point at which the difference equation (here $y_{t+1} = \frac{1}{2}y_t$) crosses the 45° line (the line along which $\Delta y_t = 0$),

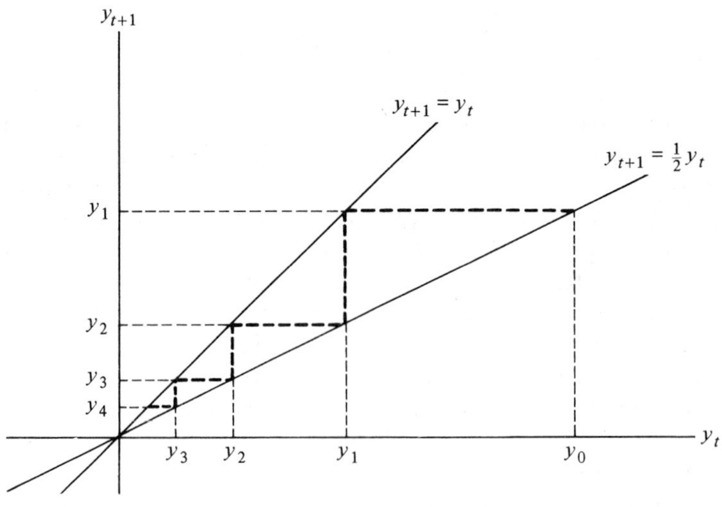

Figure C-25 $y_{t+1} = \frac{1}{2}y_t$ and $y_{t+1} = y_t$ in y_t, y_{t+1} space.

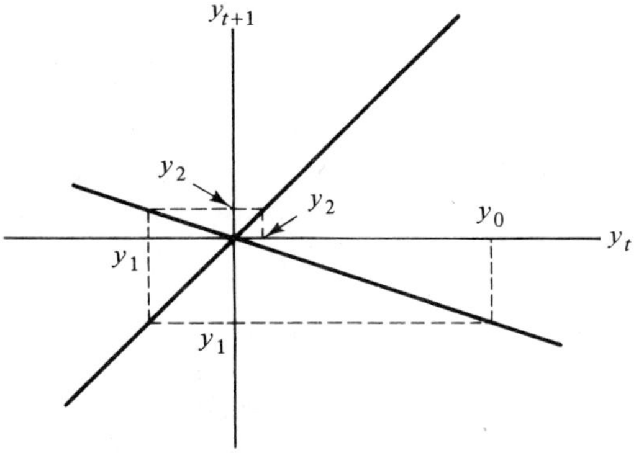

Figure C-26 $y_{t+1} = -\frac{1}{3}y_t$ in y_t, y_{t+1} space.

then y_t is approaching an equilibrium value. That is the case in Fig. C-25, where the equilibrium is at $y_t = 0$, since the original difference equation is homogeneous and therefore intersects the $y_{t+1} = y_t$ line at $y_t = 0$. The reader should trace a sequence of values of y_t following the difference equation $y_{t+1} = 3y_t$ (superimposed onto Fig. C-25) and note that y_t increases by increasing amounts, away from the origin.

Thus, for difference equation phase space, the direction of motion of y_t as t increases is leftward, in the direction of decreasing y, below the 45° line. Above it, the direction of motion is rightward (increasing y). This suggests that we might introduce arrowheads into the two-dimensional space, showing the direction in which y_t would move as t increases. Were we to do so, they would point inward along the $y_{t+1} = \frac{1}{2}y_t$ line and outward along the $y_{t+1} = 3y_t$ line in Fig. C-24. For lines with negative slopes, however, such arrowheads could be misleading.

Consider two different equations, $y_{t+1} = -\frac{1}{3}y_t$ and $y_{t+1} = -2y_t$, shown in Figs. C-26 and C-27. Beginning at y_0, y_t is seen to alternate between positive

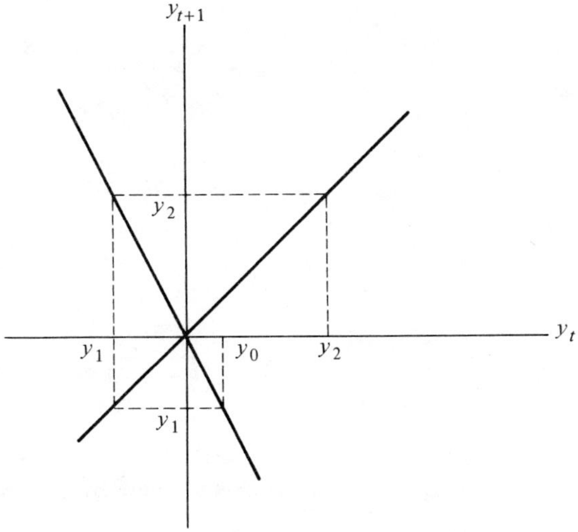

Figure C-27 $y_{t+1} = -2y_t$ in y_t, y_{t+1} space.

and negative values. Moreover, while y_t approaches zero when $y_{t+1} = -\frac{1}{3}y_t$ (Fig. C-26), the successive values of y_t are larger and larger (in absolute value) for $y_{t+1} = -2y_t$ (Fig. C-27). All of these examples are consistent with our earlier observations in Sec. C-1. Stability required $|b| < 1$; alternations occur if $b < 0$. We see, then, that the arrowheads are not always useful devices with difference equations; in particular, they suggest stability, i.e., they point toward the origin, for $y_{t+1} = -2y_t$, when in fact the time path is one of explosive alternations. The potential for confusion lies in the fact that movements in y_t, y_{t+1} space are not continuous, as they were in the differential equation $y, \dot{y}$ space. For a difference equation, the distance between successive y values is not infinitesimal. In both Figs. C-26 and C-27, any initial positive y_0 will lead to a smaller y_1, so the direction of movement from y_0 *is* leftward, as arrowheads would suggest. But in both cases y_1 is actually negative, i.e., the equilibrium value of zero has been overshot. Whether or not succeeding positive and negative y approach the origin or diverge from it depends on whether $|b| < 1$ or $|b| > 1$, as we saw earlier in Sec. C-1. (If $b = -1$, y_t will oscillate between $+y_0$ and $-y_0$.)

For nonhomogeneous equations, the effect of the constant term is simply to shift the equilibrium value rightward or leftward, away from the origin, along the 45° line. For $y_{t+1} = by_t + c$, the intersection with $y_{t+1} = y_t$ occurs at (via simple substitution) $y_t = c/(1 - b)$. Figures C-28 and C-29 illustrate this for $y_{t+1} = \frac{1}{2}y_t + 3$ and $y_{t+1} = -\frac{1}{3}y_t + 12$, respectively. (Compare Fig. C-25 for the homogeneous form of the first equation and Fig. C-26 for the second.)

Again, starting with an arbitrarily chosen y_0, successive values of y approach the equilibrium value in either figure. All that is changed is the location of the equilibrium point, i.e., the equilibrium value of y_t. By attaching a constant term to the equation represented in Fig. C-27, the reader can generate a new equation

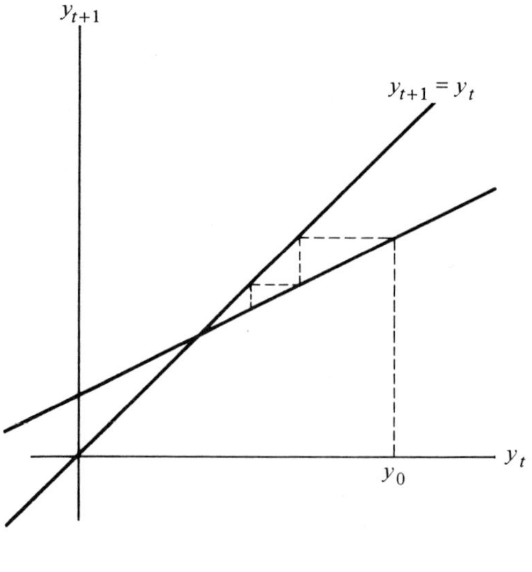

Figure C-28 $y_{t+1} = \frac{1}{2}y_t + 3$ in y_t, y_{t+1} space.

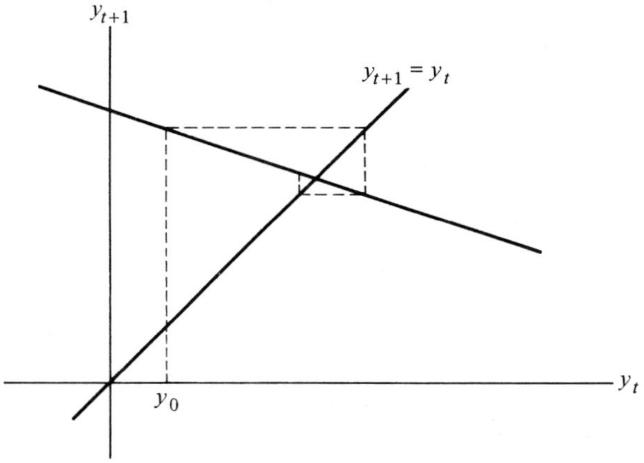

Figure C-29 $y_{t+1} = -\frac{1}{3}y_t + 12$ in y_t, y_{t+1} space.

that would still produce explosive alternations; again, only the position in y_t, y_{t+1} space would be changed.

There is no well-developed approach for pairs of first-order linear difference equations to parallel that for differential equations. The reason is fundamentally that, as we noted above for a single equation, arrowheads to represent the influence of time are not useful for the discrete motion that is implied by difference equations. For example, consider

$$\begin{aligned} y_{1,t+1} &= 2y_{1,t} + 3y_{2,t} \\ y_{2,t+1} &= 5y_{1,t} + y_{2,t} \end{aligned} \tag{C-103}$$

Letting $\Delta y_1 = y_{1,t+1} - y_{1,t}$ and $\Delta y_2 = y_{2,t+1} - y_{2,t}$, (C-103) can be rearranged to

$$\begin{aligned} \Delta y_1 &= y_{1,t} + 3y_{2,t} \\ \Delta y_2 &= 5y_{1,t} \end{aligned} \tag{C-104}$$

which is more parallel to a differential case, such as (C-95). One could then, in $y_{1,t}, y_{2,t}$ space, find the lines along which $\Delta y_1 = 0$ and along which $\Delta y_2 = 0$ (parallel to $\dot{y}_1 = 0$ and $\dot{y}_2 = 0$ for differential equations). At any point in y_1, y_2 space for differential equations, the slope of the phase curve was given by $dy_2/dy_1 = (dy_2/dt)/(dy_1/dt) = \dot{y}_2/\dot{y}_1$. However, in y_1, y_2 space for difference equations, the analogous ratio [which comes directly from the rearranged equations, as in (C-104)] is $\Delta y_2/\Delta y_1$. This only approaches dy_2/dy_1 as $\Delta y_1 \to 0$, i.e., for points "near" to the $\Delta y_1 = 0$ line. Thus the two fundamental sources of information are absent in the difference equation case: (1) the directional implications of arrow diagrams are often ambiguous and (2) conclusions about the slopes of the phase curves cannot be made throughout y_1, y_2 space.

The absence of a geometrical approach for pairs of first-order linear difference equations also means the absence of one possible representation of a second-order linear difference equation, namely, via its conversion to a pair of first-order linear equations. However, a direct approach does exist, which results in representations in y_t, y_{t+1} space for second-order linear difference equations. The interested reader should consult Baumol [3] for a complete development.

Phase Diagrams for Nonlinear Differential Equations

With ordinary algebraic equations, nonlinearities may introduce immense complexities. Questions arise with respect to existence and uniqueness of solutions and methods for finding or approximating a solution when one does exist. Similar complications arise with nonlinear difference and differential equations. Here we will briefly outline two geometrical approaches for examining the question of stability for a pair of nonlinear differential equations. More detail can be found in advanced texts.† We also introduce the approach of Liapunov, which is based on straightforward geometric reasoning.

Linear approximations Consider a pair of homogeneous nonlinear differential equations

$$\begin{aligned} \dot{y}_1 &= f_1(y_1, y_2) \\ \dot{y}_2 &= f_2(y_1, y_2) \end{aligned} \tag{C-105}$$

for which the origin is an equilibrium point, for which there are no other "nearby" equilibrium points, and in which f_1 and f_2 are differentiable functions of y_1 and y_2 near the origin. Then one can expand the right-hand side of (C-105) via the Taylor series to

$$\begin{aligned} \dot{y}_1 &= a_{11}y_1 + a_{12}y_2 + g_1(y_1, y_2) \\ \dot{y}_2 &= a_{21}y_1 + a_{22}y_2 + g_2(y_1, y_2) \end{aligned} \tag{C-106}$$

where g_1 and g_2 contain terms involving y_1^2, y_2^2, y_1y_2, and higher powers. Then, if y_1 and y_2 are "small," i.e., for y_1 and y_2 near to the origin, the g_1 and g_2 terms in (C-106) can be ignored, and we have

$$\begin{aligned} \dot{y}_1 &\cong a_{11}y_1 + a_{12}y_2 \\ \dot{y}_2 &\cong a_{21}y_1 + a_{22}y_2 \end{aligned} \tag{C-107}$$

and all of the analysis for pairs of linear differential equations applies *for this region near to the origin.*

That this analysis does not apply *in the large* is illustrated by the following pair of nonlinear differential equations for which the origin is an equilibrium point:

$$\begin{aligned} \dot{y}_1 &= y_2 \\ \dot{y}_2 &= -y_1 + y_2 - \tfrac{1}{3}y_2^3 \end{aligned} \tag{C-108}$$

† See, for example, Cunningham [7], Davis [8, especially chaps. 10 to 12], Davis and James [9], Ritger and Rose [16, especially chap. 10], or Sanchez [18, sec. 4.4].

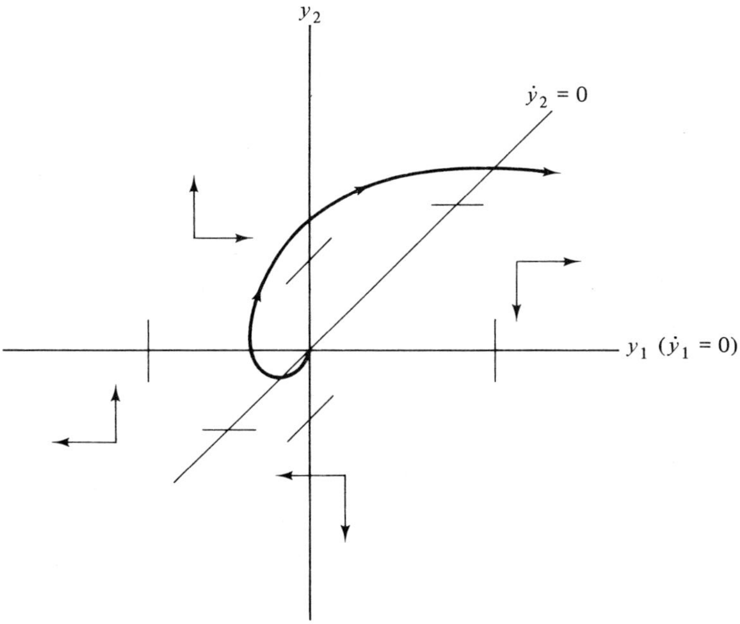

Figure C-30 The phase diagram for system (C-109).

whose linearized version would be

$$\begin{aligned} \dot{y}_1 &\cong 0y_1 + y_2 \\ \dot{y}_2 &\cong -y_1 + y_2 \end{aligned} \tag{C-109}$$

The boundaries of the arrow diagram are easily found to be: (1) $\dot{y}_1 = 0$ when $y_2 = 0$ and (2) $\dot{y}_2 = 0$ when $y_1 = y_2$. In Fig. C-30 we sketch these boundaries, the directional arrows in each area, and the phase curve slopes, $\dot{y}_2/\dot{y}_1$, along the horizontal axis (where the slope is vertical), the vertical axis (where the slope is 1), and the line $y_1 = y_2$ (where the slope is horizontal). The geometry suggests an unstable spiral with the origin as the spiral point.†

If we now return to the complete nonlinear system in (C-108), we see that the actual phase curve slope anywhere in the phase plane is given by $\dot{y}_2/\dot{y}_1 = [(y_2 - \frac{1}{3}y_2^3) - y_1]/y_2$. This means that in place of the line $y_2 = y_1$, which in Fig. C-30 represented the locus of $\dot{y}_2 = 0$ points, we really have the curve $y_2 - \frac{1}{3}y_2^3 = y_1$. In Fig. C-31 we show the true locus of $\dot{y}_2 = 0$ points, along which the slope of the phase curve is horizontal. While the slope remains vertical along the y_1 axis, note that it is no longer constant along the y_2 axis. This is because

† This is consistent with the complete solution of the linear system in (C-109), for which the eigenvalues are complex conjugates with $\alpha > 0$.

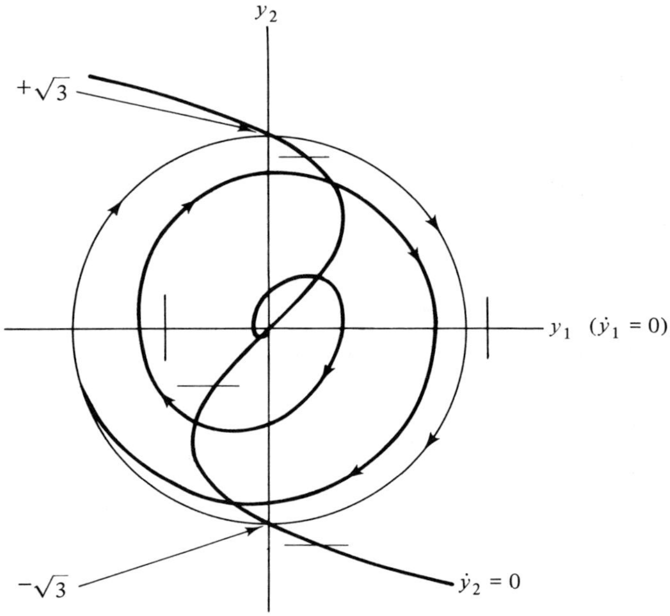

Figure C-31 The phase diagram for system (C-108).

$\dot{y}_2/\dot{y}_1$, when $y_1 = 0$, is now $(1 - \frac{1}{3}y_2^2)$; i.e., it is $+1$ at the origin (when $y_2 = 0$), becomes horizontal at $y_2 = \pm\sqrt{3}$, and is negative above $y_2 = \sqrt{3}$ and below $y_2 = -\sqrt{3}$. We sketch this information in Fig. C-31, along with a typical curve. The situation here is that we have a *limit cycle*, i.e., a closed phase curve which is approached from inside (and from outside as well). Such cycles can be approached from one side only (semistable) or, as here, from both sides (orbitally stable, or just stable).† Thus, while the behavior of the point in phase space over time *is* correctly given by an expanding spiral near to the origin, as suggested by the linear approximation in (C-109), values of y_1 and y_2 do not explode indefinitely.

Geometric approximations For nonlinear differential equations, it is often possible to derive at least the general characteristics of the $\dot{y}_1 = 0$ and $\dot{y}_2 = 0$ curves. For example, in certain kinds of applications in economic theory, convexity or concavity may be assumed. Then, once the phase space is divided into regions, the arrow diagrams can often be constructed by referring to the equations directly.‡ For example, in Figs. C-32 and C-33, we represent the same boundary curves ($\dot{y}_1 = 0$ and $\dot{y}_2 = 0$) but different arrow diagram orientations.§

† Limit cycles can occur with a single linear difference equation in the rather special case where there is a kink on the 45° line.

‡ For a detailed example of this kind of reasoning, see Arrow and Kurz [1, pp. 64–69].

§ Adapted from Burmeister and Dobell [6, pp. 86–87].

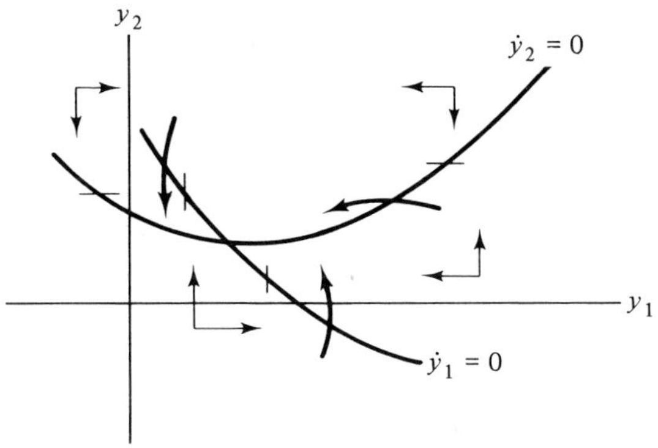

Figure C-32 A phase diagram for nonlinear equations.

The longer, heavy arrows indicate the only kinds of phase space trajectories that are compatible with these figures. In the first case, then, the $\dot{y}_1 = 0$, $\dot{y}_2 = 0$ intersection represents a stable equilibrium. In the second, we see that it is a saddle point in which only initial y_1 and y_2 values that lie along the one curve through the $\dot{y}_1 = 0$, $\dot{y}_2 = 0$ intersection will approach the equilibrium; all others approach infinitely large values for at least one of the two variables.

Liapunov's direct method We mention briefly the direct (or second) method of Liapunov. While essentially algebraic in nature, the underlying notion comes from geometric considerations in phase space.† Using as an example the pair of homogeneous nonlinear differential equations in (C-105), for which the origin is an equilibrium point, imagine any point (y_1^*, y_2^*) in y_1, y_2 space. If the *distance* of y_1^*, y_2^* from the origin decreases as t increases, then the origin is a stable

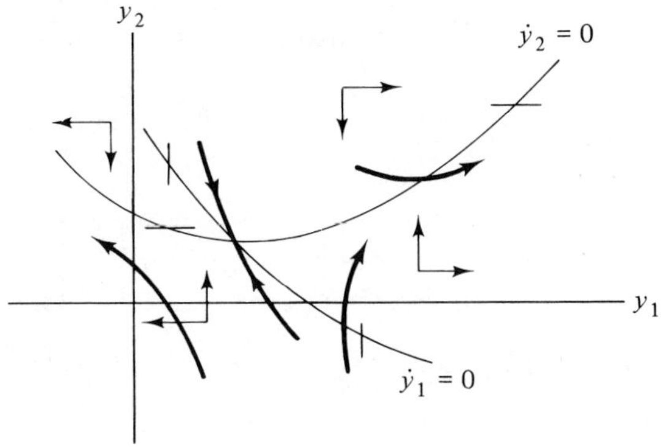

Figure C-33 A phase diagram for nonlinear equations.

† The indirect (or first) method requires that we have the actual solutions to the equations. As we shall see, the second method employs the equations themselves directly and not their solutions.

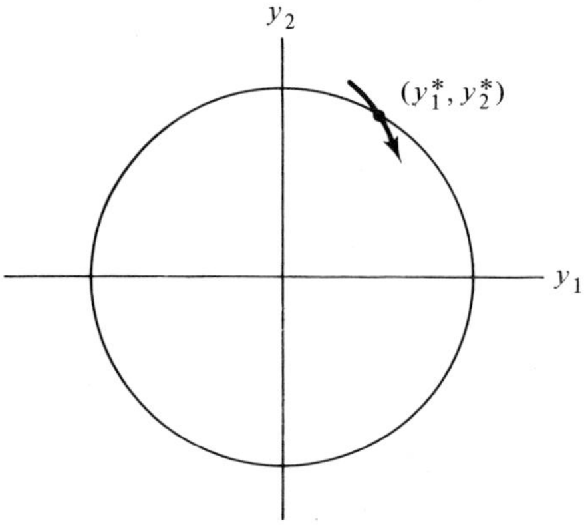

Figure C-34 Possible solution curve orientation at y_1^*, y_2^* in the stable case.

equilibrium point. For $\mathbf{Y}^* = \begin{bmatrix} y_1^* \\ y_2^* \end{bmatrix}$, the length or norm of the vector, $\|\mathbf{Y}^*\|$, is just the distance of y_1^*, y_2^* from the origin, since $\|\mathbf{Y}^*\| = +\sqrt{(y_1^*)^2 + (y_2^*)^2}$. To simplify notation and also to conform later with the general Liapunov results, denote $\|\mathbf{Y}\|$ for any y_1, y_2 by V, that is, $V = +\sqrt{y_1^2 + y_2^2}$. Then the stability argument made above is that if (1) dV/dt (or $\dot{V}$) < 0 for all $y_1 \neq 0$ and $y_2 \neq 0$ and (2) $dV/dt = 0$ when and only when $y_1 = y_2 = 0$, then the origin is stable.

Geometrically, to require that the distance of the point from the origin be decreasing as $t \to \infty$ means that at any given $y_1^* \neq 0$, $y_2^* \neq 0$, the solution curve in the phase plane must at that point cut through the circle (centered at the origin) on whose circumference y^*, y^* lies, and the direction of motion must be inward, as Fig. C-34 suggests. That is, after a short period of time, the new y_1^*, y_2^* must lie on a circle of smaller radius, which means that the point y_1^*, y_2^* must be closer to the origin. Note that it is not necessary that both $\dot{y}_1 < 0$ and $\dot{y}_2 < 0$ (in Fig. C-34, at y_1^*, y_2^*, $\dot{y}_2 < 0$ but $\dot{y}_1 > 0$). Since $V = +\sqrt{y_1^2 + y_2^2}$ and since the solution to the equations would give y_1 and y_2 as functions of t, dV/dt is found by the usual chain rule:

$$\frac{dV}{dt} = \frac{\partial V}{\partial y_1}\frac{dy_1}{dt} + \frac{\partial V}{\partial y_2}\frac{dy_2}{dt} \tag{C-110}$$

or, using the usual gradient notation, $\mathbf{\nabla V}$, for $\begin{bmatrix} \partial V/\partial y_1 \\ \partial V/\partial y_2 \end{bmatrix}$ and using $\dot{\mathbf{Y}}$ for $\begin{bmatrix} \dot{y}_1 \\ \dot{y}_2 \end{bmatrix}$,

$$\dot{V} = [\mathbf{\nabla V}] \cdot [\dot{\mathbf{Y}}] \tag{C-111}$$

and the basic requirement for stability is $\dot{V} < 0$.

Since the cosine of the angle included between two vectors, **A** and **B**, emanating from the same point, is given by $[\mathbf{A}] \cdot [\mathbf{B}] / \|\mathbf{A}\| \, \|\mathbf{B}\|$, and since the denominator is always positive, the sign of the cosine will be governed completely by the inner product, $[\mathbf{A}] \cdot [\mathbf{B}]$. For an angle ϕ in the range $0° \leq \phi \leq 180°$ (which is necessary if it is to qualify as an *included* angle between two vectors), $\cos\phi < 0$ when $90° < \phi \le 180°$ (see Fig. C-4 and Table C-1). Thus, from (C-111), the basic requirement for stability

$$[\nabla \mathbf{V}] \cdot [\dot{\mathbf{Y}}] < 0 \tag{C-112}$$

means that the two vectors $\nabla \mathbf{V}$ and $\dot{\mathbf{Y}}$ must meet at an angle greater than 90° and no more than 180°. Recall that the gradient for any function f, $\nabla \mathbf{f}$, evaluated at a particular point, gives the direction of the outward-pointing normal to the function at that point (i.e., the line perpendicular to the tangent at that point). The equation of a circle, centered at the origin and passing through y_1^*, y_2^*, is $y_1^2 + y_2^2 = r^2$, where r^2 is the constant given by $(y_1^*)^2 + (y_2^*)^2$. The gradient along the circle is $\begin{bmatrix} 2y_1 \\ 2y_2 \end{bmatrix}$ or $2\begin{bmatrix} y_1 \\ y_2 \end{bmatrix}$. The *direction* is given by $\begin{bmatrix} y_1 \\ y_2 \end{bmatrix}$, i.e., by $\mathbf{Y}$, evaluated at any point; the scalar, 2, affects only the magnitude. For our distance function V, $\nabla \mathbf{V} = \begin{bmatrix} y_1/\sqrt{y_1^2 + y_2^2} \\ y_2/\sqrt{y_1^2 + y_2^2} \end{bmatrix} = (1/\sqrt{y_1^2 + y_2^2})\begin{bmatrix} y_1 \\ y_2 \end{bmatrix}$. Again the *direction* is given by $\begin{bmatrix} y_1 \\ y_2 \end{bmatrix}$, i.e., by $\mathbf{Y}$, evaluated at any point; the scalar $(1/\sqrt{y_1^2 + y_2^2})$ only changes the magnitude. Thus $\nabla \mathbf{V}$ at y_1^*, y_2^* gives the direction of the outward-pointing normal to the circle through y_1^*, y_2^*.

As we are now well aware, the slope of the solution curve in phase space at a given point is $\dot{y}_2/\dot{y}_1$, evaluated at that point. This is the slope indicated by the vector $\dot{\mathbf{Y}}\left(= \begin{bmatrix} \dot{y}_1 \\ \dot{y}_2 \end{bmatrix}\right)$ at that point.† Therefore, the requirement, (C-112), that $[\nabla \mathbf{V}] \cdot [\dot{\mathbf{Y}}] < 0$ simply means that at y_1^*, y_2^* the outward-pointing normal on the circle through that point and the vector which indicates the slope of the solution curve at that point must meet at an obtuse angle.‡ Figure C-35 illustrates this for $y_1^*, y_2^* = (1, 2)$.

The Liapunov direct method is a generalization of (C-112).

Liapunov's theorem If a function $V(y_1, \ldots, y_n)$—a so-called Liapunov function—can be found such that (1) $V > 0$ if at least one $y_i \neq 0$, i.e., if $\|\mathbf{Y}\| \neq 0$, and $V = 0$ if and only if all $y_i = 0$, i.e., if $\|\mathbf{Y}\| = 0$, (2) $V \to \infty$ as $\|\mathbf{Y}\| \to \infty$, and (3) $\dot{V} < 0$ if at least one $y_i \neq 0$ and $\dot{V} = 0$ if and only if all $y_i = 0$, then the origin is a stable equilibrium point.

The converse is also true: if the origin is stable, then a Liapunov function can be found with properties (1) through (3). Therefore the existence of a Liapunov

† The reader should make a simple sketch, if this does not seem obviously true.

‡ The reader who is familiar with gradient methods for constrained nonlinear programming problems may recall a similar kind of requirement to assure that directions of movement toward an optimum are always feasible, i.e., do not violate any constraints.

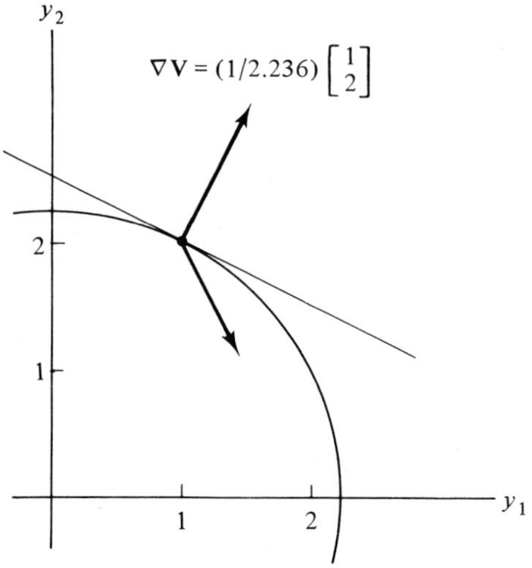

Figure C-35 The geometry of $[\nabla \mathbf{V}]\cdot[\dot{\mathbf{Y}}] < 0$.

function is a necessary and sufficient condition for stability. Moreover, if a function V with properties (1) and (2) can be found for which $\dot{V} > 0$ if at least one $y_i \neq 0$, then the origin is unstable.

The generalization involved is that the Liapunov function need not be exactly the distance function—$+\sqrt{y_1^2 + \cdots + y_n^2}$ in the n-dimensional case. By the same token, it is clear that the ordinary distance function—or, for that matter, its square, $(y_1^2 + \cdots + y_n^2)$—will always satisfy properties (1) and (2); if a problem arises, it will be with respect to the sign of $\dot{V}$. In particular, if the sign of $\dot{V}$ is not unambiguously negative (or positive) when $V = \sqrt{y_1^2 + \cdots + y_n^2}$ or when $V = (y_1^2 + \cdots + y_n^2)$, then one must look for other possible Liapunov functions, and the procedure for finding them is not easy to specify for the general case.† [For difference equations, the rules (1) through (3) in the Liapunov theorem apply, except that, in (3), $\dot{V}$ is replaced by ΔV.]

A few examples illustrate how the Liapunov approach can be used. Let

$$\begin{aligned} \dot{y}_1 &= -y_1^3 - y_2 \\ \dot{y}_2 &= y_1 - y_2^3 \end{aligned} \tag{C-113}$$

and try $V = +\sqrt{y_1^2 + y_2^2}$. The question of stability hinges on the sign of $\dot{V}$, since (1) and (2) of the theorem are met. Here

$$\nabla \mathbf{V} = \begin{bmatrix} y_1/\sqrt{y_1^2 + y_2^2} \\ y_2/\sqrt{y_1^2 + y_2^2} \end{bmatrix} = \left(1/\sqrt{y_1^2 + y_2^2}\right) \begin{bmatrix} y_1 \\ y_2 \end{bmatrix}$$

† "Modified" distance functions and further refinements can be found in more advanced texts. See, for example, Benavie [4, especially sec. 4.4], Gandolfo [10, pp. 371–375], and LaSalle and Lefschetz [14].

and the elements of $\dot{\mathbf{Y}}$ are given by (C-113). This is why the method is referred to as a direct one; we utilize the given differential equations and not their solution. Therefore, since $\dot{V} = [\nabla V] \cdot [\dot{\mathbf{Y}}]$,

$$\dot{V} = \frac{1}{\sqrt{y_1^2 + y_2^2}} [y_1(-y_1^3 - y_2) + y_2(y_1 - y_2^3)]$$

$$= \frac{1}{\sqrt{y_1^2 + y_2^2}} (-y_1^4 - y_2^4)$$

which is clearly negative for any $y_1 \neq 0$ and/or $y_2 \neq 0$. Hence (C-113) has a stable equilibrium at the origin.

Note that using $V = (y_1^2 + y_2^2)$ would avoid the square-root term in $\dot{V}$. It would also satisfy requirements (1) and (2) of the Liapunov theorem, and furthermore, since $\nabla V = \begin{bmatrix} 2y_1 \\ 2y_2 \end{bmatrix} = 2\begin{bmatrix} y_1 \\ y_2 \end{bmatrix}$,

$$\dot{V} = 2(-y_1^4 - y_2^4)$$

which is clearly negative for $y_1 \neq 0$ and/or $y_2 \neq 0$. Hence $(y_1^2 + y_2^2)$ is also a valid Liapunov function for (C-113).

For less immediate success, consider

$$\begin{aligned} \dot{y}_1 &= -y_1^3 - 4y_2 \\ \dot{y}_2 &= 3y_1 - y_2^3 \end{aligned} \tag{C-114}$$

and $V = y_1^2 + y_2^2$. Here

$$\begin{aligned} \dot{V} &= (2y_1)(-y_1^3 - 4y_2) + (2y_2)(3y_1 - y_2^3) \\ &= -2y_1^4 - 8y_1y_2 + 6y_1y_2 - 2y_2^4 \\ &= -2y_1^4 - 2y_1y_2 - 2y_2^4 \end{aligned}$$

whose sign is ambiguous, because of the term involving the product of y_1 and y_2, since the sign of this term depends on the signs of both y_1 and y_2. Looking at the second line of $\dot{V}$, we see that the problem arises because the two coefficients on y_1y_2 terms, namely, (-8) and $(+6)$, do not sum to zero. Looking further back, to the first line of $\dot{V}$, we also realize that this is because of the (-4) on y_2 and the $(+3)$ on y_1 in the expressions for $\dot{y}_1$ and $\dot{y}_2$, respectively. Thus our Liapunov function should give weights other than $2y_1$ to $\dot{y}_1$ and $2y_2$ to $\dot{y}_2$. Try $V = 3y_1^2 + 4y_2^2$, which still clearly satisfies (1) and (2) of the theorem. Now

$$\begin{aligned} \dot{V} &= (6y_1)(-y_1^3 - 4y_2) + (8y_2)(3y_1 - y_2^3) \\ &= -6y_1^4 - 24y_1y_2 + 24y_1y_2 - 8y_2^4 \\ &= -6y_1^4 - 8y_2^4 \end{aligned}$$

which is clearly negative for $\mathbf{Y} \neq \mathbf{0}$, and hence the origin is a stable equilibrium point. Although the squared-distance function does not qualify as a Liapunov function, we found that $V = 3y_1^2 + 4y_2^2$ does. This is all that is needed; if *any* function can be found to satisfy the theorem, stability is proven.

Finally, we look for a Liapunov function for the pair of nonlinear differential equations in (C-108), where we found a limit cycle (Fig. C-31). Using the squared-distance function $V = y_1^2 + y_2^2$, we have

$$\begin{aligned}\dot{V} &= (2y_1)(y_2) + (2y_2)(-y_1 + y_2 - \tfrac{1}{3}y_2^3)\\ &= 2y_2^2 - \tfrac{2}{3}y_2^4\\ &= 2y_2^2(1 - \tfrac{1}{3}y_2^2)\end{aligned}$$

which is clearly positive for $(1 - \frac{1}{3}y_2^2) > 0$, i.e., for $y_2 < \pm\sqrt{3}$. This tells us that the origin is an unstable point and suggests the presence of the limit cycle passing through $y_2 = \pm\sqrt{3}$.

There are many examples of the use of phase diagrams for analysis of the systems of nonlinear differential equations that govern the motion of variables in dynamic economic models. Such equations, or their discrete difference equation counterparts, are at the heart of models of economic growth. In this role, these equations are part of the descriptive internal content of the model. In addition, as already noted, application of the maximum principle of Pontryagin to questions of optimality in dynamic growth models often leads to a pair of nonlinear differential equations which constitute necessary conditions for maximum or minimum functions. Here, then, the equations constitute external optimality criteria imposed upon the model. In either case, it is essential that a person reading the current growth literature be familiar with at least the fundamentals of the geometry of analysis in the phase plane.†

PROBLEMS

C-1 Solve the following difference equations:

(*a*) $y_{t+2} = 6y_{t+1} - 8y_t$, with $y_0 = 3$ and $y_1 = 2$
(*b*) $y_{t+2} = 3y_{t+1} - 2y_t$, with $y_0 = 1$ and $y_1 = 2$
(*c*) $y_{t+1} = \frac{1}{2}y_t - \frac{1}{2}$, with $y_0 = 0$
(*d*) $y_{t+2} + 4y_{t+1} + 4y_t = 0$, with $y_0 = 1$ and $y_1 = 0$

C-2 Examine each of the equations given in Prob. C-1 for stability, using the Schur theorem where appropriate. Verify your results by examining the solutions to each of the equations.

C-3 Solve the following differential equations:

(*a*) $\ddot{y} - 6\dot{y} + 8y = 0$, with $y = 3$ and $\dot{y} = 2$ (at $t = 0$)
(*b*) $\ddot{y} + 2\dot{y} = 3$, with $y = 3$ and $\dot{y} = 2$ (at $t = 0$)
(*c*) $\ddot{y} + \dot{y} - 6y = 0$, with $y = 10$ and $\dot{y} = 1$ (at $t = 0$)
(*d*) $d^3y/dt^3 - dy/dt = 1$, with $y = 6$, $dy/dt = 2$, and $d^2y/dt^2 = 1$ (at $t = 0$)
(*e*) $\ddot{y} - 2\dot{y} + 10y = 0$, with $y = 2$ and $\dot{y} = 2$ (at $t = 0$)

C-4 Examine each of the equations given in Prob. C-3 for stability. Verify your results by examining the solutions to each of the equations.

† Examples can be found, for example, in Arrow and Kurz [1], Burmeister and Dobell [6], Hadley and Kemp [12], and Shell [19].

C-5 Rewrite each of the following problems as a system of first-order linear equations and then solve. Verify your results by comparison with the solutions to the original problems:

(*a*) Prob. C-1(*a*)

(*b*) Prob. C-3(*c*)

(*c*) Prob. C-3(*d*)

C-6 Analyze each of the systems of equations in Prob. C-5 for stability, using the necessary conditions on tr(**A**) and $|\mathbf{A}|$ from Secs. C-6 and C-7. Compare the results with those in Prob. C-2 [for Prob. C-1(*a*)] and Prob. C-4 [for Probs. C-3(*c*) and C-3(*d*)].

C-7 Consider $y_{t+2} - cy_{t+1} + cy_t = 0$, where c is a positive constant. For what values of c will the solution to this second-order linear homogeneous difference equation exhibit explosive cyclical behavior?

C-8 Confirm the instability of the system in Prob. C-5(*b*) by showing that a Liapunov function cannot be found.

C-9 Examine the following nonlinear system for stability:

$$\dot{x}_1 = -x_1^3 + 6x_2$$

$$\dot{x}_2 = -x_1 - 2x_2$$

C-10 (*a*) Rewrite Prob. C-3(*a*) as a pair of first-order linear differential equations and sketch the phase diagram for the system, thereby examining the question of stability. Compare with the outcome of the analysis in Prob. C-4.

(*b*) Sketch the phase diagram for the first-order system of Prob. C-5(*b*) and compare the stability results with those of Prob. C-4.

(*c*) Rewrite Prob. C-3(*e*) as a pair of first-order linear differential equations and sketch the phase diagram for the system. Compare the stability results with the outcome in Prob. C-4.

REFERENCES

1. Arrow, K. J., and M. Kurz: "Public Investment, the Rate of Return, and Optimal Fiscal Policy," Johns Hopkins Press for Resources for the Future, Baltimore, 1970. Examples of phase diagrams and their usefulness in optimal economic growth model analysis are contained in chaps. III and IV.
2. Baumol, W. J.: "Economic Dynamics," 3d ed., Macmillan, New York, 1970. An extremely readable text covering difference and differential equations and their role in economics.
3. ———: Topology of Second Order Linear Difference Equations with Constant Coefficients, *Econometrica*, vol. 26, pp. 258–285, April, 1958. A thorough analysis of the algebra and geometry of second-order linear difference equations.
4. Benavie, A.: "Mathematical Techniques for Economic Analysis," Prentice-Hall, Englewood Cliffs, N.J., 1972. Difference and differential equations and stability analysis are covered in chaps. 3 and 4; moderate to fairly advanced level of mathematics.
5. Boyce, W. E., and R. C. di Prima: "Elementary Differential Equations and Boundary Value Problems," 2d ed., Wiley, New York, 1969. A thorough, standard text on differential equations.
6. Burmeister, E., and A. R. Dobell: "Mathematical Theories of Economic Growth," Macmillan, New York, 1970. Examples of phase diagrams and their usefulness in optimal economic growth model analysis are contained in chap. 11.
7. Cunningham, W. J.: "Introduction to Nonlinear Analysis," McGraw-Hill, New York, 1958. Contains a very readable, although mathematically advanced, discussion of stability theory for nonlinear differential equations.
8. Davis, H. T.: "Introduction to Nonlinear Differential and Integral Equations," Dover, New York, 1962. Chapters 10 to 12 deal with stability for nonlinear differential equations at a fairly advanced level; extensive use of phase diagrams.
9. Davis, T. V., and E. M. James: "Nonlinear Differential Equations," Addison-Wesley, Reading, Mass., 1962. Includes discussion of stability analysis for nonlinear differential equations.

10. Gandolfo, G.: "Mathematical Methods and Models in Economic Dynamics," American Elsevier, New York, 1971. A very readable and thorough account of difference and differential equations and their usefulness in economic applications.
11. Goldberg, S.: "Introduction to Difference Equations," Science eds., Wiley, New York, 1961. An exposition of difference equations and some areas of application in economics at a modest mathematical level.
12. Hadley, G., and M. C. Kemp: "Variational Methods in Economics," American Elsevier, New York, 1971. There are several examples of phase diagrams and their usefulness in economic applications throughout this text.
13. Krieder, D. L., R. G. Kuller, and D. R. Ostberg: "Elementary Differential Equations," Addison-Wesley, Reading, Mass., 1968. A thorough introduction to differential equations at a moderate level of mathematical difficulty.
14. LaSalle, J., and S. Lefschetz: "Stability by Liapunov's Direct Method, with Applications," Academic Press, New York, 1961. A relatively advanced text on stability analysis.
15. Levy, H., and F. Lessman: "Finite Difference Equations," Pitman, London, 1959. A thorough and readable text on difference equations; moderate level of mathematical difficulty.
16. Ritger, P. D., and N. J. Rose: "Differential Equations with Applications," McGraw-Hill, New York, 1968. A standard text on differential equations; fairly advanced mathematical level; stability analysis for nonlinear differential equations is contained in chap. 10.
17. Samuelson, P. A.: "Foundations of Economic Analysis," Harvard University Press, Cambridge, Mass., 1947. Appendix B contains a very thorough discussion of difference equations.
18. Sanchez, D. A.: "Ordinary Differential Equations and Stability Theory: An Introduction," Freeman, San Francisco, 1968. Contains many proofs and extensive analysis of stability questions for differential equations; advanced mathematical level.
19. Shell, K. (ed.): "Essays on the Theory of Optimal Economic Growth," MIT Press, Cambridge, Mass., 1967. This collection of papers has numerous examples of the use of phase diagrams in analysis of models of optimal economic growth.

APPENDIX

D

DISCRETE APPROXIMATIONS AND DISCRETE MODELS

The connection between a discrete approach to a particular problem and a continuous approach to the same problem is often an obvious one. The area under a curve is an example. That is, the notion that the area under a smooth, continuous curve $f(x)$—above the horizontal axis and between two vertical boundaries at $x = a$ and $x = b$ $(b > a)$—can be approximated by summing the areas of a number of rectangles (App. A, Sec. A-3) illustrates the relationship between a continuous and a discrete solution to a problem. The trapezoidal rule and Simpson's rule, for example, are computational devices for approximating the continuous problem using a discrete approach. Conversely, in some situations, an exact definite integral (continuous approach) may be used to approximate an inherently discrete problem (e.g., the sum of a large number of values at many discrete points in the future, each discounted back to the present).

As another example, it is clear in principle that a curve in two-dimensional space can be approximated to any desired degree of accuracy by a large enough number of straight-line segments. In the same vein, the distinction between a difference equation model and one consisting of differential equations is fundamentally a function of the way in which the independent variable (or variables) are measured; generally this means whether time is considered to be a discrete or a continuous variable (App. C). The choice between a discrete and a continuous model, then, is often made on the basis of operational, i.e., computational, convenience. If a function is easily integrated, a definite integral is easily computed; if a function is impossible to integrate exactly, a discrete approximation to the definite integral would be used.

A large class of numerical methods in the calculus of variations use discrete methods as an approach to approximating the definite integral which is the objective functional or to solving the Euler-Lagrange (differential) equation, which constitutes a necessary condition that an optimizing function must satisfy. Some of these approaches are presented in Sec. D-1, below. These procedures use discrete methods to approximate a solution to the exact (continuous) version of the problem. On the other hand, the original optimization problem could be approximated by a discrete version, with a summation replacing the integration and with difference equations replacing differential equations in the constraints. Exact solution methods could then be employed on the discrete approximation of the problem. The discrete maximum principle illustrates this point of view; it is discussed in Sec. D-2.

Dynamic programming is the general term for an alternative approach that can be taken for dynamic optimization problems of the calculus of variations and maximum principle type. Although there is a continuous formulation of the dynamic programming methodology, the greatest usefulness of the technique appears to be in its discrete form. These matters are investigated briefly in Sec. D-3. Finally, in Sec. D-4, we note the kind of "dynamic" optimization problem for which recursive programming is designed.

D-1 DISCRETE METHODS IN THE CALCULUS OF VARIATIONS†

In the standard approach to the simplest calculus of variations problems (Chap. 2), the Euler-Lagrange equation constitutes the first necessary condition to be dealt with. Generally this equation will be subject to boundary conditions. Thus, from the mathematical standpoint, the boundary-value differential equation problem is equivalent to the variational optimization problem for which the differential equation is the first-order condition. This suggests that a direct method that solved the optimization problem would also be a method for solving boundary-value differential equations. Conversely, a direct method for solving boundary-value differential equation problems will also solve an associated variational optimization problem. In what follows we consider only a small subset of the methods that attempt to make operational this connection. The purpose here is simply to illustrate the computational advantages of direct methods.

As an example of the connection between variational problems and differential equations, we consider the fact that *any* second-order linear differential equation can be viewed as the Euler-Lagrange equation for a variational problem of the type

$$I[y] = \int_{x_0}^{x_1} F(x, y, \dot{y})\, dx = \int_{x_0}^{x_1} [\phi(x)\dot{y}^2 + \omega(x)y^2 + 2\psi(x)y]\, dx \tag{D-1}$$

† I am indebted to a former student, W.S.P. doVale, for the examples in this section.

To establish this connection, take the general second-order linear differential equation (where we use x throughout for the independent variable—instead of t, as in App. C—to conform with the notation used for calculus of variations problems in the text)

$$p(x)\ddot{y} + q(x)\dot{y} - r(x)y = s(x) \tag{D-2}$$

Multiply both sides by $\exp\left(\int\{[q(x) - \dot{p}(x)]/p(x)\}\,dx\right)$ or, for notational simplicity, by $\exp\left\{\int[(q - \dot{p})/p]\,dx\right\}$. This gives

$$p(x)\exp\left(\int\frac{q-\dot{p}}{p}\,dx\right)\ddot{y} + q(x)\exp\left(\int\frac{q-\dot{p}}{p}\,dx\right)\dot{y}$$
$$- r(x)\exp\left(\int\frac{q-\dot{p}}{p}\,dx\right)y = s(x)\exp\left(\int\frac{q-\dot{p}}{p}\,dx\right) \tag{D-3}$$

Equation (D-3) can be simplified by noting (using the rule for derivatives of products and rearranging) that

$$\begin{aligned}\frac{d}{dx}p(x)\exp\left(\int\frac{q-\dot{p}}{p}\,dx\right)\dot{y} &= \dot{p}(x)\exp\left(\int\frac{q-\dot{p}}{p}\,dx\right)\dot{y}\\ &\quad + p(x)\exp\left(\int\frac{q-\dot{p}}{p}\,dx\right)\left(\frac{q-\dot{p}}{p}\right)\dot{y}\\ &\quad + p(x)\exp\left(\int\frac{q-\dot{p}}{p}\,dx\right)\ddot{y}\\ &= p(x)\exp\left(\int\frac{q-\dot{p}}{p}\,dx\right)\ddot{y}\\ &\quad + q(x)\exp\left(\int\frac{q-\dot{p}}{p}\,dx\right)\dot{y}\end{aligned}$$

Thus (D-3) can be represented as

$$\frac{d}{dx}p(x)\exp\left(\int\frac{q-\dot{p}}{p}\,dx\right)\dot{y} - r(x)\exp\left(\int\frac{q-\dot{p}}{p}\,dx\right)y$$
$$- s(x)\exp\left(\int\frac{q-\dot{p}}{p}\,dx\right) = 0 \tag{D-4}$$

Consider next the Euler-Lagrange equation, $F_y - (d/dx)(F_{y'}) = 0$, for the integral in (D-1). Differentiation, cancellation, and multiplication by -1 lead to

$$\frac{d}{dx}\phi(x)\dot{y} - \omega(x)y - \psi(x) = 0 \tag{D-5}$$

Thus the differential equation (D-2) [rewritten in (D-4)] is the Euler-Lagrange equation to the integral in (D-1) when

$$\begin{aligned} \phi(x) &= p(x) \exp\left(\int \frac{q-\dot{p}}{p}\,dx\right) \\ \omega(x) &= r(x) \exp\left(\int \frac{q-\dot{p}}{p}\,dx\right) \\ \psi(x) &= s(x) \exp\left(\int \frac{q-\dot{p}}{p}\,dx\right) \end{aligned} \tag{D-6}$$

For example, the problem of solving

$$\ddot{y} + x\dot{y} + y = 2x \tag{D-7}$$

with boundary conditions of, say, $y(0) = 1$ and $y(1) = 0$, is equivalent to the variational problem:†

$$\text{Minimize} \quad I[y] = \int_0^1 e^{x^2/2}(\dot{y}^2 - y^2 + 4xy)\,dx \tag{D-8}$$

From (D-2) and (D-7), we find $p(x) = 1$, $q(x) = x$, $r(x) = -1$, and $s(x) = 2x$. Therefore, from (D-6), $\phi(x) = \exp\{\int [(x-0)/1]\,dx\} = \exp(\int x\,dx) = e^{x^2/2}$, $\omega(x) = -e^{x^2/2}$, and $\psi(x) = 2x\,e^{x^2/2}$. Substitution into (D-1) and factoring out $e^{x^2/2}$ leads directly to the result in (D-8).

The object of the illustration is simply to show how a method of solution for a two-point boundary-value differential equation problem will also solve an associated calculus of variations problem, and vice versa. We now consider, in turn, approximations to the integral (objective functional) and approximations to differential equation solutions (the Euler-Lagrange conditions).

Discrete Approximations to the Objective Functional

The Euler method of finite differences is representative of this class of approximations. The essence of the method is the approximation of a curve by a number of straight-line segments and hence the approximation of an integral by a sum. One of the simplest calculus of variations problems is to

$$\begin{aligned} &\text{Maximize/minimize} \quad I[y] = \int_{x_0}^{x_1} F(x, y, \dot{y})\,dx \\ &\text{where} \qquad y(x_0) = y_0 \quad \text{and} \quad y(x_1) = y_1 \end{aligned} \tag{D-9}$$

† That the integral in (D-8) is to be minimized rather than maximized is a fact to be established via added conditions, e.g., the Legendre and Jacobi conditions (Chap. 3, Sec. 3-5). Whether the integral in (D-8) is to be minimized or maximized, of course, the Euler-Lagrange equation will be the same.

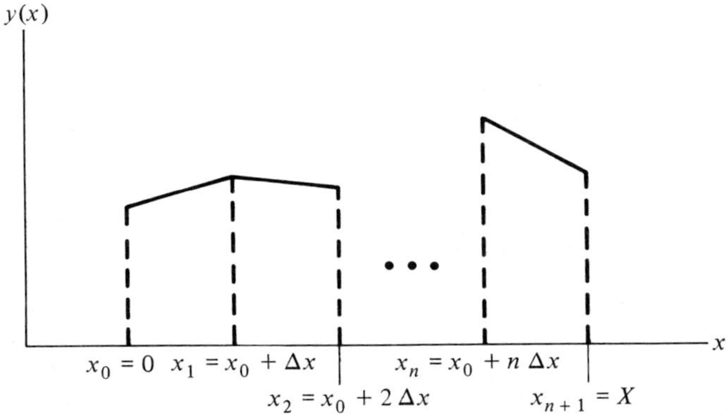

Figure D-1 Division of the interval $[x_0, x_{n+1}]$.

[This was (2-6) in Chap. 2, for example.] To avoid trivial but cumbersome notational problems, we now denote the initial and terminal values of the independent variable, x, by 0 and X. Consequently the problem in (D-9) now reads:

$$\text{Maximize/minimize} \quad I[y] = \int_0^X F(x, y, \dot{y})\, dx \qquad \text{(D-10)}$$

where $\quad y(0) = y_0 \quad \text{and} \quad y(X) = y_X$

Geometrically, the method of finite differences divides the closed interval $[0, X]$ into $n + 1$ equal subintervals, with abscissae $x_0 = 0$, $x_1 = x_0 + \Delta x$, $x_2 = x_0 + 2\,\Delta x, \ldots, x_n = x_0 + n\,\Delta x$, $x_{n+1} = X$, where $\Delta x = (X - 0)/(n + 1)$. The continuous function $y(x)$ is replaced by a set of discrete values $y_0 = y(0), y_1, \ldots, y_{n+1} = y(X)$ (see Fig. D-1). The integral of interest, in (D-10), is thus replaced by a function of the discrete set of ordinates $y_0, y_1, \ldots, y_{n+1}$:

$$I[y] = \int_0^X F(x, y, \dot{y})\, dx \cong \sum_{i=0}^{n} F\left(x_i, y_i, \frac{y_{i+1} - y_i}{\Delta x}\right) \Delta x \qquad \text{(D-11)}$$

The problem now lends itself to classical multivariable optimization techniques. We are interested in finding the y_i $(i = 1, \ldots, n)$ that maximize or minimize the summation in (D-11), and for either kind of extremum the necessary (first-order) conditions are that $\partial I/\partial y_i = 0$, that is,

$$\frac{\partial}{\partial y_i}\left\{\left[F\left(x_{i-1}, y_{i-1}, \frac{y_i - y_{i-1}}{\Delta x}\right) + F\left(x_i, y_i, \frac{y_{i+1} - y_i}{\Delta x}\right)\right]\Delta x\right\} = 0 \qquad \text{(D-12)}$$

for $i = 1, \ldots, n$.

We consider the application of this approach to the following example, for various values of n, and compare the results with the exact answer (from the Euler-Lagrange equation). Generally, of course, the method is useful when the

Euler-Lagrange equation cannot be dealt with directly:

$$\text{Minimize} \quad I[y] = \int_0^1 (\dot{y}^2 - y^2)\,dx$$
$$\text{where} \qquad y(0) = 0 \quad \text{and} \quad y(1) = 1 \tag{D-13}$$

Investigating, initially, the continuous solution from the calculus of variations approach, we find that the Euler-Lagrange equation, $F_y - (d/dx)(F_{y'}) = 0$, is $-2y - 2\ddot{y} = 0$, or

$$\ddot{y} + y = 0 \tag{D-14}$$

This is a second-order linear differential equation with complex roots (App. C, Sec. C-4). The general solution to such an equation is $y = e^{\alpha x}(A_1 \cos \beta x + A_2 \sin \beta x)$, where $\alpha = -(a_1/2a_0)$ and $\beta = \sqrt{4a_0a_2 - a_1^2}/2a_0$, found from the parameters of the original equation $a_0\ddot{y} + a_1\dot{y} + a_2 y = 0$. Here, in (D-14), $a_0 = 1$, $a_1 = 0$, $a_2 = 1$; thus $\alpha = 0$ and $\beta = 1$ and

$$y = A_1 \cos x + A_2 \sin x \tag{D-15}$$

From the boundary condition that $y(0) = 0$, and since $\cos 0 = 1$ and $\sin 0 = 0$, we have $A_1 = 0$. For $x = 1$, when $y = 1$, we therefore have $A_2 = 1/\sin 1 = 1.1884$,† and

$$y(x) = \frac{1}{\sin 1} \sin x = (1.1884) \sin x \tag{D-16}$$

constitutes the only function satisfying the Euler-Lagrange equation and hence qualifying as a solution to (D-13). [Investigation of the Legendre, Jacobi, and Weierstrass conditions (from Chap. 3) in fact shows that this represents a strong relative minimum for (D-13).]

The exact minimum value—to be used as a benchmark against which to examine the finite-difference approximations—comes from integration of (D-13), with (D-16) substituted for y. That is, from finding $\int_0^1 (\dot{y}^2 - y^2)\,dx$, with $y(x) = (1.1884) \sin x$. In particular,

$$\int_0^1 \left\{ \left[\frac{d}{dx} (1.1884)(\sin x) \right]^2 - \left[(1.1884)(\sin x) \right]^2 \right\} dx$$
$$= \int_0^1 (1.1884)^2 \left[\left(\frac{d}{dx} \sin x \right)^2 - (\sin x)^2 \right] dx$$
$$= \int_0^1 (1.412)(\cos^2 x - \sin^2 x)\,dx$$

Denote this $\int_0^1 F(x, y^*, \dot{y}^*)\,dx$; it equals

$$\int_0^1 (1.412) \cos(2x)\,dx \tag{D-17}$$

† Angles are measured in radians, since the independent variable, x, is measured linearly, not in degrees.

Since this is easily integrated, the exact minimum value is $(\frac{1}{2})(1.412)[\sin(2x)]_0^1 = (0.706)\sin 2 = 0.6419$.

It is the integral in (D-17), which incorporates the optimal $y(x)$, that is approximated by the series in (D-11) and the imposition of first-order conditions, as in (D-12). For this example, (D-12) becomes

$$\frac{\partial}{\partial y_i}\left[\left(\frac{y_{i+1}-y_i}{\Delta x}\right)^2 - (y_i)^2 + \left(\frac{y_i - y_{i-1}}{\Delta x}\right)^2 - (y_{i-1})^2\right]\Delta x$$

Taking derivatives, rearranging, and setting equal to zero, gives

$$2\,\Delta x\left\{\frac{[2-(\Delta x)^2]y_i - y_{i+1} - y_{i-1}}{(\Delta x)^2}\right\} = 0 \qquad \text{(D-18)}$$

Considering cases in which $\Delta x \neq 0$ (i.e., in which the number of intervals is not infinite), (D-18) requires that

$$-y_{i-1} + [2-(\Delta x)^2]y_i - y_{i+1} = 0 \qquad \text{(D-19)}$$

for $i = 1, \ldots, n$, with $y_0 = 0$ and $y_{n+1} = 1$.

For example, for $n = 4$, the interval between $x = 0$ and $x = 1$ would be divided into five sub-intervals. Given that $x_0 = 0$, $y_0 = 0$, $x_{n+1} = x_5 = 1$, $y_5 = 1$, and $\Delta x = \frac{1}{5}$, the four equations given in (D-19) would be (for $i = 1, 2, 3, 4$, respectively)

$$\begin{aligned}
-0 + \frac{49}{25}y_1 - y_2 \qquad\qquad\qquad &= 0\\
- y_1 + \frac{49}{25}y_2 - y_3 \qquad\quad &= 0\\
- y_2 + \frac{49}{25}y_3 - y_4 \quad &= 0\\
- y_3 + \frac{49}{25}y_4 - 1 &= 0
\end{aligned} \qquad \text{(D-20)}$$

This is a set of linear equations with a simple structure. In $\mathbf{AX} = \mathbf{B}$ form, we have

$$\mathbf{A} = \begin{bmatrix} (49/25) & -1 & 0 & 0 \\ -1 & (49/25) & -1 & 0 \\ 0 & -1 & (49/25) & -1 \\ 0 & 0 & -1 & (49/25) \end{bmatrix}$$

$$\mathbf{X} = \begin{bmatrix} y_1 \\ y_2 \\ y_3 \\ y_4 \end{bmatrix}$$

and

$$\mathbf{B} = \begin{bmatrix} 0 \\ 0 \\ 0 \\ 1 \end{bmatrix}$$

Either calculating $\mathbf{A}^{-1}$ or solving (D-20) recursively, we find that

$$\begin{bmatrix} y_1 \\ y_2 \\ y_3 \\ y_4 \end{bmatrix} = \begin{bmatrix} 0.23623 \\ 0.46302 \\ 0.67129 \\ 0.85270 \end{bmatrix} \tag{D-21}$$

The discrete approximation to $\int_0^1 (1.412) \cos(2x)\, dx$, in (D-17) is

$$\sum_{i=0}^{n} \left[\left(\frac{y_{i+1} - y_i}{\Delta x} \right)^2 - (y_i)^2 \right] \Delta x \tag{D-22}$$

For the $n = 4$ case, with $\Delta x = \frac{1}{5}$, $y_0 = 0$, $y_5 = 1$, and the y_1 through y_4 that are given in (D-21), this sum is 0.7365. Comparing this with 0.6419, the exact figure, shows clearly that $\Delta x = \frac{1}{5}$ provides a rather coarse approximation. Geometrically, the bracketed terms in (D-22) are heights of rectangles, each of whose bases is Δx. From (D-21), for the $n = 4$ case, these heights are 1.395, 1.230, 0.870, 0.372, and -0.185, respectively. They are represented, loosely, along with the actual function $F(x, y^*, \dot{y}^*) = (1.412) \cos(2x)$, from (D-17), in Fig. D-2.

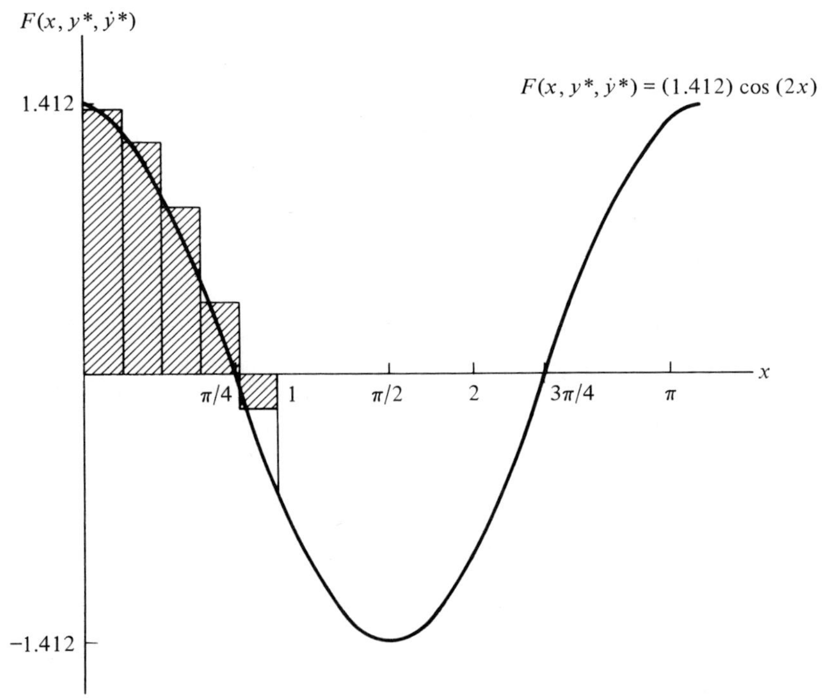

Figure D-2 $I[y^*]$ and a discrete approximation, with $\Delta x = \frac{1}{5}$.

Table D-1 Discrete approximations to area in (D-17)

n	x	Approximation to (0.6419)
0	1	1
1	$\frac{1}{2}$	0.8571
2	$\frac{1}{3}$	0.7933
3	$\frac{1}{4}$	0.7584
4	$\frac{1}{5}$	0.7365
5	$\frac{1}{6}$	0.7216
6	$\frac{1}{7}$	0.7107
7	$\frac{1}{8}$	0.7024
8	$\frac{1}{9}$	0.6959
9	$\frac{1}{10}$	0.6907

Table D-1 lists the approximated minimum values from (D-22), for $n = 0, 1, \ldots, 9$ (or $\Delta x = 1, \frac{1}{2}, \ldots, \frac{1}{10}$), i.e., for approximations utilizing one, two, ..., ten rectangles. For the interested reader, Table D-2 presents the ordinates for several other cases, namely, for $n = 0$, 1, 5, and 9. The rectangles for each case could be sketched in Fig. D-2, and the improvements in the approximations would be clear as n increases.

Discrete Approximations for Differential Equations

Since first-order conditions in calculus of variations problems require the solution of one or more differential equations, for which exact integrals may not easily be found—or, indeed, may not exist—discrete methods for such equations are sometimes useful. We consider only two examples of such approaches to illustrate the general logic involved.

The Euler method The Euler method for integrating an ordinary differential equation depends on the Taylor series expansion of a function about a point. In particular, given the differential equation

$$\dot{y} \equiv \frac{dy}{dx} = f(x, y) \tag{D-23}$$

Table D-2 Ordinates of approximating rectangles

n	x	Ordinates					
0	1	1.0					
1	$\frac{1}{2}$	1.306,	0.408				
5	$\frac{1}{6}$	1.404,	1.288,	1.029,	0.656,	0.210,	−0.258
9	$\frac{1}{10}$	1.408,	1.366,	1.269,	1.122,	0.930,	0.701
				0.444,	0.169,	−0.113,	−0.390

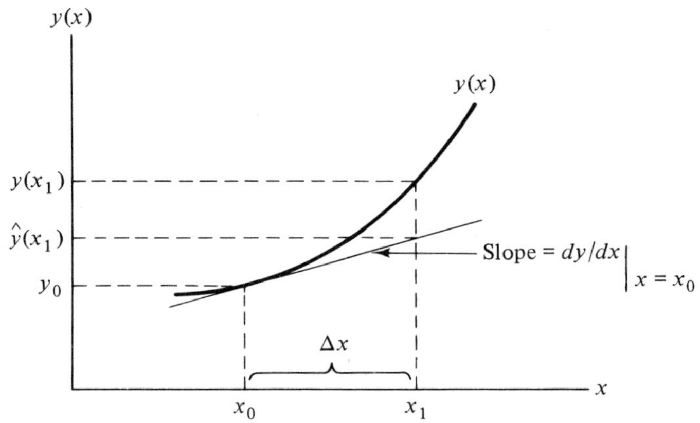

Figure D-3 Linear approximation provided by (D-25).

we know that an approximation to the value of $y(x)$ at a point x_1, "near to" x_0, namely, $x_1 = x_0 + \Delta x$, is given by

$$y(x_1) = y(x_0) + \frac{dy}{dx}(x_1 - x_0) + \frac{1}{2}\frac{d^2y}{dx^2}(x_1 - x_0)^2 + \cdots$$

or

$$y(x_1) = y(x_0) + \frac{dy}{dx}(\Delta x) + \frac{1}{2}\frac{d^2y}{dx^2}(\Delta x)^2 + \cdots \tag{D-24}$$

and that when $\Delta x = (x_1 - x_0)$ is small—in particular, so that $(\Delta x)^2 = (x_1 - x_0)^2$ is small compared with Δx—then

$$y(x_1) \cong y(x_0) + \left.\frac{dy}{dx}\right|_{x=x_0}(\Delta x) = y(x_0) + f(x_0, y_0)(\Delta x) \tag{D-25}$$

Define $\hat{y}(x_1)$ as the estimate provided by the right-hand side of (D-25) (see Fig. D-3). Thus, knowing y_0 at x_0, y at a "nearby" value, x_1, can be found from (D-25). Repeating, from the point x_1 to a "nearby" value, x_2, one eventually traces out an accompanying sequence of values of y, beginning at x_0. Hence a set of discrete approximations to points along the desired function $y = y(x)$ can be found.

For example, let

$$\dot{y} = y^2 \tag{D-26}$$

and $y = 0.5$ at $x_0 = 0$; i.e., the initial condition is $y_0 = 0.5$. Consider an approximation to the solution to (D-26) over the range $0 \leq x \leq 1$. Let $\Delta x = 0.1$; from (D-25),

$$y_{0.1} = y_0 + (y_0)^2(\Delta x) = 0.5 + (0.5)^2(0.1) = 0.525$$

and consequently

$$y_{0.2} = y_{0.1} + (y_{0.1})^2(\Delta x) = 0.525 + (0.525)^2(0.1) = 0.5526$$

Continuing in this fashion, one finds $y_{0.3}, \ldots, y_{0.9}, y_1$. These results are given in the Euler column of Table D-3. In the case of the differential equation (D-26), exact solution is straightforward—$y = 1/(2 - x)$. Table D-3 also lists the exact values for $y_0, y_{0.1}, \ldots, y_{0.9}, y_1$.

The Runge-Kutta method A more accurate approximation to the actual values of $y(x)$ is provided, at the expense of some computational complexity, by the Runge-Kutta method. The motivation behind the method is easy to appreciate. If we consider again the geometry of Fig. D-3, it is clear that for a strictly convex function (or over a strictly convex interval of a more complex function), the Euler approximation for increasing values of x underestimates the true values of $y(x)$; this of course follows from the observation that a strictly convex function lies above its tangent.† As suggested in Fig. D-4, a better approximation to $y(x_1)$ would be provided by averaging two estimates of y: one given by utilizing the tangent, AA, at x_0 (as in the Euler method) and the other provided by a line of steeper slope, BB, through the point (x_0, y_0). Denoting these two estimates by Δy_A and Δy_B, respectively, it is apparent that in this illustration the simple average $\frac{1}{2}(\Delta y_A + \Delta y_B)$—$\Delta y_{\text{avg}}$ in Fig. D-4—is closer to the true change in $y(x)$ than the simple Euler approximation, Δy_A. Clearly, the accuracy of the Δy_{avg} figure depends on how the line BB is constructed; there are endless possibilities for generating one or more lines like BB in Fig. D-4.

The Runge-Kutta method expands upon this idea in a particular way. Formally, with $x_1 = x_0 + \Delta x$, the Runge-Kutta rule for estimating $y(x_1)$ is

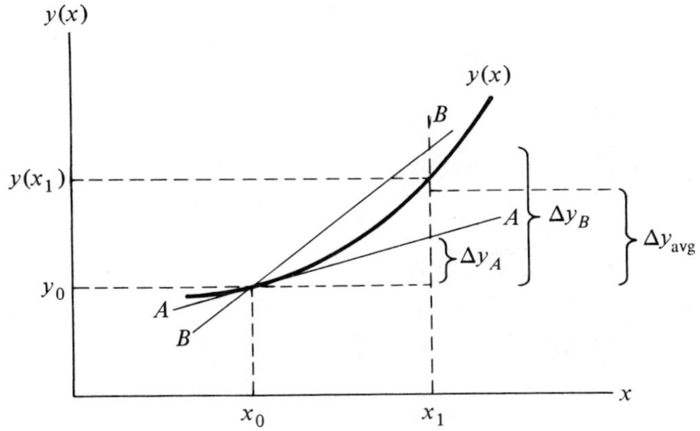

Figure D-4 An alternative approximation to $y(x_1)$.

† In all of the geometry that follows, we will deal with situations in which $x_1 > x_0$ and the function $y(x)$ is strictly convex. For strictly concave functions, the Euler method overestimates the values of $y(x)$ from x_0 to x_1, etc.

$$\hat{y}(x_1) = y(x_0) + \tfrac{1}{6}(k_1 + 2k_2 + 2k_3 + k_4)$$

or

$$\hat{y}(x_1) = y(x_0) + \tfrac{1}{6}k_1 + \tfrac{2}{6}k_2 + \tfrac{2}{6}k_3 + \tfrac{1}{6}k_4 \tag{D-27}$$

where

$$\begin{aligned} k_1 &= f(x_0, y_0)\,\Delta x \\ k_2 &= f\left(x_0 + \frac{\Delta x}{2}, y_0 + \frac{k_1}{2}\right)\Delta x \\ k_3 &= f\left(x_0 + \frac{\Delta x}{2}, y_0 + \frac{k_2}{2}\right)\Delta x \\ k_4 &= f(x_0 + \Delta x, y_0 + k_3)\,\Delta x \end{aligned} \tag{D-28}$$

Note that, in this notation, the Euler method is

$$\hat{y}(x_1) = y(x_0) + k_1$$

That is, Δy_A in Fig. D-4 is what is denoted k_1 in the Runge-Kutta procedure. Thus the Runge-Kutta technique "averages in" three additional estimates of $\Delta y(x_1)$, namely, k_2, k_3, and k_4, weighting k_2 and k_3 twice as heavily as k_1 (the Euler estimate) and k_4.

Figure D-5 suggests the geometry of the estimate provided by k_2. The point $(x_0 + \Delta x/2, y_0 + k_1/2)$, denoted P, is easily found. According to (D-28), $k_2/\Delta x = f(x_0 + \Delta x/2, y_0 + k_1/2)$, i.e., line CC is constructed through P with a slope equal to the slope that $y(x)$ would have if it went through that point, namely, $f(x_0 + \Delta x/2, y_0 + k_1/2)$. [Recall from (D-23) that we denote dy/dx by $f(x, y)$.] For small Δx, the line CC will be approximately parallel to the tangent to the true $y(x)$ at $x_0 + \Delta x/2$. Then, forming the shaded triangle with base Δx, the vertical side will be k_2. Finally, imagine the shaded triangle moved leftward and downward, so that P is located at (x_0, y_0); k_2 and k_1 will then be collinear above the

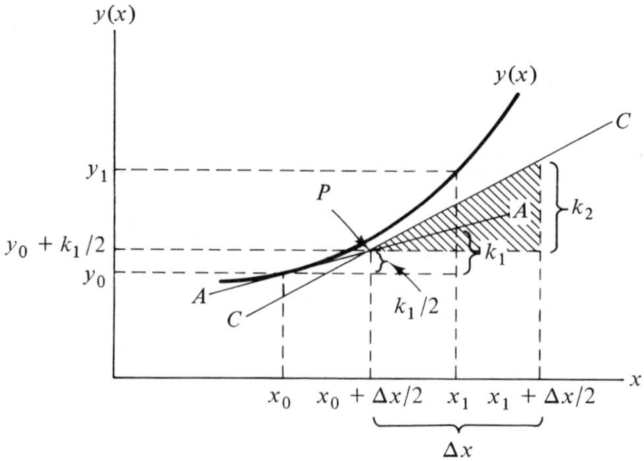

Figure D-5 The geometry of k_2 in the Runge-Kutta procedure.

point where $x = x_1$, and CC will be located similarly to BB in Fig. D-4. In summary, then, k_2 represents an estimate of $\Delta y(x_1)$ that is larger than the one provided by k_1, because it utilizes a "steeper" line through (x_0, y_0). It is certain to be steeper (when strictly convex functions are involved) because the slope of the tangent at $x_0 + \Delta x/2$ is certain to be larger than the slope of the tangent at x_0.

The geometry behind k_3 is almost identical, except that the lower left corner of the new triangle is at a different height above $x_0 + \Delta x/2$, namely, at $y_0 + k_2/2$ instead of $y_0 + k_1/2$. Since $k_2 > k_1$, this means that this triangle will be "higher" in the figure than the shaded part of Fig. D-5. Finally, k_4 is derived from a triangle whose hypotenuse slopes even more steeply, since it is parallel to the tangent to $y(x)$ at $x = x_1$.

Clearly, any number of points in the open interval from x_0 to x_1 could be chosen as locations above which to estimate the slope of the tangent. Similarly, any number of weightings in the averaging process could be used. In the Runge-Kutta approach, the logic of weighting k_2 and k_3 twice as heavily as k_1 and k_4 is that the slopes found at $x_0 + \Delta x/2$ (from which k_2 and k_3 are derived) are closer to the slope of the chord connecting (x_0, y_0) and (x_1, y_1) than are the slopes at either x_0 (for k_1) or x_1 (for k_4).

Taking the same example, (D-26), where $f(x, y) = y^2$, with $\Delta x = 0.1$ and with $y_0 = 0.5$ at $x_0 = 0$, we have, from (D-27) and (D-28),

$$y_{0.1} = y_0 + \tfrac{1}{6}(k_1 + 2k_2 + 2k_3 + k_4)$$

where

$$k_1 = (0.5)^2(0.1) = 0.025$$

$$k_2 = (0.5 + 0.0125)^2(0.1) = 0.02627$$

$$k_3 = (0.5 + 0.01314)^2(0.1) = 0.02633$$

$$k_4 = (0.5 + 0.02633)^2(0.1) = 0.02770$$

and therefore

$$y_{0.1} = 0.5 + \tfrac{1}{6}(0.1579) = 0.5263$$

Continuing:

$$y_{0.2} = y_{0.1} + \tfrac{1}{6}(k_1 + 2k_2 + 2k_3 + k_4)$$

where, now,

$$k_1 = (0.5263)^2(0.1) = 0.02770$$

$$k_2 = (0.5263 + 0.01385)^2(0.1) = 0.02918$$

$$k_3 = (0.5263 + 0.01459)^2(0.1) = 0.02926$$

$$k_4 = (0.5263 + 0.02926)^2(0.1) = 0.03086$$

and so

$$y_{0.2} = 0.5263 + \tfrac{1}{6}(0.1754) = 0.5555$$

Table D-3 Two discrete methods for $\dot{y} = y^2$

x	Euler	Runge-Kutta	Exact
0	0.5	0.5	0.5
0.1	0.525	0.5263	0.5263
0.2	0.5526	0.5555	0.5556
0.3	0.5831	0.5881	0.5882
0.4	0.6171	0.6249	0.6250
0.5	0.6552	0.6666	0.6667
0.6	0.6981	0.7142	0.7143
0.7	0.7468	0.7691	0.7692
0.8	0.8026	0.8332	0.8333
0.9	0.8670	0.9089	0.9091
1.0	0.9422	0.9997	1.0000

Table D-3 summarizes the Runge-Kutta results as well as the earlier Euler estimates, and it also shows the exact figures, obtained from integration of (D-26) to $y = 1/(2 - x)$. Clearly, iterative procedures can generate values of an unknown function whose derivative is known, as in (D-26), with a good deal of accuracy.

D-2 THE DISCRETE MAXIMUM PRINCIPLE†

Either because one feels that the "dynamic" phenomenon with which he is dealing is inherently discrete in nature or because of the computational implications of dealing with sums and difference equations instead of integrals and differential equations, a noncontinuous approach to a control problem may be useful. At the outset of Chap. 4, we noted that one of the simplest calculus of variations problems, namely:

$$\text{Maximize} \quad I[y] = \int_{x_0}^{x_1} F(x, y, \dot{y})\, dx$$

$$\text{where} \qquad y(x_0) = y_0 \quad \text{and} \quad y(x_1) = y_1 \tag{D-29}$$

could be posed in control theory terms by defining $u = \dot{y}$. That is, (D-29) could be expressed as:

$$\text{Maximize} \quad I[y, u] = \int_{x_0}^{x_1} F(x, y, u)\, dx$$

$$\text{where} \qquad y(x_0) = y_0,\ y(x_1) = y_1 \quad \text{and where} \quad \dot{y}(x) = u(x) \tag{D-30}$$

† Dorfman [8, sec. V] presents a very readable illustration of the discrete approach. For more detail and derivations, the reader should consult Benavie [4, chap. 5]. One of the most comprehensive references is Fan and Wang [10]. The connection between discrete optimal control problems and nonlinear programming problems is thoroughly covered in Canon, Cullum, and Polak [6]. I am indebted to a graduate student, Asao Ando, for helpful observations on notation.

As far as appearance is concerned, $\dot{y}(x)$ has been replaced in (D-30) in the integrand by $u(x)$, and the maximization in (D-30) is carried out subject to the added equality constraint $\dot{y}(x) = u(x)$.

Consistent with the relationship between integrals and summation signs and between differential and difference equations, it is apparent that a discrete form of the problem in (D-30) would be to find the values of u_i for $i = 0, 1, \ldots, n-1$ which will

$$\text{Maximize} \quad S[y, u] = \sum_{i=0}^{n-1} F(x_i, y_i, u_i)\, \Delta x$$

where $\qquad y_0$ and y_n are specified and where $\qquad$ (D-31)

$$\frac{y_{i+1} - y_i}{\Delta x} = u_i \qquad i = 0, \ldots, n-1$$

The standard Lagrange-multiplier approach to an equality-constrained problem, such as (D-31), would be to form the augmented lagrangian function $L(x_i, y_i, u_i, \lambda_i)$ and impose the usual requirements that its first partial derivatives equal zero.† That is, let

$$L = \sum_{i=0}^{n-1} \left[F(x_i, y_i, u_i)\, \Delta x - \lambda_i \left(\frac{y_{i+1} - y_i}{\Delta x} - u_i \right) \right] \tag{D-32}$$

and then require that

$$\frac{\partial L}{\partial y_i} = \frac{\partial F}{\partial y_i} \Delta x - \frac{\lambda_{i-1}}{\Delta x} + \frac{\lambda_i}{\Delta x} = 0 \qquad (i = 1, \ldots, n-1) \tag{D-33}$$

$$\frac{\partial L}{\partial u_i} = \frac{\partial F}{\partial u_i} \Delta x + \lambda_i = 0 \qquad (i = 0, \ldots, n-1) \tag{D-34}$$

$$\frac{\partial L}{\partial \lambda_i} = -\left(\frac{y_{i+1} - y_i}{\Delta x} - u_i \right) = 0 \qquad (i = 0, \ldots, n-1) \tag{D-35}$$

Define a hamiltonian function, H, as

$$H(x_i, y_i, u_i, \lambda_i) = \sum_{i=0}^{n-1} [F(x_i, y_i, u_i)\, \Delta x + \lambda_i u_i] \tag{D-36}$$

and thus

$$L = H - \sum_{i=0}^{n-1} \lambda_i \frac{y_{i+1} - y_i}{\Delta x}$$

We see, then, that $\partial L/\partial y_i = \partial H/\partial y_i - \lambda_{i-1}/\Delta x + \lambda_i/\Delta x$, $\partial L/\partial u_i = \partial H/\partial u_i$, and

† For a review of this standard approach, see, for example, Miller [15, secs. 4.4 to 4.6].

$\partial L/\partial \lambda_i = \partial H/\partial \lambda_i - y_{i+1}/\Delta x + y_i/\Delta x$. Thus (D-33) to (D-35) can be reexpressed as:

$$\frac{\partial H}{\partial y_i} = \frac{\lambda_{i-1} - \lambda_i}{\Delta x} \quad \text{or} \quad -\frac{\partial H}{\partial y_i} = \frac{\lambda_i - \lambda_{i-1}}{\Delta x} \tag{D-37}$$

$$\frac{\partial H}{\partial u_i} = 0 \tag{D-38}$$

$$\frac{\partial H}{\partial \lambda_i} = \frac{y_{i+1} - y_i}{\Delta x} \tag{D-39}$$

The results for the continuous case were given in (4-8) to (4-10) in Chap. 4; these are repeated here:

$$-\frac{\partial H}{\partial y} = \dot{\lambda} \tag{D-40}$$

$$\frac{\partial H}{\partial u} = 0 \tag{D-41}$$

$$\frac{\partial H}{\partial \lambda} = \dot{y} \tag{D-42}$$

The parallels are clear, since the derivatives on the right-hand sides of (D-40) and (D-42) become finite differences in the discrete case [(D-37) and (D-39)]. Subject to the two difference equations in (D-37) and (D-39), with initial and terminal values for y_i, (D-38) suggests that the optimal u_i will be such as to maximize the value of the hamiltonian for $i = 0, \ldots, n-1$.†

Complications of the basic problem (e.g., with respect to alternative endpoint conditions and/or inequality constraints) can be handled in discrete form. Consider the case of a free right-hand boundary, i.e., where y_n is not specified. This means that in (D-33) there will not only be a $\partial L/\partial y_i$ for $i = 1, \ldots, n-1$, but also that there will be an equation for $\partial L/\partial y_n$, since y_n is no longer fixed. However, since y_n does not appear in S, we have $\partial L/\partial y_n = -\lambda_{n-1}/\Delta x = 0$. In this case, then, the difference equation for y_i has a specified initial value, namely y_0, and the difference equation for λ_i has a specified terminal value, $\lambda_{n-1} = 0$. Again, as expected, this is completely analogous to the continuous case (Chap. 4, Sec. 4-2).

When inequality constraints are present, an approach to the discrete version of the problem is to employ Kuhn-Tucker results.‡ If there are boundaries on the u_i, of course, the results in (D-38) are replaced by the requirement that the maximization of H subject to the constraints on the u_i, i.e., boundary maxima

† As was discussed in Chap. 4, whether one maximizes or minimizes the hamiltonian function can depend on the exact form in which the problem is posed. As in the bulk of Chap. 4, we will associate the maximization of the hamiltonian with the objective of maximizing a sum, as in (D-32).

‡ Again, for a review, see Miller [15, secs. 4.8 and 8.2].

may result, where $\partial H/\partial u_i \neq 0$. In general, developments from the Kuhn-Tucker approach can be shown to be the discrete parallels to the results in Chap. 4, Sec. 4-4. A good deal depends, as usual, on the kinds of assumptions that one is willing or able to make about the convexity of sets and functions involved; e.g., sufficient conditions from the Kuhn-Tucker results parallel those in Chap. 4, Sec. 4-4, which depend on concavity/convexity assumptions.

D-3 DYNAMIC PROGRAMMING†

A true dynamic optimization problem (i.e., where the independent variable is time), in discrete form, can be thought of as one in which a sequence of decisions is made at discrete points over time. As usual in the discrete-continuous connection, when the interval between decisions becomes very small, the sequence becomes a continuous function. The dynamic programming approach was originally developed to deal with such multistage or sequential decision processes. The notation and terminology that has grown up around dynamic programming seems cumbersome and potentially confusing in the abstract, and for this reason the fundamental ideas are often developed in an illustration. The underlying philosophy of dynamic programming is contained in the principle of optimality, which states: an optimal policy (i.e., set of rules for making the sequence of decisions) has the property that, whatever the initial state and initial decision may be, the remaining decisions must constitute an optimal policy with respect to the state (i.e., outcome) resulting from the first decision. The idea is simple enough; it says that if the minimum-driving-time automobile route from Seattle to San Francisco goes through Portland, Oregon, then the minimum-driving-time automobile route from Portland to San Francisco will be along the (final) part of the optimal Seattle-San Francisco route.‡

Dynamic programming is a type of stepwise optimization procedure. As such, t is only useful when the complete objective can be expressed as some kind of combination of objectives at each discrete time point. Clearly a summation of individual outcomes would satisfy such a criterion, as when total welfare over an interval of time is expressed as the sum of the welfare measured at each point in the interval. There are a number of more subtle kinds of objectives that dynamic programming can handle, but they must satisfy certain fundamental separability properties.§

† In addition to texts such as those by Gluss [11] and Nemhauser [17], the dynamic programming approach has been developed fully in Bellman's books, e.g., Bellman [2] or Bellman and Dreyfus [3].

‡ A classic "translation" of the formal statement of the principle of optimality is due to Aris [1, p. 27]: ". . . if you don't do the best you can with what you happen to have got, you'll never do the best you might have done with what you should have had."

§ See, for example, Nemhauser [17, especially secs. 2.6 and 2.9] or Gluss [11, chap. 3].

Discrete Dynamic Programming

The basic dynamic programming terminology and way of thinking are illustrated in the following rather general example. Suppose that a given amount of resource is to be allocated to several activities, where the returns differ among activities. Let there be n activities, with $f_i(x_i)$ the return expected from allocation of an amount x_i of the resource to activity i; furthermore, let the total return be the sum of the returns in each activity, that is,

$$R(x_1, \ldots, x_n) = \sum_{i=1}^{n} f_i(x_i) \tag{D-43}$$

Suppose that the total amount of resource is c, and that it is to be completely allocated, so that

$$x_1 + \cdots + x_n = c \tag{D-44}$$

becomes a constraint, along with $x_i \geq 0$, subject to which (D-43) is to be maximized. When the f_i in (D-43) are nonlinear functions, this is a nonlinear programming problem with an equality constraint as well as nonnegativity requirements. Standard approaches, e.g., via Kuhn-Tucker reasoning, would seek a set of necessary (and possibly sufficient) conditions for the entire problem, i.e., for the $x_1, \ldots, x_n$ simultaneously. The "dynamism" of dynamic programming consists of the viewpoint that the optimal values of x_1 through x_n can be selected sequentially, as if the process were evolving over time and required, at each point in time, only one decision. That is, a single n-dimensional problem is viewed as n one-dimensional problems.

Notationally, it is convenient to denote the total amount of resource available for the n activities by c_n; (D-44) becomes $x_1 + \cdots + x_n = c_n$. The logical steps in the dynamic programming approach are:

1. Allocate $0 \leq x_n \leq c_n$ to the nth activity. This brings a return of $f_n(x_n)$, and it leaves $c_n - x_n = c_{n-1}$ for the remaining activities.
2. Allocate the remaining c_{n-1} *optimally* among all of the remaining $n - 1$ activities. This is the principle of optimality: do the best you can with what you have left. Denote this optimal return from the remaining $n - 1$ activities by $M_{n-1}(c_{n-1})$—for maximum or minimum.

The total return from this procedure, given the choice of x_n, is

$$f_n(x_n) + M_{n-1}(c_{n-1}) \tag{D-45}$$

Thus the *optimal* choice of the original x_n is the one that maximizes (D-45). That is, x_n should be chosen to

$$\underset{0 \leq x_n \leq c_n}{\text{Maximize}} \left[f_n(x_n) + M_{n-1}(c_{n-1}) \right]$$

Consistent with the definition of $M_{n-1}(c_{n-1})$ in (2), above, this expression is $M_n(c_n)$, the optimal return from allocation of resources in amount c_n to the n activities:

$$M_n(c_n) = \max_{0 \leq x_n \leq c_n} [f_n(x_n) + M_{n-1}(c_{n-1})] \tag{D-46}$$

This illustrates the so-called fundamental recurrence relation of dynamic programming. Similarly,

$$M_{n-1}(c_{n-1}) = \max_{0 \leq x_{n-1} \leq c_{n-1}} [f_{n-1}(x_{n-1}) + M_{n-2}(c_{n-2})] \tag{D-47}$$

This says that the amount left over from c_n after an allocation has been made to activity n should be divided optimally between the $(n-1)$th activity and the other remaining ones.

Continuing, then,

$$\begin{aligned} M_{n-2}(c_{n-2}) &= \max_{0 \leq x_{n-2} \leq c_{n-2}} [f_{n-2}(x_{n-2}) + M_{n-3}(c_{n-3})] \\ &\vdots \\ M_2(c_2) &= \max_{0 \leq x_2 \leq c_2} [f_2(x_2) + M_1(c_1)] \end{aligned} \tag{D-48}$$

but, finally,

$$M_1(c_1) = f_1(c_1) \tag{D-49}$$

That is, when there is c_1 left to allocate to activity 1 (the "last" one being considered), the return is just $f_1(c_1)$; no optimization is involved since there is no choice about how much to allocate to activity 1. In this sense, then, one works "backwards" through the problem. More compactly, the fundamental dynamic programming relations are:

$$M_k(c_k) = \max_{0 \leq x_k \leq c_k} [f_k(x_k) + M_{k-1}(c_{k-1})] \tag{D-50}$$

for $k = 2, \ldots, n$, and

$$M_1(c_1) = f_1(c_1) \tag{D-51}$$

We make these relationships more concrete in the following example.

Assume that a state government is faced with the problem of deciding how to allocate \$10,000 in funds for unemployment relief among four economically depressed counties. Estimates are available on the new employment (in terms of new payroll dollars) in each of the counties that can be expected for various levels of state investment in each of those counties. Assume that the state plans to make allocations only in units of \$1000. These estimates are shown in Table D-4 and in Fig. D-6.

Table D-4 Expected new payroll generated ($000)

Investment ($000)	County 1	County 2	County 3	County 4
0	0	0	0	0
1	2.8	2.5	1.5	2.0
2	4.5	4.1	2.5	3.3
3	6.5	5.5	4.0	4.2
4	7.8	6.5	5.0	4.8
5	9.0	7.5	6.2	5.3
6	10.2	8.0	7.3	5.6
7	11.3	8.5	8.2	5.8
8	12.3	8.8	9.0	6.0
9	13.2	9.0	9.6	6.0
10	13.8	9.0	10.0	6.0

Suppose, then, that the problem is to decide how to distribute the $10,000 among the counties so as to maximize total expected new payroll generated. (In fact, suppose that, in addition, it would be useful to find the optimal regional distributions for total investments of $1000 through $9000.) This would be a very

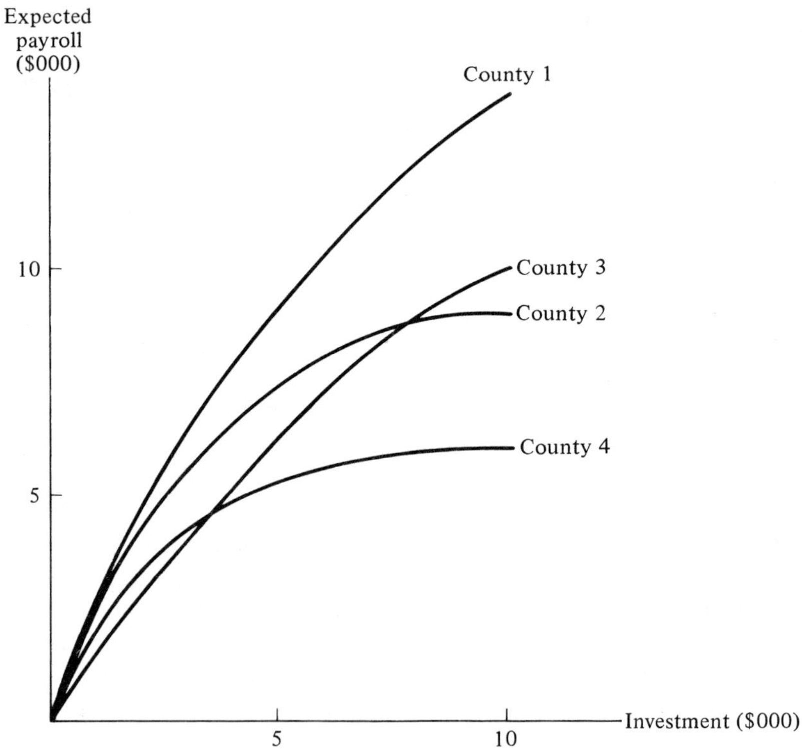

Figure D-6 Expected new payroll as functions of investment in each county.

large problem if a complete enumeration were worked out for all possible alternatives among the four counties.

Consider, instead, a sequential approach to the solution. Define $M_2(c_2)$ to be the maximum expected new payroll that results when $\$c_2$ are *optimally* invested in regions 1 and 2 combined; $M_3(c_3)$ to be the maximum when $\$c_3$ are optimally invested in regions 1, 2, and 3 combined; and $M_4(c_4)$ similarly. Let $f_i(x_i)$ denote the expected new payroll from investing $\$x_i$ in region i; this comes from Table D-4 directly. Thus, $M_1(c_1) = f_1(c_1)$, and the objective is to maximize $\sum_{i=1}^{4} f_i(x_i)$, subject to $x_1 + x_2 + x_3 + x_4 = 10{,}000$, and the restrictions on each x_i that it be $0 \leq x_i \leq 10$ and integer. (Recall that the x_i are in units of \$1000.)

In the notation already developed, then, $M_2(c_2) = \max_{0 \leq x_2 \leq c_2} [f_2(x_2) + M_1(c_1)]$ or, since $c_2 - x_2 = c_1$, $M_2(c_2) = \max_{0 \leq x_2 \leq c_2} [f_2(x_2) + M_1(c_2 - x_2)]$. The constraint on x_i—that it be one of the numbers listed in the left column of Table D-4—simplifies the maximization procedure, since only 11 values need be considered.

For example, to find $M_2(2)$ requires selecting the maximum of $[f_2(2) + M_1(0)]$, $[f_2(1) + M_1(1)]$, $[f_2(0) + M_1(2)]$. From Table D-4,

$$f_2(2) + M_1(0) = 4.1 + 0 \quad = 4.1$$

$$f_2(1) + M_1(1) = 2.5 + 2.8 = 5.3$$

$$f_2(0) + M_1(2) = 0 \quad + 4.5 = 4.5$$

Thus $M_2(2) = 5.3$; similarly, $M_2(0), M_2(1), \ldots, M_2(9), M_2(10)$ can be found. If we were *only* interested in allocating \$10,000, only $M_2(10)$ would be needed. The information necessary for these calculations is contained in the county 1 and county 2 columns of Table D-4. These are reproduced in Table D-5.

Note that the fact that each expected payroll figure in county 1 is larger than the corresponding figure in county 2 does *not* imply that one should always

Table D-5 $M_2(c_2) = \max [f_2(x_2) + M_1(c_2 - x_2)]$

c_2 (\$000)	$f_1(c_2 - x_2)$	$f_2(x_2)$	$M_2(c_2)$	Optimal investment policy (counties 1, 2)
0	0	0	0	(0, 0)
1	2.8	2.5	2.8	(1, 0)
2	4.5	4.1	5.3	(1, 1)
3	6.5	5.5	7.0	(2, 1)
4	7.8	6.5	9.0	(3, 1)
5	9.0	7.5	10.6	(3, 2)
6	10.2	8.0	12.0	(3, 3)
7	11.3	8.5	13.3	(4, 3)
8	12.3	8.8	14.5	(5, 3)
9	13.2	9.0	15.7	(6, 3)
10	13.8	9.0	16.8	(7, 3)

invest only in county 1. Both the actual numbers and the *differences* between them in each column are important. For example, while the first \$1000 is best invested in county 1 ($2.8 > 2.5$), \$2000 is best divided equally between them, since the increase in county 1 in going from \$1000 to \$2000 is 1.7, whereas the new \$1000 invested in county 2 brings an expected 2.5.

Next consider $M_3(c_3)$, the optimal distributions of $\$c_3$ (in thousands) between counties 1, 2, and 3. $M_3(c_3) = \max[f_3(x_3) + M_2(c_3 - x_3)]$. The information necessary for these calculations comes from the $M_2(c_2)$ column of Table D-5 and the county 3 column of Table D-4. To find $M_3(2)$, for example, requires selecting the maximum of $[f_3(2) + M_2(0)]$, $[f_3(1) + M_2(1)]$, $[f_3(0) + M_2(2)]$. From Tables D-4 and D-5,

$$f_3(2) + M_2(0) = 2.5 + 0 \quad = 2.5$$

$$f_3(1) + M_2(1) = 1.5 + 2.8 = 4.3$$

$$f_3(0) + M_3(2) = 0 \quad + 5.3 = 5.3$$

Hence $M_3(2) = 5.3$, which is achieved when nothing is invested in county 3 and \$2000 is optimally allocated between counties 1 and 2. (Note that, although three regions are involved, comparisons are only necessary between *two* columns of numbers: the expected new payroll in county 3 and the *optimal* expected new payroll for counties 1 and 2 in combination.) The results of all of these comparisons are shown in Table D-6.

Finally, in a completely analogous way, $M_4(c_4) = \max[f_4(x_4) + M_3(c_4 - x_4)]$ must be found. These calculations require data from the $M_3(c_3)$ column in Table D-6 and the county 4 column in Table D-4. The results are shown in Table D-7.

Thus optimal interregional investment policies for possible total investments of \$1000 through \$10,000 have been found. In particular, \$10,000 would be best invested as: \$4000 in county 1, \$3000 in county 2, \$1000 in county 3, and \$2000

Table D-6 $M_3(c_3) = \max[f_3(x_3) + M_2(c_3 - x_3)]$

c_3 (\$000)	$M_2(c_3 - x_3)$	$f_3(x_3)$	$M_3(c_3)$	Optimal investment policy (counties 1, 2, 3)
0	0	0	0	(0, 0, 0)
1	2.8	1.5	2.8	(1, 0, 0)
2	5.3	2.5	5.3	(1, 1, 0)
3	7.0	4.0	7.0	(2, 1, 0)
4	9.0	5.0	9.0	(3, 1, 0)
5	10.6	6.2	10.6	(3, 2, 0)
6	12.0	7.3	12.1	(3, 2, 1)
7	13.3	8.2	13.5	(3, 3, 1)
8	14.5	9.0	14.8	(4, 3, 1)
9	15.7	9.6	16.0	(5, 3, 1) or (3, 3, 3)
10	16.8	10.0	17.3	(4, 3, 3)

Table D-7 $M_4(c_4) = \max[f_4(x_4) + M_3(c_4 - x_4)]$

c_4 (\$000)	$M_3(c_4 - x_4)$	$f_4(x_4)$	$M_4(c_4)$	Optimal investment policy (counties 1, 2, 3, 4)
0	0	0	0	(0, 0, 0, 0)
1	2.8	2.0	2.8	(1, 0, 0, 0)
2	5.3	3.3	5.3	(1, 1, 0, 0)
3	7.0	4.2	7.3	(1, 1, 0, 1)
4	9.0	4.8	9.0	(3, 1, 0, 0) or (2, 1, 0, 1)
5	10.6	5.3	11.0	(3, 1, 0, 1)
6	12.1	5.6	12.6	(3, 2, 0, 1)
7	13.5	5.8	14.1	(3, 2, 1, 1)
8	14.8	6.0	15.5	(3, 3, 1, 1)
9	16.0	6.0	16.8	(4, 3, 1, 1) or (3, 3, 1, 2)
10	17.3	6.0	18.1	(4, 3, 1, 2)

in county 4. Expected new payroll would be \$18,100. It is to be noted that the presence of only one constraint equation connecting the x_i is what allowed the very simple forms of expressions such as $M_n(c_n) = \max[f_n(x_n) + M_{n-1}(c_n - x_n)]$. M_n (and M_{n-1}) depend on the right-hand side of the single constraint, namely on c_n. A second constraint of this sort would require a whole *series* of tables, similar to Table D-4, one for each possible value of the right-hand side of the second constraint. With several such constraints, the dynamic programming approach falls under, as Bellman has described it, the "curse of dimensionality," and the usefulness of the technique is reduced tremendously. On the other hand, constraints on the individual x_i—as in the problem above, that they be $0 \le x_i \le 10$ and integer—serve, generally, to simplify the optimization calculation at each step by reducing the number of values that have to be investigated.

Dynamic Programming in Continuous Form

The dynamic programming approach is most often applied to discrete problems although the connection to continuous problems requires only, as always, passing to the limit. The close connection between dynamic programming and the more classical calculus of variations approach to "dynamic" problems is illustrated for a continuous problem.† The simplest calculus of variations problem (Chap. 2) was illustrated by:

$$\text{Minimize} \quad I[y] = \int_{x_0}^{x_1} F(x, y, y')\,dx$$

$$\text{where} \qquad y(x_0) = y_0 \quad \text{and} \quad y(x_1) = y_1 \tag{D-52}$$

† There are many references in which the connections between dynamic programming, the calculus of variations, and the maximum principle are presented and explored in detail. See, among others, Dreyfus [9] or Bellman and Dreyfus [3, chap. V], Kirk [13, sec. 7.1] or MacCausland [14, secs. 7.4 and 7.6].

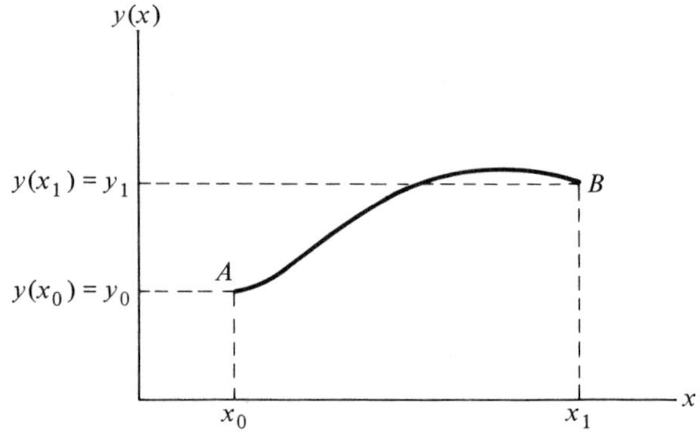

Figure D-7 Geometry of the simplest calculus of variations problem.

Geometrically, the problem was to find the curve joining the fixed initial and terminal points $A = (x_0, y_0)$ and $B = (x_1, y_1)$ that also minimized the integral; the brachistochrone problem was a particular example (see Fig. D-7).

The dynamic programming view of such a problem breaks it up into a sequence of smaller problems as follows. Consider the right-hand endpoint still fixed at $B = (x_1, y_1)$ and imagine the problem of optimally connecting to B some arbitrary point $G = (x, y)$, where $x_0 < x < x_1$ (Fig. D-8). The criterion integral from G to B depends of course on the location of G:

$$I[x, y] = \int_x^{x_1} F(x, y, y')\, dx$$

$$\text{where} \qquad y(x) = y \quad \text{and} \quad y(x_1) = y_1 \tag{D-53}$$

Consistent with the dynamic programming notation above, define by $M(x, y)$ the minimum of $I[x, y]$ for any particular location of G. Geometrically, the optimal path from G to B can be approximated by a (brief) straight-line segment, from G to H, and then an optimal path from H to B, as in Fig. D-9. The location of H is $(x + \Delta x, y + \Delta y)$; for some line with slope $\Delta y/\Delta x = y'$ at G, $\Delta y = y' \Delta x$

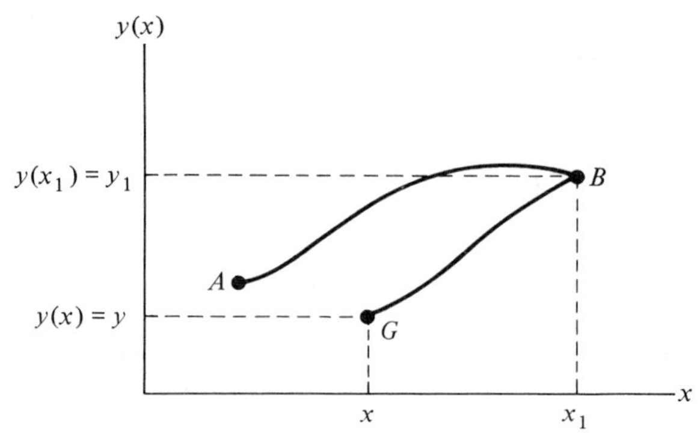

Figure D-8 Beginning the dynamic programming approach to the simplest calculus of variations problem.

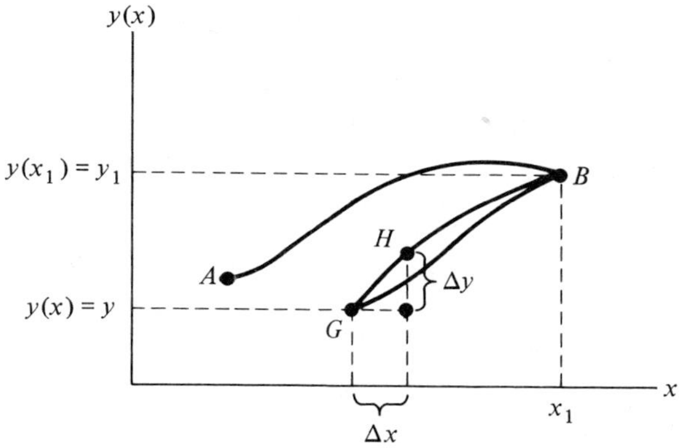

Figure D-9 Details of the dynamic programming approach to the simplest calculus of variations problem.

and the location of H is $(x + \Delta x, y + y' \Delta x)$. For an appropriate choice of y', H achieves a position on the optimal path from G to B and the path from H to B is therefore part of the optimal one from G to B. Thus we can express the minimum of $I[x, y]$ from G to B as depending on the choice of y':

$$M(x, y) = \min_{y'} [F(x, y, y')\Delta x + M(x + \Delta x, y + y' \Delta x)] \qquad \text{(D-54)}$$

[Compare the recursive relation in the discrete case, as in (D-50), for example.] The connection to classical (calculus of variations) theory now comes through mathematical manipulation. From the Taylor series,

$$M(x + \Delta x, y + y' \Delta x) = M(x, y) + \frac{\partial M}{\partial x} \Delta x + \frac{\partial M}{\partial y} y' \Delta x + 0(\Delta x) \qquad \text{(D-55)}$$

where $0(\Delta x)$ represents the sum of terms involving Δx squared or raised to higher powers. Putting this into (D-54), noting that $M(x, y)$ does not involve y' and thus can be subtracted from both sides of (D-54), we have

$$0 = \min_{y'} \left[F(x, y, y') \Delta x + \frac{\partial M}{\partial x} \Delta x + \frac{\partial M}{\partial y} y' \Delta x + 0(\Delta x) \right]$$

Dividing by Δx, denoting $\partial M/\partial x$ by M_x and $\partial M/\partial y$ by M_y, and letting $\Delta x \to 0$, gives

$$0 = \min_{y'} [F(x, y, y') + M_x + M_y y'] \qquad \text{(D-56)}$$

This is an example of the fundamental nonlinear partial differential equation of dynamic programming. The right-hand side of (D-56) says (because of the minimization operation) that the partial derivative of the bracketed expression with respect to y' must be zero. Moreover, the equation itself, in (D-56), says that, when the optimal y' is found, the expression in brackets itself will be zero. This leads to the following two equations:

$$F_{y'} + M_y = 0 \qquad \text{(D-57)}$$

$$F + M_x + M_y y' = 0 \tag{D-58}$$

Consider the derivative of (D-57) with respect to x (using the chain rule and recognizing that M_y must be considered a function of both y and x):

$$\frac{d}{dx} F_{y'} + \frac{d}{dx}\frac{\partial M}{\partial y} = \frac{d}{dx} F_{y'} + M_{yy}y' + M_{yx} = 0 \tag{D-59}$$

Take the partial derivative of (D-58) with respect to y:

$$F_y + F_{y'}\frac{\partial y'}{\partial y} + M_{xy} + M_{yy}y' + M_y\frac{\partial y'}{\partial y} = 0 \tag{D-60}$$

From (D-57), $M_y = -F_{y'}$; substituting into (D-60) gives

$$F_y + F_{y'}\frac{\partial y'}{\partial y} + M_{xy} + M_{yy}y' - F_{y'}\frac{\partial y'}{\partial y} = 0 \tag{D-61}$$

or

$$F_y + M_{xy} + M_{yy}y' = 0 \tag{D-62}$$

From (D-62), $M_{xy} + M_{yy}y' = -F_y$, and putting this into (D-59) gives, finally, $(d/dx)(F_{y'}) - F_y = 0$, or, alternatively,

$$F_y - \frac{d}{dx} F_{y'} = 0 \tag{D-63}$$

which is precisely the Euler-Lagrange equation from the calculus of variations approach [e.g., (2-25) in Chap. 2].

The object of this manipulation is to indicate that the calculus of variations procedures and the dynamic programming approach come around to the same mathematical basis. Operationally, however, the approaches are quite different; the calculus of variations, e.g., in the Euler-Lagrange equation, specifies an overall characteristic that an optimizing curve must have throughout its length. Dynamic programming, on the other hand, approaches the problem by building up the optimizing curve, piece by piece, starting at the right-hand endpoint and working backward toward the left-hand point of origin. This distinction is not unlike that in nonlinear programming, where the Kuhn-Tucker conditions set forth a complete set of necessary conditions for an optimal point while, for example, gradient methods approach the optimum in a series of well-designed steps. As with nonlinear programming problems, the Euler-Lagrange results for the calculus of variations approach may be difficult to utilize operationally, in which case some sort of discrete approximation may be needed.

D-4 RECURSIVE PROGRAMMING

The "dynamism" inherent in the recursive programming methodology is essentially less global than that in the calculus of variations, dynamic programming, or maximum principle approaches. The philosophy is that, because of the increasing uncertainty of events further into the future, planning over a time horizon should be done in a series of optimizing steps, but beginning with the initial point.

To continue with the Seattle-to-San Francisco example,† the calculus of variations or maximum principle approaches would specify a complete set of characteristics simultaneously for all parts of the optimal route. Dynamic programming would begin consideration at the destination, San Francisco, and then back up to all possible distinguishably different points (towns) just north of San Francisco, through which one might drive, calculating driving time from each to San Francisco. (Call these the first-level towns.) Then, for each of these towns, one would consider the towns north of them (second-level towns), through which one might come, on the way to San Francisco, and, in particular, the fastest route from each second-level town via some first-level town to San Francisco, etc. In the last step, the $(n-1)$th-level towns would be connected to Seattle and the fastest route determined. The recursive programming point of view proceeds in the other direction, making a locally best southbound decision out of Seattle to $(n-1)$th-level towns, then a locally best southbound decision from there to $(n-2)$th-level towns, and so on, into San Francisco. Clearly this approach will not, generally, lead to an overall optimal route; the justification is that the uncertainty surrounding facts further away (temporally or spatially) makes them unreliable as inputs for current decision making.‡ To emphasize this suboptimality, some authors prefer the term recursive programs (rather than programming), emphasizing a sequence of choices and not an overall, global optimal program.§

As an example, the recursive programming methodology for a set of linear programming maximizing problems is to:

$$\text{Maximize} \quad \mathbf{P}'(t)\mathbf{X}(t)$$

$$\text{subject to} \qquad \mathbf{A}(t)\mathbf{X}(t) \le \mathbf{C}(t) \tag{D-64}$$

$$\text{and} \qquad \mathbf{X}(t) \ge \mathbf{0}$$

where $\mathbf{P}(t)$ = an $(n \times 1)$ vector of objective function parameters at time t
$\mathbf{A}(t)$ = an $(m \times n)$ matrix of constraint coefficients at time t
$\mathbf{C}(t)$ = an $(m \times 1)$ vector of constraining amounts at time t
and $\mathbf{X}(t)$ = an $(n \times 1)$ vector of primal decision variables at time t

Also, let

$\mathbf{U}(t)$ = an $(m \times 1)$ vector of dual variables from the primal program at time t.

† The spatial rather than temporal nature of the example should not cause problems. All of the techniques considered in this book are just as valid for optimization over space as they are for optimization over time (and ultimately, of course, for optimization over both space and time, as illustrated in Chap. 5, Sec. 5-5).

‡ Obviously, this kind of reasoning is inappropriate for some of the classical calculus of variations problems such as minimal surfaces of revolution, the brachistochrone, etc., but it is germane for more modern concerns dealing with growth (e.g., of an economy) over time and/or space.

§ Compare, for example, Day [7] and Nelson [16, especially p. 34].

The recursive programming framework recognizes that $\mathbf{P}(t)$, $\mathbf{A}(t)$, and/or $\mathbf{C}(t)$ may be functions of past decisions and exogenous variables. These relationships are expressed as a set of difference equations of order s:

$$\begin{aligned}\mathbf{P}(t) &= G_1[\mathbf{X}^*(t-1),\ldots,\mathbf{X}^*(t-s),\mathbf{U}^*(t-1),\ldots,\mathbf{U}^*(t-s),\mathbf{H}_1(t)]\\ \mathbf{A}(t) &= G_2[\mathbf{X}^*(t-1),\ldots,\mathbf{X}^*(t-s),\mathbf{U}^*(t-1),\ldots,\mathbf{U}^*(t-s),\mathbf{H}_2(t)]\\ \mathbf{C}(t) &= G_3[\mathbf{X}^*(t-1),\ldots,\mathbf{X}^*(t-s),\mathbf{U}^*(t-1),\ldots,\mathbf{U}^*(t-s),\mathbf{H}_3(t)]\end{aligned} \quad \text{(D-65)}$$

where asterisks indicate optimal values of previously determined primal and dual variables and $\mathbf{H}_1(t)$, $\mathbf{H}_2(t)$, and $\mathbf{H}_3(t)$ represent vectors of exogenous variables. The essence of a particular application, of course, is the specification of the feedback relationships in (D-65). Once these are determined, the time-dependency of current decisions on past decisions is clear. In this sense, then, the model is a "dynamic" one, but in general it is not appropriate for the more forward-looking, global optimization problems with which the calculus of variations, maximum principle, and dynamic programming approaches deal effectively.

PROBLEMS

D-1 Write the equivalent calculus of variations problem for each of the following second-order linear differential equations (all from App. C):

(*a*) Prob. C-3(*a*)
(*b*) Prob. C-3(*b*)
(*c*) Prob. C-3(*c*)
(*d*) Prob. C-3(*e*)

D-2 (*a*) Construct a discrete approximation to the objective functional in Prob. D-1(*c*), above, letting $n = 4$ and thus $\Delta x = 0.2$. In particular, find the approximating values for $y_1, \ldots, y_4$ and compare with the actual y values for the solution function, found for Prob. C-3(*c*) in App. C. Compare, also, the value of the integral for the solution to that problem with the approximating area found here.

(*b*) Redo part (*a*), above, letting $n = 9$ and hence $\Delta x = 0.1$. Again, compare the y values and the approximating area with those from the solution found in Prob. C-3(*c*) in App. C. Compare also with the approximating values found in part (*a*) of this problem.

D-3 Using $\Delta x = 0.1$, compare an Euler approximation and a Runge-Kutta approximation to the differential equation in Prob. C-3(*c*) in App. C over the range $0 \le x \le 1$, using the form found in Prob. C-5(*b*) (namely, a pair of first-order linear differential equations). Compare the y values for the two approximations with the exact values, found from the solution to Prob. C-3(*c*). Also, compare the total area under the exact solution function with the total area under the ten trapezoids in each of the two approximations.

D-4 Formulate the discrete form of the following problem: minimize $I[y, u] = \int_0^1 \frac{1}{2}(3y^2 + 5u^2)\,dx$ where $y' = y + 4u$ and $y(x_0) = 1$ (this is Prob. 4-6 of Chap. 4). Solve the problem using the approach of the discrete maximum principle.

D-5 (*a*) Formulate and solve the discrete version of Prob. 4-7(*a*) in Chap. 4. This is Prob. D-4, above, with the added condition that $y_n = 0.5$.

(*b*) Consider Prob. D-4 with the terminal value of the state variable constrained to be nonnegative. [The continuous version of this problem is Prob. 4-7(*b*) in Chap. 4.]

(*c*) Consider Prob. D-4 with the new terminal requirement that $y_1 \ge 0.5$. [Again, compare Prob. 4-7(*c*) in Chap. 4.]

D-6 A classic example illustrating the usefulness of the dynamic programming approach is the following: maximize $x_1x_2x_3$, subject to $x_1 + x_2 + x_3 = c$ and $x_i \geq 0$ ($i = 1, 2, 3$). Solve this problem via dynamic programming.

REFERENCES

1. Aris, R.: "Discrete Dynamic Programming," Blaisdell, New York, 1964. An introduction to dynamic programming at a moderate level of mathematical difficulty.
2. Bellman, R.: "Dynamic Programming," Princeton University Press, Princeton, 1957. The classic reference on dynamic programming by the person who originated the idea.
3. ——— and S. Dreyfus: "Applied Dynamic Programming," Princeton University Press, Princeton, 1962. A readable introduction to the subject of dynamic programming and to its connections to the calculus of variations and the maximum principle.
4. Benavie, A.; "Mathematical Techniques for Economic Analysis," Prentice-Hall, Englewood Cliffs, N.J., 1972. Chapter 5 contains a thorough exposition of the discrete maximum principle and its connection to Kuhn-Tucker theory.
5. ——— and F. J. Gould: The Discrete Maximum Principle—A Correction, *Western Economic Journal*, vol. 8, pp. 266–269, September, 1970. A mathematical correction of Holmes [12].
6. Canon, M. D., C. D. Cullum, Jr., and E. Polak: "Theory of Optimal Control and Mathematical Programming," McGraw-Hill, New York, 1970. A mathematically advanced discussion of the interrelations between variational methods and mathematical programming.
7. Day, R. H.: "Recursive Programming and Production Response," North-Holland, Amsterdam, 1963. An introduction to the approach of recursive programming, with applications; moderate level of mathematical difficulty.
8. Dorfman, R.: An Economic Interpretation of Optimal Control Theory, *American Economic Review*, vol. 59, pp. 817–831, December, 1969. A discrete version of the maximum principle is discussed in sec. V.
9. Dreyfus, S.: "Dynamic Programming and the Calculus of Variations," Academic Press, New York, 1965. Provides a thorough discussion of the connections between dynamic programming, the calculus of variations, and the maximum principle.
10. Fan, L. T., and C. S. Wang: "The Discrete Maximum Principle," Wiley, New York, 1964. At an advanced mathematical level, this provides a complete reference to the fundamentals of the discrete maximum principle.
11. Gluss, B.: "An Elementary Introduction to Dynamic Programming," Allyn and Bacon, Boston, 1972. A thorough and readable introduction to dynamic programming techniques.
12. Holmes, W. L.: Derivation and Application of a Discrete Maximum Principle, *Western Economic Journal*, vol. 6, pp. 385–394, December, 1968. An investigation of the mathematical bases of a discrete version of the maximum principle, with an application in macroeconomics.
13. Kirk, D. E.: "Optimal Control Theory, an Introduction," Prentice-Hall, Englewood Cliffs, N.J., 1970. An engineering text at a fairly advanced level of detail. Chapters 3, 4, and 5 cover dynamic programming, the calculus of variations, and the Pontryagin principle, respectively.
14. MacCausland, I.: "Introduction to Optimal Control," Wiley, New York, 1969. Connections between dynamic programming, the calculus of variations, and the maximum principle are discussed in chap. 7.
15. Miller, R. E.: "Modern Mathematical Methods for Economics and Business," Holt, Rinehart and Winston, New York, 1972. Standard Lagrange multiplier techniques for equality constraints are discussed in secs. 4.4 to 4.6; the Kuhn-Tucker approach to inequality-constrained optimization problems is covered in secs. 4.8 and 8.2.
16. Nelson, J. P.: An Interregional Recursive Programs Model of Production, Investment, and Technological Change, *Journal of Regional Science*, vol. 11, pp. 33–47, April, 1971. A brief summary of the recursive programs approach with an application; comments on "programs" versus "programming" terminology.
17. Nemhauser, G.: "Introduction to Dynamic Programming," Wiley, New York, 1966. A standard and readable introduction to dynamic programming; modest level of mathematical difficulty.

ANSWERS TO PROBLEMS

CHAPTER 2

2-1 (*a*) Continuous (*b*) Discontinuous at $x = 1$ (*c*) Continuous (*d*) Continuous
(*e*) Continuous, with a kink at $x = 2$

2-2 (*a*) $y'' = -\frac{7}{2}x$ (*b*) $-2x = 0$ (*c*) $y' + xy'' = 0$ (*d*) $y'' = \frac{1}{2}x^3$

2-3 (*a*) $2y_1'' + y_2'' = 0$ and $y_1'' = 1$
(*b*) $x + y_2 - y_2'' = 0$ and $x + y_1 - y_1'' = 0$
(*c*) $xy_2y_3 = 0$, $xy_1y_3 = 2$, and $xy_1y_2 - 2y_3'' = 0$
(*d*) $2y(x_1 + x_2) - 2 = 0$

2-4 (*a*) $y = -\frac{7}{12}x^3 + \frac{67}{12}x$
(*b*) $y = -\frac{7}{12}x^3 + 65.306x - 64.723$
(*c*) $y = -\frac{7}{12}x^3 + \frac{6007}{12}x$

CHAPTER 3

3-1 (*a*) $y = -\frac{7}{12}x^3 + \frac{7}{4}x$ (*b*) $y = -\frac{7}{12}x^3 - 4.134x$ and $y = -\frac{7}{12}x^3 + 1.719x$
(*c*) $y = -\frac{7}{12}x^3 + 2.162x$

3-2 (*a*) $y = 0.2x$ (*b*) $y = 0.2x - 4.75$
(*c*) Orthogonality at the right-hand end requires $y'(x_1) = -1/\sigma'(x_1) = c_1$. At the left-hand end, the orthogonality requirement is that $y'(x_0) = -1/\rho'(x_0) = c_1$. Thus when $\sigma'(x) \neq \rho'(x)$, which is to say when the initial and terminal lines are not parallel, there are conflicting requirements on the value of c_1 in the general solution $y = c_1x + c_2$. In this case, of course, the

initial and terminal lines will intersect at some point and hence the minimum distance between them is zero. On the other hand, when $\sigma'(x) = \rho'(x)$, so that the lines are parallel, then $-1/\sigma'(x_1) = c_1 = -1/\rho'(x_0)$ and the extremal line will be orthogonal to both initial and terminal lines, but c_2 is indeterminate, since the minimum distance between two parallel lines is measured by a perpendicular transversal located anywhere.

3-3 (*a*) $y = -\frac{7}{12}x^3 - 44.125x^2 + 49.708x$

(*b*) $y = -\frac{7}{12}x^3 - 38.125x^2 + 43.709x$, when the right-hand side of the constraint is 9; $y = -\frac{7}{12}x^3 - 50.125x^2 + 55.709x$, when the right-hand side of the constraint is 11. The associated values of $I[y]$ are -497.565 and -850.534, respectively. For part (*a*), $I[y]$ evaluated for the optimal $y(x)$ is -662.064. Thus when the right-hand side of the constraint increases from 10 to 11, the optimal value of $I[y]$ decreases by 188.47; when the right-hand side decreases from 10 to 9, the optimal value of $I[y]$ increases by 164.499. The average of the absolute values of these changes for a unit change in the right-hand side of the constraint is 176.485. The value of λ in part (*a*) was -176.5.

3-4 (*a*) $y_1(x) = -\frac{7}{24}x^3 + 5.292x$ and $y_2(x) = \frac{7}{24}x^3 - 5.292x + 100$

(*b*) $y_1(x) = -\frac{7}{12}x^3 + 5.583x$ and $y_2(x) = -5x + 100$

(*c*) Using the extremals from part (*a*), $I[y_1, y_2] = -38.20$. Using the extremals from part (*b*), $I[y_1, y_2] = -38.06$. The difference is 0.14 units. Since in the unconstrained case $y_1(x) + y_2(x) = -0.583x^3 + 0.583x + 100$, it is clear that for x in the range $0 \le x \le 1$ this sum is close to 100. It is exactly 100 when $x = 0$ and when $x = 1$, and it is slightly larger than 100 for x in the range $0 < x < 1$.

3-5 $y_1(x) = -\frac{7}{24}x^3 + 5.292x$ and $y_2(x) = \frac{7}{24}x^3 - 5.292x + 100$

3-6 (*a*) For the objective functional in Probs. 3-1 and 3-3, the condition in (3-62) requires $y'_- = y'_+$. This is a requirement that $y(x)$ be smooth at any x_c, since the derivative of $y(x)$ must be the same to the left and to the right of x_c; since $y'(x)$ is continuous at x_c, $y(x)$ is smooth.

(*b*) The objective functional in Prob. 3-2 is $F = \sqrt{1 + (y')^2}$. Here $F_{y'} = y'\sqrt{1 + (y')^2}$ and again it is clear that for $F_{y'}$ to be continuous across a corner (for $F_{y'_-} = F_{y'_+}$) y' itself must be continuous and hence $y(x)$ must be smooth.

(*c*) The objective functional for Prob. 3-4 (and 3-5) is $F = 7xy_1 - (y'_1)^2 - (y'_2)^2$. The extension of the corner conditions to functionals of more than one variable is given in (3-67) through (3-70). Here the conditions for $y_1(x)$ will be exactly those given in part (*a*) of this problem; thus $y_1(x)$ must be smooth. For $y_2(x)$, (3-67) leads to $y'_{2_-} = y'_{2_+}$, again requiring continuity of y'_2 across a corner and hence smoothness of $y_2(x)$.

3-7 (*a*) For Prob. 3-1, $F_{y'y'} = -2$, satisfying the Legendre condition in (3-76) for a maximum. The form of the solutions for all parts of Prob. 3-1 is $y(x) = -\frac{7}{12}x^3 + c_1x + c_2$, from which $\psi_1 = x$, $\psi_2 = 1$, and $\psi_1/\psi_2 = x$, which is clearly monotonic increasing and hence the Jacobi condition in (3-91) is satisfied. Finally, the Weierstrass E function, (3-92), is $E = -(z' - y')^2$, which is clearly negative for all $z' \neq y'$.

(*b*) For Prob. 3-2, the integrand is $F = \sqrt{1 + (y')^2}$. This was examined in the text and all three conditions were seen to be met.

(*c*) For Prob. 3-3, the Legendre and Weierstrass conditions are identical to part (*a*), above, since the objective functional integrand here is the same as in part (*a*). The solutions are of the form $y = -\frac{7}{12}x^3 + (\lambda/4)x^2 + (c_1/2)x + c_2/2$, and hence $\psi_1/\psi_2 = x$, which, as before, is monotonic increasing and hence (3-91) is satisfied.

(*d*) For Probs. 3-4 and 3-5, $F = 7xy_1 - (y'_1)^2 - (y'_2)^2$. Hence $F_{y'_1y'_1} = -2$, $F_{y'_2y'_2} = -2$, and $F_{y'_1y'_2} = F_{y'_2y'_1} = 0$ so that $\partial^2 F/\partial \dot{\mathbf{Y}}^2 = \begin{bmatrix} -2 & 0 \\ 0 & -2 \end{bmatrix}$, which is negative definite, since the principal minors alternate in sign, beginning negative. The ratios ψ_1/ψ_2 for both y_1 and y_2 are equal to x and, as before, since this is monotonic increasing, the Jacobi condition is satisfied. Here, $E = -(z'_1 - y'_1)^2 - (z'_2 - y'_2)^2$, which is always strictly negative for $z'_1 \neq y'_1$ and $z'_2 \neq y'_2$.

3-8 $y = \frac{1}{3}e^{2x}$

CHAPTER 4

4-1 The hamiltonian for this problem is $H = 7xy - u^2 + \lambda u$, and the solution, as in Chap. 2, is $y = -\frac{7}{12}x^3 + \frac{67}{12}x$.

4-2 (*a*) $y = -\frac{7}{12}x^3 + \frac{7}{4}x$ (*b*) $y = -\frac{7}{12}x^3 - 4.134x$ and $y = -\frac{7}{12}x^3 + 1.719x$
(*c*) $y = -\frac{7}{12}x^3 + 2.162$

4-3 (*a*) $y = 0.2x$ (*b*) $y = 0.2x - 4.75$

4-4 (*a*) The unconstrained solution, $y = -\frac{7}{12}x^3 + \frac{67}{12}x$, satisfies the constraint over $0 \le x \le 1$.
(*b*) $y = 5.3x$ for x in the range $0 \le x \le 0.697$ and $y = -\frac{7}{12}x^3 + \frac{67}{12}x$ for x in the range $0.697 \le x \le 1$; i.e., there is a corner at $x = 0.697$.

4-5 (*a*) $y_1(x) = -\frac{7}{12}x^3 + 5.583x$ and $y_2(x) = -5x + 100$
(*b*) $y_1(x) = 5x$ and $y_2(x) = -5x + 100$

4-6 $y(x) = 0.0028\,e^{3.256x} + 0.9972\,e^{-3.256x}$. In addition, $\lambda(x) = -0.0020\,e^{3.256x} + 1.3262\,e^{-3.256x}$ and $u(x) = -(0.8)\lambda(x) = 0.0016\,e^{3.256x} - 1.0610\,e^{-3.256x}$

4-7 (*a*) $y(x) = 0.0179\,e^{3.256x} + 0.9822\,e^{-3.256x}$; $\lambda(x) = -0.0126\,e^{3.256x} + 1.3061\,e^{-3.256x}$; $u(x) = -(0.8)\lambda(x) = 0.0101\,e^{3.256x} - 1.0449\,e^{-3.256x}$
(*b*) Same solution as Prob. 4-6.
(*c*) Same solution as Prob. 4-7(*a*).

4-8 (*a*) Same solution as Prob. 4-1.
(*b*) There is no solution to this problem.

APPENDIX A

A-1 (*a*) $x + \frac{1}{3}x^3 + \frac{3}{5}x^5 + c$ (*b*) $x^5 - 2x + c$ (*c*) $-\frac{1}{3}e^{-3x} + c$
(*d*) $\frac{3}{2}e^{2x}(x^2 - x + \frac{1}{2}) + c$ (*e*) $\frac{1}{12}x^4 + \frac{1}{9}e^{3x} + c_1x + c_2$

A-2 (*a*) 358/15 (*b*) 329/15 (*c*) −2 (*d*) −6.36 (*e*) 273.56

A-3 (*a*) 358/15 (*b*) 29/15 (*c*) 5 (*d*) 2 (*e*) 733/30 (*f*) 9/2

A-4 (*a*) 1 (*b*) 1/2*e* (*c*) Undefined

A-5 (*a*) 7106.82 (*b*) 7062.20 (*c*) 7046.88

APPENDIX B

B-1 (*a*) $\mathbf{A} = \begin{bmatrix} -1 & \frac{1}{2} & 0 \\ \frac{1}{2} & -1 & 1 \\ 0 & 1 & -4 \end{bmatrix}$ (*b*) $\mathbf{A} = \begin{bmatrix} 2 & -3 \\ -3 & 6 \end{bmatrix}$

(*c*) $\mathbf{A} = \begin{bmatrix} 1 & -\frac{1}{2} & -\frac{1}{2} \\ -\frac{1}{2} & 1 & -\frac{1}{2} \\ -\frac{1}{2} & -\frac{1}{2} & 1 \end{bmatrix}$ (*d*) $\mathbf{A} = \begin{bmatrix} 5 & 0 & 0 \\ 0 & 0 & -3 \\ 0 & -3 & 1 \end{bmatrix}$

B-2 (*a*) Negative definite (*b*) Positive definite (*c*) Neither (*d*) Neither

B-3 (*a*) $d^2f > 0$ (*b*) $d^2f < 0$
(*c*) d^2f is neither strictly positive nor strictly negative.
(*d*) Same as (*c*).

APPENDIX C

C-1 (*a*) $y_t = -2(4)^t + 5(2)^t$ (*b*) $y_t = (2)^t$
(*c*) $y_t = (\frac{1}{2})^t - 1$ (*d*) $y_t = (-2)^t(1 - t)$

C-2 (*a*) Unstable (*b*) Unstable (*c*) Stable (*d*) Unstable

C-3 (*a*) $y = -2e^{4t} + 5e^{2t}$ (*b*) $y = \frac{13}{4} - \frac{1}{4}e^{-2t} + \frac{3}{2}t$
(*c*) $y = \frac{19}{5}e^{-3t} + \frac{31}{5}e^{2t}$ (*d*) $y = 5 + 2e^t - e^{-t} - t$ (*e*) $y = e^t(2 \cos 3t)$

C-4 (*a*) Unstable (*b*) Unstable (*c*) Unstable (*d*) Unstable (*e*) Unstable

C-5 (*a*) The pair of equations is $y_{t+1} = x_t$ and $x_{t+1} - 6x_t + 8y_t = 0$.
(*b*) The pair of equations is $\dot{y} = x$ and $\dot{x} + x - 6y = 0$.
(*c*) The three equations are $x = \dot{y}$, $z = \dot{x}$, and $\dot{z} - x = 1$.

C-6 (*a*) Unstable (*b*) Unstable (*c*) Unstable

C-7 Explosive behavior when c is in the range $1 < c < 4$

C-8 Try $V = x^2 + y^2$. This gives $\dot{V} = -2x^2 + 12xy + 2xy$ and one cannot in any way "balance" the $12xy$ and $2xy$ terms so that they cancel, since both have positive signs; and introduction of a negative sign into the V function is not possible because of the required $V > 0$ property.

C-9 Stable; use $V = x_1^2 + 6x_2^2$.

C-10 (*a*) The pair of equations is $x = \dot{y}$ and $\dot{x} = 6x - 8y$.
The following phase diagram results.

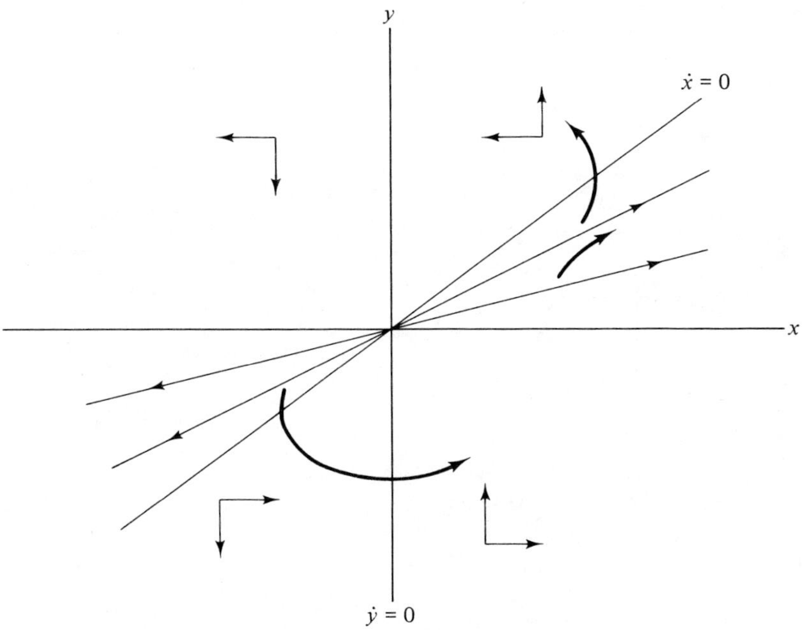

Phase diagram 1 for the unstable system $\dot{y} = x$ and $\dot{x} = 6x - 8y$.

(b) The pair of equations is $x = \dot{y}$ and $\dot{x} = -x + 6y$.
The following phase diagram results.

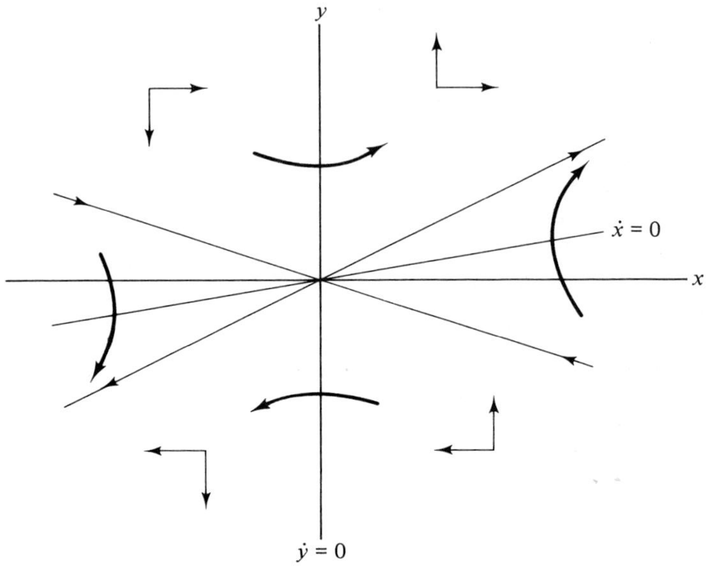

Phase diagram 2 for the unstable system $\dot{y} = x$ and $\dot{x} = -x + 6y$.

(c) The pair of equations is $x = \dot{y}$ and $\dot{x} = 2x - 10y$.
The following phase diagram results.

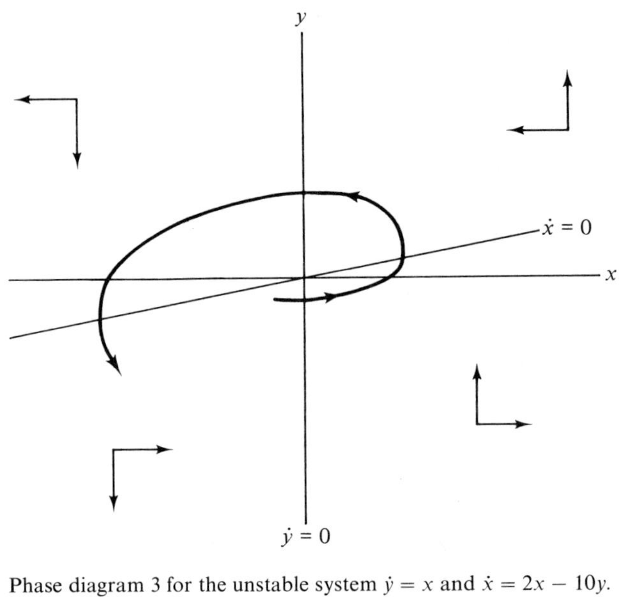

Phase diagram 3 for the unstable system $\dot{y} = x$ and $\dot{x} = 2x - 10y$.

APPENDIX D

D-1 (*a*) $I[y] = \int_{x_0}^{x_1} e^{-6x}(\dot{y} - 8y^2)\,dx$

(*b*) $I[y] = \int_{x_0}^{x_1} e^{2x}(\dot{y}^2 + 6y)\,dx$

(*c*) $I[y] = \int_{x_0}^{x_1} e^{x}(\dot{y}^2 + 6y^2)\,dx$

(*d*) $I[y] = \int_{x_0}^{x_1} e^{-2x}(\dot{y}^2 - 10y^2)\,dx$

D-2 (*a*) Actual values for $y_1, \ldots, y_4$ are 11.33, 14.94, 21.21, and 31.05, respectively; the approximating values are 10.92, 14.30, 20.50, and 30.50, respectively. The value of the integral is approximately 11,376; the total area under the approximating rectangles is 8010.

(*b*) The y values are:

	y_1	y_2	y_3	y_4	y_5	y_6	y_7	y_8	y_9
Exact	10.39	11.33	12.84	14.94	17.70	21.21	25.61	31.05	37.76
Approximate	10.25	11.10	12.53	14.58	17.30	20.80	25.22	30.73	37.57

The value of the integral is approximately 11,376; the total area under the approximating rectangles is now 9579.

D-3 The y values are:

	y_0	y_1	y_2	y_3	y_4	y_5	y_6	y_7	y_8	y_9	y_{10}
Exact	10	10.39	11.34	12.84	14.94	17.70	21.21	25.61	31.05	37.76	46.00
Euler	10	10.1	10.79	12.02	13.77	16.07	18.96	22.53	26.88	32.15	38.50
Runge-Kutta	10	10.39	11.34	12.84	14.94	17.70	21.21	25.60	31.05	37.76	46.00

The areas are: exact = 21.01; Euler = 18.82; Runge-Kutta = 21.08.

D-4 Letting $\Delta x = 0.1$ and thus $n = 10$, we find

$$y_i = 0.0053(1.362)^i + 0.9947(0.734)^i.$$

D-5 Letting $\Delta x = 0.1$ and thus $n = 10$, as above, the solutions are:

(*a*) $y_i = 0.0207(1.362)^i + 0.9793(0.734)^i$.

(*b*) Same solution as in Prob. D-4.

(*c*) Same solution as in part (*a*) of this problem.

D-6 Let $M_3(c_3) = \max_{0 \le x_3 \le c_3}[f_3(x_3)M_2(c_2)] = \max_{0 \le x_3 \le c_3}[x_3 M_2(c_2)]$,
$M_2(c_2) = \max_{0 \le x_2 \le c_2}[f_2(x_2)M_1(c_1)] = \max_{0 \le x_2 \le c_2}[x_2 M_1(c_1)]$,
and $M_1(c_1) = f_1(c_1) = c_1$. Thus, since $M_1(c_1) = c_1$, $M_2(c_2) = \max_{0 \le x_2 \le c_2}[x_2 M_1(c_2 - x_2)] = \max_{0 \le x_2 \le c_2}[x_2(c_2 - x_2)]$. This leads to $x_2 = c_2/2$ and $M_2(c_2) = c_2^2/4$. Similarly, one finds that $x_3 = c_3/3$, from which $x_2 = c_3/3$ and $x_1 = c_3/3$.

NAME INDEX

SUBJECT INDEX